Cultural Anthropology

Cultural Anthropology

A Perspective on the Human Condition

Emily A. Schultz
St. Cloud State University

Robert H. Lavenda
St. Cloud State University

Seventh Edition

New York   Oxford
OXFORD UNIVERSITY PRESS
2009

Oxford University Press, Inc., publishes works that further Oxford University's
objective of excellence in research, scholarship, and education.

Oxford New York
Auckland   Cape Town   Dar es Salaam   Hong Kong   Karachi
Kuala Lumpur   Madrid   Melbourne   Mexico City   Nairobi
New Delhi   Shanghai   Taipei   Toronto

With offices in
Argentina   Austria   Brazil   Chile   Czech Republic   France   Greece
Guatemala   Hungary   Italy   Japan   Poland   Portugal   Singapore
South Korea   Switzerland   Thailand   Turkey   Ukraine   Vietnam

Published by Oxford University Press, Inc.
198 Madison Avenue, New York, New York 10016
http://www.oup.com

Oxford is a registered trademark of Oxford University Press

Library of Congress Cataloging-in-Publication Data

Schultz, Emily A. (Emily Ann), 1949–
  Cultural anthropology : a perspective on the human condition / Emily A. Schultz,
Robert H. Lavenda.—7th ed.
    p. cm.
  ISBN 978-0-19-533850-8 (pbk.)
1. Ethnology. I. Lavenda, Robert H. II. Title.

  GN316.S38 2009
  306—dc22

                                                              2007051450

Printing number: 9 8 7 6 5 4 3 2 1

Printed in the United States of America
on acid-free paper

For Daniel and Rachel

Contents

Chapter 4
Anthropology in History and the Explanation of Cultural Diversity   75

Part II   The Resources of Culture

Chapter 5
Language   101

Chapter 6
Culture and Individuals   131

Chapter 7
Play, Art, Myth, and Ritual   165

Chapter 8
Worldview   199

Part III   The Organization of Material Life

Chapter 9
Culture and Power   231

Chapter 10
Making a Living   259

Part IV   Systems of Relationships

Chapter 11
Imagined Communities: Kinship and Other Forms of Relatedness   287

Chapter 12
Marriage and Family   325

Chapter 13
Dimensions of Inequality in the Contemporary World   359

Chapter 14
A Global World   393

Preface

The women on the cover of this book are returning from the market. On the face of it, this looks like a classic anthropological image—women in colorful outfits, living their traditional lives, heading back to the village—an image of difference and the exotic. But there's more there than meets the eye. These are women in Darfur, the site of terrible persecution and suffering in these opening years of the twenty-first century. The caption provided by the photo agency gives us some details: "Internally displaced women return to Hamadiya camp from the market in Zallingi, in West Darfur, February 2007. Since the beginning of the war in Darfur, over two million people have been displaced from their villages throughout the region, and hundreds of thousands have been killed." These are women who, whether they wished it or not, found themselves swept up in what is often called global-ization, but not the globalization of high finance, the Internet, and global flows of capital and images. They are part of the underside of globalization, the part that has brought suffering, death, and dislocation to mil-lions of people. How can we make sense of the bar-rage of images such as these that confront us daily? How can we understand the suffering, but also the joy, that characterizes their lives? How are these women of Darfur connected to the readers of this book? As citizens of the twenty-first century, we need to learn to pay attention to the local contexts situated in a broader social, cultural, and political matrix that now encompasses the globe. This is the work of con-temporary cultural anthropology.

ORGANIZATION AND CONTENT

Cultural Anthropology: A Perspective on the Human Con-dition, Seventh Edition, consists of fifteen chapters in five parts:

▼ Part I, The Tools of Cultural Anthropology, con-sists of three introductory chapters on the concept of culture; ethnographic fieldwork; and history, anthropology, and the explanation of cultural diversity.

▼ Part II, The Resources of Culture, is a set of four chapters on the key dimensions and products of human creativity: language; cognition; play, art, myth, and ritual; and worldview.

▼ Part III, The Organization of Material Life, consists of two chapters—one on power, and one on mak-ing a living—that deal with the ways human cul-tural creativity is channeled and circumscribed by political and economic constraints.

▼ Part IV, Systems of Relationships, looks at the organization of human interdependence. Chapters about relatedness, and marriage and the family allow us to emphasize how people make use of cultural resources as they struggle to pursue their personal projects within contexts of political and material constraints.

▼ Part V, From Local to Global, concludes the text by asking students to contemplate the globalizing, transnational context in which all human beings live at the beginning of the twenty-first century, and the ever-intensifying political, economic, and cul-tural forces with which all societies must cope. We do this through chapters that examine dimensions of inequality in the contemporary world (covering gender, class, caste, race, ethnicity, and nationalism), global processes, and anthropology in everyday life.

WHAT'S NEW IN THE SEVENTH EDITION

1. Based on continuing feedback from students and the help of insightful users of the book and reviewers, we have continued to streamline or rewrite throughout the book to improve readabil-ity and accessibility. This is the clearest and most

readable version of this text yet, and we have made the presentation more appealing by offering it in full color.

2. The book now has fifteen chapters, the better to correspond with the academic calendar. We shortened the discussions of non-kin relationships and incorporated them into the chapters on relatedness and marriage and family.

3. We incorporated a section on gender inequality into the chapter on social inequality.

4. There are extensive new examples from contemporary Native American societies.

5. There is a new section on the inadequacies of the race concept from the perspective of biological anthropology, to complement the discussion of the cultural construction of race later in the book.

6. We have increased our coverage of medical anthropology, including examples from critical medical anthropology on trauma and social suffering, as well as research published in the summer of 2007 on health care of infibulated women in Norway.

7. The broader world context continues to shape the lives of both the peoples anthropologists have studied and anthropologists themselves. We have drawn attention to new ways that anthropologists address questions of inequality and struggles over meaning in our coverage of such phenomena as transnational flows of people, wealth, images, and ideologies, including new assertions of transborder identities and struggles over human rights.

8. We have substantially modified several chapters, particularly those dealing with the anthropological perspective, culture, history and theory in anthropology, making a living, relatedness, and globalization in the world system.

Throughout the text, we continue to highlight the way human beings use culture to adapt to and transform the world. This has been quite an extensive revision, and most chapters have seen noteworthy changes:

▼ *Chapter 1: The Anthropological Perspective.* Significantly revised, this chapter includes a new discussion of holism as well as new material on medical anthropology.

▼ *Chapter 2: Culture and the Human Condition.* Also extensively revised, this chapter includes a new example of cultural relativism: African female genital cutting, an example that now reappears in other places in the text. The streamlined and clarified discussion of writing against culture now features a discussion of Luke Eric Lassiter's collaborative work on Kiowa Christianity.

▼ *Chapter 3: Fieldwork.* We have included new material on collaborative research—Luke Eric Lassiter's work again is discussed—and there is more on multisited, "multipositional" fieldwork, based on Sawa Kurotani's *Home Away from Home.*

▼ *Chapter 4: Anthropology in History and the Explanation of Cultural Diversity.* This chapter has again been extensively revised. It now includes new material on ethnography and Native American peoples, a new section on the biology of "race," extensive revisions of theoretical sections, a revised section on anthropology and colonialism, and new material on the comparative study of processes, based on work by Sally Falk Moore.

▼ *Chapter 5: Language.* There is a new section on language loss and language revitalization and a new example in the language and gender section from work by Joel Kuipers.

▼ *Chapter 7: Play, Art, Myth, and Ritual.* We have included material on baseball and masculinity in Cuba in the discussion of sport, and there is also a new discussion of hip-hop in Japan.

▼ *Chapter 8: Worldview.* The discussion of shamanism has been expanded, and the discussion of ideology has been revised.

▼ *Chapter 9: Culture and Power*. We have changed the title of this chapter to better suit the contents, and have provided a new introductory section on the peace process in Guatemala, which we then use again to discuss agency and hegemony.

▼ *Chapter 10: Making a Living*. We have extensively rewritten the economic anthropology section, based on the work of Richard Wilk and Lisa Cliggett.

▼ *Chapter 11: Imagined Communities: Kinship and Other Forms of Relatedness.*There are extensive changes in this chapter. There is a new discussion of systems of relatedness and an expanded discussion of kinship and practice. That section now includes new material on assisted reproduction and Jewish kinship in Israel from the work of Susan Martha Kahn, as well as a discussion of Lesley Sharp's work on the development of relatedness in organ recipients and the families of the organ donors. We have incorporated material on friendship, sodalities, and secret societies in West Africa (from the "Beyond Kinship" chapter in earlier editions).

▼ *Chapter 12: Marriage and Family*. This chapter features modifications to the definition of marriage as well as a new discussion of the effect on family and gender dynamics in middle- and upper middle-class Japanese executive families who are sent to the United States by the husband's company for assignments that last several years.

▼ *Chapter 13: Dimensions of Inequality in the Contemporary World*. There is a major new section on gender inequality in this chapter.

▼ *Chapter 14: A Global World*. An extensively rewritten discussion of Cold War—and post–Cold War—era theories opens this chapter. The discussion of multiculturalism and the New Europe has been moved from its position in earlier editions in the last chapter. There is now a new discussion of Anna Lowenhaupt Tsing's *Friction*.

▼ *Chapter 15: Anthropology in Everyday Life*. We have rewritten the introductory section. There is a substantial new applied medical anthropology section on caring for infibulated Somali women giving birth in Norway based on R. Elise B. Johansen's work. This discussion connects to the discussion of cultural relativism in Chapter 2. There is also a new section on indigenous activism and the United Nations Permanent Forum on Indigenous Issues, based on work by Ronald Niezen.

FEATURES AND LEARNING AIDS

▼ *We take an explicitly global approach in the text*. We systematically point out the extent to which the current sociocultural situation of particular peoples has been shaped by their particular histories of contact with capitalism, and we highlight ways that the post–Cold War global spread of capitalism has drastically reshaped the local contexts within which people everywhere live their lives.

▼ *We incorporate current anthropological approaches to power and inequality into the text*. We explore how power is manifested in different human societies, how it permeates all aspects of social life, and how it is deployed, resisted, and transformed. We discuss issues of trauma, social suffering, and human rights.

▼ *Material on gender and feminist anthropology is featured throughout the text*. Discussions of gender are tightly woven into the fabric of the book, and include (for example) material on supernumerary sexes and genders, genital cutting, varieties of human sexual practices, language and gender, dance and gender politics, women and colonialism, and gender inequality. In fact, extensive material on gender is now found in every chapter in this text.

▼ *New voices, including those of indigenous peoples, anthropologists, and nonanthropologists, are presented in the* In Their Own Words *boxes.* These short commentaries provide alternative perspectives—always readable and sometimes controversial—on topics featured in the chapter in which they appear.

▼ *EthnoProfiles.* These text inserts provide a consistent, brief information summary for each society discussed at length in the text. Each *EthnoProfile* also contains a map of the area in which the society is found. The inserts emerged from our desire as teachers to supply our students with basic geographical, demographic, and political information about the peoples anthropologists have worked with. They are not intended to be a substitute for reading ethnographies or for in-class lectures, nor are they intended to reify or essentialize the "people" or "culture" in question. Their main purpose is simply to provide a consistent orientation for readers. At the same time, as it becomes more and more difficult to attach peoples to particular territories in an era of globalization, the orienting purpose of the *EthnoProfile* is also undermined. How does one calculate population numbers or draw a simple map to locate a global diaspora? How does one construct an *EthnoProfile* for overseas Chinese or transborder Haitians? We did not know the answer to these questions, which is why *Ethno-Profiles* for those groups will not be found in the textbook.

▼ *Additional learning aids.* Key terms are boldfaced in the text and defined in a running glossary on the page on which they appear. Each chapter ends with a list of the key terms in the order they appeared in the text, a numbered chapter summa-

ry, and annotated suggested readings. Maps are featured extensively throughout the text.

▼ *In our discussions, we have tried to avoid being omniscient narrators by making use of citations and quotations in order to indicate where anthropological ideas come from.* In our view, even first-year students need to know that an academic discipline like anthropology is constructed by the work of many people; no one, especially not textbook authors, should attempt to impose a single voice on the field. We have avoided, as much as we could, predigested statements that students must take on faith. We try to give them the information that they need to see where particular conclusions come from.

ANCILLARIES

▼ *Student online resources* are available for this text, including glossary flashcards, self-quizzes, a list of Web links to professional resources and organizations, as well as a frequently requested feature from earlier editions—Guest Editorials. These are brief essays by well-known anthropologists written especially for our text. Also available online is an *Anthropology Study Skills Guide.* The guide is filled with hints and suggestions on improving study skills and strategies for studying this text, organizing information, writing essay exams, taking multiple-choice exams, and much more. Written by the long-time director of a university study skills center in collaboration with the authors, this guide will help students, even the best-prepared, be more successful in their college classes. All these materials can be found at the website for this book: www.oup.com/us/culturalanthro.

▼ *Online Reviews* give students the opportunity to test themselves about each chapter's content;

these reviews offer a key terms review and multiple choice questions to assess students' knowledge of the reading.

▼ *Instructors' Resources* are available both online and on disk. Online resources for instructors are available at the book site, www.oup.com/us/culturalanthro, and include Guest Editorials, links to professional resources and organizations, and links to new and noteworthy Oxford anthropology titles. An extensive test bank is available on CD-ROM.

A FINAL NOTE

We take students seriously. In our experience, although students may sometimes complain, they are also pleased when a course or a textbook gives them some credit for having minds and being willing to use them. We have worked hard to make this book readable and to present anthropology in its diversity as a vibrant, lively discipline full of excitement, contention, and intellectual value. We do not run away from the meat of the discipline with the excuse that it's too hard for students. We are aware that instant messaging, text messaging, and social networks and live journals have changed the ways in which students communicate, spend their time, and interact with their courses, especially their textbooks. We believe that a clear, straightforward, uncluttered presentation of cultural anthropology works well. Our collective teaching experience has ranged from highly selective liberal arts colleges to multi-purpose state universities, to semi-rural community colleges. We have found students at all of these institutions willing to be challenged and to make an effort when it is clear to them that anthropology has something to offer, be it intellectual, emotional, or practical. It is our hope that this new edition will continue to be a useful tool in challenging students and convincing them of the value of anthropology as a way of thinking about, and dealing with, the world in which they live.

ACKNOWLEDGMENTS

We would like to thank Jan Beatty, our editor at Oxford University Press, for her confidence, friendship, support, advice, and sure eye. We very much appreciate her eagerness to publish this book. We also appreciate the dedication of Assistant Editors Cory Schneider and Lauren Mine, and the Oxford production team, headed by Lisa Grzan. Developmental Editor John Haber's contributions are also much appreciated.

We continue to be impressed by the level of involvement of the reviewers of this book. Our reviewers recognize that they are important not only to us, the authors of this book, but also to the users of textbooks—students and colleagues both. They also recognize that authors have invested more than time in their work, and their thoughtfulness in their comments is much valued. We have found that even when we didn't follow their suggestions, their work caused us to think and rethink the issues they raised—it is safe to say that we have discussed every point they mentioned. We would like therefore to recognize Richard Adams, University of Texas at San Antonio; Joseph Alter, University of Pittsburgh; Michael Alvard, Texas A&M University; Ana Aparicio, University of Massachusetts, Boston; Diane Baxter, University of Oregon; John Beatty, Brooklyn College; Stephen Beckermann, Pennsylvania State University; Andrew Buckser, Purdue University; Howard Campbell, University of Texas at El Paso; Peter Castro, Syracuse University; Victor Garcia, Indiana University of Pennsylvania; Jane Granskog, California State University, Bakersfield; Ray Hames,

University of Nebraska; Teresa Holmes, York University; Alice James, Shippensburg University; Adam King, University of South Carolina; Ann Kingsolver, University of South Carolina; William Leons, University of Toledo; Walter E. Little, State University of New York at Albany; Robert Mucci, Indiana University, Northwest; Amy Ninetto, Rice University; Nicole Oretsky, Colorado State University; Frances Purifoy, University of Louisville; Jeannette E. Sherbondy, Washington College; Michael Simonton, Northern Kentucky University; Jill Smith, University of Wisconsin, Eau Claire; Pauline Turner Strong, University of Texas at Austin; Kenneth Tankersley, Northern Kentucky University; Bradley Tatar, University of North Carolina at Greensboro; Gerry Tierney, Webster University; Olessia P. Vovina, Montclair State University; and Cassandra White, Georgia State University. We owe a special debt to Ivan Karp, who was our most important source of intellectual stimulation and support for this project in its early days.

Our children, Daniel and Rachel, have grown up with our textbooks. As they have grown, they have become increasingly concerned with the issues we raise in the book, as well they should: These are issues that affect the future of us all.

Chapter 1

The Anthropological Perspective

This chapter introduces the field of anthropology. We look at what anthropology is and explore its different subfields. We touch on anthropology's key concept—culture—as well as its key research method—fieldwork. We conclude with a discussion of the ways anthropological insights are relevant in everyday life.

In early 1976, the authors of this book traveled to northern Cameroon, in western Africa, to study social relations in the town of Guider, where we rented a small house. In the first weeks we lived there, we enjoyed spending the warm evenings of the dry season reading and writing in the glow of the house's brightest electric fixture, which illuminated a large, unscreened veranda. After a short time, however, the rains began, and with them appeared swarms of winged termites. These slow-moving insects with fat, two-inch abdomens were attracted to the light on the veranda, and we soon found ourselves spending more time swatting at them than reading or writing. One evening, in a fit of desperation, we rolled up old copies of the international edition of *Newsweek* and began an all-out assault, determined to rid the veranda of every single termite.

The rent we paid for this house included the services of a night watchman. As we launched our attack on the termites, the night watchman suddenly appeared beside the veranda carrying an empty powdered milk tin. When he asked if he could have the insects we had been killing, we were a bit taken aback but warmly invited him to help himself. He moved onto the veranda, quickly collected the corpses of fallen insects, and then joined us in going after those termites that were still airborne. Although we became skilled at thwacking the insects with our rolled-up magazines, our skills paled beside those of the night watchman, who simply snatched the termites out of the air with his hand, squeezed them gently, and dropped them into his rapidly filling tin can. The three of us managed to clear the air of insects—and fill his tin—in about 10 minutes. The night watchman thanked us and returned to his post, and we returned to our books.

The following evening, soon after we took up our usual places on the veranda, the watchman appeared at the steps bearing a tray with two covered dishes. He explained that his wife had prepared the food for us in exchange for our help in collecting termites. We accepted the food and carefully lifted the lids. One dish contained *nyiri*, a stiff paste made of red sorghum, a staple of the local diet. The other dish contained another pasty substance with a speckled, salt-and-pepper appearance, which we realized was termite paste prepared from the insects we had all killed the previous night.

The night watchman waited at the foot of the veranda steps, an expectant smile on his face. Clearly, he did not intend to leave until we tasted the food his wife had prepared. We looked at each other. We had never eaten insects before or considered them edible in the North American, middle-class diet we were used to. To be sure, "delicacies" like chocolate-covered ants exist, but such items are considered by most North Americans to be food fit only for eccentrics. However, we understood the importance of not insulting the night watchman and his wife, who were being so generous to us. We knew that insects were a favored food in many human societies and that eating them brought no ill effects. So we reached into the dish of *nyiri*, pulling off a small amount. We then used the ball of *nyiri* to scoop up a small portion of termite paste, brought the mixture to our mouths, ate, chewed, and swallowed. The watchman beamed, bid us goodnight, and returned to his post.

We looked at each other in wonder. The sorghum paste had a grainy tang that was rather pleasant. The termite paste tasted mild, like chicken, not unpleasant at all. We later wrote to our families about this experience. When they wrote back, they described how they had told friends about our experience. Most of their friends had strong negative reactions. But one friend, a home economist, was not shocked at all. She simply commented that termites are a good source of clean protein.

▼ WHAT IS ANTHROPOLOGY?

This anecdote is not just about us, but also illustrates some of the central elements of the anthropological experience. Anthropologists want to learn about as many different human ways of life as they can. The people they come to know are members of their own society or live on a different continent, in cities or in rural areas. Their ways of life may involve patterns of regular movement across international borders, or they may make permanent homes in the borderlands themselves. Archaeologists reconstruct ancient ways of life from traces left behind in the earth that are hundreds or thousands of years old; anthropologists who strive to reconstruct the origin of the human species itself make use of fossil remains that reach back millions of years into the past. Whatever the case may be, anthropologists are sometimes exposed to practices that startle them. However, as they take the risk of getting to know such ways of life better, they are often treated to the sweet discovery of familiarity. This shock of the unfamiliar becoming familiar—as well as the familiar becoming unfamiliar—is something anthropologists come to expect and is one of the real pleasures of the field. In this book, we share aspects of the anthropological experience in the hope that you, too, will come to find pleasure, insight, and self-recognition from an involvement with the unfamiliar.

Anthropology can be defined as the study of human nature, human society, and the human past (Greenwood and Stini 1977). It is a scholarly discipline that aims to describe in the broadest possible sense what it means to be human. Anthropologists are not alone in focusing their attention on human beings and their creations. Human biology, literature, art, history, linguistics, sociology, political science, economics—all these scholarly disciplines and many more—concentrate on one or another aspect of human life. Anthropologists are convinced, however, that explanations of human activities will be superficial unless they acknowledge that human lives are always entangled in complex patterns of work and family, power and meaning. What is distinctive about the way anthropologists study human life? As we shall see, anthropology is holistic, comparative, field based, and evolutionary. First, it emphasizes that all the aspects of human life intersect with one another in complex ways. They shape one another and become integrated with one another over time. Anthropology is thus the integrated, or *holistic*, study of human nature, human society, and the human past. This **holism** draws together anthropologists whose specializations might otherwise divide them. At the most inclusive level, we may thus think of anthropology as the integrated (or holistic) study of human nature, human society, and the human past. Holism has long been central to the anthropological perspective and remains the feature that draws together anthropologists whose specializations might otherwise divide them.

Second, in addition to being holistic, anthropology is a discipline interested in **comparison**. To generalize about human nature, human society, and the human past requires evidence from the widest possible range of human societies. It is not enough, for example, to observe only our own social group, discover that we do not eat insects, and conclude that human beings as a species do not eat insects. When we compare human diets in different societies, we discover

that insect eating is quite common and that our North American aversion to eating insects is nothing more than a dietary practice specific to our own society.

Third, anthropology is also a field-based discipline. That is, for almost all anthropologists, the actual practice of anthropology—its data collection—takes place away from the office and in direct contact with the people, the sites, or the animals that are of interest. Whether they are biological anthropologists studying chimpanzees in Tanzania, archaeologists excavating a site high in the Peruvian Andes, linguistic anthropologists learning an unwritten language in New Guinea, or cultural anthropologists studying ethnic identity in West Africa or small-town festivals in Minnesota, anthropologists are in direct contact with the sources of their data. For most anthropologists, the richness and complexity of this immersion in other patterns of life is one of our discipline's most distinctive features. Field research connects anthropologists directly with the lived experience of other people or other primates or to the material evidence of that experience that they have left behind. Academic anthropologists try to intersperse field research with the other tasks they perform as university professors. Other anthropologists—applied anthropologists—regularly spend most or all of their time carrying out field research. All anthropology begins with a specific group of people (or primates) and always comes back to them as well.

Finally, anthropologists try to come up with generalizations about what it means to be human that are valid across space and over time. Because anthropologists are interested in documenting and explaining change over time in the human past, **evolution** is at the core of the anthropological perspective.

---

anthropology The study of human nature, human society, and the human past.

holism A characteristic of the anthropological perspective that describes, at the highest and most inclusive level, how anthropology tries to integrate all that is known about human beings and their activities.

comparison A characteristic of the anthropological perspective that requires anthropologists to consider similarities and differences in as wide a range of human societies as possible before generalizing about human nature, human society, or the human past.

evolution A characteristic of the anthropological perspective that requires anthropologists to place their observations about human nature, human society, or the human past in a temporal framework that takes into consideration change over time.

Anthropologists examine the *biological evolution* of the human species, which documents change over time in the physical features and life processes of human beings and their ancestors. Topics of interest include both human origins and genetic variation and inheritance in living human populations. If evolution is understood broadly as change over time, then human societies and cultures may also be understood to have evolved from prehistoric times to the present.

Anthropologists have long been interested in *cultural evolution*, which concerns change over time in beliefs, behaviors, and material objects that shape human development and social life. As we will see in chapter 4, early discussions of cultural evolution in anthropology emphasized a series of universal stages. However, this approach has been rejected by contemporary anthropologists who talk about cultural evolution, like William Durham (1991) and Robert Boyd (e.g., Richerson and Boyd 2006). Theoretical debates about culture change and about whether it ought to be called "cultural evolution" or not are very lively right now, not only in anthropology but in related fields like evolutionary biology and developmental psychology. In the midst of this debate, one of anthropology's most important contributions to the study of human evolution remains the demonstration that biological evolution is not the same thing as cultural evolution. Distinction between the two remains important as a way of demonstrating the fallacies and incoherence of arguments claiming that everything people do or think can be explained biologically, for example, in terms of "genes" or "race" or "sex."

▼ WHAT IS THE CONCEPT OF CULTURE?

A consequence of human evolution that had the most profound impact on human nature and human society was the emergence of **culture**, which can be defined as sets of learned behavior and ideas that hu-

> **culture** Sets of learned behavior and ideas that human beings acquire as members of society. Human beings use culture to adapt to and to transform the world in which they live.
>
> **biocultural organisms** Organisms (in this case, human beings) whose defining features are codetermined by biological and cultural factors.

man beings acquire as members of society. Human beings use culture to adapt to and transform the world in which we live.

Culture makes us unique among living creatures. Human beings are more dependent than any other species on learning for survival because we have no instincts that automatically protect us and help us find food and shelter. Instead, we have come to use our large and complex brains to learn from other members of society what we need to know to survive. Learning is a primary focus of childhood, which is longer for humans than for any other species.

From the anthropological perspective, the concept of *culture* is central to explanations of why human beings are what they are and why they do what they do. Anthropologists are frequently able to show that members of a particular social group behave in a particular way *not* because the behavior was programmed by their genes, but because they observed other people and copied what they did. For example, North Americans typically do not eat insects, but this behavior is not the result of genetic programming. Rather, North Americans have been told as children that eating insects is disgusting, have never seen any of their friends or family eat insects, and do not eat insects themselves. As we discovered personally, however, insects can be eaten by North Americans with no ill effects. This difference in dietary behavior can be explained in terms of culture rather than biology.

However, to understand the power of culture, anthropologists must also know about human biology. Anthropologists in North America traditionally have been trained in both areas so that they can understand how living organisms work and become acquainted with comparative information about a wide range of human societies. As a result, they can better evaluate how biology and culture contribute to different forms of human behavior. Indeed, most anthropologists reject explanations of human behavior that force them to choose either biology or culture as the unique cause. Instead, they emphasize that human beings are **biocultural organisms**. Our biological makeup—our brain, nervous system, and anatomy—is the outcome of developmental processes to which our genes and cellular chemistry contribute in fundamental ways. It also makes us organisms capable of creating and using culture. Without these biological endowments, human culture as we know it would not exist. At the same time, our survival as biological organisms depends on learned ways of thinking and acting that help us find food, shelter, and mates and that teach us how to rear our children. Our biological endowment, rich as it is, does not provide us with instincts that would automatically take care of these survival needs. Human biology makes culture possible; human culture makes human biological survival possible.

▼ WHAT MAKES ANTHROPOLOGY A CROSS-DISCIPLINARY DISCIPLINE?

Because of its diversity, anthropology does not easily fit into any of the standard academic classifications. The discipline is usually listed as a social science, but it spans the natural sciences and the humanities as well. What it is *not*, as we will see, is the study of the "exotic," the "primitive," or the "savage," terms that anthropologists reject. Figure 1.1 brings some order to the variety of interests found under the anthropological umbrella.

Traditionally, North American anthropology has been divided into four subfields: *biological anthropology*, *cultural anthropology*, *linguistic anthropology*, and *archaeology*. Because of their commitment to holism, many anthropology departments try to represent most or all of the subfields in their academic programs. However, universities in other parts of the world, such as Europe, usually do not bring all these specialties together. Even some North American anthropologists, such as Daniel Segal and Sylvia Yanagisako (2005), have argued that the traditional holistic "four-field" approach to the discipline should be abolished. They worry that this tradition's nineteenth-century origins in the era of scientific racism can never be overcome. They are also concerned that the four-field framework may restrict interdisciplinary collaborations. Other anthropologists, however, associate holistic four-field North American anthropology with the successful repudiation of nineteenth-century scientific racism by Franz Boas and other early 20th-century anthropologists. They also value four-field anthropology as a protected "trading zone" within which anthropologists are encouraged to bring together fresh concepts and knowledge from a variety of research traditions. North American anthropologist Rena Lederman, for example, has stressed that four-field anthropology does not insist on a single way of bringing the subfields together (2005).

Anthropological holism is attractive even to those who were not trained in North America. British

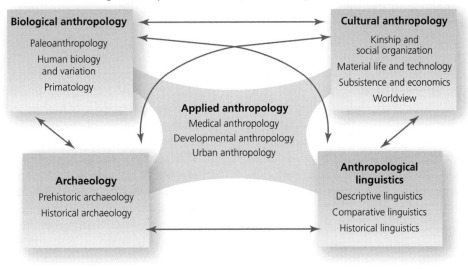

Anthropology
The intergrated study of human nature, human society, and human history.

Biological anthropology
Paleoanthropology
Human biology and variation
Primatology

Cultural anthropology
Kinship and social organization
Material life and technology
Subsistence and economics
Worldview

Applied anthropology
Medical anthropology
Developmental anthropology
Urban anthropology

Archaeology
Prehistoric archaeology
Historical archaeology

Anthropological linguistics
Descriptive linguistics
Comparative linguistics
Historical linguistics

FIGURE 1.1 In the United States, anthropology is traditionally divided into four specialties: biological anthropology, cultural anthropology, anthropological linguistics, and archaeology. Applied anthropology draws on information provided by the other four specialties.

anthropologist Tim Ingold, for example, argues, "The best anthropological writing is distinguished by its receptiveness to ideas springing from work in subjects far beyond its conventional boundaries, and by its ability to connect these ideas in ways that would not have occurred to their originators, who may be more enclosed in their particular disciplinary frameworks" (1994, xvii). We share the views of Lederman and Ingold: Trained in holistic, four-field anthropology, we continue to value the unique perspective it brings to the study of human nature, human society, and the human past. Indeed, as the organizers of a recent anthropological conference observed, "Even those who were the least persuaded that the traditional four-field organization of American anthropology was still viable (if it ever was) came away with a strong sense that the subfields had a great deal to say to one another and indeed needed one another" (McKinnon and Silverman 2005; viii).

▼ BIOLOGICAL ANTHROPOLOGY

Since the nineteenth century, when anthropology was developing as an academic field, anthropologists have studied human beings as living organisms in order to discover what makes us different from or similar to other animals. Early interest in these matters was a by-product of centuries of exploration. Western Europeans had found tremendous variation in the physical appearance of peoples around the world and had long tried to make sense of these differences. Some researchers developed a series of elaborate techniques to measure different observable features of human populations, including skin color, hair type, body type, and so forth, hoping to find scientific evidence that would allow them to classify all the peoples of the world into a set of unambiguous categories based on distinct sets of biological attributes. Such categories were called **races**, and many scientists were convinced that clear-cut criteria for racial classification would be discovered if careful measurements were made on enough people from a range of different populations.

European scientists first applied racial categories to the peoples of Europe itself, but their classifications soon included non-European peoples, who were coming under increasing political and economic domination by expanding European and European American capitalist societies. These peoples differed from "white" Europeans not only because of their darker skin color but also because of their unfamiliar languages and customs. In most cases, their technologies were also no match for the might of the West. In the early eighteenth century, for example, the European biologist Carolus Linnaeus (Carl von Linne, 1707–1778) classified known human populations into four races (American, European, Asian, and Negro) based on skin color (reddish, white, yellow, and black, respectively). Linnaeus also connected racial membership with the mental and moral attributes of group members. Thus, he wrote, Europeans were "fickle, sanguine, blue-eyed, gentle, and governed by laws," whereas Negros were "choleric, obstinate, contented, and regulated by custom" and Asians were "grave, avaricious, dignified, and ruled by opinion" (Molnar 2001, 5–6).

In the nineteenth century, influential natural scientists such as Louis Agassiz, Samuel George Morton, Francis Galton, and Paul Broca built on this idea of race, ranking different populations of the world in terms of brain size; unsurprisingly, the brains of "white" Europeans and North Americans were found to be larger, and the other races were seen to represent varying grades of inferiority, with Africans ranked at the bottom (Gould 1996). These findings were used to justify the social practice of **racism**: the systematic oppression of members of one or more socially defined "races" by another socially defined "race" that is justified in terms of the supposed inherent biological superiority of the rulers and the supposed inherent biological inferiority of those they rule.

Biological or physical anthropology as a separate discipline had its origins in the work of scholars like these, whose training was in some other discipline, often medicine. Johann Blumenbach (1752–1840), for example, whom some have called the "father of physical anthropology," was trained as a physician. Blumenbach identified five different races

---

races Social groupings that allegedly reflect biological differences.

racism The systematic oppression of one or more socially defined "races" by another socially defined "race" that is justified in terms of the supposed inherent biological superiority of the rulers and the supposed inherent biological inferiority of those they rule.

Anthropology as a Vocation
Listening to Voices

James W. Fernandez (Ph.D., Northwestern University) is a professor of anthropology at the University of Chicago. He has worked among the Fang of Gabon and among cattle keepers and miners of Asturias, Spain. This is an excerpt from an essay about the anthropological vocation.

For me, the anthropological calling has fundamentally to do with the inclination to hear voices. An important part of our vocation is "listening to voices," and our methods are the procedures that best enable us to hear voices, to represent voices, to translate voices.

By listening carefully to others' voices and by trying to give voice to these voices, we act to widen the horizons of human conviviality. If we had not achieved some fellow feeling by being there, by listening carefully and by negotiating in good faith, it would be the more difficult to give voice in a way that would widen the horizons of human conviviality. Be that as it may, the calling to widen horizons and increase human conviviality seems a worthy calling—full of a very human optimism and good sense.

Who would resist the proposition that more fellow feeling in the world is better than less, and that to extend the interlocutive in the world is better than to diminish it?

At the same time, there is a paradox here, one that demands of us a sense of proportion. Although the anthropologist is called to bring diverse people into intercommunication, he or she is also called to resist the homogenization that lies in mass communication. We are called by our very experience to celebrate the great variety of voices in the human chorus. The paradox is that we at once work to amplify the scale of intercommunication—and in effect contribute to homogenization—while at the same time we work to insist on the great variety of voices in communication. We must maintain here too a sense of proportion. We must recognize the point at which wider and wider cultural intercommunication can lead to dominant voices hidden in the homogenizing process. Human intercommunication has its uses and abuses.

Source: Fernandez 1990, 14–15.

(Caucasoid, Mongoloid, American, Ethiopian, and Malayan), and his classification was influential in the later nineteenth and twentieth centuries (Molnar 2001, 6). He and his contemporaries assumed that the races of "mankind" (as they would have said) were fixed and unchaning subdivisions of humanity.

However, as scientists learned more about biological variation in human populations, some of them came to realize that traits traditionally used to identify races, such as skin color, did not correlate well with other physical and biological traits, let alone mental and moral traits. Indeed, scientists could not even agree about how many human races there were or where the boundaries between them should be drawn.

By the early twentieth century, some anthropologists and biologists were arguing that "race" was a cultural label invented by human beings to sort people into groups and that races with distinct and

unique sets of biological attributes simply did not exist. Anthropologists like Franz Boas, for example, who in the early 1900s founded the first department of anthropology in the United States, at Columbia University, had long been uncomfortable with racial classifications in anthropology. Boas and his students devoted much energy to debunking racist stereotypes, using both their knowledge of biology and their understanding of culture. As the discipline of anthropology developed in the United States, students were trained in both human biology and human culture to provide them with the tools to fight racial stereotyping. After World War II, this position gained increasing strength in North American anthropology, under the forceful leadership of Sherwood Washburn. The "new" physical anthropology Washburn developed at the University of California, Berkeley, repudiated racial classification and shifted attention to patterns

FIGURE I.2 Some biological anthropologists are primatologists, such as Jane Goodall (*a*). Other biological anthropologists are paleoanthropologists, such as Matthew Tornow, who studies ancient primate ancestors (*b*).

of variation and adaptation within the human species as a whole. This shift in emphasis led many of Washburn's followers to define their specialty as **biological anthropology**, a move that highlighted their differences with the older "physical anthropology" devoted to racial classification.

Some biological anthropologists work in the fields of **primatology** (the study of the closest living relatives of human beings, the nonhuman primates), **paleoanthropology** (the study of fossilized bones and teeth of our earliest ancestors), and human skeletal biology (measuring and comparing the shapes and sizes—or morphology—of bones and teeth using skeletal remains from different human populations)

> **biological anthropology (or physical anthropology)** The specialty of anthropology that looks at human beings as biological organisms and tries to discover what characteristics make them different from other organisms and what characteristics they share.
>
> **primatology** The study of nonhuman primates, the closest living relatives of human beings.
>
> **paleoanthropology** The search for fossilized remains of humanity's earliest ancestors.

(Figure 1.2). Newer specialties focus on human adaptability in different ecological settings, on human growth and development, or on the connections between a population's evolutionary history and its susceptibility to disease. Forensic anthropologists use their knowledge of human skeletal anatomy to aid law enforcement and human rights investigators. Molecular anthropologists trace chemical similarities and differences in the immune system, an interest that has led to active research on the virus that causes HIV/AIDS. Moreover, new analytic techniques, such as biostatistics, three-dimensional imaging, and electronic communication and publishing, have revolutionized the field. In all these ways, biological anthropologists can illuminate what makes human beings similar to and different from one another, other primates, and other forms of life (Boaz and Wolfe 1995; Weinker 1995).

Whether they study human biology, primates, or the fossils of our ancestors, biological anthropologists clearly share many methods and theories used in the natural sciences—primarily biology, ecology, chemistry, and geology. What tends to set biological anthropologists apart from their nonanthropological colleagues is the holistic, comparative, and evolutionary perspective that has been part of their anthropological training. That perspective reminds them always to consider their work as only part of the overall study of human nature, human society, and the human past.

▼ CULTURAL ANTHROPOLOGY

The second specialty within anthropology is **cultural anthropology**, which is sometimes called *sociocultural anthropology*, *social anthropology*, or *ethnology*. Once anthropologists realized that racial biology could not be used to explain why everyone in the world did not dress the same, speak the same language, pray to the same god, or eat insects for dinner, they knew that something else must be responsible for these differences. They suggested that this "something else" was culture. Because people everywhere use culture to adapt to and transform everything in the wider world in which they live, the field of cultural anthropology is vast.

Cultural anthropologists tend to specialize in one or another domain of human cultural activity (Figure 1.3). Some study the ways particular groups of human beings organize themselves to carry out collective tasks, whether economic, political, or spiritual. This focus within cultural anthropology bears the closest resemblance to the discipline of sociology, and from it has come the identification of anthropology as one of the social sciences.

Sociology and anthropology developed during the same period and share similar interests in social organization. What differentiated anthropology from sociology was the anthropological interest in comparing different forms of human social life. In the racist framework of nineteenth- and early-twentieth-century European and North American societies, some people viewed sociology as the study of "civilized" industrial societies and labeled anthropology as the study of all other societies, lumped together as "primitive." Today, by contrast, anthropologists are concerned with studying *all* human societies, and they reject the labels *civilized* and *primitive* for the same reason they reject the term *race*. Contemporary anthropologists do research in urban and rural settings around the world and among members of all societies, including their own.

FIGURE 1.3 Cultural anthropologist Robert Laughlin with members of the Sna Jtz'ibajom group puppet theater in San Cristóbal de las Casas, Mexico. Cultural anthropologists talk to many people, observe their actions, and participate as fully as possible in a group's way of life.

Anthropologists discovered that people in many non-Western societies do not organize bureaucracies or churches or schools, yet they still manage to carry out successfully the full range of human activity because they developed institutions of relatedness that enabled them to organize social groups through which they could live their lives. One form of relatedness, called *kinship*, links people to one another on the basis of birth, marriage, and nurturance. The study of kinship has become highly developed in anthropology and remains a focus of interest today. In addition, anthropologists have described a variety of forms of social groups organized according to different principles, such as secret societies, age sets, and numerous forms of complex political organization, including states. In recent years, cultural anthropologists have studied contemporary issues of gender and sexuality, transnational labor migration, urbanization, globalization, the post–Cold War resurgence of ethnicity and nationalism around the globe, and debates about human rights.

Cultural anthropologists have investigated the patterns of material life found in different human groups. Among the most striking are worldwide variations in clothing, housing, tools, and techniques for getting

cultural anthropology The specialty of anthropology that shows how variation in the beliefs and behaviors of members of different human groups is shaped by sets of learned behaviors and ideas that human beings acquire as members of society—that is, by culture.

food and making material goods. Some anthropologists specialize in the study of technologies in different societies or in the evolution of technology over time. Those interested in material life also describe the natural setting for which technologies have been developed and analyze the way technologies and environments shape each other. Others have investigated the way non-Western people have responded to the political and economic challenges of colonialism and the capitalist industrial technology that accompanied it.

People everywhere are increasingly making use of material goods and technologies produced outside their own societies. Anthropologists have been able to show that, contrary to many expectations, non-Western people do not slavishly imitate Western ways. Instead, they make use of Western technologies in ways that are creative and often unanticipated but that make sense in their own local cultural context. For example, some anthropologists are currently tracing the various ways in which populations both inside and outside the West make use of cybertechnology for their own social and cultural purposes.

As cultural anthropologists have become increasingly aware of the socio-cultural influences that stretch across space to affect local communities, they have also become sensitive to those that stretch over time. As a result, many contemporary cultural anthropologists make serious efforts to place their cultural analyses in detailed historical context. Cultural anthropologists who do comparative studies of language, music, dance, art, poetry, philosophy, religion, or ritual often share many of the interests of specialists in the disciplines of fine arts and humanities.

Cultural anthropologists, no matter what their area of specialization, ordinarily collect their data during an extended period of close involvement with

the people in whose language or way of life they are interested. This period of research, called **fieldwork**, has as its central feature the anthropologists' involvement in the everyday routine of those among whom they live. People who share information about their culture and language with anthropologists have traditionally been called **informants**; however, anthropologists use this term less today and some prefer to describe these individuals as *respondents*, *collaborators*, *teachers*, or simply as *"the people I work with"* because these terms emphasize a relationship of equality and reciprocity. Fieldworkers gain insight into another culture by participating with members in social activities and by observing those activities as outsiders. This research method, known as *participant-observation*, is central to cultural anthropology.

Cultural anthropologists write about what they have learned in scholarly articles or books and sometimes document the lives of the people they work with on film or video. An **ethnography** is a description of "the customary social behaviors of an identifiable group of people" (Wolcott 1999, 252–3); **ethnology** is the comparative study of two or more such groups. Thus, cultural anthropologists who write ethnographies are sometimes called *ethnographers*, and anthropologists who compare ethnographic information on many different cultural practices are sometimes called *ethnologists*. But not all anthropological writing is ethnographic. Some anthropologists specialize in reconstructing the history of our discipline, tracing, for example, how anthropologists' fieldwork practices have changed over time and how these changes may be related to wider political, economic, and social changes within the societies from which they came and within which they did their research.

▼ LINGUISTIC ANTHROPOLOGY

Perhaps the most striking cultural feature of our species is **language**: the system of arbitrary vocal symbols we use to encode our experience of the world and of one another. People use language to talk about all areas of their lives, from material to spiritual. **Linguistic anthropology** therefore studies language, not only as a form of symbolic communication, but also as a major carrier of important cultural information. Many early anthropologists were the first people to transcribe non-Western languages

fieldwork An extended period of close involvement with the people in whose language or way of life anthropologists are interested, during which anthropologists ordinarily collect most of their data.

informants People in a particular culture who work with anthropologists and provide them with insights about their way of life. Also called *respondents, teachers,* or *friends*.

ethnography An anthropologist's written or filmed description of a particular culture.

ethnology The comparative study of two or more cultures.

language The system of arbitrary vocal symbols used to encode one's experience of the world and of others.

linguistic anthropology The specialty of anthropology concerned with the study of human languages.

and to produce grammars and dictionaries of those languages (Figure 1.4). Contemporary linguistic anthropologists and their counterparts in sociology (called *sociolinguists*) study the way language differences correlate with differences in gender, race, class, or ethnic identity. Some have specialized in studying what happens when speakers are fluent in more than one language and must choose which language to use under what circumstances. Others have written about what happens when speakers of unrelated languages are forced to communicate with one another, producing languages called *pidgins*. Some linguistic anthropologists study sign languages. Others look at the ways children learn language or the styles and strategies followed by fluent speakers engaged in conversation. More recently, linguistic anthropologists have paid attention to the way political ideas in a society contribute to people's ideas of what may or may not be said and the strategies speakers devise to escape these forms of censorship. Some take part in policy discussions about literacy and language standardization and address the challenges faced by speakers of languages that are being displaced by international languages of commerce and technology such as English.

In all these cases, linguistic anthropologists try to understand language in relation to the broader cultural, historical, or biological contexts that make it possible. Because highly specialized training in linguistics as well as anthropology is required for people who

practice it, linguistic anthropology has long been recognized as a separate subfield of anthropology. Contemporary linguistic anthropologists continue to be trained in this way, and many cultural anthropologists also receive linguistics training as part of their professional preparation.

▼ ARCHAEOLOGY

Archaeology, another major specialty within anthropology, is a cultural anthropology of the human past involving the analysis of material remains. Through archaeology, anthropologists discover much about human history, particularly *prehistory*, the long stretch of time before the development of writing. Archaeologists look for evidence of past human cultural activity, such as postholes, garbage heaps, and settlement patterns. Depending on the locations and ages of sites they are digging, archaeologists may also have to be experts on stone-tool manufacture, metallurgy, or ancient pottery. Because archaeological excavations frequently uncover remains such as bones or plant pollen, archaeologists often work in teams with other scientists who specialize in the analysis of these remains.

Archaeologists' findings complement those of paleoanthropologists. For example, archaeological information about successive stone-tool traditions in a particular region may correlate with fossil evidence of prehistoric occupation of that region by ancient human populations. Archaeologists can use dating techniques to establish ages of *artifacts*, portable objects modified by human beings. They can create distribution maps of cultural artifacts that allow them to make hypotheses about the ages, territorial ranges, and patterns of sociocultural change in ancient societies. Tracing the spread of cultural inventions over time from one site to another allows them to hypothesize about the nature and degree of social contact between different peoples in the past. The human past that they investigate may be quite recent: Some contemporary archaeologists dig through layers of garbage deposited by human beings within the last two or three decades, often uncovering surprising information about contemporary consumption patterns.

FIGURE 1.4 Linguist Alan Rumsey listens to a warrior from highland New Guinea.

archaeology A cultural anthropology of the human past involving the analysis of material remains left behind by earlier societies.

FIGURE 1.5 Members of the Argentine Forensic Anthropologists Team work on the biggest dictatorship-era mass grave to date, where around 40 suspected victims of the 1976–1983 military junta were buried in a local cemetery in Cordoba, 800 km (500 miles) northwest of Buenos Aires.

▼ APPLIED ANTHROPOLOGY

Applied anthropology is the subfield of anthropology in which anthropologists use information gathered from the other anthropological specialties to propose solutions to practical problems (Figure 1.5). Some may use a particular culture's ideas about illness and health to introduce new public health practices in a way that makes sense to and will be accepted by followers of that culture. Other applied anthropologists may use knowledge of traditional social organization to ease the problems of refugees trying to settle in a new land. Still others may use their knowledge of traditional and Western methods of cultivation to help farmers increase their crop yields. Given the growing concern throughout the world with the effects of different technologies on the environment, this kind of applied anthropology holds promise as a way of bringing together Western knowledge and non-Western knowledge in order to create sustainable technologies that minimize pollution and environmental degradation. Some applied

---

applied anthropologists Specialists who use information gathered from the other anthropological specialties to solve practical cross-cultural problems.

---

anthropologists have become management consultants or carry out market research, and their findings may contribute to the design of new products.

In recent years, some anthropologists have become involved in policy issues, participating actively in social processes that attempt to shape the future of those among whom they work (Moore 2005, 3), and this has involved a transmutation in their understanding of what applied anthropology is. Les W. Field, for example, has addressed the history of applied anthropology on Native American reservations—"Indian Country"—in the United States. He observes that by the end of the twentieth century, a major transformation had occurred, "from applied anthropology in Indian Country to applications of anthropological tools in Indian country to accomplish tribal goals" (2004, 472). This often draws anthropologists into work in the legal arena, as when, for example, they have lent their expertise to arguments in favor of legislation mandating the repatriation of culturally significant artifacts and tribal lands in North America or to efforts by tribal groups to reclaim official government-recognized status (Field 2004), or to defending indigenous land rights in Latin America (Stocks 2005).

Although many anthropologists believe that applied work can be done within any of the traditional four fields of anthropology, increasing numbers in

FIGURE 1.6 Medical anthropologist Andrea Wiley is shown here in a high-altitude setting in the Himalayas of Ladakh (India), where she studied maternal and child health.

recent years have come to view applied anthropology as a separate field of professional specialization (see Figure 1.1). More and more universities in the United States have begun to develop courses and programs in a variety of forms of applied anthropology. Anthropologists who work for government agencies or nonprofit organizations or in other nonuniversity settings often describe what they do as the *anthropology of practice*. In the twenty-first century, it has been predicted that more than half of all new Ph.D.s in anthroplogy will become practicing anthropologists rather than take up positions as faculty in university departments of anthropology.

▼ MEDICAL ANTHROPOLOGY

Medical anthropology is one of the most rapidly growing branches of anthropology. Beginning half a century ago as a form of applied anthropology, it has developed into an important anthropological specialty that has offered new ways to link biological and cultural anthropology. Medical anthropology concerns itself with human health—the factors that contribute to disease or illness and the ways that human populations deal with disease or illness (Baer et al. 2003, 3). Medical anthropologists may consider

the physiological variables that are involved with human health and disease, the environmental features that affect human well-being, and the way the human body adapts to various environments. Contemporary medical anthropologists engage in work that directly addresses the anthropological proposition that human beings must be understood as biocultural organisms (Figure 1.6).

Particularly significant has been the development of *critical medical anthropology*, which links questions of human health and illness in local settings to social, economic, and political processes operating on a national or global scale. Indeed, critical medical anthropologists have been among the most vocal in pointing out how various forms of suffering and disease cannot be explained only by the presence of microbes in a diseased body, but may depend on—or be made worse by—the presence of social inequality and a lack of access to health care. According to anthropologist Merrill Singer, critical medical anthropology "is committed to the 'making social' and the 'making political' of health and medicine" (1998,

medical anthropology The specialty of anthropology that concerns itself with human health—the factors that contribute to disease or illness and the ways that human populations deal with disease or illness.

195). Thus, critical medical anthropologists pay attention to the way social divisions based on class, "race," gender, and ethnicity can block access to medical attention or make people more vulnerable to disease and suffering. They draw attention to the way traditional Western biomedicine "encourages people to fight disease rather than to make the changes necessary to prevent it," for example, by linking low birth weight in newborn babies to poor nutrition, but failing to note that poor nutrition "may be a major health factor among impoverished social classes and oppressed ethnic groups in developed countries despite an abundance of food in society generally" (Singer 1998, 106, 109).

One of the most important insights of critical medical anthropologists has been to point out that "various practices that bioculturalist anthropologists have traditionally called 'adaptations' might better be analyzed as social adjustments to the consequences of oppressive sociopolitical relationships" (M. Singer 1998, 115). Gavin Smith and R. Brooke Thomas, for example, draw attention to situations where "social relations compromise people's options" for attaining biological well-being and cultural satisfaction but where people do not passively accept this situation and choose instead to "try to escape or change these relations"; Smith and Thomas call these practices "adaptations of resistance" (G. Smith and Thomas 1998, 466). In later chapters we cite case studies by medical anthropologists that illustrate the complex and nuanced views they are able to bring to the explanation and treatment of human suffering.

▼ THE USES OF ANTHROPOLOGY

Why take a course in anthropology? An immediate answer might be that human fossils or broken bits of ancient pots or the customs of faraway peoples inspire a fascination that is its own reward. But the experience of being dazzled by seemingly exotic places and peoples carries with it a risk. As you become increasingly aware of the range of anthropological data, including the many options that exist for living a satisfying human life, you may find yourself wondering about the life you are living. Contact with the unfamiliar can be liberating, but it can also be threatening if it undermines your confidence in the absolute truth and universal rightness of your previous understanding of the way the world works.

The contemporary world is increasingly interconnected. As people from different cultural backgrounds come into contact with one another, learning to cope with cultural differences becomes crucial. Anthropologists experience both the rewards and the risks of getting to know how other people live, and their work has helped to dispel many harmful stereotypes that sometimes make cross-cultural contact dangerous or impossible. Studying anthropology may help prepare you for some of the shocks you will encounter in dealing with people who look different from you, speak a different language, or do not agree that the world works exactly the way you think it does.

Anthropology involves learning about the kinds of living organisms we human beings are, the various ways we live our lives, and how we make sense of our experiences. Studying anthropology can equip you to deal with people with different cultural backgrounds in a less threatened, more tolerant manner. You may never be called on to eat termite paste. Still, you may one day encounter a situation in which none of the old rules seem to apply. As you struggle to make sense of what is happening, what you learned in anthropology class may help you relax and dare to try something totally new to you. If you do so, perhaps you too will discover the rewards of an encounter with the unfamiliar that is at the same time unaccountably familiar. We hope you will savor the experience.

CHAPTER SUMMARY

I. Anthropology aims to describe in the broadest sense what it means to be human. The anthropological perspective is holistic, comparative, and evolutionary and has relied on the concept of culture to explain the diversity of human ways of life. Human beings depend on cultural learning for successful biological survival and reproduction, which is why anthropologists consider human beings to be biocultural organisms. Anthropology is also a field-based discipline. In the United States today, anthropology is considered to have five major subfields: biological anthropology, archaeology, cultural anthropology, linguistic anthropology, and applied anthropology.

2. Biological anthropology began as an attempt to classify all the world's populations into different races. By the early twentieth century, however, most anthropologists had rejected racial classifications as scientifically unjustifiable and objected to the ways in which racial classifications were used to justify the social practice of racism. Contemporary anthropologists who are interested in human biology include biological anthropologists, primatologists, and paleoanthropologists.

3. Cultural anthropologists study cultural diversity in all living human societies, including their own. Linguistic anthropologists approach cultural diversity by relating varied forms of language to their cultural contexts. Both gather information through fieldwork, by participating with their informants in social activities, and by observing those activities as outsiders. They publish accounts of their research in ethnographies. Archaeology is a cultural anthropology of the human past, with interests ranging from the earliest stone tools to twenty-first-century garbage dumps. Applied anthropologists use information from the other anthropological specialities to solve practical cross-cultural problems. Medical anthropology overlaps biological anthropology, cultural anthropology, and applied anthropology and concerns itself with human health and illness, suffering, and well-being.

KEY TERMS

anthropology	biological anthropology (or physical anthropology)	ethnology
holism		language
comparison	primatology	linguistic anthropology
evolution	paleoanthropology	archaeology
culture	cultural anthropology	applied anthropology
biocultural organisms	fieldwork	medical anthropology
races	informants	
racism	ethnography	

SUGGESTED READINGS

Ashmore, Wendy, and Robert J. Sharer. 2000. *Discovering our past: A brief introduction to archaeology*, 3d ed. Mountain View, CA: Mayfield. *An engaging introduction to the techniques, assumptions, interests, and findings of modern archaeology.*

Besteman, Catherine, and Hugh Gusterson (eds). 2005. *Why America's top pundits are wrong: Anthropologists talk back.* Berkeley: University of California Press. *According to the editors, "pundits" are media personalities—conservative and liberal—who lack authoritative knowledge on important issues but whose confident, authoritative, and entertaining pronouncements attract large audiences, especially when they defend simplified views of issues that reinforce rather than challenge popular prejudices. Twelve anthropologists offer critical assessments of the writings of pundits Samuel Huntington, Robert Kaplan, Thomas Friedman, and Dinesh D'Sousa and also explore questionable popular accounts of the origins of racial inequality and sexual violence.*

Feder, Kenneth L. 1999. *Frauds, myths and mysteries: Science and pseudoscience in archaeology*, 3d ed. Mountain View, CA: Mayfield. *An entertaining and informative exploration of fascinating frauds and genuine archaeological mysteries that also explains the scientific method.*

Kidder, Tracy. 2004. *Mountains beyond mountains: The quest of Dr. Paul Farmer, a man who would cure the world.* New York, Random House. *Kidder follows Dr. Farmer, an anthropologist and physician, relating his efforts to enlist powerful funders, the World Health Organization, and ordinary people in neglected communities in a quest to bring the best modern medicine to those who need it most.*

Relethford, John. 2004. *The human species: An introduction to biological anthropology*, 6th ed. New York: McGraw-Hill. *An excellent, clear introduction to biological anthropology.*

Chapter 2

Culture and the Human Condition

This chapter examines in greater detail the concept of culture, one of the most influential ideas that anthropologists have developed. We survey different ways that anthropologists have used the culture concept to expose the fallacies of biological determinism. We also discuss the reasons why some anthropologists believe that continuing to use the culture concept today may be a problem.

Anthropologists have long argued that the human condition is distinguished from the condition of other living species by *culture*. Other living species learn, but the extent to which human beings depend on learning is unique in the animal kingdom. Because our brains are capable of open symbolic thought and our hands are capable of manipulating matter powerfully or delicately, we interact with the wider world in a way that is distinct from that of any other species. Before we explore more closely the ways anthropologists study living societies, however, it is worth reviewing the anthropological understanding of culture in more detail.

▼ HOW DO ANTHROPOLOGISTS DEFINE CULTURE?

In chapter 1, we defined **culture** as patterns of learned behavior and ideas acquired by people as members of society. Culture is not reinvented by each generation; rather, we learn it from other members of the social groups we belong to, although we may later modify this heritage in some way. Therefore, culture is *shared* as well as *learned*. Many things we learn, such as table manners and what is good to eat and where people are supposed to sleep, are never explicitly taught but rather are absorbed in the course of daily practical living. This kind of cultural learning is sometimes called *habitus*. The cultural practices shared within social groups always encompass the varied knowledge and skills of many different individuals. For example, space flight is part of North American culture, and yet no individual North American could build a space shuttle from scratch.

Human cultures also appear *patterned*; that is, related cultural beliefs and practices show up repeatedly in different areas of social life. For example, in North America individualism is highly valued, and its influence can be seen in child-rearing practices (babies are expected to sleep alone, and children are reared with the expectation that they will be independent at the age of 18), economic practices (individuals are urged to get a job, to save their money, and not

---

culture Sets of learned behaviors and ideas that humans acquire as members of society. Humans use culture to adapt to and transform the world in which they live.

---

to count on other people or institutions to take care of them; many people would prefer to be in business for themselves; far more people commute to work by themselves in their own cars than carpool), and religious practices (the Christian emphasis on personal salvation and individual accountability before God). Cultural patterns can be traced through time: That English and Spanish are widely spoken in North America, whereas Fulfulde (a language spoken in West Africa) is not, is connected to the colonial conquest and domination of North America by speakers of English and Spanish in past centuries. Cultural patterns also vary across space: In the United States, for example, the English of New York City differs from the English of Mississippi in style, rhythm, and vocabulary ("What? You expect me to schlep this around all day? Forget about it!" is more likely to be heard in the former than the latter!).

It is this patterned cultural variation that allows anthropologists (and others) to distinguish different "cultural traditions" from one another. But separate cultural traditions are often hard to delineate. That is because, in addition to any unique elements of their own, all contain contradictory elements, and they also share elements with other traditions. First, customs in one domain of culture may contradict customs in another domain, as when religion tells us to share with others and economics tells us to look out for ourselves alone. Second, people have always borrowed cultural elements from their neighbors, and many increasingly refuse to be limited in the present by cultural practices of the past. Why, for example, should literacy not be seen as part of Ju/'hoansi culture once the children of illiterate Ju/'hoansi foragers learn to read and write (see EthnoProfile 11.2: Ju/'hoansi). Thus, cultural patterns can be useful as a kind of shorthand, but it is important to remember that the boundaries between cultural traditions are always fuzzy. Ultimately, they rest on someone's judgment about how different one set of customs is from another set of customs. As we will see shortly, these kinds of contradictions and challenges are not uncommon, leading some anthropologists to think of culture not in terms of specific customs but in terms of rules that become "established ways of bringing ideas from different domains together" (Strathern 1992, 3).

Culture is learned, shared, and patterned, and cultural traditions are reconstructed and enriched,

IN THEIR OWN WORDS

The Paradox of Ethnocentrism

Ethnocentrism is usually described in thoroughly negative terms. As Ivan Karp points out, however, ethnocentrism is a more complex phenomenon than we might expect.

Anthropologists usually argue that ethnocentrism is both wrong and harmful, especially when it is tied to racial, cultural, and social prejudices. Ideas and feelings about the inferiority of blacks, the cupidity of Jews, or the lack of cultural sophistication of farmers are surely to be condemned. But can we do without ethnocentrism? If we stopped to examine every custom and practice in our cultural repertoire, how would we get on? For example, if we always regarded marriage as something that can vary from society to society, would we be concerned about filling out the proper marriage documents, or would we even get married at all? Most of the time we suspend a quizzical stance toward our own customs and simply live life.

Yet many of our own practices are peculiar when viewed through the lenses of other cultures. Periodically, for over fifteen years, I have worked with and lived among an African people. They are as amazed at our marriage customs as my students are at theirs. Both American students and the Iteso of Kenya find it difficult to imagine how the other culture survives with the bizarre, exotic practices that are part of their respective marriage customs.

Ethnocentrism works both ways. It can be practiced as much by other cultures as by our own.

Paradoxically, ethnographic literature combats ethnocentrism by showing that the practices of cultures (including our own) are "natural" in their own setting. What appears natural in one setting appears so because it was constructed in that setting—made and produced by human beings who could have done it some other way. Ethnography is a means of recording the range of human creativity and of demonstrating how universally shared capacities can produce cultural and social differences.

This anthropological way of looking at other cultures—and, by implication, at ourselves—constitutes a major reason for reading ethnography. The anthropological lens teaches us to question what we assume to be unquestionable. Ethnography teaches us that human potentiality provides alternative means of organizing our lives and alternative modes of experiencing the world. Reading ethnographies trains us to question the received wisdom of our society and makes us receptive to change. In this sense, anthropology might be called the subversive science. We read ethnographies in order to learn about how other peoples produce their world and about how we might change our own patterns of production.

Source: Karp 1990, 74–75.

---

generation after generation, primarily because human biological survival depends on culture. Thus, culture is also *adaptive*. Human newborns are not born with "instincts" that would equip them to survive on their own. On the contrary, they depend utterly on support and nurturance from adults and other members of the group in which they live. It is by learning the cultural practices of those around them that human beings come to master appropriate ways of thinking and acting that promote their own survival as biological organisms (Figure 2.1). Culture allows us both to adapt to and to transform the environments in which we live.

Finally, culture is *symbolic*. A **symbol** is something that stands for something else. The letters of an alphabet, for example, symbolize the sounds of a spoken language. There is no necessary connection between the shape of a particular letter and the speech sound it represents. Indeed, the same or similar sounds are represented symbolically by very different letters in the Latin, Cyrillic, Hebrew, Arabic, and Greek alphabets, to name but five. Even the sounds

symbol Something that stands for something else.

FIGURE 2.1 Of all living organisms, humans are the most dependent on learning for their survival. From a young age, girls in northern Cameroon learn to carry heavy loads on their heads and also learn to get water for their families.

of spoken language are symbols for meanings a speaker tries to express. The fact that we can translate from one language to another suggests that the same or similar meanings can be expressed by different symbols in different languages. But language is not the only domain of culture that depends on symbols. Everything we do in society has a symbolic dimension, from how we conduct ourselves at the dinner table to how we bury the dead. It is our heavy dependence on symbolic learning that sets human culture apart from the apparently nonsymbolic learning on which other species rely.

Human culture, then, is *learned*, *shared*, *patterned*, *adaptive*, and *symbolic*. And the contemporary human capacity for culture has also evolved, over millions of years. Culture's beginnings can perhaps be glimpsed among Japanese macaque monkeys who invented the custom of washing sweet potatoes and among wild chimpanzees who invented different grooming postures or techniques to crack open nuts or to gain access to termites or water (Boesch-Ackerman and Boesch 1994; Wolfe 1995, 162–63). Our apelike ancestors surely shared similar aptitudes when they started walking on two legs some 6 million years ago. By 2.5 million years ago, their descendants were making stone tools. Thereafter, our hominid lineage

gave birth to a number of additional species, all of whom depended on culture more than their ancestors had. By the time *Homo sapiens* appeared some 200,000 years ago, a heavy dependence on culture had long been a part of our evolutionary heritage.

Thus, as Rick Potts puts it, "an evolutionary bridge exists between the human and animal realms of behavior. . . . Culture represents continuity" (1996, 197). Potts urges us to think of the modern human capacity for culture not as a uniform monolith but rather as a structure whose various pieces were added at different times in our evolutionary past (Figure 2.2). Potts identifies five elements that seem to be prerequisites for human symbolic culture: (1) *transmission*, copying behavior by observation or instruction; (2) *memory*, because traditions cannot develop unless the new behavior is remembered; (3) *reiteration*, the ability to reproduce or imitate behavior or information that has been learned; (4) *innovation*, the ability to invent new behaviors; and (5) *selection*, the ability to select which innovations to keep and which to discard. Monkeys and apes possess many of these elements to varying degrees, which is why they can be said to possess simple

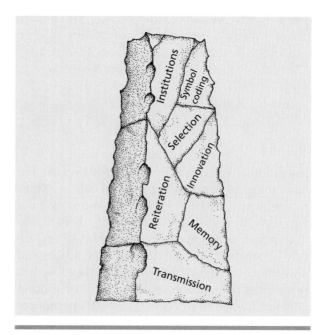

FIGURE 2.2 The modern human capacity for culture did not appear all at once; rather, the various pieces that make it up were added at different times in our evolutionary past.

cultural traditions. Certainly our earliest hominid ancestors were no different.

Apes apparently also possess a rudimentary capacity for *symbolic coding*, or symbolic representation, something our ancestors undoubtedly possessed as well. But new species can evolve new capacities not found in their ancestors. This occurred in the human past when our ancestors first developed a capacity for *complex symbolic representation*, including the ability to communicate freely about the past, the future, and the invisible. This ability distinguishes human symbolic language, for example, from the vocal communication systems of apes (see chapter 5). Biological anthropologist Terrence Deacon argues that evolution produced in *Homo sapiens* a brain "that has been significantly overbuilt for learning symbolic associations" such that "we cannot help but see the world in symbolic categories" (1997, 413, 416). Moreover, the enormous adaptive value of complex symbolic representation for our ancestors appears to have created a new set of selective pressures that favored genetic changes that improved our brain's symbolic capacities. Put another way, culture and the human brain *coevolved*, each furnishing key features of the environment to which the other needed to adapt (Deacon 1997, 44; Odling-Smee 1994). We have used our complex symbolic abilities, moreover, to create *institutions*—complex, variable and enduring forms of cultural practice that organize social life, also unique to our species. As a result, for *Homo sapiens*, culture has become "the predominant manner in which human groups vary from one another . . . it *swamps* the biological differences among populations" (Marks 1995, 200). We are truly biocultural organisms.

▼ WHAT IS THE PLACE OF CULTURE IN EXPLANATIONS OF THE HUMAN CONDITION?

Dualism, Idealism, and Materialism

What is the world like? And what is the human condition within the world? Indeed, does it make sense to speak of a *single* "condition" shared by all human beings? Not just anthropologists but members of all societies pose questions like these. And all societies develop their own answers. If asked what they believe about human nature, for example, many North Amer-

icans would answer that human nature has two parts: sometimes called *mind* and *matter*, *soul* and *body*, or *spirit* and *flesh*. The belief that human nature, or reality as a whole, is made up of two radically different forces is called **dualism**. Dualistic thinking is deeply rooted in Western thought; for millennia, people have debated the importance of each half of our nature. Perhaps the oldest attempt to resolve this debate can be traced to the ancient Greek philosopher Plato.

Plato divided all reality into mind and matter: Mind is higher and finer and belongs to the celestial realm of ideal forms; matter is lower and cruder and corruptible, belonging to the earthly realm. Human nature is dualistic because each person is made up of an earthly material body inhabited by a mind whose true home is the realm of ideal forms. According to Plato, the drama of human existence consists of the internal struggle between the body, drawn naturally to base, corruptible matter, and the mind or soul, drawn naturally to pure, unchanging forms. Christian theology later incorporated the view that each human being consists of a soul that seeks God and a physical body that is tempted by the material world. This view of earthly life as a struggle between flesh and spirit is sometimes called *conflict dualism*.

Dualistic accounts of human nature do not satisfy everyone, however. Many Western thinkers have tried to show that only one of the two phenomena recognized in dualistic accounts is actually responsible for making us what we are. For example, Platonic and Christian theories of human nature emphasize that, although human beings are equipped with material bodies, their true nature is spiritual, not material; the body is a material impediment that frustrates the full development of the mind or spirit. This view is known as **idealism**. However, it is equally possible to make the contrary argument: that matter—the material activities of our physical bodies in the material world—makes human beings what they are. From this perspective, human existence becomes the struggle to exercise our physicality as fully as we can; to put spiritual values above bodily needs

---

dualism The philosophical view that reality consists of two equal and irreducible forces.

idealism The philosophical view (dating back at least as far as Plato in Western thought) that ideas—or the mind that produces such ideas—constitute the essence of human nature.

Culture and Freedom

Finding a way to fit human agency into a scientific account of culture has never been easy. Hoyt Alverson describes some of the issues involved.

One's assumptions concerning the existence of structure in culture, or the existence of freedom in human action, determine whether one believes that there can be a science of culture or not. Note that the possibility of developing a science of culture has nothing to do with the use of mathematics, the precision of one's assertions, or the elegance of one's models. If a phenomenon actually has structure, then a science of that phenomenon is at least conceivable. If a phenomenon exhibits freedom and is not ordered, then a science of that phenomenon is inconceivable. The human sciences, including anthropology, have been debating the issue of structure versus freedom in human cultural behavior for the past two hundred years, and no resolution or even consensus has emerged.

Some persuasive models of culture, and of particular cultures, have been proposed, both by those working with scientific, universalist assumptions, and by those working with phenomenological, relativistic assumptions.

To decide which of these approaches is to be preferred, we must have a specific set of criteria for evaluation. Faced with good evidence for the existence of both structure and freedom in human culture, no coherent set of criteria for comparing the success of these alternative models is conceivable. The prediction of future action, for example, is a good criterion for measuring the success of a model that purports to represent structure: it must be irrelevant to measuring the success or failure of a model that purports to describe freedom. For the foreseeable future, and maybe for the rest of time, we may have to be content with models that simply permit us to muddle through.

Source: Alverson 1990, 42–43.

would "go against human nature." People would not seek spiritual salvation, it is sometimes argued, if their material needs were satisfied. This view is known as **materialism**.

Thus, both idealism and materialism attempt to explain human nature by attributing it to a single causal force. That is, idealists claim that human nature is *nothing but* mind, or nothing but spirit; materialists claim that human nature is *nothing but* genes or anatomy or biology. Put another way, idealism and materialism are both forms of **determininism**: Idealists claim that human nature is *determined by* the causal force of mind or spirit; materialists argue that human nature is *determined by* the causal force of physical matter.

---

materialism The philosophical view that the material activities of our physical bodies in the material world constitute the essence of human nature.

determinism The philosophical view that one simple force (or a few simple forces) causes (or determines) complex events.

▼ CULTURE, HISTORY, AND HUMAN AGENCY

The human condition is rooted in time and shaped by history. As part of the human condition, culture is also historical, being worked out and reconstructed in every generation. At the same time, anthropologists have differed in their approach to human history. Nineteenth-century thinkers such as Herbert Spencer argued that the evolution of social structures over time from simple to complex was central to the study of the human condition. Other anthropologists, sensitive to the excesses of people like Spencer, were not interested in change over time. Still other anthropologists had no interest in history for a different reason. Western capitalist culture, with its eye on the future and its faith in progress, has had little use for the past. It is therefore no wonder that some anthropologists built clockwork models of social structures that could be trusted to run reliably without "losing time." In these models, human beings and societies are both likened to machines. If a living organism is used as the model of society and if organisms are nothing but machines, then a machine model of society, with individuals as robotlike moving parts, is not at all far-fetched. A holistic and dialectical approach to human history, however, rejects these clockwork models. Culture is part of our biological heritage. Our biocultural heritage has produced a living species that uses culture to surmount biological and individual limitations and is even capable of studying itself and its own biocultural evolution.

This realization, however, raises another question: Just how free from limitations are humans? Opinion in Western societies often polarizes around one of two extremes: Either we have *free will* and may do just as we please, or our behavior is completely determined by forces beyond our control. Many social scientists, however, are convinced that a more realistic description of human freedom was offered by Karl Marx, who wrote, "Men make their own history, but they do not make it just as they please; they do not make it under circumstances chosen by themselves, but under circumstances directly encountered, given and transmitted by the past" (1963, 15). That is, people regularly struggle, often against great odds, to exercise some control over their lives. Human beings active in this way are called *agents* (Figure 2.3). Human agents cannot escape from the cultural and historical context within which they act. However, they must frequently select a course of action when the "correct" choice is unclear and the outcome uncertain. Some anthropologists even liken human existence to a mine field that we must painstakingly try to cross without blowing ourselves up. It is in such contexts, with their ragged edges, that human beings exercise their **human agency** by making interpretations, formulating goals, and setting out in pursuit of them.

▼ WHAT DOES IT MEAN TO BE HUMAN?

Deterministic accounts of human nature—whether idealist or materialist—aim to strip away attributes of the thing we are examining that seem extraneous or unnecessary, in order to reveal an unchanging core of fea-

FIGURE 2.3 People regularly struggle, often against great odds, to exercise some control over their lives. During the "Dirty War" in Argentina in the 1970s and early 1980s, women whose children had been disappeared by secret right-wing death squads began, at great personal risk, to stand every Thursday in the Plaza de Mayo, the central square of Buenos Aires, with photographs of their missing children. Called the Mothers of Plaza de Mayo, they continue their weekly vigil today. They were a powerful rebuke to the dictatorship and to subsequent governments that were not forthcoming about providing information about the disappeared.

tures, or **essence**, that is unique to things of the same kind (whether those are chairs, cows, ideas, or people) and that makes them what they are. Many debates in Western philosophy and anthropology about human nature have assumed that our species has an essence but have disagreed about just what that essence is. In this respect, idealism, materialism, and dualism can be understood as attempts by Western thinkers to pinpoint the essence of *what it means to be human*.

But other thinkers have argued that human beings come into the world with *no fixed essence*. For them, our sense of what it means to be human is the outcome of experiences we undergo over the course of our lives, as we are shaped by various forces we encounter along the way. Frequently, however, thinkers disagree about just what those outside forces might be, how many there are, and which of them is the most powerful. For

human agency The exercise of at least some control over their lives by human beings.

essence An unchanging core of features that is unique to things of the same kind and that makes them what they are.

example, some nineteenth-century thinkers argued that the most powerful material forces that shape human nature were to be found outside our bodies in the surrounding *natural environment*. Rich soil, a temperate climate, too little rainfall, and the absence of domesticable animals are examples of the environmental factors understood to shape the societies we lived in and, ultimately, our sense of who we were. The followers of Karl Marx, by contrast, argued that forces shaping human beings' self-understanding were rooted in social relations shaped by the mode of economic production that sustained their society. Because different groups, or *classes*, played different roles in that production process, members of each group would develop different senses of what human life was all about.

An extreme idealist reaction against such materialist thinking, influential in cultural anthropology, has argued that human beings have no fixed essence when they come into the world but that they become different kinds of human beings as a result of the particular ideas, meanings, beliefs, and values they absorb as members of particular societies. Optimistic versions of this view place no limits on the abilities of human beings to be or do whatever they want. Pessimistic versions, however, rule this out: "You are what you learn" becomes "You are what you are conditioned to be," something over which you have no control.

A recurring difficulty with all these views, in fact, has been the way in which the apparently optimistic "liberating" assumption that "frees" our species from the burden of being born with a fixed essence regularly turns into a pessimistic account in which the burden returns. Even when human beings are assumed to begin with no fixed essence, they are regularly portrayed as passive, pliable creatures wholly molded by the forces of either nature, society, history, culture, or something else.

Holistic Explanations

Materialists and idealists have battled with one another for centuries, in an obsessive and apparently irresolvable search for an inner essence of human nature, and

---

holism Perspective on the human condition that assumes that mind and body, individuals and society, and individuals and the environment interpenetrate and even define one another.

the end results seem rigid and one-dimensional. Many anthropologists have long argued that there is yet another point of view on the human condition that is less distorting than dualism, less simplistic than materialism or idealism, and that does not reduce human beings to passive lumps of clay totally molded by totalitarian forces completely beyond their control. The anthropological point of view called *holism* assumes that no sharp boundaries separate mind from body, body from environment, individual from society, my ideas from our ideas, or their traditions from our traditions (Figure 2.4). Rather, holism assumes that mind and body, body and environment, and so on, interpenetrate each other and even define each other. From a holistic perspective, attempts to divide reality into mind and matter at most isolate and pin down certain aspects of a process that, by its very nature, resists isolation and dissection. Anthropologists who have struggled to develop this holistic perspective on the human condition have made a contribution of unique and lasting value. Holism holds great appeal for those who seek a theory of human nature that is rich enough to do justice to its complex subject matter.

One traditional way of defining **holism** is to say that the whole (for example, a human being, a society, a cultural tradition) is greater than the sum of its parts. Individual human organisms are not just x percent genes and y percent culture added together. Rather, human beings are what they are because the mutual shaping of genes and culture and experience living in the world produces something new, something that cannot be reduced to the materials used to construct it. That new something—a symbol-making human organism—is, to be sure, closed off from the wider world in some ways by the material configurations that bind our cells, tissues, and organs into a single body. At the same time, like all living organisms, human beings are open to the world in other ways: they absorb energy and matter from the environment, excrete waste products, and learn from experience (see Deacon 2003, 296–97). Similarly, a society is not just the sum of the behaviors of its individual members, and a cultural tradition is not just a list of beliefs, values, and practices. Cultural traditions are identified by patterned configurations of beliefs, values, and practices that have accumulated over time and been passed on

Human-Rights Law and the Demonization of Culture

Sally Engle Merry is professor of anthropology at Wellesley College.

Why is the idea of cultural relativism anathema to many human-rights activists? Is it related to the way international human-rights lawyers and journalists think about culture? Does this affect how they think about anthropology? I think one explanation for the tension between anthropology and human-rights activists is the very different conceptions of culture that these two groups hold. An incident demonstrated this for me vividly a few months ago. I received a phone call from a prominent radio show asking if I would be willing to talk about the recent incident in Pakistan that resulted in the gang rape of a young woman, an assault apparently authorized by a local tribal council. Since I am working on human rights and violence against women, I was happy to explain my position that this was an inexcusable act, that many Pakistani feminists condemned the rape, but that it was probably connected to local political struggles and class differences. It should not be seen as an expression of Pakistani "culture." In fact, it was the local Islamic religious leader who first made the incident known to the world, according to news stories I had read.

The interviewer was distressed. She wanted me to defend the value of respecting Pakistani culture at all costs, despite the tribal council's imposition of a sentence of rape. When I told her that I could not do that, she wanted to know if I knew of any other anthropologists who would. I could think of none, but I began to wonder what she thought about anthropologists.

Anthropologists, apparently, made no moral judgments about "cultures" and failed to recognize the contestation and changes taking place within contemporary local communities around the world. This also led me to wonder how she imagined anthropologists thought about culture. She seemed to assume that anthropologists viewed culture as a coherent, static, and unchanging set of values.

Apparently cultures have no contact with the expansion of capitalism, the arming of various groups by transnational superpowers using them for proxy wars, or the cultural possibilities of human rights as an emancipatory discourse. I found this interviewer's view of culture wrongheaded and her opinion of anthropology discouraging. But perhaps it was just one journalist, I thought.

However, the recent article "From Skepticism to Embrace: Human Rights and the American Anthropological Association" by Karen Engle in *Human Rights Quarterly* (23: 536–60) paints another odd portrait of anthropology and its understanding of culture. In this piece, a law professor talks about the continuing "embarrassment" of anthropologists about the 1947 statement of the AAA Executive Board, which raised concerns about the Universal Declaration of Human Rights. Engle claims that the statement has caused the AAA "great shame" over the last fifty years (p. 542). Anthropologists are embarrassed, she argues, because the statement asserted tolerance without limits. While many anthropologists now embrace human rights, they do so primarily in terms of the protection of culture (citing 1999 AAA Statement on Human Rights at www.aaanet.org). Tensions over how to be a cultural relativist and still make overt political judgments that the 1947 Board confronted remain. She does acknowledge that not all anthropologists think about culture this way. But relativism, as she describes it, is primarily about tolerance for difference and is incompatible with making moral judgments about other societies.

But this incompatibility depends on how one theorizes culture. If culture is homogenous, integrated and consensual, it must be accepted as a whole. But anthropology has developed a far more complex way of understanding culture over the last two decades, focusing on its historical production, its porosity to outside influences and pressures, and its incorporation of competing repertoires of meaning and action. Were this conception more widely

(continued on next page)

Human-Rights Law and the Demonization of Culture *(continued)*

recognized within popular culture as well as among journalists and human-rights activitists, it could shift the terms of the intractable debate between universalism and relativism. Instead, culture is increasingly understood as a barrier to the realization of human rights by activists and a tool for legitimating noncompliance with human rights by conservatives.

One manifestation of the understanding of culture prevalent in human-rights law is the concept of harmful traditional practices. Originally developed to describe female genital mutilation or cutting, this term describes practices that have some cultural legitimacy yet are designated harmful to women, particularly to their health. In 1990, the committee monitoring the Convention on the Elimination of All Forms of Discrimination Against Women (CEDAW), an international convention ratified by most of the nations of the world, said that they were gravely concerned "that there are continuing cultural, traditional and economic pressures which help to perpetuate harmful practices, such as female circumcision," and adopted General Recommendation 14, which suggested that state parties should take measures to eradicate the practice of female circumcision. Culture equals tradition and is juxtaposed to women's human rights to equality. It is not surprising, given this evolving understanding of culture within human-rights discourse, that cultural relativism is seen in such a negative light. The tendency for national elites to defend practices oppressive to women in the name of culture exacerbates this negative view of culture.

Human-rights activists and journalists have misinterpreted anthropology's position about relativism and difference because they misunderstand anthropology's position about culture. Claims to cultural relativism appear to be defenses of holistic and static entities. This conception of culture comes from older anthropological usages, such as the separation of values and social action advocated in the 1950s by Talcott Parsons. Since "culture" was defined only as values, it was considered inappropriate to judge one ethical system by another one. For Melville Herskovits,

the leader of the AAA's relativist criticism of the Universal Declaration of Human Rights in 1947, cultural relativism meant protecting the holistic cultures of small communities from colonial intrusion (AAA 1947 Statement, AA 49: 539–43).

If culture is understood this way, it is not surprising that cultural relativism appears to be a retrograde position to human-rights lawyers. Nor is it puzzling that they find anthropology irrelevant. As human-rights law demonizes culture, it misunderstands anthropology as well. The holistic conception of culture provides no space for change, contestation or the analysis of the links between power, practices and values. Instead, it becomes a barrier to the reformist project of universal human rights. From the legal perspective on human rights, it is the texts, the documents and compliance that matter. Universalism is essential while relativism is bad. There is a sense of moral certainty which taking account of culture disrupts. This means, however, that the moral principle of tolerance for difference is lost.

When corporate executives in the U.S. steal millions of dollars through accounting fraud, we do not criticize American culture as a whole. We recognize that these actions come from the greed of a few along with sloppy institutional arrangements that allow them to get away with it. Similarly, the actions of a single tribal council in Pakistan should not indict the entire culture, as if it were a homogeneous entity. Although Pakistan and many of its communities have practices and laws that subordinate women, these are neither homogeneous nor ancient. Pakistan as a "culture" can be indicted by this particular council's encouragement to rape only if culture is understood as a homogenous entity whose rules evoke universal compliance. Adopting a more sophisticated and dynamic understanding of culture not only promotes human-rights activism, but also relocates anthropological theorizing to the center of these issues rather than to the margins, where it has been banished.

Source: Merry 2003.

FIGURE 2.4 Perspectives on the human condition.

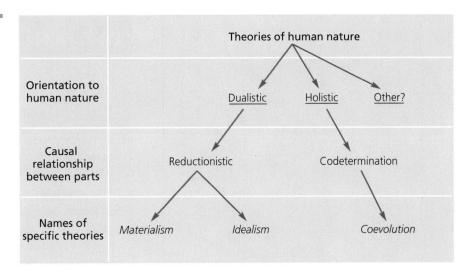

to others. Moreover, all societies and cultural traditions are vulnerable to outside influences.

Human beings who develop and live together in groups shaped by cultural patterns are so deeply affected by shared cultural experiences that they become different from what they would have been had they matured in isolation; they also become different from other people who have developed in the context of different social and cultural patterns. Social scientists have long known that human beings who grow up isolated from meaningful social interactions with others do not behave in ways that appear recognizably human. As anthropologist Clifford Geertz observed long ago, such human beings would be neither failed apes nor "natural" people stripped of their veneer of culture; they would be "mental basket cases" (1973, 40). Social living and cultural sharing are necessary for individual human beings to develop what we recognize as a *human* nature.

One useful way of thinking about the relationships among the parts that make up a whole is in terms of **coevolution**. A coevolutionary approach to the human condition emphasizes that human organisms, their physical environments, and their symbolic practices *codetermine* one another; with the passage of time, they can also *coevolve* alongside one another. A coevolutionary view of the human condition also sees human beings as organisms whose bodies, brains, actions, and thoughts are equally involved in shaping what they become. Coevolution produces a human nature embedded in a wider world and pro-

foundly shaped by culture. Embeddedness in the world makes us vulnerable over the courses of our lives to influences that our ancestors never experienced. The open, symbolic, meaning-making properties of human culture make it possible for us to respond to those influences in ways that our ancestors could not have anticipated.

▼ WHY DO CULTURAL DIFFERENCES MATTER?

The same objects, actions, or events frequently mean different things to people with different cultures. In fact, what counts as an object or event in one tradition may not be recognized as such in another. This powerful lesson of anthropology was illustrated by the experience of some Peace Corps volunteers working in southern Africa.

In the early 1970s, the Peace Corps office in Botswana was concerned by the number of volunteers who seemed to be "burned out," failing in their assignments, leaving the assigned villages, and increasingly hostile to their Tswana hosts. (See Figure 2.5 and EthnoProfile 2.1: Tswana.) The Peace Corps asked American anthropologist Hoyt Alverson, who

coevolution The dialectical relationship between biological processes and symbolic cultural processes, in which each makes up an important part of the environment to which the other must adapt.

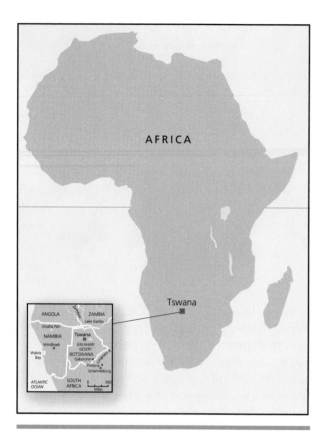

EthnoProfile 2.1

Tswana

Region: Southern Africa

Nation: Botswana

Population: 1,200,000 (also 1,500,000 in South Africa)

Environment: Savanna to desert

Livelihood: Cattle raising, farming

Political organization: Traditionally, chiefs and headmen; today, part of a modern nation-state

For more information: Comaroff, Jean. 1985. *Body of power, spirit of resistance: The culture history of a South African people.* Chicago: University of Chicago Press.

FIGURE 2.5 Location of Tswana. For more information, see EthnoProfile 2.1.

was familiar with Tswana culture and society, for advice. Alverson (1977) discovered that one major problem the Peace Corps volunteers were having involved exactly this issue of similar actions having very different meanings. The volunteers complained that the Tswana would never leave them alone. Whenever they tried to get away and sit by themselves for a few minutes to have some private time, one or more Tswana would quickly join them. This made the Americans angry. From their perspective, everyone is entitled to a certain amount of privacy and time alone. To the Tswana, however, human life is social life; the only people who want to be alone are witches and the insane. Because these young Americans did not seem to be either, the Tswana who saw them sitting alone naturally assumed that there

had been a breakdown in hospitality and that the volunteers would welcome some company. Here, one behavior—a person walking out into a field and sitting by himself or herself—had two very different meanings (Figure 2.6).

Human experience turns out to be inherently ambiguous. Even within a single cultural tradition, the meaning of an object or an action may differ, depending on the context. Quoting philosopher Gilbert Ryle, anthropologist Clifford Geertz (1973, 6) noted that there is a world of difference between a wink and a blink, as anyone who has ever mistaken one for the other has undoubtedly learned. To resolve the ambiguity, experience must be interpreted, and human beings regularly turn to their own cultural traditions in search of an interpretation that makes sense. They do this daily as they go about life among others with whom they share traditions. Serious misunderstandings may arise, however, when individuals confront the same ambiguous situation without realizing that their cultural ground rules differ.

Ethnocentrism

Ethnocentrism is the term anthropologists use to describe the opinion that one's own way of life is natural or correct, indeed the only way of being fully human. Ethnocentrism is one solution to the inevitable

ethnocentrism The opinion that one's own way of life is natural or correct and, indeed, the only true way of being fully human.

FIGURE 2.6 For Tswana, human life is social life. It was difficult for Peace Corps volunteers from the United States accustomed to having "private time" to adjust to Tswana practices.

tension between one cultural self and another cultural self. It reduces the other way of life to a version of one's own. Sometimes we correctly identify meaningful areas of cultural overlap. But other times, we are taken aback by the differences we encounter. We may conclude that if our way is right, then their way can only be wrong. (Of course, from their perspective, our way of life may seem to be a distortion of theirs.)

The members of one society may go beyond merely interpreting another way of life in ethnocentric terms. They may decide to do something about the discrepancies they observe. They may conclude that the other way of life is wrong but not fundamentally evil and that the members of the other group need to be converted to their own way of doing things. If the others are unwilling to change their ways, however, the failed attempt at conversion may enlarge into an active dualism: we versus they, civilization versus savagery, good versus evil. The ultimate result may be war and *genocide*—the deliberate attempt to exterminate an entire group based on race, religion, national origin, or other cultural features.

The Cross-Cultural Relationship

Is it possible to avoid ethnocentric bias? One way to address this quesiton is to view relationships between individuals with different cultural backgrounds as not being fundamentally different from relationships between individuals with very similar cultural backgrounds (we pursue this further in chapter 15). Although relationships are often much more difficult to negotiate between people who can take very little for granted about each other, they are possible. Like all human relationships, they affect all parties involved in the encounter, changing them as they learn about each other. People with a cultural background very different from your own may help you see possibilities for belief and action that are drastically at odds with everything your tradition considers possible. By becoming aware of these unsuspected possibilities, you become a different person. People from the other cultural backgrounds are likely to be affected in the same way.

Learning about other cultures is at once enormously hopeful and immensely threatening; once it occurs, we can no longer claim that any single culture has a monopoly on truth. Although this does not mean that the traditions in question must therefore be based entirely on illusion or falsehood, it does mean that the truth embodied in any cultural tradition is bound to be partial, approximate, and open to further insight and growth.

Cultural Relativism

Anthropologists must come to terms with the consequences of learning about cultural differences as they do their fieldwork. One result has been the formulation of the concept of cultural relativism. Definitions of cultural relativism have varied as different anthropologists have tried to draw conclusions based on their own experience of other ways of life.

For example, **cultural relativism** can be defined as "understanding another culture in its own terms sympathetically enough so that the culture appears to be a coherent and meaningful design for living" (Greenwood and Stini 1977, 182). According to this holistic definition, the goal of cultural relativism is to promote understanding of cultural practices, particularly of those that an outsider finds puzzling, incoherent, or morally troubling. These practices range from trivial (like eating insects) to horrifying (like genocide), but most are likely to be located somewhere between these extremes.

▼ HOW CAN CULTURAL RELATIVITY IMPROVE OUR UNDERSTANDING OF CONTROVERSIAL CULTURAL PRACTICES?

Rituals initiating girls and boys into adulthood are widely practiced throughout the world. In some parts of Africa, this ritual includes genital cutting (Figure 2.7). For example, ritual experts may cut off the foreskins of the penises of adolescent boys, who are expected to endure this operation without showing fear or pain. In the case of girls, ritual cutting may involve little more than nicking the clitoris with a knife blade to draw blood. In other cases, however, the surgery is more extreme. The clitoris itself may be cut off (or *excised*), a procedure called *clitoridectomy*. In some parts of eastern Africa, however, the surgery is even more extreme: The labia are excised along with the clitoris, and remaining skin is fastened together, forming scar tissue that partially closes the vaginal opening. This version is often called *pharaonic circumcision* or *infibulation*. When young women who have undergone this operation marry, they may require further surgery to widen the vaginal opening; if this is not done, brides experience severe pain when they engage in sexual intercourse with their husbands for the first time. Surgery may be necessary again to widen the vaginal opening when a woman gives birth; and after she has delivered her child, she

cultural relativism Understanding another culture in its own terms sympathetically enough so that the culture appears to be a coherent and meaningful design for living.

FIGURE 2.7 Among many East African people, including the Maasai, female genital cutting is an important part of the transformation of girls into women. These young women are recovering from the operation.

may expect to be closed up again. Many women who have undergone these procedures repeatedly can develop serious medical complications involving the bladder and colon later in life.

The removal of the male foreskin—or *circumcision*—has long been a familiar practice in Western societies, not only among observant Jews, who perform it for religious reasons, but also among physicians, who have encouraged circumcision of male newborns as a hygienic measure. The ritual practice of female genital cutting, by contrast, has been unfamiliar to most people in Western societies until recently, even though clitoridectomy has been promoted in the past by some Western physicians as a cure for "female problems" (Sheehan 1997). And although clitoridectomy is sometimes called "female circumcision," excision of the clitoris is anatomically analogous to cutting off the entire penis, not just removing the male foreskin, the typical procedure in "male circumcision."

Genital Cutting, Gender, and Human Rights

In 1978, radical feminist Mary Daly grouped "African female genital mutilation" together with practices such as foot binding in China and witch burning in medieval Europe and labeled all these practices patriarchal "Sado-Rituals" that destroy "the Self-affirming be-ing of women" (1978, 111). Feminists and other cultural critics in Western societies spoke out against such practices in the 1980s. In 1992, African American novelist Alice Walker published a best-selling novel *Possessing the Secret of Joy*, in which the heroine is an African woman who undergoes the operation, suffers psychologically and physically, and eventually pursues the female elder who performed the ritual on her. Walker also made a film, called *Warrior Marks*, that condemned female genital cutting. While many Western readers continue to regard the positions taken by Daly and Walker as formidable and necessary feminist assertions of women's resistance against patriarchal oppression, other readers—particularly women from societies in which female genital cutting is an ongoing practice—have responded with far less enthusiasm.

Does this mean that these women are in favor of female genital cutting? Not necessarily; in fact, many of them are actively working to discourage the practice in their own societies. But they find that when outsiders publicly condemn traditional African rituals like clitoridectomy and infibulation, their efforts may do more harm than good. As members of societies where these practices continue, the proclamations of a Mary Daly or an Alice Walker sound too much like the ethnocentric, reductionist critiques of "barbaric" African customs that western Europeans offered in the past, in order to justify colonial conquest. Women anthropologists who come from African societies where female genital cutting is traditional point out that Western women who want to help are likely to be more effective if they pay closer attention to what the African women themselves have to say about the meaning of these customs: "Careful listening to women helps us to recognize them as political actors forging their own communities of resistance. It also helps us to learn how and when to provide strategic support that would be welcomed by women who are struggling to challenge such traditions within their own cultures" (Abusharaf 2000).

A better understanding of female genital cutting is badly needed in places like the United States and the European Union, where some immigrants and refugees from Africa have brought traditions of female genital cutting with them. Since the mid-1990s, growing awareness and public condemnation of the

practice has led to the passage of laws that criminalize female genital cutting in 15 African states and 10 industrialized nations, including the United States and Canada (http://www.crlp.org/pub_fac_fgmicpd.html). Nonprofit legal advocacy organizations such as the Center for Reproductive and Legal Rights consider female genital cutting (which they call *female genital mutilation*, or FGM) to be a human rights violation. They acknowledge: "Although FGM is not undertaken with the intention of inflicting harm, its damaging physical, sexual, and psychological effects make it an act of violence against women and children" (http://www.crlp.org/pub_fac_fgmicpd.html). Some women have been able successfully to claim asylum or have avoided deportation by claiming that they have fled their home countries to avoid the operation. However, efforts to protect women and girls may backfire badly when immigrant or refugee mothers in the United States who seek to have their daughters ritually cut are stigmatized in the media as "mutilators" or "child abusers" and find that this practice is considered a felony punishable by up to five years in prison (Abusharaf 2000). Indeed, as we will see in chapter 15, such efforts can backfire even when members of the receiving society attempt to be culturally sensitive.

Genital Cutting as a Valued Ritual

Anthropologists can help clarify matters by doing ethnographic work that illuminates the cultural meanings that turn female genital cutting into a valued ritual. As Abusharaf writes, "Debates swirling around circumcision must be restructured in ways that are neither condemnatory nor demeaning, but that foster perceptions illuminated by careful study of the nuanced complexities of culture" (Abusharaf 2000, 17). One ethnographic study that aims to achieve these goals has been written by Janice Boddy, a cultural anthropologist who has carried out field research since 1976 in the Muslim village of Hofriyat in rural northern Sudan, where female genital surgery is traditionally performed in childhood. She writes that "nothing . . . had adequately prepared me for what I was to witness" when she first observed the operation; nevertheless, "as time passed in the village and understanding deepened I came to regard this form of female circumcision in a very different light" (1997, 309). Circumcisions in Hofriyat were traditionally performed on both boys and girls, but the ritual had a different meaning for boys than it did for girls. Once circumcised, a boy takes a step toward manhood, but a girl will not become a woman until she marries. Female circumcision is required, however, to make a girl marriageable, making it possible for her "to use her one great gift, fertility" (1997, 310).

Boddy encountered a number of different explanations by scholars and other observers about the purpose of female genital cutting: to ensure chastity and protect women from rape; as a form of birth control; as a way to increase male sexual pleasure by making the vaginal opening smaller; as a way of reducing excessive female sexual desire; and as a practice designed to prevent female vaginal infection. Of all these explanations, Boddy found that preserving chastity and curbing female sexual desire made the most sense in rural northern Sudan, where women's sexual conduct is the symbol of family honor. But in practical terms, infibulation ensures "that a girl is a virgin when she marries for the first time" (313). And women who undergo the procedure do indeed suffer a lot, not only at the time of circumcision, but whenever they engage in sexual intercourse, whenever they give birth, and, over time, as they become subject to recurring urinary infections and difficulties with menstruation. What cultural explanation could make all this suffering meaningful to women?

The answer lies in the connection rural northern Sudanese villagers make between the infibulated female body and female fertility. Boddy believes that the women she knew equated the category of "virgin" more with fertility than with lack of sexual experience and believed that a woman's virginity and her fertility could be renewed and protected by the act of reinfibulation after giving birth. Women she knew described infibulated female bodies as clean and smooth and pure (313). Boddy concluded that the ritual was best understood as a way of socializing female fertility "by dramatically de-emphasizing their inherent sexuality" and turning infibulated women into potential "mothers of men." This means they are eligible, with their husbands, to found a new lineage section by giving birth to sons. Women who become "mothers of men" are more than mere sexual partners or servants of their husbands and may attain high status, their name remembered in village genealogies (314).

Boddy discovered that the purity, cleanliness, and smoothness associated with the infibulated female body is also associated with other activities, concepts, and objects in everyday village customs. For example, pigeons and other waterbirds were considered "pure": "Young unmarried girls who dance at wedding parties are often referred to as . . . (pigeons going to market)" (315). Chickens, by contrast, were considered filthy; yet chicken *eggs* were considered "clean food" (315), and Boddy found that women collected and displayed ostrich eggshells in their rooms: "My friends said that ostrich eggshells . . . are so placed because the woman who sleeps in that room wishes to become pregnant. . . . They are fertility objects" (316). A man's testes are called his "eggs," and gourds shaped like ostrich eggshells are also associated with fertility. Cleanliness and purity are associated with whiteness, and foods like eggs, goat's milk, goat's milk cheese, cow's milk, fish, rice, sugar, and white flour are all considered "clean" foods. Tinned foods, associated with "white-skinned" Europeans and Lebanese, "are thought of being especially clean because they are all, so to speak, 'contained' or enclosed and protected from dirt and dryness" (316). A woman's cosmetic preparations are designed to whiten her skin, and indeed "a woman's body shares several qualities with the ostrich egg fertility object: Both are smooth, both are clean and 'white,' and both are pure. What is more, the shape of the ostrich egg, with its tiny orifice, corresponds to the idealized shape of the circumcised woman's womb" (317).

Because the ability of an object to retain moisture is likened to its ability to retain fertility, additional objects and structures are drawn into the same symbolic universe. Fetching water is traditionally considered women's work. A dried egg-shaped gourd with seeds that rattle inside is like the womb of infibulated women that contains and mixes her husband's semen with her own blood. Women prepare their family's staple food, *kisra*, by mixing flour and water by hand in a *gulla*, a "squat, rounded pottery jar, about the size of an average pumpkin, having an opening at the top slightly larger than a woman's fist" that "must not allow anything inside of them to seep out" (318). If a woman miscarries late in pregnancy, the midwife will wrap the fetus in a cloth; "then it is placed in a *gulla* and buried somewhere within the confines of . . . the house enclosure" (319). Indeed, the house enclosure itself seems to be a symbol for the womb: "Generally speaking, all enclosed areas in the village are considered clean and protected places" and "clean spaces,

spaces that are inside, are social areas" (319). Social areas, in turn, are bounded by a series of concentric circles: household within neighborhood/village, surrounded by farmlands, beyond which is the graveyard, and beyond that, the edge of the desert.

A human face "is considered beautiful if it is characterized by a small mouth and by narrow nostrils," but all bodily orifices are dangerous, vulnerable to *djinn* and other evil phenomena: "Thus, while orifices of the human body are necessary for sustaining life, they are dangerous, not aesthetically pleasing if large, and not to be left open after death" (320). Finally, "nonanatomical terms are often applied to parts of the anatomy. . . . The word 'house' is explictly associated with the womb" which is called "the 'house of childbirth' . . . and the vaginal opening is its . . . door or mouth" (321). In the same way that the household enclosure "protects a man's descendants, so the enclosed womb protects a woman's fertility . . . the womb of an infibulated woman is an oasis, the locus of appropriate human fertility" (321).

Evidence like this leads Boddy to insist that, for the women of Hofriyat, pharaonic circumcision is "an assertive symbolic act." The experience of infibulation, as well as other traditional curing practices teach girls to associate pure female bodies with heat and pain, making them meaningful. Such experiences become associated with the chief purpose women strive for—to become mothers of men—and the lesson is taught them repeatedly in a variety of ways when they look at waterbirds or eggs or make food or move around the village. Boddy's relativistic account demonstrates how the meanings associated with female infibulation are reinforced by so many different aspects of everyday life that girls who grow up, marry, and bear children in Hofriyat come to consider the operation a dangerous but profoundly necessary and justifiable procedure that enables them to help sustain all that is most valued in their own world.

Culture and Moral Reasoning

A relativistic understanding of female genital cutting, therefore, accomplishes several things. It makes the practice comprehensible and even coherent. It reveals how a physically dangerous procedure can appear perfectly acceptable—even indispensable—when placed in a particular context of meaning. It can help us see how some of the cultural practices

that we take for granted, such as the promotion of weight loss and cosmetic surgery among women in our own society, are equally dangerous—from "Victorian clitoridectomy" (Sheehan 1997) to twenty-first century cosmetic surgery. In the March 1, 2007, issue of the *New York Times*, for example, reporter Natasha Singer observes, "Before braces, crooked teeth were the norm. Is wrinkle removal the new orthodontics?" (Singer 2007, 3). Media and marketing pressure for cosmetic treatments that stop the visible signs of aging bombard middle-aged women. People are living longer, and treatments like Botox injections are becoming more easily available, with the result that "the way pop culture perceives the aging face" is changing, leaving women "grappling with the idea of what 60 looks like" (2007, E3). Moreover, pressure to undergo antiaging treatments, including plastic surgery, is not simply a matter of vanity. "At the very least, wrinkles are being repositioned as the new gray hair—another means to judge attractiveness, romantic viability, professional competitiveness and social status" (2007, E3). Singer quotes a 33-year-old real estate broker who has had Botox injections, chemical peels and laser treatments who said, "If you want to sell a million-dollar house, you have to look good . . . and you have to have confidence that you look good" (2007, E3). In Sudan, people say that virgins are "made, not born" (Boddy 1997, 313); perhaps in the United States, youth is also "made, not born." In the United States today, the media message to women is that success in life requires not an infibulated body, but a face that never ages. In both cases, cultural practices recommend surgical intervention in the female life cycle to render permanent certain aspects of youthful female bodies that are otherwise transient (fertility and unlined faces, respectively).

Did Their Culture Make Them Do It?

Do these examples imply that women support "irrational" and harmful practices simply because "their culture makes them do it?" For some people, this kind of cultural determinism is plausible, even preferable, to alternative explanations, because it absolves individual people of blame. How can one justify accusing immigrant African women of being mutilators or abusers of children and throw them into prison if they had no choice in the matter, if their cultures conditioned them into believing that female circumcision was necessary and proper and they are powerless to resist?

Nevertheless, invoking cultural determinism to account for the continued practice of infibulation in Hofriyat is too simplistic. Cultural determinism requires us to accept three assumptions about human nature and human society: first, that cultures have neat boundaries between them and are sealed off from one another; second, that every culture offers people only one way to interpret experience, that cultures are monolithic and permit no variety, harbor no contradictions, and allow no dissent; and third, that people living in these closed cultural worlds are passively molded by culture, helpless to resist indoctrination into a single worldview, and incapable of inventing alternatives to that view. Boddy's account makes clear that, for women and men in villages like Hofriyat, none of these assumptions is justified.

First, the villages of northern Sudan are not sealed off from a wider, more diverse world. Northern Sudan has experienced a lively and often violent history as different groups of outsiders, including the British, have struggled to control the land; Boddy describes the way rural men regularly leave the village as migrant workers and mix with people whose customs—including sexual customs—are very different from the ones they left behind; and outsiders, like anthropologists, also may come to the village and establish long-lasting relationships with those whom they meet. Second, Boddy's account makes clear that the culture of Hofriyat allows peole more than one way to interpret their experiences. For example, she notes that although men in Sudan and Egypt are supposed to enjoy sexual intercourse with infibulated women more than with noninfibulated women, in fact these men regularly visit brothels where they encounter prostitutes who have not undergone the surgery.

Perhaps most significantly, Boddy observes that a less radical form of the operation began to gain acceptance after 1969, and not only are women who have undergone this version finding husbands, but "men are now marrying—and what is more, saying that they prefer to marry—women who have been less severely mutilated," at least in part because they find sexual relations to be more satisfying (312). Finally, as these observations also show, Boddy's account emphatically rejects the view that women or men in Hofriyat are passive beings, helpless to resist cultural indoctrination. As Abusharaf would wish, Boddy listened to women in Hofriyat and recognized them "as political actors forging their own communities of resistance." Specifically, Boddy showed how increasing numbers of women (and men) continued to connect female genital cutting with properly socialized female fertility—but they no longer believed that infibulation was the only procedure capable of achieving that goal.

Understanding something is not the same as approving of it or excusing it. People everywhere may be repelled by unfamiliar cultural practices when they first encounter them. Sometimes when they understand these practices better, they change their minds. They may conclude that the practices in question are more suitable for the people who employ them than their own practices would be. They might even recommend incorporating practices from other cultures into their own society. But the opposite may also be the case. It is possible to understand perfectly the cultural rationale behind such practices as slavery, infanticide, headhunting, and genocide—and still refuse to approve of these practices. Insiders and outsiders alike may not be persuaded by the reasons offered to justify these practices, or they may be aware of alternative arrangements that could achieve the desired outcome via less drastic methods. In fact, changing practices of female circumcision in Hofriyat seem to be based precisely on the realization that less extreme forms of surgery can achieve the same valued cultural goals. This should not surprise us: It is likely that any cultural practice with far-reaching consequences for human life will have critics as well as supporters within the society where it is practiced. This is certainly the case in the United States, where abortion and capital punishment remain controversial issues.

A sensitive ethnographic account of a controversial cultural practice, like Boddy's account of female genital cutting in Hofriyat, will address both the meaningful dimensions of the practice and the contradictions it involves. As Boddy concludes,

> Those who work to eradicate female circumcision must, I assert, cultivate an awareness of the custom's local significances and of how much they are asking people to relinquish as well as gain. The stakes are high and it is hardly surprising that efforts to date have met with little success. It is, however, ironic that a practice that—at least in Hofriyat—emphasizes female fertility at a cultural level can be so destructive of it physiologically and so damaging to women's health overall. That paradox has analogies elsewhere, in a world considered "civilized," seemingly far re-

moved from the "barbarous East." Here too, in the west from where I speak, feminine selfhood is often attained at the expense of female well-being. In parallels like these there lies the germ of an enlightened approach to the problem (322).

Cultural relativism makes moral reasoning more complex. It does not, however, require us to abandon every value our own society has taught us. Every cultural tradition offers more than one way of evaluating experience. Exposure to the interpretations of an unfamiliar culture forces us to reconsider the possibilities our own tradition recognizes in a new light and to search for areas of intersection as well as areas of disagreement. What cultural relativism does discourage is the easy solution of refusing to consider alternatives from the outset. It also does not free us from sometimes facing difficult choices between alternatives whose rightness or wrongness is less than clear-cut. In this sense, "cultural relativism is a 'toughminded' philosophy" (Herskovits 1973, 37).

▼ DOES CULTURE EXPLAIN EVERYTHING?

We believe that our view of the concept of culture as presented in this chapter is widely shared among contemporary cultural anthropologists. Nevertheless, in recent years the concept of culture has become controversial in anthropology; in fact, anthropologist Lila Abu-Lughod published a critical article entitled "Writing Against Culture" (1991). What is behind this controversy? The issues are complex and are more fully explored in later chapters, but we offer here a brief account to provide some historical context.

Writing against Culture

For at least the past 50 years, many anthropologists have distinguished between Culture (with a capital C) and cultures (plural with a lowercase c). *Culture* has been used to describe an attribute of the human species as a whole—its members' ability, in the absence of highly specific genetic programming, to create and to imitate patterned, symbolically mediated ideas and activities that promote the survival of our species. By contrast, the term *cultures* has been used to refer to particular, learned *ways of life* belonging to specific groups of human beings. Given this distinc-

tion, the human species as a whole can be said to have Culture as a defining attribute, but actual human beings would only have access to particular human cultures—either their own or other people's.

It is the plural use of cultures with a lowercase c that has become controversial. By and large, those who advocate "writing against culture" continue to defend the validity of Culture with a capital C. But some of them find the issue so serious that they recommend dropping the term *culture* from the anthropological vocabulary altogether.

The controversy is heated because many anthropologists have viewed the plural use of the culture concept not only as analytically helpful but as politically progressive. Their view reflects a struggle that developed in nineteenth-century Europe: Supporters of the supposedly progressive, universal civilization of the Enlightenment, inaugurated by the French Revolution and spread by Napoleonic conquest, were challenged by inhabitants of other European nations, who resisted both Napoleon and the Enlightenment in what has been called the Romantic Counter-Enlightenment. Romantic intellectuals in nations like Germany rejected what they considered to be the imposition of "artificial" Enlightenment *civilization* on the "natural" spiritual traditions of their own distinct national *cultures* (Kuper 1999; Crehan 2002).

This political dynamic, which pits a steamroller civilization against vulnerable local cultures, carried over into the usage that later developed in anthropology, particularly in North America. The decades surrounding the turn of the twentieth century marked the period of expanding European colonial empires as well as westward expansion and consolidation of control in North America by European settlers. At that time, the social sciences were becoming established in universities, and different fields were assigned different tasks. Anthropology was allocated what Michel-Rolph Trouillot (1991) has called "the savage slot"— that is, the so-called "primitive" world that was the target of colonization. Anthropologists thus became the official academic experts on societies whose members suffered appalling racist denigration as "primitives" and whose ways of life were being undermined by contact with Western colonial "civilization."

Anthropologists were determined to denounce these practices and to demonstrate that the "primitive" stereotype was false. Some found inspiration in the work of English anthropologist E. B. Tylor, who, in

1871, had defined "culture or civilization" as "that complex whole which includes knowledge, belief, art, morals, law, custom, and any other capabilities and habits acquired by man as a member of society" (1958 [1871]:1). This definition had the virtue of blurring the difference between "civilization" and "culture," and it encouraged the view that even "primitives" possessed "capabilities and habits" that merited respect. Thus, in response to stereotypes of "primitives" as irrational, disorganized, insensitive, or promiscuous, anthropologists like Franz Boas and Bronislaw Malinowski were able to show that, on the contrary, so-called "primitives" possessed "cultures" that were reasonable, orderly, artistically developed, and morally disciplined. The plural use of culture allowed them to argue that, in their own ways, "primitives" were as fully human as "civilized" people.

By the end of the twentieth century, however, the plural use of culture began to appear pernicious rather than progressive. To some, the boundary that once was thought to protect vulnerability now looked more like a prison wall, condemning those within it to live according to "their" culture, just as their ancestors had done, like exhibits in a living museum, whether they wanted to or not. Critics argue that the plural concept of culture not only highlights the differences between groups of people but also assumes that group members uncritically accept those differences, want to preserve them, and naturally view cultural change as the loss of authenticity. Consequently, if group members disagree with one another publicly or challenge traditional ways by, for example, protesting against a custom like female genital cutting, they may be condemned, by insiders and outsiders alike, as having sold out to powerful outsiders who are trying to portray their traditional customs as barbaric. As we have seen, however, this overlooks the possibility that alternatives to a controversial practice might already exist *within* the cultural tradition and that followers of that tradition may *themselves* decide that some alternatives make more sense than others in today's world. The issue then becomes not just which traditions have been inherited from the past—as if "authentic" cultures were monolithic and unchanging—but, rather, which traditional practices *ought* to continue in a contemporary world—and who is entitled to make that decision.

Culture Change and Cultural Authenticity

It is no secret that colonizing states have regularly attempted to determine the cultural priorities of those whom they conquered. Sending missionaries to convert colonized peoples to Christianity is one of the best-known practices of Western cultural imperialism. In North America in the 1860s, for example, escalating struggles between settlers and Native American groups led federal policymakers to place federal Indian policy in the hands of Christian reformers "who would embrace the hard work of transforming Indians and resist the lure of getting rich off the system's spoils" (Lassiter et al. 2002, 22). And although missionaries were initially resisted, eventually they made many converts, and Christianity remains strong among indigenous groups like the Comanches and Kiowas today. But how should this religious conversion be understood? As Luke Eric Lassiter notes, "Much of the American Studies literature lacks serious attention to Christian experience in general; scholars more often than not choose either to dismiss it altogether or pose it as mere assimilation to the American mainstream" (2002, 5). Yet Lassiter's own work among the Kiowa people in Oklahoma challenged the assimilationist view. Lassiter discovered that Kiowa singer Ralph Kotay and other Kiowa Christians who place a high value on their tradition of Kiowa hymns were concerned that it might die out, taking Kiowa cultural identity with it.

Doesn't the fact that Kiowas are Christians today show that federal officials and missionaries succeeded in their policies of Western Christian cultural imperialism? Maybe not: "Taking the 'Jesus Way' is not necessarily the story of how one set of beliefs replace another one wholesale, or of the incompatibility of Kiowa practices with Christian ones. Rather, it is a more complex encounter in which both sides make concessions" (Lassiter et al. 2002,19). True, missionaries arrived as the buffalo were disappearing and Kiowa people were being confined to reservations, and in 1890 the U.S. government used military force to put an end to the Kiowa Sun Dance, the centerpiece of Kiowa ceremonies. And yet, Lassiter tells us, "For many Kiowas—as for Indian people generally—Christianity has been, and remains, a crucially important element in their lives as Native people. Its concern for community needs, its emphasis on shared beliefs, and its promise of salvation have helped to mediate life in a region long buffeted by limited economic development, geographic isolation, and cultural stress" (Lassiter et al. 2002, 18).

One reason it succeeded was that missionaries did not insist that the Kiowa give up all traditional ways (2002, 53). Prominent individuals adopted Christianity, and Kiowa converts were trained to become missionaries and ministers, which proved attractive (2002, 57; Figure 2.8). Especially persuasive were women missionaries who "lived in the Kiowa camps, ate their food, and endured the privations of life on the plains with impressive strength" (2002, 59). Missionaries, in turn, actively sought to adapt Christian practices to traditional Kiowa ways. For example, "Missions were historically located in and around established camps and communities," with the result that "churches were the natural extension of traditional Kiowa camps" and eventually took their place at the center of Kiowa life (2002, 61). "People would often camp on the grounds or stay with relatives for weeks at a time. . . . Services with Kiowa hymns and special prayers often extended into the evening" (2002, 62).

It might be as accurate to say that the Kiowa "kiowanized" Christianity, therefore, as it would be to say that missionaries "Christianized" the Kiowa. One of Lassiter's Kiowa collaborators, Vincent Bointy, insists that Christianity is not the same as "the white man's way" and explains that "the elders didn't say 'Christian.' . . . They said 'this is the way of God'" (Lassiter et al. 2002, 63). Kiowa identity and Christian values are so closely intertwined for Bointy that "he believes that he can express the power of Christianity better in Kiowa than in English." And this is why Kiowa hymns are so important. Unlike other Kiowa songs, Kiowa hymns are sung in the Kiowa language, which is spoken less and less in other settings. Kiowa hymns "give life to a unique Kiowa experience, preserve the language, and affirm an ongoing (and continually unfolding) Kiowa spirituality. Indeed, Kiowa Indian hymns are as much Kiowa (if not more) as they are Christian (Lassiter 2004, 205).

The way in which Kiowa Christians have been able to transform what began as an exercise in cultural imperialism into a reaffirmation of traditional Kiowa values challenges the presumption that "authentic cultures" never change. This presumption, in turn, exposes the plural concept of culture as a rigid, "totalitarian" concept of culture (Hann 2002, 260) that endorses a kind of oppressive cultural determinism.

FIGURE 2.8 Among the Kiowa, prominent individuals, like Chief Lone Wolf, adopted Christianity and invited missionaries to train Kiowa ministers.

Such an inflexible concept of culture can accommodate neither the agency of Kiowa Christians nor the validity of the "ongoing" and "continually unfolding" cultural traditions they produce.

Culture and the Politics of "Difference"

Christian missionizing on Indian reservations in the nineteenth and twentieth centuries was part of U.S. government policy to turn Native Americans into individualistic, Christian, capitalist farmers. It might seem, in retrospect, that a federal policy that recognized and valued cultural differences would have been more enlightened. And yet much depends on the political circumstances within which cultural differences are promoted. One of the most damning critiques of the plural use of culture has come from anthropologist Adam Kuper, who shows how the rulers in twentieth-century *apartheid* South Africa made use of the plural concept of culture in order to control indigenous African populations. Kuper explains that some Afrikaner intellectuals argued that "not race but culture was the true basis of difference, the sign of destiny. And cultural differences were to be valued" (1999, xiii). Kuper quotes one spokesman who justified apartheid as a policy aiming at encouraging "'higher Bantu culture and not at producing black Europeans'" (1999, xiii). From Kuper's perspective, and contrary to the goals of the American anthropologists who first developed it, "the idea of culture could actually reinforce a racial theory of difference" (1999, 14).

A century ago, as Trouillot reminds us, the anthropological concept of culture was developed in the United States "as race repellent." Culture was "not only what race is not, but it is what prevents race from occupying in anthropological discourse the defining place that it otherwise occupies in larger American society" (2002, 40). For similar reasons, Kuper wants to prevent the plural concept of culture from occupying in anthropological discourse the defining place that it came to occupy in apartheid South African society.

Trouillot and Kuper also agree that for anthropologists to continue to use "culture" as a part of their professional analytic vocabulary risks lending credibility to the way the concept has been used to oppress rather than to liberate. This is a serious position with which we sympathize. Implementing it, however, is complicated by the fact that a variety of groups, from indigenous activists in Amazonia to immigrant activists in Europe, have incorporated the plural use of culture into their own self-definitions, and in some cases anthropologists defend this move as valuable and progressive. In addition, scholarly disciplines outside anthropology, from cultural studies to cognitive science, have incorporated "culture"

into their own technical vocabularies. On the one hand, this can be seen (perhaps ironically) as a measure of the success of earlier generations of anthropologists in demonstrating the value of the culture concept. On the other hand, it means that today, "culture" is sometimes used in ways that anthropologists find objectionable but that they cannot control.

Attempts by anthropologists to deal with these complications are a focus in future chapters, especially in our discussions of anthropological approaches to ethnicity and nationalism (chapter 13), globalization and multiculturalism (chapter 14), and democracy and identity politics (chapter 15).

▼ THE PROMISE OF THE ANTHROPOLOGICAL PERSPECTIVE

The anthropological perspective on the human condition is not easy to maintain. It forces us to question the commonsense assumptions with which we are most comfortable. It only increases the difficulty we encounter when faced with moral and political decisions. It does not allow us an easy retreat, for once we are exposed to the kinds of experience that the anthropological undertaking makes possible, we are changed. We cannot easily pretend that these new experiences never happened to us. There is no going back to ethnocentrism when the going gets rough, except in bad faith. So anthropology is guaranteed to complicate your life. Nevertheless, the anthropological perspective can give you a broader understanding of human nature and the wider world, of society, culture, and history, and thus help you construct more realistic and authentic ways of coping with those complications.

CHAPTER SUMMARY

1. Anthropologists have argued that culture distinguishes the human condition from the condition of other living species. Human culture is learned, shared, patterned, adaptive, and symbolic. It did not emerge all at once but evolved over time. The role of culture in human life is

often debated in the Western world using concepts rooted in philosophy. Mind–matter dualism is deeply rooted in Western thought, dating back to such figures as Plato. Because culture includes ideas, it is often associated with the mind and sometimes thought to control the material body. Those who emphasize matter rather than mind, by contrast, often try to reduce culture to a simple by-product of material factors such as genes, hormones, biology, the environment, or history. Dualist views of human nature can engender extremist positions that reduce human cultural practices to single determining causes. Most anthropologists find this way of explaining human action seriously inadequate.

2. In preference to dualism, reductionism, and determinism, many anthropologists have long thought holistically about human culture. Anthropological holism argues that objects and environments interpenetrate and even define each other. Thus, the whole is more than the sum of its parts. Human beings and human societies are open systems that cannot be reduced to the parts that make them up. The parts and the whole mutually define, or codetermine, each other and coevolve. This book adopts a coevolutionary approach to human nature, human society, and the human past. Human beings depend on symbolic cultural understandings to help them resolve the ambiguities inherent in everyday human experience.

3. Ethnocentrism is a form of reductionism. Anthropologists believe it can be countered by a commitment to cultural relativism, an attempt to understand the cultural underpinnings of behavior. Cultural relativism does not require us to abandon every value our society has taught us; however, it does discourage the easy solution of refusing to consider alternatives from the outset. Cultural relativism makes moral decisions more difficult because it requires us to take many things into account before we make up our minds.

4. Human history is an essential aspect of the human story, a dialectic between biology and culture. Culture is worked out over time and passed on from one generation to the next. The cultural beliefs and practices we inherit from the past or borrow from other people in the present make some things easier for us and other things more difficult. At the same time, culture provides resources human beings can make use of in the pursuit of their own goals. Thus, the anthropological understanding of human life recognizes the importance of human agency.

5. Many anthropologists have criticized using the term *cultures* to refer to particular, learned ways of life belonging to specific groups of human beings. Critics argue that this way of talking about culture seems to endorse a kind of oppressive cultural determinism. Supporters, however, argue that in some cases this version of the culture concept can be used to defend vulnerable social groups against exploitation and oppression by outsiders.

KEY TERMS

culture	idealism	human agency	coevolution
symbol	materialism	essence	ethnocentrism
dualism	determinism	holism	cultural relativism

SUGGESTED READINGS

Gamst, Frederick, and Edward Norbeck. 1976. *Ideas of culture: Sources and uses.* New York: Holt, Rinehart & Winston. *A useful collection of important articles about culture. The articles are arranged according to different basic approaches to culture.*

Geertz, Clifford. 1973. Thick description: Towards an interpretive theory of culture *and* The impact of the concept of culture on the concept of man. In *The interpretation of cultures.* New York: Basic Books. *Two classic discussions of culture from a major figure in American anthropology. These works have done much to shape the discourse about culture in anthropology.*

Kuper, Adam. 1999. *Culture: The anthropologists' account.* Cambridge, MA: Harvard University Press. *A critical history of the use of the culture concept in anthropology, which traces its links to earlier Western ideas about culture and analyzes the work of several late twentieth-century anthropologists who made the concept central to their scholarship. Based on his experience with the abuse of the culture concept in* apartheid *South Africa, Kuper recommends that anthropologists drop the term entirely from their professional vocabulary.*

Voget, Fred. 1975. *A history of ethnology.* New York: Holt, Rinehart & Winston. *A massive, thorough, and detailed work. For the student seeking a challenging read.*

Chapter 3

Fieldwork

One of the hallmarks of cultural anthropology is close, first-hand knowledge of the ways of life of people all over the world. This chapter describes how cultural anthropologists become familiar with other ways of life by engaging in participant-observation in the course of ethnographic fieldwork. It also considers some of the effects of the fieldwork experience on anthropologists, the people they work with, and the discipline of anthropology itself.

Roger Lancaster is an anthropologist who carried out intensive research in a Nicaraguan working-class neighborhood during the 1980s (Figure 3.1; see EthnoProfile 3.1: Managua). In June 1985, he went to Don Pablo's *tienda popular* (a "popular store" that carried government-subsidized food basics) to buy a chicken. On his way into the store, he was stopped by a drunken old man who wanted to talk. They exchanged greetings in Spanish and then the old man "uttered a string of vowels and consonants that proved entirely unintelligible." Lancaster explained in Spanish that he did not understand what the man was saying and then entered the store to buy chicken. He relates the rest of the encounter:

> I was trying to decide how large the chicken should be when the drunk old man appeared in the doorway, waving his arms and raving that he had caught an agent of the CIA trying to spy on Nicaragua. "*¡La CIA!*" he kept shouting. I turned and realized he was talking about me. . . .
>
> Now it was Don Pablo's turn to speak. "Now what makes you think this *joven* [youth] is CIA?" "Because," replied the old man with a flourish of cunning, "I spoke to him in English, and he pretended that he didn't understand what I was saying! Now why else would he do that unless he were trying to conceal his nationality? And why would he conceal his nationality unless he were trying to hide something? He must be CIA. Arrest him!"

I was growing concerned because the old man was now blocking the doorway, and it would scarcely have been appropriate for me to push my way past him. I was trying to figure out how to prevent this from becoming an even more unpleasant scene when Don Pablo's wife walked over to the meatbox, pulled out a chicken, and asked me if it were acceptable. I said that it was, and she put it on the scales. "Two and a half pounds," she observed, and then turned to address the old man. With an air of authority, she announced, "Listen, compañero, this isn't a spy from the CIA. This is Róger Lancaster, a friend of Nicaragua from the United States. He's an anthropology student at the University of California at Berkeley—not Los Angeles, there's another one in Berkeley, which doesn't have a basketball team. He's working on his doctoral dissertation, and he's here studying the role of religion in our revolution, especially the Popular Church. When he goes back, he's going to tell the truth about Nicaragua, and our revolution, and it will be good for us."

I listened with amazement. I had never been inside the popular store before, and I didn't even know either the proprietor or his wife by their names. I had seen them only in passing, and we had never been introduced. Yet here was Doña Carmen, accurately describing my credentials and my research topic. Gossip moves quietly but quickly on the streets of the neighborhoods. (Lancaster 1992, 76)

Unfortunately, Lancaster's experience is not unique—other anthropologists have been suspected

FIGURE 3.1 A shopkeeper in a neighborhood store in Managua, Nicaragua, in 1986.

EthnoProfile 3.1

Managua

Region: Central America

Nation: Nicaragua

Population: 1,000,000 (1995 est.)

Environment: Tropical city

Livelihood: Modern stratified city

Political organization: City in modern nation-state

For more information: Lancaster, Roger. 1992. *Life is hard: Machismo, danger, and the intimacy of power in Nicaragua.* Berkeley: University of California Press.

and sometimes accused of being CIA agents. Almost always, they have been able to reassure the people they are working with that this is not the case, but the accusation makes clear that ethnographic research is not carried out in a vacuum. People's understanding of world politics at a particular moment in history can determine whether they welcome or are suspicious of ethnographers from the United States or elsewhere who suddenly appear in their midst.

Even when they do not suspect the ethnographer of covert activities, however, many people around the world find something unusual about ethnographic fieldwork. Here is someone who shows up in the community, plans to be there for a year or more, claims to be interested in their way of life, and then spends all of his or her time observing, talking to people, and taking notes! In this chapter we will consider why anthropologists put themselves into these situations, as well as the effect field research has on anthropologists and the people whose lives they study.

▼ WHY DO FIELDWORK?

Ethnographic **fieldwork** is an extended period of close involvement with the people whose way of life interests the anthropologist. This is the period in which anthropologists collect most of their data. Fieldwork deliberately brings together people from different cul-

tural backgrounds, an encounter that makes misunderstandings, understandings, and surprises likely. It is nevertheless through such encounters that fieldwork generates much of what anthropologists come to know about people in other societies.

Gathering data while living for an extended period in close contact with members of another social group is called **participant-observation**. Cultural anthropologists also gather data by conducting interviews and administering surveys as well as by consulting archives and previously published literature relevant to their research. But participant-observation, which relies on face-to-face contact with people as they go about their daily lives, was pioneered by cultural anthropologists and remains characteristic of anthropology as a discipline. Participant-observation allows anthropologists to interpret what people say and do in terms of cultural beliefs and values, social interactions, and the wider political context within which people live. Sometimes anthropologists administer questionnaires and psychological tests as part of their fieldwork, but they would never rely solely on such methods because, by itself, the information they produce cannot be contextualized and may be misleading. Participant-observation is perhaps the best method available to scholars who seek a holistic understanding of culture and the human condition.

▼ THE FIELDWORK EXPERIENCE

For most cultural anthropologists, ethnographic fieldwork is the experience that characterizes the discipline. Anthropologists sometimes gain field experience as undergraduates or early in their graduate studies by working on research projects or in field schools run by established anthropologists. An extended period of fieldwork is the final phase of formal anthropological training, but most anthropologists hope to incorporate additional periods of field research into their subsequent careers.

fieldwork An extended period of close involvement with the people in whose language or way of life an anthropologist is interested, during which anthropologists ordinarily collect most of their data.

participant-observation The method anthropologists use to gather information by living as closely as possible to the people whose culture they are studying while participating in their lives as much as possible.

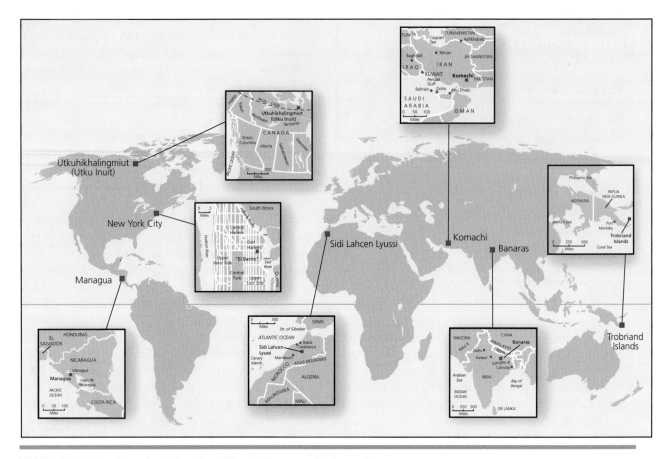

FIGURE 3.2 Locations of societies whose EthnoProfiles appear in chapter 3.

Beginning anthropologists usually decide during graduate school where and on what topic they wish to do their research. Success depends on being able to obtain both permission to work in a particular place in the form of approvals from academic and governmental offices in the host country and the funds to support one's research. Getting grants from private or government agencies involves, among other things, persuading them that your work will focus on a topic of current interest within anthropology and is connected to their funding priorities. As a result, "field sites end up being defined by the crosshatched intersection of visa and clearance procedures, the interests of funding agencies, and intellectual debates within the discipline and its subfields" (Gupta and Ferguson 1997, 11). Because there is a great demand for grants, not all topics of current interest can be funded, and so some anthropologists pay for their research themselves by getting a job in the area where they

want to do fieldwork or by supplementing small grants out of their own pockets.

Classic anthropological fieldwork emphasized working "abroad"—that is, doing fieldwork in societies that were culturally and geographically distant from that of the ethnographer. This orientation bears undeniable traces of its origins under European colonialism, but it continues to be a valuable means of drawing attention to ways of life and parts of the world that elite groups in powerful Western nations have traditionally dismissed and marginalized. It also forces the fieldworker to recognize differences that might not be so obvious at home.

More recent discussions of anthropological fieldwork, however, have drawn attention to the significance of working "at home"—including paying attention to the forms of social differentiation and marginalization present in the society to which the ethnographer belongs. This orientation has the virtue of emphasizing ethnographers' ethical and political accountability to those among whom they work, especially when the anthropologists are themselves members of the groups they study. Such an orientation incorporates traditions of anthropological research that have developed in countries like Mexico, Brazil, India, and Russia, where fieldwork at home has long been the norm. At the beginning of the twenty-first century, these developments are helping to create "decolonized anthropology in a deterritorialized world" that will be enriched by varied contributions of anthropologists trained in different traditions, working at home and abroad, who seek to forge "links between *different* knowledges that are possible from different locations" (Gupta and Ferguson 1997, 35, 38).

Participant-observation requires living as closely as possible to the people whose culture you are studying. Anthropologists who work among remote peoples in rain forests, deserts, or tundra may need to bring along their own living quarters. In other cases, an appropriate house or apartment in the village, neighborhood, or city where the research is to be done becomes the anthropologist's home.

A Meeting of Cultural Traditions

In any case, living conditions in the field can themselves provide major insights into the culture under study. This is powerfully illustrated by the experiences of Charles and Bettylou Valentine, whose field site was a poor neighborhood they called *Blackston*, located in a large city in the northern United States (see EthnoProfile 3.2: Blackston). The Valentines lived for the last field year on one-quarter of their regular income; during the final six months, they matched their income to that of welfare families:

> For five years we inhabited the same decrepit rat- and roach-infested buildings as everyone else, lived on the same poor quality food at inflated prices, trusted our health and our son's schooling to the same inferior institutions, suffered the same brutality and intimidation from the police, and like others made the best of it by some combination of endurance, escapism, and fighting back. Like the dwellings of our neighbors, our home went up in flames several times, including one disaster caused by the carelessness or ill will of the city's "firefighters." For several cold months we lived and worked

EthnoProfile 3.2

Blackston

Region: North America

Nation: United States

Population: 100,000

Environment: Urban ghetto

Livelihood: Low-paying full-time and temporary jobs, welfare

Political organization: Lowest level in a modern nation-state

For more information: Valentine, Bettylou. 1978. *Hustling and other hard work.* New York: The Free Press.

in one room without heat other than what a cooking stove could provide, without hot water or windows, and with only one light bulb. (C. Valentine 1978, 5)

Not all field sites offer such a stark contrast to the middle-class backgrounds of many fieldworkers, and indeed some can be almost luxurious. But physical and mental dislocation and stress can be expected anywhere. People from temperate climates who find themselves in the tropics have to adjust to the heat; fieldworkers in the Arctic have to adjust to the cold. In hot climates especially, many anthropologists encounter plants, animals, insects, and diseases with which they have had no previous experience. In any climate, fieldworkers need to adjust to local water and food.

In addition, there are the cultural differences—which is why the fieldworkers came. Yet the immensity of what they will encounter is difficult for them to anticipate. Initially, just getting through the day—finding a place to stay and food to eat—may seem an enormous accomplishment; but there are also data to gather, research to do!

Sometimes, however, the research questions never become separate from the living arrangements. Philippe Bourgois, who studied drug dealers in East Harlem in New York City, had to learn to deal not only with the violence of the drug dealers but also with the hostility and brutality that white police

EthnoProfile 3.3

El Barrio

Region: North America

Nation: United States
(New York City)

Population: 110,000 (1990 census)

Environment: Urban ghetto

Livelihood: Low-paying full-time and temporary jobs,
selling drugs, welfare

Political organization: Lowest level in a modern nation-
state

For more information: Bourgois, Philippe. 1995. *In
search of respect: Selling crack in El Barrio.* New York:
Cambridge University Press.

officers directed toward him, a white man living in
El Barrio (see EthnoProfile 3.3: *El Barrio*; Figure 3.3).
His experiences on the street pressed him to consider
how the situation he was studying was a form of
what he calls "inner-city apartheid" in the United
States (Bourgois 1995, 32).

Early in their stay, it is not uncommon for fieldworkers to feel overwhelmed. With time, however,
they discover that the great process of human survival begins to assert itself: They begin to adapt. The
rhythms of daily activity become familiar. Their use
of the local language improves. Faces of the local inhabitants become the faces of neighbors. They are
participating and observing—and doing a lot of writing as well. It seems as though fieldworkers always
have a notebook somewhere handy and, whenever
possible, jot down notes on what they are seeing,
hearing, doing, or wondering. These days, laptops,
digital cameras, video cameras, and digital recorders
are usually considered essential to the accurate
recording of field data. We cannot really trust our
memories to keep track of the extraordinary range of
information that comes at us in the field. But note taking is not sufficient. The quickly jotted scrawls in

notebooks must be turned into field notes; as a result,
anthropologists spend a lot of their time in front of
their computers, writing as complete and coherent a
set of notes as possible. Most ethnographers try to
write up field notes on a daily basis, and they also try
to code the information so that they can find it later.
There are very useful field manuals for neophyte
ethnographers to consult to assist them in developing
workable and straightforward coding systems (e.g.,
Bernard 2006; DeWalt and DeWalt 2002). As fieldworkers type up their notes, places for further inquiry
become plain and a back-and-forth process begins.
The ethnographer collects information, writes it down,
thinks about, analyzes it, and then takes new questions
and interpretations back to the people with whom he
or she is working to see if these questions and interpretations are more accurate than the previous ones.

It is important to realize that even the best field
notes, however, are not **ethnographies**, published
books or articles based on anthropological fieldwork.
Writing about the cultural practices one has learned
is not as straightforward as it may seem to nonanthropologists. Over the last century, anthropologists'
ideas about what ethnographies ought to look like—
how long they ought to be, how much and what
kinds of details they should contain, whether they
should be addressed to audiences of other professionals or to popular audiences or to members of the
societies being studied—have undergone revision.
Contemporary ethnographers try to be explicit about
who they are and how they came to do their research
and try to take into account who the various intended
(and unintended) readers of their work might be.
They search for sensitive and insightful ways to include multiple points of view besides their own in
their texts. When the topics of their research are socially or politically sensitive and could put vulnerable people at risk, they need to be vigilant about their
disclosures in order to protect the identity of those
with whom they worked.

▼ ETHNOGRAPHIC FIELDWORK: HOW HAS ANTHROPOLOGISTS' UNDERSTANDING CHANGED?

When anthropology began to take on its own identity
as an intellectual discipline during the nineteenth century, it aspired to be scientific. Anthropology still aims

---

ethnography An anthropologist's written or filmed description of a
particular culture.

FIGURE 3.3 *El Barrio*, the part of New York City in which Philippe Bourgois did his research, is a socially complex, dynamic urban neighborhood.

to be scientific in its study of human nature, human society, and human history. For several decades, however, scientists, philosophers, historians and increasing numbers of social scientists have been reexamining some deeply rooted assumptions about what science is and how it works. This research effort has challenged many popular understandings about science. One outcome of this work has been the demonstration that the so-called hard sciences (such as physics, chemistry, and biology) and the so-called soft sciences (such as psychology, sociology, and anthropology) actually have more in common with each other than previously recognized (e.g., Barad 1999; Pickering 1995). Another outcome has been to show that instead of a single Scientific Method, there are actually a variety of different scientific methods that have been developed to produce reliable knowledge in different scientific disciplines that focus on different aspects of the world (e.g., Knorr Cetina 2000). Anthropologists have joined

in this effort to reconsider what science is all about. Sarah Franklin, a pioneer in this effort, writes: "Anthropology is a science and has the tools to understand science as a form of culture" (1995, 165).

Cultural anthropologists have made many efforts over the years to understand the scientific status of the data gathered during participant-observation–based fieldwork. This research strategy came into its own in the early decades of the twentieth century, in the work of such pioneer ethnographers as Bronislaw Malinowski (who, it is often said, invented long-term participant-observation–based fieldwork), Franz Boas, and Boas's best-known student, Margaret Mead. Since that time, the conditions within which fieldwork has been carried out have changed, and with these changed conditions, anthropologists have been prompted to rethink and revise their basic views about fieldwork, both in terms of its scientific status and as a form of human interaction (Figure 3.4). We

FIGURE 3.4 Participant-observation has characterized cultural anthropology from its earliest days, although "fieldwear" may have changed between Malinowski's day (top) and Wolf Schiefenhövel's in the 1990s (below). There are other important differences as well in how fieldwork is carried out.

will briefly review three approaches to ethnographic fieldwork that have developed over the last hundred years. These are the positivist approach, the reflexive approach, and multisited fieldwork, which is the most recent, and is discussed later in the chapter.

positivism The view that there is a reality "out there" that can be known through the senses and that there is a single, appropriate set of scientific methods for investigating that reality.

The Positivist Approach

The traditional method of the physical sciences, which early social scientists tried to imitate, is now often called *positivistic science*. Its proponents based their view of science on a set of principles most fully set out in the writings of a group of influential thinkers known as positivists, who were active in the late nineteenth and early twentieth centuries. Today, **positivism** has become a label for a particular way of looking at and studying the world scientifically.

Positivism aims to explain how the material world works, and in terms of material causes and processes that we can detect using our five senses (sight, smell, touch, hearing, and taste). Second, to achieve this goal, positivists also are committed to a scientific methodology that separates facts from values. This separation is justified on the grounds that facts relate to the nature of physical, material reality—what *is*—whereas, in their view, values are based on speculation about what *ought to be*. To the positivist, scientific research is concerned only with what is. As a result, all valid scientific inquiry, from subatomic structure, to genetic engineering, to in vitro fertilization, or human sexual response should be understood as different aspects of a single, disinterested quest for knowledge, a quest that cannot be compromised simply because it offends some people's moral or political sensibilities. Truth remains the truth, whether people like it or not, whether it conforms to their idea of what is good and proper or not. These examples point to a third feature of positivism: the conviction that a single scientific method can be used to investigate any domain of reality, from planetary motion to chemical reactions to human life. The most ambitious positivists are convinced that all scientific knowledge will ultimately be unified in a "theory of everything."

Based on these commitments, the traditional goal of the positivist program has been to produce **objective knowledge**, knowledge about reality that is true for all people in all times and places. Positivist science has been viewed as the route to that objective knowledge, precisely because of its disciplined determination to describe the way the material world actually is, unobscured by any webs of meaning and value that human beings might ascribe to it. For the positivist, there is a single structure to material reality, and the positivist method can lay it bare.

Applying Positivist Methods to Anthropology

For the positivist, the prototypical research scenario involves a physical scientist in a laboratory. This prototype creates obstacles for those who study human life by means of participant-observation in a natural setting. Early cultural anthropologists were aware of these obstacles, and they tried to devise ways to get

around them. Their first step was to approximate lab conditions by testing hypotheses in different cultural settings. These settings were carefully selected to exhibit naturally the same range of variation that a laboratory scientist could create artificially. As a result, the field could be seen as a living laboratory. Each research setting would correspond to a separate experimental situation, a method called *controlled comparison*. Margaret Mead used this method in the 1930s, when she studied four different societies in an attempt to discover the range and causes of gender roles.

Positivist anthropologists were encouraged by the enormous successes that the physical scientists had attained by following these principles. From the middle of the nineteenth century to the middle of the twentieth century, positivistically inclined anthropologists recorded as faithfully as they could the ways of life of peoples their contemporaries had neither heard of nor cared to know. Rejecting the slipshod, impressionistic work of an earlier period, they produced accounts of other cultures that were systematic and accurate—and sometimes insensitive.

What does it mean to accuse scientists of insensitivity? Anthropologists can be charged with insensitivity when their reports treat their human subjects as if they are no different from rocks or molecules. After all, the subject matter of the social sciences is human beings who belong to the same species (and possibly to the same society) as the social scientists. Anthropologists found themselves confronting a paradox. Although they regularly developed close personal ties to the people among whom they worked, defending their full humanity to outsiders and sometimes intervening on their behalf with the government, none of this showed up in their ethnographies. Instead, they wrote as if they had been invisible observers recording objective facts about a way of life in which they were not personally involved.

Questioning the Positivist Approach

The 1960s and 1970s mark a turning point in anthropological understandings of fieldwork. This was a period of social and political turmoil throughout the world, as struggles for civil rights, women's rights,

objective knowledge Knowledge about reality that is absolute and true.

and independence from colonial control called into question many assumptions about the way the world worked. This included questioning the nature of science. Anthropologists began to reconsider the ethics and politics of positivist science in general and of participant-observation in particular. In the 1970s and 1980s anthropologists began to write ethnographies highlighting the ways their own involvement with others in the field had contributed to the growth of cross-cultural knowledge. They were able to show how different observers, working from different assumptions, often produce different knowledge about the same society. At the same time, differently situated fieldworkers also sometimes draw similar conclusions, which allows them to link up their work in productive ways.

Consider the fieldwork of Annette Weiner in the Trobriand Islands carried out in the 1970s, nearly 60 years after Bronislaw Malinowski did his original and celebrated fieldwork there. Weiner and Malinowski were anthropologists of different nationalities and different genders working in different villages with different informants during different historical periods. Weiner made an important contribution to our understanding of Trobriand life by describing and explaining activities involving Trobriand women's "wealth" that were absolutely central to the continued healthy functioning of Trobriand life—but about which Malinowski had written nothing (see chapter 10). Weiner might have published her findings by declaring that Malinowski had got it wrong. But this route did not appeal to her, primarily because, as she put it, he got so very much right. Malinowski's own preoccupations led him to write about aspects of Trobriand life different from those that interested Weiner. As a result, he left behind a portrait of Trobriand society that Weiner later felt obliged to supplement. Nevertheless, Weiner found that much of Malinowski's work remained valid and insightful in her day. She quoted long passages from his ethnographies in her own writings about the Trobriands, in tribute to him (see Weiner 1976, 1988; see also EthnoProfile 3.4: Trobriand Islanders).

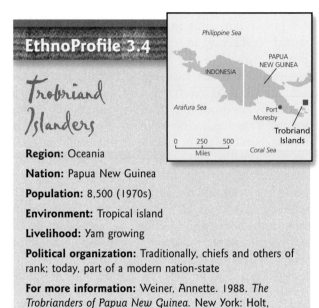

EthnoProfile 3.4

Trobriand Islanders

Region: Oceania

Nation: Papua New Guinea

Population: 8,500 (1970s)

Environment: Tropical island

Livelihood: Yam growing

Political organization: Traditionally, chiefs and others of rank; today, part of a modern nation-state

For more information: Weiner, Annette. 1988. *The Trobrianders of Papua New Guinea.* New York: Holt, Rinehart and Winston.

But the reconsideration of fieldwork looked not only at the way the backgrounds of ethnographers shaped their fieldwork. It also began to pay closer attention to the ethical and political dimensions of the relationships that anthropologists develop with the people whose way of life they study, usually referred to as **informants**. Anthropologists in the 1960s and 1970s began to reexamine the laboratory model of fieldwork. In geology and chemistry, for example, it is fairly easy to justify a hierarchy elevating the inquiring intelligence of the scientists over their subject matter. It seems difficult to imagine ethical obligations that the geologist might have to a mineral, or the political differences that might complicate chemists' relationships with the molecules in their test tubes.

But matters are otherwise when the subject matter of science is other human beings. Anthropologists wanting to do scientific fieldwork cannot avoid the realization that they share crucial commonalities with their subject matter that geologists and chemists do not share with theirs. Human beings *do* have ethical obligations to other human beings; political factors *can* complicate the relationships ethnographers are able to develop with their informants. Scientific accuracy therefore requires that anthropologists regard their informants as full human beings. Their subjects may be as eager to learn about the anthropologist as

---

informants People in a particular culture who work with anthropologists and provide them with insights about their way of life. Also called teachers or friends.

the anthropologist is to learn about them, and they may have their own motives for engaging in ethnographic fieldwork. Anthropologists must also see themselves as full human beings, not as impersonal recording machines, and acknowledge that human involvement with their informants is central to cross-cultural understanding. This is why, for example, many contemporary ethnographers no longer use the word *informant* to refer to those with whom they work, preferring a term like *consultants*, *guides*, *advisors*, or, more generally, *the people with whom I work*.

But these requirements for scientific fieldwork mean that anthropologists can no longer accept the basic assumptions of positivist research without question. Such questioning of positivist science is not taken lightly, especially by other scientists committed to it. Often those who question positivist methods are accused of abandoning scientific discipline entirely, allowing material facts to be obscured by their own, individual *subjective* values and preferences. This is a serious charge. Does the rejection of positivism turn fieldwork into just one person's subjective impressions of other people?

Most anthropologists would answer with a firm "no," because the fieldwork is a *dialogue* between ethnographers and their informants. The fact that ethnographer and informant are both human beings means that scientist and subject matter *both* possess inquiring intelligences. Ethnographers engage in real, literal, conversations with their informants in order to learn about their informants' way of life. These dialogues are often patient and painstaking collaborative attempts to sort things out, to piece things together. When successful, the outcome is a new understanding of the world that both anthropologist and informant can share. This means that field data are not subjective, but *intersubjective:* They are the product of long dialogues between researcher and informant. The focus of fieldwork is the range of **intersubjective meanings** that informants share. Fieldworkers can come to understand these meanings by sharing activities and conversations with their informants. This is what participant-observation is all about.

The Reflexive Approach

The intersubjective meanings on which informants rely are public, not private. Informants take them for granted, but they may not be obvious to an outsider.

In order to make these meanings explicit, anthropologist and informant together must occasionally step back from the ordinary flow of daily life and examine them critically. They must think about the way members of the culture normally think about their lives. This thinking about thinking is known as **reflexivity**; thus, fieldwork in cultural anthropology is a reflexive experience. Reflexive fieldwork retains a respect for detailed, accurate information gathering (Figure 3.5), but it also pays explicit attention to the ethical and political context of research, the background of researchers, the full partnership of informants, and the collaborative relationships that produce anthropological knowledge.

Reflexive fieldwork takes into consideration a broader range of contextual information than does positivistic fieldwork. But consideration of these factors is seen to be essential in order to produce knowledge about human beings that is scientifically valid. Ethnographers have come to recognize that the reliability of their knowledge of other cultures depends on explicit recognition of the ethical and political dimensions of fieldwork, and acknowledgement of how these may have shaped that knowledge. Thus, ethnographic knowledge, shaped by the reflexivity of the ethnographer, has to be understood as *situated knowledge* (Haraway 1991). The "situating" to which Donna Haraway refers involves making explicit exactly who you are as an ethnographer, i.e., your nationality, your class background, your gender, your ethnic background, your educational background, your political preferences, why you undertook this research project, and so forth.

While it might seem that these factors are irrelevant to science and ought to be suppressed, Haraway and others stress that it is precisely these kinds of factors that will shape the kinds of interactions ethnographers will be able to enter into with their informants. In some societies, being a male ethnographer may bar you from studying certain social activities that are seen as inappropriate for men. If these activities are central to the ongoing viability of the local culture, and you end up not being able to learn about them, your ethnographic account of that culture is

---

intersubjective meanings The shared, public symbolic systems of a culture.

reflexivity Critically thinking about the way one thinks; reflecting on one's own experience.

FIGURE 3.5 Anthropologists use different technologies for different research purposes. Anthropologist Ryan Cook videotapes the spectators and ritual performers at the Popocatepetl volcano in Mexico.

bound to be incomplete. On the one hand, this can be seen as a weakness if only a complete discussion meets the test of positivist "scientific objectivity." On the other hand, to present a detailed and accurate account of what you were able to learn, together with an explicit acknowledgement of its limitations (based on who you are, what you are competent to write about, and what you were permitted to study) can be seen as far more reliable, despite the fact that it is partial. This is because it accurately reflects the objective fact that you did not talk to everybody, or see everything, and therefore refuse to make sweeping generalizations about an entire social group on the basis of limited knowledge. Thus, reflexivity promotes explicit recognition that any ethnographic account must be understood as situated knowledge produced by the partial understandings of particular ethnographers working with particular informants, whose relationships to one another are shaped by particular ethical and political contexts. Far from making ethnographic knowledge subjective, however, reflexivity generates what philosopher of science Sandra Harding calls *strong objectivity*, which she contrasts with the *weak objectivity* produced by traditional positivistic approaches (1991, 149ff.). We would argue that the best ethnographies have always been reflexive, whether they were done in 1937 or 2007 and whether or not the ethnographers

realized it. Moreover, ethnographic understanding of the culture of the Trobriand Islanders is richer and more reliable when the partial, situated knowledges of Malinowski and Weiner are acknowledged, juxtaposed, and eventually supplemented by the work of other, differently situated participant-observers.

The commitment to reflexivity has had far-reaching implications for the ways anthropologists carry out their research. Fieldworkers do not merely participate and observe and let it go at that. They consider themselves scientifically and ethically obligated to make public the way in which they gather data. Some anthropologists have argued that they must also share their conclusions with their informants and include their informants' reflections on those conclusions in their published ethnographies. Bettylou Valentine, for example, persuaded several of her informants to comment on her manuscript before publication. She visited them for lengthy discussions and found that, in general, they agreed with her conclusions. In the published volume, Valentine states her own conclusions, based on her own research and analysis. She also allows her informants a voice, permitting them, in a final chapter, to state where and why they disagree with her. Valentine's ethnography presents a vivid example of the open-endedness of the dialogue between anthropologist and informant: No single interpretation of human experience is final. Overall, a focus on reflexivity in anthropology has led to a more complex understanding of the ethical challenges anthropologists face as they carry out research. Pat Caplan, who edited a recent collection of essays exploring the relationship between anthropology and ethics, has noted that this commitment to reflexivity requires that we ask who we are before we ask what we ought to do. She adds that "the ethics of anthropology must be *critical*, both of ourselves and of our discipline, . . . obliging us to grapple with difficult and complex issues, and to pose again and again the fundamental question: What's it all for?" (2003, 27).

▼ WHAT IS THE DIALECTIC OF FIELDWORK?

Fieldwork is a risky business. Fieldworkers not only risk offending their informants by misunderstanding their way of life, but they also face the shock of the unfamiliar and their own vulnerability. Indeed, they must embrace this shock and cultivate this vulnerability if they are to achieve any kind of meaningful understanding of their informants' culture.

In the beginning, fieldworkers can be reassured by some of the insights that anthropological training has provided. Since all human beings are members of the same biological species, ethnographers can expect to find in all human groups the same range of variation with regard to such human potentialities as intelligence. This can fortify them against ethnocentric impulses by recalling "that if what we observe appears to be odd or irrational, it is probably because we do not understand it and not because it is a product of a 'savage' culture in which such nonsense is to be expected" (Greenwood and Stini 1977, 185).

Anthropologist Michael Agar uses the expression *rich points* for unexpected moments when problems in cross-cultural understanding emerge. Rich points may be words or actions that signal the gaps between the local people's out-of-awareness assumptions about how the world works and those of the anthropologist. For Agar, rich points are the raw material of ethnography. As he says, "It is this distance between two worlds of experience that is exactly the problem that ethnographic research is designed to locate and resolve" (Agar 1996, 31). Ethnographers work hard to situate rich points within the local cultural world, continually testing their interpretations in a variety of settings and with different people in order to see whether those interpretations are or are not confirmed.

Interpretation and Translation

How does one go about interpreting the actions and ideas of other human beings? We need a form of interpretation that does not turn our informants into objects. That is, we need a form of interpretation based on reflexivity rather than objectivity. Paul Rabinow addresses this problem in a book based on reconsideration of his own fieldwork experiences. In *Reflections on Fieldwork in Morocco* (1977), Rabinow suggested that what goes on in ethnographic research was described well by French philosopher Paul Ricoeur: "Following Ricoeur, I define the problem of hermeneutics (which is simply Greek for 'interpretation') as 'the comprehension of the self by the detour of the comprehension of the other.' It is vital to stress that this is not psy-

chology of any sort. . . . The self being discussed is perfectly public. . . . [It is] the culturally mediated and historically situated self which finds itself in a continuously changing world of meaning" (Rabinow 1977, 5–6). For the anthropologist in the field, then, interpretation becomes a task of coming to comprehend the *cultural self* by the detour of comprehending the *cultural other*. In other words, the anthropologist's understanding of the cultural other is intersubjectively constructed, using elements drawn from the cultural systems of anthropologist and informant alike. As we come to grasp the meaning of the other's cultural self, we simultaneously learn something of the meaning of our own cultural identity.

The gulf between self and other may seem unbridgeable in the context of cross-cultural ethnography. Yet anthropologists and informants engaged in participant-observation do share one thing: the fieldwork situation itself. They are face to face, observing and discussing the same objects and activities. At first, they may talk past one another, as each describes activities from a different perspective and using a different language. However, all cultures and languages are open enough to entertain a variety of viewpoints and a variety of ways to talk about them. Continued discussion allows anthropologist and informant to search for ways to communicate about what is going on around them. Any overlap or intersection that promotes mutual understanding, however small, can form the foundation on which anthropologist and informant may then build a new intersubjective symbolic language of their own.

This process of building a bridge of understanding between self and other is what Rabinow refers to as the **dialectic of fieldwork** (1977, 39). Both fieldworker and informant may begin with little or nothing in the way of shared experience that could allow them to figure one another out with any accuracy. But if they are motivated to make sense of one another and willing to work together, steps toward valid interpretation and mutual understanding can be made.

For example, traditional fieldwork often begins with collecting data on how people in the local

dialectic of fieldwork The process of building a bridge of understanding between anthropologist and informants so that each can begin to understand the other.

community believe themselves to be related to each other. A trained anthropologist comes to the field with knowledge of a variety of possible forms of social organization in mind. These ideas derive in part from the anthropologist's own experience of social relations, but they will also be based on research and theorizing about social relations by other anthropologists. As the fieldworker begins to ask questions about social relations, he or she may discover that the informants have no word in their language that accurately conveys the range of meaning carried by a term like *kinship* or *ethnic group*. This does not mean that the anthropologist must give up. Rather, the anthropologist must enter into the dialectic process of *interpretation* and *translation*.

The process works something like this. The anthropologist asks about "ethnic groups" using a term in the informants' language that seems close in meaning to the term *ethnic group* in English. Informants then try to interpret the anthropologist's question in a way that makes sense to them. That is, each informant has to be reflexive, thinking about how people in his or her society think about the topic that the anthropologist is addressing. Having formulated an answer, the informant responds in terms he or she thinks the anthropologist will understand. Now it is the anthropologist's turn to interpret this response, to decide if it makes sense and carries the kind of information he or she was looking for.

In the dialectic of fieldwork, both anthropologist and informant are active agents. Each party tries to figure out what the other is trying to say. If there is goodwill on the part of both, each party also tries to provide responses that make sense to the other. As more than one anthropologist has remarked (see, for example, Crick 1976; Rabinow 1977), anthropological fieldwork is translation, and translation is a complicated and tricky process, full of false starts and misunderstandings. Moreover, the informant is just as actively engaged in translation as the anthropologist. As time passes and the partners in this effort learn from their mistakes and successes, their ability to communicate increases. Each participant learns more about the other: The anthropologist gains skill at asking questions that make sense to the informant, and the informant becomes more skilled at answering those questions in terms relevant to the anthropologist. The validity of this ongoing translation is an-

chored in the ongoing cultural activities in which both anthropologist and informant are participant-observers. Out of this mutual activity comes knowledge about the informant's culture that is meaningful to both anthropologist and informant. This is new knowledge, a hybrid product of common understandings that emerges from the collaboration of anthropologist and informant.

Informants are equally involved in this dialogue and may end up learning as much or more about anthropologists as anthropologists learn about them. But it is important to emphasize that in field situations *the dialogue is initiated by anthropologists*. Anthropologists come to the field with their own sets of questions, which are determined not by the field situation but by the discipline of anthropology itself (see Karp and Kendall 1982, 254). Furthermore, when anthropologists are finished with a particular research project, they are often free to break off the dialogue with informants and resume discussions with fellow professionals. The only link between these two sets of dialogues—between particular anthropologists and the people with whom they work and among anthropologists in general—may be the particular anthropologists themselves.

Beyond the Dialectic

As we noted earlier, anthropologists feel strongly that their informants' identities should be protected, all the more so when they belong to marginal and powerless groups that might suffer retaliation from more powerful members of their society. Some informants, however, wish to express their identity and their ideas openly, and some anthropologists have experimented with forms of ethnographic writing in which they serve primarily as translators and editors of the voices and opinions of individual informants (see, for example, Keesing 1983; Shostak 1981). Anthropologists working in their own societies have written about their fieldwork both as observers of others and as members of the society they are observing (see, for example, Foley 1989; Kumar 1992). In recent years, members of indigenous societies have begun to speak powerfully on their own behalf, as political advocates for their people, as lawyers, as organizers, and as professional scholars. Nevertheless, it is often the case that the people with whom anthropologists

IN THEIR OWN WORDS

Japanese Corporate Wives in the United States

Anthropologist Sawa Kurotani writes about the "breakthrough" in her research with Japanese corporate wives living in the United States while their husbands were on assignment there.

The fact that I did not have children was perhaps the most significant factor that made my working relationships with Japanese corporate wives awkward. I was Japanese, I was female, and I came from a family background that was very similar to that of many of the women. However, I did not take the typical path of a woman from such a habitus, namely, to work for a few years after college, marry a man with a stable job, quit my job, have a child or two, and become a full-time wife/mother. Instead, I moved to the United States, went on to graduate school, married a foreigner, and postponed having children. If I were, say, an American woman, they could have attributed all our differences to the difference in sociocultural norms; but with me, that was not an option. I was, in a way, a freak of a middle-class Japanese woman, who turned her back on the respectable life that she was supposed to live; that made my character somewhat questionable. The combination of similarities and differences made it difficult for my female informants to relate to my choices and experiences. Among the mothers with young children, there were also more pragmatic issues with having a childless woman around. They were often afraid that their children would do something to offend those who were not used to having children—often crying, whining, and messy children—around. In fact, many of Kawagoe-san's friends apologized to me every time their children tried to get on my knees, or tugged at my clothes, or even looked in my direction. I repeatedly told them that I liked children (which was true) and that their children were not bothering me at all (which was usually true), but I could see that they found it cumbersome as much as I did to have to worry so much about their children all the time. This went on for a couple of months, until the chicken incident.

One day, I was sitting in Kawagoe-san's living room over take-out Chinese lunch with several other women and their children. Although I was becoming a familiar face at Kawagoe-san's, I felt that most of Kawagoe-san's friends were still somewhat unsure about me. They continued to talk to me in polite language, and they rarely initiated a conversation with me. The only exception was Irie-san, who, on a number of occasions, sat next to me and engaged in conversation about my work and my experience in the United States, That day, too, she and her son Yohei were sitting next to me; suddenly, Yohei grabbed a piece of chicken from his plate and handed it to me. The chicken had been pushed around on his plate for a while, and perhaps was even chewed on a couple of times. I took it anyway and immediately threw it into my mouth. I did so partly because I did not want to disappoint the child and also because, somewhere in my mind, I calculated its effect on the mothers. Irie-san was first to speak.

"You know, my husband won't eat the food from Yohei's plate, let alone from his hands," she said. "Men simply can't do that. After all, they are not like women, they are not mothers."

"That's so true," Kawagoe-san chimed in, "but I can't blame them, either. I couldn't have done that before I had my own kids!"

From the way other women chuckled, it seemed to be the same with their husbands. They went on citing instances of men's inability to deal with the filth and dirt (kitanaimono) generated by children: half-eaten food, spilled drinks on the floor, runny noses, and dirty diapers.

The chicken incident was a critical turning point in two ways. First, it gave me an invaluable insight into the problem of my marginality; second, it became the beginning of our negotiation to establish me, the childless woman, as mother material (if my true potential was untested). Irie-san and other women distinguished between themselves and their husbands by the way they physically related to their children, in particular, through their reaction to the filth and dirt that, in their mind, necessarily came with small children. It suddenly dawned on me that this was, for them, an important criterion of gender categories: those who could

(continued on next page)

Japanese Corporate Wives in the United States *(continued)*

handle the filth are (potential) mothers, thus necessarily female. The gender of nonmother females, who could not deal with it, was more ambiguous; it was certainly not the same as that of the mothers. The problem of female academicians, according to these women's stereotype at least, was their lack of motherly ability to take care of the dirty things that children produce and, thus, a fatal flaw in their

femininity. The gender category of these (biological) women was left unclear when they could not perform the motherly function. In the eyes of my female Japanese informants, I crossed the threshold into womanhood/motherhood with that gooey piece of chicken in my mouth.

Source: Kurotani 2005, 132–133.

work may be prohibited by language and other barriers from speaking to an audience of professional scholars on complex topics, nor are their interests necessarily the same as those of professional scholars. Fieldwork regularly involves differences of power and places a heavy burden of responsibility on researchers. They are accountable not only to their informants but also to the discipline of anthropology, which has its own theoretical and practical concerns and ways of reasoning about ethnographic data.

For these reasons, a number of anthropologists have begun to call for forms of ethnographic research and writing that go beyond the dialectic of fieldwork. Luke Eric Lassiter, for example, observes that "anthropologists and American Indian scholars alike" are searching for collaborative ways to "write texts both responsive and relevant to the public with whom they work" (2001, 139). Lassiter used a collaborative methodology as he wrote and rewrote first the text of his Ph.D. dissertation on Kiowa song and, later, the book based on his dissertation. One of the key issues he faced was how to write about "a felt entity encountered in song called, in Kiowa, *daw* and in English *power* or, more precisely, *Spirit* (2001, 140). Most academically oriented ethnographers tend to write about such entities "from a position of disbelief," but for Kiowa singers like Ralph Kotay, "Spirit is not a concept. It is a very real and tangible thing" (2001, 140). And so Lassiter struggled in his ethnography

to shift my focus form situating Spirit within an academic sacred/secular dichotomy (based on distance and disbelief) to that of emphasizing the phenome-

nological questions about Spirit (based in proximity and belief) emergent in our collaborative conversations. Discussions about the ethnographic text itself powerfully reshaped and redefined the book's evolution and further shifted the authority and control of the text from the ethnographer to the *dialogue* between ethnographer and consultants (2001, 140).

Lassiter's work with Ralph Kotay and other Kiowa consultants raised a further issue as well (Figure 3.6). At one point, Kotay had told him, "I'm always willing to give out information like this. But . . . I don't want anything else said *above* this" (2001, 143). Lassiter suggests that Kotay's comment is not just about the obligation to report Kotay's views accurately but also implies that Lassiter should "draw my interpretation of Kiowa song from his perspective rather than my own, and that I will privilege any public representations of Kiowa song (i.e., in texts, essays, etc.) from that same perspective. For Kotay and many other Kiowa consultants, the issue . . . is truly about who has control and who has the 'last word'" (2001, 143). To produce collaborative ethnographies of this kind would require anthropologists to resist the deeply rooted Western academic practice of writing texts for which they claimed sole authorship; this could have repercussions in university settings where scholars are expected to publish as individuals. But it would also transform "the role of the so-called informant—where collaborators appear only to inform the production of knowledge—to that of 'consultant,' of 'co-intellectual,'" and would introduce into their ethnographic writings forms of activism that

IN THEIR OWN WORDS

The Situation of the Brazilian Anthropologist

Contemporary anthropologists come from many places other than Europe or the United States. Anthropologist Roberto da Matta explores what it means for him to be a Brazilian anthropologist working in Brazil.

In order to grasp deep motivations in ethnographic styles, one has to deal with how natives are represented as "others"—as different, as distinct—in divergent national contexts. In Brazil, the "other" is incarnated by a small native population, scattered in the empty Amazon and Central Brazil, a population generically called by the name, "êndio" (Indian). But the "Indian" is not alone, for with the category "Negro" they form the basis of a singular and intriguing view of the immediate human diversity for Brazilians. The "Negro" (who is fundamentally the ex-slave) is an intrinsic element of Brazilian social structure, haunting with his massive presence the "whiteness" of a bourgeois lifestyle. The "Indian" is an outsider, giving rise to the romantic fantasies of the noble savage who has to be either isolated and protected from the evils of civilization or be eliminated from the national landscape for incapacity to take part in modern progress.

In this context, to be with "Indians" is, for a Brazilian anthropologist, more than having the opportunity of living with another humanity. It is also to have the privilege of getting in touch with a mythical other. And by doing so, have the honor of being the one to overcome all manner of discomforts in order to describe a new way of life in the midst of Brazilian civilization. Thus, for Brazilian anthropologists, "to be there" is also an opportunity of being a witness to the way of life of a different society. This is particularly true when that way of life runs the risk of succumbing to a contact situation that is brutally unequal in political terms.

Source: da Matta 1994, 122–23.

already engage many ethnographers in other contexts (2001, 145).

In a similar fashion, Arjun Appadurai has called for a "deparochialization of the research ethic" that would involve collaboration with colleagues outside the United States, such as grassroots activists, who often lack the kinds of institutional resources and professional experience that scholars in the United States take for granted. With the right support, such colleagues could become equal partners in "a conversation about research" in which they "bring their own ideas of what counts as new knowledge" as well as their own ideas of how to measure the researcher's accountability to those among whom they work (2002, 281).

The Dialectic of Fieldwork: Some Examples

Daniel Bradburd writes about the give and take of cross-cultural learning in his discussion of fieldwork among the Komachi, a nomadic people in Iran with whom he and his wife, Anne Sheedy, lived in the mid-1970s (see EthnoProfile 3.5: Komachi). Bradburd had gone to Iran to study the process of active decision making among nomadic herding people, and he was therefore quite interested in when people would move their camps and why they would do it (Figure 3.7). His first experience with moving was not what he had expected. After a month in one place, he started to hear talk about moving. Why? he asked. To be closer to the village and because the campsite was dirty. When? Soon. When is soon? When Tavakoli comes. This answer made no sense until further questioning revealed that Tavakoli was the son of the leader of the camp.

Eventually their hosts told them that the move would be the next day, but when the next day came, there were no signs of activity in the camp. Finally, when it became clear that they would not be moving that day, Bradburd began asking why they hadn't moved. The answer was *"ruz aqrab."* When they

FIGURE 3.6 Anthropologist Luke Eric Lassiter (on the right) and Kiowa collaborator Ralph Kotay.

looked up *aqrab* in the dictionary, the answer made even less sense than the previous one: they weren't moving because it was the day of the scorpion. "As was often the case, we felt as though we had moved one step forward and two steps back. We had an answer, but we hadn't the faintest idea what it meant. We were pretty certain it didn't have anything to do

with real scorpions, because we hadn't seen any. We were also pretty certain that we hadn't heard any mention of them. So back we trudged to Qoli's tent, and we started asking more questions. Slowly it became clear. The scorpion was not a real, living one; it was the constellation Scorpio, which Qoli later pointed out to us on the horizon" (Bradburd 1998, 41).

After more questioning and more thinking, Bradburd and Sheedy finally concluded that the Komachi believed it was bad luck to undertake a new activity on days when it appeared that Scorpio would catch the rising moon. On checking back with their informants, they found that their conclusion was correct, but they were still puzzled. On the day that they had been told that the move would be the next day, the Komachi in their camp had been fully aware that Scorpio and the rising moon would be in conjunction the next day. Eventually, Bradburd and Sheedy decided that *ruz aqrab* was a reasonable excuse for not moving, but they never did figure out the real reason for not moving that day. In fact, over the course of many such experiences, Bradburd and Sheedy came to realize that the Komachi didn't have specific reasons for not moving. Rather, they still had one or another thing to do where they were, or the weather was uncertain, or the route to take wasn't clear yet, and so on. As a result of Bradburd's questions and the Komachi's responses, his interpretations and their responses to them, he gradually concluded that the Komachi decision-making process was an attempt to minimize the risks they had to take. Rather than being heroic nomads, masters of their fate, the Komachi made decisions only when they had to.

Nita Kumar is an anthropologist from Delhi, India, who chose to do fieldwork in her own country, but in a region of India very different from the one where she grew up: "Banaras was such a mystery to me when I arrived there in 1981 ironically *because* I was an Indian and expected to have a privileged insight into it. In fact, from Banaras I was *thrice* removed: through my education and upbringing, than which there is no greater molder of attitudes; by language and linguistic culture; and by region and regional culture" (1992, 15) (see EthnoProfile 3.6: Banaras). Although her social connections smoothed the way for her in official circles, she had no special advantage when trying to make contact with the artisans in Banaras whose way of life interested her.

EthnoProfile 3.5

Komachi
(mid-1970s)

Region: Southwest Asia

Nation: Iran

Population: 550

Environment: Varied—mountain valleys, lowland wooded areas

Livelihood: Nomadic herders

Political organization: Part of modern nation-state

For more information: Bradburd, Daniel. 1998. *Being there: The necessity of fieldwork.* Washington DC: Smithsonian Institution Press.

FIGURE 3.7 Daniel Bradburd and Komachi camels packed for moving.

Finding informants and establishing rapport with them has always been seen as an indispensable first step in fieldwork, but there are no foolproof procedures that guarantee success. In her fieldwork memoir, *Friends, Brothers, and Informants* (1992), Kumar shares the four failed attempts she made to contact weavers. The first time, the weavers turned out to have well-established ties to rickshaw pullers and taxi drivers who regularly brought tourists to visit their shop and buy souvenirs. Not wishing to become just another business contact, she left. Her second contact was with the Muslim owner of a weaving establishment whose suspicions of her motives caused her to turn elsewhere. Her third attempt was made through a sari salesman who took her to a market where silk weavers sold their wares. Unfortunately for her, he would periodically announce to all assembled who she was and invite weavers to come up and speak with her, a procedure she found deeply embarrassing. Her fourth attempt followed the accidental discovery that two members of a family selling firecrackers were also weavers. When she was invited to see one brother's loom, however, she grew "uncomfortable with all the obvious evidence of bachelor existence and their readiness to welcome me into it. . . . I just went away and never came back" (99). On her fifth attempt, she was introduced by a silk-yarn merchant to weavers living in a government-subsidized housing project next to his house. In the home of a weaver named Shaukatullah, surrounded by members of his family, she finally found a setting in which she felt welcome and able to do her work.

"In a matter of weeks I was given the status of a daughter of Shaukatullah" (105). That status of daughter was not only important to Kumar's research, but it was also a congenial status to her, one with which she was familiar.

Ruptures in Communication

Jean Briggs is an anthropologist who was also adopted by a family of informants. Briggs worked among the Utkuhikhalingmiut (Utku, for short), an Inuit group in Alaska (see EthnoProfile 3.7:

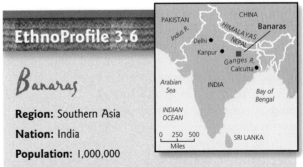

EthnoProfile 3.6

Banaras

Region: Southern Asia

Nation: India

Population: 1,000,000

Environment: Tropical monsoon region

Livelihood: Arts, weaving silk, handicrafts; pilgrimage center; urban occupations, education

Political organization: City in a modern nation-state

For more information: Kumar, Nita. 1992. *Friends, brothers, and informants: Fieldwork memories of Banaras.* Berkeley: University of California Press.

EthnoProfile 3.7

*Utkuhikhaling-
miut
(Utku Inuit)*

Region: North America

Nation: Canada (Northwest Territories)

Population: 35

Environment: Tundra

Livelihood: Nomadic fishing, hunting, gathering

Political organization: Communal

For more information: Briggs, Jean. 1970. *Never in anger: Portrait of an Eskimo family.* Cambridge, MA: Harvard University Press.

Utkuhikhalingmiut [Utku Inuit]). There were several steps her informants took in order to figure her out once she took on the role of daughter in the home of her new "father," Inuttiaq, and "mother," Allaq: "From the moment that the adoption was settled, I was 'Inuttiaq's daughter' in the camp. [They] drilled me in the use of kin terms appropriate to my position, just as they drilled [Inuttiaq's] three-year-old daughter, who was learning to speak" (Briggs 1980, 46). The context of their interactions had clearly changed as a result of the adoption, and Briggs's family had new expectations both of Briggs and of themselves: "Allaq, and especially Inuttiaq . . . more and more attempted to assimilate me into a proper adult parent-daughter relationship. I was expected to help with the household work . . . and I was expected to obey unquestioningly when Inuttiaq told me to do something. . . . Inevitably, conflicts, covert but pervasive, developed" (47).

Briggs found herself feeling increasingly uncomfortable and began to analyze her situation. She began to realize that part of the problem had to do with differences between her ideas of how parents ought to relate to their daughters and Utku beliefs on these matters. She also experienced contradictions between

her roles as daughter and anthropologist. The dialectic of fieldwork brought sharply to awareness—aided in the construction of—her understanding of the meaning of those roles in her own culture. Moreover, Briggs was not the only person who had to be reflexive. Her Utku informants were forced to reconsider how they had been dealing with her since her arrival. As she was able to reconstruct it, their understanding of her went through three stages. At first, her informants thought she was strange, anomalous. After her adoption, they saw her as educable. But when the communication breakdown occurred, they concluded that she was "uneducable in important ways . . . a defective person" (60–61). Unlike Kumar, Briggs found that assuming the role of daughter was uncomfortable for her personally. While it initially provided her with an opportunity to "fit into" the community she was studying, it also posed challenges to the very continuation of her fieldwork.

Briggs's experience among the Utku also illustrates how, despite strenuous efforts at mutual understanding and translation, the dialectic of fieldwork is not always smooth, and how, despite one's best efforts, the ethnographer may fail to perceive how the same behavior in different cultural circumstances can be interpreted differently. Briggs understood from her informants that anger was dangerous and must never be shown. She also became aware of the various ways her informants diverted or diffused angry feelings. Nevertheless, she remained ignorant of the full power of this value in Utku culture until she found herself having seriously violated it.

Beginning a few years before her fieldwork, Briggs relates, sportsmen from the United States and Canada had begun to fly into the inlet where her informants lived during July and August. Once there, they borrowed canoes belonging to the Utku. Although there had at one time been several usable canoes in the community, only two remained when Briggs arrived. That summer some sportsmen borrowed one canoe, but ran it onto a rock. They then asked the Utkus if they could borrow the one remaining canoe, which happened to belong to Briggs's "father," Inuttiaq.

Briggs became the translator for the sportsmen. She was annoyed that their carelessness had led to the ruin of one of the last two good canoes. Because canoes are used for getting food and are not pleasure craft, the loss had serious economic consequences for her informants. When the outsiders asked to use the last canoe afloat, Briggs says, "I exploded." She lectured the sportsmen about their carelessness and insensitivity and explained how important canoes were to the Utku. Then, remembering Inuttiaq's often-repeated admonition never to lend his canoe, she told the sportsmen that the owner of the one remaining canoe did not want to lend it. When Inuttiaq insisted that the canoe be lent, she was not only surprised, she was shocked.

But this was only the beginning. Briggs discovered that, following her outburst, her informants seemed to turn against her rather than against the sportsmen. "I had spoken unbidden and in anger. . . . Punishment was a subtle form of ostracism. . . . I was isolated. It was as though I were not there. . . . But . . . I was still treated with the most impeccable semblance of solicitude" (56–57). Briggs discovered just how much at odds her breaking point was with Utku cultural style. This breach might well have ended her fieldwork if a Westernized Utku friend, Ikayuqtuq, had not come to her rescue. "I had written my version of the story to Ikayuqtuq, had told her about my attempt to protect the Utku from the impositions of the kaplunas [white men] and asked her if she could help to explain my behavior to the Eskimos" (58). Ikayuqtuq did write to Allaq and Inuttiaq, although the letter did not arrive until three months later. During that time, Briggs seemed to be frozen out of Utku society.

Once the letter arrived, everything changed. Briggs's friend had found a way to translate her intentions into terms that Allaq and Inuttiaq could understand. As Briggs recalls, "the effect was magical." Inuttiaq began to tell the others what a dangerous task Briggs had taken on to defend the Utkus against the white men. The ice melted. And Briggs knew that relationships had been restored (and perhaps deepened) when Inuttiaq called her "daughter" once again.

The struggle that ensued when Briggs tried to be a good Utku daughter stems in part from what happens when ethnographers struggle to keep in check the full expression of their own cultural selves, in an effort to avoid offending their informants. The situation is complicated by the fieldworker's imperfect awareness of the sorts of behavior that are likely to offend informants. As a result, the fieldworkers have frequently felt that their motto ought to be "The in-

formant is always right." Many fieldworkers therefore forbid themselves to express anger or disgust or disagreement. But this behavior is likely to cause problems for both them and their informants. After all, what sort of person is always smiling, never angry, without opinions? Anthropologists who refuse to challenge or be challenged by their informants dehumanize both themselves and their informants. Clearly, it takes a good deal of diplomatic skill to walk a fine line between ethnocentrism and depersonalization. Sometimes, as in Briggs' case, this may not be possible, and the fieldwork itself may be put in jeopardy.

Paul Rabinow reflected on the consequences of his own commitment to the fieldworkers' motto in his relations with his informant Ali, who had agreed to take Rabinow to a wedding at some distance from the town where they lived; they were to go in Rabinow's car. Unfortunately, Rabinow was ill the day of the wedding. He did not want to break his promise and perhaps offend Ali and ruin any future chances to attend weddings, but he felt terrible. Ali agreed to stay only a short time at the wedding and then leave. Once they arrived, however, Ali disappeared for long stretches, returning to announce that they would definitely be leaving soon only to wander off again. Rabinow found himself feeling worse, trying to smile at members of the wedding party, and growing angrier and angrier with Ali. At last, many hours after their arrival, Rabinow managed to get Ali into the car and they headed for home. Things did not improve. Rabinow was certain that his annoyance must be obvious to Ali as they drove along, yet Ali kept asking him if he was happy, which was the sign of a pleased guest and a good host. When Rabinow steadfastly refused to answer him, Ali then declared that if Rabinow was unhappy, he, Ali, was insulted and would get out of the car and walk back to town. Rabinow had had enough. He stopped the car to let his companion out and drove on without him.

Rabinow was sure he had sabotaged his fieldwork completely. In retrospect, he acknowledged that this event led him to question seriously whether or not the informant is always right. He said, "If the informant was always right, then by implication the anthropologist had to become a sort of non-person. . . . He had to be willing to enter into any situation as a smiling observer. . . . One had to completely subordinate one's own code of ethics, conduct, and world view, to 'suspend disbelief' . . . and sympathetically and accurately record events" (1977, 46). The quarrel with Ali forced him to drop the anthropologist's all-accepting persona and allow the full force of his personality through. Rabinow chose to be true to himself on this occasion, regardless of the consequences for his fieldwork.

The results could have been disastrous, as they were for Briggs, but Rabinow was lucky. This rupture of communication with Ali was the prelude to Rabinow's experiencing one of his most significant insights into Moroccan culture. After his anger had cooled, he attempted to make up with Ali. To his great surprise, after only a few hours of warm apologies, his relationship with Ali was not only restored but even closer than before! How was this possible? Rabinow had unwittingly behaved toward Ali in the only manner that would impress him, in Moroccan terms. Rabinow learned that Moroccan men test each other all the time to see how far they can assert dominance before their assertions are challenged. In this world, a man who is all-accepting, such as an anthropologist, is not respected or admired but viewed as weak. "There was a fortuitous congruence between my breaking point and Moroccan cultural style. Perhaps in another situation my behavior might have proved irreparable. . . . By standing up to Ali I had communicated to him" (49).

Ruptures of communication between anthropologists and their informants can ultimately lead to a deepening of insight and a broadening of mutual understanding. This is what all fieldworkers hope for—and dread—because, as in Briggs' case, negotiating the rupture can be dangerous, and no positive outcome is ensured. The risks may seem greater when the informants' culture is very different from the anthropologist's, and consequently, it might seem that the resulting insights must also be more startling. Yet Bettylou Valentine discovered that fieldwork in the United States, among African Americans like herself, also held surprises: "At the start of fieldwork I assumed at a subconscious level that my college education . . . would enable me, unlike many ghetto residents, to handle successfully any problem resulting from the impact of the larger society on my family, myself, or any less-skilled ghetto resident I chose to help. This assumption was proved totally wrong many, many times" (1978, 132).

These examples of ethnographic fieldwork illustrate, each in its own way, the effects of reflexive awareness on the production of anthropological knowledge by means of participant-observation rooted in the dialectic of fieldwork. These commitments also affect the kind of ethnography anthropologists write. Unlike earlier ethnographies committed to the positivist approach, in reflexive ethnographies, the presence, the personalities, and the voices of ethnographers and informants alike become vivid elements.

All these accounts highlight the complications and misunderstandings that are a regular part of the dialectic of fieldwork, while Bourgois's, Kumar's, and the Valentines' accounts illustrate the particular opportunities and challenges that arise when doing fieldwork in your own society. In these respects, all these ethnographic accounts would seem to mark a clear advance over positivistic ethnographies in which such matters are never addressed or are ruled out of bounds. As a result, each account can lay claim to strong objectivity.

In other ways, however, the fieldwork of all five of these ethnographers is very much in keeping with the fieldwork tradition inherited from Malinowski and Boas. That is, all of them engaged in what remains the most common form of fieldwork in anthropology: "the intensively-focused-upon single site of ethnographic observation and participation" (Marcus 1995, 96). Much valuable work of this kind continues to be done. But changes in the world as a whole, particularly in the 1980s and 1990s, have led many anthropologists to undertake fieldwork projects that include more than one single site.

▼ HOW HAVE GLOBAL CHANGES AFFECTED FIELDWORK?

Changes in the world as a whole, particularly in the 1980s and 1990s, led many anthropologists to conclude that their ethnographic understandings would be incomplete if they confined their research to a single setting, even if they were committed to the reflexive approach. Indeed, developments within anthropology and related social sciences increasingly suggested that important factors would be missed unless ethnographers took explicit efforts to situate their work within a global context. In 1974, for example, sociologist Immanuel Wallerstein published a highly influential two-volume study called, *The Modern World System*, in which he argued that the rise and expansion of the European capitalist economy between 1450 and 1750 had incorporated vast regions of the world into a world system held together by the capitalist market. His account had important implications for anthropologists, for he argued that many parts of the world where anthropologists worked today had long ago been remade to occupy specialized niches within the capitalist world system. Thus, anthropological attempts to account for the current beliefs and practices of small-scale societies in these parts of the world could not ignore the historical impact on them of world-system influences such as European colonialism.

Wallerstein's work was followed by anthropologist Eric Wolf's monumental *Europe and the People Without History* (1982). Wolf's title is to be taken ironically: The non-European people about whom he wrote did indeed have histories of their own that were profoundly affected by European expansion. Tracing some of the same world-system interconnections discussed by Wallerstein, Wolf regularly would abandon the abstract view of the overall system in order to focus on the historical ethnographic details of specific societies affected by that system. In Wolf's discussion, indigenous peoples of North America appear as actors creatively coping with the challenge of the fur trade and European settlement, developing some of their characteristic forms of social organization (such as the League of the Iroquois) to ward off European threats or coming together to form new societies and new rituals in new territories (e.g., the Ojibway of the Great Lakes) after having been pushed off their old ones by settler expansion.

Multisited Fieldwork

The influence of the work of Wallerstein and Wolf upon ethnographers was profound. George Marcus notes that single-site fieldwork continued, but it was now conceived from the perspective of the world system (1995, 96). Anthropologists began to supplement their own data gathering with archival research that allowed them to situate the society they encountered historically, and they began to rethink existing social arrangements and cultural understandings as the products of active response to outside pressures rather than as timeless practices. Such work reanimated their awareness of the *lack* of isolation of the societies they studied, both in the past and in the present, and reinforced their awareness of their informants' agency that had been emphasized in the reflexive approach. The result was that neat boundaries between particular societies and the larger world system of which they were parts began to dissolve, as ethnographers were contextualizing their own field data in the context of places and processes that stretched far beyond their original field site. By the early 1990s, after the breakup of the Soviet Union, the successful move of capitalism into China, and the extraordinary surge of migrants around the world because of war and economic dislocation, all traditional boundaries seemed on the verge of dissolution. Wallerstein's world system no longer seemed so systemic, and the attention of many anthropologists shifted to the mapping of disconnected, fragmentary cultural processes in a disorganized, globalized world. These are the issues with which all contemporary ethnographic fieldwork must somehow come to terms.

The multisited approach to ethnography seems particularly well suited for the challenges of fieldwork in a world characterized by disorderly global processes. **Multisited fieldwork** focuses on cultural processes that are not contained by social, ethnic, religious or national boundaries, and the ethnographer follows the process from site to site, often doing fieldwork in sites and with persons that traditionally were never subject to ethnographic analysis (Figure 3.8). As Marcus describes it, "Multi-sited research is designed around chains, paths, threads, conjunctions, or juxtapositions of locations" as ethnographers trace "a complex cultural phenomenon . . . that turns out to be contingent and malleable as one traces it" (1995, 105–6). Multisited ethnographers follow *people, things, metaphors, plots* and *lives* (Marcus 1995, 107).

multisited fieldwork Ethnographic research on cultural processes that are not contained by social, ethnic, religious, or national boundaries, in which the ethnographer follows the process from site to site, often doing fieldwork at sites and with persons who traditionally were never subjected to ethnographic analysis.

FIGURE 3.8 Multisited field research is increasingly important in contemporary anthropology. As part of her research in Bolivia, Michelle Bigenho played violin with an ensemble in La Paz (left) and also spent time in participant-observation—here helping with planting—while studying music in the small town of Yura (right).

Examples of this kind of ethnography will appear throughout the book, but here are a few:

Ethnographers who follow people include those who study tourists or migrants. Philippe Bourgois's research in Spanish Harlem (1995) involved this kind of work: Although his day-to-day fieldwork was mostly focused on the neighborhood where the crack dealers lived, he followed them outside *El Barrio* when they sought employment in other parts of New York City. He also visited the sites in Puerto Rico from which their parents and grandparents had emigrated to the United States, in order to gain a first-hand understanding of that setting. And he supplemented present-day participant-observation with research on the history of Spanish Harlem from its first settlement up to the present day, thus locating it within the changing context of New York City, and shaped by wider processes of immigration and employment and job loss.

Michelle Bigenho (2002) was interested in "authenticity" in Bolivian musical performances and in how Bolivian identities and music were connected. Studying this topic took her to Bolivia for two years plus several subsequent summers, where she per-

formed with one musical ensemble in La Paz, studied a nongovernmental organization in La Paz dedicated to cultural projects related to music, and worked in two highland indigenous communities in the south. She also traveled to France to perform at an international folk festival with the Bolivian ensemble in which she played. This kind of topic could not have been pursued except as a multi-sited ethnography. As she herself puts it, "I moved through multiple places to conduct research on the narratives of Bolivian nations as experienced through several music performance contexts" (2002, 7).

Emily Martin's multisited ethnography—*Flexible Bodies: Tracking Immunity in American Culture from the Days of Polio to the Age of AIDS* (1995)—illustrates a different kind of achievement that can result when fieldwork is carried out in a range of different sites. Rather than follow people or music, Martin followed a metaphor—flexibility—which appeared to become popular in a variety of seemingly unconnected contexts in North American society. The project began when Martin reflected on the ways the immune system was discussed and understood in different settings; she then undertook systematic research in several such settings to pursue possible connections between them. Martin looked at the way the immune system was presented in the media and in the understandings of ordinary citizens "on the street," of practitioners of "alternative" medicine, and among professional scientists. This led her to reflect on the parallels she found in all these settings, in terms of what made bodies healthy and what made them sick, and realized that the same understanding informed the kinds of things business leaders were saying about what made businesses healthy and what made them sick. In all these cases, the goal is to achieve *flexibility*. Indeed, the book begins with a quotation from a business leader offering advice about how to "manage chaos" which will be echoed in the discussions about managing illness that she discusses later in her book. Martin's research involved a lot of reading, but it also involved interviewing, and participant observation as an AIDS volunteer, as a medical student, and as a management trainee. It is unlikely that the depth and nuances Martin is able to reveal in her book would have been possible had she been unable to pursue connections wherever they led her.

The complexities of the present are well illustrated by the research of Sawa Kurotani (see In Their Own Words, pp. 55–56; chapter 3). Kurotani is a Japanese anthropologist who went to college and graduate school in the United States and did her field research with Japanese corporate wives who had accompanied their husbands to the husbands' job assignments at three separate locations in the United States—New York City, the Research Triangle area of North Carolina, and for the longest period, in a small city (kept anonymous) in the midwest where a major Japanese auto company had an assembly plant. Kurotani carried out multisited fieldwork that enabled her to see a variety of different strategies that expatriate Japanese women employed for creating a home. But at the same time, she also was sometimes an insider to the women she worked with, sometimes an outsider. She was born and raised in Japan, and she, like they, was living in the United States. But she was also pursuing a doctorate, married to a non-Japanese man from the United States, with no children, and intending to stay in the United States. Not only was her research multisited, we could also say it was "multipositional."

▼ THE EFFECTS OF FIELDWORK

How Does Fieldwork Affect Informants?

Fieldwork changes both anthropologists and informants. What kinds of effects can the fieldwork experience have on informants? Anthropologists have not always been able to report on this. In some cases, the effects of fieldwork on informants cannot be assessed for many years. In other cases, it becomes clear in the course of fieldwork that the anthropologist's presence and questions have made the informants aware of their own cultural selves in new ways that are both surprising and uncomfortable.

As he reflected on his own fieldwork in Morocco, Rabinow recalled some cases in which his informants' new reflexivity led to unanticipated consequences (Figure 3.9). One key informant, Malik, agreed to help Rabinow compile a list of landholdings and other possessions of the villagers of Sidi Lahcen Lyussi (see EthnoProfile 3.8: Sidi Lahcen Lyussi). As a first step in tracing the economic status of the middle stratum in society, Rabinow suggested that Malik list his own possessions. Malik appeared to be neither rich nor poor; in fact, he considered himself "not well off." "As we began to make a detailed list of his possessions, he became touchy and defensive. . . . It was clear that he was not as impoverished as he had portrayed himself. . . . This was confusing and troubling for him. . . . Malik began to see that there was a disparity between his self-image and my classification system. The emergence of this 'hard' data before his eyes and through his own efforts was highly disconcerting for him" (1977, 117–18).

Malik's easy understanding of himself and his world had been disrupted, and he could not ignore the disruption. He would either have to change his self-image or find some way to assimilate this new information about himself into the old self-image. In the end Malik managed to reaffirm his conclusion that he was not well-off by arguing that wealth lay not in material possessions alone. Although he might be rich in material goods, his son's health was bad, his own father was dead, he was responsible for his mother and unmarried brothers, and he had to be constantly vigilant in order to prevent his uncle from stealing his land (117–19).

FIGURE 3.9 Paul Rabinow's reflections on his fieldwork experiences in a Moroccan village much like this one led him to reconceptualize the nature of anthropological fieldwork.

Bettylou Valentine was determined from the outset to acknowledge the point of view of her informants in Blackston. Yet before the publication of her ethnography, she discovered that some informants were not pleased with what she had said about them. One woman read in the manuscript about her own illegal attempts to combine work and welfare to bet-ter her family's standard of living. Angry, she denied to Valentine that she had ever done such a thing. Valentine talked to her informant at some length about this matter, which was well documented in field notes. It gradually became clear that the woman was concerned that if the data about her illegal activities were published, her friends and neighbors on the block would learn about it. In particular, she was afraid that the book would be sold on corner newsstands. Once Valentine explained how unlikely this was, her informant relaxed considerably: "The exchange made clear how different interests affect one's view. From my point of view, corner newsstand distribution would be excellent because it would mean the possibility of reaching the audience I feel needs to read and ponder the implications of the book. Yet Bernice and Velma [the informant and her friend] specified that they wouldn't mind where else it was distributed, even in Blackston more generally, if it could be kept from people on Paul Street and the surrounding blocks" (B. Valentine 1978, 122).

How Does Fieldwork Affect the Researcher?

What does it feel like to be in the field, trying to figure out the workings of an unfamiliar way of life? What are the consequences of this experience for the

EthnoProfile 3.8

Sidi Lahcen Lyussi

Region: Northern Africa

Nation: Morocco

Population: 900

Environment: Mountainous terrain

Livelihood: Farming, some livestock raising

Political organization: Village in a modern nation-state

For more information: Rabinow, Paul. 1977. *Reflections on fieldwork in Morocco.* Berkeley: University of California Press.

fieldworker? Graduate students in anthropology who have not yet been in the field often develop an idealized image of field experience: at first, the fieldworker is a bit disoriented and potential informants are suspicious, but uncertainty soon gives way to understanding and trust as the anthropologist's good intentions are made known and accepted. The fieldworker succeeds in establishing rapport. In fact, the fieldworker becomes so well loved and trusted, so thoroughly accepted, that he or she is accepted as an equal and allowed access to the culture's secrets. Presumably, all this happens as a result of the personal attributes of the fieldworker. If you have what it takes, you will be taken in and treated like one of the family. If this doesn't happen, you are obviously cut out for some other kind of work.

But much more than the anthropologist's personality is responsible for successful fieldwork. Establishing rapport with the people being studied is an achievement of anthropologist and informants together. Acceptance is problematic, rather than ensured, even for the most gifted fieldworkers. After all, fieldworkers are often outsiders with no personal ties to the community in which they will do their research. According to Karp and Kendall (1982), it is therefore not just naive to think that the locals will accept you as one of them without any difficulty, but it is also bad science.

Rabinow recalled the relationship he formed with his first Moroccan informant, a man called Ibrahim, whom he hired to teach him Arabic. Rabinow and Ibrahim seemed to get along well together, and, because of the language lessons, they saw each other a great deal, leading Rabinow to think of Ibrahim as a friend. When Rabinow planned a trip to another city, Ibrahim offered to go along as a guide and stay with relatives. This only confirmed Ibrahim's friendliness in Rabinow's eyes. But things changed once they arrived at their destination. Ibrahim told Rabinow that the relatives with whom he was to stay did not exist, that he had no money, and that he expected Rabinow to pay for his hotel room. When Rabinow was unable to do so, however, Ibrahim paid for it himself. Rabinow was shocked and hurt by this experience, and his relationship with Ibrahim was forever altered. Rabinow remarks: "Basically I had been conceiving of him as a friend because of the seeming personal relationship we had established.

But Ibrahim, a lot less confusedly, had basically conceptualized me as a resource. He was not unjustly situating me with the other Europeans with whom he had dealings" (1977, 29).

Rabinow's experience illustrates what he calls the "shock of otherness." Fieldwork institutionalizes this shock. Having to anticipate **culture shock** at any and every turn, anthropologists sometimes find that fieldwork takes on a tone that is anything but pleasant and sunny. For many anthropologists, what characterizes fieldwork, at least in its early stages, is anxiety—the anxiety of an isolated individual with nothing familiar to turn to, no common sense on which to rely, and no relationships that can be taken for granted. There is a reason anthropologists have reported holing up for weeks at a time reading paperback novels and eating peanut butter sandwiches. One of the authors (EAS) recalls how difficult it was every morning to leave the compound in Guider, Cameroon. Despite the accomplishments of the previous day, she was always convinced that no one would want to talk to her *today* (see EthnoProfile 8.1: Guider).

The move to multisited fieldwork can bring additional anxieties. George Marcus (1995) notes that the special value of single-sited fieldwork comes from its ability to offer insights that can only come from long-term, intense involvement in a single locale, which would seem to suggest that it is not the kind of research strategy best suited to investigating "global" phenomena. But attempting to carry out fieldwork in more than one setting would appear to dilute the intensity of involvement fieldworkers are able to develop with their informants in each site studied, thereby limiting the depth of understanding and insight. As well, some anthropologists are activists who use their ethnography as a way of drawing public attention to the plight of those whose lives they study, and multisited research would seem to undercut or call into question their political commitments to their primary informants.

Marcus recognizes these drawbacks, but does not see them as fatal. Even multisited fieldwork usually is based in one primary site, as in the past; its major

---

culture shock The feeling, akin to panic, that develops in people living in an unfamiliar society when they cannot understand what is happening around them.

IN THEIR OWN WORDS

The Relationship between Anthropologists and Informants

Many anthropologists have developed warm, lasting relationships with their informants. However, as Allyn Stearman points out, the nature of the anthropologist–informant relationship is not always unproblematic.

While doing fieldwork among the Ik (pronounced "eek") of Uganda, Africa, anthropologist Colin Turnbull challenged the old anthropological myth that the researcher will like and admire the people he or she is studying. A corollary of this assumption is that to the uninformed outsider who does not "understand" the culture, a group may seem hostile, unresponsive, or stoic, or may have any number of less admirable characteristics; but to the trained observer who truly knows "his or her" people, these attributes are only a façade presented to outsiders. What Turnbull finally had to concede, however, was that overall the Ik were not a very likable people. His portrait of the Ik as selfish, uncaring, and uninterested even in the survival of their own children is understandable when he describes their history of displacement, social disruption, and the constant threat of starvation. Nonetheless, an intellectual understanding of the factors contributing to Ik personality and behavior did not make it any easier for Turnbull to deal emotionally with the day-to-day interactions of fieldwork.

For me, knowing of Turnbull's situation alleviated some of my own anxieties in dealing with the Yuqu'. As was Turnbull's, my previous field experiences among other peoples had been very positive. In the anthropologist's terms, this meant that I was accepted quite rapidly as a friend and that my informants were open and cooperative.

The Yuqu' did not fit any of these patterns. But like Turnbull, I understood something of the Yuqu' past and thus on an intellectual level could comprehend that since they were a hunted, beleaguered people being threatened with extinction I could not expect them to be warm, friendly, and welcoming. Still, on an emotional level it was very difficult to cope with my frequent feelings of anger and resentment at having to put up with their teasing, taunting, and testing on an almost daily basis. My only consolation was that while I was often the brunt of this activity, so were they themselves. I am uncertain whether I finally came to understand the Yuqu', or simply became hardened to their particular way of dealing with the world. By doing favors for people, I incurred their indebtedness, and these debts could be translated into favors owed. How I chose to collect was up to me. As favors mounted, I found that relationships with individual Yuqu' were better. Then came the challenges. Could I be easily duped or taken advantage of? At first, I extended kindnesses gratuitously and was mocked. I learned to show my anger and stubbornness, to demand something in return for a tool lent or a service provided. Rather than alienate the Yuqu', this behavior (which I found difficult and distasteful throughout my stay) conferred prestige. The more I provided and then demanded in return, the more the Yuqu' were willing to accept me. In the Yuqu' world, as in any other, respect must be earned. But unlike many other peoples, for the Yuqu', kindness alone is not enough. In the end it is strength that is valued and that earns respect.

Source: Stearman 1989, 7–10.

---

innovation involves doing some fieldwork in additional sites and bringing information from all these sites together in a single study that is able to argue for their relationships "on the basis of first-hand ethnographic research" (Marcus 1995, 100). However, concerns about the way multisited ethnography may dilute one's ability to adopt an unequivocal position as

defender of a single group is an issue with no easy resolution. Multisited ethnography is a form of fieldwork that highlights the multi-centered, complex conflicts of the contemporary world, in which clear-cut "good guys" and "bad guys" are increasingly hard to identify. When individuals can legitimately claim, or be accorded, multiple identities, some of which conflict, innocent "identity politics" becomes impossible (Haraway 1991, 192). For example, to defend the views of working-class women in a single site is to downplay or ignore the points of view of middle-class women, or unemployed women; it may gloss over differences *among* those women based on class or "race" or ethnicity or religion; and it ignores entirely the points of view of men. Moreover, the spread of industrial capitalism across the globe means that the growth of an urban immigrant workforce in one place is probably connected to a lack of employment somewhere else. A multisited ethnography offers the possibility of juxtaposing more than one place and more than one point of view, thereby bringing to light connections among them that would otherwise remain undetected.

Something like this seems to have inspired Paul Rabinow, who shifted his ethnographic focus from Morocco to study Western scientists at work. His book *Making PCR* (1996) as well as an earlier article, "Reflections on Fieldwork in Alameda" (1993), explores the culture of a private start-up biotechnology firm in the San Francisco Bay area, one of whose members, Kary Mullis, was awarded the Nobel Prize in 1988 for coming up with the technique of polymerase chain reaction (PCR), a technique that enabled biologists to produce vast quantities of genetic material quickly and cheaply. Rabinow's work had a historical dimension, since the key events he was analyzing had ended years earlier. But he was curious about the scientists who worked at the Cetus Corporation during the years when PCR was made. His methodology was to "follow the life" by interviewing key members of the research team about how they came to be scientists and their understandings about how their collaboration in the lab had led to the invention of PCR. Rabinow sees his book as "an experiment in posing the problem of who has the authority—and responsibility—to represent experience and knowledge" (1996, 17). Transcribed interviews—the dialogue of fieldwork in textual form—make up a large part of the book. Multisited ethnography of this kind clearly enabled him to seek in the biographies of scientists the clues that might help explain how scientists are made. And this is what he sees as the goal of ethnography: "In my view, the task of the human sciences is neither glorification nor unmasking, nor is it to embody some phantom neutrality. The anthropologically pertinent point is the fashioning of the particularity of practices" (1996, 17)—how people in particular places at particular moments engage with one another and the world.

The Humanizing Effects of Fieldwork

Anthropological knowledge is the fruit of reflexivity produced by the mutual attempts of anthropologist and informant to understand each other. As a result, anthropological knowledge ought to be able to provide answers to questions about human nature, human society, and the human past. Somehow, good ethnography should not only persuade its readers, on intellectual grounds, that the ethnographer's informants were human beings. It should also allow readers to *experience* the informants' humanity. This privileged position, the extraordinary opportunity to experience "the other" as human beings while learning about their lives, is an experience that comes neither easily nor automatically. It must be cultivated, and it requires cooperation between and effort from one's informants and oneself. We have made an important first step if we can come to recognize, as Paul Rabinow did, that "there is no primitive. There are other [people] living other lives" (1977, 151).

Multisited ethnography can complicate the picture by simultaneously offering rich, fieldwork-based portraits of other people living other lives as variously situated as AIDS patients and corporate managers, and by demonstrating, moreover, that members of these groups share important cultural commitments. In the best ethnographic writing, we can grasp the humanity—the greed, compassion, suffering, pleasure, confusions and ambivalences—of the people who have granted the anthropologist the privilege of living with them for an extended period of time. Because of such experiences, it may also become more natural for us to talk about cultural differences by saying "not 'they,' not 'we,' not 'you,' but some of us are thus and so" (W. Smith 1982, 70).

▼ WHERE DOES ANTHROPOLOGICAL KNOWLEDGE COME FROM?

The dialectic of fieldwork often involves extended discussions about just what counts as "the facts" that constitute anthropological knowledge. Anthropologist

IN THEIR OWN WORDS

The Skills of the Anthropologist

Anthropologists cannot avoid taking their own cultural and theoretical frameworks into the field. However, as Stephen Gudeman observes, fieldwork draws their attention in unanticipated directions, making them aware of new phenomena that constantly challenge those frameworks.

According to the accepted wisdom, poets should be especially facile with language and stretch our vision with freshly cut images. Historians, with their knowledge of past events, offer a wise and sweeping view of human change and continuities. Physical scientists, who have analytical yet creative minds, bring us discoveries and insights about the natural world.

What about anthropologists? Have we any finely honed talents and gifts for the world?

Because anthropology is the study of human life, the anthropologist needs to know a little something about everything—from psychology to legal history to ecology. Our field equipment is primitive, for we rely mainly on the eye, the ear, and the tongue. Because ethnographers carry few tools to the field and the tools they have can hardly capture the totality of the situation, the background and talents of the researcher strongly determine what is "seen" and how it is understood. But the field experience itself has a special impact, too. I studied economic practices in Panama because I was trained to do so, but the field research forced me to alter all the notions I had been taught. Most of them were useless! Anthropologists try to open themselves up to every facet of their field situation and to allow its richness to envelop them. In this, the tasks of the anthropologist are very unlike those of the normal laboratory scientist: the anthropologist can have no predefined hypothesis and testing procedures. The best equipment an ethnographer can possess is a "good ear" and patience to let the "data talk."

This is not all. In the field, anthropologists carry out intense and internal conversations with themselves. Every observation, whether clearly seen or dimly realized, must be brought to consciousness, shuffled about, and questioned. Only by recognizing and acknowledging their own incomprehension can anthropologists generate new questions and lines of inquiry. In the solitude of the field, the anthropologist must try to understand the limits of her or his knowledge, have the courage to live with uncertainty, and retain the ambition to seize on openings to insight.

But field studies constitute only a part of the total research process. Once home, the field notes have to be read and reread, put aside, and then rearranged. The anthropologist is a pattern seeker, believing that within the data human designs are to be found. The task is like solving a puzzle, except that there is no fixed solution and the puzzle's pieces keep changing their shapes! With work and insight, however, a picture—an understanding or an explanation—begins to emerge.

Eventually, the results of all these efforts are conveyed to others, and so anthropologists also need to have expository skills and persuasive powers, for they have to convince others of their picture and their viewpoint about how cultures and social lives are put together.

Source: Gudeman 1990, 458–59.

---

fact A widely accepted observation, a taken-for-granted item of common knowledge. Facts do not speak for themselves; only when they are interpreted and placed in a context of meaning do they become intelligible.

David Hess defines **fact** as a widely accepted observation, a taken-for-granted item of common knowledge (1997, 101–2). Ethnographers' field notebooks will be full of facts collected from different informants, as well as facts based on their own cultural experiences and professional training. But what happens when facts from these various sources contradict one another?

Producing Knowledge

Facts turn out to be complex phenomena. On the one hand, they assert that a particular state of affairs about the world is true. On the other hand, reflexive analysis has taught us that *who* tells us that *x* is a fact is an extremely important thing to know. This is because facts do not speak for themselves. They speak only when they are interpreted and placed in a context of meaning that makes them intelligible. What constitutes a cultural fact is ambiguous. Anthropologists and informants can disagree; anthropologists can disagree among themselves; informants can disagree among themselves. The facts of anthropology exist neither in the culture of the anthropologist nor in the culture of the informant. "Anthropological facts are cross-cultural, because they are made across cultural boundaries" (Rabinow 1977, 152). In short, facts are not just out there, waiting for someone to come along and pick them up. They are made and remade (1) in the field, (2) when fieldworkers reexamine field notes and reflect on the field experience at a later time, and (3) when the fieldworkers write about their experiences or discuss them with others.

For Daniel Bradburd, fieldwork begins with "being there." But simply being there is not enough. As Bradburd puts it, "my experiences among the Komachi shaped my understanding of them, and that part of field experience consists of a constant process of being brought up short, of having expectations confounded, of being forced to think very hard about what is happening, right now, with me and them, let alone the thinking and rethinking about those experiences when they have—sometimes mercifully—passed" (1998, 161–62). After all, fieldwork is field*work*—there are notes to be taken, interviews to be carried out, observations to make, interpretations to be made. There is also the transformation of the experiences of being there into what Bradburd calls "elements of an understanding that is at once incomplete and impossible to complete, but also wonderfully capable of being improved" (1998, 164). According to Harry Wolcott (1999, 262), it is what ethnographers *do* with data—"making considered generalizations about how members of a group tend to speak and act, warranted generalizations appropriate for collectivities of people rather than the usual shoot-from-the-hip stereotyping adequate for allowing us to achieve our individual purposes"—that makes field-work experience different from just experience and turns it into doing ethnography. Multisited fieldwork elaborates upon and further complicates this experience, because it involves being "here and there." In the course of the movement from site to site, new facts come into view that would otherwise never be known, adding a further layer to the thinking and rethinking that all fieldwork sets in motion. What happens if you find that your activism in support of the urban poor at one site works against the interests of the indigenous people you have supported at a different site? "In conducting multisited research," Marcus says, "one finds oneself with all sorts of cross-cutting commitments" that are not easily resolved. Unlike positivists, however, who might have found "refuge in being a detached anthropological scholar," Marcus suggests that the multisited journey will itself shape the "circumstantial activism" of ethnographers doing fieldwork in a variety of sites. "If that sounds contradictory or ambivalent, it is nevertheless faithful to key features of the contemporary world in which we all live" (Marcus 1995).

Anthropological Knowledge as Open-Ended

We have suggested that there is no such thing as purely objective knowledge and that when human beings are both the subject and object of study, we must speak in terms of reflexivity rather than objectivity. Cultivating reflexivity allows us to produce less distorted views of human nature and the human condition, and yet we remain human beings interpreting the lives of other human beings. We can never escape from our humanity to some point of view that would allow us to see human existence and human experience from the outside. Instead, we must rely on our common humanity and our interpretive powers to show us the parts of our nature that can be made visible.

If there truly is "no primitive," no subsection of humanity that is radically different in nature or in capacity from the anthropologists who study it, then the ethnographic record of anthropological knowledge is perhaps best understood as a vast commentary on human possibility. As with all commentaries, it depends on an original text—in this case, human experience. But that experience is ambiguous, speaking with many voices, capable of supporting more than one interpretation. Growth of anthropological knowledge is no different, then, from the growth of human self-understanding in general. It ought to contribute to the domain of human wisdom that concerns who we are as a species, where we have come from, and where we may be going.

Like all commentaries, the ethnographic record is and must be unfinished: Human beings are open systems; human history continues; and problems and their possible solutions change. There is no one true version of human life. For anthropologists, the true version of human life consists of all versions of human life. This is a sobering possibility. It makes it appear that "the anthropologist is condemned to a greater or lesser degree of failure" in even trying to understand another culture (Basham 1978, 299). Informants would equally be condemned to never know fully even their own way of life. And the positivistic orientation resists any admission that the understanding of anything is impossible. But total pessimism does not seem warranted. We may never know everything, but it does not follow that our efforts can teach us nothing. "Two of the fundamental qualities of humanity are the capacity to understand one another and the capacity to be understood. Not fully certainly. Yet not negligibly, certainly. . . . There is no person on earth that I can fully understand. There is and has been no person on earth that I cannot understand at all" (W. Smith 1982, 68–69).

Moreover, as our contact with the other is prolonged and as our efforts to communicate are rewarded by the construction of intersubjective understanding, we can always learn more. Human beings are open organisms, with a vast ability to learn new things. This is significant, for even if we can never know everything, it does not seem that our capacities for understanding ourselves and others are likely to be exhausted soon. This is not only because we are open to change but also because our culture and our wider environment can change, and all will continue to do so as long as human history continues. The ethnographic enterprise will never be finished, even if all nonindustrial ways of life disappear forever, all people move into cities, and everyone ends up speaking English. Such a superficial homogeneity would mask a vast heterogeneity beneath its bland surface. In any case, given the dynamics of human existence, nothing in human affairs can remain homogeneous for long.

CHAPTER SUMMARY

1. Anthropological fieldwork traditionally involved participant-observation, extended periods of close contact at a single site with members of another society. Anthropologists were expected to carry out research in societies different from their own, but in recent years increasing numbers have worked in their own societies. Each setting has its own advantages and drawbacks for ethnographers.

2. Early anthropologists who wanted to be scientific tried to remake fieldwork in the image of controlled laboratory research. According to positivist scientists and philosophers, laboratory research was the prototype of scientific investigation. Following this positivist model, anthropologists systematically collected highly accurate data on societies in many parts of the world.

3. When human beings study other human beings, scientific accuracy requires that they relate to one another as human beings. Successful fieldwork involves anthropologists who think about the way they think about other cultures. Informants also must reflect on the way they and others in their society think and they must try to convey their insights to the anthropologist. This is basic to the reflexive approach to fieldwork, which sees participant-observation as a dialogue about the meaning of experience in the informant's culture. Fieldworkers and informants work together to construct an intersubjective world of meaning.

4. When communication between anthropologist and informant is ruptured, learning about another culture is often greatest. Ruptures occur when current intersubjective understandings prove inadequate to account for experience. A rupture always carries the possibility of bringing

research to an end. But when the reasons for the rupture are explored and explanations for it are constructed, great insights are possible.

5. In recent years, a number of anthropologists have begun to carry out fieldwork that takes them to a number of different sites. Such multisited fieldwork is usually the outcome of following cultural phenomena wherever they lead, often crossing local, regional, and national boundaries in the process. Such fieldwork allows anthropologists to understand better many cultural processes that link people, things, metaphors, plots, and lives that are not confined to a single site.

6. Taking part in ethnographic fieldwork has the potential to change informants and researchers in sometimes-unpredictable ways. In some cases, anthropologists have worked with their informants to effect social change, although not all anthropologists agree that this is appropri-

ate. In other cases, anthropologists argue that their main task is to figure out and explain to others how people in particular places at particular moments engage with one another and with the world.

7. Because cultural meanings are intersubjectively constructed during fieldwork, cultural facts do not speak for themselves. They speak only when they are interpreted and placed in a context of meaning that makes them intelligible. Multisited fieldwork complicates this because it involves the anthropologist in cross-cutting commitments in different contexts, where the same cultural facts may be differently understood or valued.

8. The ethnographic record of anthropological knowledge is perhaps best understood as a vast unfinished commentary on human possibility. We may never learn all there is to know, but we can always learn more.

KEY TERMS

fieldwork
participant-observation
ethnographies
positivism

objective knowledge
informants
intersubjective meanings
reflexivity

dialectic of fieldwork
multisited fieldwork
culture shock
fact

SUGGESTED READINGS

Bigenho, Michelle. 2002. *Sounding indigenous: Authenticity in Bolivian musical performance*. New York: Palgrave Macmillan. *A recent multisited ethnography that follows Bolivian and non-Bolivian members of a Bolivian musical ensemble through different settings on more than one continent, chronicling varied understandings of what counts as "indigenous" Bolivian music.*

Bradburd, Daniel. 1998. *Being there: The necessity of fieldwork*. Washington, DC: Smithsonian Institution Press. *An engaging personal study of how the many seemingly small details of experience during field research add up to anthropological understanding.*

Briggs, Jean. 1970. *Never in anger: Portrait of an Eskimo family*. Cambridge, MA: Harvard University Press. *A moving, insightful study of fieldwork and of an Utku family.*

Kumar, Nita. 1992. *Friends, brothers, and informants: Fieldwork memories of Banaras*. Berkeley: University of California Press. *A moving and thought-provoking reflection on the experience of fieldwork in the author's own country but in a culture quite different from her own.*

Levi-Strauss, Claude. 1974. *Tristes Tropiques*. New York: Pocket Books. *Originally published in French in 1955, this book (with an untranslatable title) is considered by some to be the greatest book ever written by an anthropologist (although not necessarily a great anthropology book). This is a multifaceted work about voyaging, fieldwork, self-knowledge, philosophy, and much more. It is a challenging read in some parts but highly rewarding overall.*

Martin, Emily. 1995. *Flexible bodies*. Boston: Beacon Press. *A classic multisited ethnography, in which the ethnographer follows the metaphor of flexibility from scientific research laboratories to businesses to political demonstrations to support groups.*

Rabinow, Paul. 1977. *Reflection on fieldwork in Morocco*. Berkeley: University of California Press. *An important, brief, powerfully written reflection on the nature of fieldwork. Very accessible and highly recommended.*

Valentine, Bettylou. 1978. *Hustling and other hard work* New York: Free Press. *A classic, innovative, provocative study of African American inner-city life. Reads like a good novel.*

Chapter 4

Anthropology in History and the Explanation of Cultural Diversity

Like any field of scholarship, anthropology has a history. In this chapter, we look at how cultural anthropology developed in Europe and the United States and how anthropology's explanations of cultural diversity have varied over time. In particular, we highlight the way in which cultural anthropologists and biological anthropologists joined forces in the twentieth century to demonstrate that biological races do not exist and therefore cannot explain why human populations differ from one another.

In Chinese tradition, five elements are said to make up the world: water, fire, wood, metal, and earth. This theory, which dates to the third century B.C.E. was one of the bases of all Chinese scientific thought. These elements were understood not as substances but as *processes*, differentiated by the kinds of changes they underwent. Water was associated with soaking, dripping, and descending. Fire was allied with heating, burning, and ascending. Wood was connected with that which accepted form by submitting to cutting and carving instruments. Metal was affiliated with that which accepted form by molding when in the liquid state and had the capacity to change form by remelting and remolding. Earth was associated with the production of edible vegetation.

In Han times (about 200 B.C.E. to 200 C.E.), the theory achieved a final form, which has been passed down through the ages. According to Colin Ronan and Joseph Needham in their *Shorter Science and Civilisation in China*, "one aspect of the theory, the mutual conquest order, described the series in which each element was supposed to conquer its predecessor. It was based on a logical sequence of ideas that had their basis in everyday scientific facts: for instance, that Wood conquers Earth because, presumably, when in the form of a spade, it can dig up earth. Again, Metal conquers Wood since it can cut and carve it; Fire conquers Metal for it can melt or even vaporize it; Water conquers Fire because it can extinguish it; and, finally, Earth conquers Water because it can dam it and contain it—a very natural metaphor for people to whom irrigation and hydraulic engineering were so important. This order was also considered significant from the political point of view; it was put forward as an explanation for the course of history, with the implication that it would continue to apply in the future and was, therefore, useful for prediction. . . . The Five Elements gradually came to be associated with every conceivable category of things in the universe that it was possible to classify in fives" (1978, 151;153). This included the seasons, the points of the compass, tastes, smells, numbers, kinds of musical notes, heavenly bodies, planets, weather, colors, body parts, sense organs, affective states, and human psychological functions. It also included the periods of dynastic history, the ministries of government, and styles of government, which included relaxed, enlightened, careful, energetic, and quiet, corresponding respectively to wood, fire, earth, metal, and water.

"As we might imagine," Ronan and Needham conclude, "these correlations met with criticism, sometimes severe, because they led to many absurdities. . . . Yet in spite of such criticisms, it seems that in the beginning these correlations were helpful to scientific thought in China. They were certainly no worse than the Greek theory of the elements that dominated European medieval thinking, and it was only when they became overelaborate and fanciful, too far removed from the observation of Nature, that they were positively harmful" (1978, 156–57).

These observations are relevant to any apt metaphor or good scientific theory. They apply to anthropology as well. Like the Chinese sages, anthropologists began by sorting human cultures into different categories based on what they believed to be their similarities and differences. Over time, the purposes of classification have been questioned, and the categories have been modified or discarded, reflecting changes in the wider world and changing research interests among anthropologists. This chapter considers some of the influential classifications, placing them in the context of the development of anthropology as a discipline within the political and economic influence of the West.

▼ WHERE DO CULTURAL TRADITIONS BEGIN?

We argued in chapter 2 that culture is an aspect of human nature that is as much a source of freedom as it is a requirement for our survival. Human imagination can suggest which aspects of the material world to pay attention to, and these suggestions can become part of a cultural tradition. At the same time, once a group commits itself to paying attention to some parts of the material world, it locks itself into a set of relationships that it may not be able to abandon freely. These relationships can and do exert a determinant pressure on future choices. This is the paradox of the human condition.

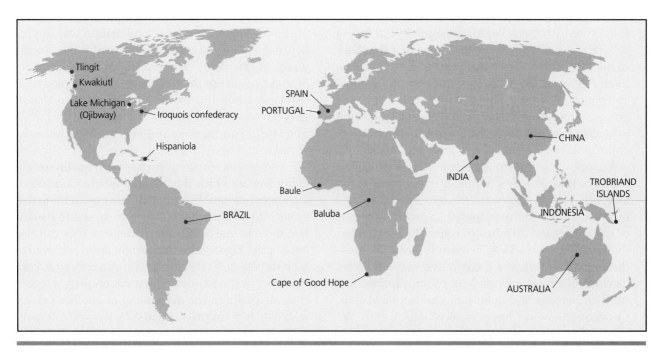

FIGURE 4.1 Locations of societies and places discussed in chapter 4.

What parts of the material world do human beings pay attention to, and what parts do they ignore? To answer this question, we can begin by considering how the need to make a living in different natural environments has led to the development of a range of different forms of human social organization. At the same time, because people can make a living in different ways in the same environment, or in much the same way in different environments, we must also pay attention to those cultural and social factors that cannot be predicted on the basis of natural environment alone. Some of these factors arise out of the internal traditions of the group itself; others depend on external and unpredictable historical encounters with other human groups. By looking at both sets of factors, we will understand better the interplay of forces shaping human society and human history. When we further situate the discipline of anthropology within the social and historical contexts which have shaped its development, we also gain a clearer understanding of the kinds of situated knowledge (see chapter 3, p. 51) anthropologists have produced in different times and places.

▼ CAPITALISM, COLONIALISM, AND THE ORIGINS OF ETHNOGRAPHY

As we mentioned in chapter 3, anthropology became organized as a university discipline in the nineteenth century, at the height of European colonial expansion, and in the division of labor between the new social sciences, it was assigned "the savage slot." What this meant was that anthropologists would be conducting research on societies that either had already been, or soon would become, dominated territories within one or another European empire. In the United States, attention was focused on the indigenous inhabitants of the continent who were being subdued as the country followed its "manifest destiny" to occupy the continent from Atlantic to Pacific.

Writing about the encounter between anthropologists and Native Americans, Peter Whiteley observes, "Ethnography in the New World is coterminous with Europeans in the New World; ethnography is a deeply *cultural* and politically *structural* matter, that goes back in one way or another to Columbus" (2004, 435–6). Even though ethnographies written by professional anthropologists did not appear until fairly late in this process—the late nineteenth century—it is important to realize that the development of the discipline of anthropology is closely intertwined with the history of European (and Euro-American) imperialism. At the same time, however, Whiteley insists that "in the long run, Native American ethnography has been—by no means always consciously—a principal means of subverting the premises of colonial reason rather than one of its tools. Despite its multiple problems—discursive, ethical, and interpretive—ethnography has been the most powerful contributor to intercultural knowledge and important philosophical complication the world has ever seen" (2004, 460). We think Whiteley is correct, but to make sense of his claims, we need to review key historical developments that made both European expansion and anthropological scholarship possible.

By the end of the Middle Ages, centralized monarchies had come into existence in several different European territories. Since the fall of the Roman Empire, Europe had never been politically unified, which meant that, beginning in the fifteenth century, fledgling European states could strike out on their own without being answerable to any central authority (Gledhill 1994, 58–59). At the same time, Europeans were working out a new kind of society with a new kind of economy whose development was aided by trade and conquest—namely, **capitalism**.

Capitalism and Colonialism

The term *capitalism* refers to at least two things: an economic system dominated by the supply-demand-price mechanism called *the market*, and the way of life that grew up in response to and in service to that

---

capitalism An economic system dominated by the supply-demand-price mechanism called the market; an entire way of life that grew in response to and in service of that market.

---

market. This new way of life changed the face of Europe and transformed other regions as well.

There had been expansive empires before the rise of capitalism, but capitalist exploitation was unique because it derived from a new worldview. In the words of Eric Wolf, "The guiding fiction of this kind of society—one of the key tenets of its ideology—is that land, labor, and wealth are commodities, that is, goods produced not for use, but for sale" (1969, 277). The world is a market, and everything within the world has, or should have, its price.

The genius of capitalism has been the thoroughgoing way in which those committed to the marketing metaphor have been able to convert anything that exists into a commodity; they turn land into real estate and material objects into inventory. They can also attach price tags to ideas (copyright laws) and even to human beings. The slave in Western society is considered "first and foremost a commodity. He is a chattel, totally in the possession of another person who uses him for private ends" (Miers and Kopytoff 1977, 3). Even human beings who are not slaves are nevertheless reduced to their labor power by the capitalist market and become worth whatever price the laws of supply and demand determine.

To be sure, complex commercial activity was not invented by Western capitalists. In China and India, for example, the use of trade, money, and markets by stratified state societies was highly developed by the time the first representatives of Western capitalism arrived on the scene. Elites in such societies were well prepared to take advantage of new economic opportunities.

However, the consequences of capitalism were often negative for ordinary members of these societies, who lost many traditional socioeconomic supports. Capitalism was even more devastating in small-scale societies existing outside the control of these complex states. Members of these societies saw the land they had always used turned into a commodity for sale on the capitalist market. They experienced the devaluation of their traditional social identities based on descent, alliance, and residence and the erosion of traditional obligations that protected them from destitution. Before the introduction of capitalism, multipurpose money did not exist, exchanges were hedged about by social restrictions, and there was no single standard according to which anything could be assigned a value. Capitalism changed all this.

What began as trade contracts with European nations was followed nearly everywhere by European conquest. **Colonialism** refers to a social system in which political conquest by one society of another leads to "cultural domination with enforced social change" (Beidelman 1982, 2). Western conquest of non-Western societies created European colonial empires in two historical phases. The first phase of European colonialism, involving Spain, Portugal, and Holland, required colonies to pay tribute to the empire through trading companies, but the second phase, led by England and France, was based on industrial capitalism (Gledhill 1994, 74). When capitalist practices were imposed on non-Western societies through colonialism, indigenous life was forever altered. To function intelligibly within the capitalist world order, colonized peoples had to begin to see the world as a storehouse of potential commodities. Much of recent world history can usefully be viewed as a narrative of non-Western responses to this new worldview and the practical actions it encouraged and justified. Some people's responses were enthusiastic, others were resentful but accommodating, still others were violent in repudiation or took action to protect themselves.

In western Africa, first the Portuguese and later the Dutch, British, and French found themselves confined for more than 400 years to trading posts built on the coast or on offshore islands. During this period, local peoples living along the coast procured the goods sought by their European trading partners. This long-lasting arrangement shows that western African societies were resilient enough to adapt to the European presence and strong enough to keep Europeans and their commercial interests at arm's length for several centuries. The European presence also reshaped societies of the western African coast, stimulating the growth of hierarchical social forms in some areas where there had been none before. These changes had repercussions farther inland, as the new coastal kingdoms sought trade goods from the people of the African hinterland. Only in the second half of the nineteenth century did this relationship between Europeans and western Africans change.

The situation in southern Africa was different. The Dutch community on the Cape of Good Hope was founded to service Dutch ships on the route to India, but it soon attracted settlers who had moved

FIGURE 4.2 In the late fifteenth and sixteenth centuries, Western explorers such as Columbus ventured beyond the boundaries of the world known to Europe. This sixteenth-century engraving depicts Columbus meeting the inhabitants of Hispaniola, the first territory colonized by Spain in the New World.

inland by the late seventeenth century. Their arrival led to the subjugation and destruction of indigenous peoples, both by warfare and by disease. In western Africa, the situation was often just the reverse; Europeans succumbed to tropical maladies such as malaria to which coastal African populations had greater resistance.

In America, the complex civilizations of Mexico and Peru had been conquered within thirty years of the arrival of Columbus (see Figure 4.2). Indigenous American populations, like those of southern Africa, were laid waste more by European-borne diseases such as measles and smallpox than by armed conflict. They suffered further dislocation after Spanish colonial administration was established. Spain was

colonialism Cultural domination with enforced social change.

determined to keep control of the colonies in its own hands, and it checked the attempts of colonists to set themselves up as feudal lords commanding local indigenous groups as their peasants. These efforts, however, were far from successful. Conquered indigenous people were put to work in mines and on plantations. Hard labor further reduced their numbers and fractured their traditional forms of social organization. By the time the worst of these abuses were finally curtailed, in the early seventeenth century, indigenous life in New Spain had been drastically reshaped. Indeed, in the areas of greatest Spanish penetration and control, indigenous groups were reduced to but one component in the complex hierarchy of colonial society.

The Fur Trade in North America

The fur trade had important consequences for indigenous societies in North America. When the Dutch first began to trade with indigenous Americans for furs, they already had trading links to Russia, where fur collecting and fur processing had been established for centuries (Wolf 1982, 158ff.). The fur trade was thus an international phenomenon, and the strong stimulus that indigenous American populations felt to seek fur was shaped by the demand of the fur-processing industry in eastern Europe. The most eagerly sought fur was beaver, used to make felt for cloth and especially hats.

Involvement in the fur trade significantly modified the traditional ways that indigenous North American groups made a living. While the beaver supply lasted, they could obtain many of the material items they needed by exchanging pelts for them at the trading post. This gave them a strong incentive to neglect or even abandon the activities that previously had supplied those items and to devote themselves to fur trapping. Once the beaver were gone, however, people discovered that their highly successful new adaptation had become obsolete. They also discovered that a return to the old ways was impossible, either because those ways had been forgotten or because the new circumstances of life made them impossible to carry out. The result often was severe social dislocation.

In all cases, however, they responded actively, reimagining their relations with the material world, and with each other; struggling to rework their traditional understandings and practices to minimize the negative impact of European pressures.

The Iroquois confederacy was the outcome of one such struggle. Wolf argues that the indigenous members of the confederacy tried to create a form of society that could effectively counter the power of the European trading companies with which they dealt. In forming the confederacy, however, the groups did not simply borrow the social organization of the European traders. Rather, they drew on traditional kinship forms and reworked these into new and broader-reaching structures that, for a time at least, kept the Europeans at bay. The Iroquois confederacy, like the coastal trading kingdoms in Africa, was a creative response to the opportunities and challenges initiated by European contact.

The Slave and Commodities Trades

The fur trade was followed by the slave trade and the trade in commodities such as sugar and cotton, both of which accompanied the rise of capitalist industry. These ventures continued to reshape social life throughout the world even as they drew parts of that world ever closer together into an interdependent economic network centered on the growing power and influence of capitalist markets centered in Europe. The slave trade dominated commerce between Europeans and coastal Africans by the eighteenth century. The nature of the merchandise sought for this trade—people—had a devastating effect on the societies of the African hinterland whose members were captured and sold to meet European demand. The survivors actively sought refuge beyond the slavers' reach, regrouping themselves into new societies with new names and reworking their collective traditions into new forms. The slave trade did not alter social relations in Africa alone. The presence of slaves in the New World profoundly reshaped the lives of both local indigenous peoples and European colonists. The growth of plantation economies in areas that had been used by hunters or gatherers or small-scale farmers altered the local ecology as well as local society. And the wealth produced in these economies transformed both the local gentry and the European nations who claimed sovereignty over them. As a result, Africa, America, and

Europe became inextricably intertwined in one another's fate.

Colonialism and Modernity

The period of history that followed the Enlightenment and includes the rise of European nation-states and colonial empires is traditionally called "modernity." Life in European industrial cities has often been seen as the prototype of social life under modernity. In the colonial context, however, being modern has often been understood as nothing more than adopting the practices and worldview of Western capitalism. As a result, the so-called backward rural peoples often turned out to be either those who escaped capitalism's embrace or those who actively opposed it. For many of them, the colonial city and the life it represented symbolized everything wrong with the colonial order.

Cities were centers of commerce, and rural areas were sources of raw materials for industry. Systems set up by colonial authorities to extract raw materials disrupted indigenous communities and created new ones. The mining towns of Bolivia and South Africa, for example, are outgrowths of this process. Labor for such enterprises was recruited, sometimes by force, from local populations. Little by little, in an effort to streamline the system of colonial exploitation, society was restructured.

The Colonial Political Economy

Because the colonial order focused on the extraction of material wealth, it might be said that its reason for existence was economic. Yet this new economic order did not spring up painlessly by itself. It was imposed and maintained by force. For that reason, many anthropologists describe the colonial order as a **political economy**—a holistic term that emphasizes the centrality of material interest in the organization of society and the use of power to protect and enhance that interest. The colonial political economy created three kinds of links, connecting conquered communities with one another within a conquered territory; different conquered territories with one another; and all conquered territories with the country of the colonizers. Wolf describes a particularly striking example of this linkage: Silver mined in Spanish colonies in America was shipped to a Spanish colony in Asia—the Philippines—where it was used to buy textiles from the Chinese (1982, 153).

More commonly, colonial enterprises drew labor from neighboring regions, as in South Africa. Here, indigenous Africans were recruited from some distance to work in the mines; money earned in one area was thus remitted for the economic support of families in another area. Again, these linkages did not come about spontaneously. In the beginning, Africans were still largely able to guarantee their own subsistence through traditional means. They were unwilling to work for wages in the mines except on a short-term basis. Profitability in mining required, therefore, that African self-sufficiency be eliminated so that Africans would have no choice but to work for whatever wages mine owners chose to offer. This goal was achieved in two ways. First, taxes were imposed on conquered African populations, but the taxes could only be paid in cash. Second, the colonial government deliberately prevented the growth of a cash economy in African areas. Thus, the only way Africans could obtain the cash needed to pay their taxes was by working for wages in the mines.

Although there were no professional anthropologists on the scene until the middle of the nineteenth century, contemporary observers of these historical processes—soldiers, traders, colonial administrators, missionaries—wrote about these developments and the peoples whom they affected. Often these ethnographic reports contain detailed, accurate information that has proved of lasting value. Nevertheless, it was widely assumed that people in the non-Western world were "people without history," people who lived as they had always lived until forced to change by contact with the West. As Eric Wolf demonstrated, however, the notion that non-Western peoples had no history was a pernicious Western stereotype; in fact, many of the "tribes" or "peoples" whom anthropologists later would study—the North American Ojibway and the African Baluba, for example—are relatively recent creations, forged in the contact between indigenous populations and Europeans (Wolf 1982).

---

political economy A holistic term that emphasizes the centrality of material interest (economy) and the use of power (politics) to protect and enhance that interest.

Another widespread assumption was that the cultures of peoples dominated by the West were doomed to disappear and that members of such societies would have to adopt Western ways or perish. This view was shared by many American anthropologists into the early twentieth century. Their work was described as "salvage ethnography": an attempt to document the "memory cultures" of indigenous people who remembered the old ways, before it was too late. But the assumption that non-Western ways of life were doomed to disappear has also turned out to be false. As we will see in chapter 15, one of the most dynamic political institutions at the beginning of the twenty-first century is the United Nations Permanent Forum on Indigenous Issues.

▼ ANTHROPOLOGY AND THE COLONIAL ENCOUNTER

In 1973, anthropologist Talal Asad edited a collection of articles entitled *Anthropology and the Colonial Encounter*. This book was the first high-profile work by anthropologists willing to consider directly the connections between their discipline and colonialism. In 2002, Asad reflected on what had been learned from this attempt by anthropologists to reflect critically on the context in which so much ethnographic fieldwork had been undertaken. He concluded that "the process of European global power has been central to the anthropological task of recording and analyzing the way of life of subject populations" and therefore must be recognized as having been "always part of the reality anthropologists sought to understand, and the way they sought to understand it" (2002, 134). Anthropologists sometimes were hired to provide specific information about particular societies, research that would help conquered peoples adjust to life under colonial rule. European anthropologists sometimes played an equivocal role in the colonial setting: They were valued for the expert knowledge they could provide, but they were also viewed with suspicion because their expert knowledge might easily contradict or undermine administrative goals. But even for anthropologists whose goal was to resist or mitigate the effects of colonial rule on subject peoples, the colonial context itself constituted a space within which anthropologists were obliged to maneuver.

Charges have sometimes been made, by those within and outside the discipline, that anthropology has been nothing more than a form of "applied colonialism." Asad disagrees, for two reasons. First, anthropological findings were too specialized to be used by colonial administrators, especially compared to the enormous amount of information supplied to them by merchants, missionaries, and other government functionaries. Second, the motives that led anthropologists to carry out work under colonial conditions were complex and variable (2002, 134). Peter Whiteley makes a similar point when he describes the history of ethnographic work among Native Americans:

> The sheer proliferation of ethnographic materials, in the [Bureau of American Ethnology] and other institutional publications, together with their orientation toward salvage, provides the best argument against ethnography's complicity with colonialism. These accounts were not assembled for federal agents to better control subjected populations. . . . As ethnographic research and publications on Native American cultures became more detailed and more complex, they increasingly opened up a space of challenge to the colonial consciousness of domination (2004, 447).

One way of coping with colonial power was to address it indirectly. In the middle part of the twentieth century, a number of North American anthropologists tried to clarify what their role should be in the expanding world of capitalist colonialism. Two documents (Redfield, Linton, and Herskovits 1936 and Broom et al. 1954) bracket the period that Bohannan and Plog (1967, x) called the "high period" of the study of culture. The anthropologists involved promoted an impartial and scientific program of research that would discover the laws of culture change. They had a broad view of culture change. They considered situations encountered under colonialism, but they also considered situations where contact and change occurred in the absence of political conquest. The latter cases involved autonomous groups whose members could be freer about what they selected and rejected. The anthropologists did not see themselves supporting any particular political position in advocating that culture change be approached in this way; however, they were sympathetic to the plight of colonial subjects. Melville Herskovits, in particular, was

IN THEIR OWN WORDS

The Anthropological Voice

Anthropologist Annette Weiner traces the history of anthropological challenges to colonialism and Western capitalism, pointing out why the perspective of anthropologists has so often been ignored.

Colonialism brought foreign governments, missionaries, explorers, and exploiters face-to-face with cultures whose values and beliefs were vastly different. As the harbingers of Western progress, their actions were couched in the rhetoric of doing something to and for "the natives"—giving them souls, clothes, law—whatever was necessary to lift them out of their "primitive" ways. Anthropologists were also part of the colonial scene, but what they came to "do" made them different from those who were carrying out the expectations of missions, overseas trade, and government protectorates. Anthropologists arrived in the field determined to understand the cultural realities of an unfamiliar world. The knowledge of these worlds was to serve as a warning to those in positions of colonial power by charging that villagers' lives were not to be tampered with arbitrarily and that changing the lives of powerless people was insensitive and inhumane, unless one understood and took seriously the cultural meanings inherent in, for example, traditional land ownership, the technologies and rituals surrounding food cultivation, myths, magic, and gender relations.

All too often, however, the anthropologist's voice went unnoticed by those in power, for it remained a voice committed to illuminating the cultural biases under which colonialists operated. Only recently have we witnessed the final demise of colonial governments and the rise of independent countries. Economically, however, independence has not brought these countries the freedom to pursue their own course of development. In many parts of the world, Western multinational corporations, often playing a role not too dissimilar from colonial enterprises, now determine the course of that freedom, changing people's lives in a way that all too often is harmful or destructive. At the same time, we know that the world's natural resources and human productive capabilities can no longer remain isolates. Developed and developing countries are now more dependent on one another than ever before in human history. Yet this interdependency, which should give protection to indigenous peoples, is often worked out for political ends that ignore the moral issues. Racism and the practice of discrimination are difficult to destroy, as evidenced by the United States today, where we still are not completely emancipated from assumptions that relegate blacks, women, Asians, Hispanics, and other minorities to second-class status. If we cannot bridge these cultural differences intellectually within our own borders, then how can we begin to deal politically with Third World countries—those who were called "primitives" less than a century ago—in a fair, sensitive, and meaningful way?

This is the legacy of anthropology that we must never forget. Because the work of anthropology takes us to the neighborhoods, villages, and campsites—the local level—we can ourselves experience the results of how the world's economic and political systems affect those who have no voice. Yet once again our voices too are seldom heard by those who make such decisions. Anthropologists are often prevented from participating in the forums of economic and government planning. Unlike economists, political scientists, or engineers, we must stand on the periphery of such decision making, primarily because our understanding of cultural patterns and beliefs forces on others an awareness that ultimately makes such decisions more formidable.

At the beginning of the twentieth century, anthropologists spoke out strongly against those who claimed that "savage" societies represented a lower level of biological and social development. Now, as we face the next century, the anthropological approach to human nature and human societies is as vital to communicate as ever. We face a difficult, potentially dangerous, and therefore complex future. A fundamental key to our future is to make certain that the dynamic qualities of human beings in all parts of the world are recognized and that the true value of cultural complexities is not ignored. There is much important anthropology to be done.

Source: Weiner 1990, 392–93.

FIGURE 4.3 Native American communities continue to struggle for social justice. In October 2002, the National Congress of American Indians held a rally at the United States Supreme Court building to protest Supreme Court decisions that they claim have eroded Indian sovereignty rights.

outspoken in his defense of the right of indigenous African peoples to control their own destinies.

In the years following World War II, European colonial powers were increasingly forced to come to terms with colonial subjects who rejected the role they had been forced to play as students of civilization. The colonial order was no longer a given, and its ultimate benevolence was sharply questioned. This critical attitude persisted after independence was granted to most European colonies in the 1950s and 1960s. It became clear that formal political independence could not easily undo the profound social and economic entanglements linking the former colonial territories to the countries that had colonized them, a phenomenon that came to be called **neocolonialism**. In North America, this same period witnessed the civil rights movement in the United States, which stimulated activism by women and Native Americans and others who felt their rights had been violated by the state. Many Native American communities continue to struggle for social justice, by using the courts to pursue the fulfillment of treaty obligations and international human

rights law to press for the recognition of tribal sovereignty (Figure 4.3).

▼ WHAT EXPLAINS HUMAN CULTURAL VARIATION?

How have these changing historical contexts shaped the theories anthropologists have devised to explain human cultural variation? Three points seem particularly clear. First, most of the societies studied by anthropologists, even one hundred years ago, were not leading timeless, unchanged ways of life that had been unaffected by the presence of others, especially by the presence of Europeans. The cultural patterns we find have everywhere been affected by the arrival of Europeans or the transformations of the world set in motion by the spread of European capitalism and colonialism. Second, in the face of these powerful outside forces, many groups shaped new identities and devised new social forms to deal with the effects of contact and conquest. In some cases, these new social forms drew on very ancient traditions, reworked to meet the demands of new experiences. In other cases, a contemporary ethnographer can glimpse ways of life that were invented long ago and continue to prove their worth by being reproduced today. Sometimes, modes of living that have endured successfully for

neocolonialism The persistence of profound social and economic entanglements linking former colonial territories to their former colonial rulers despite political sovereignty.

IN THEIR OWN WORDS

The Ecologically Noble Savage?

Part of the stereotype of the "primitive," as Paul Rabinow pointed out, includes the belief that "primitives" live in total harmony with their environment. Kent Redford explores how this stereotype has been recycled in recent years into the image of an idealized "ecologically noble savage."

To live and die with the land is to know its rules. When there is no hospital at the other end of the telephone and no grocery store at the end of the street, when there is no biweekly paycheck nor microwave oven, when there is nothing to fall back on but nature itself, then a society must discover the secrets of the plants and animals. Thus indigenous peoples possess extensive and intensive knowledge of the natural world. In every place where humans have existed, people have received this knowledge from their elders and taught it to their children, along with what has been newly acquired. . . . Writings of several scientists and indigenous rights advocates echo the early chroniclers' assumption that indigenous people lived in "balance" with their environment. Prominent conservationists have stated that in the past, indigenous people "lived in close harmony with their local environment." The rhetoric of Indian spokespersons is even stronger: "In the world of today there are two systems, two different irreconcilable 'ways of life.' The Indian world—collective, communal, human, respectful of nature, and wise—and the western world—greedy, destructive, individualist, and enemy of nature" (from a report to the International NGO Conference on Indigenous Peoples and the Land, 1981). The idealized figure of centuries past had been reborn, as the ecologically noble savage.

The recently accumulated evidence, however, refutes this concept of ecological nobility. Precontact Indians were not "ecosystem men"; they were not just another species of animal, largely incapable of altering the environment, who therefore lived within the "ecological limitations of their home area." Paleobiologists, archaeologists, and botanists are coming to believe that most tropical forests had been severely altered by human activities before European contact. Evidence of vast fires in the northern Amazonian forests and of the apparently anthropogenic origins of large areas of forest in eastern Amazonia suggests that before 1500, humans had tremendously affected the virgin forest, with ensuing impacts on plant and animal species. These people behaved as humans do now: they did whatever they had to to feed themselves and their families.

"Whatever they had to" is the key phrase in understanding the problem of the noble savage myth in its contemporary version. Countless examples make it clear that indigenous people can be either forced, seduced, or tempted into accepting new methods, new crops, and new technologies. No better example exists than the near-universal adoption of firearms for hunting by Indians in the Neotropics. Shotguns or rifles often combined with the use of flashlights and outboard motors, change completely the interaction between human hunters and their prey.

There is no cultural barrier to the Indians' adoption of means to "improve" their lives (i.e., make them more like Western lives), even if the long-term sustainability of the resource base is threatened. These means can include the sale of timber and mining rights to indigenous lands, commercial exploitation of flora and fauna, and invitations to tourists to observe "traditional lifestyles." Indians should not be blamed for engaging in these activities. They can hardly be faulted for failing to live up to Western expectations of the noble savage. They have the same capacities, desires, and perhaps, needs to overexploit their environment as did our European ancestors. Why shouldn't Indians have the same right to dispose of the timber on their land as the international timber companies have to sell theirs? An indigenous group responded to the siren call of the market economy in just this spirit in Brazil in 1989, when Guajajara Indians took prisoners in order to force the government Indian agency, FUNAI, to grant them permission to sell lumber from their lands.

Source: Redford 1993, 11–13.

centuries are at last falling before the advance of Western technology and the rigors of market capitalism (see, for example, Lee 2002, 1992a, 1992b). Far from being static survivors of a timeless past, however, the members of these societies are people coping actively with contemporary problems and opportunities, people whose history is also our history. Finally, in spite of everything, human societies around the world continue to generate and retain an impressive variety of cultural forms in response to the changing circumstances under which they live.

Colonial empires no longer exist, but global influences today are having if anything an even more powerful effect on the populations of the world. This means that making sense of the variety of forms of human society that exist across space and time is an ongoing task for anthropologists. One important technique that anthropologists have used in this effort has been to devise a **typology** in order to classify the societies they study according to their similarities and differences. In the rest of the chapter, we will briefly examine some of the most influential typologies that anthropologists have devised. We will also show how the colonial context of ethnographic research shaped the kinds of typologies that became influential in the discipline, and discuss some of the reasons why, eventually, these typologies fell out of favor.

Evolutionary Typologies: The Nineteenth Century

A system of classification reflects the features that its creator believes to be most significant. As a result, different assessments of what is significant can lead to different classifications. In the early years of anthropology, most Westerners who compared non-Western societies with their own were struck by certain features that set apart Europeans from the various peoples they conquered. Westerners identified these differences between themselves and others as *deficiencies:* lack of a state, lack of sophisticated technology, lack of organized religion, and so forth. Perhaps without realizing it, observers took Western industrial capitalist society as the universal standard against which to measure all other human societies. Having done this, they often

assumed that the alleged defects of non-Western societies were too obvious to require comment.

This approach to cultural differences was persuasive to nineteenth-century Westerners. It spoke directly to the cross-cultural experience that Western nations were having with the non-Western peoples they had colonized or with whom they traded. A colonial ruler eager to establish a smoothly working administration in New Spain or the operator of a trading post anxious to maximize profits in the fur trade would be most aware of the facets of a people's life that kept him from reaching his goals. How do you successfully collect taxes in a colony that has poor roads, lacks government officials who can read and write, and is populated by subjects who do not speak your language? How do you "pay" for beaver pelts when the "sellers" are not interested in money? Europeans faced with such practical problems were bound to see life outside Europe in terms of a series of deficiencies compared with what they could count on in the home country.

Observers of a more philosophical nature, too, were bound to wonder why there should be such deficiencies in societies outside western Europe (or in the more provincial areas of Europe outside the capital cities). Although their research rarely took them outside their libraries, they studied the reports of travelers and missionaries as well as history. They learned that many of the social and technological patterns they took for granted had not always existed, even in Europe. They became aware of the "advances" that had occurred and were continuing in all areas of European social life since the Middle Ages. It seemed clear that their ancestors too had once lacked the tools and ideas and social forms that made them powerful today. If they went back far enough, perhaps they would discover that their more distant ancestors had lived much as many peoples of America or Africa were living at that time. Indeed, ancient writers such as Julius Caesar had painted a picture of indigenous life in early Europe that resembled the contemporary customs of indigenous Americans and Africans. As archaeology developed, particularly in the nineteenth century, researchers could supplement written records with ancient artifacts presumably made by the primitive ancestors of modern Europeans.

Unilineal Cultural Evolutionism   For many nineteenth-century thinkers, the experience of social change, together with historical and archaeological evidence of

---

typology A classification system based on, in this case, forms of human society.

past social change, was suggestive. Perhaps the ways of life of the non-Western peoples they were reading about were similar to, and even repeats of, the ways of life of European generations long past. That is, perhaps the West had already moved through periods of history in which ways of life had been the same as those of contemporary non-Western societies. According to these scholars, if non-Western societies were left to themselves and given enough time, they would make the same discoveries and change socially the same way that western Europe had.

This way of thinking about social and cultural change has been called **unilineal cultural evolutionism**. It reached its most elaborate development in the nineteenth century, when evolutionary ideas were popular in all areas of Western thought (Figure 4.4). Unilineal cultural evolutionism was one way to explain the widespread cultural diversity that Europeans had been finding since the Age of Exploration. It proposed to account for this diversity by arguing that different kinds of society represented different stages of cultural evolution through which every human society either had passed or would pass, if it survived. Unilineal evolutionists viewed their own late-nineteenth-century European capitalist industrial society as the most advanced stage of cultural evolution yet. Living societies that had not already reached this level were seen as relics of more primitive stages that the West had already left behind.

Today, anthropologists find this approach to the classification of forms of human society to be inadequate—if not totally misleading. Nevertheless, it is a powerful scheme, and its continuing popularity among ordinary members of Western societies is not difficult to understand: It offers a coherent framework for classifying all societies.

For example, unilineal cultural evolutionism provided scholars who worked in museums an analytic framework for organizing artifacts collected from different types of living societies into a sequence based on the discoveries of history and archaeology. Thus, contemporary groups who made a living by gathering, hunting, and fishing were assumed to represent the way of life that had once existed universally, before farming and herding were invented. By the nineteenth century, however, it was clear that agriculture and animal husbandry had been invented only a few thousand years ago, whereas human beings had been around far longer than that. Re-

FIGURE 4.4 E. B. Tylor (1832–1917), one of the founders of anthropology in Great Britain, was convinced that societies moved through a series of unilineal stages.

searchers concluded that contemporary foragers had somehow gotten stuck in the earliest stage of human cultural development, whereas other societies had managed to move upward by domesticating plants and animals. Many of the non-Western groups with which nineteenth-century Europeans and Americans were familiar did farm or herd for a living, however. Their societies were usually larger than those of the foragers and technologically more complex. Farmers usually also built permanent structures and made pottery and woven cloth, goods that were unknown among foragers. Their social patterns too were often more elaborate. These peoples clearly seemed to be a

unilineal cultural evolutionism A nineteenth-century theory that proposed a series of stages through which all societies must go (or had gone) in order to reach civilization.

rung above the foragers. But they were also very different from Europeans. Most did not have writing, and their societies were not organized in anything resembling a European nation-state. For such reasons, this group of societies, midway between the foragers and modern Europeans, were given their own category. They seemed to typify the stage through which gatherers and hunters had to pass—through which Europe's ancestral populations had already passed—before attaining modern civilization.

In this manner, the first important anthropological typology of human social forms emerged. It had three basic categories, corresponding to the preceding distinctions. But the labels given these categories indicated more than objective differences; they also carried moral implications. The foragers—peoples who neither farmed nor herded—were called *savages.* Groups that had domesticated plants and animals but had not yet invented writing or the state were called *barbarians. Civilization* was limited to the early states of the Mediterranean basin and southwestern Asia (such as Mesopotamia and Egypt), their successors (such as Greece and Rome), and certain non-Western societies boasting a similar level of achievement (such as India and China). However, the advances that Europe had experienced since antiquity were seen to be unique, unmatched by social changes in other civilizations, which were understood to be declining. That decline seemed proven when representatives of Western civilization found they could conquer the rulers of such civilizations, as the English had done in India.

As we noted in chapter 1, this way of classifying different societies into stages also involved a classification of the peoples who were members of those societies into different categories called "races." A major disagreement developed in the nineteenth century between those who saw movement from lesser to greater cultural complexity as the result of the efforts of only one or a few "races" and those who believed that all peoples everywhere were equally inventive and might, under favorable circumstances, advance from lower to higher stages of cultural accomplishment. It would not be until the second half of the twentieth century, however, after the establishment of evolutionary theory in biology and the joining of genetics to studies of natural selection, that anthropologists would develop the theoretical and practical tools to demonstrate the fallacy of biological race.

Social Structural Typologies: The British Emphasis

As time passed, better and more detailed information on more societies led anthropologists to become dissatisfied with grand generalizations about cultural diversity and cultural change. This change in perspective was the outcome of improved scholarship and better scientific reasoning, but it was also a consequence of the changes taking place in the world itself.

Origins in the Colonial Setting   As we have seen, the last quarter of the nineteenth century ushered in the final phase of Western colonialism. Most of Africa and much of Asia, which until then had remained nominally independent, were divided up among European powers. At the same time, the United States assumed a similarly powerful and dominating role in its relationships with the indigenous peoples in its territory and with the former colonies of Spain. Unilineal cultural evolutionism may have justified the global ambitions of Europe and made colonial rule appear inevitable and just. However, it was inadequate for meeting the practical needs of the rulers once they were in power.

Effective administration of subject peoples required accurate information about them. For example, one goal of a colonial administrator in Africa was to keep peace among the various groups over which he ruled. To do so, he needed to know how those people were accustomed to handling disputes. Most colonies included several societies with various customs for dispute resolution. Administrators had to be aware of the similarities and differences among their subjects in order to develop successful government policies. At the same time, colonial officials planned to introduce certain elements of European law and political economy uniformly throughout the colony. Common examples were commercial laws permitting the buying and selling of land on the open market. They also tried to eliminate practices like witchcraft accusations or local punishment for capital crimes. Reaching these goals without totally disrupting life in the colony required firsthand understanding of local practices. The earlier "armchair anthropology" was wholly incapable of providing that understanding.

These changes in the relationships between the West and the rest of the world encouraged the development of a new kind of anthropological research. Under the colonial "peace," anthropologists found

FIGURE 4.5 Colonial officers often relied on traditional rulers to keep the peace among their subjects through traditional means. This 1895 photograph shows the British governor of the Gold Coast (seated on the right) together with a contingent of native police.

that they could carry out long-term fieldwork. Unsettled conditions had made such work difficult in earlier times. Anthropologists also found that colonial governments would support their research when persuaded that it was scientific and could contribute to effective colonial rule. This did not mean that anthropologists who carried out fieldwork under colonial conditions supported colonialism. To the contrary, their sympathies often lay with the colonized peoples with whom they worked. For example, Sir E. E. Evans-Pritchard, who worked in central Africa for the British government in the 1920s and 1930s, saw himself as an educator of colonial administrators. He tried to convey to them the humanity and rationality of Africans. His goal was to combat the racism and oppression that seemed an inevitable consequence of colonial rule. For these reasons, colonial officials were often wary of anthropologists and distrustful of their motives. It was all too likely that the results of anthropological research might make colonial programs look self-serving and exploitative.

Colonial officials quickly learned that the task of administering their rule would be easier if they could rely on traditional rulers to keep the peace among

their traditional subjects through traditional means (Figure 4.5). Thus developed the British policy of *indirect rule*. Colonial officials were at the top of the hierarchy. Under them, the traditional rulers (elders, chiefs, and so on) served as intermediaries with the common people. How could anthropologists contribute to the effectiveness of indirect rule? Perhaps the information they gathered about the traditional political structures of different groups might offer insights into the best way to adapt indirect rule to each group. As a result, anthropologists—especially British ones—developed a new way of classifying forms of human society. Their focus was on the **social structure**, especially the political structure, of groups under colonial rule. That British anthropologists came to call themselves *social anthropologists* reflects these developments.

In 1940, in a classic work on African political systems, Meyer Fortes and E. E. Evans-Pritchard distinguished between state and stateless societies. This distinction is similar to Morgan's unilineal evolutionary

social structure The enduring aspects of the social forms in a society, including its political and kinship systems.

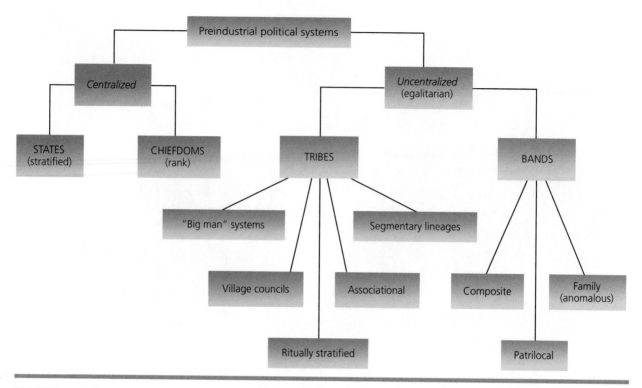

FIGURE 4.6   A typical classification of forms of human society. (From Lewellen 1983, 16)

classifications in terms of ethnical periods. However, there is a significant difference in the terminology used by Evans-Pritchard and Fortes: It makes no mention of "progress" from "lower" to "higher" forms of society. To be sure, the labels "savagery," "barbarism," and "civilization" were still part of the vocabulary of anthropology. Bronislaw Malinowski, for example, was quite comfortable sometimes referring to the inhabitants of the Trobriand Islands as *savages*. But the emphasis on contemporary social structures was bringing rich new insights to anthropology. Questions of evolution and social change took a back seat as social anthropologists concerned themselves with figuring out the enduring traditional structures of the societies in which they worked. A detailed knowledge of social structures was supposed to allow the anthropologist to identify the social type of any particular society. These types were treated as unchanging. They were compared for similarities and differences, and out of this comparison emerged a new classification of social forms.

The Classification of Political Structures   A contemporary example of a typical social-structural classification of forms of human society is shown in Figure 4.6. Here, the major distinction is between *centralized* and *uncentralized*, or *egalitarian*, political systems. This distinction is similar to the one Evans-Pritchard and Fortes made between state societies and stateless societies; only the labels have been changed, perhaps so that societies without states can be identified in a positive fashion rather than in terms of what they lack. Uncentralized systems have no distinct, permanent institution exclusively concerned with public decision making. This is another way of saying that groups (and perhaps even individuals) within egalitarian systems enjoy relative autonomy and equal status and are not answerable to any higher authority.

In this scheme, egalitarian political systems can be further subdivided into two types. A **band** is a

band The characteristic form of social organization found among foragers; a small group of people usually with 50 or fewer members. Labor is divided according to age and sex, and social relations are highly egalitarian.

small social group whose members neither farm nor herd but depend on wild food sources. A **tribe** is a group that lies somewhere between a band and a centralized political system. A tribe is generally larger than a band and has domesticated plants and animals, but its political organization remains largely egalitarian and uncentralized. Ted Lewellen refers to three subtypes of band, including the *family band*, which are cases that do not fit into the other two subtypes. He also identifies five subtypes of tribe but comments that they hardly exhaust the variety of social arrangements that tribes display (Lewellen 1993, 26).

Centralized political systems differ from egalitarian systems because they have a central, institutionalized focus of authority such as a chief or a king. These systems also involve hierarchy; that is, some members of centralized societies have greater prestige, power, or wealth than do other members. Centralized systems are divided into two types. In a **chiefdom**, usually only the chief and the chief's family are set above the rest of society, which remains fairly egalitarian. In a **state**, different groups suffer permanent inequality of access to wealth, power, and prestige, which signals the presence of social stratification.

Lewellen's typology does not attempt to make any hypotheses about evolutionary relationships. Tracing change over time is not its purpose. Instead, the focus is on structural differences and similarities observed at one point in time: now. This is not accidental. Remember that classifications of this kind were made in response to practical needs in European colonies. Colonial rulers assumed that they were civilized and that their colonial subjects were primitive, but they cared little about such matters as the origin of the state. The pressing questions for them were more likely, "How do African states work today?" and "What do we need to know about them to make them work for us?"

Structural-Functional Theory The theories of British social anthropologists dealt increasingly with how particular social forms function from day to day in order to reproduce their traditional structures. Such **structural-functional theory** was perhaps most highly developed by A. R. Radcliffe-Brown, whose major theoretical work was done in the 1930s and 1940s. Social anthropologists began to ask why things stayed the same rather than why they changed. Why

do some social structures last for centuries (the Roman Catholic Church) and others disappear quickly (the utopian communities of nineteenth-century America)? Why did some societies abandon foraging for agriculture thousands of years ago, while others are still gathering and hunting in the twenty-first century? Both kinds of questions are equally puzzling. However, an emphasis on social stability tends to downplay or ignore questions of change, just as an emphasis on social change tends to downplay or ignore questions of stability. This new focus in British social anthropology produced a succession of nonevolutionary classifications of human social forms. As data on more and more varieties of social structure grew, however, these typologies seemed to overflow with more and more subtypes. It is not surprising that some anthropologists began to question the point of it all.

Doing without Typologies: Culture Area Studies in America

Anthropologists in the United States became dissatisfied with unilineal evolutionism at about the same time as their British colleagues, and for similar reasons. The most important figure in this movement was Franz Boas, the man usually referred to as the father of American anthropology. Boas and his students worked primarily among the indigenous peoples of North America. They began to collect more and better data about these societies, especially data relating to the histories of individual groups. Change over time had not progressed through uniform stages for all these societies. For example, two societies with similar forms of social organization might have arrived at

tribe A form of social organization generally larger than a band; members usually farm or herd for a living. Social relations in a tribe are relatively egalitarian, although there may be a chief who speaks for the group or organizes group activities.

chiefdom A form of social organization in which the leader (a chief) and the chief's close relatives are set apart from the rest of the society and allowed privileged access to wealth, power, and prestige.

state A stratified society that possesses a territory that is defended from outside enemies with an army and from internal disorder with police. A state, which has a separate set of governmental institutions designed to enforce laws and collect taxes and tribute, is run by an elite that possesses a monopoly on the use of force.

structural-functional theory A position that explores how particular social forms function from day to day in order to reproduce the traditional structure of the society.

that status through different historical routes: one through a process of simplification, the other through a process of elaboration.

Boas also emphasized that new cultural forms were more often borrowed from neighboring societies than invented independently. He and his followers were quick to note that if cultural borrowing, rather than independent invention, played an important role in culture change, then any unilineal evolutionary scheme was doomed. However, a focus on cultural borrowing also emphasized the porous boundaries around different societies that made such borrowing possible.

The view of society that developed in the United States was therefore quite different from the one that developed in Great Britain. Boas and his followers rejected the cultural evolutionists' view of societies as isolated representatives of universal stages, closed to outside influences, responsible on their own for progressing or failing to progress. But they were also critical of the structural-functional view of societies as bounded, atemporal social types. Instead, they saw social groups as fundamentally open to the outside world; change over time was considered more a result of idiosyncratic local invention or contingent borrowing from neighbors than of inevitable, law-governed progress. Consequently, the Boasians focused their attention on patterns of cultural borrowing over time, a form of research called *cultural area studies*. They developed lists of **culture traits**, or features characteristic of a particular group: a particular ritual, for example, or a musical style. They then determined how widely those cultural traits had spread into neighboring societies. A **culture area** was defined by the limits of borrowing, or the diffusion, of a particular trait or set of traits (Figure 4.7).

This emphasis in anthropological research had consequences for typologies of social forms. If borrowing allowed societies to skip evolutionary stages entirely, then any classification of universal stages was meaningless. Furthermore, even timeless classificatory schemes, like those of the social anthropologists, were of limited value. They depended on the assumption that societies were clear-cut entities with internally consistent social structures. But if societies are perpetually open to cultural borrowing, it may be impossible to describe their structures in clear-cut terms. Area studies created cultural classifications that were either broader than an individual society (culture areas) or narrower than an individual society (culture traits). The end product was a list of traits and a map of cultural areas in which the traits are found. Boundaries around particular societies were ignored.

If people, practices, or artifacts could move in this way across social boundaries, then the social boundaries could not be impermeable. And if this were the case, then nineteenth-century ideas about the supposedly firm boundaries around biological "races" were also vulnerable to critique. In the first decades of the early twentieth century, Boas and his students were already arguing that races, languages, and cultures varied independently from one another. In the United States, a "nation of immigrants" that also included the descendants of conquered indigenous peoples and former African slaves, the mixing of linguistic and cultural practices accompanied the biological mixing of peoples. For the Boasians, this meant that any particular association of linguistic and cultural practices with a particular human population was an artifact of history and was vulnerable to further change.

The Biology of Human Variation

As we noted in chapter 1, this orientation within North American anthropology was strengthened after World War II by new developments in evolutionary theory that distinguished between macroevolution and microevolution. *Macroevolution* focuses on long-term evolutionary changes, especially the origins of new species and their diversification across space and over millions of years. Macroevolutionary changes revealed in the fossil record of human ancestors were of primary interest to paleoanthropologists. *Microevolution,* by contrast, concentrates on short-term evolutionary changes that occur within a given species over relatively few generations. Microevolutionary studies in evolutionary biology were made possible by the *modern evolutionary synthesis*, a major theoretical innovation accomplished in the 1930s and 1940s that integrated genetics and Darwinian natural selection into the expanded framework of *population*

---

culture traits Particular features or parts of a cultural tradition, such as a dance, a ritual, or a style of pottery.

culture area The limits of borrowing, or the diffusion, of a particular cultural trait or set of traits.

FIGURE 4.7 This map shows the Native American culture area for North America north of Mexico.

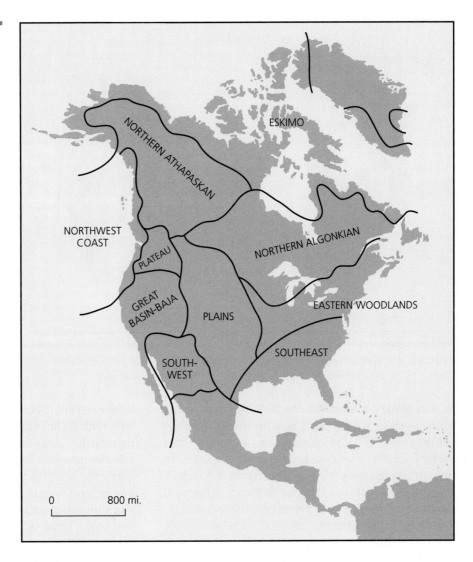

NORTHERN ATHAPASKAN

ESKIMO

NORTHWEST COAST

PLATEAU

NORTHERN ALGONKIAN

GREAT BASIN-BAJA

PLAINS

EASTERN WOODLANDS

SOUTH-WEST

SOUTHEAST

0   800 mi.

genetics. After World War II, "new physical anthropologists" (or biological anthropologists) discarded the old "race"-based physical anthropology and began to use concepts and methods drawn from population genetics to address questions about *patterns of biological variation within the human species as a whole.*

The modern synthesis defined a **species** as "a reproductive community of populations (reproductively isolated from others) that occupies a specific niche in nature" (Mayr 1982, 273). The ability of human beings from anywhere in the world to interbreed successfully is one measure of our membership in a single species. In addition, as we saw earlier, geneticists had demonstrated that most genes come in a variety of forms, called *alleles*. Population genetics has shown that genetic variation in human populations is mostly a matter of differences in the relative proportions of the same sets of alleles and that the distribution of particular phenotypes shifts gradually from place to place across populations, as the frequencies of some alleles increase while others decrease or stay the same. These observations lead to an inescapable conclusion: "Humankind . . . is not divided into a series of genetically distinct units" (Jones 1986, 324). Put another way, the boundaries said to define human "races" have been culturally imposed on shifting and unstable clusters of alleles (Marks 1995, 117). In addition, the distributions of some traits (such

species A reproductive community of populations (reproductively isolated from others) that occupies a specific niche in nature.

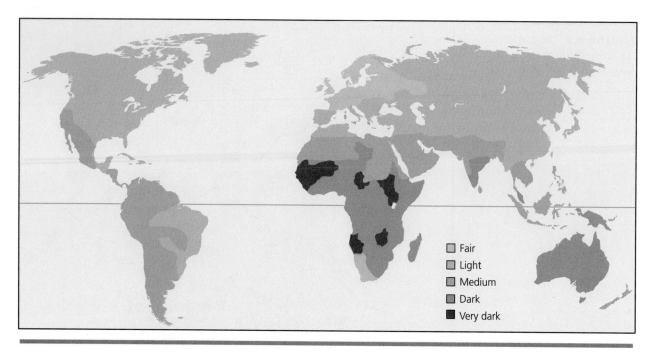

FIGURE 4.8 When the unexposed skin of indigenous people is measured and mapped according to the degree of pigmentation, skin shades tend to grow progressively lighter the farther one moves from the equator.

as skin color) do not match the distributions of other traits (such as hair type). The pattern of gradually shifting geographic frequency of a phenotypic trait across human populations is called a **cline**. Clines can be represented on maps such as Figure 4.8, which shows the gradually shifting distribution of differences in human skin color from the equator to the poles.

Phenotypic contrasts are greatest when people from very different places are brought together and compared while ignoring the populations that connect them (Marks 1995, 161). This is what happened when Europeans arrived in the New World, conquered the indigenous peoples, and imported slaves from Africa to work on their plantations. But if you were to walk from Stockholm, Sweden, to Cape Town, South Africa (or from Singapore to Beijing, China), you would perceive gradual changes in average skin color as you moved from north to south (or vice versa). Evolutionary biologists argue that skin pigmentation is distributed in this way as a consequence of natural selection: Individuals in tropical populations with darker skin pigmentation had a se-

lective advantage in equatorial habitats over individuals with light pigmentation. By contrast, populations farther away from the equator faced less intense selection pressure for darkly pigmented skin and perhaps even selective pressures in favor of lighter skins. But *different* selection pressures would have been at work on other traits, such as stature and hair type, within the same population, which is why the geographical distributions of these traits do *not* match up neatly with the distribution of skin pigmentation. To make things even more complex, different genes may be involved in the production of similar phenotypic traits in different populations. For example, although different ancestral populations of humans living near the equator all have dark skin, the identity and the number of alleles involved in the production of this phenotypic trait may be different in different populations (see below).

Evidence of intergradation in human phenotypes led biological anthropologist Frank Livingstone to declare 40 years ago, "There are no races, there are only clines" (1964, 279). Clinal variation explains why people searching for "races" have never been able to agree on how many there are or how they can be identified. *Clines are not groups.* The only group involved in clinal mapping is the entire human species. Each cline is a

---

cline The gradual intergradation of genetic variation from population to population.

map of the distribution of a *single* trait. Biologists might compare the clinal maps of trait A and trait B to see if they overlap and, if so, by how much. But the more clines they superimpose, the more obvious it becomes that the trait distributions they map *do not coincide* in ways that neatly subdivide into distinct human subpopulations. Since the biological concept of race predicts exactly such overlap, the biological concept of race cannot be correct. In other words, *clinal analysis tests the biological concept of race and finds nothing in nature to match it*. And if biological races cannot be found, then the so-called "races" identified over the years can only be symbolic constructs, based on cultural elaboration of a few superficial phenotypic differences— skin color, hair type and quantity, skin folds, lip shape, and the like. In short, early race theorists "weren't extracting races from their set of data, they were imposing races upon it" (Marks 1995, 132).

Many anthropologists hoped that the cultural category of "race" would disappear once its supposed biological underpinnings were exposed as false. During the 1960s and 1970s, anthropologists and others replaced racial explanations for social differences with cultural explanations. In the last 30 years, however, we have witnessed in the United States and elsewhere a resurgence of attempts to explain group differences in terms of race. Sometimes it is the powerful who engage in such practices, in controversial books like *The Bell Curve* (Herrnstein and Murray, 1994). Sometimes it is members of politically and economically marginalized groups who do so, as a calculated move in political struggles with those who dominate them (see chapter 14).

Genetic and other biological evidence alone cannot dismantle oppressive sociopolitical structures, but it can provide an important component in the struggle to eliminate racist practices from our societies. As we show in chapter 13, anthropologists can make a strong case when they combine the lack of biological justification for racial categories with powerful ethnographic evidence to show how racial categories have been socially, culturally, and politically constructed in the course of human history. Of course, to deny the existence of biological race is not to deny the existence of human biological or genetic diversity. It is, rather, to deny that the patterns of human diversity can be usefully sorted into a handful of mutually exclusive categories. As Jonathan Marks reminds us, it was the recognition that human varia-

tion did not come in neat divisions called races that "began to convert racial studies into studies of human microevolution" (1995, 117).

Postcolonial Realities

Then the world changed again. World War II was closely followed by the breakup of European colonial empires in Africa and Asia and by the civil rights movement in the United States. Former colonies were now independent states. Their citizens rejected the traditional Western view of them as savages or barbarians, asserting that they could govern their countries in a manner as civilized as that of Western nations.

Political realities thus created for Westerners new experiences of the non-Western other. These experiences made the pretensions of unilineal evolutionism even less plausible. As well, the leaders of the new states set out to consolidate national consciousness among the supposedly structurally separate societies within their borders. This effort made the structural focus of preindependence social anthropologists seem increasingly misguided, leading many Western anthropologists to recognize that the traditional societies they had been studying had not, in fact, been structurally separate even under colonialism. Decolonization allowed anthropologists to pay direct attention to colonialism as a form of political domination that eliminated the autonomy of indigenous social groups and forcibly restructured them into subordinate positions within a larger entity. We will take up this thread again in chapter 15.

At the same time, anthropologists with roots in the non-Western world began to add their voices to those of Western anthropologists (Figure 4.9). They were and continue to be highly critical of the cultural stereotypes institutionalized by unilineal evolutionism and structural-functionalism. But this does not mean that typologies have disappeared altogether in contemporary cultural and social anthropology.

Studying Forms of Human Society Today

Opinions about the importance of classifying forms of human society vary greatly among contemporary anthropologists. Some anthropologists, especially those interested in political and economic issues, continue to find typologies useful. Still, most anthropologists would agree that an emphasis on similarities or

FIGURE 4.9 At the beginning of the twenty-first century, increasing numbers of anthropologists are coming from regions of the world outside the West. Sri Lankan anthropologist Arjun Guneratne converses with some of his informants in Nepal.

differences in different types of society is closely related to the questions anthropologists are investigating and the theoretical assumptions they bring to their research.

For example, let us turn again to Lewellen's classification of social types. How meaningful is it? What does it reflect? Lewellen argues that it is designed to reflect structural, organizational similarities and differences. To defend such criteria, he employs a house metaphor: "Two houses built of different materials but to the same floor plan will obviously be much more alike than two houses of the same materials but very different designs (say, a town house and a ranch house). . . . In short, a house is defined in terms of its organization, not its components, and that organization will be influenced by its physical environment and the level of technology of the people who designed it" (1983, 17).

Because he assumes that structural similarities and differences are both significant and obvious, Lewellen seems to be affiliated with the tradition of British social anthropology. Similarities and differences concerning the materials out of which the houses are made can safely be ignored. For certain purposes, and for certain observers, this may be true. But is a house's organization manifested in its floor plan or in the way the various rooms are *used* regardless of floor plan? Is

a bedroom still a bedroom, whether in a town house or a ranch house, when the people living in that house use it to cook in? Does a family's ideas about how living space should properly be used change when the family moves from a thatched hut to an apartment with wooden floors and plaster walls?

Structural similarities and differences that seemed obvious to many political anthropologists in the British tradition led those anthropologists to set off states and chiefdoms sharply from tribes and bands. Would these similarities and differences seem so sharp to an anthropologist interested in classifying the ways different societies make a living? As we shall see, anthropologists interested in making such a classification employ concepts like *subsistence strategy* or *mode of production* to order their typologies, focusing on the strategies and technologies for organizing the production, distribution, and consumption of food, clothing, housing, tools, and other material goods. They therefore define a different domain of relevance, and different domains yield different typologies.

Since the end of colonialism, anthropologists have had to contend with new forms of classification, as the "peoples" of an earlier period were now being turned into citizens of postcolonial states. During the Cold War (between 1948 and 1989), a new set of categories came into existence that classified these states into either the First (or "developed") World, the Second (or "communist") World, or the Third (or "underdeveloped") World. Anthropologists adjusted to this transmuted context; many of them eventually became highly critical of the way "development" and "underdevelopment" were understood and addressed by scholars and government officials alike. With the passing of the Cold War, these distinctions have become even more problematic.

The Comparative Study of Processes

The kinds of typologies we have considered were valued at different times because they promised to allow useful comparisons to be made between different kinds of societies or cultures. But such typologies presume that societies or cultures are clearly defined entities that can be easily placed into a single category. If societies or cultures turn out to have contradictory structures or blurry boundaries and fail to fit into the available categories, then the usefulness of classification is called into question. Once anthropologists rejected the idea that social changes are fated to go in one direction only—the presumption of the unilineal evolutionists—it also became clear that typologies offer no principled way of addressing processes of social change. This would seem to suggest that classifying the forms of human societies, and perhaps anthropological comparison itself, is no longer a worthwhile activity for anthropologists.

Sally Falk Moore, however, would disagree. In the early twenty-first century, she says, a new form of anthropological comparison has emerged that focuses on the *comparative study of processes*:

> What matters to the anthropological observer is to follow the shifting form and the trajectory of the moving, interacting, social parts and the ideas that accompany them. The dynamic that sets things in motion is a major concern, for example, the growing interest in the reaction to political or economic shocks. These may be changes of regime such as the end of apartheid or the dismemberment of the former Soviet Union. These may be disruptions that create refugee streams or such economic transformations as the current expansion of Chinese industry. But mundane processes are also of interest. Although the specifics of time, place, and population are scrupulously reported, one ubiquitous puzzle is to discern the connections between local practices and larger-scale systems (2005, 2).

Comparisons of processes "involve before and after accounts" in which anthropologists "treat ongoing activities in an observable social field as an object of fieldwork" and, at the same time, "incorporate, as part of the interpretation, a wide sociopolitical context that is not necessarily observed" (2005, 9). One example of this kind of ethnographic comparison, cited by Moore, is Richard Wilson's collection of articles investigating human rights struggles in different parts of the world. "Human rights" are ordinarily taken to be universal—and universally identifiable—everywhere in the world, but the essays in Wilson's collection show that the task of making universal categories relevant in a local setting in Guatemala may be very different from the challenges encountered in a local setting in Hawaii. The comparative study of processes of human rights implementation, therefore, reveals that "human rights doctrine does get reworked and transformed in different contexts" (1997, 23). These matters are more fully explored in chapters 14 and 15.

It is sometimes easy to emphasize the shortcomings of past theoretical schemes in anthropology, but it is important not to overlook the lasting contributions they have made. Despite its excesses, unilineal cultural evolutionism highlights the fact that cultures change over time and that our species has experienced a broad sequence of cultural developments. Structural-functionalist typologies may seem overly rigid and static, but the structural-functionalist ethnographies show just how intricate the social institutions and practices of so-called simple societies can be.

The culture area studies of Boas and his students deemphasize boundaries between separate societies and run the risk of erecting boundaries around culture areas instead. Still, the attention they paid to the movement of cultural objects and practices *across* social boundaries makes clear that indigenous people have never been unthinking slaves to tradition. On the contrary, they have been alert to their surroundings, aware of cultural alternatives, and ready to adopt new ways from other people when it has suited them. Indeed, Boasian attention to forms of social and cultural mixing also highlighted the *biological* mixing that always takes place when human groups meet, providing a context within which biological anthropologists were eventually able to demonstrate the fact that biological races do not exist.

A focus on "underdeveloped" and "developed" societies may have raised more problems than it solved, but it was in the very attempt to explain why those problems existed that new anthropological understandings were achieved. Finally, it is the continuing cultural creativity of all human beings, in all societies, that keeps anthropologists especially busy today: The comparative study of cultural processes highlights the fact that differently situated populations, confronted with similar challenges, are not likely to respond in the same way and indeed may respond in ways that are unexpected and surprising. This is certainly revealed in the work of anthropologists who explore the effects of globalization on different local populations. But these are matters we attend to in the chapters to come.

CHAPTER SUMMARY

1. Modern Western history has been characterized by the rise of capitalism. The key metaphor of capitalism is that the world is a market and everything within the world—including land, material objects, and human beings—can be bought and sold. Such a view was unknown in noncapitalist societies before Western contact, even in those with highly developed economic institutions. The European capitalist penetration of non-Western societies was frequently followed by political conquest, which then reshaped conquered societies in ways that promoted economic exploitation. Colonial empires drew together economically and politically vast and previously unconnected areas of the world. To function intelligibly within the capitalist world order, colonized peoples had to begin to see the world as a storehouse of potential commodities.

2. The populations anthropologists would later study did not escape the historical processes of colonization and incorporation into a capitalist world economy. Indigenous groups lost their autonomy, and attempts were made to reintegrate them within the new colonial political economy. Many new groups came into existence in the course of commercial and political contacts between indigenous populations and Europeans. The continued existence of descendants of colonized peoples shows that conquered peoples can actively cope to reshape their own social identities despite oppression and exploitation.

3. Ethnography began at least at the time of Columbus, when Europeans had to come to terms with the ways of life of people whom they had conquered and incorporated into colonial empires. After anthropology emerged as a formal discipline in the late nineteenth century, the context of European or Euro-American colonialism was an ever-present reality within which anthropologists were obliged to maneuver. Many hoped that the dismantling of colonial empires after World War II would restore sovereignty and dignity to colonized peoples. However, independence did not free former colonies from deeply entangling neocolonial ties with their former masters. In North America and elsewhere, indigenous groups continue to seek social justice for the losses they have sustained as a consequence of colonization.

4. Although the colonial setting within which many anthropologists worked must always be taken into account, there is little evidence to suggest that anthropologists who worked in colonial settings were trying to further colonial domination. Anthropological findings were often too specialized to be used by colonial administrators, especially compared to the enormous amount of information supplied to them by merchants, missionaries, and other government functionaries. Also, the motives that led anthropologists to carry out work under colonial conditions were complex and variable.

5. A survey of the typologies used by anthropologists over the past century and a half to make sense of human cultural variation is illuminated by the historical circumstances surrounding contact between anthropologists and those with whom they have worked. Depending on an anthropologist's analytical purposes, the same social forms can be classified in different ways. The earliest important anthropological typology of forms of human society was proposed by

unilineal cultural evolutionists in the nineteenth century. They tried to explain contemporary cultural diversity by arguing that different kinds of society existing in the nineteenth century represented different stages of societal evolution. Every human society either had passed or would pass through the same stages. British anthropologists doing research in colonial settings in the first half of the twentieth century paid attention to the social structural forms of contemporary communities and showed how these structures enabled the communities to function successfully over time. They produced a succession of nonevolutionary classifications of human social forms. Following Boas, North American anthropologists rejected unilineal cultural evolutionism on the grounds that societies could easily borrow cultural forms from one another, thus skipping supposedly universal evolutionary stages. Boasian attention to forms of social and cultural mixing also highlighted the *biological* mixing that always takes place when human groups meet, providing a context within which biological anthropologists were eventually able to demonstrate the fact that biological races do not exist. Consequently, the aim of much research shifted to making lists of culture traits and mapping the culture areas through which they had spread as a result of cultural borrowing.

6. Since the end of colonialism, new classifications have appeared, such as the Cold War division of nation-states into First, Second, and Third Worlds, and the contrast between "developed" First World societies and "underdeveloped" Third World societies. While some anthropologists were always dissatisfied with these distinctions, they have become increasingly problematic since the end of the Cold War. Although some anthropologists still find some typologies useful for investigating some issues, classifying forms of human society is not an ultimate goal for most anthropologists today, and this would seem to suggest that the basis for anthropological comparison is also disappearing. But a shift in contemporary ethnography to the study of ongoing social and cultural processes has led to the emergence of work that focuses on comparisons of similar processes as they unfold over time in different social and cultural settings.

KEY TERMS

capitalism	unilineal cultural	chiefdom	culture traits
colonialism	evolutionism	state	culture area
political economy	social structure	structural-functional	species
neocolonialism	band	theory	cline
typology	tribe		

SUGGESTED READINGS

Kuper, Adam. 1996. *Anthropology and anthropologists: The modern British school*, 3rd ed. New York: Routledge. *A rich discussion of the heyday of British social anthropology, from the 1920s to the 1970s, carefully tracing developments in theory and method and locating these developments in the personal and political contexts out of which they emerged.*

Lewellen, Ted. 1993. *Political anthropology*, 2d ed. South Hadley, MA: Bergin and Garvey. *Contains much useful information about the different kinds of societies that different scholars have identified.*

Weatherford, Jack. 1988. *Indian givers: How the Indians of the Americas transformed the world*. New York: Fawcett Columbine.

————. 1991. *Native roots: How the Indians enriched America*. New York: Fawcett Columbine.

————. 1994. *Savages and civilization*. New York: Random House. *All three of these books are engaging accounts of the consequences of contact between the Old World and New World in the past and in the present.*

Whiteley, Peter. 2004. Ethnography. In *A companion to the anthropology of American Indians*, ed. Thomas Biolsi, 435–71. Malden, MA: Blackwell. *A thoughtful, thorough, critical account of the history of ethnographic practice in North America, from the arrival of Columbus to the present.*

Wolf, Eric. 1982. *Europe and the people without history*. Berkeley: University of California Press. *A classic text about the connection of European expansion to the rest of the world. This work also discusses the effect of European contact on indigenous societies.*

Chapter 5

Language

Only human beings have symbolic language, and it is so deeply part of our lives that we rarely even think about how unusual it is. In this chapter, you learn about what makes human symbolic language different from other forms of animal communication, about the building blocks of language, about linguistic inequality, and about the death and revitalization of human languages.

The system of arbitrary vocal symbols human beings use to encode and communicate about their experience of the world and of one another is called **language**. It is a unique faculty that sets human beings apart from other living species. It provides basic tools for human creativity, making possible the cultural achievements that we view as monuments to our species' genius. The number of languages spoken in the world today is difficult to determine.

According to David Crystal, author of *The Cambridge Encyclopedia of Language*, estimates range between 3,000 and 10,000, although he believes that it is unlikely that there are fewer than 4,000. Yet these estimates are problematic because new languages are regularly being identified while old languages continue to disappear (1987, 284–5). Language is a slippery phenomenon, and its tools are double-edged (Figure 5.1). This chapter explores the ambiguity, limitations, and power of human language.

▼ WHY DO ANTHROPOLOGISTS STUDY LANGUAGE?

Human language is a *biocultural* phenomenon. The human brain and the anatomy of our mouth and throat make language a biological possibility for us. At the same time, every human language is clearly a cultural product. It is shared by a group of speakers, encoded in symbols, patterned, and historically transmitted through teaching and learning, thus making communication possible.

Language and Culture

Language is of primary interest to anthropologists for at least three reasons: as a means to communicate in the field, as an object of study in its own right, and for what it reveals about cultures. First, anthropologists often do fieldwork among people whose language is different from theirs. In the past these languages were often unwritten and had to be learned without formal instruction.

---

language The system of arbitrary vocal symbols we use to encode our experience of the world.

linguistics The scientific study of language.

Second, anthropologists can transcribe or tape-record speech and thus lift it out of its cultural context to be analyzed on its own. The grammatical intricacies revealed by such analysis suggested to many that what was true about language was true about the rest of culture. Indeed, some schools of anthropological theory have based their theories of culture explicitly on ideas taken from **linguistics**, the scientific study of language.

Third, and most important, all people use language to encode their experience, to structure their understanding of the world and of themselves, and to engage one another interactively. By learning another society's language, we learn something about its culture as well. In fact, learning another language inevitably provides unsuspected insights into the nature of our own language and culture, often making it impossible to take language of any kind for granted ever again.

As with the culture concept, the concept of "language" has regularly involved a distinction between *Language* and *languages*. *Language* with a capital *L* (like *Culture* with a capital *C*) was viewed as an abstract property belonging to the human species as a whole, not to be confused with the specific *languages* of concrete groups of people. This distinction initially enabled the recognition that all human groups possessed fully developed *languages* rather than "primitive," "broken," or otherwise defective forms of vocal communication. Today, however, linguistic anthropologists realize that totalitarian views of "languages" can be as problematic as totalitarian views of "cultures." The difficulties associated with demarcating the boundaries between one language and another, or with distinguishing between dialects and languages, become particularly obvious in studies of pidgins and creoles, as we will see.

It remains useful, however, to distinguish *language* from *speech* and *communication*. We usually think of spoken language (speech) when we use the term *language*, but English can be communicated in writing, Morse code, or American Sign Language, to name just three nonspoken media. *Human communication* can be defined as the transfer of information from one person to another, which can take place without the use of words, spoken or otherwise. People communicate with one another nonverbally all the time, sending messages with the clothes they

by George Herriman

FIGURE 5.1 In 1918, Krazy Kat asks the question "Why is 'lenguage'?"

wear, the way they walk, or how long they keep other people waiting for them.

In fact, even linguistic communication depends on more than words alone. Native speakers of a language share not just vocabulary and grammar but also a number of assumptions about how to speak that may not be shared by speakers of a different language. Students learning a new language discover early on that word-for-word translation from one language to another does not work. Sometimes there are no equivalent words in the second language; but even when there appear to be such words, a word-for-word translation may not mean in language B what it meant in language A. For example, when English speakers have eaten enough, they say, "I'm full." This may be translated directly into French as *Je suis plein*. To a native speaker of French, this sentence (especially when uttered at the end of a meal) has the nonsensical meaning "I am a pregnant [male] animal." Alternatively, if uttered by a man who has just consumed a lot of wine, it means "I'm drunk."

Speaking a second language is often frustrating and even unsettling; someone who once found the world simple to talk about suddenly turns into a babbling fool. Studying a second language, then, is less a matter of learning new labels for old objects than it is of learning how to identify new objects that go with new labels. The student must also learn the appropriate contexts in which different linguistic forms

may be used: A person can be "full" after eating in English, but not in French. Knowledge about context is cultural knowledge. The linguistic system abstracted from its cultural context must be returned to that context if a holistic understanding of language is to be achieved.

Talking about Experience

Language, like the rest of culture, is a product of human attempts to come to terms with experience. Each natural human language is adequate for its speakers' needs, given their particular way of life. Speakers of a particular language tend to develop larger vocabularies to discuss those aspects of life that are of importance to them. The Aymara, who live in the Andes of South America, have invented hundreds of different words for the many varieties of potato they grow (see EthnoProfile 7.1: Aymara). By contrast, speakers of English have created an elaborate vocabulary for discussing computers. However, despite differences in vocabulary and grammar, all natural human languages ever studied by linguists prove to be equally complex. Just as there is no such thing as a "primitive" human culture, there is no such thing as a "primitive" human language.

Traditionally, languages are associated with concrete groups of people called *speech communities*. Nevertheless, because all languages possess alternative

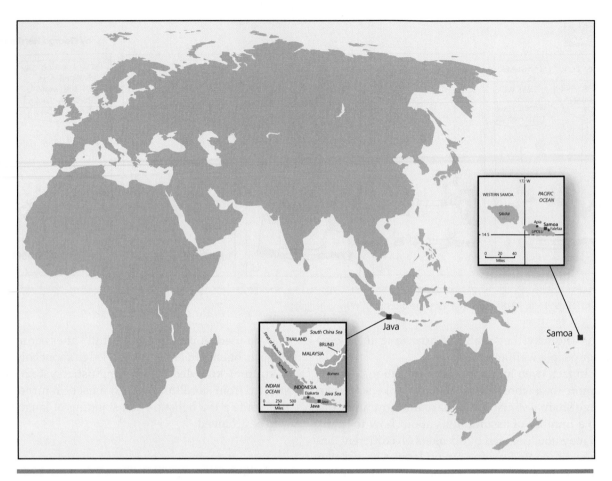

FIGURE 5.2 Locations of societies whose EthnoProfiles appear in chapter 5.

ways of speaking, members of particular speech communities do not all possess identical knowledge about the language they share, nor do they all speak the same way. Individuals and subgroups within a speech community make use of linguistic resources in different ways. Consequently, there is a tension in language between diversity and commonality. Individuals and subgroups attempt to use the varied resources of a language to create unique, personal voices. These efforts are countered by the pressure to negotiate a common code for communication within the larger social group. In this way, language is produced and reproduced through the activity of its speakers. Any particular language that we may identify at a given moment is a snapshot of a continuing process.

There are many ways to communicate our experiences, and there is no absolute standard favoring one way over another. Some things that are easy to say in language A may be difficult to say in language B, yet other aspects of language B may appear much simpler than equivalent aspects of language A. For example, English ordinarily requires the use of determiners (*a*, *an*, *the*) before nouns, but this rule is not found in all languages. Likewise, the verb *to be*, called the *copula* by linguists, is not found in all languages, although the relationships we convey when we use *to be* in English may still be communicated. In English, we might say "There *are* many people in the market." Translating this sentence into Fulfulde, the language of the Fulbe of northern Cameroon, we get *Him'be boi 'don nder luumo*, which, word-for-word, reads something like "people-many-there-in-market" (Figure 5.3). No single Fulfulde word corresponds to the English *are* or *the*.

FIGURE 5.3 *Him'be boi 'don nder luumo.*

▼ WHAT MAKES HUMAN LANGUAGE DISTINCTIVE?

In 1966, anthropological linguist Charles Hockett listed sixteen different **design features** of human language that, in his estimation, set it apart from other forms of animal communication. Six of these design features seem especially helpful in defining what makes human language distinctive: openness, displacement, arbitrariness, duality of patterning, semanticity, and prevarication.

Openness, probably the most important feature, emphasizes the same point that the linguist Noam Chomsky emphasized (1965, 6): Human language is creative. Speakers of any given language not only can create new messages but also can understand new messages created by other speakers. Someone may have never said to you, "Put this Babel fish in your ear," but knowing English, you can understand the message. Openness might also be defined as "the ability to understand the same thing from different points of view" (Ortony 1979, 14). In language, this means being able to talk about the same experiences from different perspectives, to paraphrase using different words and various grammatical constructions. Indeed, it means that the experiences themselves can be differently conceived, labeled, and discussed. In this view, no single perspective would necessarily emerge as more correct in every respect than all others.

The importance of openness for human verbal communication is striking when we compare, for example, spoken human language to the vocal communication systems (or *call systems*) of monkeys and apes. This point is stressed in the recent work of biological anthropologist Terrence Deacon (1997), who points out that modern human beings still possess a set of six calls: laughing, sobbing, screaming with fright, crying with pain, groaning, and sighing. These calls, together with gestures and the changes in speech rhythm, volume, and tonality that linguists call *speech prosody*, all appear to have coevolved alongside symbolic language, which is probably why they integrate with one another so smoothly when we speak. Deacon emphasizes, however, that primate call systems do *not* map onto any of the elements of human symbolic language and are even controlled by different parts of the brain.

Nonhuman primates can communicate in rather subtle ways using channels of transmission other

design features Those characteristics of language that, when taken together, differentiate it from other known animal communication systems.

than voice. However, these channels are far less sophisticated than, say, American Sign Language. The number of calls in a call system range from 15 to 40, depending on the species, and are produced only when the animal finds itself in a situation including such features as the presence of food or danger; friendly interest and the desire for company; or the desire to mark the animal's location or to signal pain, sexual interest, or the need for maternal care. If the animal is not in the appropriate situation, it does not produce the call. At most, it may refrain from uttering a call in a situation that would normally trigger it. In addition, nonhuman primates cannot emit a signal that has some features of one call and some of another. For example, if the animal encounters food and danger at the same time, one of the calls takes precedence. For these reasons, the call systems of nonhuman primates are said to be *closed* when compared to open human languages.

Closed call systems also lack *displacement*, our human ability to talk about absent or nonexistent objects and past or future events as easily as we discuss our immediate situations. Although nonhuman primates clearly have good memories, and some species, such as chimpanzees, seem to be able to plan social action in advance (such as when hunting for meat), they cannot use their call systems to discuss such events.

Closed call systems also lack *arbitrariness*, the absence of any link between sound and meaning in language. For example, the sound sequence /*boi*/ refers to a "young male human being" in English, but means "more" or "many" in Fulfulde. One aspect of linguistic creativity is the free, creative production of new links between sounds and meanings. Thus, arbitrariness is the flip side of openness: If all links between sound and meaning are open, then the particular link between particular sounds and particular meanings in a particular language must be arbitrary. In primate call systems, by contrast, links between the sounds of calls and their meanings appear to be fixed and under considerable direct biological control.

Arbitrariness is evident in the design feature of language that Hockett called *duality of patterning*. Human language, Hockett claimed, is patterned on two different levels: sound and meaning. On the first level, the small set of significant sounds (or *phonemes*) that characterize any particular language are not random but are systematically patterned. On the second level of patterning, however, grammar puts the sound units

together according to an entirely different set of rules: The resulting sound clusters are the smallest meaning-bearing units of the language, called *morphemes*.

Since Hockett first wrote, many linguists have suggested that there are more than just two levels of patterning in language. (We will discuss some additional levels later in the chapter.) In all cases, the principle relating levels to each other is the same: Units at one level, patterned in one way (sounds), can be used to create units at a different level, patterned in a different way (morphemes, or units of meaning). The rules governing morphemes, in turn, are different from the rules by which morphemes are combined into sentences, which are different from the rules combining sentences into discourse. Today, linguists recognize many levels of patterning in human language, and the patterns that characterize one level cannot be reduced to the patterns of any other level. By contrast, ape call systems lack multilevel patterning (Wallman 1992).

Arbitrariness shows up again in the design feature of *semanticity*—the association of linguistic signals with aspects of the social, cultural, and physical world of a speech community. People use language to refer to and make sense of objects and processes in the world. Nevertheless, any linguistic description of reality is always somewhat arbitrary because all linguistic descriptions are selective, highlighting some features of the world and downplaying others. For example, a trained primatologist would distinguish "apes" (like chimpanzees) from "monkeys" (like baboons), and both apes and monkeys from "prosimians" (like lemurs). By contrast, a person with no special knowledge of primates might use the words "monkey" and "ape" interchangeably to refer to chimpanzees, and might never have heard of prosimians. Each speaker links the same words to the world in different ways.

Perhaps the most striking consequence of linguistic openness is the design feature *prevarication*. Hockett's remarks about this design feature deserve particular attention: "Linguistic messages can be false, and they can be meaningless in the logician's sense." In other words, not only can people use language to lie, but in addition, utterances that seem perfectly well formed grammatically may yield semantic nonsense. As an example, Chomsky offered the following sentence: "Colorless green ideas sleep furiously" (1957, 15). This is a grammatical sentence

IN THEIR OWN WORDS

Cultural Translation

Linguistic translation is complicated and beset with pitfalls, as we have seen. Cultural translation, as David Parkin describes, requires knowledge not just of different grammars but also of the various different cultural contexts in which grammatical forms are put to use.

Cultural translation, like translation from one language to another, never produces a rendering that is semantically and stylistically an exact replica of the original. That much we accept. What is not often recognized, perhaps not even by the translators themselves, is that the very act of having to decide how to phrase an event, sentiment, or human character engages the translator in an act of creation. The translator does not simply represent a picture made by an author. He or she creates a new version, and perhaps in some respects a new picture—a matter that is often of some great value.

So it is with anthropologists. But while this act of creation in reporting on "the other" may reasonably be regarded as a self-sustaining pleasure, it is also an entry into the pitfalls and traps of language use itself. One of the most interesting new fields in anthropology is the study of the relationship between language and human knowledge,

both among ourselves as professional anthropologists and laypeople, and among peoples of other cultures. The study is at once both reflexive and critical.

The hidden influences at work in language use attract the most interest. For example, systems of greetings have many built-in elaborations that differentiate subtly between those who are old and young, male and female, rich and poor, and powerful and powerless. When physicians discuss a patient in his or her presence and refer to the patient in the third-person singular, they are in effect defining the patient as a passive object unable to enter into the discussion. When anthropologists present elegant accounts of "their" people that fit the demands of a convincing theory admirably, do they not also leave out [of] the description any consideration of the informants' own fears and feelings? Or do we go too far in making such claims, and is it often the anthropologist who is indulged by the people, who give him or her the data they think is sought, either in exchange for something they want or simply because it pleases them to do so? If the latter, how did the anthropologist's account miss this critical part of the dialogue?

Source: Parkin 1990, 90–91.

---

on one level—the right kinds of words are used in the right places—but on another level it contains multiple contradictions. The ability of language users to prevaricate—to make statements or ask questions that violate convention—is a major consequence of open symbolic systems. Apes using their closed call systems can neither lie nor formulate theories.

▼ WHAT DOES IT MEAN TO "LEARN" A LANGUAGE?

Years ago, studies of child language amounted to a list of errors that children make when attempting to gain what Chomsky calls **linguistic competence**, or mastery of adult grammar. Today, however, linguists study children's verbal interactions in social and cul-

tural context and draw attention to what children can do very well. "From an early age they appear to communicate very fluently, producing utterances which are not just remarkably well-formed according to the linguist's standards but also appropriate to the social context in which the speakers find themselves. Children are thus learning far more about language than rules of grammar. [They are] acquiring communicative competence" (Elliot 1981, 13).

Communicative competence, or mastery of adult rules for socially and culturally appropriate speech, is

---

linguistic competence A term coined by linguist Noam Chomsky to refer to the mastery of adult grammar.

communicative competence A term coined by anthropological linguist Dell Hymes to refer to the mastery of adult rules for socially and culturally appropriate speech.

a term coined by American anthropological linguist Dell Hymes (1972). As an anthropologist, Hymes objected to Chomsky's notion that linguistic competence consisted only of being able to make correct judgments of sentence grammaticality (Chomsky 1965, 4). Hymes observed that competent adult speakers do more than follow grammatical rules when they speak. They are also able to choose words and topics of conversation appropriate to their social position, the social position of the person they are addressing, and the social context of interaction.

Language and Context

Anthropologists are powerfully aware of the influence of context on what people choose to say. For example, consider the issue of using personal pronouns appropriately when talking to others. For native speakers of English, the problem almost never arises with regard to pronoun choice because we address all people as "you." But any English speaker who has ever tried to learn French has worried about when to address an individual using the second-person plural (*vous*) and when to use the second-person singular (*tu*). To be safe, most students use *vous* for all individuals because it is the more formal term and they want to avoid appearing too familiar with native speakers whom they do not know well. But if you are dating a French person, at which point in the relationship does the change from *vous* to *tu* occur, and who decides? Moreover, sometimes—for example, among university students—the normal term of address is *tu* (even among strangers); it is used to indicate social solidarity. Native speakers of English who are learning French wrestle with these and other linguistic dilemmas. Rules for the appropriate use of *tu* and *vous* seem to have nothing to do with grammar, yet the choice between one form and the other indicates whether the speaker is someone who does or does not know how to speak French.

But French seems quite straightforward when compared with Javanese, in which all the words in a sentence must be carefully selected to reflect the social

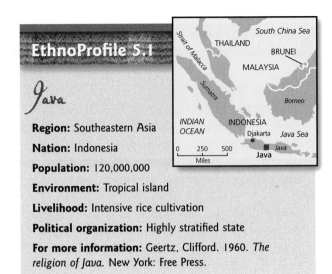

EthnoProfile 5.1

Java

Region: Southeastern Asia

Nation: Indonesia

Population: 120,000,000

Environment: Tropical island

Livelihood: Intensive rice cultivation

Political organization: Highly stratified state

For more information: Geertz, Clifford. 1960. *The religion of Java.* New York: Free Press.

relationship between the speaker and the person addressed (see EthnoProfile 5.1: Java). It is impossible to say anything in Javanese without also communicating your social position relative to the person to whom you are speaking. Even a simple request like, "Are you going to eat rice and cassava now?" requires that speakers know at least five different varieties of the language in order to communicate socially as well as to make the request (Figure 5.4). This example illustrates the range of diversity present in a single language and how different varieties of a language are related to different subgroups within the speech community.

▼ DOES LANGUAGE AFFECT HOW WE SEE THE WORLD?

During the first half of the twentieth century, two American anthropological linguists noted that the grammars of different languages often described the same situation in different ways. Edward Sapir and Benjamin Whorf were impressed enough to conclude that language has the power to shape the way people see the world. This claim has been called the **linguistic relativity principle**, or the Sapir-Whorf hypothesis. This hypothesis has been highly controversial because it is difficult to test and the results of testing have been ambiguous.

The so-called strong version of the Sapir-Whorf hypothesis is also known as *linguistic determinism*. It

linguistic relativity principle A position, associated with Edward Sapir and Benjamin Whorf, that asserts that language has the power to shape the way people see the world.

Speaking to persons of:	Level	"Are	you	going	to eat	rice	and	cassava	now?"	Complete sentence
Very high position	3a		pandjenengan		ḍahar					Menapa pandjenengan baḍé ḍahar sekul kalijan kaspé samenika?
		menapa		baḍé			kalijan		samenika	
High position	3					sekul				Menapa sampéjan baḍé neḍa sekul kalijan kaspé samenika?
Same position, not close	2	napa	sampéjan	adjéng	neḍa			kaspé	saniki	Napa sampéjan adjéng neḍa sekul lan kaspé saniki?
Same position, casual acquaintance	1a							lan		Apa sampéjan arep neḍa sega lan kaspé saiki?
		apa		arep		sega			saiki	
Close friends of any rank; also to lower status (basic language)	1		kowé		mangan					Apa kowé arep mangan sega lan kaspé saiki?

FIGURE 5.4 The dialect of nonnoble, urbanized, somewhat-educated people in central Java in the 1950s. (From Geertz 1960)

is a totalitarian view of language that reduces patterns of thought and culture to the patterns of the grammar of the language we speak. If a grammar classifies nouns in male and female gender categories, for example, linguistic determinism concludes that speakers of that language are forced to think of males and females as radically different kinds of beings. By contrast, a language that makes no grammatical distinctions on the basis of gender presumably trains its speakers to think of males and females as exactly the same. If linguistic determinism is correct, then a change in grammar should change thought patterns: If English speakers replaced *he* and *she* with a new, gender-neutral, third-person singular pronoun, such as *te*, then, linguistic determinists predict, English speakers would begin to treat men and women as equals.

There are a number of problems with linguistic determinism. In the first place, there are languages such as Fulfulde in which only one third-person pronoun is used for males and females (*o*); however, male-dominant social patterns are quite evident among Fulfulde speakers. In the second place, if language determined thought in this way, it would be impossible to translate from one language to another or even to learn another language with a different grammatical structure. Because human beings do learn foreign languages and translate from one language to another, the strong version of the Sapir-Whorf hypothesis cannot be correct. Third, even if it were possible to draw firm boundaries around speech communities (which it isn't), every language provides its native speakers with alternative ways of describing the world. Finally, in most of the world's societies, monolingualism is the exception rather than the rule, yet people who grow up bilingual do not also grow up schizophrenic, as if trying to reconcile two contradictory views of reality

FIGURE 5.5 Canada is officially a bilingual country, and signs are in both French and English. People in Canada who are bilingual do not grow up schizophrenic.

(Figure 5.5). Indeed, bilingual children ordinarily benefit from knowing two languages, do not confuse them, can switch readily from one to another, and even appear to demonstrate greater cognitive flexibility on psychological tests than do monolinguals (Elliot 1981, 56).

In the face of these objections, other researchers offer a "weak" version of the Sapir-Whorf hypothesis that rejects linguistic determinism but continues to claim that language shapes thought and culture. Thus, grammatical gender might not determine a male-dominant social order, but it might facilitate the acceptance of such a social order because the grammatical distinction between *he* and *she* might make separate and unequal gender roles seem "natural." Because many native speakers of English also are strong promoters of gender equality, however, the shaping power of grammar would seem far too weak to merit any scientific attention.

Neither Sapir nor Whorf favored linguistic determinism. Sapir argued that language's importance lies in the way it directs attention to some aspects of experience rather than to others. He was impressed by the fact that "it is generally difficult to make a complete divorce between objective reality and our linguistic symbols of reference to it" (E. Sapir [1933] 1966, 9, 15). Whorf's views have been more sharply criticized by later scholars. His discussions of the linguistic relativity principle are complex and ambiguous. At least part of the problem arises from Whorf's attempt to view grammar as the linguistic pattern that shapes culture and thought. Whorf's contemporaries understood grammar to refer to rules for combining sounds into words and words into sentences. Whorf believed that grammar needed to be thought of in broader terms (Schultz 1990), but he died before working out the theoretical language to describe such a level.

Eskimo Words for Snow

Word-for-word translation from one language to another is often difficult because the vocabulary referring to a given topic may be well developed in one language and poorly developed in another. However, as Laura Martin shows, we may draw erroneous conclusions from these differences without a deeper knowledge of the grammars of the languages concerned.

The earliest reference to Eskimos and snow was apparently made by Franz Boas. Among many examples of cross-linguistic variation in the patterns of form/meaning association, Boas presents a brief citation of four lexically unrelated words for snow in Eskimo: aput "snow on the ground," qana "falling snow," piqsirpoq "drifting snow," and qimuqsuq "a snow drift." In this casual example, Boas makes little distinction among "roots," "words," and "independent terms." He intends to illustrate the noncomparability of language structures, not to examine their cultural or cognitive implications.

The example became inextricably identified with Benjamin Whorf through the popularity of "Science and Linguistics," his 1940 article. . . .exploring the same ideas that interested Boas, lexical elaboration not chief among them. Although for Boas the example illustrated a similarity between English and "Eskimo," Whorf reorients it to contrast them. . . . It is a minor diversion in a discussion of pervasive semantic categories such as time and space, and he develops it no further, here or elsewhere in his writings.

Of particular significance is Whorf's failure to cite specific data, numbers, or sources. His English glosses suggest as many as five words, but not the same set given by Boas. Although Whorf's source is uncertain, if he did rely on Boas, his apparently casual revisions of numbers and glosses are but the first mistreatments to which the original data have been subjected.

Anthropological fascination with the example is traceable to two influential textbooks, written in the late 1950s by members of the large group of language scientists familiar with "Science and Linguistics," and adopted in a variety of disciplines well into the 1970s. One or both of these were probably read by most anthropologists trained between 1960 and 1970, and by countless other students as well during that heyday of anthropology's popularity.

In the first, *The Silent Language*, Edward Hall mentions the example only three times, but his treatment of it suggests that he considered it already familiar to many potential readers. Hall credits Boas, but misrepresents both the intent and extent of the original citation. Even the data are misplaced. Hall inexplicably describes the Eskimo data as "nouns" and, although his argument implies quite a large inventory, specific numbers are not provided. Hall introduces still another context for the example, using it in the analysis of cultural categories.

At approximately the same time, Roger Brown's *Words and Things* (1958) appeared, intended as a textbook in the "psychology of language." Here the example is associated with Whorf and thoroughly recast. Brown claims precisely "three Eskimo words for snow," an assertion apparently based solely on a drawing in Whorf's paper. Psychological and cognitive issues provide still another context in Brown's discussion of a theory about the effects of lexical categorization on perception.

Brown's discussion illustrates a creeping carelessness about the actual linguistic facts of the example; this carelessness is no less shocking because it has become so commonplace. Consider Brown's application of Zipf's Law to buttress arguments about the relationship between lexicon and perception. Since Zipf's Law concerns word length, Brown's hypothesis must assume something about the length of his "three" "Eskimo" "snow" words; his argument stands or falls on the assumption that they must be both short and frequent. Eskimo words, however, are the products of an extremely synthetic morphology in which all word building is accomplished by multiple suffixation. Their length is well beyond the limits of Zipf's calculations. Furthermore, precisely identical whole "words" are unlikely to recur because the particular combination of

(continued on next page)

IN THEIR OWN WORDS

Eskimo Words for Snow
(continued)

suffixes used with a "snow" root, or any other, varies by speaker and situation as well as by syntactic role.

A minimal knowledge of Eskimo grammar would have confirmed the relevance of these facts to the central hypotheses, and would, moreover, have established the even more relevant fact that there is nothing at all peculiar about the behavior or distribution of "snow words" in these languages. The structure of Eskimo grammar means that the number of "words" for snow is literally incalculable, a conclusion that is inescapable for any other root as well.

Any sensible case for perceptual variation based on lexical inventory should, therefore, require reference to distinct "roots" rather than to "words," but this subtlety has escaped most authors. Brown, for example, repeatedly refers to linguistic units such as "verbal expression," "phrase," and "word" in a way that underscores the inadequacy of his understanding of Eskimo grammar. His assumption that English and "Eskimo" are directly comparable, together with his acceptance of pseudo-facts about lexical elaboration in an unfamiliar language, cause him to construct a complex psychocultural argument based on cross-linguistic "evidence" related to the example with not a single item of Eskimo data in support. This complete absence of data (and of accurate references) sets a dangerous precedent because it not only prevents direct evaluation of Brown's claims but suggests that such evaluation is unnecessary.

Source: L. Martin 1986, 418–19.

▼ WHAT ARE THE COMPONENTS OF LANGUAGE?

Linguistic study involves a search for patterns in the way speakers use language; linguists aim to describe these patterns by reducing them to a set of rules called a **grammar**. Over time linguists came to recognize a growing number of components that form part of the grammar of any language. The most widely acknowledged components of language are phonology, morphology, syntax, semantics, and pragmatics.

Phonology: Sounds

The study of the sounds of language is called **phonology**. The sounds of human language are special because they are produced by a set of organs, the speech organs, that belong only to the human species (Figure 5.6). The actual sounds that come out of our mouths are called *phones*, and they vary continuously in acoustic properties. Speakers of a particular language hear all the phones within a particular range of variation as functionally equivalent versions of the "same" sound. Each class of functionally equivalent sounds is called a *phoneme* of the language, and the variant phones within each class are called *allophones* of that phoneme. All the phonemes of a particular language can be identified and distinguished from each other based on their complementary patterns of distribution with other phonemes in the language. Part of the phonologist's job is to map out possible arrangements of speech organs or acoustic perception that human beings may use to create and understand the sounds of language. Another part is to examine individual languages to discover the particular sound combinations they contain and the patterns into which those sound combinations are organized. No language makes use of all the many sounds the human speech organs can produce, and no two languages use exactly the same set. American English uses only 38 sounds (more or less depending on the dialect). Most work in

grammar A set of rules that aim to describe fully the patterns of linguistic usage observed by members of a particular speech community.

phonology The study of the sounds of language.

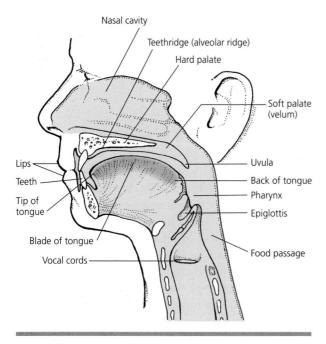

FIGURE 5.6 The speech organs.

phonology has been done from the perspective of the speaker, who produces, or articulates, the sounds of language using the speech organs.

Although all languages rely on only a handful of phonemes, no two languages use exactly the same set. That is, the range of variation among phones mentioned above may be organized into different phonemes in different languages. Furthermore, different speakers of the same language often differ from one another in the way their phonemes are patterned, producing "accents," which constitute one kind of variety within a language. This variety is not random; the speech sounds characteristic of any particular accent follow a pattern. Speakers with different accents are usually able to understand one another in most circumstances, but their distinctive articulation is a clue to their ethnic, regional, or social class origins.

Morphology: Word Structure

Morphology is the study of how words are put together. The study of the indigenous languages of North America by linguistic anthropologists like Sapir and Whorf revealed many kinds of word structures that were not found in European languages.

What is a word? English speakers tend to think of words as the building blocks of sentences and of sentences as strings of words. But words are not all alike: Some words (*book*), cannot be broken down into smaller elements; even though we might think that *boo* is a word, the remaining *k* is not. The word *bookworm*, however, can be broken down into *book* and *worm*. The puzzle deepens when we try to translate words from one language into another. Sometimes expressions that require only one word in one language (*préciser* in French) require more than one word in another (*to make precise* in English). Other times, we must deal with languages whose utterances cannot easily be broken down into words at all. Consider the utterance *nikookitepeena* from Shawnee (an indigenous North American language), which translates into English as "I dipped his head in the water" (Whorf 1956, 172). Although the Shawnee utterance is composed of parts, the parts do not possess the characteristics we attribute to words in, say, English or French (Table 5.1).

To make sense of the structure of languages such as Shawnee, anthropological linguists needed a concept that could refer to both words (like those in the English sentence above) and the parts of an utterance that could not be broken down into words. This led to the development of the concept of *morphemes*, traditionally defined as "the minimal units of meaning in a language." The various parts of a Shawnee utterance can be identified as morphemes, and so can many English words. Describing minimal units of meaning as morphemes, and not as words, allows us to compare the morphology of different languages.

Morphemic patterning in languages like Shawnee may seem hopelessly complicated to native English speakers, yet the patterning of morphemes in English is also complex. Why is it that some morphemes can stand alone as words (*sing*, *red*) and others cannot (*-ing*, *-ed*)? What determines a word boundary in the first place? Words, or the morphemes they contain, are the minimal units of meaning. Thus, they represent the fundamental point at which the arbitrary pairing of sound and meaning occurs.

morphology In linguistics, the study of the minimal units of meaning in a language.

TABLE 5.1	Morphemes of Shawnee Utterance and Their Glosses			
ni	*kooki*	*tepe*	*en*	*a*
I	immersed in water	point of action at head	by hand action	cause to him

Syntax: Sentence Structure

A third component of language is **syntax**, or sentence structure. In languages like English, for example, rules governing word order cannot explain what is puzzling about the following English sentence: "Smoking grass means trouble." For many native speakers of American English, this sentence exhibits what linguists call *structural ambiguity*. That is, we must ask ourselves what kind of *trouble* is involved: the illegal act of smoking grass (marijuana) or the danger of a prairie fire. In the first reading, smoking is a gerund working as a noun; in the second, it is a gerund working as an adjective.

We can explain the existence of structurally ambiguous sentences if we assume that the role a word plays in a sentence depends on the overall structure of the sentence in which the word is found and not on the structure of the word itself. Thus, sentences can be defined as ordered strings of words, and those words can be classified as parts of speech in terms of the function they fulfill in a sentence. But these two assumptions cannot account for the ambiguity in a sentence like "The father of the girl and the boy fell into the lake." How many people fell into the lake? Just the father, or the father and the boy? Each reading of the sentence depends on how the words of the sentence are grouped together. Linguists discovered numerous other features of sentence structure that could not be explained in terms of morphology alone, leading to a growth of interest in the study of syntactic patterns in different languages. Although theories of syntax have changed considerably since Chomsky's early work, the recognition that syntax is a key component of human language structure remains central to contemporary linguistics.

syntax　The study of sentence structure.
semantics　The study of meaning.

Semantics: Meaning

Semantics, the study of meaning, was avoided by linguists for many years because *meaning* is a highly ambiguous term. What do we mean when we say that a word or a sentence means something? We may be asking about what each individual word in the sentence means, or what the sentence as a whole means, or what I mean when I utter the sentence, which may differ from what someone else would mean even if uttering the same sentence.

In the 1960s, a formal analysis of semantics was prompted by Chomsky's argument that grammars needed to represent all of a speaker's linguistic knowledge, including word meanings, as sets of abstract rules. Formal semanticists focused attention on how words are linked to each other within a language, exploring such relations as *synonymy*, or "same meaning" (*old* and *aged*); *homophony*, or "same sound, different meaning" (*would* and *wood*); and *antonymy*, or "opposite meaning" (*tall* and *short*). They also defined words in terms of *denotation*, or what they referred to in the "real world."

The denotations of words like *table* or *chair* seem fairly straightforward, but this is not the case with words like *truth* or *and*. Moreover, even if we believe a word can be linked to a concrete object in the world, it may still be difficult to agree on exactly what the term should refer to. (We saw this earlier when we discussed Hockett's design feature of *semanticity*.) Formal semantics studies the meaning relations among the words of a language as they might appear in a dictionary, whereas semanticity refers to the way actual speakers use those words to talk about things in the world. And, as Hockett stressed, the link between the vocabulary items in a dictionary and objects in the world is open, never determined once and for all.

This suggests that meaning must be constructed in the face of ambiguity. Formal semantics, however, tries to deal with ambiguity by eliminating it, by "disambiguating" ambiguous utterances. To find a word's "unambiguous" denotation, we might consult a dictionary. According to the *American Heritage Dictionary*, for example, a pig is "any of several mammals of the family Suidae, having short legs, cloven hoofs, bristly hair, and a cartilaginous snout used for digging." A formal definition of this sort does indeed relate the word *pig* to other words in English, such as *cow* and *chicken*, and these meaning relations would hold even if all real pigs, cows, and chickens were wiped off the face of the earth. But words also have *connotations*, additional meanings that derive from the typical contexts in which they are used in everyday speech. In the context of antiwar demonstrations in the 1960s, for example, a pig was a police officer.

From a denotative point of view, to call police officers *pigs* is to create ambiguity deliberately, to muddle rather than to clarify. It is an example of **metaphor**, a form of figurative or nonliteral language that links together expressions from unrelated semantic domains. A **semantic domain** is a set of linguistic expressions with interrelated meanings; this metaphor links the domain of law enforcement to the domain of livestock. Metaphors are used all the time in everyday speech, however. Does this mean, therefore, that people who use metaphors are talking nonsense? What can it possibly mean to call police officers *pigs*?

We cannot know until we place the statement into some kind of context. If we know, for example, that protesters in the 1960s viewed the police as the paid enforcers of racist elites responsible for violence against the poor, and that pigs are domesticated animals, not humans, who are often viewed as fat, greedy, and dirty, then the metaphor "police are pigs" begins to make sense. This interpretation, however, does not reveal the "true meaning" of the metaphor for all time. In a different context, the same phrase might be used, for example, to distinguish the costumes worn by police officers to a charity function from the costumes of other groups of government functionaries. Our ability to use the same words in different ways (and different words in the same way) is the hallmark of openness, and formal semantics is powerless to contain it. This suggests that much of the referential meaning of language escapes us if we neglect the context of language use.

Pragmatics: Language in Contexts of Use

Pragmatics can be defined as the study of language in the context of its use. Each context offers limitations and opportunities concerning what we may say and how we may say it. Everyday language use is thus often characterized by a struggle between speakers and listeners over definitions of context and appropriate word use.

Formal linguistic pragmatics developed during the 1970s and 1980s; it has been described as the "last stand" of formal linguists who wanted to explain speech entirely in terms of invariant grammatical rules (Hanks 1996, 94). Indeed, both language use and context are narrowly defined in formal pragmatics, bearing only on those uses and contexts that are presumably common to all speakers of all languages, a problematic assumption. Formal pragmatics more closely resembles formal logic than patterns of everyday language use.

Michael Silverstein (1976, 1985) was one of the first linguistic anthropologists to argue that the referential meaning of certain expressions in language cannot be determined unless we go beyond the boundaries of a sentence and place the expressions in a wider context of use. Two kinds of context must be considered. *Linguistic context* refers to the other words, expressions, and sentences that surround the expression whose meaning we are trying to determine. The meaning of *it* in the sentence "I really enjoyed it" cannot be determined if the sentence is considered on its own. However, if we know that the previous sentence was "My aunt gave me this book for my birthday," we have a linguistic context that allows us to deduce that *it* refers to *this book*. *Nonlinguistic context* consists of objects and activities that are present in the situation of speech at the same time we are speaking. Consider the sentence, "Who is that standing by the door?" We need to inspect the actual physical context at the moment this sentence is uttered to find the door and the person standing by the door and thus give a referential meaning to the words

metaphor A form of thought and language that asserts a meaningful link between two expressions from different semantic domains.

semantic domain A set of linguistic expressions with interrelated meanings.

pragmatics The study of language in the context of its use.

who and *that* (Figure 5.7). Furthermore, even if we know what a door is in a formal sense, we need the nonlinguistic context to clarify what counts as a door in this instance (for example, it could be a rough opening in the wall).

By forcing analysts to go beyond syntax and semantics, pragmatics directs our attention to **discourse**, which is formally defined as a stretch of speech longer than a sentence united by a common theme. Discourse includes a spoken one-word greeting, a series of sentences uttered by a single individual, a conversation among two or more speakers, or an extended narrative. Many linguistic anthropologists accept the arguments of M. M. Bakhtin and V. N. Voloshinov (see, for example, Voloshinov [1929] 1986) that the series of rejoinders in conversation are the primary form of discourse. In this view, the speech of any single individual, whether a simple *yes* or a book-length dissertation, is only one rejoinder in an ongoing dialogue.

Ethnopragmatics

Linguistic anthropologists analyze the way discourse is produced when people talk to one another. But they go far beyond formal pragmatics, paying attention not only to the immediate context of speech, linguistic and nonlinguistic, but also to broader cultural contexts that are shaped by unequal social relationships and rooted in history (Brenneis and Macauley 1996; Hill and Irvine 1992). Alessandro Duranti calls this **ethnopragmatics**, "a study of language use which relies on ethnography to illuminate the ways in which speech is both constituted by and constitutive of social interaction" (Duranti 1994, 11). Such a study focuses on *practice*, human activity in which the rules of grammar, cultural values, and physical action are all conjoined (Hanks 1996, 11). Such a perspective locates the source of meaning in everyday routine social activity, or habitus, rather than in grammar. As a result, phonemes, morphemes, syntax, and semantics are viewed as linguistic resources people

FIGURE 5.7 To answer the question "What is that on the door?" requires that we examine the actual physical context at the moment we are asked the question in order to try to determine what "that" refers to. Is it the locks? the door handles? the studs on the door? Also, what part of the structure is the "door"?

---

discourse A stretch of speech longer than a sentence united by a common theme.

ethnopragmatics A study of language use that relies on ethnography to illuminate the ways in which speech is both constituted by and constitutive of social interaction.

---

can make use of, rather than rigid forms that determine what people can and cannot think or say.

If mutual understanding is shaped by shared routine activity and not by grammar, then communication is possible even if the people interacting with one another speak mutually unintelligible languages. All they need is a shared sense of "what is going on here" and the ability to negotiate successfully who will do what (Hanks 1996, 234). Such mutually coengaged people shape *communicative practices* that involve spoken language but also include values and shared habitual knowledge that may never be put into words. Because most people in most societies regularly engage in a wide range of practical activities with different subgroups, each one will also end up knowledgeable about a variety of different communicative practices and the linguistic habits that go with them. For example, a college student might know the linguistic habits appropriate to dinner with her parents, to the classroom, to worship services, to conversations in the dorm with friends, and to her part-time job in a restaurant. Each set of linguistic habits she knows is called a discourse genre. Because our student simultaneously knows a multiplicity of different discourse genres she can use in speech, her linguistic knowledge is characterized by what Bakhtin called *heteroglossia* (Bakhtin 1981).

For Bakhtin, heteroglossia is the normal condition of linguistic knowledge in any society with internal divisions. Heteroglossia describes a coexisting multiplicity of linguistic norms and forms, many of which are anchored in more than one social subgroup. Because we all participate in more than one of these subgroups, our language use is complex, even if the only language we know is English! Our capacity for heteroglossia is another example of Hockett's linguistic openness: It means that our thought and speech are not imprisoned in a single set of grammatical forms, as linguistic determinists argued. Indeed, if our college student reflects on the overlap as well as the contrasts between the language habits used in the dorm and those used in the restaurant, she might well find herself raising questions about what words really mean. To the extent, however, that her habitual ways of speaking are deeply rooted in everyday routine activity, they may guide the way she typically thinks, perceives, and acts. And to that extent, linguistic relativity may be seen to operate on the level of discourse (Hanks 1996, 176, 246; Schultz 1990).

A practice approach to language use aims to show how grammar, human action, and human values are all inextricably intertwined. But this does not mean that formal grammar can be ignored. As William Hanks puts it, "The system of language does

have unique properties, and we do better to recognize this than to try to pretend it isn't so" (1996, 232). Each language, as a system, has a particular set of formal possibilities that can be mobilized as resources when people talk to one another. At the same time, "context saturates linguistic forms, right down to the semantic bones" (142). Meaning is the outcome, thus, both of the formal properties of language uttered and the contextual situation in which it is uttered. And context always includes understandings about social relationships and previous history that may never be put into words.

How all this works is best illustrated with an example. One of the most obvious ways that context influences speech is when speakers tailor their words for a particular audience. Advertising agencies, for example, are notorious for slanting their messages to appeal to the people they want to buy their clients' products or services. Alessandro Duranti learned that a sense of audience is highly cultivated among the professional orators who argue cases before the titled people, called *matai*, who meet regularly in the Samoan village council, or *fono* (see EthnoProfile 5.2: Samoa). Orators make use of a discourse genre midway in formality between everyday speech and ceremonial speech. Because the fono renders judgments that assign praise and blame, the

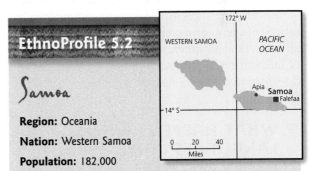

EthnoProfile 5.2

Samoa

Region: Oceania

Nation: Western Samoa

Population: 182,000

Environment: Tropical island

Livelihood: Horticulture, fishing, wage labor in capital

Political organization: Ranked, with linguistic markers for high- and low-status people; now part of a modern nation-state

For more information: Duranti, Alessandro. 1994. *From grammar to politics. Linguistic anthropology in a western Samoan village.* Berkeley: University of California Press.

main struggle between orators for different sides is "often centered on the ability to frame the reason for the meeting as involving or not involving certain key social actors" (Duranti 1994, 3). Of all the grammatical resources used by orators, one particular form, called the *ergative Agent*, most attracted Duranti's attention.

In semantic terms, an ergative Agent can be understood as a "willful initiator of an event that may be depicted as having consequences" for either an object or a passive recipient of the event (125). In Samoan, ergative Agents are marked by the preposition *e*, to distinguish them grammatically. Other forms of agency are marked by different prepositions: For example, *i* or *ia* frames the human agent as the source of the transaction, rather than as its willful initiator; and the possessive marker *o* or *a* attached to an agent focuses attention not on the possessor, but on the object possessed, that is, on John's *food* rather than on *John's* food. These ways of framing agency in grammatical terms are common in the fono, as disputants argue over who should be held accountable for some act. Possible agents include God, particular individuals, or groups. It is perhaps not surprising that the speaker who produced the highest number of ergative Agents in his speech was the senior orator, who ran the meetings and often served as prosecutor. "Powerful actors are more likely to define others as ergative Agents when they want to accuse them of something. Less powerful actors can try to resist such accusations by suggesting alternative linguistic definitions of events and people's roles in them" (133). In all cases, final judgments are the outcome of talk, but of talk saturated with sociopolitical awareness and deeply rooted in local historical context.

▼ WHAT HAPPENS WHEN LANGUAGES COME INTO CONTACT?

The Samoan village fono is a setting in which speakers and listeners are able, for the most part, to draw upon knowledge of overlapping language habits in

order to struggle verbally over moral and political issues. In some instances, however, potential parties to a verbal exchange find themselves sharing little more than physical proximity to one another. Such situations arise when members of communities with radically different language traditions and no history of previous contact with one another come face to face and are forced to communicate. There is no way to predict the outcome of such enforced contact on either speech community, yet from these new shared experiences, new forms of practice, including a new form of language—**pidgin**—may develop.

"When the chips are down, meaning is negotiated" (Lakoff and Johnson 1980, 231). The study of pidgin languages is the study of the radical negotiation of new meaning, the dialectical production of a new whole (the pidgin language) that is different from and reducible to neither of the languages that gave birth to it. The shape of a pidgin reflects the context in which it arises—generally one of colonial conquest or commercial domination. Vocabulary is usually taken from the language of the dominant group, making it easy for that group to learn. Syntax and phonology may be similar to the subordinate language (or languages), however, making it easier for subordinated speakers to learn. Morphemes that mark the gender or number of nouns or the tenses of verbs tend to disappear (Holm 1988).

Pidgins are traditionally defined as reduced languages that have no native speakers. They develop, in a single generation, between groups of speakers of distinct native languages. When speakers of a pidgin language pass that language on to a new generation, linguists traditionally referred to the language as a *creole*. The creolization of pidgins involves increased complexity in phonology, morphology, syntax, semantics, and pragmatics, such that the pidgin comes to resemble a conventional language.

Pidgins and Creoles

This traditional view suggested to Derek Bickerton (1981) that the way in which pidgins form could shed light on the universal biological bases of human language. He found that Hawaiian Pidgin English differed in many ways from Hawaiian Creole, which descended from it. Because, in his view, none of these differences could be connected to any of the

---

pidgin A language with no native speakers that develops in a single generation between members of communities that possess distinct native languages.

languages available to those who invented Hawaiian Creole, he concluded that they were produced by the innate linguistic "bioprogram" of the creole creators, and he claimed that these same forms could be found in other unrelated creoles as well.

Other students of pidgins and creoles tried to test his hypotheses. While their work did not confirm his views, it did reveal other important data. One discovery was that the old distinction between pidgins and creoles was more complex than previously thought. In the Pacific, for example, linguists have discovered pidgin dialects, pidgin languages used as main languages of permanently settled groups, and pidgins that have become native languages. Moreover, creolization can take place at any time after a pidgin forms, creoles can exist without having been preceded by pidgins, pidgins can remain pidgins for long periods and undergo linguistic change without acquiring native speakers, and pidgin and creole varieties of the same language can coexist in the same society (Jourdan 1991, 192ff.). In fact, it looks as if heteroglossia is as widespread among speakers of pidgins and creoles as among speakers of other languages.

Negotiating Meaning

More information has been gathered about the historical and sociocultural contexts within which pidgins first formed. Here as elsewhere in linguistic anthropology, the focus has turned to practice. Awareness of heteroglossia in pidgin/creole speech communities has led to redefinition of a pidgin as a shared secondary language in a speech community where speakers also use some other main language in smaller groups, and a creole as a main language in a speech community, whether or not it has native speakers. According to the new view, creolization is likely when pidgin speakers find themselves in new social contexts requiring a new language for *all* the practical activities of everyday life; without such a context, it is unlikely that creoles will emerge (Jourdan 1991, 196).

Viewing pidgin creation as a form of communicative practice means that attention must be paid to the role of pidgin creators as agents in the process (Figure 5.8). As we negotiate meaning across language barriers, it appears that all humans have intu-

Dispela i wanpela long aidia Radio Australia Papua Niugini Sevis i laik putim aut Nius.

Ol bikpela nius bilong wik, Mande igo nap long Fraide

April 12-16, 1997

1. RACE RALLIES (12-4-97)
Sampela hundred pipal ibin kamap long ol RALLY oa bung bilong toktok ino laikim "RACIST" pasin insait long Sydney na Brisbane long Australia.

FIGURE 5.8 Tok Pisin, a pidgin language that developed in New Guinea following colonization by English speakers, has become a major medium of communication in New Guinea. The news in Tok Pisin is available on the Internet at http://www.abc.net.au/ra/tokpisin/.

itions about which parts of our speech carry the most meaning and which parts can be safely dropped. Neither party to the negotiation, moreover, may be trying to learn the other's language; rather, "speakers in the course of negotiating communication use whatever linguistic and sociolinguistic resources they have at their disposal, until the shared meaning is established and conventionalized" (Jourdan 1991, 200).

▼ LINGUISTIC INEQUALITY

Pidgins and creoles turn out to be far more complex and the result of far more active human input than we used to think, which is why they are so attractive to linguists and linguistic anthropologists as objects of study. Where they coexist, however, alongside the language of the dominant group (e.g., Hawaiian Pidgin English and English), they are ordinarily viewed by members of society as defective and inferior languages. Such views can be seen as an outgrowth of the situation that led to the formation of most of the pidgins we know about: European colonial domination. In a colonial or postcolonial setting, the colonizer's language is often considered to be superior to pidgin or creole languages, which the colonizers characterize as broken, imperfect versions of their own

Varieties of African American English

The school board of Oakland, California, gained national attention in December 1996 when its members voted to recognize Ebonics as an official second language. What they called Ebonics is also known as Black English Vernacular (BEV), Black English (BE), African American English Vernacular (AAEV), and African American English (AAE). The school board decision generated controversy both within and outside the African American community because it seemed to be equating Ebonics with other "official second languages," such as Spanish and Chinese. This implied that Standard English was as much a "foreign language" to native speakers of Ebonics as it was to native speakers of Spanish and Chinese and that Oakland school students who were native speakers of Ebonics should be entitled not only to the respect accorded native Spanish- or Chinese-speaking students but also, perhaps, to the same kind of funding for bilingual education. The uproar produced by this dispute caused the school board to amend the resolution a month later. African American linguistic anthropologist Marcyliena Morgan's commentary highlights one issue that many disputants ignored: namely, that the African American community is not monoglot in Ebonics but is in fact characterized by heteroglossia.

After sitting through a string of tasteless jokes about the Oakland school district's approval of a language education policy for African American students, I realize that linguists and educators have failed to inform Americans about varieties of English used throughout the country and the link between these dialects and culture, social class, geographic region and identity. After all, linguists have been a part of language and education debates around AAE and the furor that surrounds them since the late 1970s. Then the Ann Arbor school district received a court order to train teachers on aspects of AAE to properly assess and teach children in their care.

Like any language and dialect, African American varieties of English—ranging from that spoken by children and some adults with limited education to those spoken by adults with advanced degrees—are based on the cultural, social, historical and political experiences shared by many US people of African descent. This experience is one of family, community and love as well as racism, poverty and discrimination. Every African American does not speak AAE. Moreover, some argue that children who speak the vernacular, typically grow up to speak both AAE as well as mainstream varieties of English. It is therefore not surprising that the community separates its views of AAE, ranging from loyalty to abhorrence, from issues surrounding the literacy education of their children. Unfortunately, society's ambivalent attitudes toward African American students' cognitive abilities, like Jensen's 1970s deficit models and the 1990s' The Bell Curve, suggest that when it comes to African American kids, intelligence and competence in school can be considered genetic.

African American children who speak the vernacular form of AAE may be the only English-speaking children in this country who attend community schools in which teachers not only are ignorant of their dialect but refuse to accept its existence. This attitude leads to children being marginalized and designated as learning disabled. The educational failure of African American children can, at best, be only partially addressed through teacher training on AAE. When children go to school, they bring not only their homework and textbooks but also their language, culture and identity. Sooner rather than later, the educational system must address its exclusion of cultural and dialect difference in teacher training and school curriculum.

Source: M. Morgan 1997, 8.

language. The situation only worsens when formal education, the key to participation in the European-dominated society, is carried out in the colonial language. Speakers of a pidgin or creole or indigenous language who remain illiterate may never be able to master the colonial tongue and may find themselves effectively barred from equal participation in the civic life of their societies.

To take one language variety as the standard against which all other varieties are measured might be described as linguistic ethnocentrism, and such a standard may be applied to any language, not just pidgins and creoles. This is one kind of linguistic inequality: making value judgments about other people's speech in a context of dominance and subordination. A powerful example of the effects of linguistic inequality is found in the history and controversies surrounding African American English in the United States.

Language Habits of African Americans

In the 1960s, some psychologists claimed that African American children living in urban areas of the northern United States suffered from linguistic deprivation. They argued that these children started school with a limited vocabulary and no grammar and thus could not perform as well as European American children in the classroom—that their language was unequal to the challenges of communication. Sociolinguist William Labov and his colleagues found such claims incredible and undertook research of their own (Labov 1972), which demonstrated two things. First, they proved that the form of English spoken in the inner city was not defective pseudolanguage. Second, they showed how a change in research context permitted inner-city African American children to display a level of linguistic sophistication that the psychologists had never dreamed they possessed.

When African American children were in the classroom (a European American–dominated context) being interrogated by European American adults about topics of no interest to them, they said little. This did not necessarily mean, Labov argued, that they had no language. Rather, their minimal responses were better understood as defensive at-

tempts to keep threatening European American questioners from learning anything about them. For the African American children, the classroom was only one part of a broader racist culture. The psychologists, due to their ethnocentrism, had been oblivious to the effect this context might have on their research.

Reasoning that reliable samples of African American speech had to be collected in contexts where the racist threat was lessened, Labov and his colleagues conducted fieldwork in the homes and on the streets of the inner city. They recorded enormous amounts of speech in African American English (AAE) produced by the same children who had had nothing to say when questioned in the classroom. Labov's analysis demonstrated that AAE was a variety of English that had certain rules not found in Standard English. This is a strictly linguistic difference: Most middle-class speakers of Standard English would not use these rules but most African American speakers of AAE would. However, neither variety of English should be seen as "defective" as a result of this difference. This kind of linguistic difference, apparent when speakers of two varieties converse, marks the speaker's membership in a particular speech community. Such differences can exist in phonology, morphology, syntax, semantics, or pragmatics (Figure 5.9). Indeed, similar linguistic differences distinguish the language habits of most

FIGURE 5.9 The language habits of African Americans are not homogeneous; they vary according to gender, social class, region, and situation.

social subgroups in a society, like that of the United States, that is characterized by heteroglossia.

What is distinctive about African American English from a practice perspective, however, are the historical and sociocultural circumstances that led to its creation. For some time, linguists have viewed AAE as one of many creole languages that developed in the New World after Africans were brought there to work as slaves on plantations owned by Europeans. Dominant English-speaking elites have regarded AAE with the same disdain that European colonial elites have accorded creole languages elsewhere. Because African Americans have always lived in socially and politically charged contexts that questioned their full citizenship, statements about their language habits are inevitably thought to imply something about their intelligence and culture. Those psychologists who claimed that inner-city African American children suffered from linguistic deprivation, for example, seemed to be suggesting either that these children were too stupid to speak or that their cultural surroundings were too meager to allow normal language development.

The work of Labov and his colleagues showed that the children were not linguistically deprived, were not stupid, and participated in a rich linguistic culture. But this work itself became controversial in later decades when it became clear that the rich African American language and culture described was primarily that of adolescent males. These young men saw themselves as bearers of authentic African American language habits and dismissed African Americans who did not speak the way they did as "lames." This implied that everyone else in the African American community was somehow not genuinely African American, a challenge that those excluded could not ignore. Linguists like Labov's team, who thought their work undermined racism, were thus bewildered when middle-class African Americans, who spoke Standard English, refused to accept AAE as representative of "true" African American culture (Morgan 1995, 337).

From the perspective of linguistic anthropology, this debate shows that the African American community is not homogeneous, linguistically or culturally, but is instead characterized by heteroglossia and a range of attitudes regarding AAE. At a minimum, language habits are shaped by social class, age cohort, and gender. Moreover, members of all of these subgroups use both Standard English and AAE in their speech. Morgan reports, for example, that upper-middle-class African American students at elite colleges who did not grow up speaking AAE regularly adopt many of its features and that hip-hop artists combine the grammar of Standard English with the phonology and morphology of AAE (1995, 338). This situation is not so paradoxical if we recall, once again, the politically charged context of African American life in the United States. African Americans both affirm and deny the significance of AAE for their identity, perhaps because AAE symbolizes both the oppression of slavery and resistance to that oppression (339). A quarter of a century ago, Claudia Mitchell-Kernan described African Americans as "bicultural" and struggling to develop language habits that could reconcile "good" English and AAE (1972, 209). That struggle continues at the beginning of the twenty-first century, while whites continue to adopt words and expressions from AAE as "hip."

Language Ideology

Building on earlier work on linguistic inequality, linguistic anthropologists in recent years have developed a focus on the study of **language ideology:** ways of representing the intersection "between social forms and forms of talk" (Woolard 1998, 3). While the study of language ideology discloses speakers' sense of beauty or morality or basic understandings of the world, it also provides evidence of the ways in which our speech is always embedded in a social world of power differences. Language ideologies are markers of struggles between social groups with different interests, revealed in what people say and how they say it. The way people monitor their speech to bring it into line with a particular language ideology illustrates that language ideologies are "active and effective . . . they transform the material reality they comment on" (Woolard 1998, 11). In settings with a

---

language ideology A marker of struggles between social groups with different interests, revealed in what people say and how they say it.

history of colonization, where groups with different power and different languages coexist in tension, the study of language ideologies has long been significant (Woolard 1998, 16). The skills of linguistic anthropologists especially suit them to study language ideologies because their linguistic training allows them to describe precisely the linguistic features (phonological, morphological, or syntactic, for example) that become the focus of ideological attention, and their training in cultural analysis allows them to explain how those linguistic features come to stand symbolically for a particular social group.

Linguistic anthropologist Marcyliena Morgan has studied the language ideology held by African Americans about African American English. Her research reveals that perhaps the key element of African American language ideology is the importance of *indirectness* (2002, 25). Indirectness of communication was vital for African Americans living under conditions of slavery and legal segregation. In conditions of extreme political inequality, African Americans had to contend with a set of unwritten rules that governed how they were supposed to communicate with whites, such as speaking only when permission was granted, without questioning or contradicting what whites said to them, and bowing their heads and saying "yes, sir" or "yes, ma'am." Following these rules publicly confirmed the subordinate status of African Americans in the racial hierarchy, while breaking the rules was severely punished.

African Americans spoke differently when not in the company of whites. But they also developed ways of speaking when whites were present that allowed them to demonstrate their agency in a way that was "very much above ground . . . cloaked and unseen by those in power" (2002, 23). That is, African Americans developed a *counterlanguage* based on indirectness that could only be fully enacted before an audience that included both people who had been socialized within the African American setting and outsiders who had not. The most highly valued instances of this counterlanguage were ambiguous speech performances that were usually puzzling or unintelligible to outsiders, but easily understood by the African Americans who were present. Successful performances depend on participation by the audience as well as the speaker, and on everyone's mastery of local heteroglossia: "the knowledge that language varieties exist and represent different positions of power, politics, and history" (2002, 38).

Morgan collected samples of African American discourse and drew upon African American language ideology to explain the significance of what is said and what is not said. For example, she examined a narrative provided by Rose and Nora, two elderly African American women, whom she interviewed about the 1919 race riot in Chicago. Morgan reproduced the transcript of their conversation, and then pointed to significant passages that reveal the disciplined indirectness of these women's speech. For example, when Morgan asked them *how* the riot started, Nora replied by saying *where* it started, *on the beach*. While to an outsider this answer may seem unrelated to the question, in fact it is an indirect response that signals the correct answer to listeners in the know: "The location is in fact the reason for the riot. The 31st Street beach included an imaginary line in the water separating black and white swimmers. A young white man accused a young black man of swimming across the border" (2002, 109). Rose and Nora referred only to "the whites" as being the attackers, although historical sources suggest that the main group involved were Irish. At the same time, the women explicitly stated that "the Italians" living on certain named streets helped to calm things down. Again, to those in the know, the named streets indirectly signal that Italians were living on some of the same streets as African Americans, which also indirectly suggests why they might have been motivated to calm things down.

Finally, when Morgan asked the two women why the riot happened, Rose answered that she still hasn't figured it out, that the type of mattress they were sleeping on must have caused it (2002, 109). This answer seems completely inappropriate, but Morgan is able to show that such explanations for the horrors of life under white supremacy conform to another pattern of indirectness: Statements like this at the end of a narrative of this kind signify "that there is no explanation for racist acts. . . . The riot happened because white supremacy exists. If one does not want the truth, the mattress is as good an explanation as any" (2002, 110).

Language Habits of Women and Men

Differences in language habits not only distinguish ethnic groups from one another but also distinguish the speech habits of women and men. Indeed, one of the early objections to work on African American English was that it focused on the discourse genres of men only. Since the 1970s, the language habits of African American women and girls have figured in numerous studies, to which Morgan's work is a recent contribution (see also Morgan 1995, 336ff.).

Sociolinguist Deborah Tannen (1990) gained much popular attention in the media with her study of speech patterns of men and women in the United States. Tannen focuses on typical male and female styles of discourse, arguing that men and women use language for different reasons: Men tend to use language as a competitive weapon in public settings, whereas women tend to use language as a way of building closeness in private settings. Tannen shows what happens when men and women each assume that their rules are the only rules without realizing that the other gender may be defining appropriate language use from a different perspective. For example, when a husband and wife get home from work at the end of the day, she may be eager to talk while he is just as eager to remain silent. She may interpret his silence as a sign of distance or coldness and be hurt. He, by contrast, may be weary of the day's verbal combat and resent his wife's attempts at conversation, not because he is rejecting her personally but because he believes he has a right to remain silent.

As you would expect by now, however, these kinds of gender-based distinctions are not universal. They vary cross-culturally, not only in terms of the different styles of speaking recognized in different societies, but also in terms of the extent to which different styles are or are not allocated to speakers based on locally recognized gender categories. This is illustrated in the research of linguistic anthropologist Joel Kuipers, who worked in the Weyéwa highlands on the island of Sumba in Indonesia (Kuipers 1986). Previous ethnographers had reported very little gender difference in Indonesian societies, and Kuipers found this to be true in Weyéwa society as well. The main exception, however, occurred in important ritual settings, where the speech performances of men and women differed sharply.

The Weyéwa people used numerous varieties of both colloquial and ritual speech, but Kuipers found that their ritual speech was distinctive. First, ritual speech involved the use of elaborate metaphors and had to be delivered in pairs of poetic couplets, "in which the second line parallels the first line in rhythm and meaning" (1986, 450). Second, some varieties of ritual speech are so demanding that experts—both women and men—may be paid for performing them in other people's rituals. Still, the ritual speech in which women specialize is often not performed for pay and includes funeral laments, work songs, humorous storytelling, and the production of trilling sounds (called *ululations*) to support the ritual speech performances of men. "In short, women's communication is focused on evoking immediate, usually emotional, responses in the audience, often with practical results, for example, getting a particular job done" (1986, 451). By contrast, men have special responsibilities for communicating with the spirits of ancestors to whom they are related through their fathers (see chapter 11, on kinship and relatedness). This communication takes place by means of ritual speech in performances in rites of prayer, divination, placation, lament, and blessing. If men lack the skills to perform these verbal tasks properly, they must hire an expert to perform in their place; otherwise, they run the risk of offending the ancestral spirits and possibly being fined.

Misfortunes such as crop failure, sudden death, and house fires are common on the island of Sumba. Weyéwa people explain such calamities as punishments sent by ancestral spirits who are angry because their living descendants have neglected them. When such events occur, both men and women respond with open emotion, in one or another form of colloquial speech. But as the extent of the calamity becomes clear, people engage in a more formal ritual response: first divination, to determine the cause; then a placation rite in which proper relations to the spirits are restored; and finally—for those who can afford it—an elaborate celebration to obtain a blessing from the formerly angry spirits.

Kuipers discovered that gendered differences in speech were important in these postcalamity rituals. Men's ritual speech is organized in the form of a narrative in paired couplets that recapitulates the story of neglect that led to ancestral anger that led to misfortune and then to the healing of relations between ancestral spirits and their descendants. This speech is extremely indirect, offering an account that will be discussed and analyzed later to determine who was to blame for the misfortune and must therefore foot the bill for feasts or temple-building activities that will soothe the ancestors' anger. Should anyone in the audience detect an error of poetic structure in this performance, the ritual speaker may be fined and required to pay an item such as a chicken or a cloth to the client's ancestors. Women's speech on these ritual occasions does not have this narrative function. For example, women are silent during divination rites, but they support the male speaker during placation rites with high-pitched ululations that are supposed to encourage him, and other men in the audience will scold them if their efforts are not perceived to be sufficiently energetic. During mourning rites, women perform laments that emphasize the complexity of mourners' grief, and their performances are evaluated afterwards in terms of how successful they were in provoking emotional responses from the audience.

Why does the speech of women and men vary in this way? One hypothesis might be that women specialize in laments and other emotion-provoking speech styles because women are more emotionally expressive than men, but Kuipers does not find this kind of circular reasoning persuasive. Another hypothesis might be that different gendered speech styles are related to differences in the gendered division of labor in Weyéwa society, but Kuipers found no real division of labor by gender: Men and women share nearly all productive work. Kuipers concluded that the most persuasive explanation relates women's and men's speech performances to the roles of women and men in the Weyéwa social and symbolic order. Weyéwa organize themselves into lineages traced through men, and when women marry they go to live with their husbands. This move breaks a woman's ties to her own kinship group, and she will not be fully incorporated into her husband's group for many years. Thus, it is only the men who are seen to have the local, temporal continuity to know and master the history of their kinship group—but this also means that it is they, not their wives, who are re-

sponsible for communication with the sacred spirits to repair relations after calamity. Nevertheless, women's speech has its own power in these rites: "Through systematic violation of couplets, repetitions, and evocative interjections, women's speech evokes immediate and powerful responses in their immediate social environment" (1986, 460).

▼ WHAT IS LOST IF A LANGUAGE DIES?

At the beginning of the twenty-first century, many anthropologists and linguists have become involved in projects to maintain or revive languages with small numbers of native speakers. These languages are in danger of disappearing as younger people in the speech community stop using the language or never learn it in the first place. Communities concerned about **language revitalization** can range from Irish speakers in the United Kingdom to Kiowa speakers in Oklahoma to users of indigenous sign languages in Australia.

And the threats to these languages range widely as well. They include the spread of "world" languages like English and the marginalization of one dialect in favor of a neighboring dialect. They also include support for a "national" sign language in Thailand instead of local, "indigenous" sign languages used by small communities, and (as is the case in places like the United States, Australia, and Norway) the spread of technologies that can "save" people from being deaf (Walsh 2005). How seriously different "small languages" are endangered depends on what counts as "small" and how imminent the threat is perceived to be—and experts can differ in their evaluation of these matters.

Linguistic anthropologists have paid particular attention to "indigenous" languages spoken by small communities who have experienced a history of colonization by outsiders and who are minorities within states where colonial languages dominate. At the

---

language revitalization Attempts by linguists and activists to preserve or revive languages with few native speakers that appear to be on the verge of extinction.

same time, as Michael Walsh explains, indigenous language situations are not all alike. In Guatemala, for example, "Mayan languages are spoken among a majority of the populations, and the languages are all closely related; so it is possible to have a more unified approach to Mayan language revitalization. Mayas in Guatemala are now using their languages in schools, and they are taking steps toward gaining official recognition of their languages" (2005, 296). Sometimes, however, colonial borders separate members of an indigenous language community, meaning that speakers on one side of the border may be better supported in their language revitalization efforts than speakers on the other side of the border. Examples include Ojibwe speakers (who are better supported in Canada than in the United states) and Quichua speakers (who receive different levels of support in Ecuador, Bolivia, and Peru) (Walsh 2005, 296). And sometimes the ethnolinguistic practices of speakers can interfere with language retention: Among Ilgar speakers in northern Australia, for example, conversation between opposite-sex siblings is forbidden. This means that a man finds himself "talking his mother tongue to people who don't speak it, and not talking it with the couple of people who do" (Evans 2001, 278; cited in Walsh 2005, 297).

Attempts to implement language revitalization have met with mixed success. Methods that work for literate groups (e.g., French speakers in Quebec) may be inappropriate for programs of language revival among speakers of languages that lack a long tradition of literacy, which is often the case with indigenous languages in the Americas and Australia (Figure 5.10). In some cases, where prospects for revitalization are poor, it has been suggested that the functions of the endangered language can be transferred to a different language. This is a phenomenon well known in the case of colonial languages like Spanish and English, which have all experienced "indigenization" as the communities who adopt them tailor them to fit their own local communicative practices. Other scholars have pointed out that language loss is nothing new. In the ancient world, for example, the spread of Latin led to the extinction of perhaps 50 of the 60 or so languages spoken in the Mediterranean prior to 100 B.C.E. However, the extension of Latin into ancient Europe also led to the birth of the Romance languages, some of whose native speakers (e.g., the French) express concern that the survival of their mother tongue is also threatened by the spread of global English (Walsh 2005, Sonntag 2003). New languages emerging from the processes of pidginization and creolization also continue to appear. For example, Copper Island Aleut is a hybrid of Russian and Aleut (Walsh 2005, 297).

FIGURE 5.10 Students at the Ojibwe Immersion School in the Hayward Elementary School, where they are taught culture and language. The school is part of a program to revive the language, by immersing children in their native language.

Maintaining or reviving endangered languages faces many obstacles, not the least of which is the concern of many parents who care less about preserving their dying language than they do about making sure their children become literate in a world language that will offer them a chance at economic and social mobility. Some indigenous groups are concerned that loss of language will mean loss of access to traditional sources of religious power, which can only be addressed in the traditional tongue. Yet other indigenous speakers would not like to see what was once a fully functioning mode of communication reduced to nothing but ceremonial use. Clearly, language endangerment is a very delicate topic of discussion. This is unfortunate, in Walsh's view, since practical solutions require "frank and forthright discussions of the issues . . . and good clear statements of advice" (2005, 308). But Walsh also believes that concerned people who want to save their languages ought to try to do what they can and not wait until scholarly experts arrive at consensus.

▼ LANGUAGE AND TRUTH

For the late Thomas Kuhn, a philosopher of science, metaphor lay at the heart of science. He argued that changes in scientific theories were "accompanied by a change in some of the relevant metaphors and in corresponding parts of the network of similarities through which terms attach to nature" (1979, 416). Kuhn insisted that these changes in the way scientific terms link to nature are not reducible to logic or grammar. "They come about in response to pressures generated by observation or experiment"—that is, by experience and context. And there is no neutral language into which rival theories can be translated and subsequently evaluated as unambiguously right or wrong (416). Kuhn asks the question, "Is what we refer to as 'the world' perhaps a product of mutual accommodation between experience and language?"

If our understanding of reality is the product of a dialectic between experience and language (or, more broadly, culture), then ambiguity will never be permanently removed from any of the symbolic systems that human beings invent. Reflexive consciousness makes humans aware of alternatives. The experience of doubt, of not being sure what to believe, is never far behind.

This is not merely the experience of people in Western societies. When E. E. Evans-Pritchard lived among the Azande of Central Africa in the early twentieth century, he found that they experienced a similar form of disorientation (see EthnoProfile 8.4: Azande). The Azande people, he wrote, were well aware of the ambiguity inherent in language, and they exploited it by using metaphor (what they called *sanza*) to disguise speech that might be received badly if uttered directly. For example, "A man says in the presence of his wife to his friend, 'Friend, those swallows, how they flit about in there.' He is speaking about the flightiness of his wife and in case she should understand the allusion, he covers himself by looking up at the swallows as he makes his seemingly innocent remark" (Evans-Pritchard 1963, 211). Evans-Pritchard later observed that *sanza* "adds greatly to the difficulties of anthropological inquiry. Eventually the anthropologist's sense of security is undermined and his confidence shaken. He learns the language, can say what he wants to say in it, and can understand what he hears, but then he begins to wonder whether he has really understood . . . he cannot be sure, and even they [the Azande] cannot be sure, whether the words do have a nuance or someone imagines that they do" (228).

However much we learn about language, we will never be able to exhaust its meanings or circumscribe its rules once and for all. Human language is an open system, and as long as human history continues, new forms will be created and old forms will continue to be put to new uses.

CHAPTER SUMMARY

1. Language is a uniquely human faculty that both permits us to communicate and sets up barriers to communication. It is a part of culture that people use to encode their experience, structure their understanding of the world and of themselves, and to engage one another interactively. The study of different languages reveals the shared nature of language and culture and the contextual assumptions that speakers make and use.

2. There are many ways to communicate our experiences, and there is no absolute standard favoring one way over another. Individual efforts to create a unique voice are countered by pressures to negotiate a common code within the larger social group.

3. Of Charles Hockett's sixteen design features of language, six are particularly important: openness, arbitrariness, duality of patterning, displacement, semanticity, and prevarication.

4. Early linguistic anthropologists like Edward Sapir and Benjamin Whorf suggested that language has the power to shape the way people see the world. This is called the linguistic relativity principle.

5. Today formal linguistic analysis is usually subdivided into five specialties: phonology, the study of the sounds of language; morphology, the study of minimal units of meaning in language; syntax, the study of sentence structure; semantics, the study of meaning patterns; and pragmatics, the study of language in context of use. These formal analyses, however, often more closely resemble formal logic than patterns of everyday language use.

6. Ethnopragmatics pays attention both to the immediate context of speech and to broader contexts that are shaped by unequal social relationships and rooted in history. It locates meaning in routine practical activities, which turn grammatical features of language into resources people can make use of in their interactions with others.

7. Because linguistic meaning is rooted in practical activity, which carries the burden of meaning, the activity and the linguistic usage together shape communicative practices. Different social groups generate different communicative practices. The linguistic habits that are part of each set of communicative practices constitute discourse genres. People normally command a range of discourse genres, which means that each person's linguistic knowledge is characterized by heteroglossia.

8. The study of pidgin languages is the study of the radical negotiation of new meaning. In pidgins, two groups of language speakers who come in contact (often as a result of colonization or commercial domination) invent a new language different from either parent language. Pidgin languages exhibit many of the same linguistic features as nonpidgin languages. Studies of African American English illustrate the historical circumstances that can give rise to creoles, and also provide evidence of the ways in which our speech is always embedded in a social world of power differences. Linguists and anthropologists have described differences in the gender-based communicative practices of women and men.

9. Language ideologies are unwritten rules shared by members of a speech community concerning what kinds of language are valued. Language ideologies develop out of the cultural, social, and political histories of the groups to which they belong. Knowing the language ideology of a particular community can help listeners make sense of speech that otherwise would seem inappropriate or incomprehensible to them.

10. Many linguistic anthropologists have become involved in projects to maintain or revive languages with small numbers of native speakers, especially "indigenous" languages spoken by small communities who have experienced a history of colonization by outsiders and who are minorities within states where colonial languages dominate. These languages may disappear if younger generations do not learn them and end up speaking instead a regionally or globally dominant language such as Spanish or English. Maintaining or reviving threatened languages is complex and controversial, but such efforts are ongoing in many parts of the world.

KEY TERMS

language
linguistics
design features
linguistic competence
communicative competence
linguistic relativity principle
grammar

phonology
morphology
syntax
semantics
metaphor
semantic domain
pragmatics

discourse
ethnopragmatics
pidgin
language ideology
language revitalization

SUGGESTED READINGS

Akmajian, A., R. Demers, A. Farmer, and R. Harnish. 2001. *Linguistics*. 5th ed. Cambridge, MA: MIT Press. *A fine introduction to the study of language as a formal system.*

Brenneis, Donald, and Ronald K. S. Macauley, eds. 1996. *The matrix of language*. Boulder, CO: Westview. *A wide-ranging collection of essays by anthropologists studying linguistic habits in their sociocultural contexts.*

Lakoff, George, and Mark Johnson. 1980. *Metaphors we live by*. Berkeley: University of California Press. *An important, clear, and very accessible book that presents a radical and persuasive view of metaphor and has now become a classic.*

Ottenheimer, Harriet. 2005 *The anthropology of language: An introduction to linguistic anthropology*. Belmont, CA: Wadsworth. *Topics covered in this recent introductory textbook range from the analysis of formal features of languages to the discussion of language ideologies. It comes with a companion workbook.*

Smitherman, Geneva. 1977. *Talkin and testifyin: The language of Black America*. Detroit: Wayne State University Press. *A classic introduction to Black English Vernacular, for native and nonnative speakers alike, with exercises to test your mastery of the grammar of African American English.*

Chapter 6

Culture and Individuals

In this chapter, we explore the way symbolic cultural practices shape your patterns of thought, your sense of self, and even your personality. However, we also consider the active role individuals play in the making of cultural meanings, particularly when challenged by experiences of trauma and social suffering.

If human culture is learned, it is ultimately individual human beings who engage in that learning. They do not all learn the same things, even if they live in the same society, because of socially, culturally, and politically shaped differences in status and experience. But it is because patterns can be detected in learned ways of thinking and ways of acting that anthropologists become interested in cultural learning by individuals. Historically, psychological anthropology addressed this phenomenon by seeking answers for a series of persistent questions: "What characteristics of our species are found in all times and places? What features are limited to specific groups of humans? How can we best take account of individual uniqueness?" (Bock 1994, ix).

Philip Bock notes that "An anthropology that takes account of individuals must make use of ideas from neighboring disciplines" (1994, ix), primarily from different kinds of psychological theories. To some extent this has involved anthropological adoption and cross-cultural evaluation of a series of different theoretical orientations in psychology. For example, some of the first twentieth-century anthropologists to take an interest in psychological matters, such as Margaret Mead and Bronislaw Malinowski, were influenced by the psychoanalytic views of Sigmund Freud, and attempted to test in non-Western settings certain ideas about personality development based on Freud's work in late-nineteenth-century Viennese society.

These early studies initiated a pattern of analysis that has remained central to much psychological anthropology: that of critically examining universal claims about human nature produced by Western psychologists, especially claims that are based on research done in Western societies only. This critical role is especially important in those situations where researchers make extreme claims about all members of the human species. Such claims frequently get a lot of publicity and tend to generate a lot of controversy. Early tests of Freudian theory are a good example. Is the pattern of early childhood development described by Freud universal in all human groups—"found in all times and places"? Or, conversely is it an example of "individual uniqueness," characteristic perhaps of individuals with disturbed childhoods but not of everyone else?

In Euro-American societies claims about universal human psychology compete with assertions of individual uniqueness. One of the most deeply entrenched debates opposes "biology" to "culture" as alternative, mutually exclusive explanations for some particular aspect of human psychological functioning. Such extreme claims and counterclaims seem never to be resolved, perhaps because they are too crude to illuminate much of lasting interest in human psychology.

Most psychological anthropologists would agree that human beings are biocultural organisms. But finding a way to explain the connection between human biology and human culture that avoids an either-or option is often elusive. It is for this reason, as Bock says, that anthropologists have typically concentrated on "the intermediate zone of group differences" where it becomes possible to identify relationships between specific features of a given culture and specific individuals (1994, ix). This sort of demonstration has done a great deal to undermine ethnocentric prejudices, such as the assumption that all people are (or ought to be) "just like us," or that some of us are "rational" while others of us are "irrational."

One of the more promising directions recognized by Bock, and taken by some psychological anthropologists in recent years (e.g., Ingold 2000) has been influenced by the work of developmental psychologist Susan Oyama (1985). Now becoming known as Developmental Systems Theory (DST), this perspective has made great strides in rethinking the relationship between evolving species and the development of individual members of those species. DST recognizes that a developing organism is subject to many environments, identifiable at different levels of analysis, as it lives out its life cycle. From the perspective of DST, a proper account of development requires taking into account the reciprocal influences of organisms and their environments at all steps in this ongoing process. It involves recognizing, furthermore, that environments as well as genes are passed on from parents to offspring, from the cytoplasm of the mother's egg, to the cellular products produced within the developing embryo, to the mother's uterus, to the postnatal setting which provides (or fails to provide) the amounts and kinds of resources the organism needs to continue to develop in one direction or another.

Social, economic, and political environments thus become relevant factors shaping individual development for human beings, and enduring features of socially constructed environments get passed on to subsequent generations as faithfully as genes, thus influencing the developmental trajectory of future life cycles, and potentially, evolutionary selection pressures that impinge on the species itself. This is the case for many kinds of organisms, but is particularly obvious for human beings. Human beings live in social groups that intensively rework their material environments, bequeath social, economic, and political resources to subsequent generations, and so shape in decisive ways the directions of their lives. Much recent work by psychological anthropologists implicitly if not explicitly adopts the DST approach in addressing various issues in human psychology, as we will see below.

Still, the field of psychological anthropology is complex and not easy to summarize because its practitioners have pursued and continue to pursue a wide variety of research problems and theoretical orientations. According to Bock, however, the work of psychological anthropologists can be grouped into three basic areas of human experience: perception, cognition, and motivation (1994, x). We will look at each area in turn, drawing together classic and more recent work that has demolished stereotypes about the factors responsible for individual thought and action, and that has provided more detailed, nuanced explanations in the intermediate zone.

As we will see, this evidence overwhelmingly sustains the view put forth in our discussion of language: that is, human psychological processes are open to a wide variety of influences. Like language, human psychology is an open system. Human beings not only talk about the world in a variety of ways, but they also think and feel about it in a variety of ways; and if no one way of thinking or feeling is obligatory, then any particular way of thinking or feeling is shaped by factors encountered in the course of development. Human psychology routinely develops in the context of culturally shaped activities that draw our attention to some parts of the world while ignoring others.

Because what we think or feel about something depends greatly on what we have learned to pay attention to in the past and the values we have learned to associate with it, different groups in a society—with different histories and experiences—are likely to develop unique points of view, pay attention to different things, and feel differently about them. When we learn from this culturally shaped experi-

ence, we can use preexisting categories to help us interpret new experiences. This is a version of the linguistic design feature called *displacement*. Because we all simultaneously belong to more than one social group, we often face the need to juggle competing points of view and to struggle with sometimes-conflicting feelings about them. This is a version of the linguistic phenomenon called *heteroglossia*. All our senses can play tricks on us, moreover, and if they are artful enough, people can trick other people into perceiving something that "does not exist." *Prevarication*, or deception, is thus a built-in feature of general human psychological processes, just as it is of language.

Human psychological processes are also heavily influenced by symbols. Language and visual perception, for example, both push human beings to construct symbolic representations of their experiences in order to make sense of them. As a result, the meaning of what we see, touch, smell, taste, or hear depends on context. As with language, two contexts are normally invoked: the immediate context of the perception itself and the displaced context stored in memory and shaped by culture and history. As with sentences, so too with the objects of perception. The "same" object can mean different things in different contexts. Consider what seeing a butcher knife means (1) lying on a cutting board in your kitchen next to a pile of mushrooms or (2) wielded by an intruder who has cornered you in your kitchen at midnight.

▼ PERCEPTION

Perception can be defined as the "processes by which people organize and experience information that is primarily of sensory origin" (Cole and Scribner 1974, 61). Perception as a psychological process has been thought to link people to the world around them or within them: We perceive size, shape, color, pain, and so on. Studies of perception flourished in the 1950s and 1960s, but their results remain significant today as a means of correcting persistent misunderstandings about the way human perception works.

perception The processes by which people organize and experience information that is primarily of sensory origin.

FIGURE 6.1   Locations of societies whose EthnoProfiles appear in chapter 6.

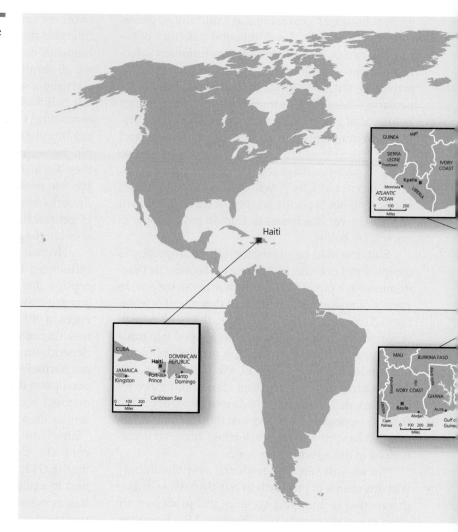

Intellect and emotion have referred to the two principal ways in which perceptions might be dealt with: rationally and logically on the one hand, passionately and intuitively on the other. Anthropologists and some psychologists suggest, however, that this approach is highly problematic. Particularly troubling is the traditional split between reason and emotion, which has often been accompanied by the overvaluing of one at the expense of the other. But at least as problematic is the assumption, frequently made by psychologists who are not anthropologists, that perception occurs in a culture-free vacuum. Anthropologists have always insisted that, as Bock puts it, "culture enters into every step of the perceptual process, initially by providing patterned material for perception . . . and later, through verbal and non-verbal means, by suggesting (or insisting on) the proper labeling of and responses to perceived patterns" (1994, xi). It is often difficult to pinpoint the effects of a particular cultural background on perception when the cultural shaping is general and not explicit (1994, xii). At the same time, researchers have been able to identify some of the ways in which meaning is mapped onto our experiences.

Schemas and Prototypes

Chunks of experience that appear to hang together as wholes, exhibiting the same properties in the same configuration whenever they recur, are called schemas. As human beings grow up, they gradually become aware of the schemas that their culture (or subculture) recognizes. Such schemas are often embedded in practical activities and labeled linguistically, and they may serve as a focus for discourse. People living in the United States, for example, cannot avoid a schema called *Christmas*, a chunk of experience that recurs once every year. The Christmas schema can include features like cold and snowy weather and activities like baking cookies, singing carols, going to church, putting up a Christmas tree, and buying and wrapping gifts. In the experience of a child, all these elements may appear to be equally relevant parts of a seamless whole. It may take time and conditioning for Christian parents to persuade children what the "true meaning of Christmas" really is. Some adults who celebrate Christmas disagree about its true meaning. Non-Christians living in the United States must also come to terms with this schema and may struggle to explain to their children why the activities associated with it are not appropriate for them.

People take for granted most of the schemas that their culture recognizes, using them as simplified interpretive frameworks for judging new experiences as typical or not, human or not (D'Andrade 1992, 48).

---

schemas Patterned, repetitive experiences.

That is, they learn to use schemas as **prototypes**. Prototypes of various sorts appear to be central to the way meaning is organized in human language. The words we use refer to typical instances, typical elements or relations, and are embedded, as we saw in chapter 5, in genres of discourse associated with routine cultural practices.

When we organize experience and assign meaning on the basis of prototypes, however, the categories we use have fuzzy boundaries. And because our experiences do not always neatly fit our prototypes, we are often not sure which prototype applies. Is a tossed salad a prototypical tossed salad if in addition to lettuce and tomatoes and onions it also contains raisins and apple slices? Is a library a prototypical library when it contains fewer books than DVDs, videotapes, and electronic databases? In cases like this, suggests linguist R. A. Hudson (1980), a speaker must simply recognize the openness of language and apply linguistic labels creatively.

Similarly, we may be confronted with novel perceptions and experiences with no ready-made cultural interpretation. Thinking and feeling human beings must then extrapolate creatively to make sense of what is going on around them. As we will see, such psychological creativity and resiliency are particularly urgent when people are subjected to extreme social suffering or violent trauma.

Perception and Convention

As we saw in Chapter 3, the only evidence recognized by traditional positivist science is the evidence of our five senses. In this view, a suitably objective observer should be able to see and describe the world as it truly is. If other people describe the world differently, then their perceptions must in some way be distorted. Either they are not being objective, or their ability to discriminate among sensations is impaired, or they are attempting to trick and mislead. Most modern researchers are far less certain about what perception entails. True, our perception is sometimes impaired, either for physical reasons (we aren't wearing our glasses) or because our observations aren't disinterested (our child's forehead feels cool because

we are afraid he or she might have a fever). And people do sometimes play jokes on one another, insisting that they have seen things they really have not seen. But what about people whose physiological equipment is functioning properly, who have no stake in the outcome, and who are not trying to deceive, and yet who perceive things differently?

Classic research on variations in perception attempted to relate people's descriptions of their experiences, or their performances on psychological tests, to their understandings of *context*. For example, nonliterate South African mine workers were tested using two-dimensional line drawings of three-dimensional objects (Figure 6.2). The test results indicated that the mine workers consistently interpreted the drawings in two dimensions. When asked at which animal the man was pointing his spear on Card 1, subjects would usually respond, "the elephant." The elephant is, in fact, directly in line with and closest to the spear point in the drawing. However, the elephant ought to be seen as standing on top of the distant hill if the subjects interpret the drawings three-dimensionally. Did their responses mean that these Africans could not perceive in three dimensions?

J. B. Deregowski devised the following test. He presented different African subjects with the same drawings, asked them to describe what they saw, and got two-dimensional verbal reports. Next, he presented the same subjects with the line drawings in Figure 6.3. This time, he asked his subjects to construct models based on the drawings using materials he provided. His subjects had no difficulty producing three-dimensional models.

In these tests, the "correct" solution depended on the subject's mastery of a Western convention for interpreting two-dimensional drawings and photographs. For the drawings in Figure 6.2, the Western convention includes assumptions about perspective that relate the size of objects to their distance from the observer. Without such a convention in mind, it is not obvious that the size of a drawn object has any connection with distance. Far from providing us with new insights about the African perceptual abilities, perhaps the most interesting result of such tests is what they teach us about Western perceptual conventions. That is, drawings do not necessarily speak for themselves. They can make sense to us only once we accept certain rules for interpreting them (Cole and Scribner 1974).

---

prototypes Examples of a typical instance, element, relation, or experience within a culturally relevant semantic domain.

FIGURE 6.2 Pictures used for the study of depth perception in Africa.

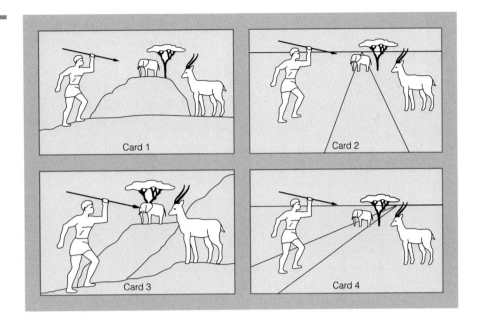

FIGURE 6.3 Drawings used for the construction of models in the depth-perception test in Africa.

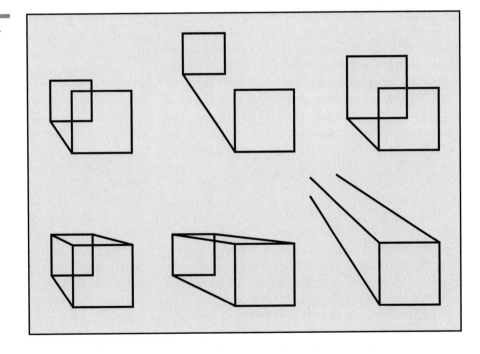

Illusion

If you examine Figure 6.4, you will see that marks on a piece of paper can be ambiguous. The signals we receive from the outside world tend to be open to more than one interpretation, be they patterns of light and dark striking the retinas of our eyes, or smells, tastes, shapes, or words. Just as studies of metaphor provide insight into the nature of literal language, so studies of visual illusions provide insight into the nature of visual perception. Indeed, the contrast between literal and metaphorical language is not unlike the contrast between reality and illusion as it relates to perception. In both cases, knowledge of

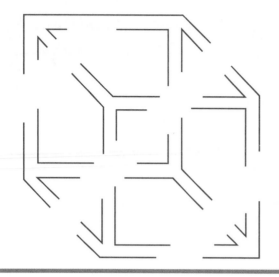

FIGURE 6.4 Ambiguous marks.

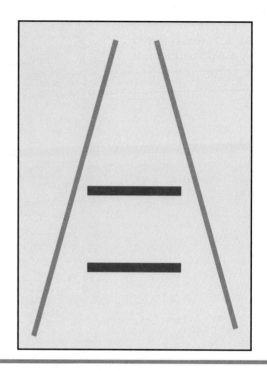

FIGURE 6.5 An example of distortion: the Ponzo illusion.

context permits us to distinguish between the literal and the metaphorical, the real and the illusory.

Richard Gregory is a cognitive psychologist who has spent most of his career studying visual illusions. In his view, illusions are produced by *misplaced procedures*: perfectly normal, ordinary cognitive processes that have somehow been inappropriately selected and applied to a particular set of visual signals. For him, perceptions are symbolic representations of reality, not direct samples of reality. Perceivers must often work very hard to make sense of the visual signals they receive. When they are wrong, they are subject to illusion.

Consider the visual illusion Gregory (R. 1981) calls *distortion:* What you see appears larger or smaller, longer or shorter, and so on, than it really is. Look at the Ponzo illusion in Figure 6.5. Typically, the upper parallel line appears to be longer than the lower one when, in fact, they are equal. The standard explanation of this illusion is that we are looking at a two-dimensional drawing but interpreting it as if it were in three dimensions. In other words, the Ponzo illusion plays on our ability to see three-dimensional space in a two-dimensional drawing.

This explanation helps us understand the responses of the African mine workers to the drawings reproduced in Figure 6.2. Western observers interpret these drawings as two-dimensional representations of three-dimensional reality. In the Ponzo illusion, the shapes trick us because they are very similar to what

we perceive when we stand on a railroad track and look toward its vanishing point on the horizon. Africans are also familiar with railroad tracks, but they did not attempt to interpret the Ponzo-like lines on Card 2 of Figure 6.2 as representations of three-dimensional reality. On the contrary, they seemed to work very hard to keep the relationships between objects in two dimensions, even if this meant that the sizes of the objects themselves appeared distorted. When we compare the Western interpretation of the Ponzo illusion with the African interpretation of the pictures in Figure 6.2, we discover something important: Both sets of drawings are ambiguous, and both are potentially open to distortion. How people interpret them depends on preexisting experiences and cultural conventions.

Colin Turnbull was an anthropologist who worked for many years among the Mbuti of northeastern Democratic Republic of the Congo (Zaire) (see EthnoPro-file 6.1: Mbuti). He discovered that people who live all their lives in a dense forest have no experience of distance greater than a few feet and are therefore not accustomed to taking distance into consideration when estimating the size of an object in the visual field. Turnbull took one of his informants,

EthnoProfile 6.1

Mbuti

Region: Central Africa

Nation: Democratic Republic of the Congo (Zaire)

Population: 40,000

Environment: Dense tropical forest

Livelihood: Nomadic hunting and gathering

Political organization: Traditionally, communal bands of 7 to 30 families (average 17 families); today, part of a modern nation-state

For more information: Turnbull, Colin. 1961. *The forest people.* New York: Simon & Schuster.

Kenge, on a trip that brought them out of the forest and into a game park. For the first time in his life, Kenge faced vast, rolling grasslands nearly empty of trees. Kenge's response to this experience was dramatic: "When Kenge topped the rise, he stopped dead. Every smallest sign of mirth suddenly left his face. He opened his mouth but could say nothing. He moved his head and eyes slowly and unbelievingly" (1961, 251). When Kenge finally saw the far-off animals grazing on the plain, he asked Turnbull what insects they were. When told that they were buffalo, Kenge laughed and accused Turnbull of lying. Then he strained to see better and inquired what kind of buffalo could be so small. Later, when Turnbull pointed out a fishing boat on the lake, Kenge scoffed at him and insisted it was a floating piece of wood (252).

When people in another culture fail to see similarities between people or objects that we think ought to be obvious to any observer, we are apt to become impatient. Yet in the United States, where racist stereotypes influence perceptions of people of mixed ancestry, many of us are subject to similar blindness. Puerto Ricans, for example, experience racial distinctions in Puerto Rico in terms of a continuum of phenotypes and skin shades. When they move to the United States, however, they often find that their cultural identity as Puerto Ricans is ignored and they are classified as either "white" or "black" (Rodriguez 1994).

Visuality: Learning to Look

Susan Vogel has studied the sculpture of the Baule people of Ivory Coast since the early 1970s (see EthnoProfile 6.2), and her research taught her that looking and seeing are culturally learned modes of sensory perception (1997, 108–11). She uses the term **visuality** to refer to the ways that individuals from different societies learn to interpret what they see and to construct mental pictures using the visual practices that their cultural system favors. Vogel notes that, for the Baule, objects are powerful and affect the people who see them. Spiritually significant objects, which includes much of what Westerners would call sculpture, are thus potentially dangerous. "Even an inadvertent glimpse of a forbidden object can make a person sick, can expose them to huge fines or sacrifices, or can even be fatal" (110).

For the Baule, looking is the most important of all perceptual activities: Seeing something is potentially more significant and more dangerous than touching something or eating or drinking something. Even looking at an object thought to be good, safe, or pure is not beneficial, according to the Baule, and ought to be avoided. Indeed, there is an explicit etiquette governing how one ought to look at things, and staring is highly disapproved of. It is disrespectful for younger people to look directly at their elders, for example (110), and the rules for looking actually limit the "visibility" of sculpture.

For example, Western worshippers in a medieval Christian cathedral might gaze directly and intently at the altar, paying special attention to the elaborate painting or sculpture with which it has been adorned. For the Baule, however, analogous behavior would be highly improper:

> If someone stopped and looked for a whole minute at the altar erected in plain view in Nguessan's courtyard, they would be called before the chief to explain. The fact that the altar stands in a public place, where a hundred people pass daily, does not mean it can be stared at. In fact the only motives for looking hard at such an object would be malevolent: a desire to kill someone in the courtyard, or to nullify the altar's powers. The stare itself is not the means of achieving either of these ends; it merely accumulates information for later use. (111)

visuality The ways that individuals from different societies learn to interpret what they see and to construct mental pictures using the visual practices that their own cultural system favors.

EthnoProfile 6.2

Baule

Region: Western Africa

Nation: Ivory Coast

Population: 2,760,000

Environment: Savanna

Livelihood: Farming (yams in particular) and cloth production

Political organization: In the precolonial period, no state and no clear stratification; today, part of a modern nation-state

For more information: Etienne, Mona. 1980. Women and men, cloth and colonization: The transformation of production-distribution relations among the Baule (Ivory Coast). In *Women and colonization: Anthropological perspectives*, edited by Mona Etienne and Eleanor Leacock, 270–93. New York: Praeger.

In chapter 5, we noted that speakers of a language shape its vocabulary to reflect their cultural preoccupations. This can be seen in the ways Baule speakers talk about visuality. Vogel notes that there are four words in the Baule language for looking and seeing in general. These terms distinguish among objects that anyone can look at, objects that must never be deliberately looked at, and all degrees in between (91). The most common verb translated as "to look" is *nian*, which can also mean "to watch." It connotes intentional watching, and is used for watching mask dances intended for entertainment and for watching television. The noun *nyin* means "a stare," or a good hard look. The phrase *nyin kpa*, "a real stare," is used to describe looking at a useful decorated object with no sacred meaning. Two more words are commonly used for the secret glances that people steal of personal sculptures that are behind the closed doors of sleeping rooms: *kanngle*, a noun meaning "evil looks

from the corner of the eye," and *nian klekle*, "to look clandestinely, to cast a rapid glance" (91). The most awesome objects and events—the men's sacred masks, divination dances, and funerals—are not spoken of with any of those words. "One never says one has seen or looked at these potent things; one merely says *N'wo se bo*, "I went to the funeral," or *N'su ko awebo*, "I went to the divination dance" (92).

For the Baule, life is lived knowing that sculpture—powerful objects—are present but cannot be examined, cannot be looked at closely. As a result, when these objects are visible, even though they are incompletely seen, they make an extraordinary impression on people, who use memory and imagination to construct lasting images in their minds, remembering their experiences of seeing sculpture in great detail for the rest of their lives. Such experiences make important contributions to the perception of a particular Baule worldview (see chapter 8).

▼ COGNITION

The study of illusion demonstrates that there can be a gulf between what we see and what we know, what we perceive and what we conceive. Nevertheless, in the ordinary contexts of everyday life, these discrepancies seem to be manageable: There is coherence between perceptions and conceptions. Moreover, because our link with the world is a dialectical one, there is no sharp boundary between what we perceive and what we conceive. Not only can new perceptions lead us to modify our conceptions (that is, we learn), but new conceptions can also lead us to perceive aspects of the world around us that we didn't pay attention to before. We are active meaning-makers, striving to make sense of our experiences. As a result, **cognition** is perhaps best understood as "a nexus of relations between the mind at work and the world in which it works" (Lave 1988, 1).

The study of cognition began in the 1960s with growing interest by anthropologists in the ways different peoples classified cultural knowledge. Using the native language of their informants, anthropologists doing what was called *ethnoscience* elicited the indigenous categories in terms of which cultural information was organized in different areas of life. Pursuing links between language and culture, they

---

cognition (1) The mental process by which human beings gain knowledge; (2) the nexus of relations between the mind at work and the world in which it works.

focused on such topics as basic color terms, or kinship terminologies, or ways of labeling and classifying different parts of the natural world. More recently, cognitive anthropologists have become more interested in the mental processes people use to make sense of their experiences in the world, some of which we review below.

Cognitive Capacities and Intelligence

What makes it possible for human beings to receive signals from the outside world (or from within our own bodies) and then interpret those signals in a way that makes appropriate action possible? One traditional answer has been that every person either possesses at birth or develops over time certain basic cognitive capacities. At one time, these hypothetical capacities were thought of as substances or properties, and the goal of psychological testing was to measure how much of each cognitive capacity an individual had. Consequently, intelligence has traditionally been "measured" using an "instrument" called the *intelligence test*; the "amount" of intelligence measured is assigned a number called the *Intelligence Quotient*, or *IQ*. In the past, some researchers were quick to equate differences in performance on intelligence tests with differences in intelligence. Today, such a reductionist approach is subjected to intense scrutiny.

If it is difficult to identify and measure cognitive capacities in individuals, it may be impossible to do so for entire groups. Michael Cole is a scholar who has spent several decades trying to combine psychology and anthropology in his own work (Cole 1994, 329). Beginning in the 1960s, he and Sylvia Scribner developed extensive experience in cross-cultural psychological testing. In their fieldwork, they repeatedly encountered situations in which the same psychological test produced results that differed between Western and non-Western subjects. They rejected the idea that non-Western subjects were just less intelligent, because, outside the laboratory setting, in the routine contexts of everyday life, their informants' intelligence and full humanity were obvious.

So why do intelligent informants often perform poorly on psychological tests? In the work of the Russian psychologist Lev Vygotsky, Cole and Scribner (1974) found an approach that pointed toward an answer. Vygotsky distinguished between elementary

cognitive processes and the higher systems into which these processes are organized. **Elementary cognitive processes** include the ability to make abstractions, to categorize, to reason inferentially, and so forth. All normal humans everywhere are equipped with these abilities. Different cultures, however, organize these elementary processes into different **functional cognitive systems**. Culture also assigns different functional systems to different tasks in different contexts.

Consider once again the African American children whose "speech capacity" was measured by European American psychologists (see chapter 5). When testing both African American and European American children, the same test, instructions, and controlled testing situation were used. The European American children responded easily and fluently, whereas the African American children responded in monosyllables or not at all. Following Vygotsky, we have no reason to doubt that both groups of children possessed the same range of elementary cognitive processes. The difference in group performance was related to how the members of each group combined these elementary cognitive processes to interpret the testing situation and to function within it. The European American children interpreted the test and the testing situation as a nonthreatening opportunity to display their verbal ability, and they did so. The African American children interpreted the same test and situation as a threatening personal and social attack, and they responded by refusing to respond. When interviewed in a nonthreatening context, however, these same children displayed considerable verbal ability.

In other words, there are different ways of defining tasks; once tasks are defined, there are different strategies for carrying them out; and routine strategies for carrying out (or refusing to carry out) tasks cannot be separated from the broader cultural and political contexts in which people live. As a result, administering an adequate psychological test starts to look as difficult as doing good anthropological fieldwork, with the same rewards and pitfalls.

elementary cognitive processes The ability to make abstractions, reason inferentially, categorize, and perform other mental tasks common to all normal humans.

functional cognitive systems Culturally linked sets of cognitive processes that guide perception, conception, reason, and emotion.

Cognitive Style

Cognitive style refers to a recurring pattern of perceptual and intellectual activity. Cultures provide people with a range of cognitive styles that are appropriate for different cognitive tasks in different contexts. Psychological anthropologists have attempted to compare cognitive styles cross-culturally. Some have argued that the styles of individuals and of groups can be located on a continuum between a global style and an articulated style. People who use a **global style** tend to view the world holistically; they see first a bundle of relationships and only later the bits and pieces that are related. They are said to be *field dependent*. By contrast, people who use an **articulated style** tend to break up the world into smaller and smaller pieces, which can then be organized into larger chunks. They also tend to see a sharp boundary between their own bodies and the outside world. People using an articulated style are able to consider whatever they happen to be paying attention to apart from its context and so are said to be *field independent* (Cole and Scribner 1974, 82).

Originally, most people in Western societies were thought to be field independent, whereas most people in most non-Western cultures were thought to be field dependent. However, more detailed research shows that these generalizations are misleading. For instance, the preferred cognitive style of an individual often varies from task to task and from context to context. People who use articulated styles for some tasks also use global styles for other tasks. In fact, they may bring a range of different styles to bear on a single task.

Research by Jean Lave and her colleagues (1988) demonstrated that middle-class North Americans are not field independent in all contexts, even when the task involves mathematics, which would seem to be the most field independent of all cognitive activities.

> **cognitive style** Recurring patterns of cognitive activity that characterize an individual's perceptual and intellectual activities.
>
> **global style** A way of viewing the world that is holistic. People who use such a style first see a bundle of relationships and only later see the bits and pieces that are related. They are said to be field dependent.
>
> **articulated style** A way of viewing the world that breaks it up into smaller and smaller pieces, which can then be organized into larger chunks. People who use such a style consider whatever they happen to be paying attention to apart from its context. They are said to be field independent.

Lave and her associates wanted to test the widespread assumption that cognitive style does not vary across contexts. In particular, they wanted to find out whether ordinary people use the same mathematical skills in the supermarket and the kitchen that they use in the classroom. As part of the research, subjects were given a pencil-and-paper math test to determine how well they could solve certain problems in a school-like context. Researchers also observed how the same subjects used mathematics while making buying decisions at the grocery store. Finally, the subjects were presented with paired grocery items and asked to calculate the best buy.

The results of this research were surprising. First, the subjects averaged only 59 percent correct on the pencil-and-paper test but achieved averages of 98 percent on the supermarket experiment and 93 percent on the best-buy experiment. Second, the researchers found that the high scores on the last two experiments were achieved with very little reliance on mathematics taught in school. Shoppers did occasionally use formal mathematics as an alternative to the other informal strategies. However, they did so *only* when the numbers for quantity and price were easy to transform into unit-price ratios. This did not happen very often, however, because units and prices in supermarkets are often given in prime numbers, making rapid mental calculation tedious and complicated. Rather than waste time dividing $5.27 by 13 ounces to obtain the price per ounce, the shoppers preferred to rely on other calculation strategies.

Many observers would have expected subjects trained in formal mathematics to rely on its infallible methods to help them make wise economic decisions. On the contrary, the test results suggest that shoppers were better able to make wise economic decisions using informal calculation strategies. The three most common informal strategies were *inspection* (recognizing that one item was both lower in price and larger in volume), *best-buy calculations* (comparing two quantities and two prices first and choosing the better value), and a *difference strategy* (deciding whether a marginal difference in quantity was worth the marginal difference in price; Lave 1988, 107ff.).

Lave notes that some psychologists would conclude from these results that there was something primitive or illogical about the informal strategies—and, by extension, about the people who used them (see, for example, Lave 1988, 79ff., 107ff.). In the terms we used earlier, these strategies are all closer to the global, field-dependent end of the cognitive-style continuum. Should we conclude, therefore, that ordinary middle-class North Americans fail to think rationally when they shop for groceries? This conclusion is contradicted by the experimental evidence showing that the shoppers' informal strategies were exceptionally accurate.

These strategies point to a major difference between "school" math and "grocery store" math. In school, the only purpose of a mathematical exercise is to obtain a single correct answer. "The puzzles or problems are assumed to be objective and factual. . . . Problem solvers have no choice but to try to solve problems, and if they choose not to, or do not find the correct answer, they 'fail'" (Lave 1988, 35). Matters are otherwise outside the classroom. Shoppers do not visit supermarkets as an excuse to practice formal mathematics; they go to buy food for their families. Consequently, the choices they make are influenced not merely by unit-price ratios but by the food preferences of the other family members, the amount of storage space at home, the amount of time they can spend shopping, and so on (Figure 6.6). In the supermarket, as Lave puts it, "'problems' are dilemmas to be resolved, rarely problems to be solved" (20). Formal mathematical calculations and knowledge of what costs less per unit may help resolve some dilemmas, but in other cases they may be too trou-blesome to bother with, or even irrelevant. Shoppers, unlike students in the classroom, are free to abandon calculation, to use means other than formal mathematics to resolve a dilemma (58).

One feature all Lave's subjects shared was the knowledge that pencil-and-paper tests in school-like settings required an articulated, field-independent style. In non-Western societies, attending a European- or American-style school seems to impart the same knowledge to non-Western people. But even Western subjects may reserve that cognitive style for the classroom, preferring a variety of more global strategies to resolve the dilemmas of everyday life. We have seen how some of these dilemmas can be generated by a lack of fit between the background information we take for granted and sensory signals that are ambiguous. This lack of fit may be between, say, our family's food preferences and confusing price-ratio information on two products we are comparing. It may be between our expectation that straight edges are normally continuous and surprising gaps in our visual field. In any case, our awareness of the cognitive dilemmas we face should make us more sympathetic to cognitive "errors" we see being made by people from different cultures who may be employing different cognitive styles.

These studies reinforce the conclusion that competent members of all societies employ a range of cognitive styles. We cannot speak of abstract thinking and

FIGURE 6.6 People use a range of cognitive styles in their lives. Grocery store math is not based on the same principles as school math— shopping is not a pass–fail endeavor. People are trying to figure out the better buy, not the exact answer to a "prices per ounce" problem.

concrete thinking as mutually exclusive. Anthropologists have found that many non-Western peoples are not used to thinking about things without relating them to some kind of context. Members of those societies can learn to use a context-free cognitive style if they attend school, but this does not mean that they never use abstract categories outside the classroom. As Lave's research demonstrates, the full range of her shoppers' calculating skills were displayed only when she studied mathematics in the supermarket rather than in the classroom and became aware of the range of factors in addition to price that influenced buying decisions.

Cross-cultural research in cognition is a delicate business. For the researcher, the trick is first to devise a test that will give people who use different cognitive styles an opportunity to show what they know and what they can do. The researcher must also discover whether different groups of subjects share the same understanding of tasks they are being asked to perform. In recent years, a number of researchers have worked to develop methods to assess cognition that are not bound to the traditional psychological testing laboratory or to the classroom.

Reason and the Reasoning Process

From the earliest days of the West's discovery of other societies, there has been a debate about the extent to which nonliterate non-Western peoples might be said to possess reason. Rooted in the context of Western colonialism, this debate was rarely disinterested, for domination by Europeans was often justified on the grounds that those dominated were irrational. Faced with this problematic history, how might anthropologists study rational thinking?

Most cognitive psychologists have adopted Jerome Bruner's famous definition of **thinking** as "going beyond the information given." This means that thinking is different from remembering (which refers to information already given) and also from learning (which involves acquiring information that

> **thinking** An active cognitive process that involves going beyond the information given.
>
> **syllogistic reasoning** A form of reasoning based on the syllogism, a series of three statements in which the first two statements are the premises and the last is the conclusion, which must follow from the premises.

was not given beforehand). Going beyond the information given thus implies a complex interrelationship between some information already at hand and the cognitive processes of the person who is attempting to cope with that information. This definition highlights the "nexus of relations between the mind at work and the world in which it works." Thinking is open and active, and it has no predetermined outcome.

Culture and Logic

One set of cognitive tests has to do with verbal reasoning ability. These tests present subjects with three statements in the form of a syllogism—for example, "All men are mortal, Socrates is a man, therefore Socrates is mortal." The first two propositions are called the *premises*, and the third statement is the *conclusion*. For a syllogism to be sound, the conclusion must follow from the premises.

Syllogistic reasoning is enshrined in Western culture as the quintessence of rational thought. Some researchers suggested that the rational capacities of non-Western peoples could be tested using logical problems in syllogistic form. Presumably their rationality would be confirmed if they could deduce correctly when the conclusion followed logically from the premises and when it did not.

Cole and Scribner presented logical problems involving syllogistic reasoning to their Kpelle subjects (see EthnoProfile 6.3: Kpelle). Typically, the logical problem was embedded in a folktale-like story. The experimenter read the story to the subjects and then asked them a series of follow-up questions designed to reveal whether the subjects could draw a correct conclusion from the premises given.

Here is one story Cole and Scribner prepared: "At one time Spider went to a feast. He was told to answer this question before he could eat any of the food. The question is: Spider and Black Deer always eat together. Spider is eating. Is Black Deer eating?" (1974, 162). Given the two premises, the conclusion should be that Black Deer is eating. Now consider a typical Kpelle response to hearing this story:

SUBJECT   Were they in the bush?

EXPERIMENTER   Yes.

SUBJECT   Were they eating together?

EXPERIMENTER   Spider and Black Deer always eat together. Spider is eating. Is Black Deer eating?

EthnoProfile 6.3

Kpelle

Region: Western Africa

Nation: Liberia (central and western)

Population: 86,000

Environment: Tropical forest

Livelihood: Rice farming

Political organization: Traditionally, chiefdoms; today, part of a modern nation-state

For more information: Bellman, Beryl. 1975. *Village of curers and assassins: On the production of Fala Kpelle cosmological categories.* The Hague: Mouton.

SUBJECT   But I was not there. How can I answer such a question?

EXPERIMENTER   Can't you answer it? Even if you were not there, you can answer it. (Repeats the question.)

SUBJECT   Oh, oh, Black Deer is eating.

EXPERIMENTER   What is your reason for saying that Black Deer was eating?

SUBJECT   The reason is that Black Deer always walks about all day eating green leaves in the bush. Then he rests for a while and gets up again to eat. (Cole and Scribner 1974, 162)

The subject's answer to the question and subsequent justification for that answer seem to have nothing whatever to do with the logical problem the subject is being asked to solve.

The experimenters devised this story the same way schoolteachers devise mathematical word problems. That is, the contextual material is nothing more than a kind of window dressing. Schoolchildren quickly learn to disregard the window dressing and seek out the mathematical problem it hides. In the same way, the Kpelle subjects hearing the story about Spider and Black Deer are supposed to demonstrate logic by *disregarding the contextual material* about the feast and seeking out the syllogism embedded within it. However, Kpelle subjects did not understand that they were being read this story in a testing situation for which considerations of context or meaningfulness were irrelevant. In the preceding example, the subject seemed to have difficulty separating the logical problem both from the introductory material about the feast and from the rest of his experiential knowledge.

Cole and Scribner interpreted their subject's response to this problem as being due not to irrationality but to a "failure to accept the logical task" (Cole and Scribner 1974, 162). In a follow-up study, Cole and Scribner discovered that Kpelle high school children responded "correctly" to the logical problems 90 percent of the time. This suggests a strong correlation between Western-style schooling and a willingness to accept context-free analytic tasks in testing situations (164).

But this is not all. David Lancy, one of Cole and Scribner's colleagues, discovered that Western-style syllogisms are very similar to certain forms of Kpelle riddles. Unlike syllogisms, however, those riddles have no single, "logically correct" answer. "Rather, as the riddle is posed to a group, the right answer is the one among many offered that seems most illuminating, resourceful, and convincing as determined by consensus and circumstance. This emphasis on edification as a criterion for 'rightness' is found in Kpelle jurisprudence as well" (Lancy cited in Fernandez 1980, 47–48). In other words, the "right" answer cannot be extracted from the form of the riddle by logical operations. Rather, it is the answer that seems most enlightening and informative to the particular audience in the particular setting where the riddle is posed.

Enlightening answers, moreover, appear to be rooted in shared cultural schemas. Roy D'Andrade has shown that college undergraduates at the University of California, San Diego, are unable to complete syllogisms similar to the Spider–Black Deer story when the content is arbitrary (Figure 6.7). Only 53 percent of UCSD undergraduates (a result only slightly above chance) selected the correct answer to the following syllogism:

1. *Given:* If Tom is drinking a Pepsi then Peter is sitting down.
2. *Suppose:* Peter is not sitting down.
3. Then:
   a. It must be the case that Tom is drinking a Pepsi.
   b. Maybe Tom is drinking a Pepsi or maybe he isn't.
   c. It must be the case that Tom is not drinking a Pepsi.

The Madness of Hunger

Medical anthropologist Nancy Scheper-Hughes describes how symptoms of a rural Brazilian folk ailment can be understood as a form of protest against physical exploitation and abuse.

Among the agricultural wage laborers living in the hillside shantytown of Alto do Cruzeiro, on the margins of a large, interior market town in the plantation zone of Pernambuco, Brazil, and who sell their labor for as little as a dollar a day, socioeconomic and political contradictions often take shape in the "natural" contradictions of angry, sick, and afflicted bodies. In addition to the wholly expectable epidemics of parasitic infections and communicable fevers, there are the more unexpected outbreaks and explosions of unruly and subversive symptoms that will not readily materialize under the health station's microscope. Among these are the fluid symptoms of nervos (angry, frenzied nervousness): trembling, fainting, seizures, hysterical weeping, angry recriminations, blackouts, and paralysis of face and limbs.

These nervous attacks are in part coded metaphors through which the workers express their dangerous and unacceptable condition of chronic hunger and need . . . and in part acts of defiance and dissent that graphically register the refusal to endure what is, in fact, unendurable and their protest against their availability for physical exploitation and abuse. And so, rural workers who have cut sugarcane since the age of seven or eight years will sometimes collapse, their legs giving way under an ataque de nervos, a nervous attack. They cannot walk, they cannot stand upright; they are left . . . without a leg to stand on.

In the exchange of meanings between the body personal and the body social, the nervous-hungry, nervous-angry body of the cane cutter offers itself as metaphor and metonym of the nervous sociopolitical system and for the paralyzed position of the rural worker in the current economic and political disorder. In "lying down" on the job, in refusing to return to the work that has overly determined their entire lives, the cane cutters' body language signifies both surrender and defeat. But one also notes a drama of mockery and refusal. For if the folk ailment nervos attacks the legs and the face, it leaves the arms and hands intact and free for less physically ruinous work. Consequently, otherwise healthy young men suffering from nervous attacks press their claims as sick men on their various political bosses and patrons to find them alternative work, explicitly "sitting down" work, arm work (but not clerical work for these men are illiterate).

The analysis of nervos does not end here, for nervous attack is an expansive and polysemic form of disease. Shantytown women, too, suffer from nervos—both the nervos de trabalhar muito, "overwork" nerves from which male cane cutters suffer, and also the more gender-specific nervos de sofrir muito, the nerves of those who have endured and suffered much. "Sufferers' nerves" attacks those who have endured a recent, especially a violent, tragedy. Widows of husbands and mothers of sons who have been abducted and violently "disappeared" are prone to the mute, enraged, white-knuckled shaking of "sufferers' nerves."

Source: Scheper-Hughes 1994, 236–37.

The correct answer (c) exactly parallels the correct answer to the Spider–Black Deer story. And, indeed, the reasoning processes of the undergraduates bear a striking similarity to those of Cole and Scribner's Kpelle informants: "When arbitrary relations are presented, the typical respondent does not seem to integrate the state of affairs described by the first. Respondents say . . . 'So what if *Peter* is not sitting down. That doesn't have anything to do with *Tom's* drinking a Pepsi'" (D'Andrade 1992, 49). By contrast,

86 percent of UCSD undergraduates chose the correct answer to the same kind of syllogism that involved a well-formed North American cultural schema (that cities are located within states). There is no reason to doubt that Liberians, North Americans, and other humans come equipped with the same elementary cognitive processes: the ability to make abstractions, to create conceptual categories, and to reason inferentially. The difficulty is to understand how these elementary cognitive processes are put to work within

FIGURE 6.7 If Steve is drinking coffee then Paul is sitting down. Paul is sitting down. Therefore, Steve is drinking coffee. But suppose Paul is not sitting down? Then what? This syllogism does not make sense to many U.S. college students, who want to know what Paul's sitting down has to do with Steve's drinking coffee (the answer to the new syllogism is if Paul is not sitting down, then Steve is not drinking coffee).

culturally shared schemas to produce different, functional cognitive systems known as **reasoning styles**.

▼ EMOTION

Psychological anthropologists who try to define emotion in cross-cultural terms run into a familiar problem: They discover not just that different cultures talk about emotion in different languages but also that not all languages even possess a term that might be translated as *emotion*. To get out of this tangle, they have tried to develop a theory of cognitive functioning that accounts for the experiences that some cultures recognize as emotional.

The Cultural Construction of Emotion

In traditional Western dualism, reason and thought are associated with the mind and emotion with the body. Any attempt to explain emotion must deal with the nature of the bodily arousal we associate with it. But there is more to emotion, as commonly understood, than mere bodily arousal. Recall the butcher knife referred to earlier in this chapter. What do we feel when we see a butcher knife sitting beside mushrooms on a cutting board in our kitchen? What do we feel when we see that same knife in the hands of an intruder bent on attacking us? The knife alone does not trigger our feeling. The situation, or context, in which we encounter the knife is equally important. The context itself is often ambiguous, and our emotional experience changes as our interpretation of the context changes.

Thus, emotion can be understood as the product of a dialectic between bodily arousal and cognitive interpretation. Cognitive psychologist George Mandler suggests that bodily arousal can trigger an emotional experience by attracting our attention and prompting us to seek the source of arousal (1975, 97). Conversely, a particular interpretation of our experience can trigger bodily arousal. Arousal may heighten or diminish, depending on how we interpret what is happening around us.

Mandler's discussion of emotion, like Cole and Scribner's discussion of cognition, describes emotions as *functional systems*. Each links elementary processes that involve the body's arousal system to other elementary processes that play a role in the construction of perception, conception, and reasoning. "Emotions are not something that people 'have,' they are constituted of people's states, values and arousals" (Mandler 1983, 151). Approaching emotion from this perspective accomplishes three things: (1) it integrates mind and body in a holistic fashion; (2) it acknowledges ambiguity as a central feature of emotional experience, just as we have argued it is central to linguistic, perceptual, and conceptual experience; and (3) it suggests how different cultural interpretive frameworks might shape not only what we think but

reasoning styles How we understand a cognitive task, how we encode the information presented to us, and what transformations the information undergoes as we think. Reasoning styles differ from culture to culture and from context to context within the same culture.

also what we feel. In short, **emotion** can be understood for our purposes as the product of a dialectic between bodily arousal and cognitive interpretation; it comprises states, values and arousals.

Why should we experience emotion at all? The role of emotion in human life may be rooted in the evolutionary history of a highly intelligent species that is capable of thinking before acting. Bodily arousal alerts us to something new and unexpected in our environment, something that does not easily fit into any conventional schema. Once our attention is caught in this way, the rest of our cognitive processes focus on the interrupting phenomenon. From this perspective, a person would be foolish to ignore his or her guts when trying to sort out a confusing experience. Indeed, the guts are usually what alert us to confusion in the first place. The need of "whole-body" experience for understanding also becomes more comprehensible. Mandler reminds us, "Just telling people what a situation is going to be like isn't enough, and it isn't good enough training when you encounter the real situation" (1983, 152). Generations of new spouses, new parents, and anthropological fieldworkers can testify to the overwhelming truth of this statement.

In sum, we experience bodily arousal when our familiar world is somehow interrupted. That arousal may either fade away or develop into an emotional experience depending on the meaning we assign to it. Possible meanings arise out of cultural interpretations of recurring experiential schemas. We should not be surprised to find some overlap in the categories of feeling recognized by different cultures. After all, certain experiential schemas that interrupt the familiar world—birth and death, for example—are human universals. At the same time, we should expect that the wider cultural context will in each case modify the angle from which such experiences are understood and, thus, the categories of feeling associated with them.

Emotion in an Eastern African Culture

David Parkin (1984) has studied the cultural construction of emotion among the Giriama of coastal Kenya (see EthnoProfile 6.4: Giriama). We must ex-

emotion The product of a dialectic between bodily arousal and cognitive interpretation, emotion comprises states, values, and arousals.

EthnoProfile 6.4

Giriama

Region: Eastern Africa
Nation: Kenya
Population: 150,000
Environment: Varied; coastal to desert, lush, hilly, flat
Livelihood: Farming and herding
Political organization: Traditionally, men of influence but no coercive power; today, part of a modern nation-state
For more information: Parkin, David. 1991. *Sacred void: Spatial images of work and ritual among the Giriama of Kenya.* Cambridge: Cambridge University Press.

plain several features of Giriama thinking before considering their understanding of what we call emotion. First, the Giriama theory of human nature does not recognize a mind-body dualism of the Western sort. Indeed, the Giriama are unwilling to set up sharp, mutually exclusive oppositions of any kind when discussing human nature. Parkin tells us that such behavior as spirit possession, madness, hysteria, witchcraft, persistent violence, drunkenness, and thieving are explained "as the result of what we might call imbalances in human nature. . . . I call them imbalances because the Giriama do not believe that a person can be intrinsically or irredeemably evil: At some stage, usually remarkably quickly, he will be brought back into the fold, even if he subsequently leaves it again. A large number of terms, roughly translatable as greed, lust, envy, jealousy, malice, resentment, anger, are used to refer to these imbalances of character and the accompanying behavior" (14).

As with Westerners, the Giriama associate different feelings with different parts of the body. In the West, people conventionally connect the brain with reason and the heart with emotion. For the Giriama, however, the heart, liver, kidneys, and eyes are the seat of reason and emotion. Although the Giriama may distinguish thinking from feeling in discussing the actual behavior of real people, they nevertheless presume a common origin for both (Parkin 1984, 17). Indeed, the Giriama framework for understanding human cognition has much in common with the anthropological perspective described throughout this chapter.

What about particular emotions? Although the categories of feeling recognized by Giriama overlap in some respects with the experiences labeled by English terms for emotions, Parkin suggests that there are important differences that stem from the nature of the schemas that Giriama culture conventionally recognizes and from the prototypical thoughts and feelings that are appropriate to those schemas. Consider what the term *utsungu* means as a label for a category of feeling: "Utsungu means poison, bitterness, resentment, and anger, on the one hand, but also grief on the other. It is the feeling experienced at a funeral of a loved or respected relative or friend. A man or woman is grieved at the loss but also bitter that it has happened at all, and angry with the witch who caused the death. Since the witch will be made to pay, the sentiment carried with it both the consequences of the loss of a dear one and the intention to avenge his or her death" (118).

In Western societies, people also feel "grief" at the death of a loved one. But the prototypical Western experience of grief does not contain the additional meaning involving anger at witchcraft and the desire for vengeance. Perhaps one would have to be a Giriama—or have lived in another culture in which witchcraft was understood as the usual cause of death and in which such wrongful death could be avenged—to experience the emotional configuration that Parkin describes for the Giriama.

Emotion in Oceania

Catherine Lutz (1988) is concerned with situating the way people understand emotion more fully within the social structures and social behaviors that drive it. Lutz did fieldwork among the Ifaluk of the Caroline Islands in the Pacific (see Figure 6.8; EthnoProfile 6.5: Ifaluk). While not denying the links of emotion to the body, she emphasizes how emotions can be understood as a form of social discourse (see chapter 5). That is, people's use of the language of emotion can be understood as a way of talking about social relationships. Like the Giriama, the Ifaluk do not distinguish sharply between thought and emotion; they understand events in a way that is simultaneously cognitive and affective. Saying that they are experiencing *song* (justifiable anger) is not just the description of an internal bodily state, but it is also a comment about someone else's failure to observe appropriate social behavior. That is, inappropriate social behavior interrupts the world of social expectations, producing an emotional response. The Ifaluk expect that the person who provoked *song* in another

FIGURE 6.8 The particular configuration of emotion and thought among Ifaluk people in the Caroline Islands is related to the natural and political conditions of everyday life on a small coral atoll.

EthnoProfile 6.5

Ifaluk

Region: Micronesia

Nation: Caroline Islands

Population: 430 (1988)

Environment: Coral atoll

Livelihood: Taro cultivation, government employment

Political organization: Traditionally, chiefdoms; today, a U.S. Trust Territory

For more information: Lutz, Catherine. 1988. *Unnatural emotions*. Chicago: University of Chicago Press.

[Map: PACIFIC OCEAN showing Guam, Ulithi, Fais, Sorol, Faraulep, Woleai, Eauripik, Elato, Lamotrek, Namonuito, Puluwat, Truk, Losap, Ifaluk, Satawal, Pulusuk — CAROLINE ISLANDS; scale 0 100 200 Miles]

will naturally experience *metagu* (fear/anxiety) once he or she finds out. Indeed the Ifaluk often link categories of thought/feeling in pairs: *song* and *metagu*, *gafago* (neediness) and *fago* (compassion/love/sadness).

Lutz writes, "the mental state of *any* mature individual is seen as having fundamentally social roots. Others can then be held responsible for the social conditions that produce the state" (1988, 101). Consequently, claiming to be justifiably angry is the first step in a process of negotiating the meaning of other people's actions in relation to oneself. Claims of *song* made by people of higher status or greater power (such as lineage heads and chiefs) tend to be accepted publicly, and the responsible party is expected to experience *metagu* as a result. Claims concerning others of similar status or power, however, may involve more negotiation over whether or not they have the right to apply *song* in a particular situation. Extended negotiation is also common when Ifaluk are unsure of what to feel/think about a newly introduced cultural item like cash, which does not fit into traditional schemas about proper social behavior and yet must be dealt with.

Lutz relates the Ifaluk's particular configuration of emotion/thought to the natural and political conditions of everyday life on a small coral atoll with a high rate of infant mortality and the ever-present threat of sudden devastation and death from typhoons. *Fago*, for example, motivates people to share

food, adopt one another's children, and provide close personal care to those who are ill or in some other way *gafago* (needy).

▼ MOTIVATION

Perception and cognition are psychological processes that acquaint us with the inner and outer "worlds" of our experiences and assist us in making sense of those worlds. But human life involves activity, *agency*: We set goals and pursue the means to achieve them. Even when those goals and means are culturally prescribed, we have to be induced to accept them as valid and important enough to take them on and make efforts to accomplish what our culture values.

Anthropological approaches to motivation have always embedded the sources of motivation within a cultural matrix. In the early years of the discipline, when Freudian theory was influential, many psychological anthropologists accepted Freud's idea that all human beings were motivated to seek pleasure in a world that frequently made that goal unattainable. Freud spoke of two basic kinds of "instincts," the erotic and the aggressive, which were present in all human beings. Unregulated pursuit of satisfaction of these instincts would lead to social chaos. Thus, culture entered the picture as a set of humanly invented arrangements that allowed these otherwise destructive instincts to be curbed or channeled into socially useful activities (Bock 1994, xii).

But many anthropologists have found speaking of "instinct" to be unhelpful, particularly when the culturally defined goals which people pursue in different societies seem so different from one another that tying these goals to the same instinct is implausible. In the 1930s, Ruth Benedict argued that each culture had its own sets of motives, its own models of ideal behavior, which members of a particular society adopted and which motivated them to pursue some kinds of behaviors rather than others. More recently, in work like that of Catherine Lutz, anthropologists have focused on how people interact with one another and how they talk about those interactions, in an attempt to uncover the local "ethnopsychology of motives" (Bock 1994, xii–xiii). This, in turn, requires close attention to the social and cultural contexts in which individuals learn to interact with other members of their society, learn to understand the local discourse about vice and virtue, and come to terms with these practices and values when attempting to exercise their own agency. That is, the mainsprings of motivation are to be uncovered in the study of socialization and enculturation.

Socialization and Enculturation

Children use their own bodies and brains to explore their world. But from their earliest days, other people are actively working to steer their activity and attention in particular directions. Consequently, their exploration of the world is not merely trial and error: the path is cleared for them by others who shape their experiences—and their interpretations of their experiences—for them.

Two terms in the social sciences refer to this process of culturally and socially shaped cognitive development. The first, **socialization**, is the process of learning to live as a member of a group. This involves mastering the skills of appropriate interaction with others and learning how to cope with the behavioral rules established by the social group. The second term, **enculturation**, refers to the cognitive challenges facing human beings who live together and must come to terms with the ways of thinking and feeling that are considered appropriate in their respective cultures. Becoming human involves both these processes, for children learn how to act, think, feel, and speak at the same time as they participate in the joint activities carried out by social groups to which they belong. We will use the term *socialization/enculturation* to represent this holistic experience. Socialization/enculturation produces a socially and culturally constructed *self* capable of functioning successfully in society.

Anthropologists and psychologists who seek a theory of cognitive development that is holistic have been attracted to the ideas of George Herbert Mead (1863–1931) and, more recently, to the work of Soviet psychologist Lev Vygotsky (1896–1934). Although both men were contemporaries, Vygotsky's work became influential in the West only recently. Before his early death, Vygotsky had helped to found a major school of Soviet psychology that continues to thrive. The writings of this *sociohistorical school* have in-spired some of the most interesting research in cognitive anthropology.

For Mead and Vygotsky alike, human life is social from the outset. As Vygotsky wrote, "The social dimension of consciousness is primary in time and in fact. The individual dimension of consciousness is derivative and secondary" (1978, 30). Like Vygotsky, Mead (1934) believed that human nature is completed and enhanced, not curtailed or damaged, by socialization and enculturation. Indeed, Mead argued that the successful humanization of human beings lies in people's mastery of symbols, which begins when children start to learn language. As children come to control the symbolic systems of their cultures, they gain the ability to distinguish objects and relationships in the world. Most important, they come to see themselves as *objects* as well as *subjects*.

Mead's analysis focused primarily on face-to-face interactions, but anthropologists need a theoretical framework that goes beyond such interactions. Here Vygotsky's work is important because Vygotsky's understanding of context goes beyond Mead's. Vygotsky wanted to create a psychology that was compatible with a marxian analysis of society. His ideas are far from doctrinaire; indeed, during the Stalin years in Russia, his work was censored. At the same time, his marxian orientation directed attention to the social, cultural, and historical context in which face-to-face interaction is embedded.

The Sociohistorical View

Earlier in this chapter, we introduced one of Vygotsky's theoretical contributions: the distinction between *elementary cognitive processes* and *functional cognitive systems*. This distinction allows anthropologists to describe the similarities and differences observed when we compare how people from different cultures think and feel. These differences we observe have implications for cognitive development as well.

socialization The process by which human beings as material organisms, living together with other similar organisms, cope with the behavioral rules established by their respective societies.

enculturation The process by which human beings living with one another must learn to come to terms with the ways of thinking and feeling that are considered appropriate in their respective cultures.

IN THEIR OWN WORDS

American Premenstrual Syndrome

Anthropologist Alma Gottlieb explores some of the contradictions surrounding the North American biocultural construction known as PMS.

To what extent might PMS be seen as an "escape valve," a means whereby American women "let off steam" from the enervating machine of the daily domestic grind? To some extent this explanation is valid, but it tells only part of the story. It ignores the specific contours of PMS and its predictable trajectory; moreover it puts PMS in a place that is peripheral to the American vision of womanhood, whereas my contention is that the current understanding of PMS (and, before its creation, of the menstrual period itself) is integral to how we view femininity. Even if it occupies a small portion of women's lives (although some women may see the paramenstruum as occupying half the month), and even if not all women suffer from it, I contend that the contemporary vision of PMS is so much a part of general cultural consciousness that it constitutes, qualitatively, half the female story. It combines with the other part of the month to produce a bifurcated vision of femininity whose two halves are asymmetrically valued.

Married women who suffer from PMS report that during the "normal" phase of the month they allow their husbands' myriad irritating acts to go uncriticized. But while premenstrual they are hyper-critical of such acts, sometimes "ranting and raving" for hours over trivial annoyances. Unable to act "nice" continually, women break down and are regularly "irritable" and even "hostile." Their protest is recurrent but futile, for they are made to feel guilty about it, or, worse, they are treated condescendingly. "We both know you're going to have your period tomorrow so why don't we just go to bed?" one husband regularly tells his wife at the first sign of an argument, thereby dismissing any claim to legitimate disagreement. Without legitimacy, as Weber taught us long ago, protests are doomed to failure; and so it is with PMS.

I suggest that these women in effect choose, however unconsciously, to voice their complaints at a time that they know those complaints will be rejected as illegitimate. If complaints were made during the non-premenstrual portion of the month, they would have to be taken seriously. But many American women have not found a voice with which to speak such complaints and at the same time retain their feminine allure. They save their complaints for that "time of the month" when they are in effect permitted to voice them yet by means of hormones do not have to claim responsibility for such negative feelings. In knowing when their complaints will not be taken seriously yet voicing them precisely during such a time, perhaps women are punishing themselves for their critical thoughts. In this way, and despite the surface-level aggression they display premenstrually, women continue to enact a model of behavior doomed to failure, as is consistent with what some feminists have argued is a pervasive tendency among American women in other arenas. . . .

So long as American society re-creates its unrealistic expectations of the female personality, it is inevitable that there will be a PMS, or something playing its role: a regular rejection of the stringent expectations of female behavior. But PMS masks the protest even as it embodies it: for, cast in a biological idiom, PMS is made to seem an autonomous force that is often uncontrollable . . . ; or if it can be controlled, it is only by drugs not acts of personal volition. Thus women's authorship of their own states of mind is denied them. As women in contemporary America struggle to find their voices, it is to be hoped that they will be able to reclaim their bodies as vehicles for the creation of their own metaphors, rather than autonomous forces causing them to suffer and needing to be drugged.

Source: Gottlieb 1988.

The functional systems employed by adult members of society must be acquired during childhood. For Vygotsky, acquisition takes place in a context of face-to-face interactions between, typically, a child and an adult. When children learn about the world in such a context, they are not working on their own; on the contrary, they are learning about the world as they learn the symbolic forms (usually language) that others use to represent the world.

This learning process creates in the child a new plane of consciousness resting on the dialogue-based, question-and-answer format of social interaction. From this, Vygotsky inferred that our internal thought processes would also take the format of a dialogue. Mead suggested something similar when he spoke of every person as being able to carry on internal conversations between the *I* (the unsocialized self) and the *me* (the socially conditioned self). Only on this basis can an individual's sense of identity develop as the self comes to distinguish itself from the conversational other.

One interesting Vygotskian concept is the *zone of proximal development*, which is the distance between a child's "actual development level as determined by independent problem solving" and the level of "potential development as determined through problem solving under adult guidance or in collaboration with more capable peers" (Vygotsky 1978, 86). Psychologists everywhere have long been aware that children can often achieve more when they are coached than when they work alone (Figure 6.9). Western psychologists, with their individualist bias, have viewed this difference in achievement as contamination of the testing situation or as the result of cheating. Vygotsky and his followers see it as an indispensable measure of potential growth that simultaneously demonstrates how growth is rooted in social interaction, especially in educational settings (Moll 1990).

The concept of the zone of proximal development enables anthropologists and comparative psychologists to link cognitive development to society, culture, and history, because practices of coaching or formal instruction are shaped by social, cultural, and historical factors. To the extent that these factors vary from society to society, we can expect cognitive development to vary as well.

FIGURE 6.9 The zone of proximal development is the distance between what a child can do on her own and what she can do under adult guidance. Here a woman helps a girl with Chinese calligraphy.

▼ IS COGNITIVE DEVELOPMENT THE SAME FOR EVERYONE?

Most theories, including Mead's, portray cognitive development as a progression through a series of stages. With the exception of Vygotsky's theory, these theories ordinarily assume that the stages are the same for all human beings, or at least all human beings in a particular society. A Vygotskian perspective helps us explain not only cross-cultural differences in development but also differences in the cognitive development of different subgroups in a single society.

For example, from their birth in 1973 through the late 1980s, a sample of 4,299 children were followed by a team of Cuban researchers who periodically collected information on their cognitive, social, economic, physical, and academic development (Gutierrez Muñiz, López Hurtado, and Arias Beatón n.d.). The researchers identified a series of correlations between levels of education, wage employment, living standards, and health of mothers and levels of development and achievement of the children. Put in Vygotskian terms, the data show that the zone of proximal development is greater for children of mothers with higher levels of education and participation in the paid workforce than it is for children of mothers with lower educational levels who do not work outside the home. These findings contradicted popular beliefs that the children of educated working mothers would suffer as a result of their mothers' activities (Arias Beatón, personal communication).

Carol Gilligan (1982) carried out a comparative study on the moral development of women and men in North American society. She argued that middle-class boys and girls in the United States begin their moral development in different sociocultural contexts. Boys are encouraged from an early age to break away from their mothers and families and make it on their own. In this context, they learn that independence is good, that dependency is weakness, and that their first duty is to themselves and what they stand for. By contrast, girls mature in a sociocultural context in which their bond to their mothers and families is never sharply ruptured. They learn that connection to others is good, that the destruction of relationships is damaging, and that their first responsibility in any difficult situation is to ensure that nobody gets hurt.

Gilligan did not adopt a Vygotskian perspective in this study, although she was influenced by Mead. But the Vygotskian concept of the zone of proximal development provides a useful tool for describing how the differential moral development of boys and girls is accomplished. In Vygotskian terms, the moral development of boys and girls proceeds in different directions because boys and girls are coached differently by more mature members of society. That is, when faced with the same dilemmas but unsure of how to act, boys are encouraged to make one set of choices, girls another.

In this way, each gender category builds up a different set of schemas as to what constitutes the "good." As a result, American men and women consistently see one another acting immorally. For example, when men and boys try to be true to themselves and strike out on their own, women and girls may condemn such action as being highly destructive to personal relationships. When women and girls try to encourage intimacy and closeness, men and boys may view such ties as confining and repressive.

Like Vygotsky, Gilligan situated the development of moral reasoning in sociocultural and historical context. She argued that men are able to present their moral perspective as universally correct because men as a group hold power over women as a group in American society. As American women gain power, however, their "different voice" may acquire more legitimacy, and the culturally embedded paths of moral development may themselves be altered.

▼ SELF/PERSONALITY/SUBJECTIVITY

As we discussed earlier, the experiences of socialization and enculturation produce a **self**, an individual capable of functioning successfully in society. But what sort of entity is a self? Many Western psychologists have assumed that the mature self was a bounded, independent, self-contained entity with a clear and noncontradictory sense of identity that persisted through time. Anthropologists working in other societies, however, often found that the development of such an independent self was not recognized as the goal of socialization and enculturation. On the contrary, socialization and enculturation were often designed to shape selves that did *not* think of themselves as independent and self-sufficient; the mature individual was one motivated to look out for others, work for the well-being of the family or the lineage rather than in pursuit of his or her own individual self-interest.

Early psychological anthropologists often spoke of individual **personality** rather than the self; this is seen in the name adopted by the early Culture and Personality school of the mid-twentieth century. Bock points out that in such formulations, "personality involves the relative *integration* of an individual's perceptions, motives, cognitions, and behavior within a sociocultural matrix (The subjective view of this unity is more often referred to as the *self*). The importance of consistent social feedback to individual functioning has been demonstrated. . . . Personality is thus revealed as part of a dynamic interactive system between a human organism and its physical-social environment" (1994, xiv). Many psychological anthropologists, including Bock himself, have argued that an individual's personality, understood in this

self The result of the process of socialization/enculturation for an individual.

personality The relative integration of an individual's perceptions, motives, cognitions, and behavior within a sociocultural matrix.

way, is not merely a reflection of a culturally ideal type, but is regularly shaped by such factors as "the individual's position in the social structure, including his or her social class, gender, occupational role, and even birth order. . . . These quasi-universal structural constraints cut across conventional divisions into 'cultures' and even nations" (1994, xiv).

The notion of an integrated personality, or self, harks back to Enlightenment ideas; as a result, it is hardly surprising that the postmodern critique of Enlightenment ideas questioned the existence of integrated, harmonious personalities or selves. Attention began to be paid to the different dimensions of one's personality or self that were activated (or deactivated) in different contexts, and people began to speak of "decentered" selves as the norm, rather than the exception. The idea of a centered, integrated self was viewed as an illusion or an effect of powerful political ideologies that worked to mask the heterogeneity and contradictory features of individual experience.

Contemporary scholars in many fields continue to disagree about the extent to which anyone's self is integrated or coherent, and few anthropologists would defend an unreflective Enlightenment view of the self. In psychological anthropology, this has led to the shift of focus we see in the work of Lutz, for example: rather than attempt to relate an individual's behavior to internal experiences of the self, attention is focused on social discourse about people's behavior. This suggests that "culture is (largely) created by people in the discourse justifying their behavior as rational and moral" (Bock 1994, xv). But anthropologists who recognize the uneven and contradictory features of individual self-experience also often draw attention to the attempts individuals make, even in the most difficult or bewildering situations, to impose meaning, to make sense of what is happening to them. We struggle to find patterns, strive to achieve ordered, coherent understandings of the world and of ourselves, even if the world is disorderly and even if our understandings are inevitably imperfect and partial.

In recent years, many psychological anthropologists and others have come to speak not of individual personality or individual self, but of individual **subjectivity**. Veena Das and Arthur Kleinman, for example, define subjectivity as "the felt interior experience of the person that includes his or her positions in a field of relational power" (2000, 1). To think of individuals as *subjects* has much to recommend it in a postmodern climate. First, it points to individual agency: each of us is, to some degree, the initiating subject of our actions. Second, however, individual agency is not understood as absolute: We are not free to chart our own destinies unimpeded. Quite the contrary, our agency is circumscribed by various limitations that result from the deployment of social, economic, and political power in the societies in which we live.

These limitations may be greater or lesser, depending on who we are (remember Bock's urging that we pay attention to the effect of such social variables as class, gender, occupation, or birth order and its impact on our developing sense of self). That is, we are *subject to* the workings of institutionalized power in the various *subject positions* we occupy. The fact that all people in all societies occupy a variety of different subject positions reflects our decentered selves: A particular individual may, in different contexts, be positioned in terms of gender, or ethnicity, or occupation, or class, or some combination of these positions. At the same time, however, all of us can potentially play the insights gained from each subject position off against the others and thus gain a measure of reflexive awareness and understanding of our own situations.

Socialization and enculturation heavily influence individual subjectivity. But social and cultural expectations are sometimes overturned by experiences that intrude on predictable daily routines, and these, too, will have a powerful role in shaping the subjectivities of the individuals who are affected.

▼ HOW DO VIOLENCE AND TRAUMA ALTER OUR VIEW OF OURSELVES?

Among the most powerful such experiences are those occasioned by structural violence and social trauma, two areas of social suffering that have unfortunately become all too prevalent in recent times. Processes of globalization, which displace populations or shape the contexts that allow their own governments to oppress or persecute them, have themselves become all

subjectivity The felt interior experience of the person that includes his or her positions in a field of relational power.

too frequent in the late twentieth and early twenty-first centuries. For those who live under such disordered circumstances, orderly, harmonious daily life is not taken for granted. A number of anthropologists have turned explicitly to the investigation of the sources of social suffering and the consequences of such suffering for individual subjectivity. Although the world's attention is usually drawn to large-scale *traumatic violence* that erupts in civil wars or other forms of armed conflict, anthropologists have also pointed to less spectacular forms of *structural violence*, with political and economic causes. Each in its own way is responsible for severe social suffering, and we will look at each in turn.

Structural Violence

Paul Farmer is an anthropologist and medical doctor who has worked since 1983 in Haiti (see EthnoProfile 6.6: Haiti). His activities as a physician have exposed him to extreme forms of human suffering that are part and parcel of everyday life for those at the bottom of Haitian society (Figure 6.10). As he points out, "In only three countries in the world was suffering judged to be more extreme than that endured in Haiti; each of these three countries is currently in the midst of an internationally recognized civil war" (Farmer 2002, 424). But if the suffering of poor Haitians is not the outcome of the traumatic violence of war, it can be described as a consequence of another form of violence: structural violence.

Structural violence is violence that results from the way that political and economic forces structure risk for various forms of suffering within a population. Much of this suffering is in the form of infectious and parasitic disease. But it can also include other forms of extreme suffering, such as hunger, torture, and rape (2002, 424). The operations of structural violence create circumscribed spaces in which the poorest and least powerful members of Haitian society are subjected to highly intensified risks of all kinds, increasing the likelihood that sooner or later they will experience one or more varieties of social suffering. The structural aspect of this violence is important to emphasize, since the attention of most Western out-

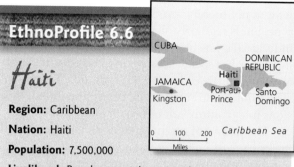

EthnoProfile 6.6

Haiti

Region: Caribbean

Nation: Haiti

Population: 7,500,000

Livelihood: Rough, mountainous terrain, tropical to semi-arid climate. About 80 percent of the population lives in extreme poverty

Political organization: Multiparty, nation-state

For more information: Farmer, Paul. 1992. *AIDS and accusation: Haiti and the geography of blame.* Berkeley, University of California Press.

side observers, even those who want to alleviate suffering, is often trained on individuals and their personal experiences, with the resulting temptation to blame the victims for their own distress.

Farmer's work as a physician allowed him to see firsthand the suffering of poor Haitians he knew, and his work as an anthropologist allowed him to link that suffering to economic and political structures in Haitian society that are often invisible in local situations, but that can be revealed through careful analysis. Farmer begins by offering the biographies of two young Haitians he treated, one a woman and one a man. Both died young, the woman of AIDS and the man of injuries inflicted on him in the course of a beating by the police. As he says, these two individuals "suffered and died in exemplary fashion," and he shows how the combined forces of racism, sexism, political violence, and poverty conspired "to constrain agency" and "crystallize into the sharp, hard surfaces of individual suffering" (2002, 425).

Acéphie Joseph was the woman who died of AIDS at 25, in 1991, one of the first in her rural village, "the latest in a string of tragedies that she and her parents readily linked together in a long lamentation, by now familiar to those who tend the region's sick" (426). Her parents had been prosperous peasant farmers selling produce in village markets until 1956, when the fertile valley in which they lived was flooded after a dam was built to generate electricity. They lost everything and became "water refugees"

structural violence Violence that results from the way that political and economic forces structure risk for various forms of suffering within a population.

FIGURE 6.10 Dr. Paul Farmer with AIDS patients at Clinique Bon Sauveur. Political and economic forces structure people's risks for various forms of suffering in Haiti and elsewhere.

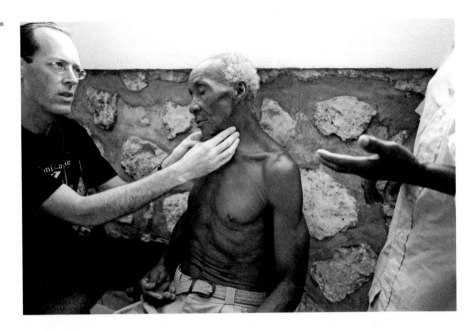

forced to try to grow crops on an infertile plot in the village where they were resettled.

Acéphie and her twin brother were born in the village and attended primary school there. Farmer writes that Acéphie's "beauty and her vulnerability may have sealed her fate as early as 1984" (426). She began to help her mother carry produce to the market along a road that went past the local military barracks, where soldiers like to flirt with the passing women, and one soldier in particular approached her. "Such flirtation is seldom unwelcome, at least to all appearances. In rural Haiti, entrenched poverty made the soldiers—the region's only salaried men—ever so much more attractive" (427). Although Acéphie knew he had a wife and children, she nevertheless did not rebuff him; indeed, he visited her family, who approved of their liaison. "'I could tell that the old people were uncomfortable, but they didn't say no . . . I never dreamed he would give me a bad illness . . . it was a way out, that's how I saw it,'" Acéphie explained.

Only a few weeks after the beginning of their sexual relationship, the soldier died, and Acéphie sought training as a cook in order to qualify for work as a servant in the city, for she had no other viable alternative. Eventually she found work as a maid and began a relationship with a young man who drove a bus whom she planned to marry. After three years as a maid, Acéphie became pregnant, and went home to her village to give birth, but she had a very difficult delivery, and when she finally sought medical help for a series of infections, she was diagnosed with AIDS. Following her death, her father hanged himself.

Chouchou Louis grew up in a village on the Central Plateau of Haiti. He attended primary school briefly and then worked with his father and older sister to raise produce after his mother died. In the 1980s, times were especially difficult under the repressive dictatorship of Jean-Claude Duvalier, and those Haitians who tried to flee by boat to the United States were termed "economic" rather than political refugees; a 1981 treaty between Duvalier and President Ronald Reagan ensured that such refugees would be promptly returned to Haiti. By 1986, a pro-democracy movement had grown powerful enough in Haiti to force Duvalier to leave the country, but he was replaced in power by the military. The U.S. government hoped that this military government would bring democracy and supplied it with over $200 million in aid. But poor peasants like Chouchou Louis and his family saw little difference between the military rulers and the dictator they had replaced, because peasants continued to be subject to violence at the hands of soldiers. An election in 1990 brought the popular leader Father Jean-Bertrand Aristide to power with over 70 percent of the vote, but in 1991 he was ousted in a coup. Anger in the countryside at this coup "was soon followed by sadness, then fear, as the country's repressive machinery, dismantled during the seven months of Aristide's tenure, was hastily reassembled under the patronage of the army" (429).

Soon thereafter Chouchou was riding in a truck when he made a remark about the poor state of the roads that might have been interpreted as a veiled criticism of the coup. On the same truck was an out-of-uniform soldier who, at the next checkpoint, had Chouchou dragged from the truck and beaten. Although he was let go, he lived in fear of another arrest, which came several months later, with no explanation, when he was visiting his sister. He was taken to the nearest military checkpoint and tortured. After three days he was dumped in a ditch, and the following day Farmer was brought in to treat him, but his injuries were too severe. He died three days later.

Acéphie and Chouchou are individuals, and so it is natural to ask how representative their experiences might be. Farmer's experience among many poor women with AIDS allowed him to recognize that all of their cases, including Acéphie's, showed "a deadly monotony." The women he interviewed "were straightforward about the nonvoluntary aspect of their sexual activity." They had been driven to it by poverty (431). Similarly, Chouchou was only one of more than 3,000 Haitian civilians, most of them poor peasants, who were killed after 1991 by military or paramilitary forces. Thus, Farmer concludes, "the agony of Acéphie and Chouchou was in a sense, 'modal' suffering. In Haiti, AIDS and political violence are two leading causes of death among young adults" (431). And all this suffering and death was the outcome of structural violence: All the key events that contributed to their deaths, from the flooding of the valley to the funding of the Haitian army, were the consequences of human agency which, in turn, severely circumscribed the agency of Acéphie and Chouchou no matter what they did.

Farmer identifies specifically the relations of power in which each of them was embedded, for these contributed to the likelihood that their suffering and death would take the forms it took. For example, "gender helps explain why Acéphie died of AIDS whereas Chouchou died from torture" (433). Race or ethnicity helps explain why illness is more likely to be suffered by the descendants of enslaved Africans, and social class helps explain why they were more likely to be poor (Figure 6.11). "These grim biographies suggest that the social and economic forces that have helped to shape the AIDS epidemic are, in every sense, the same forces that led to Chouchou's death and to the larger repression in which it was eclipsed. What is more, both were 'at risk' of such a fate long before they met the soldiers who altered their destinies. *They* were both, from the outset, victims of structural violence" (431).

Trauma

Incidents of warfare, genocide, ethnic cleansing, and other forms of large-scale collective violence were distinctive features of the twentieth century, leading not only to widespread loss of life but also to the disruption of social institutions, the destruction of economic and political arrangements, and the displacement of surviving populations into unfamiliar and often hostile new settings. These developments have not been ignored by anthropologists, many of whom have collaborated with specialists in other disciplines to investigate the causes of these events and to help treat the victims. In approaching this topic, some have chosen to speak in terms of **trauma**: "events in life generated by forces and agents external to the person and largely external to his or her control, and specifically to events generated in the setting of armed conflict and war," including such phenomena as "separation and loss, imprisonment and exile, threats of annihilation, even death and mutilation" (Apfel and Simon 2000, 103). Roberta Apfel and Bennett Simon distinguish these sorts of experiences from the less devastating "ordinary traumas" or "necessary losses" that all people are likely to face, "such as the birth of a sibling, natural death of a parent or sibling, divorce, illnesses, and accidents, whether man-made or natural" (2000, 103).

Anthropologists investigating the causes and consequences of such large-scale trauma regularly work together with other specialists, including psychoanalysts like Apfel and Simon, because such phenomena are so complex. Large-scale collective violence has complex causes involving psychic, social, political, economic, and cultural factors, and aims to destroy not just individual psychological functioning, but also the physical body and the social order. Individual and cultural factors together bring about the trauma, and are equally implicated in the ways in which survivors come to deal with trauma's aftermath (Suárez-Orozco and Robben 2000, 1).

trauma Events in life generated by forces and agents external to the person and largely external to his or her control; specifically, events generated in the setting of armed conflict and war.

FIGURE 6.11 AIDS and political violence are two leading causes of death among young people in Haiti. They leave behind other forms of social suffering for their parents and children. Here, the parents of Jean-David Droitdieu, an AIDS victim, holding his orphaned daughter, sit in front of their home and the place of his burial, surrounded by relatives and neighbors.

This means, of course, that attempts to reduce explanations of large-scale collective forms of violence to either "nature" or "culture" are bound to be inadequate. Like Bock, Suárez-Orozco and Robben seek analysis in the intermediate zone "somewhere between those two analytical dead ends" (2000, 2). For example, attributing large-scale collective forms of violence to some innate *individual* capacity for violence ignores the many differences between small-scale, face-to-face violent interchanges and the massing of armies and technology to wreak havoc on an "enemy" that is often not known personally. To grasp the complexities involved requires "processual multi-level approaches" that combine "solid understandings of the inner psychic processes as well as the social and cultural contexts of large-scale violence and trauma" (2000, 4).

Western scholarly and medical understanding of large-scale trauma developed over the course of the twentieth century. Phenomena called "shell shock" or "battle fatigue" were first identified in some soldiers during World War I. Although initially these soldiers were vilified as cowards who were morally corrupt, some researchers, including anthropologists W. H. R. Rivers and Abram Kardiner, eventually proposed that the suffering these soldiers experienced could not be attributed to individual psychological or moral deficiency, but needed to be seen as a consequence of the trauma inflicted by battlefield experience itself. The commitment in World War II to "total war" made the destruction of civilian populations and support structures as important, or more important, than the destruction of soldiers on the battlefield. "The number of civilian casualties went from 5 per cent in the First World War, and 50 per cent in the Second World War to over 80 per cent in the Vietnam War" (Suárez-Orozco and Robben 2000, 15). After World War II, attention was for the first time directed to the massive trauma to which civilians had been subjected, with particular attention focused on the experiences of those who survived Nazi concentration camps. Suárez-Orozco and Robben note that the pioneering work by psychoanalyst Bruno Bettelheim, for example, highlighted the "complex social dynamics between perpetrators and victims of violence" (2000, 17), but these dynamics were neglected in the aftermath of the Vietnam War, in which the focus was on identification and treatment of roughly one third of individual veterans suffering from what was officially designated as "post-traumatic stress disorder" (PTSD) in 1980 (20).

Suárez-Orozco and Robben emphasize the importance of promoting effective forms of healing among those who suffer such massive trauma, but they also note that societies as well as individuals need to heal. In both cases, successful healing seems to require the reestablishment of "basic trust:" Individuals need to find ways to trust other individuals, but all survivors also need to be able to find ways to develop trust in the institutions of their society which also are implicated in the management of (or in failing to manage) collective violence. Some dimensions of healing can be successfully promoted by the efforts of psychiatrists and medical specialists who focus on individuals; for example, interpreting the suffering of Vietnam era veterans in medical terms, as PTSD, acknowledged that the veterans' suffering was not a consequence of their own personal defects, but had to be traced to the trauma they had experienced in war. At the same time, medicalization of PTSD and a continuing focus on individuals diverts attention away from the socio-cultural dimensions of such trauma. "Combat trauma shatters the meaningfulness of the self and the world, and makes its sufferers put their bodies and minds on constant alert for any possible attack. They become distrustful of others, their own memories, and visual perceptions" (Suárez-Orozco and Robben 2000, 20). The taken-for-grantedness of everyday social life is destroyed, allowing "the uncanny"—"the dread and horror of social violence"—to become a recurring and unassimilable feature of their lives. "Those who experience such traumas are faced with an unbelievable and unreal reality that is incompatible with anything they knew previously. As a result, they can no longer fully believe what they see with their own eyes; they have difficulty in distinguishing between the unreal reality they have survived and the fears that spring from their own imagination. . . . When one experiences the uncanny . . . what has been hidden becomes visible, what is familiar becomes strange and frightening" (Gampel 2000, 49–50).

We all experience a mild form of "the uncanny" when we find ourselves in more manageable situations of ambiguity, for example, when learning a new language or becoming acquainted with new foods or new customs when we travel. The cultural shock of fieldwork is more jarring, but still manageable by most anthropologists. So, too, living in another society, whether as a tourist or student or immigrant, can be a struggle but may involve less trauma if the experience was chosen and the individuals involved are surrounded by supportive economic, social, and political institutions: Anthropologists who study migration have been able to document such cases, some of which we will look at in more detail in later chapters. But "the uncanny" experienced by war refugees or concentration camp survivors or victims of state repression is massively more intense. "We feel safe when we exist in a constantly affective background,

in a constant social context. The feeling of uncanniness overwhelms us when we are thrust into a fragmented, violent social context, one without any continuity and which transmits extremely paradoxical messages" (Gampel 2000, 55). The response of individuals to these experiences varies, however. For survivors of Nazi death camps, trauma was often severe and affected the children of survivors in ways that were often not made explicit, but were revealed in such behaviors as parental anxiety and overprotectiveness toward their children. Psychoanalysts can be effective in helping those who suffer from such experiences, but many believe it is naïve and overly optimistic to imagine that total "cure" is possible (Langer 1997). Other survivors exhibit (and pass on to their children) a remarkable resiliency, "the capacity to survive violence and loss, and moreover, to have flexibility of response over the course of a life time" including "a sense of agency and a sense of capacity to choose—among courses of action and among conflicting moral values" (Apfel and Simon 2000, 103).

Chosen Trauma

In still other cases, however, collective trauma can produce far more troubling responses. Some traumatized persons and groups turn to "hatred and violence as ways of coping with traumatic wounds" (Apfel and Simon 2000, 102). Vamik Volkan has described one way in which this can happen, in terms of what he calls a group's *chosen trauma*. A chosen trauma arises, Volkan argues, from experiences of collective violence and loss that survivors are unable to mourn. This can lead to a collective focus on the group's past experiences of victimization or humiliation, and the entire identity of the group's members may come to center on the chosen trauma. Moreover, the chosen trauma can be passed on to subsequent generations along with the expectation that it is up to them to right past wrongs, using violence if necessary. "While the group does not consciously choose to feel victimized, it does choose to psychologize losses, and to transform them into powerful cultural narratives which become an integral part of the social identity" (Suárez-Orozco and Robben 2000, 23). Volkan studied Christian Serbs, who elaborated and passed on for hundreds of years their chosen trauma: the loss of their empire to the Ottoman Turks in the early 1500s. Although this chosen trauma was not always in the forefront of Serbian actions during those centuries, it remained a powerful cultural resource which Slobodan Milosevic and his cronies successfully exploited for their own political purposes in the 1990s, as the former Yugoslavia broke apart (23).

The power of chosen traumas derives in large part from the fact that they remain unmourned, thus cutting off possible forms of social and cultural healing that can rebuild trust in social institutions. Suárez-Orozco and Robben note, for example, that "institutional acknowledgement—in the form of 'truth' commissions and reparations (monetary and symbolic)—and justice—in the form of trials of perpetrators—can begin partially to restore the symbolic order that is another casualty of the work of violence" (2000, 5). These kinds of institutional acknowledgement, most often initiatives taken on the level of the nation-state (as in post-apartheid South Africa), may coincide with more local actions designed to reduce the trauma of massive social disruption, through healing rituals and other collective symbolic activities designed to aid recovery and rebuild social trust (22, 24).

▼ HOW DOES INDIVIDUAL PSYCHOLOGY DEPEND ON CONTEXT?

Cross-cultural studies of human psychological functioning all stress the vital importance of *context*—not just the immediate context of the laboratory situations or fieldwork encounters, but also the displaced context of culture and history that may be invisible in local settings but present in people's habits of thought and feeling. Sometimes, however, contextual factors are made obvious. When administering a psychological test on visual illusions to the Fang, for example, James Fernandez (1980) discovered that many questioned his explanation of the "real" reason behind such a bizarre activity as psychological testing (see EthnoProfile 8.3: Fang). Years of colonial domination and exploitation at the hands of outsiders made their suspicions of the anthropologist's motives far from irrational.

Contextual factors shape human experiences in subtle ways as well, contributing to nuanced, holistic ethnographic understandings of other ways of making meaning. An excellent description of just this kind of holistic experience is given by anthropologist Michael Gilsenan (1982), who worked for a time

among urban Muslims in Cairo, Egypt (see EthnoProfile 6.7: Cairo). Gilsenan spent many hours with his informants observing their prayers in the local mosque. Along the inside wall of the mosque were verses from the Qur'an shaped out of bright green neon tubing. Green is the color of the prophet Muhammad, so finding that color used prominently in mosque decoration is not surprising. However, Gilsenan's experiences in Western culture did not include schemas in which neon light and serious worship went together, and for several months the neon interfered with his attempts to assume a properly reverential attitude. Then one day, Gilsenan reports, "I turned unthinkingly away from the swaying bodies and the rhythms of the remembrance of God and saw, not neon, but simply greenness. . . . No gaps existed between color, shape, light, and form. From that unreflecting and unsuspecting moment I ceased to see neon at all" (1982, 266).

Nothing had happened to Gilsenan's eyes or his other senses, which continued to receive the same signals they had always received, but the meaning of the signals had been altered. Gilsenan's experience in the mosque situated neon light within a new schema, and his growing familiarity with that schema made the neon seem more and more natural. Eventually, Gilsenan was noticing only the color green. He was still able to report, of course, that the green light was produced by green neon tubing; however, that fact seemed irrelevant given the new schema he used to interpret his experience.

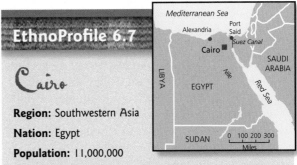

EthnoProfile 6.7

Cairo

Region: Southwestern Asia

Nation: Egypt

Population: 11,000,000

Environment: Capital city; delta and desert

Livelihood: Modern stratified society

Political organization: City in a modern nation-state

For more information: Gilsenan, Michael. 1982. *Recognizing Islam: Religion and society in the modern Arab world.* New York: Pantheon.

These transformations of perception and understanding remain mysterious, but they seem to occur whenever we have an insight of any kind. Insights, like apt metaphors, reshape the world for us, throwing new aspects into sharp focus and casting other aspects into the background. Our ability to achieve insights, like our ability to create apt metaphors, remains the most central and most mysterious aspect of human psychological processes.

CHAPTER SUMMARY

1. Anthropologists have long been interested in cultural learning by individuals. They have tried to find out what all members of our species have in common, what features are limited to specific groups of humans, and how individual uniqueness might be understood. This effort has involved cooperation with other disciplines, such as psychology. Often anthropologists have tested universal assumptions about human psychology in different cultural settings, and have found them to be problematic.

2. The field of psychological anthropology is complex and difficult to summarize, but can be grouped into three basic areas of human experience: perception, cognition, and motivation. Research overwhelmingly sustains the view that human psychological processes are open to a wide variety of influences.

3. Human psychological perception always takes place in a cultural context. Researchers use concepts like schemas and prototypes to describe some of the ways in which meaning is mapped onto our experience. Classic research on cross-cultural variations in perception showed that variation in responses to psychological tests depended on the meanings subjects brought to the testing situation, especially whether they understood the tests the same way Western subjects typically understood them. Alternative understandings are possible because of the ambiguity of many perceptual signals, a phenomenon that is illustrated in the study of visual illusions. In addition, looking and seeing are culturally learned modes of sensory perception, as illustrated in Vogel's study of Baule visuality.

4. Human beings are active meaning-makers, striving to make sense of our experiences, which is a focus of anthropological studies of cognition. Their research has been critical of so-called intelligence tests on which non-Western subjects performed poorly, because outside the laboratory setting the same individuals' intelligence and full humanity were obvious. Today, it is unclear exactly what the results of intelligence tests represent. Consequently, research has shifted its focus to cognitive processes and the way these are organized into culturally shaped functional systems.

5. Some anthropologists argue that people in different cultures have different cognitive styles that can be located on a continuum ranging from global style at one end to articulated style at the other. Research suggests that the same individual may use a global style for some tasks and an articulated style for others. In everyday situations, the goal of cognition is not to solve a problem by finding the single correct answer. Instead, people try to resolve dilemmas in a way that allows them to get on with life.

6. Several attempts have been made to measure the levels of rational thinking in non-Western populations. The results are problematic. Rational thinking is not the same as logic. Formal Western logic is better understood as a learned reasoning style characteristic of Western culture. Rules of Western logic can be useful, but other logics may be equally valid in other societies—or on other occasions in Western societies—when contextual factors are vital and must be taken into consideration.

7. Our emotions, like our thoughts, are not just something we have; they are culturally constructed of our state of mind, our cultural interpretations, and our levels of bodily arousal. Different cultures recognize different domains of experience and different categories of feeling as being appropriate to these domains. For this

reason, it is often difficult to translate the language of emotion from one culture to another.

8. Anthropological approaches to motivation have always embedded the sources of motivation within a cultural matrix. Finding the notion of "instinct" to be unhelpful, anthropologists have had greater success in studying the culturally defined goals which people pursue in different societies.

9. The mainsprings of motivation are to be uncovered in the study of socialization and enculturation. Humans must learn to pattern and adapt behavior and ways of thinking and feeling to the standards considered appropriate in their respective cultures. Vygotsky's concept of the zone of proximal development stresses that cognitive development results from a dialogue. Children progress through that process at different rates and in different directions, depending on the amount and kind of coaching they receive by others. This concept makes it possible to explain why people in different cultural subgroups are socialized and enculturated in different ways.

10. Anthropologists have been critical of ideas of the individual self that assume it to be a bounded independent entity with a clear and noncontradictory sense of identity that persists through time. Early psychological anthropologists preferred to speak of individual personality, which always assumed that an individual's psychological processes were integrated within a socio-cultural matrix. More recently, anthropologists have shifted from a concern with relating personality to an individual's internal experiences and have paid more attention to attributions about individuals that emerge in social discourse about people's behavior. Some anthropologists prefer to speak not of personality or self, but of individual subjectivity, which focuses on internal experiences of individuals as they are shaped by their positions in a field of power relations.

11. Patterns of socialization and enculturation are sometimes overturned by experiences that intrude on predictable daily routines. Among the most powerful such experiences are those occasioned by structural violence and social trauma, the investigation of which has become a significant topic for some contemporary psychological anthropologists.

KEY TERMS

perception	elementary cognitive processes	articulated style	enculturation
schemas		thinking	self
prototypes	functional cognitive systems	syllogistic reasoning	personality
		reasoning styles	subjectivity
visuality	cognitive style	emotion	structural violence
cognition	global style	socialization	trauma

SUGGESTED READINGS

Bock, Philip K. 1999. *Rethinking psychological anthropology: Continuity and change in the study of human action*, 2d ed. Prospect Heights, IL: Waveland Press. *A thorough introduction to psychological anthropology, tracing developments from the early twentieth century to current directions in the field.*

Cole, Michael, and Sylvia Scribner. 1974. *Culture and thought: A psychological introduction*. New York: Wiley. *A clear, readable survey of the literature and case studies on the cultural shaping of cognition.*

Farmer, Paul. 2003. *Pathologies of power: Health, human rights, and the new war on the poor*. Berkeley: University of California Press. *Paul Farmer, a physician and anthropologist, uses his experiences in several different parts of the world to show how patterns of disease and suffering are shaped by social and political policies that violate human rights, creating landscapes of "structural violence."*

Miller, Jonathan. 1983. *States of mind*. New York: Pantheon. *A series of interviews in which Jonathan Miller (English actor, writer, physician, director) talks to several of the most interesting scholars on the mind, including George Mandler, Richard Gregory, and Clifford Geertz. This book is witty and enjoyable.*

Schwartz, Theodore, Geoffrey M. White, and Catherine A. Lutz, eds. 1992. *New directions in psychological anthropology*. Cambridge: Cambridge University Press. *A classic survey of psychological anthropology with articles by experts in the fields of cognition, human development, biopsychological studies, and psychiatric and psychoanalytic anthropology.*

Chapter 7

Play, Art, Myth, and Ritual

Human beings are creative, not just in their use of language, but also in their manipulation of a variety of symbolic forms. We look at a range of different kinds of human symbolic creativity in this chapter, including play, art, myth, and ritual.

One of the authors of this book (RHL) was carrying out fieldwork in Caracas, Venezuela, toward the end of October 1974, when excitement about the heavy-weight boxing championship featuring George Fore-man and Muhammad Ali began to build. Boxing is extremely popular in Venezuela, and the Caracas newspapers devoted a great deal of attention to this bout. They gave Ali little chance of winning. It was late in his career, and he had already lost once to Foreman. Too old, they said, too out of shape, too big a mouth, too strong an opponent.

I (RHL) managed to resist interest in the fight un-til the last moment. I had other work to do and didn't care for boxing. Besides, I didn't have a television in my apartment. On the night the fight was to be tele-cast on the national network, I went out to dinner alone. On my way home, I was surprised to see the city almost deserted. Then I remembered that the fight was about to start. I was feeling lonely, and my curiosity got the better of me. I passed a bar that had a television, so I stopped in. The preliminaries, native dancing from Congo where the fight was being held, were just ending. The bar gradually filled up. A cou-ple of people seemed to know each other, but the rest were strangers.

As the fight began, I became aware that we were all Ali fans. As he did better and better, we be-came increasingly excited, and communication among the patrons increased. When finally, mirac-ulously, Ali won, pandemonium broke loose. The crowd seemed to explode into a paroxysm of *abra-zos* ("embraces"), tears, cries of joy, and calls for rounds of beer. Strangers before, all of us were now united in a feeling of oneness and joy. None of us had any idea who the others were or what they did, but it didn't matter—we had witnessed something wonderful and felt a comradeship that transcended our strangerness.

But what was it that we had witnessed and been part of? A sporting event? A ritual? A drama, pitting youth against age? Was there something mythic in that spectacle that so engrossed us?

---

play A framing (or orienting context) that is (1) consciously adopted by the players, (2) somehow pleasurable, and (3) systemically related to what is nonplay by alluding to the nonplay world and by transforming the objects, roles, actions, and relations of ends and means characteristic of the nonplay world.

In this chapter, we consider how anthropologists go about trying to make sense of events similar to the event in the bar. We will examine play, art, myth, and ritual—four elements of human experience in which the interplay of openness and creativity with rules and constraints enables people to produce powerful and moving phenomena.

▼ WHY PLAY?

In the previous two chapters, we explored the con-cept of *openness* in linguistic and cognitive settings. Openness was defined as the ability to talk or think about the same thing in different ways and different things in the same way. If we expand openness to in-clude all behavior—that is, the ability not just to talk or think about but also to *do* the same thing in differ-ent ways or different things in the same way—we begin to define **play**. All mammals play, and humans play the most and throughout their lives.

Robert Fagen (1981, 1992) tries to understand an-imal play as the product of natural selection. He points out that play gives young animals (including young human beings) the exercise they need to build up their bodies for the rigors of adulthood. Play trains them in activities necessary for physical sur-vival: fighting, hunting, or running away when pur-sued. During a brief period of neural development, peak brain development associated with motor skills and peak periods of play occur at the same time. Some scholars have proposed that play may be im-portant for the development of cognitive and motor skills involving the brain. In species with more com-plex brains, play seems to aid in the development of other parts of the brain as well. Playful exploration of the environment aids learning and allows for the development of behavioral versatility (see Fagen 1981, 350–55). It also seems to have a connection with the repair of developmental damage caused either by injury or trauma. All of these functions of play may have significant value for the survivability of indi-viduals of various species.

Fagen proposes an additional function of play: the communication of the message "all's well" (1992, 48–49). "It seems likely that a frequent consequence and possible biological function of play is to convey information about short-term and long-term health, general well-being, and biological fitness to parents, littermates, or other social companions" (51).

Thinking about Play

We defined play as a generalized form of behavioral openness: the ability to think about, speak about, and do different things in the same way or the same thing in different ways.

Joking, which can be verbal or physical (practical jokes, pranks, horseplay), is a good example of how play operates overall and in its cultural context. Anthropologist Andrew Miracle discusses joking behavior among Aymara people in Bolivia (see Ethno-Profile 7.1: Aymara). He notes that ordinarily Aymara do not laugh in the presence of strangers because that is considered disrespectful. They laugh and joke only within a circle of acquaintances and friends. This kind of joking reinforces existing social bonds (1991, 151).

Much of the joking Miracle observed took place on the crowded buses or trucks that transport rural people around the country. Ordinarily, Aymara personal space extends about one arm's length. Where there is any choice, people do not get any closer to one another. They also show respect and honor other people's privacy by not staring. Miracle notes that in everyday situations, "when stared at, the Aymara may yell at the one staring and become quite rude" (1991, 146). On buses or trucks, however, the context changes, and people who are strangers to one another are forced into artificial intimacy. They must sit or stand very close to one another for long periods of time, frequently looking right at one another. Their response, Miracle writes, is often to joke and laugh, behavior normally reserved for intimates. Put another way, they choose to do "different things" (passing time with close friends and passing time with strangers in unusually close quarters) in the "same way," by joking. This altered definition of context gives joking among strangers a new meaning, playfully changing strangers into friends and thus making a socially unpleasant situation more tolerable.

Moving from everyday reality to the play reality requires a radical transformation of perspective. This movement may remain hidden; to an outside observer, the switch from everyday reality to play reality may go undetected. However, sometimes the switch can have serious consequences for other people and their activities. In this case, play and nonplay must be signaled clearly, so that one is not mistaken for the other.

According to Gregory Bateson (1972), this shift requires a level of communication, called **metacommunication**, or communication about communication. It provides information about the relationship between those who are communicating. Consider the remark, "You drive." This simple statement can communicate a variety of messages about the relationship between the speakers. It can be an order: The metacommunication is "I have the right to compel you to drive." It can also be a plea: "You are able to drive. I am not." Or it can be an admission of equality: "You are now at the point of doing something that I too can do."

In play there are two kinds of metacommunication. The first, called **framing**, is a cognitive boundary that marks certain behaviors as play or as ordinary life. Dogs, for example, have a *play face*, a signal understood by other dogs (and recognizable by some human beings, dog owners in particular, perhaps) indicating a willingness to play. If dogs agree to play, they bare their fangs and one animal attacks the other. But the bite is not consummated; it becomes a nip. Both dogs have agreed to enter the *play frame*, an imaginative world in which bites don't mean bites. To put it another way, a basic element of Western logic—that $A = A$—does not apply in play; or, the same thing is being treated in different ways. Human beings have many ways of marking the play frame: a smile, a particular tone of voice, a referee's whistle, or the words "Let's play" or "Let's pretend" or "You can be the king." The marker says that "everything from now until we end this activity is set apart from everyday life."

The second kind of metacommunication involves **reflexivity**. Play offers us the opportunity to think about the social and cultural dimensions of the world in which we find ourselves. Because play suggests that ordinary life can be understood in more than one way,

---

metacommunication Communicating about the process of communication itself.

framing A cognitive boundary that marks certain behaviors as "play" or as "ordinary life."

reflexivity Critically thinking about the way one thinks; reflecting on one's own experience.

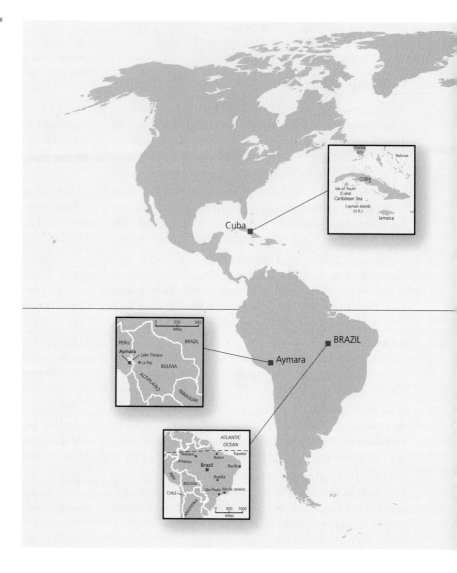

FIGURE 7.1 Locations of societies whose EthnoProfiles appear in chapter 7.

play can be a commentary on the nature of ordinary life (Handelman 1977, 186). It communicates about what can be rather than about what should be or what is (186). This is what we mean when we say that jokes keep us from taking ourselves too seriously. Through jokes, we see that there are alternative, even ridiculous, explanations for our experience.

Some Effects of Play

Some scholars see play as rehearsal for the "real world." Animals play at fighting so they will know how to fight when survival is at stake. Similarly, children play house as a way of learning the appropriate

gender roles and skills needed for adulthood (Figure 7.2). This anthropological approach commonly views children's play as an imitation of adult activities and therefore as a way of learning culture (see Schwartzman 1978, 100, 101). Others have suggested that play (especially make-believe play) increases children's creativity and originality by allowing children to overcome their limitations of age, experience, and maturity and by permitting a richer reproduction of adult life (Schwartzman 1978, 116).

But psychologist Brian Sutton-Smith—who spent decades studying children's play and games—finds this approach limiting. In his research (Sutton-Smith 1992; and summarized in Schwartzman 1978, 124ff.),

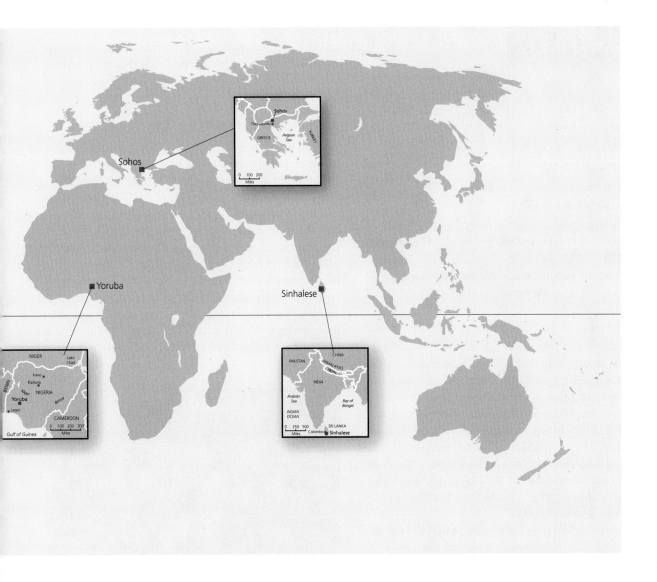

he suggests that play activities are important not because they provide a socializing force for society but because they allow for innovation, a point made by Fagen (1992) for the possible evolutionary power of play in any species. Helen Schwartzman has demonstrated how play, through satire and clowning, may allow children to comment on and criticize the world of adults (1978, 232–45). Some adult play forms, such as the pre-Lenten Carnival or Halloween, also act as a commentary on the "real world." They sanction insults and derision of authority figures, inversions of social status, clowning, parody, satire, stepping outside of everyday life, "trying on" new forms of identity, and the like (124).

A powerful example of this kind of commentary is described by anthropologist Elizabeth Chin, who studied African American girls and their dolls in Newhallville, a working-class and poor neighborhood in New Haven, Connecticut. Although "ethnically correct" dolls are on the market, very few of the girls had them, because they cost too much. The poor children Chin knew in Newhallville had white dolls. But in their play these girls transformed their dolls in a powerful way by giving them hairstyles like their own. The designers gave the dolls smooth, flowing hair to be brushed over and over again and put into a ponytail. But the girls' dolls had beads in their hair, braids held at the end with twists of aluminum foil or

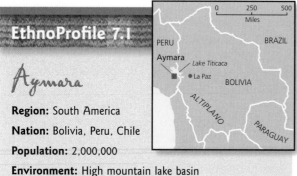

EthnoProfile 7.1

Aymara

Region: South America

Nation: Bolivia, Peru, Chile

Population: 2,000,000

Environment: High mountain lake basin

Livelihood: Peasant farmers

Political organization: Preconquest state societies conquered first by Inkas and later by Spanish; today, part of a modern nation-state

For more information: Miracle, Andrew. 1991. Aymara joking behavior. *Play and Culture* 4:144–52.

undermine the established political order. Repressive political regimes frequently attempt to censor humor critical of the rulers, with the result that such humor becomes an accepted mode of political resistance.

Alternative Views of Reality

We can easily see how humor shows an alternative view of reality, but what about nonjoking play? What about adults who climb rocks? "Is climbing a vertical face of rock at the risk of one's life play, or is it done in earnest?" (Csikszentmihalyi 1981, 16). Indeed, a rock climber risks serious consequences. Is rock climbing, then, not play? It fits a definition of play—it is consciously adopted by the player, it is somehow pleasurable, it transforms the relations of ends and means characteristic of the nonplay world—and yet "the climber is as immersed in reality as anyone can be in this world." This suggests that one's perspective on reality can vary. Each person's view

barrettes, and braids that were themselves braided together (Chin 1999, 315). As Chin observes, "In some sense, by doing this, the girls bring their dolls into their own worlds, and whiteness here is not absolutely defined by skin and hair, but by style and way of life. The complexities of racial references and racial politics have been much discussed in the case of black hair simulating the look of whiteness; what these girls are creating is quite the opposite: white hair that looks black" (315).

It is not that the girls didn't realize that their dolls were white; it is that through their imaginative and material work they were able to integrate the dolls into their own world. The overt physical characteristics of the dolls—skin color, facial features, hair—did not force the girls into treating the dolls in ways that obeyed the boundaries of racial difference. Their transformative play does not make the realities of poverty, discrimination, and racism disappear from the worlds in which they live, but Chin points out that "in making their white dolls live in black worlds, they . . . reconfigure the boundaries of race," and in so doing, "challenge the social construction not only of their own blackness, but of race itself as well" (318).

Societies contain the threat posed by play by defining it as "unserious," "untrue," "pretend," "make-believe," "unreal," and so forth (Handelman 1977, 189). Many political figures recognize that play can

FIGURE 7.2 Play enables this girl in Guider, Cameroon, to incorporate her European doll into the world she knows.

of reality "is relative to the goals that cultures and individuals create" (17). Reality is defined in terms of the goals toward which each player directs attention at any given time. In rock climbing, the goal is to find hand and toeholds in order to get to the top of the rock; it is to put one's body at risk rather than to *avoid* putting one's body at risk. In other words, people do not always submit to the rules of the paramount reality of ordinary life, which is their basic referential perspective.

Play allows us to recognize that no referential perspective is absolute. Play exists when there is an awareness of alternatives, "of two sets of goals and rules, one operating here and now, one that applies outside the given activity" (Csikszentmihalyi 1981, 19). Unless we are aware that we can act according to a set of rules that are different from those of our paramount reality, we cannot play. More important, without play there is no awareness of alternatives. Play demonstrates the openness in human experience. But openness in play is like openness in any other aspect of human life: It is ambiguous.

▼ DO PEOPLE PLAY BY THE RULES?

Sport is a kind of physical play that is constrained by rules: "a physically exertive activity that is aggressively competitive within constraints imposed by definitions and rules. A component of culture, it is ritually patterned, gamelike, and of varying amounts of play, work and leisure. In addition, sport can be viewed as having both athletic and nonathletic variations, *athletic* referring to those activities requiring the greater amount of physical exertion" (Blanchard and Cheska 1985, 60).

Play is only one component of sport. Sport can be work for the players and an investment for the owners of professional teams. It is also a form of personal and social identification for fans, who are invited into a make-believe world in which they may playfully identify with their heroes, rage at the opponents, imagine coaching the team, suffer, and rejoice. The play element in sport draws a frame around the activity. Conflict in games and sports is different from conflict in ordinary life. Competitors agree "to strive for an incompatible goal—only one

opponent can win—within the constraints of understood rules" (Lever 1983, 3). Conflict becomes the whole point of the activity rather than the means of settling a disagreement.

As with all forms of play, the relationships of means and ends in sport are altered. Sport is struggle for the sake of struggle. "Athletes and teams exist only to be rivals; that is the point of their relationship. In the world of sport, there should be no purpose beyond playing and winning. Unlike rivals in the real world, who have opposing political, economic, or social aims, sports competitors must be protected, not persuaded or eliminated" (4).

Culture and Sport

Indeed, sport is play, but it is embedded in the prevailing social order. "Even a sport that has been introduced from a foreign source is very quickly redefined and adjusted to fit the norms and values of tradition" (Blanchard and Cheska 1985, 55). Sports reflect the basic values of the cultural setting in which they are performed, and they are transformed when they are translated into a new cultural setting.

A striking example of how a sport can transform from one culture to another is found in the Trobriand Islands (see EthnoProfile 3.4: Trobriand Islanders). An English missionary introduced the sport of cricket to the Trobrianders in the very early years of the twentieth century. By the 1970s, in the more rural parts of the islands, it had become a different game. Played between two villages, it became a substitute for warfare and a way of establishing political alliances. If the hosts had 40 men ready to play and the visitors had 36, then there were 36 to a side instead of the "correct" 11. The game was always won by the home team—but not by too many runs because that would shame the visitors. War magic was employed to aid batsmen and bowlers. Teams had dances and chants for taking the field, leaving it, and celebrating outs. These dances and chants were used to comment on current events and became fertile ground

---

sport A physically exertive activity that is aggressively competitive within constraints imposed by definitions and rules. Sport is a component of culture that is ritually patterned, gamelike, and consists of varying amounts of play, work, and leisure.

for additional competition beyond that of the sporting event itself. The bat was redesigned for greater accuracy, and the entire activity was associated with the ceremonial exchange of food and other goods. Cricket, the sport of empire, was radically transformed.

From the perspective of some Trobrianders, in fact, their cricket was a way of taking the English colonizers' favorite game—a game that was supposed to teach Trobrianders how to become "civilized"— and using it to express their rejection of the colonial world. As one Trobriand leader says in the film *Trobriand Cricket* (1974), "we rubbished the white man's game; now it's our game."

Sport in the Nation-State

The full institutionalization of sport seems to have taken place in the nation-state and only fairly recently. The most important and universal feature of sport in the nation-state is that it helps complex modern societies cohere (Lever 1995, 3). In her study of soccer in Brazil, aptly titled *Soccer Madness*, Janet Lever argues that large-scale organized sport presents a mechanism for building political unity and allegiance to the nation (Figure 7.3) (see EthnoProfile 7.2: Brazil). "Sport's paradoxical ability to reinforce societal cleavages while transcending them makes soccer, Brazil's most popular sport, the perfect means of achieving a more perfect union between multiple groups . . . [by giving] dramatic expression to the strain between groups while affirming the solidarity of the whole" (5, 9).

In Brazil, there is at least one professional soccer team in every city. The larger cities have several teams, representing different social groups. In Rio de Janeiro, for example, separate teams tend to be supported by the old rich, the modern middle class, the poor, the blacks, the Portuguese, and a number of neighborhood communities. The teams come to represent these different groups in a concrete, visible fashion. Through these teams, separate groups maintain their identities. At the same time, the teams bring their opposing fans together through a shared enthusiasm for soccer. City and national championships similarly unify the socioeconomically and geographically diverse groups of Brazil.

For many Brazilians—indeed, for many people around the world—the experience of supporting a

FIGURE 7.3 In Brazil, soccer provides a mechanism for creating national unity or a sense of "Brazilianness" among fans. Here, the Brazilian national team, draped in Brazilian flags, celebrates its fifth World Cup championship in 2002.

soccer team may be their first and perhaps only experience of a loyalty beyond the local community. Unity is achieved by demonstrating that different teams, and the groups they represent, are in conflict only at one level. At a higher level, the fans of those teams are really united; for example, fans of all Rio teams support the team that goes on to represent Rio in the national championships. This process reaches a climax in international competition, as the supporters of the many local teams back the national team. At this highest level of integration, soccer provides a way of affirming one's "Brazilianness."

There is one important exception to the global mass culture of sport: It regularly separates women

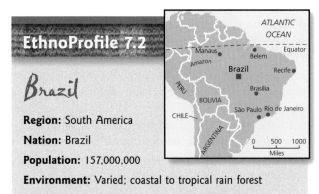

EthnoProfile 7.2

Brazil

Region: South America

Nation: Brazil

Population: 157,000,000

Environment: Varied; coastal to tropical rain forest

Livelihood: Industry, farming, mining, manufacturing, and so on

Political organization: Modern nation-state

For more information: Lever, Janet. 1983. *Soccer madness*. Chicago: University of Chicago Press.

from men. Soccer is incredibly important to Brazilian men and to many other men in the rest of the world, but it is much less important to women. The gender segregation of the sport has significant consequences for the experience of growing up male or female. It also affects relationships later in life between men and women who do not share the same experiences. There is a fundamental ambiguity in the relation of sports and integration: As sports join people together in one domain, they separate them in another. Sports can maintain and sharpen distinctions that are already significant in many other areas of a culture.

Sport as Metaphor

Why soccer? Why is it so important in Brazil and the rest of the world (outside the U.S.)? French anthropologist Christian Bromberger (1995) has written at length about soccer, based on field research in Marseille, France, and Naples and Turin in Italy. For Bromberger, soccer is fascinating because "it lays bare the major symbolic horizon of our societies: the course of a match, of a competition, resembles the uncertain fate of people in the contemporary world. Further, the combination of rules that mould the genre give this uncertainty an *acceptable* feel" (197). The outcome of a game, a tournament, even the ups and downs of a team over time can be metaphors for the fragility and the mobility of both individual and collective status.

The complexity and sudden changes of a single game or a tournament offer what Bromberger calls "a shortcut to the joys and dramas that make up a life" (197). A match or a championship season feature not only achievement on the basis of merit, but also uncertainties, introduced by strategy, luck, law and (in)justice in the form of the referee, trickery, and unfairness. It offers the fan the opportunity to compare players, to reflect, to plan, to strategize, and to be surprised. As one of Bromberger's informants put it, "At bottom, what most fascinates me is when a player chooses a solution which I had not thought of . . . and it works!" Remarks Bromberger, "The sprint or the high jump . . . don't offer the same material to reflect on" (199–200). And, as in life, the best team doesn't always win—we suspect that every soccer fan carries memories of amazing matches where a team that was outplayed for the entire game won anyway. These "Cinderella" stories, the uncertainties, the fluctuations, and the possible alternatives that the present offers, lie at the heart of a worldview that is, perhaps, uncomfortable to sports fans in the United States, who are more likely to be optimistic and less likely to embrace the quicksilver turns of fate and chance that characterize soccer.

Baseball and Masculinity in Cuba

As we have noted, sport is not just about the people who play; it is also about the spectators and their lives. Anthropologist Thomas Carter has studied baseball fans in Cuba. Baseball has been an important part of life, especially men's lives, in Cuba since the 1860s, and is now the leading sports activity in the country (see EthnoProfile 7.3: Cuba). Prior to Cuban independence, during Spanish colonial rule, baseball was banned because of its "revolutionary potential." The Spanish were not wrong: "To be a baseball fan in nineteenth-century Havana was to adopt a specific political position that asserted the modernity and independence of Cuba as a contrast to its colonial relationship with Spain" (Carter 2001, 122). This position was taken up again by the Fidel Castro government; indeed, Castro himself is a big fan. Today, there are 16 teams that play a 90-game season followed by a championship tournament, as well as a national team that represents

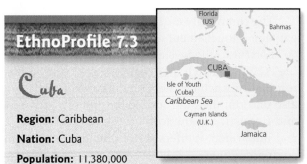

EthnoProfile 7.3

Cuba

Region: Caribbean

Nation: Cuba

Population: 11,380,000 (2006)

Environment: Large tropical island

Livelihood: Natural resource export, especially sugar; agriculture; tourism

Political organization: single-party nation-state

For more information: Carter, Thomas. 2008. *The Quality of Homeruns: Cuban Baseball, Identity and the State.* Duke University Press.

Cuba at international baseball tournaments (Cuba took second place at the World Baseball Classic in 2006).

Carter notes that to be a serious baseball fan in Cuba includes being willing and able to *discutir pelota*, to argue about baseball (Figure 7.4). Arguing implies opposition and confrontation, and confronta-

tion is a core aspect of Cuban masculinity (118). Who was the better player? Which was the better team? Which league division is the more demanding? By arguing baseball Cuban men embody and display the values of a Cuban male. These include "discipline (*disciplina*), struggle (*lucha*), and lucidity. Fans' assertive disagreements emphasize their masculinity, as evidenced by their willingness to argue and their ability to maintain self-control in the face of obvious antagonism" (118).

Carter goes on to talk about the daily *peña* in the Parque Central in Havana. In Cuban Spanish, a peña is a loose association of people, usually men, who regularly meet for a specific reason (124); in this case, this is a daily gathering of men—some regulars, some attending occasionally—in the middle of Havana's Central Park who come to argue about sports, especially baseball, both Cuban and the U.S. Major Leagues. The men are primarily urban middle class, and their reputations are built on their ability to memorize baseball knowledge, especially statistics, and the speed and accuracy with which that knowledge can be employed in rapid-fire argument (126). Women never participate in this peña, and very few women know how to (or care to) *discutir pelota*. Carter notes that in nine months of fieldwork in Cuba, he never once observed a woman approach a group of

FIGURE 7.4 Cuban men argue about baseball in Havana's Parque Central.

men involved in arguing baseball. One of his informants remarked:

> Women simply do not know anything about base-
> ball. They don't go to the stadium. They might if they
> know someone there personally, an athlete, security
> guard, or journalist who is a family member or boy-
> friend, for example. They might have *antes* ["before"
> indicating "before the Revolution"]. But even then,
> they do not grow with it. Their fathers, uncles, or
> brothers do not teach them. Besides, the language in
> a *peña* is rough, and it is not meant for a woman. It is
> not sincere [the insults] but it offends them [women].
> So, yes, the sports *peña* has only men, always (126).

Carter's point is that being able to argue about
baseball—to be a serious fan—is both to declare and
to display one's manliness. One is interested in a
male pursuit—baseball—one has the knowledge required to demonstrate that interest, and one has the
skill, self-control, and willingness to be confronta-
tional within recognized limits. But "they do not simply declare their masculinity, they demonstrate,
through their passion for baseball, that their masculinity is specifically Cuban" (136).

▼ ART

In Western societies, art includes sculpture, drawing,
painting, dance, theater, music, and literature, and
such similar processes and products as film, photog-
raphy, mime, mass media production, oral narrative,
festivals, and national celebrations. When anthropologists talk about art in non-Western societies, they begin by focusing on activities or products that resemble
art in the West. Whether non-Western peoples refer to
such activities or products as "art," the activities and
products themselves are universal. They seem rooted
in playful creativity, a birthright of all human beings.
And yet, like sport, those activities defined as "art"
differ from free play because they are circumscribed
by rules. Artistic rules direct particular attention to,
and provide standards for evaluating, the *form* of the
activities or objects that artists produce.

A Definition of Art

Anthropologist Alexander Alland defines **art** as "play
with form producing some aesthetically successful
transformation-representation" (1977, 39). For Al-

land, "form" refers to the rules of the art game: the
culturally appropriate restrictions on the way this
kind of play may be organized in time and space.

We can also think about form in terms of style
and media. A *style* is a schema (a distinctive patterning of elements) that is recognized within a culture
as appropriate to a given medium. The *media* in
which art is created and executed are culturally recognized and characterized (R. Anderson 1990, 272–
75). For example, a "painting" is a form: It is two-
dimensional; it is done with paint; it is intentionally
made; it represents or symbolizes something in the
world outside the canvas, paper, or wood on which it
is created. There are different kinds of paintings, as
well. There is the painting form called portrait—a
portrait depicts a person, it resembles the person in
some appropriate way, it is done with paint, it can be
displayed, and more.

By "aesthetic," Alland means appreciative of, or
responsive to, form in art or nature (xii). "Aesthetically successful" means that the creator of the piece of
art (and possibly its audience as well) experiences a
positive or negative response ("I like this," "I hate
this"). Indifference is the sign of something that is
aesthetically unsuccessful. It is probably the case that
the aesthetic response is a universal feature in all cultures and, as with play, may be part of the human
condition.

Aesthetic response is holistic, involving all our
faculties, including emotion, especially as these are
shaped by our social and cultural experience. V. N.
Voloshinov argued that aesthetic response to form in
a work of art is based largely on a culturally shaped
evaluation of the appropriateness of form to content.
He observed that artistic form allows both creator and
audience to exert agency: although "the form in and
of itself need not necessarily be pleasurable . . .
what it must be is a *convincing evaluation* of the content. So, for instance, while the form of 'the enemy'
might even be repulsive, the positive state, the pleasure that the contemplator derives in the end, is a consequence of the fact that the form is *appropriate to the
enemy* and that it is *technically perfect* in its realization"
([1926] 1987, 108). Evaluations of appropriateness

art Play with form producing some aesthetically successful
transformation-representation.

and of technical perfection clearly involve a broad range of intellectual, emotional, and moral judgments on the part of the viewer.

Aesthetic value judgments guide the artist's choice of form and material; they also guide the observers' evaluations. This implies that art involves more than just objects. Voloshinov argues that art is a creative "event of living communication" involving the work, the artist, and the artist's audience ([1926] 1987, 107). Artists create their works with an audience in mind, and audiences respond to these works as if the works were addressed to them. Sometimes the response is enthusiastic; sometimes it is highly critical. In either case, the aesthetic event does not leave its participants indifferent.

This view also suggests that aesthetic creation involves more than the end product, such as a painting or a poem. Art also includes the *process* through which some product is made. James Vaughan (1973, 186) points out, for example, that the Marghi of northeastern Nigeria do not appreciate a folktale as a story per se but rather enjoy the *performance* of it (see EthnoProfile 13.2: Marghi).

Transformation-Representation To understand the term **transformation-representation** in Alland's definition of art, we must recall that symbols represent something other than themselves. They are arbitrary in that they have no necessary connection with what they represent. This means that they can be cut away from the object or idea represented and appreciated for their own sake. They may also be used to represent a totally different meaning.

When a Javanese leather puppet maker makes a puppet of the great mythic hero Arjuna, he is representing the traditional form of the hero in his work, but he is also *transforming* a three-dimensional human form into a two-dimensional flat puppet made of buffalo hide, in which the colors, style, inclination of the head, and adornment stand for the internal state of the hero at a specific moment (Figure 7.5). At the same time, he is carrying out this work more or less skillfully and is embodying the meanings that

FIGURE 7.5 One of the great mythic heros of Javanese *wajang* is represented here in a beautifully painted flat leather shadow puppet. The color of the image, the angle of the head, the shape of the eye, the position of the fingers, and the style, color, and amount of clothing all represent the inner state of the hero.

Arjuna has for the Javanese in his work (see Ethno-Profile 5.1: Java).

Because transformation and representation depend on each other, Alland (1977, 35) suggests that they be referred to together (as *transformation-representation*). Transformation-representation is another way of talking about metaphor. A drawing, for example, is a metaphoric transformation of experience into visible marks on a two-dimensional surface. Similarly, a poem metaphorically transforms experience into concentrated and tightened language. This process is one place where the technical skill of the artist is involved.

transformation-representation The process in which experience is transformed as it is represented symbolically in a different medium.

"But Is It Art?"

Alland's definition of art attempts to capture something universal about human beings and their cultures. As Shelly Errington (1998, 84) observes, all human cultures have "'symbolic forms': artifacts, activities, or even aspects of the landscape that humans view as densely meaningful."

In the Western prototype of art, there is a distinction between art and nonart. Some paintings, songs, stories, carvings, dances, and the like are considered art; some are not. People who accept this perspective might argue, for example, that the *Mona Lisa* is art but paintings of Elvis Presley on black velvet are not. Why? Part of the answer may have to do with how successfully the artist has captured something that he or she considers to be important about Elvis and the culture to which both the artist and Elvis belong—that is, how aesthetically successful is the transformation-representation. But part of the answer also involves the high degree of specialization in Western societies, which has led to the emergence of an "art establishment" that includes critics, art historians, art teachers, journalists, schools, museums, and the like—as well as professional artists.

These people define what art is and what it is not, what are the appropriate styles, media, and forms. They distinguish between art and craft. That a painter may, in fact, have created an image of Elvis that is important and meaningful to the many people who have purchased the paintings—that it speaks to them both in style and medium—does not change the art establishment's opinion that the paintings are not art.

Thus, to them, Elvis on velvet is not art because it does not address problems in art theory, because it does not refer to the beautiful and the true, because it does not portray the artist's struggle to produce a new expressive style distinct from all other styles that have come before, or, indeed, because the artist seems ignorant or disdainful of the stylistic experimentation that makes up Western art history.

One dramatic example in the United States that demonstrates the power of art understood in this way is the Vietnam Veterans Memorial in Washington, DC (Figure 7.6). This work by architect Maya Lin has not only impressed the art critics but also continues to have a profound aesthetic and emotional impact on hundreds of thousands of people who visit it

each year. The memorial continues to draw offerings by visitors, not just wreaths or flowers but also messages of all kinds remembering those memorialized and even communicating with them. Letters from friends and families, a hand-lettered sign from a thirtieth high school reunion in a small Indiana town, tracings of names, intensely private grief, and respectful silence in its presence are all testimony to the success of this piece of art.

Nevertheless, many people—anthropologists included—have resisted the notion that art is only what a group of Western experts define as art. To highlight the ethnocentrism of Western art experts, they stressed that the division into categories of art and nonart is not universal. In many cultures, there is no category of art distinct from other human activities. On the other hand, convinced that all people were endowed with the same aesthetic capacities, anthropologists felt justified in speaking of art and of artists in non-Western societies. Their goal was to recognize a fully human capacity for art in all societies, but to redefine art until it became broad enough to include on an equal basis aesthetic products and activities that Western art experts would qualify, at best, as "primitive," "ethnic," or "folk" art.

For example, some anthropologists focused on the evaluative standards that artists use for their own work and other work in the same form, and how these may differ from the standards used by people who do not themselves perform such work. Anthony Forge, for example, notes that Abelam carvers in New Guinea discuss carvings in a language that is more incisive than that of noncarvers (Forge 1967). Other anthropologists pointed out that artists in traditional non-Western societies created objects or engaged in activities that presented and represented the central values of a culture. Thus, their work helped to maintain the social order, and they did not see themselves (nor were they understood to be) alienated critics of society as they are in modern Western societies.

"Primitive" and Ethnic Art

Recent work in the anthropology of art, however, has prompted many anthropologists to rethink this position. They have turned their attention to the way certain kinds of material objects made by tribal peoples flow into a global art market, where they are

FIGURE 7.6 The Vietnam Veterans Memorial is a powerfully affecting work of art that speaks directly to central issues in the culture of the United States.

transformed into "primitive" or "ethnic" art. Some anthropologists, like Shelly Errington, point out that even in the West most of the objects in fine arts museums today, no matter where they came from, were not intended by their makers to be "art." They were intended to be (for example) masks for ritual use, paintings for religious contemplation, reliquaries for holding the relics of saints, ancestor figures, furniture, jewelry boxes, architectural details, and so on. They are in fine arts museums today because at some point they were claimed to be art by someone with the authority to put them in the museum (Figure 7.7).

For these reasons, Errington distinguishes "art by intention" from "art by appropriation." Art by intention includes objects that were made to be art, such as Impressionist paintings. Art by appropria-

tion, however, consists of all the other objects that "became art" because at a certain moment certain people decided that they belonged to the category of art. Because museums, art dealers, and art collectors are found everywhere in the world today, so too it is now the case that potentially any material object crafted by human hands can be appropriated by these institutions as "art."

To transform an object into art, Errington argues, it must have *exhibition value*—someone must be willing to display it. Objects that somehow fit into the Western definition of art will be selected for the art market as "art." Looking at the collection of objects that over the years have been defined as "art," Errington sees that the vast majority show certain elements to be embedded rather deeply in the Western

FIGURE 7.7 Non-Western sculpture is transformed into art when it is displayed like Western art in a museum and viewed by a public that has the opportunity to look at it intensively (in this case, by then–French president Jacques Chirac).

definition of art: the objects are "portable (paintings, preferred to murals), durable (bronze preferred to basketry), useless for practical purposes in the secular West (ancestral effigies and Byzantine icons preferred to hoes and grain grinders), representational (human and animal figures preferred to, say, heavily decorated ritual bowls)" (1998, 116–17). In other words, for Errington, art requires that someone *intend* that the objects be art, but that someone does not have to be the object's creator.

She notes that "we humans are amazingly inventive, and we make and have always made things that we imbue with meaning, as befits creatures having both opposable thumbs and consciousness. Human artifacts are admirable. They are ingenious. They are dense with meaning. They are worthy of deep study" (1998, 103). But, she argues, they are not art until someone who carries around a particular definition of art says they are.

This is successful when the artifacts in question can be metaphorically transformed and represented as Western art objects. In their original contexts, most meaningful symbolic forms involve more than one sense: an audience hears drumming while looking at masked dancers as their own bodies respond to the dancers while feeling the warm breeze carrying the smells of palm oil and the shouts of children frightened by the dancers. But some of the sensory experiences—sounds, smells, tastes, muscular exertion, bodily response, and other sensations—that make richly symbolic performances do not last. As masks, audio recordings, and other objects are moved into the international art market, "they slough off their . . . performance contexts, . . . retaining only the durable part that can be set aside in a frame or on a pedestal" (Errington 1998, 84) or can be burned onto a CD and sold in the World Music section of a record store.

It can be fruitful to talk about art as a kind of play. Like play, art presents its creators and participants with alternative realities, a separation of means from ends, and the possibility of commenting on and transforming the everyday world. In today's global art market, however, restrictions of an entirely different order also apply. Shelly Errington observes that the people who make "primitive art" are no longer "tribal" but have become "modern-day peasants or a new type of proletariat. . . . They live in rain forests and deserts and other such formerly out-of-the-way places on the peripheries . . . within national and increasingly global systems of buying and selling, of using natural and human resources, and of marketing images and notions about products. Some lucky few of them make high ethnic art, and sell it for good prices, and obtain a good portion of the proceeds. Others make objects classed as tourist or folk art, usually for much less money, and often through a middleperson" (Errington 1998, 268). Others fulfill orders from elsewhere, "producing either masses of 'folk art' or expensive handmade items designed by people in touch with world taste and world markets" (269).

Errington points out the bitter irony that international demand for "exotic" objects is growing at the very moment when the makers of these objects are severely threatened by international economic policies and resource extraction projects that impoverish them and undermine the ways of life that give the objects they make their "exotic" allure. And, it should also be noted that what counts as fashionable decoration this year—"world taste"—may be out of fashion next year, leaving the producers with very little to fall back on.

"She's Fake": The Problem of the Authentic

Michelle Bigenho is an anthropologist and violinist whose multisited ethnography, mentioned in chapter 3, examines music performance in Bolivia, in part through her experiences performing with *Música de Maestros* (Figure 7.8). This ensemble has chosen to perform the works of master Bolivian composers and also attempts to recreate accurate performances of contemporary cultural originals that they have studied in the countryside (Bigenho 2002, 4). The ensemble was made up of both classically trained and traditionally trained musicians, as well as three foreigners: a Japanese who played the Andean flute, a Cuban who played violin, and Bigenho, from the United States, who also played violin. Along with a dance ensemble, the musicians were invited to represent Bolivia in a folklore festival in France. As the bands were lining up, a member of the Belgian delegation walked over to Bigenho and announced, in French, "She's fake." The Belgian woman then "pointed to one of the Bolivian dancers dressed in her dancing costume with her long fake braids worked into her short brown hair. As she pointed, she said, 'She's real'" (88).

In this way, Bigenho raises the question of "authenticity." What is real, when it comes to music, painting, sculpture, dance, or other "folk" art forms? How do the images that people in dominant nations have of "folk" or indigenous peoples affect the production and circulation of art? And, finally, who gets to decide what is authentic? To address these issues, Bigenho distinguishes three different forms of authenticity: experiential, cultural-historical, and unique. *Experiential authenticity* refers to "the entire sensory experience of music performances. . . . It is connected to a shared experience with others, a fleeting moment of the groove, a listener's great night at a concert" (17, 18).

Cultural-historical authenticity is connected to how music is represented: It makes a claim to a connection with the origin of the music, either in a historical or mythical past. The ensemble with which Bigenho played, *Música de Maestros*, explicitly sought to perform cultural and historically authentic renditions of Bolivian music. They performed music from the Chaco War (1932–35), as well as music from different regions and ethnic groups in Bolivia, and seemed to be quite successful in performing authentically in the

FIGURE 7.8 *Música de Maestros* in costume performing in a folklore festival in France.

different styles. (Similarly, Lynn Meisch [2002] notes that there is an ensemble in Italy that plays music from Otavalo, Ecuador, so authentically that Otavalos she knows refuse to believe that the musicians are not themselves Otavalos.) Bigenho points out that in terms of indigenous art, the power of the cultural and historical authenticity derives from the native's position in relation to the nation-state.

Unique authenticity is a term that Bigenho uses to refer to the creative activity of composing musicians. It is, as she puts it, "the founding myth of modern concepts of authorship and copyright" (20). Unique authenticity refers to the individual artist's new, innovative, and personal production. It raises the issue of who owns cultural products and whether it is possible to talk about collective creation and ownership of the music of a community, a people, an ethnic group. This is a particularly significant issue at the moment, as the politics and economics of culture raise questions about who owns experiences and representations.

Bigenho came face-to-face with this when she compiled a cassette of music from one of the villages in which she worked. She discussed with the villagers how to register the copyright on the cassette. While the villagers recognized that the music they played was composed by individuals, they felt strongly that ownership of the music was collective. In doing so, they moved from uniquely authentic individual compositions—intellectual property—to collective ownership of a "culturally authentic representation"—cultural property (217). When Bigenho went to La Paz to register the copyright, however, she found that it was impossible to register the cassette under collective authorship or ownership. In fact, *she* as the compiler could register the work, but not the people who created the work, unless they were willing to be recognized as individuals. What she discovered was that according to Bolivian law, the music on the cassette was legally folklore, "the set of literary and artistic works created in national territory by unknown authors or by authors who do not identify themselves and are presumed to be nationals of the country, or of its ethnic communities, and that are transmitted from generation to generation, constituting one of the fundamental elements of traditional cultural patrimony of the nation" (221). As a result, the music was part of the "National Patrimony," and belonged to the nation-state. But in the context of Bolivian cultural and ethnic politics, Bigenho observes,

the villagers gained visibility and connections as a collective indigenous entity, which they believed would provide them with possible economic advantages. Whether they were correct remains to be seen, but this example of the connections of art and authority is being repeated all over the world at present.

Hip-Hop in Japan

An opposite case—where global popular culture is subject to pressures from the local situation into which it is adopted—comes from anthropologist Ian Condry's work on Japanese hip-hop. Condry spent a year and a half, starting in mid-1995, studying hip-hop in Japan, which began there in the 1980s and continues to develop. It seems to be an example of the expansion of a popular culture form from the United States into another part of the world, but Condry shows how Japanese artists and fans have adapted hip-hop so that it is Japanese (Figure 7.9).

On the face of it, the Japanese hip-hop scene looks very similar to that of the United States: "It is more than a little eerie to fly from New York to Tokyo and see teenagers in both places wearing the same kinds of fashion characteristic of rap fans: baggy pants with boxers on display, floppy hats or baseball caps, and immaculate space-age Nike sneakers" (Condry 2001, 373). But the similarities disguise some important differences—most Japanese rappers and fans only speak Japanese, they live at home with their parents, and they are the products of the Japanese educational system. Their day-to-day world is Japanese.

Moreover, to understand hip-hop in Japan requires understanding where the rap scene in Japan is located. For Tokyo, this site (Condry uses the Japanese word *genba* for the "actual site") is the network of all-night clubs, where the show starts at midnight and ends at 5:00 A.M., when the trains start to run again. The largest of these clubs can accommodate over 1,000 people on the weekend. Condry describes one of the bigger clubs, called "Harlem":

> On the wall behind the DJ stage, abstract videos, *anime* clips, or edited Kung Fu movies present a background of violence and mayhem, albeit with an Asian flavor. Strobe lights, steam, and moving spotlights give a strong sense of the space, and compound the crowded, frenetic feeling imposed by the loud music. The drunken revelry gives clubs an atmosphere of excitement that culminates with the live show and the following freestyle session. (376–7)

But it is not only the music that matters. People circulate through the club, sometimes making contact, sometimes doing business (promoters, magazine writers, or record company representatives are also often there), just being part of the scene. Condry notes that he found that the time between 3:00 and 4:00 A.M. was best for his fieldwork because the clubbers had exhausted their supplies of stories and gossip and were open to finding out what he was up to.

One striking experience that Condry observed was of a concert right after the New Year. "I was surprised to see all the clubbers who knew each other going around and saying the traditional New Year's greeting in very formal Japanese: 'Congratulations on the dawn of the New Year. I humbly request your benevolence this year as well.' There was no irony, no joking atmosphere in these statements" (380). As he remarks, "Japanese cultural practices do not disappear" just because people seem to conform to the style of global hip-hop. In the same way, the topics addressed in the lyrics speak in some way to the concerns of the listeners, ridiculing school and television or celebrating video games and young men's verbal play. Most striking, perhaps, is the repeated theme that youth need to speak out for themselves. Rapper MC Shiro of Rhymester remarked, "If I were to say what hip-hop is, it would be a 'culture of the first person singular.' In hip-hop, . . . rappers are always yelling, 'I'm this'" (383). While this may not appear to be the edgy, tough lyrics of U.S. rap, in the Japanese context, where the dominant ideology is that the harmony of the group should come before individual expression, the idea that people should speak for themselves is powerful. As we will see in chapter 14, this process of localizing the global is one that many anthropologists have been interested in studying.

Sculpture and the Baule Gbagba Dance

The Baule of the Ivory Coast are renowned for their sculpture. Susan Vogel (1997), who has been studying Baule sculpture for over thirty years, identifies four forms of Baule sculpture, which she refers to as art that is watched (performances featuring carved masks), art that is seen without looking (sacred sculpture), art that is glimpsed (private sculptures of personal figures for hunting and sculpture for spirit spouses), and art that is visible to all (the profane; everyday objects that Baule see as beautiful trifles). As we saw in the last chapter, Baule visuality is distinctive; people learn to look in a way different from that of people in the West—"the more important a Baule sculpture is, the less it is displayed" (108). The Western concept of "art" in the sense that it is used in Western languages does not exist in Baule villages. Rather, "to approach art from a Baule perspective entails speaking of experiences that are not primarily visual, and of art objects that are animate presences, indistinguishable from persons, spirits, and certain prosaic things." The Baule attribute great powers to their

FIGURE 7.9 A Japanese hip-hop singer performs at 3:30 A.M. at Club Core in Tokyo's Roppongi entertainment district. While the hip-hop scene in Japan may look similar to that in the United States, Ian Condry directs attention to some significant differences.

artwork—powers that Westerners would consider incredible. The meaning of most art objects, and the emotional responses that these objects have, derive from their ability to act. For the Baule, what Western museum-goers call sculpture contain enormous powers of life and death, and Baule people do not consider their sculpture apart from these powers (85).

We will consider one use of art objects in performance, the Gbagba dance. While anthropologists have often studied dance as an independent art form (see below), we are looking here at the intersection of sculpture and dance. The Gbagba dance is an entertainment performance that lasts much of a day, and may also be performed for the funeral of an important woman. The style of mask that is used in the performance is called *Mblo*, and in the past, a village may have had as many as a dozen or more such masks, some representations of animals, some portraits of people. Portrait masks are usually of a specific woman, and the subject of the portrait always dances alongside the male dancer who dances the mask. Only the best dancers wear these masks, and they appear at the very end of the dance, sometimes right at dusk.

The Gbagba begins with skits that include non-masked performers, young dancers who are just getting started. The skits are supposed to be funny as they present scenes from everyday life from which a moral is drawn. These skits often feature masks of domestic animals—generally sheep and goats. These are followed by masks representing the large wild animals that the Baule hunt. These skits always end with the successful "killing" of the masked animal. Older, more skilled dancers are featured in these skits and there is more actual dancing.

At the same time that the first masks appear, so too does a costumed but not masked figure of a trickster figure, Ambomon, who wears a cloth hood rather than a mask and who dances in a rapid and acrobatic way, including somersaults and tumbling in his movements. Ambomon is a completely ambiguous figure, even to the Baule, who speculate as to whether or not he is a god. He has no respect for possessions, rank, and decent behavior. While comical, he also takes things from people, he sits on the ground, he gets things dirty. He never does any real damage, and people regard him as an amusing nuisance. He stands in direct contrast to the orderly vision of the world, as expressed by the masks; he is the sprit of disorder. Yet at the same time, Ambomon is the only figure in the dance that *must* appear—he can appear without any of the other masks, but the other masks cannot appear without him. When Gbagba is danced for a funeral, only Ambomon enters the courtyard to pay his respects to the deceased and to greet the mourners. Vogel suggests that the obligatory presence of Ambomon suggests that to the Baule the only certainty in life is the threat of disorder and death (167).

Vogel notes that Ambomon's style of dance is quite different from the ideal Baule dance style, which seems to minimize movement. She notes that a female solo dance moves forward very slowly in a curved line, with body and neck held upright, the hands in front, palms up. Sometimes the dancer carries something in her hand. The dancer's facial features are impassive, the eyes are downcast, and the main movement is in the neck, shoulders, and back, often marking two different rhythmic patterns in the polyrhythmic music. A male dancer may be a bit more vigorous, but "Baule dancing in general can be characterized as symmetrically balanced and essentially vertical (the dancer's knees may be flexed but the head and torso are held upright). As in so many other Baule creations, the dancer's body is closed in outline. These qualities are also characteristic of Baule sculpture, and must be recognized as expressing an aesthetic preference, with moral connotations, that is deeply embedded in Baule culture, and is expressed in myriad ways" (156).

Gbagba includes singing, and two of the songs that are repeated from time to time throughout the day refer to death. They are sung both when Gbagba is danced for women's funerals and when it is danced for entertainment. Finally, at the end of the day one or more portrait masks appear, one by one, each accompanied by its human "double." At that moment, the finest skills in the community are on display—the best dancers, the most beautiful masks, the best drummers and singers, and the distinguished women who are represented now take their places (see Figure 7.10).

The term "double" is the term that the Baule themselves use for the portrait mask and its subject. The portrait mask is considered the person's true double; the mask never performs unless the person is there to dance. Vogel tells us that the "relationships between individuals and their portrait masks are close, complex, and lifelong, and become elements of their identities" (166). When the subject of a portrait mask dies or cannot dance any more, a relative becomes the new double, or the mask is never danced again.

In sum, Vogel proposes that a Gbagba performance is a joyous occasion that brings together everyone in the village, of all ages and persuasions, in a happy celebration, the importance of which cannot be underestimated in a world with little entertainment or distractions.

> The performance teaches basic lessons about the Baule world—about hierarchies and mysteries. Each skit has a simple moral lesson, evident even to children: that humans, for example, with skill and supernatural aid, can dominate even the largest and most awesome wild animals, while the portrait masks present a model of human accomplishment and beauty. At the same time, the dance provides deeper insights about blurred boundaries—about the interpenetration of bush and village, and the complexity of gender. The subject of a portrait, most often a woman, sees herself impersonated by a man dancing "like a woman" and wearing a mask that is her double or namesake. A frequent theme of Baule art is opposite-sex doubling, meaning that two figures appear not as a pair of complementary beings but as manifestations of a single being having qualities of both sexes. The concept is too troubling to articulate openly in words, but in Gbagba it is available to wordless contemplation. (Vogel 1997, 167–68)

Dance and Gender in Northern Greece

Jane Cowan has explored how dance may play a role in the social construction of gender in northern Greece (see EthnoProfile 7.4: Sohos). She considers three different kinds of dance-events in the town of Sohos: the wedding dance, the formal evening dance, and a private dance at a home. At each dance-event, individuals present themselves publicly by eating, drinking, and talking as well as dancing, and other people at the event evaluate them. Men and women, however, do not present themselves in the same way, nor are they evaluated in the same way. They perform and experience themselves as gendered subjects— that is, as males or females, as these are defined in Sohos. "In dance-events associated with pleasure, sensual intensity, and public sociability, gender inequalities and other social hierarchies are constituted and even celebrated" (1990, 4).

Contrasting, culturally specific images of male and female sexuality in northern Greece are given a particular public form in the dance. From the perspective of women in northern Greece, dances are places where they can "escape" and "forget" their relatively restricted everyday lives. Everyone at the dance—men and women alike—encourages them to do this in order to be good, carefree celebrants. But dance presents problems for women: They are keenly aware that they are being watched, that they not

FIGURE 7.10 Portrait mask of Mya Yanso about to enter the Gbagba dance in the Baule village of Kami in 1972. The mask—an important object—is hidden by the cloths until the last moment, when the mask, its dancer, and its subject will appear dramatically in the performance.

IN THEIR OWN WORDS — Tango

Anthropologist Julie Taylor describes the traditional cultural understandings that inform the contexts in which the Argentine tanguero, or tango-man, dances the tango.

Traditionally, Argentines will not dance to a tango that is sung. If they danced they could not attend properly to the music and lyrics, or hear their own experience and identity revealed in the singer's and musicians' rendering of quintessential Argentine emotions. The singer of the tango shares his personal encounter with experiences common to them all. He does not need bold pronouncement or flamboyant gesture. His audience knows what he means and his feelings are familiar ones. They listen for the nuances—emotional and philosophical subtleties that will tell them something new about their guarded interior worlds.

When they dance to tangos, Argentines contemplate themes akin to those of tango lyrics, stimulating emotions that, despite an apparently contradictory choreography, are the same as those behind the songs. The choreography also reflects the world of the lyrics, but indirectly. The dance portrays an encounter between the powerful and completely dominant male and the passive, docile, completely submissive female. The passive woman and the rigidly controlled but physically aggressive man contrast poignantly with the roles of the sexes depicted in the tango lyrics. This contrast between two statements of relations between the sexes aptly mirrors the insecurities of life and identity.

An Argentine philosophy of bitterness, resentment, and pessimism has the same goal as a danced statement of machismo, confidence, and sexual optimism. The philosopher elaborates his schemes to demonstrate that he is a man of the world—that he is neither stupid nor naive. In the dance, the dancer acts as though he has none of the fears he cannot show—again proving that he is not

gil. When an Argentine talks of the way he feels when dancing a tango, he describes an experience of total aggressive dominance over the girl, the situation, the world—an experience in which he vents his resentment and expresses his bitterness against a destiny that denied him this dominance. Beyond this, it gives him a moment behind the protection of this facade to ponder the history and the land that have formed him, the hopes he has treasured and lost. Sábato echoes widespread feeling in Argentina when he says "Only a gringo would make a clown of himself by taking advantage of a tango for a chat or amusement."

While thus dancing a statement of invulnerability, the somber tanguero sees himself, because of his sensitivity, his great capacity to love, and his fidelity to the true ideals of his childhood years, as basically vulnerable. As he protects himself with a facade of steps that demonstrate perfect control, he contemplates his absolute lack of control in the face of history and destiny. The nature of the world has doomed him to disillusionment, to a solitary existence in the face of the impossibility of perfect love and the intimacy this implies. If by chance the girl with whom he dances feels the same sadness, remembering similar disillusion, the partners do not dance sharing the sentiment. They dance together to relive their disillusion alone. In a Buenos Aires dance hall, a young man turned to me from the fiancee he had just relinquished to her chaperoning mother and explained, "In the tango, together with the girl—and it does not matter who she is—a man remembers the bitter moments of his life, and he, she, and all who are dancing contemplate a universal emotion. I do not like the woman to talk to me while I dance tango. And if she speaks I do not answer. Only when she says to me, 'Omar, I am speaking,' I answer, 'And I, I am dancing.'"

Source: Taylor 1987, 484–85.

EthnoProfile 7.4

Sohos

Region: Europe

Nation: Greece

Population: 3,500

Environment: Rugged mountainside

Livelihood: Farming, commerce

Political organization: Commercial and administrative center within a modern nation-state

For more information: Cowan, Jane K. 1990. *Dance and the body politic in northern Greece.* Princeton: Princeton University Press.

only act but also are acted upon. So women know they must control themselves emotionally and physically. The limits of appropriate bodily expression are learned early in life and continue to be internalized throughout life. A woman's expressions of "letting go" may be at the boundaries of those limits but rarely overstep them in any fundamental way (Cowan 1990, 228).

Dance provides a place where northern Greek women play with the boundaries of "good" and "bad" female sexuality. Should she take the first position in a circle dance, or is that too forward? How intense should her *tsifte teli* (belly dance) be? Should she move closer to her partner, lean toward him, and playfully shimmy her shoulders? When a man dances an intense tsifte teli, should she break plates at his feet, a conventional statement of deep understanding of and empathy with the dancer's inner state? "In this dance space, ambivalent attitudes toward female sexuality are juxtaposed. Girls and women are not necessarily expected to mute or hide their sexuality. Flirtation, energy, the display of beauty, even subtle seduction are acknowledged and valued aspects of female performance in these events" (Cowan 1990, 228).

But there is always a potential problem: A female who is thought to lack control in these displays can be censured. "A female celebrant's experience of the dance, then, is rooted in her position in gender relations, but it is not only men who keep her 'in her place.' Women do, as well. Only when she believes that everybody is truly 'all together' can the female celebrant really feel free to let go; for girls, everybody being 'all together' is both the precondition for and the expression of collective *kefi* [high spirits]" (229).

The Mass Media: A Television Serial in Egypt

The mass media now include everything from film, radio, and television to comic books and the World Wide Web. As a result of global processes (Chapter 14), these are now central to people's lives all over the world. Anthropologists can study the mass media from a variety of perspectives. Our approach in this chapter is to consider mass media as cultural productions. We highlight the creativity of producers and consumers of media in the interpretation and incorporation of these art forms. This is, perhaps, the most important thing anthropology can add to the study of media: the fine-grained ethnographic assessment of the effects and impact of popular media among the people who watch, listen, read, and interpret (cf. Herzfeld 2001, 298), and some of whom also create those media.

In many nations in the world, soap operas or television serials are among the most popular mass entertainments, watched by millions. These programs are seen by their creators in some parts of the world not simply as entertainment, but also as tools useful for teaching certain people in their societies what they need to learn to be modern citizens. But what the intended audience gets from the program is not always the message the creators thought they were transmitting. Anthropologist Lila Abu-Lughod studied an Egyptian television serial called *Hilmiyya Nights* that was broadcast during Ramadan (the Islamic holy month) over five successful years. The serial followed the fortunes and relationships of a group of characters from the traditional Cairo neighborhood of Hilmiyya, taking them from the late 1940s, when Egypt was under the rule of King Farouk and the British, up to the early 1990s, even incorporating Egyptian reaction to the first Gulf War.

The central action revolved around the rivalry, financial wheeling-dealing, and love interests of two wealthy men—in many ways it resembles an Egyptian version of *Dallas*. What separated *Hilmiyya Nights* from prime-time serials from the United States, however, was that the Egyptian program attempted to tie the lives of its characters to Egyptian national political events. Above all, it promoted the theme of national unity. With few exceptions, all the characters were shown to be basically good and patriotic.

Abu-Lughod studied two separate groups of Egyptians during the 1990s—poor working-class women in Cairo and villagers in Upper Egypt (see EthnoProfile 6.6: Cairo). When she asked poor women in Cairo what they liked about the show, they volunteered not the serious political or social messages but two women characters: the glamorous, aristocratic femme fatale and the arrogant belly-dancer turned cabaret-owner. Although these two characters were hardly respectable and ended badly, these were nevertheless favorites because they defied the moral system that kept good women quiet. Indeed, Abu-Lughod found that both the urban women and the villagers accepted the moral stances presented in the program only when they resonated with their own worlds and ignored those aspects of the serial that were not part of their experience.

Most interestingly, she argues that television, especially for the villagers, created its own world, one that was part of, but only a small part of, the villagers' daily lives. "What they experienced through television added to, but did not displace, whatever else already existed. They treated the television world not as a fantasy escape but as a sphere unto itself with its familiar time slots and specific attitudes" (Abu-Lughod 1995, 203–4). Moreover, the villagers did not compartmentalize the "modernity" that television serials present in order to preserve a "traditional" community untouched by the outside world. On the contrary, these villagers are deeply affected in a wide variety of ways by the outside world, whether through local government policies or transnationally through the effect of advertising by multinational corporations. "Television is, in this village, one part of a complex jumble of life and the dramatic experiences and visions it offers are surprisingly easily incorporated as discrete—not overwhelming—elements in the jumble" (205).

Television in Egypt, she notes, has had measurable social effects: For example, families prefer to stay home to watch television rather than visit among households in the evenings. Television may also have increased the number of "experiences" shared across generation and gender, as young and old, men and women, now spend time together watching the television.

The intended impact of *Hilmiyya Nights* was not undermined because nobody was watching television: Both villagers and urban poor had their sets on almost constantly. Rather, the positive messages that the creators of *Hilmiyya Nights* and similar serials intended got lost because they are only part of the complex flow of programming in Egypt, which includes many kinds of other information, news, entertainment, advertising, and so on.

More important, all these messages are evaluated in terms of the life experiences of the viewers. Hence they are often neutralized or contradicted by the powerful everyday realities within which poor Egyptian villagers and urban women move. Even soap operas are contested sites, open for multiple interpretations, not simply places for the transmission of messages from the elite to the masses.

▼ MYTH

We have suggested that play lies at the heart of human creativity. However, the openness of play is random and thus just as likely to undermine the social order as to enhance it. Hence societies tend to circumscribe play with cultural rules, channeling it in directions that appear less destructive.

Rules designed to limit artistic expression are one result of this channeling process. As we have seen, artists in various media are permitted a wide range of expression as long as they adhere to rules governing the form that expression takes. Societies differ in how loose or strict the rules of artistic form may be. Artists who challenge the rules, however, are often viewed negatively by those in power, who believe they have the right to restrict artistic expressions that question social, religious, or sexual precepts that ought not to be questioned.

In fact, all societies depend on the willingness of their members *not* to question certain assumptions about the way the world works. Because the regularity and predictability of social life might collapse altogether if people were free to imagine, and act upon, alternatives to the local version of paramount reality, most societies find ways to persuade their members that the local version of reality is the only reality, period. The most venerable way of doing this is through the use of myth.

Myth as Orthodoxy

Myths are stories whose truth seems self-evident because they do such a good job of integrating personal experiences with a wider set of assumptions about the way society, or the world in general, must operate.

A conventional definition of myth emphasizes that they are stories about the sacred, as that is defined among a particular group of people. Often these are stories about beginnings—of the natural world, the social world, or the cosmos—or of endings—of time, humanity, the gods, or the cosmos. The term may also be used to refer to "ahistorical stories that are used to validate power relationships, which make the social appear natural and preexistent" (Bowie 2006, 267). As stories that involve a teller and an audience, myths are performances, products of high verbal art (and increasingly of cinematic art). Frequently the official myth tellers are the ruling groups in society: the elders, the political leaders, the religious specialists. They may also be considered master storytellers. The content of myths usually concerns past events (usually at the beginning of time) or future events (usually at the end of time). Myths are socially important because, if they are taken literally, they tell people where they have come from and where they are going and, thus, how they should live right now (Figure 7.11).

Societies differ in the degree to which they permit speculation about key myths. In complex Western societies, like that of the United States, many different groups, each with its own mythic tradition, often live side by side. Because the United States government permits freedom of conscience in such matters, it regularly prohibits one group from silencing an opposing group. But this does not mean that the United States is without myths. Consider the U.S. Declaration of Independence and its "self-evident" truths: "that all men are created equal, that they are endowed by their Creator with certain inalienable rights, that among these rights are life, liberty, and the pursuit of happiness." It is precisely in order to defend these self-evident truths that the government refuses to compromise its citizens' freedom of expression.

---

myths Stories whose truth seems self-evident because they do such a good job of integrating our personal experiences with a wider set of assumptions about the way society, or the world in general, must operate.

orthodoxy "Correct doctrine"; the prohibition of deviation from approved mythic texts.

Myths and related beliefs that are taken to be self-evident truths are sometimes codified in an explicit manner. When this codification is extreme and deviation from the code is treated harshly, we sometimes speak of **orthodoxy** (or "correct doctrine"). Societies differ in the degree to which they require members to adhere to orthodox interpretations of key myths. But even societies that place little emphasis on orthodoxy are likely to exert some control over the interpretation of key myths, because myths have implications for action. They may justify past action, explain present action, or generate future action. To be persuasive, myths must offer plausible explanations for our experience of human nature, human society, and human history. The power of myths comes from their ability to make life meaningful for those who accept them.

The success of Western science has led many members of Western societies to dismiss nonscientific myths as flawed attempts at science or history. Only recently have some scientists come to recognize the similarities between scientific and nonscientific storytelling about such events as the origin of life on earth. Scientific stories about origins—*origin myths*—must be taken to the *natural* world to be matched against material evidence; the success of this match determines whether they are accepted or rejected. By contrast, nonscientific origin myths get their vitality from how well they match up with the *social* world.

Myth as a Charter for Social Action

Early in the twentieth century, anthropologist Bronislaw Malinowski introduced a new approach to myth. He believed that to understand myths, we must understand the social context in which they are embedded. Malinowski argued that myths serve as "charters" or "justifications" for present-day social arrangements. In other words, a myth operates much like the Declaration of Independence. That is, the myth contains some "self-evident" truth that explains why society is as it is and why it cannot be changed. If the social arrangements justified by the myth are challenged, the myth can be used as a weapon against the challengers.

Malinowski's famous example is of the origin myths of the Trobriand Islanders ([1926] 1948; see EthnoProfile 3.4: Trobriand Islanders). Members of every significant kinship grouping know, mark, and retell the history of the place from which their group's ancestress and her brother emerged from the depths

FIGURE 7.11 A vase painting illustrating part of the *Popul Vuh*, the Mayan creation story.

of the earth. These origin myths are set in the time before history began. Each ancestress-and-brother pair brought a distinct set of characteristics that included special objects and knowledge, various skills, crafts, spells, and the like. On reaching the surface, the pair took possession of the land. That is why today the people on a given piece of land have rights to it. It is also why they possess a particular set of spells, skills, and crafts. Because the original sacred beings were a woman and her brother, the origin myth can also be used to endorse present-day social arrangements. Membership in a Trobriand clan depends on a person's ability to trace kinship links through women to that clan's original ancestress. A brother and a sister represent the prototypical members of a clan because they are both descended from the ancestress through female links. Should anyone question the wisdom of organizing society in this way, the myth can be cited as proof that this is indeed the correct way to live.

In Trobriand society, clans are ranked relative to one another in terms of prestige. To account for this ranking, Trobrianders refer to another myth. In the Trobriand myth that explains rank, one clan's ancestor, the dog, emerged from the earth before another clan's ancestor, the pig, thus justifying ranking the dog clan highest in prestige. To believe in this myth, Malinowski asserted, is to accept a transcendent justification for the ranking of clans. Malinowski made it clear, however, that if social arrangements change, the myth changes too—in order to justify the new arrangements. At some point, the dog clan was replaced in prominence by the pig clan. This social change resulted in a change in the

mythic narrative. The dog was said to have eaten food that was taboo. In so doing, the dog gave up its claim to higher rank. Thus, to understand a myth and its transformations, one must understand the social organization of the society that makes use of it.

Myth as a Conceptual Tool

Beginning in the mid-1950s, a series of books and articles by the French anthropologist Claude Lévi-Strauss ([1962] 1967) transformed the study of myth. Lévi-Strauss argues that myths have meaningful structures that are worth studying in their own right, quite apart from the uses to which the myths may be put. He suggested that myths should be interpreted the way we interpret musical scores. In a piece of music, the meaning emerges not just from the melody but also from the harmony. In other words, the structure of the piece of music, the way in which each line of the music contributes to the overall sound and is related to other lines carries the meaning.

For Lévi-Strauss, myths are tools for overcoming logical contradictions that cannot otherwise be overcome. They are put together in an attempt to deal with the oppositions of particular concern to a particular society at a particular moment in time. Using a linguistic metaphor, Lévi-Strauss argues that myths are composed of smaller units—phrases, sentences, words, relationships—that are arranged in ways that give both narrative (or "melodic") coherence and structural (or "harmonic") coherence. These arrangements represent and comment upon aspects of social life that are thought to oppose each other. Examples include the opposition of men to women; opposing rules of residence after marriage (living with the groom's father or the bride's mother); the opposition of the natural world to the cultural world, of life to death, of spirit to body, of high to low, and so on.

The complex syntax of myth works to relate those opposed pairs to one another in an attempt to overcome their contradictions. However, these contradictions can never be overcome; for example, the opposition of death to life is incapable of any earthly resolution. But myth can transform an insoluble problem into a more accessible, concrete form. Mythic narrative can then provide the concrete problem with a solution. For example, a culture hero may bridge the opposition between death and life by traveling from the land of the living to the land of the dead and back. Alternatively, a myth might propose that the beings who transcend death are so horrific that death is clearly preferable to eternal life. Perhaps a myth describes the journey of a bird that travels from the earth, the home of the living, to the sky, the home of the dead. This is similar to Christian thought, where the death and resurrection of Jesus may be understood to resolve the opposition between death and life by transcending death.

From this point of view, myths do not just talk about the world as it is, but they also describe the world as it might be. To paraphrase Lévi-Strauss, myths are good to think with; mythic thinking can propose other ways to live our lives. Lévi-Strauss insists, however, that the alternatives myths propose are ordinarily rejected as impossible. Thus, even though myths allow for play with self-evident truths, this play remains under strict control.

Is Lévi-Strauss correct? There has been a great deal of debate on this issue since the publication in 1955 of his article "The Structural Study of Myth" (see Lévi-Strauss [1962] 1967). But even those who are most critical of his analyses of particular myths agree that mythic structures are meaningful because they display the ability of human beings to play with possibilities as they attempt to deal with basic contradictions at the heart of human experience.

ritual A repetitive social practice composed of a sequence of symbolic activities in the form of dance, song, speech, gestures, or the manipulation of objects, adhering to a culturally defined ritual schema, and closely connected to a specific set of ideas that are often encoded in myth.

For Malinowski, Lévi-Strauss, and their followers, those who believe in myths are not conscious of how their myths are structured or of the functions their myths perform for them. More recent anthropological thinking takes a more reflexive approach. This research recognizes that ordinary members of a society often *are* aware of how their myths structure meaning, allowing them to manipulate the way myths are told or interpreted in order to make an effect, to prove a point, or to buttress a particular referential perspective on human nature, society, or history.

▼ RITUAL

Play allows unlimited consideration of alternative referential perspectives on reality. Art permits consideration of alternative perspectives, but certain limitations restricting the form and content are imposed. Myth aims to narrow radically the possible referential perspectives and often promotes a single, orthodox perspective presumed to be valid for everyone. It thus offers a kind of intellectual indoctrination, although this indoctrination may be contested within the society. But because societies aim to shape action as well as thought to orient all human faculties in the approved direction, art, myth, and ritual are often closely associated with one another.

A Definition of Ritual

Our definition of **ritual** has four elements. First, ritual is a *repetitive social practice* composed of a sequence of symbolic activities in the form of dance, song, speech, gestures, the manipulation of certain objects, and so forth. Second, it is *set off* from the social routines of everyday life. Third, rituals in any culture adhere to a characteristic, culturally defined *ritual schema*. This means that members of a culture can tell that a certain sequence of activities is a ritual even if they have never seen that particular ritual before. Finally, ritual action is closely connected to a specific set of ideas that are often *encoded in myth*. These ideas might concern the nature of evil, the relationship of human beings to the spirit world, how people ought to interact with one another, and so forth. The purpose for which a ritual is performed guides how these ideas are selected and symbolically enacted. What gives rituals their power is that the people who perform the rituals assert that the authorization for the ritual comes from outside themselves—from the state, society, God, the ancestors, or "tradition." They have not made up the ritual themselves (although they may have contributed to it, as when people create their own wedding vows); rather it connects them to a source of power that they do not control but that controls them.

The Western prototype of ritual includes the notion that it is "religious." However, in anthropological terms, ritual includes a much broader range of activities. According to the definition given in the preceding paragraph, a college graduation ceremony, procedures in a court of law, and a child's birthday party are rituals just as much as weddings, Jewish bar mitzvahs, Hmong sacrifices to the ancestors, and the Catholic Mass.

A Birthday Party as Ritual

Consider a young child's birthday party in the United States. Several children are formally invited to help celebrate the birthday. Each arrives bringing a wrapped gift, which is handed to the birthday child and then set aside. The children often put on birthday hats. They then play group games of some kind, some of which are now *only* played at birthday parties. The games culminate in the appearance of a birthday cake, illuminated by candles (one for each year of the child's life) and accompanied by the singing of "Happy Birthday." The birthday child makes a wish and blows out the candles. Following the cake and ice cream, the birthday child opens the presents. There is much commotion as the guests urge the birthday child to open theirs first. As the birthday child opens each gift, he or she examines it and thanks the guest (often with an adult's prompting). Shortly after the presents are opened, the guests' parents or guardians appear and the guests receive party favors and leave.

The ritual order of these events matters. The central events of the party—the giving of gifts; the events associated with the cake, candles, the wish, and the singing of "Happy Birthday"; and the opening of the gifts—must occur in that order. Additionally, if you, the reader, come from a tradition in which birthday parties are celebrated, it is likely that you cannot remember *learning* how to celebrate a birthday party—it is something you have always known. It's what everyone does. It's just how it is. Its authority comes from "tradition."

In the birthday party, children (both hosts and guests) learn to associate receiving gifts with important moments in life. They discover the importance of exchanging material objects in defining significant social relations. They learn to defer gratification (the presents cannot be opened immediately). They live out patterns of sociability and friendship (as anyone knows who has heard the ultimate preschool threat, "I'm not inviting you to my birthday party") while recognizing the centrality of the individual (there are few things worse than sharing your birthday party with someone else!). Finally, the children participate in patterns of sharing, of celebrating the self, and of recognizing relationships with friends and kin that are important in other areas of American life.

Ritual as Action

A ritual has a particular sequential ordering of acts, utterance, and events: That is, ritual has a *text*. Because ritual is action, however, we must pay attention to the way the ritual text is performed. The *performance* of a ritual cannot be separated from its text; text and performance shape each other dialectically. Through ritual performance, the ideas of a culture become concrete, take on a form, and, as Bruce Kapferer (1983) puts it, give direction to the gaze of participants. At the same time, ritual performance can serve as a commentary on the text to the extent of transforming it.

For example, Jewish synagogue ritual following the reading of Torah (the Five Books of Moses, the Hebrew Bible) includes lifting the Torah scroll, showing it to the congregation, and then closing it and covering it. In some Conservative synagogues, a man and a woman, often a couple, are called to lift and cover the Torah: The man lifts it and, after he seats himself, the woman rolls the scroll closed, places the tie around it, and covers it with the mantle that protects it. One of the authors (RHL) once observed a performance of this ritual in which the woman lifted the Torah and the man wrapped it; officially, the ritual text was carried out, but the performance became a commentary on the text—on the role of women in Judaism, on the Torah as an appropriate subject of attention for women as well as for men, on the roles of men and women overall, and so on. The performance was noteworthy and surprised many of the regular members of the congregation. Indeed, in Orthodox Jewish congregations, such a performance would never be allowed. However,

IN THEIR OWN WORDS

Video in the Villages

Patricia Aufderheide describes how indigenous peoples of the Amazonian rain forest in Brazil have been able to master the video camera and use it for their own purposes.

The social role and impact of video is particularly intriguing among people who are new to mass-communications technologies, such as lowlands Amazonian Indians. One anthropologist has argued persuasively that a naive disdain for commercial media infuses much well-meaning concern over the potential dangers of introducing mass media and that "indigenous media offers a possible means—social, cultural, and political—for reproducing and transforming cultural identity among people who have experienced massive political, geographic, and economic disruption." . . . In two groups of Brazilian Indians, the Nambikwara and the Kayapo, this premise has been tested.

The Nambikwara became involved with video through Video in the Villages, run by Vincent Carelli at the Centro de Trabalho Indigenista in São Paulo. This project is one example of a trend to put media in the hands of people who have long been the subjects of ethnographic film and video. . . . While some anthropologists see this resort as a "solution" to the issue of ethnographic authority, others have focused on it as part of a struggle for indigenous rights and political autonomy. . . . Many of the groups Carelli has worked with have seized on video for its ability to extensively document lengthy rituals that mark the group's cultural uniqueness rather than produce a finished product. . . .

Carelli coproduced a project with a Nambikwara leader, documenting a cultural ritual. After taping, the Nambikwara viewed the ritual and offered criticisms, finding it tainted with modernisms. They then repeated the ritual in traditional regalia and conducted, for the first time in a generation, a male initiation ceremony—taping it all. (This experience is recounted in a short tape, Girls' Puberty Ritual, produced by Carelli with a Nambikwara leader for outsiders.) Using video reinforced an emerging concept of "traditional" in contrast to Brazilian culture—a concept that had not, apparently, been part of the Nambikwara's repertoire before contact but that had practical political utility.

The Kayapo are among the best-known Brazilian Indians internationally, partly because of their video work, promoted as a tool of cultural identification by the anthropologist who works most closely with them. Like other tribes such as the Xavante who had extensive contact with Brazilian authorities and media, the Kayapo early seized on modern media technologies. . . . Besides intimidating authorities with the evidence of recording equipment . . . , the Kayapo quickly grasped the symbolic expectations of Brazilian mass media for Indians. They cannily played on the contrast between their feathers and body paint and their recording devices to get coverage. Even staging public events for the purpose of attracting television crews, they were able to insert, although not ultimately control, their message on Brazilian news by exploiting that contrast. . . . Using these techniques, Kayapo leaders became international symbols of the ironies of the postmodern age and not incidentally also the subjects of international agitation and fundraising that benefited Kayapo over other indigenous groups and some Kayapo over others.

Kayapo have also used video to document internal cultural ceremonies in meticulous detail; to communicate internally between villages; to develop an archive; and to produce clips and short documentaries intended for wide audiences. Their video work, asserts anthropologist Terence Turner, has not merely preserved traditional customs but in fact transformed their understanding of those customs as customs and their culture as a culture. Turner also found that video equipment, expertise, and products often fed into existing factional divisions. Particular Kayapo leaders used the equipment in their own interests, sometimes as a tool to subdue their enemies, sometimes as evidence of personal power. . . .

Source: Aufderheide 1993, 587–89.

precisely because it violated people's expectations, this performance directed the congregation's attention not only toward the Torah as the central symbol of the Jewish people, but also toward the changing roles of men and women in Jewish religious ritual in the United States at the end of the twentieth century.

Ritual performers are not robots but active individuals whose choices are guided by, but not rigidly dictated by, previous ritual texts (see, for example, Margaret Drewal's 1992 study of Yoruba ritual, discussed later). This is what we should expect, if human behavior is fundamentally open. Rituals highlight the fact that human understanding of the world is not just mental and not just physical but a holistic coming together of mind and body, thought and feeling. By performing our ideas, by feeling the implications of our myths, their truth becomes self-evident.

Rites of Passage

Let us examine this process by looking at one kind of ritual performance: the **rite of passage**. At the beginning of the twentieth century, the Belgian anthropologist Arnold Van Gennep noted that certain kinds of rituals around the world had similar structures. These were rituals associated with the movement (or passage) of people from one position in the social structure to another. They included births, initiations, confirmations, weddings, funerals, and the like (Figure 7.12).

Van Gennep (1960) found that all these rituals began with a period of *separation* from the old position and from normal time. During this period, the ritual passenger left behind the symbols and practices of his or her previous position. For example, military recruits leave their families behind and are moved to a new place. They are forced to leave behind the clothing, activities, and even the hair that marked who they were in civilian life.

The second stage in rites of passage involves a period of *transition*, in which the ritual passenger is neither in the old life nor yet in the new one. This period is marked by rolelessness, ambiguity, and perceived danger. Often, the person involved is subjected to ordeal by those who have already passed through. In the military service, this is the period of basic training, in which recruits (not yet soldiers but no longer civilians) are forced to dress and act alike.

They are subjected to a grinding-down process, after which they are rebuilt into something new.

During the final stage—*reaggregation*—the ritual passenger is reintroduced into society in his or her new position. In the military, this involves the graduation from basic training and the visit home, but this time in uniform, on leave, and as a member of the armed forces, a new person. Other familiar rites of passage in youth culture in the United States include high school graduation and the informal, yet significant ceremonies associated with the twenty-first birthday, both of which are understood as movements from one kind of person to another.

The work of Victor Turner has greatly increased our understanding of rites of passage. Turner concentrated on the period of transition, which he saw as important both for the rite of passage and for social life in general. Van Gennep referred to this part of a rite of passage as the liminal period, from the Latin *limen* ("threshold"). During this period, the individual is on the threshold, betwixt and between, neither here nor there, neither in nor out. Turner notes that the symbolism accompanying the rite of passage often expresses this ambiguous state. **Liminality**, he tells us, "is frequently likened to death, to being in the womb, to invisibility, to darkness, to bisexuality, to the wilderness, and to an eclipse of the sun or moon" (1969, 95). People in the liminal state tend to develop an intense comradeship with each other in which their nonliminal distinctions disappear or become irrelevant. Turner calls this modality of social relationship **communitas**, which is best understood as an unstructured or minimally structured community of equal individuals.

Turner contends that all societies need some kind of communitas as much as they need structure. Communitas gives "recognition to an essential and generic human bond, without which there could be no society" (1969, 97). That bond is the common humanity that underlies all culture and society. However, periods of communitas (often in ritual context)

---

rite of passage A ritual that serves to mark the movement and transformation of an individual from one social position to another.

liminality The ambiguous transitional state in a rite of passage in which the person or persons undergoing the ritual are outside their ordinary social positions.

communitas An unstructured or minimally structured community of equal individuals found frequently in rites of passage.

FIGURE 7.12 Rites of passage are rituals that enable people to move from one position in the social structure to another. Here, in June 2004, an Apache girl, accompanied by her godmother and a helper, moves into adulthood through the Sunrise Dance.

are brief. Communitas is dangerous, not just because it threatens structure but because it threatens survival itself. Lost in a world of communitas, the things that structure ensures—production of food and physical and social reproduction of the society—cannot be provided. Someone always has to take out the garbage and clean up after the party. Communitas gives way to structure, which in turn generates a need for the release of communitas.

The feeling of oneness reported in the earlier anecdote about the Ali-Foreman fight is communitas, and communitas is also possible in play and art. For people in contemporary nation-states the experience of communitas may well come through experiencing the climactic winning moments of a sports team, attendance at large-scale rock concerts, or participation in mass public events like Carnival in Rio, the Greenwich Village Halloween parade, or Mardi Gras in New Orleans.

Play and Ritual as Complementary

How does ritual differ from play? Play and ritual (like metaphorical and literal language) are complementary forms of metacommunication (Handelman 1977). Just as the movement from nonplay to play is

based on the premise of metaphor ("Let's make-believe"), the movement to ritual is based on the premise of literalness ("Let's believe"). From the perspective of paramount reality (the everyday social order), the result of these contrasting premises is the "inauthenticity" of play and the "truth" of ritual.

Because of the connection of ritual with self-evident truth, the metacommunication of the ritual frame ("This is ritual") is associated with an additional metacommunication: "All messages within this frame are true." It is ritual that asserts *what should be* to play's *what can be*. The ritual frame is more rigid than the play frame. Consequently, ritual is the most stable liminal domain, whereas play is the most flexible. Players can move with relative ease into and out of play, but such is not the case with ritual.

Finally, play usually has little effect on the social order of ordinary life. This permits play a wide range of commentary on the social order. Ritual is different: its role is explicitly to maintain the status quo, including the prescribed ritual transformations. Societies differ in the extent to which ritual behavior alternates with everyday, nonritual behavior. When nearly every act of everyday life is ritualized and other forms of behavior are strongly proscribed, we sometimes speak of **orthopraxy** ("correct practice"). Traditionally observant Jews and Muslims, for example, lead a highly ritualized daily life, attempting from the moment they awaken until the moment

orthopraxy "Correct practice"; the prohibition of deviation from approved forms of ritual behavior.

they fall asleep to carry out even the humblest of activities in a manner that is ritually correct. In their view, ritual correctness is the result of God's law, and it is their duty and joy to conform their every action to God's will.

Ritual may seem overwhelming and all powerful. Yet individuals and groups within a society can sometimes manipulate ritual forms to achieve nontraditional ends. This can range from pushing against tradition as far as it can go without actually destroying the ritual (as when a bride and groom have an alternative wedding outdoors, write their own vows, and still have a member of the clergy officiating) to emphasizing the importance of one ritual and ignoring or downplaying another (as when Protestant Baptists downplayed the communion ritual and emphasized the baptism ritual as a way of articulating their challenge to Roman Catholicism) to exchanging one set of rituals for another (as when lone rural migrants to the cities of northern Cameroon convert to Islam shortly after their arrival, abandoning their traditional rituals together with the rural way of life into which they were born).

Margaret Drewal argues that, at least among the Yoruba, play and ritual overlap (see EthnoProfile 7.5: Yoruba). Yoruba rituals combine spectacle, festival, play, sacrifice, and so on and integrate diverse media—music, dance, poetry, theater, sculpture (1992, 198). They are improvisatory events, spontaneous individual moves, in which the mundane order is not only inverted and reversed but may also be subverted through power play and gender play. In Yoruba life, gender roles are rigidly structured. Yoruba rituals, however, allow some cross-dressing by both men and women, providing institutionalized opportunities for men and women to cross gender boundaries and to express the traits that Yoruba consider to be characteristic of the opposite sex, sometimes as parody but sometimes seriously and respectfully (190).

▼ HOW DO CULTURAL PRACTICES COMBINE PLAY, ART, MYTH, AND RITUAL?

Many anthropologists have suggested that play, art, myth, and ritual may be, and often are, experienced together. Bruce Kapferer has made these connections clear in a study of demon exorcism in Sri Lanka (see

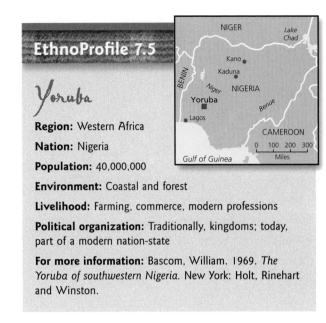

EthnoProfile 7.5

Yoruba

Region: Western Africa

Nation: Nigeria

Population: 40,000,000

Environment: Coastal and forest

Livelihood: Farming, commerce, modern professions

Political organization: Traditionally, kingdoms; today, part of a modern nation-state

For more information: Bascom, William. 1969. *The Yoruba of southwestern Nigeria.* New York: Holt, Rinehart and Winston.

EthnoProfile 7.6: Sinhalese). The demon exorcism ceremonies of the Sinhalese Buddhist working class and peasantry last an entire night and are designed to cure disease. The performance combines in "a marvelous spectacle" ritual, comedy, music, and dance. Its goal is "to change the experiential condition of [the] patients and to bring patients back into a normal conception of the world" (1983, 177, 236). In other words, the entire performance is transformative. During the course of the ceremony, a demonic reality is created and then destroyed.

At the beginning of the exorcism, the patient and the audience are in different realities. The audience is in the paramount reality of everyday life; the patient is in the alternative reality of his or her illness. In that reality, demons are central and powerful actors. During the Evening Watch, through music, song, and eventually dance, the audience becomes increasingly engaged in this alternative reality. In this part of the ceremony, the demons are portrayed as figures of horror.

At midnight, the process is complete: The audience has joined the patient's reality. The demons, played by actors, appear. At this point, the Midnight Watch begins. This part of the ceremony is a comic drama that lasts until nearly 3:00 A.M. The eruption of comedy into what had been an intensely serious ceremony transforms the demons into figures of ridicule. Through the comedy, the demonic reality begins to fragment as the gods appear and reassert

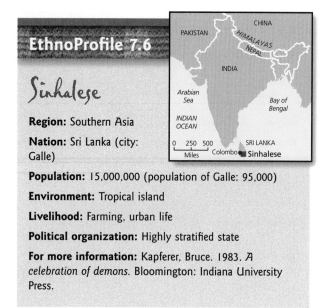

EthnoProfile 7.6

Sinhalese

Region: Southern Asia

Nation: Sri Lanka (city: Galle)

Population: 15,000,000 (population of Galle: 95,000)

Environment: Tropical island

Livelihood: Farming, urban life

Political organization: Highly stratified state

For more information: Kapferer, Bruce. 1983. *A celebration of demons.* Bloomington: Indiana University Press.

their dominance. As this occurs, the sick person begins to see that the demons are really subordinate to the gods, not superior to them.

The last part of the exorcism is the Morning Watch, which continues until 6:00 A.M. During this period, the patient and audience become reengaged

in the reality of ordinary life. The final comic drama of the performance "confirms the demonic absurdity, and destroys the demonic as powerful and relevant to normal experience in daily life" (Kapferer 1983, 220). Having played on the mind, body, and emotions of the patient and the audience, the performance ends.

To understand the performance as a whole, the interactions of all aspects of the performance must be grasped. Kapferer calls this the ceremony's *aesthetics.* He argues that the ceremony succeeds because it is composed of many different parts that fit together in a way that is satisfying to the Sinhalese. Only in the aesthetic realm are ideas, symbolic objects, and actions brought into the relationship from which their meaning comes.

Play, art, myth, and ritual are different facets of the holistic human capacity to view the world from a variety of perspectives. The human capacity to play is channeled in different directions in different cultures, but it is always present. When the products of this containment process come together in key cultural productions, such as the Sinhalese curing ceremony, they display both the opportunities and dangers that result from open human creativity.

CHAPTER SUMMARY

1. Play is a generalized form of behavioral openness: the ability to think about, speak about, and do different things in the same way or the same thing in different ways. Play can be thought of as a way of organizing activities, not merely a set of activities. We put a frame that consists of the message "this is play" around certain activities, thereby transforming them into play. Play also permits reflexive consideration of alternative realities by setting up a separate reality and suggesting that the perspective of ordinary life is only one way to make sense of experience.

2. The functions of play include exercise, practice for the real world, increased creativity in children, and commentary on the real world.

3. The fate of national sports teams can come to represent the nation itself, and the devotion of sports fans becomes a way of affirming patriotism. When sports are translated from one culture to another, they are frequently transformed to fit the patterns appropriate to the new culture.

4. Art is a kind of play that is subject to certain culturally appropriate restrictions on form and content. It aims to evoke a holistic, aesthetic response from the artist and the observer. It succeeds when the form is culturally appropriate for the content and is technically perfect in its realization. Aesthetic evaluations are culturally shaped value judgments. We recognize art in other cultures because of its family resemblance to what we call art in our own culture. Although people with other cultural understandings may not have produced art by intention, we can often successfully

appreciate what they have created as art by appropriation. These issues are addressed in ethnographic studies that call into question received ideas about what counts as "authentic" art.

5. Myths are stories whose truth seems self-evident because they do such a good job of integrating personal experiences with a wider set of assumptions about the way the world works. As stories, myths are the products of high verbal art. A full understanding of myth requires ethnographic background information.

6. Ritual is a repetitive social practice composed of sequences of symbolic activities such as speech, singing, dancing, gestures, and the manipulation of certain objects. In studying ritual, we pay attention not just to the symbols but also to how the ritual is performed. Cultural ideas are made concrete through ritual action.

7. Rites of passage are rituals in which members of a culture move from one position in the social structure to another. These rites are marked by periods of separation, transition, and reaggregation. During the period of transition, individuals occupy a liminal position. All those in this position frequently develop an intense comradeship and a feeling of oneness, or communitas.

8. Ritual and play are complementary. Play is based on the premise "Let us make-believe," while ritual is based on the premise "Let us believe." As a result, the ritual frame is far more rigid than the play frame. Although ritual may seem overwhelming and all-powerful, individuals and groups can sometimes manipulate ritual forms to achieve non-traditional ends.

KEY TERMS

play	sport	myths	liminality
metacommunication	art	orthodoxy	communitas
framing	transformation-representation	ritual	orthopraxy
reflexivity		rite of passage	

SUGGESTED READINGS

Alland, Alexander. 1977. *The artistic animal*. New York: Doubleday Anchor. *An introductory look at the biocultural bases for art. This work is very well written, very clear, and fascinating.*

Blanchard, Kendall. 1995. *The anthropology of sport*. Rev. ed. Westport, CT: Bergin and Garvey. *An excellent introduction to the field.*

Errington, Shelly. 1998. *The death of authentic primitive art and other tales of progress*. Berkeley: University of California Press. *A sharp and witty book about the production, distribution, interpretation, and selling of "primitive art."*

Fagen, Robert. 1981. *Animal play behavior*. New York: Oxford University Press. *The definitive work.*

Kapferer, Bruce. 1989. *A celebration of demons*. 2d ed. Washington, DC: Smithsonian Institution Press. *An advanced text that is well worth reading.*

Lever, Janet. 1995. *Soccer madness*. Prospect Heights, IL: Waverland Press. *A fascinating study of soccer in Brazil.*

Schwartzman, Helen. 1978. *Transformations: The anthropology of children's play*. New York: Plenum. *A superlative work that considers how anthropologists have studied children's play, with some insightful suggestions about how they might do this in the future.*

Steiner, Christopher. 1994. *African art in transit*. Cambridge: Cambridge University Press. *Steiner traces the social life of objects made in rural West African villages from their creation to their resting places in galleries, museums, tourist shops, or private Western art collections, highlighting the role of African merchants who make this transit possible.*

Turner, Victor. 1969. *The ritual process*. Chicago: Aldine. *An important work in the anthropological study of ritual, this text is an eloquent analysis of rites of passage.*

Vogel, Susan. 1997. *Baule: African art/Western eyes*. New Haven: Yale University Press. *A book of extraordinary photographs and beautifully clear text, this work explores both Baule and Western views of Baule expressive culture.*

Chapter 8

Worldview

This chapter explores the encompassing pictures of reality created by members of societies—their *worldviews*. You will learn about metaphors and how they are used to construct worldviews. We focus on one, well-known kind of worldview—religion—as well as a contending worldview—secularism—that originated in western Europe. We also explore some of the ways in which symbolic forms central to different worldviews are shaped by power relations in different social settings.

In 1976, soon after the authors of this book (EAS and RHL) arrived in Guider, Cameroon, we bought a bicycle (see EthnoProfile 8.1: Guider). About a month later, it was stolen. The thief had been seen and was well known. We went directly to the *gendarmerie*, where we swore out a complaint.

A month later, I (RHL) was talking to Amadou, a 19-year-old member of the Ndjegn ethnic group. Amadou mentioned that the Ndjegn were famous for the power of their magic (Figure 8.1). I asked him if he knew any magic. Amadou replied that he was too young but that his older brother was a powerful magician. I asked what kinds of magic his brother was best at. Amadou began to list them—one of the first types of magic was to return stolen property. "Why didn't you mention this when our bike was stolen?" I inquired. "Well, I talked it over with my best friend. We agreed that you white people don't believe in any of that and would laugh at us." But I wanted to know what would happen to the thief if Amadou's brother made the magic against him. "His stomach will begin to hurt," Amadou explained, "and if he doesn't return the bicycle within two weeks, his stomach will swell up until it explodes and he will die." I thought this was a good idea and said I wanted the magic made.

Amadou went home and told his brother, who agreed to cast the spell. Word quickly went around Guider that the two "white visitors" had caused magic to be made against the bicycle thief. The days passed, but the bicycle did not reappear. After three weeks, I asked Amadou what had happened.

"Here's the problem, Monsieur," Amadou explained. "We waited too long after the theft to cast the spell. It works better when the magic is made right after the theft. Also, the thief is in Nigeria now. He's too far away for the magic to reach him."

Why do people believe—or not believe—in magic? Amadou was bright, suspicious of fakery, far from gullible. He had attended primary and secondary school. How could he remain convinced that his brother's magic worked? Why would many Americans be convinced that he was wrong?

Anthropologists are interested in what makes magic work because it occasionally does work: People are cursed, some of them sicken, and some of them die. How can this be? The usual anthropological explanation is that magic works when the people

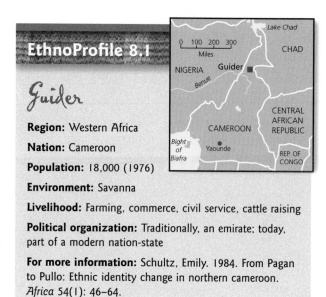

EthnoProfile 8.1

Guider

Region: Western Africa

Nation: Cameroon

Population: 18,000 (1976)

Environment: Savanna

Livelihood: Farming, commerce, civil service, cattle raising

Political organization: Traditionally, an emirate; today, part of a modern nation-state

For more information: Schultz, Emily. 1984. From Pagan to Pullo: Ethnic identity change in northern cameroon. *Africa* 54(1): 46–64.

who believe in its power find out that it has been made against them. After all, people do often get stomachaches in northern Cameroon. Many people in Guider knew that the magic had been made and by whom. Only a fool or a desperate person would take the chance of having his or her stomach swell up until it exploded. But in this case, the thief, long gone, did not know that magic had been made, and the magic's effect was neutralized by distance.

Amadou's explanation of why magic succeeds or fails is just as coherent as the traditional anthropological explanation. But each of these explanations is based on a different set of assumptions about what the world is like (see chapter 7). Where do these ideas about the world come from? Why don't all people share the same ideas? This chapter suggests some answers to these questions.

▼ WHAT IS A WORLDVIEW?

In our earlier discussions of language and cognition, we looked at some of the ways human beings use culture to construct rich understandings of everyday experiences. In this chapter, we build on those insights and describe how human beings use cultural creativity to make sense of the wider world on a comprehensive scale.

FIGURE 8.1 This man from northern Cameroon is believed to know powerful magic.

While no set of cultural beliefs or practices is perfectly integrated and without contradiction, anthropologists have good evidence that culture is not just a hodgepodge of unrelated elements. The directions in which cultural creativity goes may differ widely from one group to the next, but in any particular society, culture tends to be patterned, and an individual's everyday attempts to account for experience are not isolated efforts. Members of the same society make use of shared assumptions about how the world works. As they interpret everyday experiences in light of these assumptions, they make sense of their lives and their lives make sense to other members of the society. The encompassing pictures of reality that result are called **worldviews**. Multiple worldviews may coexist in a single society. Anthropologists are interested in how worldviews are constructed and how people use them to make sense of their experiences in the broadest contexts.

▼ WHAT IS THE ROLE OF METAPHOR, METONYMY, AND SYMBOL IN CONSTRUCTING WORLDVIEWS?

Metaphor

One way to grasp the pattern that may be found in a particular worldview is to "follow the metaphor." This strategy was adopted by Emily Martin, who followed the metaphor of "flexibility" in American culture and was able to reveal the outlines of an emergent worldview in the United States at the end of the twentieth century (see chapter 3). Following

---

worldviews Encompassing pictures of reality created by the members of societies.

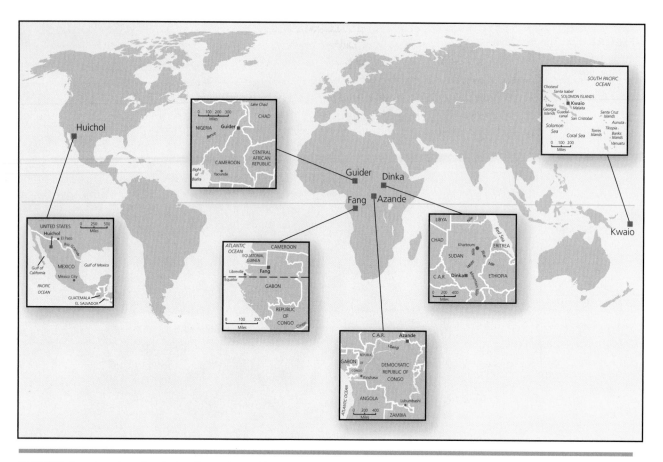

FIGURE 8.2 Location of societies whose EthnoProfiles appear in chapter 8.

metaphors successfully, however, requires understanding how metaphors work.

In chapter 5, we said that a **metaphor** asserts the existence of a meaningful link between two expressions from different sets of interrelated meanings called **semantic domains**. For example, metaphorical statements such as "Arnold is a turkey" create an ambiguity that can only be resolved in context. If we know Arnold is characteristically inept, ignorant, and annoying and that turkeys are prototypically stupid and clumsy, our metaphor becomes intelligible and apt. But why resort to metaphor to represent our opinion of Arnold? Why not simply

say, "Arnold is inept, ignorant, and annoying"? When we choose to use metaphoric language instead of literal language, it is usually because literal language is not equal to the task of expressing the meaning we intend. Perhaps it is not just that Arnold is inept, ignorant, and annoying. Perhaps we think he is funny-looking, with a tiny head and a vast, cumbersome body.

Like the AIDS patients, medical professionals, and managers who resorted to the metaphor of flexibility in describing their experiences of health and illness to Emily Martin, our experience of Arnold may be complex and difficult to pin down in literal language. That is, there is something about the image of a turkey that encompasses more of what we think about Arnold than can ever be represented by a list of adjectives. We therefore select a figurative image whose features are more familiar and use it as a tool to help us understand what kind of person Arnold is.

metaphor A form of thought and language that asserts a meaningful link between two expressions from different semantic domains.

semantic domain a set of linguistic expressions with interrelated meanings.

The metaphor does not demonstrate unequivocally that Arnold *is* a turkey, any more than Martin's informants' beliefs about flexibility exposed the final truth about how to understand the relationship between illness and health. Rather, in both cases using a particular metaphor simply asserts that a particular link exists and invites those who know both Arnold and turkeys (or who have suffered from AIDS and know what "flexibility" means) to decide (and perhaps to debate) the extent to which the metaphor is apt. Similarly, the metaphor "The Lord is my shepherd" links a subject we have trouble describing (the Lord) to an image (my shepherd) that is familiar and well understood. This metaphorical statement is an invitation to ponder what it means to be a shepherd, to be my shepherd, and then apply this knowledge to one's understanding of the Lord.

Worldviews aim to encompass the widest possible understanding of how the world works. In constructing worldviews, people tend to examine what they already know for clues that might help them make sense of what puzzles them. Metaphor is a powerful tool for constructing worldviews because it clarifies areas of human experience that are vague or poorly understood. The first part of a metaphor, the **metaphorical subject**, represents the domain of experience that needs to be clarified (the Lord). The second part of a metaphor, the **metaphorical predicate**, suggests a domain of experience that is familiar (sheepherding) and may help us understand what the Lord is all about (Figure 8.3).

To understand the metaphor, we have to list every conceivable attribute of shepherds and then decide which ones describe the Lord. These attributes of shepherds and sheep are called **metaphorical entailments** (Lakoff and Johnson 1980). They suggest what follows from, or is entailed by, our calling the Lord a shepherd. If we were to assert that "the Lord is my friend," an entirely different set of metaphorical entailments would follow: that my relationship with the Lord is a relationship between equals, for example, or that both of us have to make an effort if our friendship is to succeed.

Metonymy

Metonymy is the relationship that links the parts of a semantic domain to one another. In the metaphor "The Lord is my shepherd," the link between the metaphorical predicate shepherd and its metaphorical entailments is a link of metonymy. The word *shepherd* can stand for any and all attributes connected to the semantic domain defined by sheepherding. At the same time, any of these attributes (such as protecting sheep from wild animals) may entail the word *shepherd*. Because semantic domains are culturally defined, the meaningful elements that are linked by metonymy within any semantic domain are also culturally defined. Sheepherding occurs in many societies, and yet the range of meanings associated with sheepherding may vary: Compare a society in which shepherds are women, sheep graze freely, and mutton is primarily for family consumption with a different society in which shepherds are men, sheep graze in enclosed fields, and most animals are sold on the market for cash. Of course, members of the first society may think that theirs is the only sensible way to herd sheep, and vice versa. Put another way, in any society, semantic domains defined by links of metonymy are viewed as "natural" or "true" associations.

The links of metonymy we discover within a particular semantic domain may help us make sense of experiences that seem chaotic and meaningless. Consider what happens in the case of what some people call *religious conversion*. An individual who is troubled and confused may see his personal situation suddenly come into focus when he starts thinking of himself as a lost sheep. He may further reason that a lost sheep must have been lost by someone—the shepherd to whom it belonged. This reflection, in turn, may lead him to ask who his shepherd might be. If he learns that some people believe that the Lord is their shepherd, he may be attracted to them and want to learn more. Thus, his exploration of the links of metonymy within a particular semantic domain, in the context of his own life, may lead him to conclude

metaphorical subject The first part of a metaphor, which indicates the domain of experience that needs to be clarified.

metaphorical predicate The second part of a metaphor, which suggests a familiar domain of experience that may clarify the metaphorical subject.

metaphorical entailments All the attributes of a metaphorical predicate that relate it to the culturally defined domain of experience to which it belongs.

metonymy The culturally defined relationship of the parts of a semantic domain to the domain as a whole and of the whole to its parts.

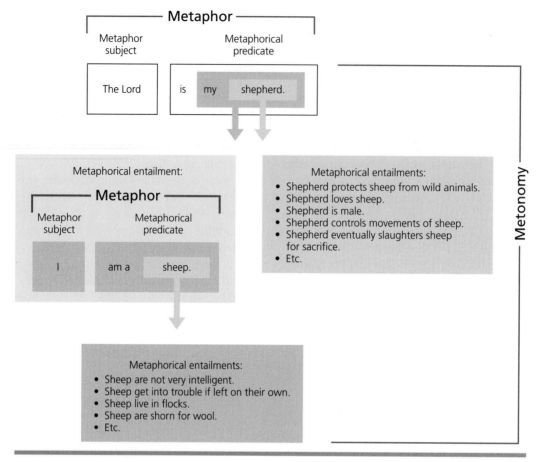

FIGURE 8.3 An analysis of the metaphor "The Lord is my shepherd," illustrating the links of metaphor and metonymy.

that the metaphor "the Lord is my shepherd" resonates with the power of divine revelation. Such reflections play an important role in religious conversion, but they are equally important in science when a new theory is adopted because it makes sense of otherwise puzzling data (see Kuhn 1970; Poewe 1989).

Symbol

As people increase their understanding of themselves and the wider world by creating apt metaphors, it is helpful to establish benchmarks that facilitate organizing this knowledge. People devise symbols to remind themselves of their significant insights and the

---

symbol Something that stands for something else. A symbol signals the presence of an important domain of experience.

---

connections between them. A **symbol**—be it a word, image, or action—is something that stands for something else. Symbols signal the presence and importance of given domains of experience. They are special cases of metonymy. Some symbols—what Sherry Ortner (1973) calls *summarizing symbols*—represent a whole semantic domain and invite us to consider the various elements within it. Others—what Ortner calls *elaborating symbols*—represent only one element of a domain and invite us to place that element in its wider semantic context.

Summarizing symbols sum up, express, represent for people "in an emotionally powerful . . . way what the system means to them" (Ortner 1973, 1339). To many people, for example, the American flag stands for the American way. But the American way is a complex collection of ideas and feelings that includes such things as patriotism, democracy, hard work, free enterprise, progress, national superiority, apple pie, and motherhood. As Ortner points out, the flag focuses our attention on all these things at once. It does not encourage us, say, to reflect on how the American way affects non-Americans. But the symbolic power of the flag is double-edged. For some people, Americans included, this same flag stands for imperialism, racism, opposition to the legitimate struggle of exploited peoples, and support for right-wing dictatorships. Perhaps stranger still, for many Americans who came of age during the 1960s, the flag sums up all these things at once, contradictory though they are!

Elaborating symbols are essentially analytic. They allow people to sort out and label complex and undifferentiated feelings and ideas into comprehensible and communicable language and action. Elaborating symbols provide people with categories for thinking about how their world is ordered. Consider the Dinka, a cattle-herding people of eastern Africa (Figure 8.4; see EthnoProfile 8.2: Dinka). According

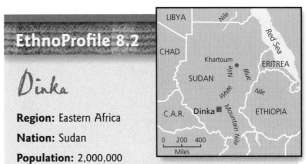

EthnoProfile 8.2

Dinka

Region: Eastern Africa

Nation: Sudan

Population: 2,000,000

Environment: Savanna

Livelihood: Principally cattle herding, also agriculture

Political organization: Traditionally, egalitarian with noble clans and chiefs; today, part of a modern nation-state

For more information: Deng, Francis Madeng. 1972. *The Dinka of the Sudan.* New York: Holt, Rinehart and Winston.

FIGURE 8.4 For pastoral people such as the Dinka and their neighbors the Nuer, cattle are elaborating symbols of paramount power.

to Godfrey Lienhardt, cattle provide the Dinka with most of the metaphors they use for thinking about and responding to experience. For instance, Dinka perceptions of color, light, and shade are connected to the colors they see in cattle. They even liken how their society is put together to how a bull is put together (Lienhardt 1961; Ortner 1973).

▼ WHAT ARE SOME KEY METAPHORS FOR CONSTRUCTING WORLDVIEWS?

Worldviews are comprehensive pictures of reality. They can be regarded as attempts to answer the following question: What must the world be like for my experiences to be what they are? Over the ages, thoughtful people in all cultural traditions have suggested various answers to this question. Often, unfamiliar worldviews become more comprehensible to us if we are able to grasp the **key metaphors** on which they are founded. Anthropologist Robin Horton suggests that people who construct a worldview are "concerned above all to show order, regularity and predictability where primary theory [that is, commonsense experience] has failed to show them." As they search for key metaphors, therefore, they look at those areas of everyday experience that are most associated with order, regularity, and predictability (1982, 237). Some worldviews seem to have tremendous staying power over time and across space, making sense of experience in a variety of circumstances and historical periods. But new worldviews based on different metaphors can emerge un-

key metaphors Metaphors that serve as the foundation of a worldview.

societal metaphors Worldview metaphors whose model for the world is the social order.

organic metaphors Worldview metaphors that apply the image of the body to social structures and institutions.

functionalism A social scientific perspective in which a society is likened to a living organism in which different systems carry out specialized tasks; functionalists identify social subsystems into which a society can be divided, identify the tasks each is supposed to perform, and describe a healthy society as one in which all the subsystems are functioning harmoniously.

der changed circumstances if they provide insight when old understandings fail.

Comparative research suggests that three important images of order and stability have regularly provided key metaphors for worldviews. The first are what we will call **societal metaphors**. In many times and places, human social relations provide great order, regularity, and predictability. In such societies, the model for the world is the social order; or, put another way, the universe (or macrocosm) and one's own society (the microcosm) are understood to operate according to the same principles. Small-scale societies organized on the basis of kinship may relate to powerful cosmic forces as if they were powerful elders; some of those forces may even be understood as the spirits of deceased elders, their ancestors. Complex societies stratified according to differences in wealth, power, and prestige may conceive of a universe in which cosmic powers are similarly stratified, and they may base their ways of dealing with cosmic forces on the skills they use to deal with powerful human beings (Figure 8.5). Societies like our own, with well-developed capitalist commercial, industrial, and financial institutions, often liken biological and social processes to operations in a capitalist market (Wolf 1969, 277).

A second image of order and stability has come from **organic metaphors**, which are based on an understanding of living organisms. The advances made by biologists in the nineteenth and early twentieth centuries led social scientists to think of societies and languages as living organisms. Many nineteenth-century theorists of linguistic or cultural evolution used organic metaphors to analyze the life histories of languages or civilizations in terms of birth, youth, maturity, reproduction, old age, and death. In the early twentieth century, by contrast, a different organic metaphor was used to develop the social scientific perspective called **functionalism**. Functionalists drew attention to the way the body of a living organism can be divided into different systems (digestive, reproductive, respiratory, and so on), each carrying out a specialized task. When all these systems are functioning in harmony with one another, the organism is said to be healthy. If society is also a living organism, we should look for the subsystems into which society can be divided, identify the tasks each is supposed to perform, and describe a healthy society

FIGURE 8.5 In a complex, hierarchically organized society like that of Renaissance Italy, the image of cosmic power was similarly organized.

as one in which all the subsystems are functioning harmoniously. *Personification* (attributing human characteristics to nonhuman entities) is another organic metaphor. The beliefs that the candy machine down the hall at the office has a personality that is both malevolent and greedy or that you can persuade your car to start on a cold morning by speaking gentle and encouraging words to it both involve personification.

Technological metaphors use machines made by human beings as metaphorical predicates. Technological metaphors became prominent with the rise of western European science, and different machine metaphors have replaced one another over time as Western science and technology have developed and changed. For instance, in the seventeenth-century world of Isaac Newton, models of the universe were based on the most complex artifact of that age: the wind-up mechanical clock. Following the industrial revolution, nineteenth-century psychologists described human cognitive and emotional processes using a steam engine metaphor (for example, Freud conceived of emotional stress building up inside people like steam in a boiler that would explode unless a social safety valve were available to release the pres-

sure without causing psychic damage). In the second half of the twentieth century, computer metaphors have become popular among some scientists investigating how the mind works (Pinker 1999).

▼ RELIGION

For many readers of this text, the most familiar form of worldview is probably **religion**. The anthropological concept of religion, like many analytic terms, began as a description of a certain domain of Western culture. As a result, it has been very difficult for anthropologists to settle on a definition of religion that is applicable in all human societies.

Scholars have often argued that a religion differs from other kinds of worldviews because it assumes the existence of a supernatural domain: an invisible world populated by one or more beings who are

---

technological metaphor A worldview metaphor that employs objects made by human beings as metaphorical predicates.

religion Ideas and practices that postulate reality beyond that which is immediately available to the senses.

more powerful than human beings and are able to influence events in the "natural" human world. The problem with this definition is that the distinction between "natural" and "supernatural" was originally made by nonreligious Western observers in order to distinguish the real "natural" world from what they took to be the imaginary "supernatural" world. Many anthropologists who study different religious traditions believe that it is less distorting to begin with their informants' statements about what exists and what does not. In this way, they are in a better position to understand the range of forces, visible and invisible, that religious believers perceive as active in their world.

For these reasons, John Bowen proposes that anthropologists approach religion in a way that begins broadly but that allows for increasing specificity as we learn more about the details of particular religious traditions. Bowen defines religion as "ideas and practices that postulate reality beyond that which is immediately available to the senses" (2002, 5). In individual societies, this may mean beliefs in spirits and gods, or awareness that ancestors continue to be active in the world of the living. In other cases, people may posit the existence of impersonal cosmic powers that may be compelled to intervene in human affairs following the correct performance of certain rituals. It is important to note that Bowen's definition of religion encompasses both practices and ideas: Religions involve *actions* as well as *beliefs* (Figure 8.6).

Indeed, anthropologist A. F. C. Wallace proposed a set of "minimal categories of religious behavior" that describe many of the practices usually associated with religions (1966). Several of the most salient are

1. *Prayer.* Where there are personified cosmic forces, there is a customary way of addressing them, usually by speaking or chanting out loud. Often people pray in public, at a sacred location, and with special apparatus: incense, smoke, objects (such as rosary beads or a prayer wheel), and so on.

2. *Physiological exercise.* Many religious systems have methods for physically manipulating psychological states to induce an ecstatic spiritual state. Wallace suggests four major kinds of manipulation: (1) drugs; (2) sensory deprivation; (3) mortification of the flesh by pain, sleeplessness, and fatigue; and (4) deprivation of food, water, or air. In many societies, the experience of ecstasy, euphoria, dissociation, or hallucination seems to be a goal of religious effort.

3. *Exhortation.* In all religious systems, certain people are believed to have closer relationships with the invisible powers than others, and they are expected to use those relationships in the spiritual interests of others. They give orders, they heal, they threaten, they comfort, and they interpret.

4. *Mana.* Mana refers to an impersonal superhuman power that is sometimes believed to be transferable from an object that contains it to one that

FIGURE 8.6 (*a*) The joint pilgrimage by Hindu worshipers to the Ganges River illustrates the social nature of religion. (*b*) Floating on the air, followed by the wind. This participant in the Hindu Thaipusam ritual pilgrimage in Singapore in 2004 has agreed to carry a kavadi for religious benefit. Kavadi can weigh 60 pounds (27 kg).

does not. The laying on of hands, in which the power of a healer enters the body of a sick person to remove or destroy an illness, is an example of the transmission of power. In Guider, some people believe that the ink used to copy passages from the Qur'an has power. Washing the ink off the board on which the words are written and drinking the ink transfers the power of the words into the body of the drinker. The principle here is that sacred things are to be touched so that power may be transferred.

5. *Taboo.* Objects or people that may not be touched are taboo. Some people believe that the cosmic power in such objects or people may "drain away" if touched or may injure the toucher. Many religious systems have taboo objects. Traditionally, Catholics were not to touch the Host during communion; Jews may not touch the handwritten text of the biblical scrolls. In ancient Polynesia, commoners could not touch the chief's body; even an accidental touch resulted in the death of the commoner. Food may also be taboo; many societies have elaborate rules concerning the foods that may or may not be eaten at different times or by different kinds of people.

6. *Feasts.* Eating and drinking in a religious context is very common. The Holy Communion of Catholics and Protestants is a meal set apart by its religious context. The Passover Seder for Jews is another religious feast. For the Huichol of Mexico, the consumption of peyote is set apart by its religious context (see EthnoProfile 8.4: Huichol). Even everyday meals may be seen to have a religious quality if they begin or end with prayer.

7. *Sacrifice.* Giving something of value to the invisible forces or their agents is a feature of many religious systems. This may be an offering of money, goods, or services. It may also be the immolation of animals or, very rarely, human beings. Sacrifices may be made in thanks to the cosmic forces, in hopes of influencing them to act in a certain way, or simply to gain general religious merit.

Religion and Communication

Those who are committed to religious worldviews are convinced of the existence and active involvement in their lives of beings or forces that are ordinarily invisible. Indeed, some of the most highly valued religious practices, such as religious ecstasy or trance, produce outer symptoms that may be perceived by others; but their most powerful effects can be experienced only by the individual who undergoes them personally.

What, then, if you wanted to know what it felt like to experience religious ecstasy? What if you were someone who had had such an experience and wanted to tell others about it? What if you were convinced that the supreme power in the universe had revealed itself to you and you wanted to share this revelation with others? How would you proceed? You might well begin by searching for metaphors based on experiences already well known to your audience.

Thus, one Hindu Tamil worshiper in Kuala Lumpur who successfully went into trance during the festival of Thaipusam described his experience as being like "floating in the air, followed by the wind" (*Floating in the Air* 1973). And the Hebrew poet who wrote the Twenty-third Psalm tried to express his experience of the power and love of his God by comparing God to his shepherd and himself to a sheep. Many contemporary theologians argue that the language human beings use to talk about God is inevitably full of everyday metaphors (see Gillman 1992, for example). Even those who claim to have had personal experience of the reality of God, or of ancestral spirits, or of witchcraft, will probably still find themselves forced to resort to poetic, metaphorical language if they want to explain that experience to other people—and perhaps even to themselves.

We saw earlier that societal metaphors are often used to gain insight into a complex phenomenon, because in many societies social relations are complex and well understood. Anthropological research suggests that members of many religious traditions apparently conceive of the structure of the universe as being the same as the structure of their society. First, members of the tradition will be likely to conceive of the force or forces at work in the universe as personified beings with many of the attributes of human agents at work in the society they know well. And because societies can be very different from one another, so the way they characterize the universe will also be different. It has long been noted by anthropologists that societies organized in strong groups based on kinship usually conceive of a universe peopled with the spirits of powerful ancestor figures who take an interest in the lives of their living descendants. By contrast, members of societies run by vast and complex bureaucracies, as was the Roman Empire, are apt to picture the universe as being run by an army of hierarchically ordered gods and spirits, all of which may be supervised by a chief god. "The Lord is my shepherd" is not likely to be accepted as an apt description of cosmic reality by people living in a society that lacks class distinctions and has no experience of sheepherding.

Organic metaphors may also figure in the construction of religious understanding. Anthropologist James Fernandez reports that organic metaphors are common in the Bwiti religion of the Fang of Gabon (see EthnoProfile 8.3: Fang). The human heart, for example, is an apt metaphor for Bwiti devotees because "(1) it is the heart which is the most alive of the bloody organs, (2) it is traditionally conceived by the Fang to be the organ of thought, and (3) in its bloodiness it is associated with the female principle. . . . Many meanings are at work in this metaphor, for that bloody organ, the heart, has a congeries of useful associations" (1977, 112).

What about technological metaphors? Their popularity in the Western world accompanied the rise of science. For example, in the seventeenth century, philosopher René Descartes popularized the notion that the human body is a machine, albeit one inhabited by an immortal soul. One of his near contemporaries, Julien La Mettrie, carried this metaphor to its radical conclusion. In his book *L'homme-machine* ("man-machine"), he argued that the concept of the human soul was superfluous because machines do not have souls.

Starting in the Renaissance, machines began to transform the world in unprecedented ways and to stimulate people's imaginations. The increasing complexity of machines, coupled with their builders' intimate knowledge of how they were put together, made them highly suggestive as metaphorical predicates. As we saw, they also give rise to a set of metaphorical entailments that are very different from the entailments of societal and organic metaphors. When we say that we are only cogs in a machine or talk about social status and roles as interchangeable parts, we are using machine metaphors (Figure 8.7).

What if people should conclude that the structure of the universe is the same as the structure of a machine—say, a clock or a computer? Would the re-

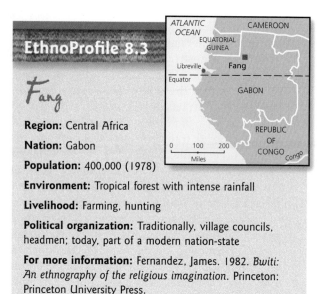

EthnoProfile 8.3

Fang

Region: Central Africa

Nation: Gabon

Population: 400,000 (1978)

Environment: Tropical forest with intense rainfall

Livelihood: Farming, hunting

Political organization: Traditionally, village councils, headmen; today, part of a modern nation-state

For more information: Fernandez, James. 1982. *Bwiti: An ethnography of the religious imagination.* Princeton: Princeton University Press.

sulting worldview still be a religion? After all, those scholars who originally distinguished the natural from the supernatural associated the supernatural with religion and declared both to be nonsense. At the same time, to view the cosmos as complex, orderly, predictable, and knowable, such that effective intervention into cosmic processes is possible, would certainly qualify as a worldview, even if the cosmos was deaf to human prayer and indifferent to human affairs. Anthropologists and other religious scholars continue to debate the matter.

Religious Organization

The most important entailment that follows from the societal metaphor is that forces in the universe are personalized. Thus, people seeking to influence those forces must handle them as they would handle powerful human beings. Communication is perhaps the central feature of how we deal with human beings: When we address each other, we expect a response. The same is true when we address personalized cosmic forces.

Maintaining contact with invisible cosmic powers is a tremendously complex undertaking. It is not surprising, therefore, that some societies have developed complex social practices to ensure that it is done properly. In other words, religion becomes *institutionalized*.

FIGURE 8.7 When we say that we are only cogs in a machine or talk about status and roles as interchangeable parts, we are using machine metaphors. Charlie Chaplin made use of technological metaphors in his film *Modern Times* (1936).

Social positions are created for specialists who supervise or embody correct religious practice.

Anthropologists have identified two broad categories of religious specialists: shamans and priests. A **shaman** is a part-time religious practitioner who is believed to have the power to contact invisible powers directly on behalf of individuals or groups. Shamans are often thought to be able to travel to the cosmic realm to communicate with the beings or forces that dwell there. They often plead with those beings or forces to act in favor of their people and may return with messages for them. The Ju/'hoansi, for example, recognize that some people are able to develop an internal power that enables them to travel to the world of the spirits—to enter "half death" (it would be called "trance" in English)—in order to cure those who are sick (see EthnoProfile 11.1: Ju/'hoansi).

In many societies, the training that a shaman receives is long, demanding, and permanent and may involve the use of powerful psychotropic substances. Repeatedly entering altered states of consciousness can produce long-lasting effects on shamans themselves, and shamans may be viewed with suspicion or fear by others in the society. This is because contacting cosmic beings to persuade them to heal embodies dangerous ambiguities: Someone who can contact such beings for positive benefits may also be able to contact them to produce a negative outcome

like disease or death. The term *shaman* comes from the Tungus of eastern Siberia, where, at a minimum, it referred to a religious specialist who has the ability to enter a trance through which he or she is believed to enter into direct contact with spiritual beings and guardian spirits for the purposes of healing, fertility, protection, and aggression, in a ritual setting (Bowie 2006, 175; Hultkrantz 1992, 10). The healing associated with Siberian shamanism was concerned with the idea that illness was caused by soul loss and healing through recovery of the soul (Figure 8.8). Thus, the shaman was responsible for dealing with spirits that were, at best, neutral and at worst actively hostile to human beings. The shaman could travel to the spirit world to heal someone by finding the missing soul that had been stolen by spirits. But a shaman who was jealous of a hunter, for example, was believed to be able to steal the souls of animals so that the hunter would fail. In these societies, shamans are dangerous.

Shamanic activity takes place in the trance séance, which can be little more than a consultation between shaman and patient, or it can be a major

---

shaman A part-time religious practitioner who is believed to have the power to travel to or contact supernatural forces directly on behalf of individuals or groups.

FIGURE 8.8 Using smoke from a juniper twig, Siberian shaman Vera heals a patient possessed by evil spirits.

public ritual, rich in drama. Becoming a shaman is not undertaken for personal development—in the societies where shamanism is important, it is said that the shaman has no choice but to take on the role; the spirits demand it. It can take a decade or more to become fully recognized as a shaman, and it is assumed that the shaman will be in service to the society (for good or ill) for the rest of his or her life.

A **priest**, by contrast, is skilled in the practice of religious rituals, which are carried out for the benefit of the group or individual members of the group. Priests do not necessarily have direct contact with

priest A religious practitioner skilled in the practice of religious rituals, which he or she carries out for the benefit of the group.

cosmic forces. Often their major role is to mediate such contact by ensuring that the required ritual activity has been properly performed. Priests are found in hierarchical societies, and they owe their ability to act as priests to the hierarchy of the religious institution (Figure 8.9). Status differences separating rulers and subjects in such societies are reflected in the unequal relationship between priest and laity.

▼ WORLDVIEWS IN PRACTICE: THREE CASE STUDIES

Anthropologists often say that people of different cultures live in different worlds. This itself is a metaphorical statement. It asserts that our understanding of reality depends on the particular point of view embodied in our culture. Of course, every culture contains subcultures that may draw pictures of reality that conflict with each other. The experience of juggling multiple points of view in our own society helps us to cope with unfamiliar perspectives in different societies.

We have been discussing how worldviews are constructed, but most of us encounter them fully formed, both in our own society and in other societies. We face a rich tapestry of symbols and rituals and everyday practices linked to one another in what often appears to be a seamless web. Where do we begin to sort things out?

Mind, Body, and Emotion in Huichol Religious Practice

Barbara Myerhoff (1974) discusses the peyote hunt of the Huichol (Figure 8.10; see EthnoProfile 8.4: Huichol). This ritual pilgrimage is a religious experience in which mind, body, and emotion all come together.

The Huichol are corn farmers who live in the Sierra Madre Occidental of northern Mexico. Annually, they travel to a desert about 350 miles from their homes to hunt peyote. Because peyote is sacred to the Huichol, this journey is also sacred, representing a pilgrimage to *Wirikuta*, the original Huichol homeland where the First People, both deities and ancestors, once lived. The journey is hard and dangerous, both physically and spiritually. The pilgrims seek to restore and experience anew the original state of unity that existed at the beginning of the world.

FIGURE 8.9 The complex organization of the Roman Catholic Church was illustrated at the funeral for Pope John Paul II in 2005.

This state of unity is symbolized by deer, maize, and peyote. The deer symbolizes the masculine, hunting past and thus connects the Huichol with their ancestors. In Huichol thought, the deer gave them peyote and appears every year in the hunt in Wirikuta. Blood from a sacrificed deer makes the maize grow and makes it nourishing to people. The deer is more powerful than human beings but not as remote as the gods. It symbolizes independence, adventure, and freedom.

Although the Huichol have only recently begun to grow maize, it is central to their present-day life. A life based on maize is tedious and precarious: The Huichol have to stay home to watch the crops, and even if they are careful, the maize may not grow. Maize symbolizes the labor of the present: food, domesticity, sharing between the sexes, routine, and persistent diligence. It also provides the Huichol with the language of beauty. "Maize," the Huichol say, "is our life."

Peyote, when gathered in the land of its origins, is sacred. It is used to induce private visions, which are not shared with others. It is also used ritually, in which case so little is eaten that no visions are produced. It seems that the purpose of ritual consumption is to reach communion with the deities. The Huichol think of peyote as plant and animal at once; and

at the climactic moments of the peyote hunt, it is hunted like the deer. "Peyote is neither mundane like maize, nor exotic and exciting, like deer. It is that solitary, ahistorical, asocial, asexual, nonrational domain without which [human beings] are not complete, without which life is a lesser affair" (Myerhoff 1974, 227). In Huichol religious thought, deer, maize, and peyote fit together: Maize cannot grow without deer blood; the deer cannot be sacrificed until after the peyote hunt; the ceremony that brings the rain cannot be held without peyote; and the peyote cannot be hunted until maize has been cleaned and sanctified. The key event, then, is the peyote hunt.

The Peyote Hunt In 1966, Barbara Myerhoff and Peter Furst accompanied Huichol pilgrims on the peyote hunt. Each pilgrim was given the name of a Huichol god for the duration of the pilgrimage. The pilgrims, under the guidance of a shaman, all followed strict rules about sexual continence and other behaviors, separating themselves from their everyday routine. Once the pilgrims entered Wirikuta, many ways of speaking and acting were reversed. "Stand up" meant "sit down"; "go away" meant "come here." The van in which they traveled became a "burro" that would stop "if he ran out of tequila." The shaman who led the pilgrimage told Myerhoff that

FIGURE 8.10 A Huichol shaman's violin and arrows, together with a basket of freshly gathered peyote.

"on the peyote hunt, we change the names of things because when we cross over there, into Wirikuta, things are so sacred that all is reversed" (Myerhoff 1974, 148).

In the sacred land, the pilgrims became hunters, searching for peyote. Once the first peyote cactus was found, it was trapped by two arrows. The pilgrims then encircled it and presented their offerings. The shaman cut it out of the ground, sliced sections, and put one section in each pilgrim's mouth. The little group was sharply etched against the desert in the late afternoon sun—motionless, soundless, the once-bright colors of their costumes now muted under layers of dust—chewing, chewing the bitter plant. So Sahagún described the ancient Indians who wept in the desert over the plant they esteemed so greatly. The success of the undertaking was unquestionable and the faces changed from quiet wonder to rapture to exaltation all without words, all at the same moment. . . . Their camaraderie, the completeness of their communion with one another was self-evident.

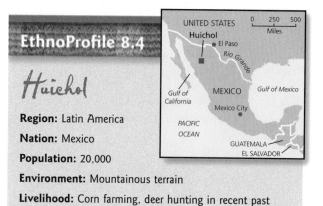

EthnoProfile 8.4

Huichol

Region: Latin America

Nation: Mexico

Population: 20,000

Environment: Mountainous terrain

Livelihood: Corn farming, deer hunting in recent past

Political organization: Traditionally, no formal organization, some men with influence; today, part of a modern nation-state

For more information: Myerhoff, Barbara. 1974. *Peyote hunt*. Ithaca, NY: Cornell University Press.

The companions were radiant. Their love for life and for one another was palpable. Though they did not speak and barely moved, no one seeing them there could call the experience anything less than collective ecstasy. (Myerhoff 1974, 155–57)

Following this moment of communitas, the pilgrims collected as much peyote as they would need for their community and hastened to depart. The reversals and other requirements remained in effect until they reached home.

The unification of deer, maize, and peyote gives the peyote hunt its power. As Myerhoff puts it, "In the climactic moments of the rituals in Wirikuta, these symbols provide the Huichols with a formulation of the large questions dealt with by religion, the questions of ultimate meaning and purpose."

She suggests that the way the Huichol's religious system answers these questions is distinctive. Some religions explain present-day moral incoherence by asserting that an original paradise was lost following an ancient sin. Other systems assert that there is an afterlife in which all the suffering of the world will be set right. But the Huichol refuse to let go of their past. "Their most precious religious heritage—their beginnings—is idealized and recovered. Even if only for a little while, by means of the peyote hunt, Paradise may be regained. Through the deer-maize-peyote complex, the deer and a life dedicated to hunting the deer is still a fact of present-day life rather than a fading, shabby memory, chewed over by old men at the end of the day" (1974, 262). In the terms we have been using so far, the deer-maize-peyote complex and the peyote hunt represent the union of mind, body, and emotion. Through a holistic ritual experience that is profoundly meaningful, deeply moving, and thoroughly physical, the Huichol reexperience the correctness of their way of life.

Witchcraft, Oracles, and Magic among the Azande

Anthropologist E. E. Evans-Pritchard, in his classic work *Witchcraft, Oracles, and Magic Among the Azande* ([1937] 1976), shows how Azande beliefs and practices concerning witchcraft, oracles, and magic are related to one another (see EthnoProfile 8.5: Azande). He describes how Azande use witchcraft beliefs to explain unfortunate things that happen to

EthnoProfile 8.5

Azande

Region: Central Africa

Nation: Sudan, Democratic Republic of Congo (Zaire), Central African Republic

Population: 1,100,000

Environment: Sparsely wooded savanna

Livelihood: Farming, hunting, fishing, chicken raising

Political organization: Traditionally, highly organized, tribal kingdoms; today, part of modern nation-states

For more information: Evans-Pritchard, E. E. [1937] 1976. *Witchcraft, oracles, and magic among the Azande,* abridged ed. Oxford: Oxford University Press.

them and how they employ oracles and magic to exert a measure of control over the actions of other people. Evans-Pritchard was impressed by the intelligence, sophistication, and skepticism of his Azande informants. For this reason, he was all the more struck by their ability to hold a set of beliefs that many Europeans would regard as superstitious.

Azande Witchcraft Beliefs   The Azande believe that *mangu* (translated by Evan-Pritchard as **witchcraft**) is a substance in the body of witches, generally located under the sternum.* Being part of the body, the witchcraft substance grows as the body grows; therefore, the older the witch, the more potent his or her witchcraft. The Azande believe that children inherit

*Beliefs and practices similar to those associated with Azande mangu have been found in many other societies, and it has become traditional in anthropology to refer to them as "witchcraft." This technical usage must not be confused with everyday uses of the word in contemporary Western societies, still less with the practices of followers of movements like Wicca, which are very different.

witchcraft The performance of evil by human beings believed to possess an innate, nonhuman power to do evil, whether or not it is intentional or self-aware.

witchcraft from their parents. Men and women may both be witches. Men practice witchcraft against other men, women against other women. Witchcraft works when its "soul" removes the soul of a certain organ in the victim's body, usually at night, causing a slow, wasting disease. Suffering such a disease is therefore an indication that an individual has been bewitched.

Witchcraft is a basic concept for the Azande, one that shapes their experience of adversity. All deaths are due to witchcraft and must be avenged by **magic**. Other misfortunes are also commonly attributed to witchcraft unless the victim has broken a taboo, has failed to observe a moral rule, or is believed to be responsible for his own problems. Suppose I am an incompetent potter and my pots break while I am firing them. I may claim that witchcraft caused them to break, but everyone will laugh at me because they know I lack skill. Witchcraft is believed to be so common that the Azande are neither surprised nor awestruck when they encounter it. Their usual response is anger.

To the Azande, witchcraft is a completely natural explanation for events. Consider the classic case of the collapsing granary. Azandeland is hot, and people seeking shade often sit under traditional raised granaries, which rest on logs. Termites are common in Azandeland, and sometimes they destroy the supporting logs, making a granary collapse. Occasionally, when a granary collapses, people sitting under it are killed. Why does this happen? The Azande are well aware that the termites chew up the wood until the supports give way, but to them that is not answer enough. Why, after all, should that particular granary have collapsed at that particular moment? To skeptical observers, the only connection is coincidence in time and space. Western science does not provide any explanation for why these two chains of causation intersect. But the Azande do: Witchcraft causes the termites to finish chewing up the wood at just that moment, and that witchcraft must be avenged.

magic A set of beliefs and practices designed to control the visible or invisible world for specific purposes.

oracles Invisible forces to which people address questions and whose responses they believe to be truthful.

Dealing with Witches   How to expose the witch? For this task, the Azande employ **oracles** (invisible forces to which people address questions and whose responses they believe to be truthful). Preeminent among these is the poison oracle. The poison is a strychnine-like substance imported into Azandeland. The oracle "speaks" through the effect the poison has on chickens. When witchcraft is suspected, a relative of the afflicted person will take some chickens into the bush along with a specialist in administering the poison oracle. This person will feed poison to one chicken, name a suspect, and ask the oracle to kill the chicken if this person is the witch. If the chicken dies, a second chicken will be fed poison, and the oracle will be asked to spare the chicken if the suspect just named is indeed the witch. Thus, the Azande double-check the oracle carefully; a witchcraft accusation is not made lightly.

People do not consult the oracle with a long list of names. They need only consider those who might wish them or their families ill: people who have quarreled with them, who are unpleasant, who are antisocial, and whose behavior is somehow out of line. Indeed, witches are always neighbors, because neighbors are the only people who know you well enough to wish you and your family ill.

Once the oracle has identified the witch, the Azande removes the wing of the chicken and has it taken by messenger to the compound of the accused person. The messenger presents the accused witch with the chicken wing and says that he has been sent concerning the illness of so-and-so's relative. "Almost invariably the witch replies courteously that he is unconscious of injuring anyone, that if it is true that he has injured the man in question he is very sorry, and that if it is he alone who is troubling him then he will surely recover, because from the bottom of his heart he wishes him health and happiness" (Evans-Pritchard [1937] 1976, 42). The accused then calls for a gourd of water, takes some in his mouth, and sprays it out over the wing. He says aloud, so the messenger can hear and repeat what he says, that if he is a witch he is not aware of it and that he is not intentionally causing the sick man to be ill. He addresses the witchcraft in him, asking it to become cool, and concludes by saying that he makes this appeal from his heart, not just from his lips (42).

People accused of witchcraft are usually astounded; no Azande thinks of himself or herself as a witch. However, the Azande strongly believe in witchcraft and in the oracles, and if the oracle says someone is a witch, then that person must be one. The accused witch is grateful to the family of the sick person for letting this be known. Otherwise, if the accused had been allowed to murder the victim, all the while unaware of it, the witch would surely be killed by vengeance magic. The witchcraft accusation carries a further message: The behavior of the accused is sufficiently outside the bounds of acceptable Azande behavior to have marked him or her as a potential witch. Only the names of people you suspect wish you ill are submitted to the oracle. The accused witch, then, is being told to change his or her behavior.

Patterns of Witchcraft Accusation

Compared with the stereotypes of European American witchcraft—old hags dressed in black, riding on broomsticks, casting spells, causing milk to sour or people to sicken—Azande witchcraft seems quite tame. People whose impression of witchcraft comes from Western European images may believe that witchcraft and witch-hunting tear at the very fabric of society. Yet anthropological accounts like Evans-Pritchard's suggest that practices such as witchcraft accusation can sometimes keep societies together.

Anthropologist Mary Douglas looked at the range of witchcraft accusations worldwide and discovered that they fall into two basic types (1970, xxvi–xxvii): In some cases, the witch is an evil outsider; in others, the witch is an internal enemy, either the member of a rival faction or a dangerous deviant. These different patterns of accusation perform different functions in a society. If the witch is an outsider, witchcraft accusations can strengthen in-group ties. If the witch is an internal enemy, accusations of witchcraft can weaken in-group ties; factions may have to regroup, communities may split, and the entire social hierarchy may be reordered. If the witch is a dangerous deviant, the accusation of witchcraft can be seen as an attempt to control the deviant in defense of the wider values of the community. Douglas concludes that how people understand witchcraft is based on social relations of their society.

Seeking Higher Consciousness among the Channelers

Anthropologist Michael F. Brown has spent several years studying the beliefs and practices of "alternative spirituality," or "New Age spirituality," focusing particularly on channeling, the use of altered states of consciousness to contact spirits, "or, as many of its practitioners say, to experience spiritual energy captured from other times and dimensions" (Brown 1997, viii). The practitioners of channeling, called channels, believe that they can "use altered states of consciousness to connect to wisdom emanating from the collective unconscious or even from other planets, dimensions, or historical eras" (6). Brown was fascinated to see how channeling brings together several important strands of North American culture: individualism, the personal recovery movement, and women-centered spirituality meld with features of nineteenth-century spiritualism to provide practitioners and followers with meaning, coherence, and a sense of control over events in what Brown refers to as "an anxious age" (Figure 8.11).

If one can speak of a theology of channeling, Brown concludes that it is based on four key assumptions. First, channels and their followers believe that human beings are in essence gods. Individuals are referred to as "fragments of the God-Head" or "Christed beings." These metaphors imply not only that humans share in the divinity that created the universe but also that we are immortal, inherently good, and fully able to create our own reality (47). Second, humans are not all fully developed beings. Channels and their clients generally believe that human beings undergo a series of reincarnations in order to acquire important learning experiences. This evolutionary process may involve previous lives lived on earth or on different planets or in different dimensions. Third, channels and their clients believe that each of us is responsible for creating our own reality. In their view, thoughts shape reality, and the impact of any thought is magnified when a critical mass of like-minded people share it (47–48). From their perspective, if enough people "Visualize World Peace," it will suddenly happen. Finally, channels and their clients believe in the transcendent value of holism. "The purpose of channeling is to bring together elements of life ripped apart by Western civilization:

FIGURE 8.11 Gerry Bowman channeling John the Baptist at the Harmonic Convergence of the Planets, celebrated in California in 1987.

male and female, reason and intuition, thought and matter. . . . Channels and their clients see the universe as a single interconnected field. Just as the thought patterns of individuals can reshape the cosmos, so shifts in the cosmos affect individuals" (48–49).

What follows from this theology is a moral framework in which the existence of evil is called into question. As we have seen, the Azande explain misfortune in terms of witchcraft. Channels and their clients explain misfortune—illness, poverty, or other forms of suffering—in one of two ways. On the one hand, misfortune occurs because the victims cannot or will not envision the world in ways that protect them from it. "Calamity originates in a failure of individual attitude or thought" (Brown 1997, 65). On the other, channels assert that victims have chosen their own fate, usually at a "deep soul level" that is beyond their own conscious awareness. The logic here is that the reincarnating soul chooses certain challenges as part of its growth process. Thus, a person who has cancer has, at some level, chosen to have it because the experience is important or necessary to the development of a higher consciousness over the course of the many lives that soul will live.

While some observers regard this as a form of blaming the victim, channels see their position as a way of asserting control. Channels see themselves "explicitly reacting against the contemporary American cult of victimhood. . . . Channeling's theological framework rejects victimhood because of its connotation of powerlessness, arguing instead that everyone suffers indignities on their way to higher consciousness. These painful episodes are important learning experiences, but nothing is gained by dwelling on them" (67).

Thus, people drawn to channeling believe that they are the authors of their own fate. If people are divine actors, then their temporary setbacks and troubles must be part of a master plan that they themselves have designed, and they are inevitably responsible to some degree for their own misfortunes (Brown 1997, 68). Among other things, this way of explaining misfortune totally rejects the social nature of human experience. As opposed to Azande witchcraft beliefs, where misfortune is due to the ill will of others, channeling is a belief system of and for individuals. Although claiming to offer a corrective to the sense of isolation that many people feel, ironically, channeling isolates individuals from one another even more, by making each of us a world unto ourselves.

IN THEIR OWN WORDS

For All Those Who Were Indian in a Former Life

Andrea Smith challenges members of the New Age movement who, in her view, trivialize the situation of women like herself "who are Indian in this life."

The New Age movement completely trivializes the oppression we as Indian women face: Indian women are suddenly no longer the women who are forcibly sterilized and tested with unsafe drugs such as Depo Provera; we are no longer the women who have a life expectancy of 47 years; and we are no longer the women who generally live below the poverty level and face a 75 percent unemployment rate. No, we're too busy being cool and spiritual.

This trivialization of our oppression is compounded by the fact that nowadays anyone can be Indian if s/he wants to. All that is required is that one be Indian in a former life, or take part in a sweat lodge, or be mentored by a "medicine woman," or read a how-to book.

Since, according to this theory, anyone can now be "Indian," then the term Indians no longer regresses specifically to those people who have survived five hundred years of colonization and genocide. This furthers the goals of white supremacists to abrogate treaty rights and to take away what little we have left. When everyone becomes "Indian," then it is easy to lose sight of the specificity of oppression faced by those who are Indian in this life. It is no wonder we have such a difficult time finding non-Indians to support our struggles when the New Age movement has completely disguised our oppression.

The most disturbing aspect about these racist practices is that they are promoted in the name of feminism. Sometimes it seems that I can't open a feminist periodical without seeing ads promoting white "feminist" practices with little medicine wheel designs. I can't seem to go to a feminist conference without the woman who begins the conference with a ceremony being the only Indian presenter. Participants then feel so "spiritual" after this opening that they fail to notice the absence of Indian women in the rest of the conference or Native American issues in the discussions. And I certainly can't go to a feminist bookstore without seeing books by Lynn Andrews and other people who exploit Indian spirituality all over the place. It seems that, while feminism is supposed to signify the empowerment of all women, it obviously does not include Indian women.

If white feminists are going to act in solidarity with their Indian sisters, they must take a stand against Indian spiritual abuse. Feminist book and record stores should stop selling these products, and feminist periodicals should stop advertising these products. Women who call themselves feminists should denounce exploitative practices wherever they see them.

Source: A. Smith 1994, 71.

▼ MAINTAINING AND CHANGING A WORLDVIEW

What makes a worldview stable? Why is a worldview rejected? These questions are related to general questions about persistence and change in human social life. Anthropologists recognize that culture change is a complex phenomenon, and they admit that they do not have all the answers.

Changes in worldview must, first of all, be related to the practical everyday experiences of people in a particular society. Stable, repetitive experiences reinforce the acceptability of any traditional worldview that has successfully accounted for such experiences in the past. When experiences become unpredictable, however, thinking people in any society may become painfully aware that past experiences can no longer be trusted as guides for the future, and traditional worldviews may be undermined (see Horton 1982, 252).

Syncretism and Revitalization

Drastic changes in experience lead people to create new interpretations that will help them cope with the changes. Sometimes the change is an outcome of local or regional struggles. The Protestant Reformation for example, adapted the Christian tradition to changing social circumstances in northern Europe during the Renaissance by breaking ties to the pope, turning church lands over to secular authorities, allowing clergy to marry, and so forth. Protestants continued to identify themselves as Christians even though many of their religious practices had changed.

In Guider, lone rural migrants to town frequently abandoned old religious practices and took on urban customs and a new identity through conversion to Islam. However, the conflict between new and old need not necessarily lead to conversion. Sometimes the result is a creative synthesis of old religious practices and new ones, a process called **syncretism**. Under the pressure of Christian missionizing, indigenous people of Central America identified some of their own pre-Christian, personalized superhuman beings with particular Catholic saints. Similarly, Africans brought to Brazil identified Catholic saints with African gods, to produce the syncretistic religion Candomblé.

Anthropologists have debated the nature of syncretistic practices, noting that while some may be viewed as a way of resisting new ideas imposed from above, others may be introduced from above by powerful outsiders deliberately making room for local beliefs within their own supralocal worldview. The Romans, for example, made room for local deities within their imperial pantheon, and post–Vatican II Catholicism explicitly urges non-European Catholics to worship using local cultural forms (Stewart and Shaw 1994).

> **syncretism** The synthesis of old religious practices (or an old way of life) with new religious practices (or a new way of life) introduced from outside, often by force.
>
> **revitalization** A conscious, deliberate, and organized attempt by some members of a society to create a more satisfying culture in a time of crisis.

When groups defend or refashion their own way of life in the face of outside encroachments, anthropologists sometimes describe their activities as **revitalization**—a deliberate, organized attempt by some members of a society to create a more satisfying culture (Wallace 1972, 75). Revitalization arises in times of crisis, most often among groups who are facing oppression and radical transformation, usually at the hands of outsiders (such as colonizing powers). Revitalization movements engage in a "politics of religious synthesis" that produces a range of outcomes (Stewart and Shaw 1994). Sometimes syncretism is embraced. Other times it is rejected in favor of nativism, or a return to the old ways. Some nativistic movements expect a messiah or prophet, who will bring back a lost golden age of peace, prosperity, and harmony, a process often called *revivalism, millennarianism*, or *messianism*.

A classic New World example of a millennarian movement was the Ghost Dance movement among indigenous peoples on the Great Plains of the United States in the 1890s. When the buffalo were exterminated, indigenous Plains dwellers lost their independence and were herded onto reservations by numerically superior and better-armed European Americans. Out of this final crisis emerged Wovoka, a prophet who taught that the existing world would soon be destroyed and that a new crust would form on the earth. All settlers and indigenous people who followed the settlers' ways would become buried. Those indigenous people who abandoned the settlers' ways, led pure lives, and danced the Ghost Dance would be saved. As the new crust formed, the buffalo would return, as would all the ancestors of the believers. Together, all would lead lives of virtue and joy.

Because the world was going to change by itself, violence against the oppressors was not a necessary part of the Ghost Dance. Nevertheless, the movement frightened settlers and the U.S. Army, who suspected an armed uprising. Those fears and suspicions led to the massacre at Wounded Knee, in which the cavalry troopers killed all the members of a Lakota (Sioux) band, principally women and children, whom they encountered off the reservation.

The Bwiti Religion A revitalization movement that has enjoyed greater longevity is the syncretistic Bwiti

FIGURE 8.12 Women rest after taking eboga during a Bwiti initiation in Libreville, Gabon, in 2005.

religion (Figure 8.12) of the Fang in Central Africa (see EthnoProfile 8.3: Fang). In the last century, the Fang have faced three important challenges to their worldview. First, the reality of "the far away," represented by French colonialism, came to challenge the reality of "the near" and familiar. Second, the protective traditional powers of "the below" were challenged by Christian missionaries' message of divinity in "the above." Third, the pluralism of colonial life was a double standard in which the colonized were treated differently from the colonizers (Fernandez 1982, 571). Bwiti allows its members to cope with the first challenge by using the drug eboga to go out to the far and convert it into the near. In the second case, the Christian god of the above and the traditional gods of the below are both incorporated into the Bwiti pantheon. For the third, Bwiti ritual promotes among members the communal feeling of "one-heartedness."

Bwiti has created a worldview that allows many Fang to cope with the strains of exploitation. Within Bwiti, some old metaphors (the forest, the body social, the kinship system) have been reanimated, some new ones (red and white uniforms, a path of birth and death, the world as a globe or a ball) have been created, and all have been fitted together in a satisfying way. This world has, however, closed itself off from the wider society of the Gabon Republic. Bwiti

represents a kind of escape from the pressures of the outside world (566).

Kwaio Religion   Nativistic movements, however, may represent resistance to, rather than escape from, the outside world, actively removing or avoiding any cultural practices associated with those who seek to dominate them. One such "anti-syncretistic" group is the Kwaio, living on the island of Malaita in the Solomon Islands (see EthnoProfile 8.6: Kwaio). Almost all their neighbors have converted to Christianity, and the nation of which they are a part is militantly Christian. Members of other groups wear clothing, work on plantations or in tourist hotels, attend schools, and live in cities. The Kwaio have refused all this: "Young men carry bows and arrows; girls and women, nude except for customary ornaments, dig taro in forest gardens; valuables made of strung shell beads are exchanged at mortuary feasts; and priests sacrifice pigs to the ancestral spirits on whom prosperity and life itself depend" (Keesing 1982, 1).

Roger Keesing (1992) admits that he does not know exactly why the Kwaio responded to colonial influence in this way. He suspects that precolonial social and political differences between the Kwaio and their coastal neighbors influenced later developments. The colonial encounter was certainly relevant. In 1927, some Kwaio attacked a British patrol, killing

EthnoProfile 8.6

Kwaio

Region: Oceania (Melanesia)

Nation: Solomon Islands (Malaita)

Population: 7,000 (1970s)

Environment: Tropical island

Livelihood: Horticulture and pig raising

Political organization: Traditionally, some men with influence but no coercive power; today, part of a modern nation-state

For more information: Keesing, Roger. 1992. *Custom and confrontation.* Chicago: University of Chicago Press.

Map: SOUTH PACIFIC OCEAN; Choiseul; Santa Isabel; SOLOMON ISLANDS; New Georgia Islands; ■ Kwaio; Malaita; Guadalcanal; San Cristobal; Santa Cruz Islands; Solomon Sea; Aunuta; Tikopia; Torres Islands; Banks Islands; Coral Sea; Vanuatu; 0 100 200 Miles

the district officer and 13 Solomon Island troops. The subsequent massacre of many Kwaio by a police force of other Malaitans and their marginalization and persecution by the colonial government contributed to Kwaio resistance.

It is important to emphasize that the Kwaio maintain their old ways deliberately, in the face of alternatives; their traditional way of life is therefore lived in a modern context. "In the course of anticolonial struggle, 'kastomu' (custom) and commitment to ancestral ways have become symbols of identity and autonomy" (Keesing 1982, 240). In the eyes of the Kwaio, the many Solomon Islanders who became Christianized and acculturated lost their cultural ties and thereby their ties to the land and to their past, becoming outsiders in their own homeland. Maintaining traditional ways is thus a form of political protest. From this perspective, many contemporary anti-syncretistic movements in the world, from various religious fundamentalisms to movements for national identity and cultural autonomy, can be understood as having aims very similar to those of the Kwaio, sparked by many of the same forces.

---

ideology A worldview that justifies the social arrangements under which people live.

▼ WORLDVIEWS AS INSTRUMENTS OF POWER

We have discussed the process that people use to build their worldviews and have noted how worldviews vary enormously from culture to culture. But within any particular cultural tradition, there are probably always different worldviews. But it is often the case that one particular account gets presented to outsiders as the "official" worldview of a given culture. How does this happen? To be in the running for the official picture of reality, a worldview must be able, however minimally, to make sense of some people's personal and social experiences. Sometimes, however, it may seem to some members of society that barely credible views of reality have triumphed over alternatives that seem far more plausible. Thus, something more than persuasive ability alone must be involved, and that something is power. As Lakoff and Johnson put it, "People in power get to impose their metaphors" (1980, 157).

When one worldview is backed by the powerful in society and alternative worldviews are censored, many social scientists would start to call the dominant worldview an ideology. An **ideology** can be defined as a cultural product of conscious reflection, such as beliefs about morality, religion, or metaphysics. As used in Marxian analysis, an ideology is a worldview used to explain and justify the social arrangements under which people live. Karl Marx argued that rulers consolidate their power by successfully persuading their subjects to accept an ideology that portrays domination by the rulers as legitimate. When such persuasion is difficult, rulers may use coercive measures to silence their critics. Dominated people may be unable to dislodge the official worldview of their society. They can, however, refuse to accept the imposition of someone else's worldview and develop an unofficial worldview based on metaphors that reflect their own condition of powerlessness (Scott 1990). Such unofficial worldviews may even suggest appropriate action for transforming that condition, as we will see in Chapter 10.

How can metaphors, or the symbols that represent them, be used as instruments of power and control? First, a symbol can be used to refer to self-evident truths when people in power seek to eliminate

Custom and Confrontation

In the following passage, the late Roger Keesing recorded the words of one of his Kwaio informants, Dangeabe'u, who defends Kwaio custom.

The government has brought the ways of business, the ways of money. The people at the coast believe that's what's important, and tell us we should join in. Now the government is controlling the whole world. The side of the Bible is withering away. When that's finished, the government will rule unchallenged. It will hold all the land. All the money will go to the government to feed its power. Once everything—our lands, too—are in their hands, that will be it.

I've seen the people from other islands who have all become Christians. They knew nothing about their land. The white people have gotten their hands on their lands.

The whites led them to forget all the knowledge of their land, separated them from it. And when the people knew nothing about their land, the whites bought it from them and made their enterprises. . . .

That's close upon us too. If we all follow the side of the Bible, the government will become powerful here too, and will take control of our land. We won't be attached to our land, as we are now, holding our connections to our past. If the government had control of our land, then if we wanted to do anything on it, we'd have to pay them. If we wanted to start a business—a store, say— we'd have to pay the government. We reject all that. We want to keep hold of our land, in the ways passed down to us.

Source: Keesing 1992, 184.

or impose certain forms of conduct. Thus, a deceased parent, whose memory must be respected, may be invoked to block some actions or to stimulate others. Holy books, like the Qur'an, may also be used in this way. For example, a legal record from Guider indicates that a son once brought suit against his father for refusing to repay him a certain amount of money. The father claimed that he had paid. Both father and son got into an increasingly heated argument in which neither would give ground. Finally, the judge in the case asked the father to take a copy of the Qur'an in his hand and swear that he was telling the truth. This he did. The son, however, refused to swear on the Qur'an and finally admitted that he had been lying. In this case, the status of the Qur'an as the unquestioned word of God, which implied the power of God to punish liars, controlled the son's behavior.

Second, a symbol may be under the direct control of a person wishing to affect the behavior of others. Consider the role of official interpreters of religious or political ideology, such as priests or kings. Their pronouncements define the bounds of permissible behavior. As Roger Keesing points out, "Senior men, in

Melanesia as elsewhere in the tribal world, have depended heavily on control of *sacred knowledge* to maintain their control of earthly politics. By keeping in their hands relations with ancestors and other spirits, by commanding magical knowledge, senior men could maintain a control mediated by the supernatural. Such religious ideologies served too, by defining rules in terms of ancient spirits and by defining the nature of men and women in supernatural terms, to reinforce and maintain the roles of the sexes—and again to hide their nature" (1982, 219).

Keesing's observations remind us that knowledge, like power, is not evenly distributed throughout a society. Just as some people speak or write or carve better than others, so too some people possess knowledge and control symbols to which others are denied access. Furthermore, this distribution of knowledge is not random: Different kinds of people know different things. In some societies, what men know about their religious system is different from what women know, and what older men know may be different from what younger men know. Such discrepancies can have important consequences. Keesing

FIGURE 8.13 Senior Dogon men carrying out fox trail divination. The knowledge and skills of elderly men, based on experience gained over a lifetime, provide their interpretations with an authority that those of people with less experience would not have.

suggested that men's control over women and older men's control over younger men are based on differential access to knowledge (1982, 14). It is not just that these different kinds of people know different things; rather, the different things they know (and don't know) enable them (or force them) to remain in the positions they hold in the society (Figure 8.13).

secularism The separation of religion and state, including a notion of secular citizenship that owes much to the notion of individual agency developed in Protestant theology.

▼ IS SECULARISM A WORLDVIEW?

The European Enlightenment gave birth to a new worldview that has come to be called "**secularism**," and the spread of this worldview has had repercussions across the globe. The development of secular ideas and practices profoundly transformed the religious and political institutions that had dominated European society in the Middle Ages. Earlier generations of anthropologists took secularism for granted, as the expected outcome of cultural evolution. More recently, however, anthropologists have been led to reconsider the nature of both the Enlightenment and of secularism, prompted most sharply by resistance to the secular institutions of Western nation-states, both by some immigrant groups living within those states and by groups in non-Western nation-states who insist that citizenship and religious identity belong together. Perhaps the most difficult have been the struggles of some Muslim groups to adjust to life in Western secular states.

Religion and Secularism

What happens when individuals and groups whose religious and political roots lay outside this European history come to live in modern, secular Europe? The distinction between what the liberal democratic state expects and what some Muslims want has recently been explored by anthropologist Talal Asad. His efforts to develop an "anthropology of secularism" highlight the ways in which notions of the secular were shaped in the course of European history, particularly by the Protestant Reformation of Christianity, the subsequent wars of religion in the sixteenth and early seventeenth centuries and by the Enlightenment and French Revolution of the eighteenth century.

Secularism is usually defined as the separation of religion and state, and is commonly understood as the Enlightenment solution to the bloody and irresolvable wars of religion that followed the Reformation. But Asad's account shows that European secularism presupposed a specific post-Reformation concept of "religion" and a very specific post-Enlightenment concept of "the state," as well as a notion of secular citizenship that owes much to the notion of individual agency developed in Protestant theology. "The secular," he argues, "is a concept that brings together certain behaviors, knowledges, and sensibilities in modern life" (2003, 25).

The particularities of modern secularism may be clarified if we return to the distinction made in chapter 7 between orthodoxy and orthopraxy. Religious disputes in the Reformation and the wars of religion concerned questions of doctrinal *orthodoxy*—that is, correct religious beliefs. In European secularism, thus, "religion" is defined primarily in terms of the beliefs to which its adherents are committed. Similarly, the secular "state" is always understood to be the modern nation-state with a capitalist economy. It is from these understandings of "religion" and "state" that the Enlightenment concept of *citizenship* develops. Secular citizenship, Asad explains, is supposed to "transcend the different identities built on class, gender, and religion, replacing conflicting perspectives by unifying experience. In a sense, this transcendent mediation *is* secularism" (2003, 5). Secular citizens are first and foremost individuals unencumbered by ties to other social groups who possess *within themselves* the motivation to formulate goals, the resources to initiate action to pursue those goals, and who are responsible for the consequences of their actions. This concept of agency, absolutely crucial to the successful functioning of democratic government and the capitalist market, was itself the product of Protestant theology. In the religious context, independent, self-motivating individuals were responsible before God; in their role as citizens of a liberal secular state, they are individually responsible before the law.

Thus, secularism as a political doctrine clearly developed as a response to specific religious, political, and economic developments in early modern Europe. Secularism depends, for example, on the notion that a domain of social life exists that is "worldly," distinct from a realm in which religion holds sway. In Christian Europe, this domain was recognized when proponents of what would become "science," such as Francis Bacon and Robert Boyle, successfully argued that the "supernatural" spiritual realm of God was separate and distinct from the "natural" material world of lifeless, inert matter (Keller 1997). The distinction between supernatural and natural worlds "signals the construction of a secular space that begins to emerge in early modernity" (Asad 2003, 27). This secular space would be the ground to which the modern nation-state would lay claim.

Religion and state remained entangled after the wars of religion, however, since "religious freedom" was left in the hands of the states themselves. That is, citizens were to profess the faith of their princes, and if their princes changed allegiance, the allegiance of citizens was to follow. But this arrangement created in every state religious minorities of "dissenters" whose rights as citizens were regularly curtailed. Protest against these inequalities fueled the secular democratic political theory of the Enlightenment, embodied in the "Declaration of the Rights of Man and the Citizen" and secured by the French Revolution. Now religious affiliation was a matter of individual conscience and could not be imposed by the state. But at the time, as Asad notes, "the decisive movements that helped to break the allegiance of church and state seem to have been religious . . . aimed at securing the freedom of Christ's church from the constraints of earthly power" (2003, 174). One consequence of this change "was the eventual emergence of 'minority rights.' But this consequence contained a paradox. Religious minorities in a secular state were at once equal to other citizens [and] . . . unequal to the majority, requiring special protection" (2003, 174).

Secularism is "not a simple matter of absence of 'religion' in the public life of the modern nation-state. For even in modern secular countries the place of religion varies" (Asad 2003, 5–6). But Asad's analysis suggests that adaptation to life in a liberal secular state is likely to be difficult and painful for those whose religious commitments are rooted primarily in forms of religious *orthopraxy*—correct practice. "Many traditions," he writes, "attribute to the living human body the potential to be shaped (the power to shape itself) for good or ill. . . . The living body's materiality is regarded as an essential means for cultivating what such traditions define as virtuous conduct and for discouraging what they consider as vice. The role of fear and hope, of felicity and pain, is central to such practices . . . the more one exercises a virtue the easier it becomes . . . the more one gives into vice, the harder it is to act virtuously" (2003, 89–90). Islamic religious traditions are rooted in such orthopraxy, and cultivation of correct practice depends upon one's embeddedness within a community of like-minded practitioners.

When successful, such orthopraxy is understood to produce "the virtue of faithfulness, [which is] an unquestioning habit of obedience." Faithfulness is "a disposition that has to be cultivated like any other, and that links one to others who are faithful, through mutual trust and responsibility" (90). Religious orthopraxy of this kind can only be sustained by faithful practitioners whose entire way of life is informed by, and acts to reinforce, these unquestioning habits of obedience. If this is the case, then such forms of orthopraxy would appear to be incompatible with secularism. "For many Muslim minorities (though by no means all) being Muslim is more than simply belonging to an individual faith whose private integrity needs to be publicly respected by the force of law and being able to participate in the public domain as equal citizens. It is more than the cultural identity recognized by the liberal democratic state. It is being able to live as autonomous individuals in a collective life that extends beyond national borders" (2003, 180). It was precisely this apparent incompatibility that was made visible in the recent "affair of the headscarves" in France.

Muslim Headscarves in France: A Case Study

In recent decades, many immigrants to France have come from Muslim countries, particularly in North Africa. By the late 1980s, some French public schools had high proportions of Muslim students. As their numbers increased, controversy developed when some of the women students were denied the right to wear their traditional headcoverings in school. From the point of view of the Muslim families, wearing headcoverings in public was a religiously required mode of dress necessary to protect female modesty in public. Controversy erupted when the French government insisted that the headscarves could not be worn in school.

Understanding why the French government was so adamant in its refusal depends on understanding what secularism means in the French republic. Anthropologist John Bowen (2002, 283–84) describes the history of the relation between religion and state that developed in France after the French Revolution in 1789. As noted, a major consequence of the Revolution was the elimination of special privileges for the Catholic Church, which until that time had been the official religion of the French state. Since the Revolution, the French state has been resolutely secular, requiring that all French citizens, whether students or employees of the state, refrain from drawing atten-

tion in public to their religious affiliations. Although Catholic students were allowed to wear necklaces with Catholic crosses, male Jewish students wishing to wear a kippah (headcovering) and female Muslim students wishing to wear headscarves were told to remove their headcoverings or they would be prohibited from attending school.

By 1989, religious groups claiming the right to exercise their religious values in public were ready to test the French secular ideal. In October 1989, three Muslim French girls of North African descent wore headcoverings to their public school. The school insisted that they remove the scarves and dress like the other girls. The girls and their families refused, claiming that wearing the scarf was part of their religious practice. Some of the students also refused to attend biology classes, on the grounds that studying biological evolution contradicted their religious beliefs, or to attend coed physical education classes, since they were immodest. Other schools around the country were challenged in the same way; and in November 1989 the government ruled that the Muslim girls' right to religious expression included wearing a headscarf. But after the French government changed from socialist to center-right, the issue arose again in 1993; this time the government banned the wearing of headcoverings in schools.

The government's decision to ban the headscarves was not merely a political response to the xenophobic far right in French politics, which claims that immigration has caused all of the economic problems that France faces and is opposed to "non-French" practices. Rather, the decision follows from the secular worldview of the French state, and it was supported by many people on the political left, not just those on the right. Bowen observes that the French state grants full citizenship rights to the children of immigrants, but in return, the "social contract" assumes that the children will be educated to be culturally French. In the official French view, students are to see themselves as identical in all respects except for achievement in school. If certain groups within the system should be allowed to argue that they are in some way fundamentally different from all other citizens, especially if the difference is defined as religious, the resolutely secular identity of the French state is called into question, raising issues that were presumed to have been properly settled long ago. Clearly those who allied in opposition to, or in support of, the wearing of headscarves assumed very different things about the character of the state and what counted as religious toleration.

The Muslim girls were supported by some conservative Catholics and some antiracism activists, while many on the extreme right wing and many on the left opposed the decision to permit headscarves to be worn. In fact, in 1996, some teachers in the town of Albertville, in the French Alps, organized a street protest march in opposition to the wearing of the headscarf, and the minister of education stated that the Republic imposes on citizens a common space of secularity (Ferenczi 1996). This is one of the major arguments that has been raised: Secularism is challenged by the scarves. The French left has long seen itself as guardian of the secular, anticlerical tradition that began with the French Revolution, and public education was the means by which the power of the Church was to be combated. Many of the partisans of the left also argued that the scarves were the symbol of the oppression of women. "Putting on jeans is an act of freedom; putting on the scarf is an act of submission" (Bowen 2002, 284, citing Moruzzi 1994). The political right agreed with that argument but placed it in the context of "the battle between Christianity and Islam, and the general threat to French identity posed by immigrants" (250).

Although France's highest administrative court reaffirmed the ban on headscarves in public schools in October 1999 (J. Gregory 1999), the controversy has continued. In February and March 2004, the French national assembly and senate voted overwhelmingly to ban "conspicuous" religious symbols in the schools. Although this law is presented as necessary to protect the secular state from the divisiveness of religious particularism, and prohibits the Jewish kippa and large Christian crosses as well as Muslim headscarves, many argue that the Muslin headscarf is its real target. The law, which affects about 1,200 of the 250,000 Muslim students in French schools, has provoked heated debate in France. Some analysts insist that this law will prompt a hardening of positions on all sides; others argue that it will take the pressure off girls who may feel forced by others to wear the scarf against their will; still others insist that the real issue concerns the preservation of the secular French state against inroads by any form of religion. As philosopher Elizabeth Badinter explains, "Because of the nature of the secularist state, you will never see a policeman wearing a Sikh's turban. While he represents the state's authority, he cannot express his religious affiliation. The terms multi-racial and multi-cultural are not the same. In France, as citizens, we adhere to a social contract, and in doing so we step back from the symbols of our private affiliations" (quoted in A. Smith 2004).

Muslims around the world have protested passage of the French law, and thousands of women have marched in Paris in support of it. The outcome of this struggle remains unclear (Figure 8.14).

FIGURE 8.14 Muslim women, some wearing headscarves, others not, rally in Paris in 2004 against the ban on headscarves in schools.

Worldviews represent comprehensive ideas about the structure of the world and the place of one's own group, or one's own self, within that world. The ethnographic record offers a broad array of different worldviews, each testifying to the imaginative, meaning-making cultural capacity of humans. These models of the world, moreover, do not exist apart from everyday social practices or political relations. When entangled beliefs, social practices, and differences in power provoke a crisis, humans struggle to make the crisis appear meaningful and therefore manageable. We are meaning-making, meaning-using, meaning-dependent organisms, and that is nowhere more clear than when a meaningful way of life is under assault.

CHAPTER SUMMARY

1. People attempting to account for their experiences make use of shared cultural assumptions about how the world works. The encompassing pictures of reality that result are called *worldviews*. Metaphors are valuable tools for constructing worldviews by directing attention to certain aspects of experience and downplaying or ignoring others.

2. The distinction between metonymy and metaphor may be said to correspond to the distinction between semantic linkages viewed as literal or true and semantic linkages viewed as hypothetical or false. If the relationships asserted in metaphors fit the rest of our experience, they may be converted into accepted relationships of metonymy.

3. As people create apt metaphors that are transformed into metonymic structures of their world view, they mark the resulting semantic domains by symbols. Symbols that sum up an entire semantic domain are called summarizing symbols. Elaborating symbols, by contrast, are analytic and allow people to sort out complex and undifferentiated feelings and ideas.

4. Differences in worldview derive from differences in experience that people try to explain by means of metaphor. People use at least three kinds of metaphors as foundations for particular worldviews: societal metaphors, organic metaphors, and technological metaphors.

5. A single society may have members who subscribe to different worldviews. Knowledge, like power, is not evenly distributed throughout a society. More powerful individuals and groups often promote ideologies, imposing their preferred worldview on the rest of society. Those without power can resist this imposition by creating their own contrasting metaphors and constructing alternative worldviews.

6. Anthropological studies of religion tend to focus on the social institutions and meaningful processes with which it is associated. Followers of religions can address personalized forces symbolically and expect them to respond. Maintaining contact with cosmic forces is very complex, and societies have complex social practices designed to ensure that this is done properly. Two important kinds of religious specialists are shamans and priests.

7. Many anthropologists have attempted to display the rich, coherent tapestries of symbols, rituals, and everyday practices that make up particular worldviews, and to demonstrate the high degree to which worldviews vary from one another. They have also studied the ways in which drastic changes in people's experiences lead them to create new meanings to explain the changes and to cope with them. This can be accomplished through elaboration of the old system to fit changing times, conversion to a new worldview, syncretism, revitalization, or resistance.

8. Some anthropologists have begun to study the relationship between religion and secularism as these developed following the European Enlightenment. Earlier generations of anthropologists took secularism for granted as the

expected outcome of cultural evolution. Contemporary resistance to secular institutions by religious groups in Western and non-Western nation-states, however, has prompted a reconsideration of secularism. An important issue is the extent to which life in a liberal secular state is likely to be difficult and painful for those whose religious practices do not recognize any domain of life in which religious considerations do not hold sway.

KEY TERMS

worldviews	key metaphors	witchcraft
metaphor	societal metaphor	magic
semantic domains	organic metaphor	oracles
metaphorical subject	functionalism	syncretism
metaphorical predicate	technological metaphor	revitalization
metaphorical entailments	religion	ideology
metonymy	shaman	secularism
symbol	priest	

SUGGESTED READINGS

Bowen, John. 2004. *Religions in practice: An approach to the anthropology of religion*, 3rd ed. Needham Heights, MA: Allyn & Bacon. *An up-to-date introduction of the anthropology of religion focusing on religious practice and interpretation, with a very wide range of case studies.*

Evans-Pritchard, E. E. [1937] 1976. *Witchcraft, oracles, and magic among the Azande*. Abridged ed. Oxford: Oxford University Press. *An immensely influential and very readable anthropological classic.*

Fernandez, James. 1982. *Bwiti: An ethnography of the religious imagination in Africa*. Princeton: Princeton University Press. *A book that is tremendously rewarding and demanding. A major study of a religious movement and its associated rituals in context.*

Keesing, Roger. 1992. *Custom and confrontation: The Kwaio struggle for cultural autonomy*. New York: Columbia University Press. *Based on 30 years of research, Keesing's final book provides a clear, readable, and committed discussion of Kwaio resistance.*

Klass, Morton. 1995. *Ordered universes: Approaches to the anthropology of religion*. Boulder, CO: Westview Press. *A brief introduction to the issues involved in the anthropological study of religion, with an emphasis on an operational definition of religion.*

Lambek, Michael. 2002. *A reader in the anthropology of religion*. Malden, MA: Blackwell. *An excellent collection of classic and contemporary readings in the anthropology of religion.*

Myerhoff, Barbara. 1974. *Peyote hunt*. Ithaca, NY: Cornell University Press. *A remarkable account of the worldview and sacred journey of the Huichol Indians of Mexico, a journey in which the author participated. This work is accessible, very well written, and theoretically sophisticated.*

Chapter 9

Culture and Power

Human beings are social animals, but how we organize our interdependence is open to cultural shaping. Furthermore, which cultural forms should prevail among members of particular social groups is often a contentious issue that is affected by power differences among group members. This chapter introduces some of the ways anthropologists have thought about power in cross-cultural perspective; it also shows how the unequal exercise of power in society can promote some cultural forms while censoring others.

In December of 1996, following 36 years of civil war, peace accords were signed in Guatemala between an umbrella organization representing the rebel forces and the Guatemalan military (Figure 9.1). The war began in the 1950s, after a CIA-supported coup that ousted a democratically elected, socialist-leaning president, Jacobo Arbenz Guzmán. Left-wing guerilla groups battled the national army and right-wing death squads, and the death toll was enormous—especially in the highlands, where indigenous Mayan peoples were the most frequent targets. A United Nations truth commission declared the violence to be genocide (Fischer and Benson 2006, 94).

The peace accords drew international media attention and strong support. According to anthropologists Ted Fischer and Peter Benson, the postwar phase has been characterized by "a new attitude toward Maya peoples that sought to provide new opportunities for a historically excluded group, and a sharp decline in massacres and other large-scale military actions." However, things did not improve across the board. The postwar period ushered in "famine brought about by droughts and declining coffee prices, as well as a sharp increase in street crimes, gang violence, kidnappings, and robberies, along with a resurgence of right-wing political activity" (Fischer and Benson 2006, 100).

Even listing the successes and failures of the peace process is complicated and problematic because the forces responsible for the "successes" are often the same ones responsible for the "failures." For example, Fischer and Benson conclude, "the waning of a certain type of violence might be considered a 'success,' even though new and subtler forms of economic and symbolic injustices may have emerged. Likewise, the strengthening of indigenous political rights might be seen as a 'success,' even though, at the same time, bureaucratic authority has been extended. It all depends on where one is standing."

Not only are failures and successes hard to identify; it is also hard to determine who actually made the peace accords happen. To be sure, Maya peasants and other victims of government genocide wanted the killing to stop, and the army, which had failed for 36 years to achieve its objectives, might have had its own reasons for deciding to negotiate for peace. At the same time, an end to the violence was by no means in their hands alone. The United States had strongly supported the Guatemalan army during the Cold War, and the army, together with the ruling elite, had justified the violence by labeling its victims Communist subversives. But things changed once the Cold War ended and the United States looked elsewhere. As Fischer and Benson point out (2006, 111):

> In the 1990s, foreign military aid to Guatemala dropped precipitously. With the Berlin Wall demolished, . . . U.S. strategic interests shifted dramatically to eastern Europe. Meanwhile, in Guatemala the revolutionaries and the government continued their low-intensity conflict, which dwindled down until the peace accords were signed in December 1996. After 1996, military aid dropped further and the Guatemalan government began a major reduction in the size of its armed forces. Between 1999 and 2005 the number of troops was reduced by half and several major bases . . . were closed.

As this suggests, the power to wage war or to negotiate for peace does not lie just with individuals, such as generals, or groups, such as Mayan rebels and the Guatemalan army. During the Cold War, the Guatemalan army and ruling class found common interests with the United States, whose resources sustained the violence and made genocide in the Highlands possible. With the end of the Cold War, however, conditions changed. Now the United States cut off the flow of resources, and the political options facing Guatemalans were also transformed. As Fischer and Benson insist, even with the peace accords, violence did not end; in fact, it had new opportunities to resume. The United States government resumed sending military aid in 2005 (2006, 111).

The varied sources of power in the course of this tragic, 36-year civil war raise questions about power itself. How can we understand the dynamics of power, structural violence, and the way they operate? These questions have interested anthropologists, and this chapter explores some of their answers.

▼ WHO HAS THE POWER TO ACT?

Human beings actively work to reshape the environments in which they live to suit their own purposes. Because the resources available in any environment can be used to sustain more than one way of life,

FIGURE 9.1 Guatemalan President Alvero Arzu (center) lights a peace torch with Guatemalan National Revolutionary Unity (URNG) commander Rolando Moran (second from right) as a girl, victim of the war, looks on, December, 29, 1996. Anthropologists are interested in the different forces that went into making the peace accords happen.

however, human beings must choose which aspects of the material world to depend on. Thus, the ability to choose implies the ability to transform a given situation. Thus, the ability to choose implies **power**, which may be understood broadly as "transformative capacity" (Giddens 1979, 88). When the choice affects an entire social group, we speak of *social power*.

Kinds of Social Power

Eric Wolf describes three different modes of social power. The first, *interpersonal power*, involves the ability of one individual to impose his or her will on another individual. The second, *organizational power*, highlights how individuals or social units can limit the actions of other individuals in particular social settings. The third, *structural power*, organizes social settings themselves and controls the allocation of social labor (1994). To lay bare the patterns of structural power requires paying attention to the large-scale and increasingly global division of labor among regions and social groups, the unequal relations between these regions and groups, and the way these relations are maintained or modified over time. The way in which clothing is manufactured now—in factories in Indonesia or El Salvador, Romania or China—for markets in Europe, the United States, and Japan, is an example of structural power. People are hired

to work long hours for low wages in unpleasant conditions to make clothing that they cannot afford to buy, even if it were available for sale in the communities where they live.

The study of social power in human society is the domain of **political anthropology**. In an overview, Joan Vincent has argued that political anthropology continues to be vital because it involves a complex interplay between ethnographic fieldwork, political theory, and critical reflection on political theory (2002, 1). Vincent divides the history of political anthropology into three phases. The first phase, from 1851 to 1939, she considers the "formative" era in which basic orientations and some of the earliest anthropological commentary on political matters was produced. The second phase, from 1942 to about 1971, is the "classic" era in the field. It is most closely associated with the flourishing of British social anthropology rooted in structural-functionalist theory, and produced well-known works by such eminent figures as E. E. Evans-Pritchard, Max Gluckman, Fredrik Barth, and Edmund Leach. This period developed under conditions of the post–World War II

power Transformative capacity; the ability to transform a given situation.

political anthropology The study of social power in human society.

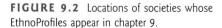

FIGURE 9.2 Locations of societies whose EthnoProfiles appear in chapter 9.

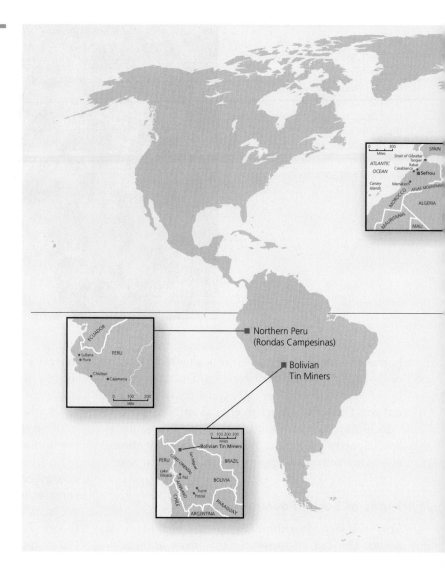

British Empire through the period of decolonization in the 1950s and 1960s. Topics of investigation during this period were also the "classic" topics of political anthropology: the classification of preindustrial political systems and attempts to reconstruct their evolution; the characteristic features of different kinds of preindustrial political systems and how these functioned to produce political order; and local processes of political strategizing by individuals in non-Western societies (see, e.g., Lewellyn 1983).

Decolonization drew attention to emerging national level politics in new states and the effects of "modernization" on the "traditional" political structures that had formerly been the focus of anthropological investigation. But the turbulent politics of the 1960s and early 1970s called into question not only received social forms but also received forms of anthropological scholarship. Beginning in the 1960s, political anthropologists developed new ways of thinking about political issues and new theoretical orientations to guide them, inaugurating in the 1970s and 1980s a third phase in which the anthropology of politics poses broader questions about power and inequality (Vincent 2002, 3). Under conditions of globalization, anthropologists interested in studying power have joined forces with scholars in other disciplines who share their concerns and have adopted ideas from influential political thinkers such as Antonio Gramsci

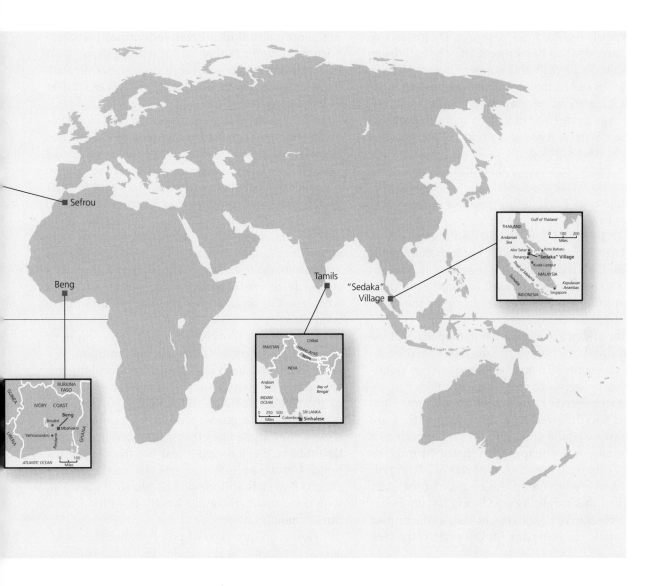

and Michel Foucault to help them explain how power shapes the lives of those on whom their ethnographies focus.

The cross-cultural study of social power reveals the paradox of the human condition. On one hand, open cultural creativity allows humans to imagine worlds of pure possibility; on the other hand, we all live in material circumstances that make many of those possibilities profoundly unrealistic. We can imagine many different ways to organize ourselves into groups, but, as Marx claims, the past weighs like a nightmare on the brain of the living—and the opportunity to remake social organization is ordinarily quite limited.

Beginning in this chapter, we will look closely at the ways in which the material circumstances of everyday life generate fields of power that channel and inhibit agency and cultural creativity—and how human beings can sometimes creatively exercise power and agency in order to evade or subvert restrictions.

The Role of the State

In the beginning, political anthropologists were strongly influenced by other Western thinkers who had investigated the same topics. Many of these earlier thinkers had assumed that the state was the prototype of "civilized" social power. The absence of a state therefore had to represent anarchy and disorder—what the English philosopher Thomas Hobbes (1588–1679) called the "war of all against all." Although the state often perpetrated injustice or exploitation as a side effect of its monopoly of force, this could be viewed as a necessary price for social order.

Early anthropologists such as Lewis Henry Morgan, however, showed that kinship institutions organized social life in societies without states. A later generation of political anthropologists showed how different kinship institutions distribute power among their members, and how nonkin institutions such as secret societies sometimes carry out important political roles. They were able to show repeatedly that societies without states can reach and carry out decisions affecting the entire social group by means of orderly traditional processes.

In the absence of a state that monopolizes physical force and can punish the disobedient, why do people cooperate? To answer this question, political anthropologists have had to reconsider many traditional Western assumptions about human nature and social power. As a consequence, they are keenly aware of the ambiguity of power both as a concept and as a phenomenon threaded into the fabric of everyday life. The emphasis of anthropologists on everyday life in the absence of the state has served them well in considering the organization of power in nation-states, as well as the impact of the state on everyday political activity (see Herzfeld 1987, 2001 118–32).

▼ HOW DOES A STATE EXERCISE POWER?

The Role of Physical Force

The traditional Western prototype of power in human social relations is based on physical coercion. A fistfight might be seen as the typical "natural" manifestation of physical coercion. This prototype is based on an exceedingly pessimistic, even cynical, view of human nature. It argues that cooperative social liv-

ing is not natural for human individuals, who are born with instincts that lead them to pursue their own self-interest above everything else and to challenge one another for dominance. This is the power of **free agency**.

Discussions of power as coercion tend to see political activity as competition between individual free agents over political control. When free agents make decisions, no larger groups, no historical obligations, no collective beliefs can or ought to stand in their way. In this view, cultural evolution took a giant leap forward when our ancestors first realized that sticks and stones could be used as weapons, not only against nonhuman predators but especially against human enemies. In this view, human history is a chronicle of the production of better and better weapons. The civilizations we are so proud of have been born and sustained in violence.

Some political anthropologists agree, more or less, with this approach to the human condition. As a result, they approach non-Western political organization in a characteristic way. They recognize that many stateless societies did not have governments with the ability to punish those who deviate. Nevertheless, they argue that other institutions had a similar function. Such societies fear not the king or the police but the ancestors, witchcraft, or the lineage elders. Power is still viewed as physical coercion, with cooperation resulting largely from the fear of punishment.

However, this view of power in nonstate societies was rejected by E. E. Evans-Pritchard, based on his work among the Azande. Evans-Pritchard ([1937] 1976) argued that the Azande were not in a constant state of fear even though they lived in a stateless society and held a complex set of beliefs about witchcraft, oracles, and magic (see EthnoProfile 8.5: Azande). He observed that Zande people discussed witchcraft openly. If they believed they were bewitched, they were likely to be angry rather than afraid and so did not feel helpless. This kind of attitude made sense because most Azande subscribed to a worldview in which witchcraft had a meaningful place. Most people believed that witchcraft would not be directed against them, and in any case they had remedies to fight their own victimization. In such a context, the belief system and the institutionalization of power it implies seem natural and rational. For that reason, ordinary, rational people support it.

free agency The freedom of self-contained individuals to pursue their own interests above everything else and to challenge one another for dominance.

Legitimate Coercion in Postcommunist Russia

Anthropologist Anatoly Khazanov reports on the political choices facing Russians following the collapse of the Soviet Union. He describes how their opportunity to choose new ways of organizing political life is constrained by old political traditions.

In some respects the situation in Russia is different from that in Central Asia and the Caucasus in that it has glimmers of hope. The highly industrialized and urbanized Russian society has a working class which has during the last years demonstrated much more maturity than might be expected; its post-Communist period has opened new avenues of economic and social mobility to many of its youth; and, last but not least, it has numerous educated middle strata. For many members of the latter, the economic hardships are still tolerable, while the liberalization of political life is an indisputable achievement. These people alone represent the guarantee for the continuation of the democratization process much better than the Russian political elite, even those parts of it who are in Yeltsin's camp but who nevertheless demonstrate some inclinations toward authoritarianism.

One should also take into account another circumstance. Most Russian families at present consist of only one or, at best, two children. This leads to an increasing appreciation of human life and to an aversion to bloody violence in all of its forms. To prove this point I can refer to the extreme unpopularity of military service or to the widespread resentment with the Russian army's involvement in inter-ethnic conflicts in the CIS [Commonwealth of Independent States] countries.

These are the positive factors. However one should not dismiss the negative ones. The Reds and Browns in Russ-ian political parlance, i.e., the broad coalition of Communists, fascists, and all kinds of chauvinists, is actively propagandizing violence as a way of changing the existing political, social, and economic conditions and restoring the Russian imperial glory of old. They find a receptive audience in a growing number of disoriented, pauperized, and lumpenized people to whom reforms turned out to be detrimental. Anti-democratic sentiments are very strong in the army, the Cossack movement, the Russian Orthodox church, and some other segments of Russian society.

The most dangerous moment in this development is that the society is again considering violence as an inevitable concomitant of the political process. Again the dispute is not over the question whether violence is legitimate but over who exactly has the legitimate right to use it.

Thus we face a vicious circle: the virtual absence of civil society and traditions and mechanisms for solving political, social, and ethnic conflicts through negotiation and compromise facilitates the spread of violence, and violence, in turn, makes the emergence of civil society much more difficult. Some recent events in Moscow prove this point. The opponents of Yeltsin's rule are certainly adversaries of the liberalization process, but they were suppressed by undemocratic means which soon resulted in violence. Thus the door is open for more violence or for essentially authoritarian rule. Only the future will tell whether Russia is capable of getting out of this circle.

Source: Khazanov 1993

Domination and Hegemony

Here we encounter an ambiguity about power in human affairs. Perhaps people do submit to institutionalized power because they have been coerced and fear punishment. But perhaps they submit because they believe that the power structures in their society are legitimate, given their understandings about the way the world works. What could lead people to accept coercion by others as legitimate (Figure 9.3)?

A worldview that justifies the social arrangements under which people live is sometimes called

FIGURE 9.3 Prior to colonial conquest by outsiders, Muslim emirs from northern Cameroon had coercive power.

an **ideology**. As we saw in chapter 8, an ideology can be defined as a cultural product of conscious reflection, such as beliefs about morality, religion, or metaphysics, that is used to explain and justify the social arrangements under which people live. Some Marxian thinkers have emphasized that rulers can consolidate their power by persuading their subjects to accept an ideology that portrays ruling-class domination as

---

ideology A worldview that justifies the social arrangements under which people live.

domination Coercive rule.

hegemony Persuading subordinates to accept the ideology of the dominant group by mutual accommodations that nevertheless preserve the rulers' privileged position.

---

legitimate. They argue that groups who accept such a ruling-class ideology suffer from "false consciousness." But the notion of false consciousness is problematic, since it views people as passive and unable to withstand indoctrination. As we discussed in chapter 2, this is not a persuasive view of human nature.

More promising was the approach taken by Antonio Gramsci (1971). Writing in the 1930s, Gramsci pointed out that coercive rule—what he called **domination**—is expensive and unstable. Rulers do better if they can persuade the dominated to accept their rule as legitimate. To do so, they may provide some genuine material benefits to their subjects and also use schools and other cultural institutions to disseminate an ideology justifying their rule. If they achieve all this—while also ensuring that none of these concessions seriously undermine their privileged position—they have established what Gramsci called **hegemony**.

Hegemony is never absolute, but always vulnerable to challenges: Struggles may develop between rulers trying to justify their domination and subordinate groups who exercise agency by challenging "official" ideologies and practices that devalue or exclude them. Hegemony may be threatened if subordinate groups maintain or develop alternative, or *counterhegemonic*, cultural practices. Successful hegemony, by contrast, involves linking the understandings of dominant and subordinate groups into what appears to be mutual accommodation.

The concept of hegemony is attractive to many anthropologists because it draws attention to the central role of cultural beliefs and symbols in struggles to consolidate social organization and political control. Gramsci's contrast between domination (rule by coercive force) and hegemony (rule by persuasion) was central to his own analysis of the exercise of power (Crehan 2002, 153), and it has helped anthropologists who study the exercise of power in societies with and without traditional state institutions. In attempting to extend Gramsci's insights to nonstate settings, anthropologists are able to avoid some of the tortuous and implausible accounts of power that depend on fear of punishment or false consciousness. Instead, they draw attention to the verbal skills and personal charisma of leaders who can persuade others to follow them without relying on coercive force. Charismatic leaders must skillfully align shared meanings, values, and goals with a particular interpretation of events or proposed course of action.

Consider, for example, the Zande belief that people use witchcraft only against those they envy. The psychological insight embodied in this belief makes it highly plausible to people who experience daily friction with their neighbors. At the same time, however, this belief makes it impossible to accuse Zande chiefs of using witchcraft against commoners—because, as Zande themselves say, why would chiefs envy their subjects? In this way, hegemonic ideology deflects challenges that might be made against those in power.

In other settings, however, hegemonic ideology may justify social action in some individuals that would be condemned in others. Consider the connection between witchcraft and kingship among the Beng of Ivory Coast (see EthnoProfile 9.1: Beng). The Beng are organized into two regions, each ruled by a king and a queen, who come from a specific matrilineal clan. The king is said to be the owner of the Earth, which is the primary focus for worship among the Beng. Violations of taboos concerning the Earth are believed to endanger the entire region and therefore must be dealt with by the king of the region. The king is also said to have the power to foresee those natural calamities that are punishment for sins committed. In general, "the king is responsible not only for the legal but also the moral and spiritual well-being of the people living in this region" (Gottlieb 1989, 249).

The legitimate power of the king is in direct contrast to the power of witches, who are considered to be utterly immoral. Using illegitimate power, working in secret, they kill and "consume" their close matrilineal kin. Nevertheless, when a man becomes king, he has one year to bewitch three close relatives in his matriline. If he fails to do so, he himself will die. Rather than destroying his power, this exercise of illegitimate power legitimates his rule. By killing three close matrilineal relatives, the king shows his commitment to the greater public "good." He is demonstrating his control over, and independence from, the narrow interests of his own kinship group. Operating on a plane beyond that of common morality, the king, a man who has sacrificed part of himself, will rule the kingdom fairly. From the point of view of the Beng, including members of his own matrilineal clan, his actions are not only legitimate but also make it possible for him to rule.

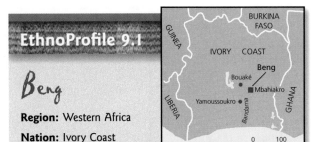

EthnoProfile 9.1

Beng

Region: Western Africa

Nation: Ivory Coast

Population: 10,000+

Environment: Savanna and forest

Livelihood: Farming, both subsistence and cash; hunting; gathering

Political organization: Traditionally, a kingdom; today, part of a modern nation-state

For more information: Gottlieb, Alma. 1989. Witches, kings, and the sacrifices of identity or The power of paradox and the paradox of power among the Beng of Ivory Coast. In *Creativity of power: Cosmology and action in African societies*, edited by W. Arens and I. Karp, 245–72. Washington, DC: Smithsonian.

Power and National Identity: A Case Study

Gramsci himself, however, was particularly interested in how hegemony is (or is not) successfully established in state societies. In a postcolonial and globalizing world, where all people are presumed to be citizens of one or another nation-state, understanding the effects of decisions and actions of state authorities becomes crucial for making sense of many events at a local level. Anthropologists have often focused on the processes by which ruling groups in former colonies attempt to build national identity.

For example, the British colony of Ceylon became independent in 1948, later changing its name to Sri Lanka. The residents of Ceylon belonged to two major populations: the Tamils concentrated in the northern part of the island and the larger population of Sinhalese who lived elsewhere (EthnoProfile 9.2: Tamils; see EthnoProfile 7.6: Sinhalese). After independence, however, new Sinhalese rulers worked to forge a national identity rooted in their version of local history, which excluded the Tamils. In 1956, Sinhala was made the only official language; in the 1960s and 1970s, Tamils' access to education was restricted and they were barred from the civil service and the army (Daniel 1997, 316). When some Tamils began to agitate for a separate state of their own, the Sri Lankan government responded in 1979 with severe, violent repression against Tamils, sending many into exile and simulating the growth of the Tamil nationalist Liberation Tigers of Tamil Eelam (LTTE), which grew "into one of the most dreaded militant organizations in the world" (Daniel 1997, 323). Since the 1980s, thousands have died in ethnic violence, although peace negotiations begun in 2001 suggest some hope for a conclusion to hostilities.

The exclusion of the Tamil residents from the Sri Lankan state has thus been pursued by means of violent coercion (Figure 9.4). But violence has also been used by the government against Sinhalese citizens who objected to state policies. Between 1987 and 1990, Indian troops were brought into Sri Lanka to supervise a peace agreement between Tamils and Sinhalese. These troops found themselves fighting the LTTE in the north, but they were also resisted violently in Sinhalese areas:

> the rest of the country was convulsed by a wave of terror as young members of a group called the JVP (Janata Vimukti Peramuna, or People's Liberation Front) attacked the government not only for betraying the nation by allowing the Indian presence, but

FIGURE 9.4 The exclusion of Tamil residents of Sri Lanka has included a move to evict Tamils living in the capital as part of a crackdown against the Tamil Liberation Tigers. Sri Lankan activists demonstrated in Colombo in June 2007 in opposition to the eviction. The Sri Lankan Supreme Court halted the eviction and set a date for a hearing on the violation of human rights.

> also for its own unjust political and economic policies. . . . The government responded with a wave of terror, directed at young males in particular, which reached its climax with the capture and murder of the JVP leadership in late 1989. As far as we can tell, the government won the day by concentrated terror—killing so many young people, whether JVP activists or not, that the opposition ran out of resources and leadership. (Spencer 2000, 124–25)

After 1990, violence directed by the state against Sinhalese lessened, and in 1994, a new government promised to settle the ethnic conflict by peaceful means. But even before then, Sri Lankan government efforts at nation-building had not rested entirely on violence. Leaders also tried to exercise persuasive power to convince Sinhalese citizens that the state had their welfare in mind and was prepared to take steps to improve their lives.

For example, anthropologist Michael Woost (1993) has described how the government of Sri Lanka has used a wide range of cultural media (television, radio, newspapers, the school system, public rituals, and even a lottery) to link the national identity to development. National development strategies are presented as attempts to restore Sinhalese village society to its former glory under the precolonial rule of Sinhalese kings. The ideal village, in this view, is engaged in rice paddy cultivation carried out according to harmonious principles of Sinhala Buddhist doctrine. The villagers Woost knew could hardly escape this nationalist development discourse, but they did not resist it as an unwelcome imposition from the outside. On the contrary, all of them had incorporated development goals into their own values and had accepted that state-sponsored development would improve their lives. This might suggest that the state's attempt to establish hegemony had succeeded.

But collaboration with the state was undermined as three different village factions selectively manipulated development discourse in their struggle to gain access to government resources. For example, nationalistic rhetoric connected development with "improvement of the land." One village faction claimed it had been the first in the village to "improve the land" by building houses or planting tree crops. A second faction claimed that it had "improved the land" first by introducing paddy cultivation in the village. A third faction claimed it had "improved the land" first since its members had intermarried with other early settlers who had planted a large mango tree, a sign of permanent residence. Each faction made what the other factions interpreted as unjust claims, and each blamed the lack of village unity on the un-Buddhist greed of its opponents. These disagreements eventually led the state to withdraw its offer of resources, ultimately preventing the implementation of a village development scheme that all factions wanted!

Woost argues that the outcome of this political wrangling demonstrates the contradictory and fragile nature of the hegemonic process: Paradoxically, the villagers' active appropriation of nationalist ideology undermined efforts to establish the very social order it was supposed to create. Gramsci himself was well aware that establishing successful hegemony in a nation-state was a difficult process whose outcome was not assured; indeed, it was the very inability of Italians to achieve this goal that stimulated many of his reflections on domination and hegemony. Indeed, Gramsci's own description of a *colonial* state, emphasized by Indian historian Ranajit Guha, as dominance *without* hegemony (Crehan 2002, 125) is brought to mind by the repeated resort of the Sri Lankan state to violent coercion.

By contrast, Fischer and Benson, working in Guatemala after the 1996 peace accords, show how agency can still be exercised under dangerous and ambiguous circumstances (see the opening of this chapter) as people, such as Mayan farmers, identify "limit points" beyond which their desire for change must not be allowed to go. Mayan farmers discipline themselves to avoid thinking about all the ways in which the peace accords have failed to live up to their expectations. Instead, farmers identify, work for, and express satisfaction with limited goals they can actually reach, given the uncertain and volatile circumstances under which they must live. For example, when Mayan farmers who grow broccoli for North American consumers earn less profit than they had hoped for, they often observe that "at least" raising broccoli on your own land is better than having to leave your family to earn cash as a migrant laborer. "At least" statements of this kind "provide a seemingly commonsensical resting place between what 'is' and what 'ought to be'" (2006, 14). By defining satisfaction in terms of limit points they themselves identify, Mayan farmers are able to see themselves as having successfully satisfied at least *some* desires of their own choosing, dissipating their dissatisfaction with and resistance to the circumstances of their lives. And it is precisely their ability to produce such a calming effect that makes the hegemonic process powerful and durable. At the same time, when farmers who hope to use income from broccoli farming to provide "something more" for their families are forced, again and again, to settle for less profit than they feel entitled to, it is difficult for them to avoid the conclusion that they are being shortchanged: "It is precisely this grounding in everyday life . . . that makes the hegemonic process an ambivalent, open-ended, never fully closed field of struggle" (2006, 15).

Biopower and Governmentality

Is there a set of skills that would bring into existence and sustain a peaceful, prosperous nation-state in places like Sri Lanka and Guatemala? This question was addressed by the French philosopher Michel Foucault, who looked at the way European thinkers from the end of the Middle Ages onward had posed (and attempted to answer) similar questions. Together with colleagues, he identified the emergence of a new form of power in the nineteenth century. This form of power he called *biopower* or *biopolitics*, and it was preoccupied with bodies—both the bodies of citizens but also the social body itself (Hacking 1991, 183). As Colin Gordon summarizes, biopower refers to "forms of power exercised over persons specifically insofar as they are thought of as living beings; a politics concerned with subjects as members of a *population*, in which issues of individual sexual and reproductive conduct interconnect with issues of national policy and power" (1991, 4–5).

According to Foucault, a state based on biopolitics is very different from states in the Middle Ages based on the rule of law or administrative states of the fifteenth and sixteenth centuries based on regulation and discipline. A major concern in those states especially was making sure that the ruler maintained control of the state. Machiavelli's famous treatise *The Prince* is the best known of a series of handbooks explaining what such an absolute ruler needed to do to maintain himself in power. But by the seventeenth century, this approach to state rule was proving increasingly inadequate. Machiavelli's critics began to speak instead about *governing* a state, likening such government to the practices that preserved and perpetuated other social institutions: "a household, souls, children, a province, a convent, a religious order, a family" (Foucault 1991, 90). The example of

household management, called at that time *economy*, was a preferred model of government, and debate concerned how to incorporate "the correct manner of managing individuals, goods and wealth within the family . . . into the management of the state" (Foucault 1991 [1980], 92). Thus was born the concept of *political economy*.

But running the state in terms of political economy—managing citizens and their relations with goods and resources, with the territory, with customs, and coping with misfortunes such as famines, epidemics and death—could not be undertaken effectively until rulers possessed adequate knowledge about such things. In the eighteenth century, such knowledge was produced by state bureaucracies that began to count and measure people and things subject to state control, giving birth to the discipline of *statistics*. Statistics suggested that populations had unique attributes, and rulers concluded that management of the population through the use of statistics was the proper task of government.

Rulers want to preserve and prolong the stability of the state and the institutions it manages, including its population, but this had been undermined in the past by calamities such as famines, wars, and the death of princes. The art of governing appropriate to biopolitics—what Foucault calls **governmentality**—relies on tactics of measuring and intervening to prevent such calamities or to blunt their effects by using statistics to identify a series of possible and probable events, calculate their cost, and prescribe a form of intervention that would render such events tolerable, such that they would not undermine the security of the state. For example, such interventions include forms of insurance that protect economic activities in the event of catastrophic events that would otherwise curtail or destroy them (Gordon 1991, 18–20).

To the extent that governmentality is a form of power at work in the contemporary world, institutions that rely on it will be counting and measuring their members in a variety of ways (Figure 9.5). Although, as Ian Hacking insists, not all bureaucratic applications of such statistical knowledge are evil (1991, 183), the fact remains that providing the government (or any bureaucratic institution) with detailed vital statistics can be very threatening, especially in cases where people are concerned that the state does not have their best interests at heart. After all, states want to tax citizens,

---

governmentality The art of governing appropriate to promoting the welfare of populations within a state.

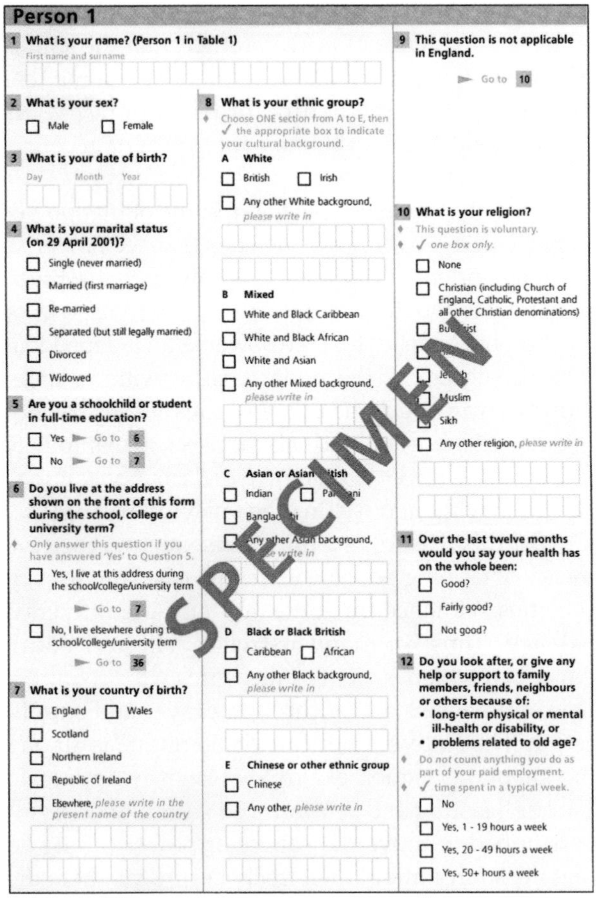

Person 1

1 **What is your name? (Person 1 in Table 1)**
First name and surname

2 **What is your sex?**
☐ Male   ☐ Female

3 **What is your date of birth?**
Day   Month   Year

4 **What is your marital status (on 29 April 2001)?**
☐ Single (never married)
☐ Married (first marriage)
☐ Re-married
☐ Separated (but still legally married)
☐ Divorced
☐ Widowed

5 **Are you a schoolchild or student in full-time education?**
☐ Yes ➤ Go to 6
☐ No ➤ Go to 7

6 **Do you live at the address shown on the front of this form during the school, college or university term?**
◆ Only answer this question if you have answered 'Yes' to Question 5.
☐ Yes, I live at this address during the school/college/university term
➤ Go to 7
☐ No, I live elsewhere during the school/college/university term
➤ Go to 36

7 **What is your country of birth?**
☐ England   ☐ Wales
☐ Scotland
☐ Northern Ireland
☐ Republic of Ireland
☐ Elsewhere, please write in the present name of the country

8 **What is your ethnic group?**
◆ Choose ONE section from A to E, then
✓ the appropriate box to indicate your cultural background.

A White
☐ British   ☐ Irish
☐ Any other White background, please write in

B Mixed
☐ White and Black Caribbean
☐ White and Black African
☐ White and Asian
☐ Any other Mixed background, please write in

C Asian or Asian British
☐ Indian   ☐ Pakistani
☐ Bangladeshi
☐ Any other Asian background, please write in

D Black or Black British
☐ Caribbean   ☐ African
☐ Any other Black background, please write in

E Chinese or other ethnic group
☐ Chinese
☐ Any other, please write in

9 **This question is not applicable in England.**
➤ Go to 10

10 **What is your religion?**
◆ This question is voluntary.
◆ ✓ one box only.
☐ None
☐ Christian (including Church of England, Catholic, Protestant and all other Christian denominations)
☐ Buddhist
☐ Hindu
☐ Jewish
☐ Muslim
☐ Sikh
☐ Any other religion, please write in

11 **Over the last twelve months would you say your health has on the whole been:**
☐ Good?
☐ Fairly good?
☐ Not good?

12 **Do you look after, or give any help or support to family members, friends, neighbours or others because of:**
• **long-term physical or mental ill-health or disability, or**
• **problems related to old age?**
◆ Do not count anything you do as part of your paid employment.
◆ ✓ time spent in a typical week.
☐ No
☐ Yes, 1 - 19 hours a week
☐ Yes, 20 - 49 hours a week
☐ Yes, 50+ hours a week

FIGURE 9.5 In order to govern, a state must know whom it is governing. Censuses are one way in which the information a state believes it needs can be collected.

vaccinate and educate their children, restrict their activities to those that benefit the state, control their movements beyond (and sometimes within) state borders, and otherwise manage what citizens do. In a globalizing world full of nation-states, anthropologists are increasingly likely in their fieldwork to encounter both the pressures of governmentality and attempts to evade or manipulate governmentality.

Trying to Elude Governmentality: A Case Study

This was the experience of Aihwa Ong (2002), who carried out research among a dispersed population of wealthy Chinese merchant families. In explaining how these Chinese became so successful, Ong focused on the different forms of governmentality characteristic of nation-states, the capitalist market, and Chinese kinship and family. All three of these institutional contexts possess rules for disciplining individual conduct in ways that are connected to the exercise of power within the institutions themselves. Ong argues that in the late nineteenth century, some Chinese managed to evade the governmentality of Chinese kinship and family by moving physically out of China and into merchant cities of European imperial possessions in Asia and Southeast Asia.

Under these circumstances, the obligations to one's lineage were effectively severed, and the individual family and its members, under the control of males, became the virtually unique focus of loyalty among kin. But such families have had to deal with two other forms of governmentality in this new setting. One of these was the governmentality of particular states. Moving from one state to the next involved making oneself or one's family subject to different forms of biopower: For example, for wealthy residents of Hong Kong, "citizenship becomes an issue of handling the diverse rules or 'governmentality' of host societies where they may be economically correct in terms of human capital, but culturally incorrect in terms of ethnicity" (2002, 340).

Finally, the prosperity of these overseas Chinese families depends on doing business according to the governmentality of the capitalist market. This form of governmentality was least susceptible to evasion or manipulation, which meant that families would try whenever possible to move family members from country to country, as needed, to take advantage of fresh opportunities for business. Such mobility, in turn, depended on being able to evade or manipulate the bureaucratic rules of state governmentality whenever these threatened to limit mobility. Thanks to their wealth, this sort of evasion was frequently possible: "international managers and professionals have the material and symbolic resources to manipulate global schemes of cultural difference, racial hierarchy, and citizenship to their own advantage . . . in environments controlled and shaped by nation-states and capitalist markets" Ong (2002, 339).

The Ambiguity of Power

The contrast between domination and hegemony and Foucault's explorations of the machinery of governmentality demonstrate that the exercise of power cannot be equated with physical violence alone. Moreover, the occasional violent outburst of one member of a foraging society against another is not the same thing as the organized violence of one army against another in a conflict between modern nation-states. No one can deny that human beings can be violent with one another. But is this the whole story?

Anthropologist Richard Newbold Adams has said: "It is useful to accept the proposition that, while men have in some sense always been equal (i.e., in that each always has some independent power), they have in another sense never been equal (in that some always have more power than others)" (1979, 409). Political anthropologists who think of power as coercion have traditionally emphasized the universality of human inequality. Others have concentrated on the first part of Adams's observation. Some have focused on power in societies without states, whereas others have taken a more Gramscian approach and reconsidered the nature of independent power available to individuals living in societies with states. The first focus involves looking at power as an independent entity. The second looks at the power of the human imagination to define the nature of social interactions and to persuade other actors to accept these definitions of the situation.

▼ POWER AS AN INDEPENDENT ENTITY

In some of the traditionally stateless societies of native North and South America, power is understood to be an entity existing in the universe independent of human beings. As such, it cannot be produced and accumulated through the interactions of human beings with one another. Strictly speaking, power does not belong to human beings at all. At most, people can hope to *gain access* to power, usually through rit-

---

resistance The power to refuse being forced against one's will to conform to someone else's wishes.

consensus An agreement to which all parties collectively give their assent.

persuasion Power based on verbal argument.

---

ual means. From this point of view, "control over resources is evidence of power, rather than the source of power" (Colson 1977, 382). If people assume that power is part of the natural order of things yet is independent of direct human control, certain consequences seem to follow.

First, they may be able to tap some of that power if they can discover how. Societies that see power as an independent entity usually know, through tradition, how to tap it.

Second, societies that see power as an independent force usually embed this understanding within a larger worldview in which the universe consists of a balance of different forces. Individuals may seek to manipulate those natural forces to their own ends, but only if they can do so without upsetting the universal balance.

For this reason, as a third consequence, coercive means of tapping power sources are ruled out in such societies. Violence threatens to undo the universal balance. Thus, in many native North and South American societies, gentler measures were required. One approached power through prayer and supplication. The Native American vision quest (as among the Lakota) is a good example of such an approach: Through fasting and self-induced suffering, individuals hoped to move the source of power to pity so that the source might then freely bestow on them the power they sought in the form of a vision or a song or a set of ritual formulas. Power freely bestowed would not disrupt the balance of the universe.

This leads to a fourth consequence: in such a worldview, violence and access to power are mutually contradictory. As our discussion of worldview leads us to expect, cultures that conceive of cosmic power in this way also tend to view individual human beings as independent entities who cannot be coerced but must be supplicated. Individuals in such societies are not free agents in the Western sense—free of social ties and responsibilities—but they are free in the sense that they can refuse to be forced against their will to conform to someone else's wishes. They exercise the power of **resistance**.

The power of individuals to resist affects how stateless societies arrive at decisions. A fifth consequence of viewing power as an independent entity is an emphasis on **consensus** as the appropriate means to decide issues affecting the group. In seeking consensus, proponents of a particular course of action must use **persuasion**, rather than coercion, to get other members of the group to support their cause. They resort to verbal argument, not physical intimidation. As a result, the most respected members of stateless societies, those sometimes given the title "chief" by outsiders, are persuasive speakers. Indeed, as Pierre Clastres (1977) pointed out, such respected individuals are often referred to by other members of their society as "those who speak for us." The shamans (or *mara'akate*) of the Huichol Indians of northern Mexico serve this function (see EthnoProfile 8.4: Huichol). By virtue of their verbal ability, they see themselves (and are seen by their fellows) as especially well suited to negotiate for all the Huichol with outsiders, especially representatives of the Mexican state.

This attitude toward power and leadership is also found elsewhere in the world. A classic example comes from the Pacific: the Big Man. Roger Keesing describes his Kwaio friend 'Elota as a *man with influence:* "When he spoke, in his hoarse voice, it was never loudly; he never shouted, never spoke in anger, never dominated conversation. Yet when he spoke people paid attention, deferred to his wisdom or laughed at his wit" (1983, 3; see EthnoProfile 8.6: Kwaio). He owed part of his influence to an extraordinary memory. Keesing thinks 'Elota could recall genealogical information about some 3,000 to 4,000 people, as well as the details of 50 years' worth of the financial transactions that are at the heart of Kwaio feasts and marriages. In addition, "his wit and wisdom were a continuing guide towards the virtues of the past, towards thinking before rushing into action."

Keesing tells us that 'Elota was "a master gamesman, in a system where prestige derives from manipulating investments and publicly giving away valuables." Finally, 'Elota also realized that the road to prominence lay in hard work devoted to producing goods that other Kwaio wanted. Those goods included taro for feasts, pigs, cane bracelets and anklets, and bark-cloth wrapping for valuables. For 'Elota, and for the Kwaio, prestige and influence come from giving away valued things. A Big Man is a master of this, especially in financing marriages and giving feasts (Figure 9.6).

Pierre Clastres suggested that stateless forms of social organization are strongly resistant to the emergence of hierarchy (1977, 35). Indeed, he argues that members of stateless societies struggle to prevent such authority from emerging. They sense that the rise of state power spells the end of individual au-

FIGURE 9.6 A Huli man from Papua New Guinea preparing food in an earth oven. The Huli are among the people in Papua New Guinea who recognize that some men are Big Men—men with influence.

tonomy and disrupts beyond repair the harmonious balance between human beings and the forces of the wider world.

Richard Lee agrees, arguing that band societies, and some farmers and herders, have found ways to limit "the accumulation of wealth and power. Such societies operate within the confines of a metaphorical ceiling and floor: a ceiling above which one may not accumulate wealth and a floor below which one may not sink. These limits . . . are maintained by powerful social mechanisms known as leveling devices. . . . Such societies therefore have social and political resources of their own and are not just sitting ducks waiting to adopt the first hierarchical model that comes along" (1992a, 39–40). Leveling devices, such as institutionalized sharing, will be discussed in chapter 10.

▼ THE POWER OF THE IMAGINATION

We have considered a variety of attempts to understand power. Finding a focus on coercion alone to be inadequate, we have seen that Gramsci's discussion of the interplay between coercion and persuasion and Foucault's discussions of governmentality and biopolitics all offer more nuanced understandings of the different levels on which social power can operate. Still, no system of social power is ever totally successful in imposing itself. Individual human beings, though not free agents, are nevertheless empowered to resist having another's will imposed on them by force. Many anthropologists would feel that a discussion of social power is incomplete if it does not also pay attention to the way individuals make sense of and use the constraints and opportunities for action open to them, however limited they may be. That is, it is necessary to take into account the imagination—the power of all human beings to invest the world with meaning.

All people everywhere have the power to interpret their experiences, regardless of the complexity of a social system and whether or not the power of coercion is monopolized by a central authority. People retain this power even under totalitarian dictatorship. It is notoriously difficult to erase from human consciousness. Hoyt Alverson has argued that "a belief in one's power to invest the world with meaning (the 'will to believe') and a belief in the adequacy of one's knowledge for understanding and acting on personal experience are essential features of all human self-identity" (1978, 7).

The power of the human imagination to invest the world with meaning is also the power to resist outside influences, to reject alternative choices that others want to impose. This does not mean that individuals work out the meanings of their experiences in isolation. All human activities, including the growth and development of self-identity, take place in a social, cultural, and historical context. Still, each individual

anomie A pervasive sense of rootlessness and normlessness in a society.

alienation A term used by Karl Marx to describe the deep separation that workers seemed to experience between their innermost sense of identity and the labor they were forced to perform in order to earn enough money to live.

retains the power to interpret that context from his or her unique vantage point, in terms of his or her unique experiences.

The Power of the Weak

Cynics might argue that the power of the imagination must in the real world be restricted to private opinions; the mind can resist, but the body must conform. From this perspective, for example, the actions of a miner who labors underground daily for a meager wage are clear-cut and unmistakable: He works for money to buy food for his family. However, ethnographic data suggest that this may not be the whole story.

The twentieth-century prototype of the downtrodden and exploited human being was the industrial laborer. In western Europe and the United States, the Industrial Revolution of the eighteenth and nineteenth centuries brought profound social and cultural dislocation. Social scientists at that time observed those changes and tried to describe them. Emile Durkheim used the term **anomie** to refer to the pervasive sense of rootlessness and normlessness that people appeared to be experiencing. Karl Marx used the term **alienation** to describe the deep separation workers seemed to experience between their innermost sense of identity and the labor they were forced to do in order to earn enough money to live.

Do industrial workers in what used to be called the Third World similarly suffer from anomie and alienation? The issue has been hotly debated. Some argue that their condition should be far worse than that of Western workers because the context of non-Western industrialization is so much more backward. This has been called the "scars of bondage" thesis. This thesis predicts that the more complete the political domination and exploitation of a people, the more deeply they will be scarred by the experience, brutalized, and dehumanized. For people suffering the twin exploitations of colonialism and industrialism, the outcome could only be the most bitter, unrelieved tragedy.

Hoyt Alverson (1978) set out to test the "scars of bondage" thesis in the field. He focused on migrant workers and their experiences in the gold mines of South Africa. His informants were Tswana living in the independent nation of Botswana, which forms part of South Africa's northern border (see Ethno-Profile 2.1: Tswana). Botswana in the 1960s and 1970s was a poor country, and most of its families were supported only by the wages men received for working in South African mines. Here was a colonized population forced into industrial exploitation in order to survive. If the "scars of bondage" thesis was correct, the Tswana ought to be an alienated, brutalized, dehumanized lot.

Without question, the material standard of living of most of Alverson's Tswana informants was low (Figure 9.7). Without question, life in the South African mines was brutal. Without question, the difficulties families had to face when one or more of their male members was absent for months on a mining contract were considerable. And yet, for most of his informants, there was little evidence of alienation, brutalization, and dehumanization. On the contrary, his informants led coherent, meaningful lives. Despite their bondage to an exploitative system, they remained relatively unscarred. How could this be?

As it turned out, the mine experience simply did not mean to the Tswana what outside observers assumed it meant: "All phenomena, including towns and gold mines, are ambiguous and can therefore be invested with manifold meanings" (Alverson 1978, 215). In most cases, Alverson's informants had managed to come to terms with their experiences in a meaningful way. This was true both for those who were grateful to the mines and for those who hated the mines. Coming to terms with one's experiences

involves mental effort. It is largely a question of finding an apt metaphor that links a person's traditional understandings with new experiences. Different people may choose different metaphors. "One Tswana may equate the relations of bosses and workers in the mine to the relationship of parent and child. If he authentically believes this analogy, then the meaning he invests in this 'inequality' will be different from that invested in it by a Tswana who defines the relationship in terms of a set of contractual exchanges made among people bound by the same set of general rights and duties" (1978, 258).

The Tswana encountered brutal inequality and discrimination outside the mines as well. Here again, however, many successfully drew on resources from their traditional culture to make sense of, and thereby transform, these experiences. For the migrant workers Alverson knew, the figure of the *Trickster* provided them with a prototype of the kind of person one had to be to survive in South Africa. The Trickster is a stock character in Tswana folklore. As his name implies, he lives by his wits, is basically amoral, and is happy to hoodwink anyone who tries to take advantage of him. Older informants, recounting their life histories, saw themselves as Tricksters. Their greatest pride lay in the way they had managed to get by despite the traps and snares all around them. According to Alverson, the strength and genius of Tswana culture was highlighted by his informants'

FIGURE 9.7 South African gold miner. Tswana miners draw on their own cultural resources to survive the brutal conditions in the mines.

ability to make sense of their experiences in terms of traditional Tswana narratives.

June Nash (1979), working among Bolivian tin miners, has made similar observations about the power of human imagination to transform experiences by investing them with meaning (see Ethno-Profile 9.3: Bolivian Tin Miners). If anything, the conditions under which these miners labor is worse than those encountered by Tswana migrants. The labor force in Bolivian mines has been drawn from local indigenous populations who, unlike the Tswana, have been effectively separated from their involvement in traditional indigenous communities. But like the Tswana of Botswana, the tin miners of Bolivia have been able creatively to combine elements of the dominant industrial culture with elements drawn from indigenous traditions. Bolivian miners have created new, cohesive cultural patterns; far from being dissonant and alienating, the miners' culture provides an intact sense of self and belonging and an ability to celebrate life because it is viewed as meaningful.

How can we explain—in the lives of Bolivian miners or Tswana migrants—this combination of what appears to be both genuine suffering and genuine celebration? Exploitation certainly leaves its mark on its victims: poor health, high infant mortality, intrafamilial abuse, shattered hopes. Yet many Bolivian miners and Tswana migrants have not been irrevocably brutalized by these experiences. Their powers to invest their experiences with meaning remain intact, despite crushing conditions of exploitation.

This is the point: "The power the Tswana will think he has will not be defined in terms of what he can get the boss to do and vice versa, but rather in terms of how freely and effectively he invests his experience with the meaning *he chooses*" (Alverson 1978, 258). This power was noted by Nash for the Bolivian miners as well: "My experience living in mining communities taught me more than anything else, how a people totally involved in the most exploitative, dehumanizing form of industrialization managed to resist alienation" (Nash 1979, 319–20). Like Alverson, Nash argues that the events people experience are less important than how they interpret those events. Nash concludes that the ethnocentrism of Western observers has kept them from recognizing the creative, revolutionary potential embodied in hybrid cultures like that of the Bolivian tin miners.

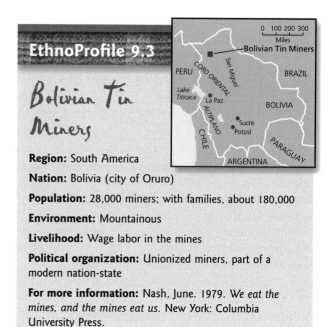

EthnoProfile 9.3

Bolivian Tin Miners

Region: South America

Nation: Bolivia (city of Oruro)

Population: 28,000 miners; with families, about 180,000

Environment: Mountainous

Livelihood: Wage labor in the mines

Political organization: Unionized miners, part of a modern nation-state

For more information: Nash, June. 1979. *We eat the mines, and the mines eat us.* New York: Columbia University Press.

Bargaining for Reality

The power that people have to invest their experiences with meanings of their own choosing suggests that a ruler's power of coercion is limited, which was Gramsci's key insight. Thought alone may be unable to alter the material circumstances of coercion, yet it has the power to transform the meaning of those material circumstances.

Any hegemonic establishment runs the risk that the dominated may create new, plausible accounts of their experiences of domination. Political scientist James Scott (1990) refers to these unofficial accounts as *hidden transcripts.* Occasionally, those who are dominated may be able to organize themselves socially in order to transform their hidden transcripts into a counterhegemonic discourse aimed at discrediting the political establishment. Those who are dominated may be able to persuade some or all of those around them that their counterhegemonic interpretation of social experience is better or truer than the hegemonic discourse of the current rulers. Such challenges to incumbent political power are frequently too strong to be ignored and too widespread to be simply obliterated by force. When coercion no longer works, what remains is a struggle between alternative accounts of experience.

Anthropologist Lawrence Rosen worked in the Moroccan city of Sefrou (see EthnoProfile 9.4: Sefrou). As he listened to his informants discussing and defining their relationships with each other, he realized that none of the traditional concepts they used could be said to have a fixed meaning. Any definition offered by one person would be verbally challenged by another. Rosen concluded that political and social life in Sefrou could not be understood unless one accepted that, for his informants, negotiation was the norm. Rosen (1984) calls this sociopolitical negotiation *bargaining for reality*.

The reality bargained for is not an impersonal, unchangeable set of truths about the world. Moroccans aim to persuade one another to accept alternative ways of understanding a particular situation. Persuasive accounts must be *coherent:* They must explain events and processes central to the experience of those to whom they are addressed; they must be expressed in language that other members of society can understand; and they must hang together in a way that is not blatantly contradictory.

Bargaining over Marriage in Morocco   The power relationship between men and women in Sefrou illustrates this process. Men view women as less intelligent, less self-controlled, and more selfish than men, and they expect women to obey them. Although women often assent to the male account of this relationship, they do not accept it in all circumstances. Women have developed an alternative account that explains elements in their lives that the male account either overlooks or interprets differently.

Women in Sefrou depend on men—first their fathers and later their husbands—for material support. But marriages are fragile, and women often have to rely on brothers or sons when their husbands divorce them (a wife cannot legally divorce her husband). Consequently, security for women depends on strengthening their positions within their families. In particular, women attempt to influence marriage negotiations because marriage automatically rearranges social relationships within the family. Women are eager to protect themselves and their daughters from oppressive demands by a husband and his kin. They view their action as sensible and compassionate, not as misplaced interference. Nor do they accept the men's view that men are superior

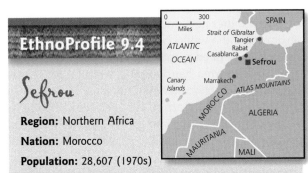

EthnoProfile 9.4

Sefrou

Region: Northern Africa

Nation: Morocco

Population: 28,607 (1970s)

Environment: Well-watered oasis in foothills

Livelihood: Agriculture, commerce, bureaucratic service, artisanship

Political organization: Part of a modern nation-state

For more information: Rosen, Lawrence. 1984. *Bargaining for reality: The construction of social relations in a Muslim community.* Chicago: University of Chicago Press.

to women intellectually and morally. Indeed, they often view men as self-centered and childish.

In effect, Moroccan men and women live side by side in different worlds. They share experiences but interpret those experiences differently. Because neither gender has much direct contact with the other during everyday life, these different interpretations of experience do not constantly come into conflict. But marriage negotiations inevitably bring these different perspectives into contention. The outcome is reality bargaining, as several different actors attempt to make their definitions of the situation prevail.

Rosen describes one marriage negotiation that he encountered in Sefrou (1984, 40–47). A girl refused to marry the suitor her family chose, and her continued resistance had disrupted the harmony of her father's household. Rosen visited the household in the company of a respected male informant who was an old friend of the family. During their visit, the family friend and the girl's mother discussed the betrothal and the girl's refusal to consent to it. Both parties interpreted the girl's refusal differently. The family friend described the girl's behavior as a typical case of female selfishness and immorality. What other reason could there be for her refusing to obey her father, as dutiful daughters should? He spoke harshly of her and repeatedly asserted that when her father returned they would force her to come to her senses and make the marriage.

Her mother never openly contradicted these assertions. All the while, however, she quietly and insistently continued to make counterassertions of her own. She reported her daughter's reason for rejecting the match: Her intended husband came from a distant city. If she married him she would have to leave her family behind and go live among strangers. It was not that she objected to an arranged marriage; rather, she did not want to marry this particular man because to do so would take her so far away from home. From a woman's perspective, the daughter's anxieties were entirely rational, given the powerlessness and isolation that a new Moroccan wife must endure in her husband's family.

As it turned out, the young girl was eventually persuaded to marry the intended spouse, but only after a year and a half of successful resistance. She only changed her mind when she became convinced that consenting to the marriage was an economically sound move, not a submission to patriarchal authority. So women may agree with the male position in general terms and yet successfully dispute its relevance in a particular situation. Men may get women to comply with their wishes, and yet the women's reasons for doing so may have nothing to do with the reasons men offer to justify their demands.

Peasant Resistance in Malaysia   Political scientist James Scott carried out two years of ethnographic research among peasant rice farmers in a Malaysian village called "Sedaka" (a pseudonym). (See EthnoProfile 9.5: "Sedaka" Village.) Poor Malaysian peasants are at the bottom of a social hierarchy dominated locally by rich farmers and nationally by a powerful state apparatus (Figure 9.8). These peasants are not kept in line by some form of state-sponsored terrorism; rather, the context of their lives is shaped by what Scott calls *routine repression:* "occasional arrests, warnings, diligent police work, legal restrictions, and an Internal Security Act that allows for indefinite preventive detention and proscribes much political activity" (1985, 274).

Scott wanted to find out how this highly restrictive environment affected political relations between members of dominant and subordinate classes in the village. He quickly realized that the poor peasants of "Sedaka" were not about to rise up against their oppressors. But this was not because they accepted their poverty and low status as natural and proper. One reason was that organized overt defense of their in-

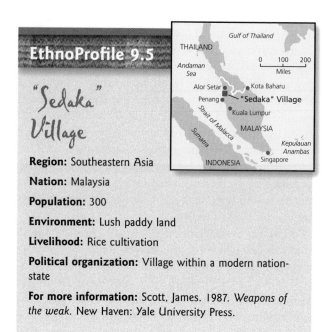

EthnoProfile 9.5

"Sedaka" Village

Region: Southeastern Asia

Nation: Malaysia

Population: 300

Environment: Lush paddy land

Livelihood: Rice cultivation

Political organization: Village within a modern nation-state

For more information: Scott, James. 1987. *Weapons of the weak.* New Haven: Yale University Press.

terests would have been difficult given the conflicting loyalties generated by local economic, political, and kinship ties. For another, the peasants knew that overt political action in the context of routine repression would be foolhardy. And they had to feed their families. Their solution was to engage in what Scott calls *everyday forms of peasant resistance:* this included "foot dragging, dissimulation, desertion, false compliance, pilfering, feigned ignorance, slander, arson, sabotage, and so forth" (1985, xvi). These actions may have done little to alter the peasants' situation in the short run; however, Scott argues, in the long run they may have been more effective than overt rebellion in undercutting state repression.

What we find in everyday forms of peasant resistance are indirect attempts to challenge local hegemony. Scott says, "The struggle between rich and poor in Sedaka is not merely a struggle over work, property rights, grain, and cash. It is also a struggle over the appropriation of symbols, a struggle over how the past and present shall be understood and labeled, a struggle to identify causes and assess blame" (1985, xvii). When peasants criticize rich landowners or rich landowners find fault with peasants, the parties involved are not just venting emotion. According to Scott, each side is simultaneously constructing a worldview. Rich and poor alike are offering "a critique of things as they are as well as a vision of things as they should be. . . . [They are

The Struggle for Indigenous Rights in Ecuador

Historian Peter Winn describes the recent history of CONAIE (Confederation of Ecuadorian Indigenous Nationalities), the first South American organization to unite indigenous highland and rain forest peoples in a common political struggle against a national government.

By 1980, when Fabián Muenala joined fifty-two educated young Indians in a bilingual Catholic University program in Quito, Ecuador's sierra Indians were ready to unite their efforts with those of the Amazonian Indians about whom they knew little.

During the early 1980s, that bilingual education project, based in part on the Shuar experience, served as a frame within which Ecuador's Indians became familiar with each other's cultures and histories. They also spent these same years working out common positions on controversial issues. "It was a difficult process," Muenala said. "There were many outside influences that tried to bend our interests to suit theirs: The Marxists wanted us to be part of a class-based peasant organization, the Christians wanted us to be part of a religious movement, the indigenistas wanted us to become dependent on foreign aid agencies, and the indianistas wanted us to reject everything Western and re-create the Inca empire. [But] in the end, we developed our own positions, in accordance with our own criteria and experience." After studying the examples of the United States, the Soviet Union, Canada, and Switzerland, the Ecuadorian Indians decided that they were "nationalities"—each with their own language, history, and "cosmovision"—living in a country that should recognize it was a multinational state. In 1986, they joined together in the Confederation of Ecuadorian Indigenous Nationalities (CONAIE), the first organization in South America to unite highland and rain forest Indians despite the many differences between them. "In the Amazon, we are trying to defend the lands of our ancestors," said Leonardo Viteri. "In the sierra they are trying to recover the lands taken from their ancestors. We agreed to support each other's struggle."

The formation of such a confederation was an historic event, but it marked the beginning of their struggle, not its end. The 1988 election of a center-left reform government led by Rodrigo Borja sparked Indian hopes: Borja had agreed during his campaign to CONAIE demands for the recognition of Ecuador as a multinational state and Quichua as one of its official languages, as well as to bilingual education, agrarian reform in the highlands, and the demarcation of Indian lands in the rain forest. Once in office, however, Borja dragged his feet on fulfilling his promises to CONAIE.

As a result, CONAIE decided on a dramatic protest. It began as a hunger strike in Quito's Santo Domingo church by two hundred Indian leaders, "to protest the government's refusal to grant our demands or even to discuss them with us," Fabián Muenala explained. The government responded by sealing off the church with troops. It backed down in the face of Church mediation and international pressure, but then refused to recognize the accord. In response, CONAIE called for peaceful protest marches throughout the country. The result was the Indian Uprising of June 1990, which galvanized Ecuador's indigenous people in Cayambe and other communities in the sierra and the rain forest. CONAIE's leaders "hadn't realized what the magnitude of response to its call would be," Muenala said. "The people exploded against the injustices they were suffering, and their energy and force paralyzed the entire country."

The scope and effectiveness of the Indian protests took Ecuador by surprise. The Church was sympathetic and offered to mediate with the government. Support from labor, women's, and peasant organizations poured in, along with expressions of solidarity from ordinary Ecuadorians—including mestizo taxi drivers, chola marketwomen, and creole intellectuals. Only the government refused to recognize the popular rebellion for what it was, accusing the Indians of being "agitators without a sense of nationality who want to divide the country." But after three days, "the cities were dying of hunger" and the

(continued on next page)

IN THEIR OWN WORDS   *The Struggle for Indigenous Rights in Ecuador*
(continued)

government was forced to agree to a Church-brokered ac-cord that committed it to negotiating Indian demands.

The Indian rebellion had brought the Ecuadorian gov-ernment to the bargaining table, but had not persuaded it to compromise on substantive issues. As one official in-sisted on condition of anonymity: "The government can not allow a small group of Indians to control its develop-ment policies and oil revenues." Nor was the Borja govern-ment willing to confront the creole elite that controlled Ecuadorian politics over land reform in order to placate its Indians. A year later, CONAIE occupied the Chamber of Deputies to protest the slow pace of reform, the jailing of Indian leaders, and the failure to declare Ecuador a multi-national state. In April 1992, a two-week march of seven thousand Shuar, Ashuar, and Quichua activists from the Amazon to Quito—retracing the 180-mile ascent of the Andes undertaken a century ago by indigenous chiefs for a similar purpose—dramatized the lack of progress on several of these issues.

By then it was clear that the struggle for indigenous rights in Ecuador was going to be a very long march. It was also evident that it was going to be an increasingly violent struggle. The government had intensified its repression, jailing leaders and harassing organizations. Even more omi-nous was the formation of paramilitary death squads by local landholders threatened with Indian land invasions. Kidnappings and murders of Indian activists confronted the movement with a new situation. "We do not want violence," Leonardo Viteri insisted. But neither he nor other Indian leaders would rule out violence in response to violence. "Indians have been dying for centuries," af-firmed Shuar leader Rafael Pandam. "We are not afraid to die for our people." Viteri was conscious of the parallels to the experience of indigenous people elsewhere in the region: "We do not want another Guatemala," he stressed, "but it may not be up to us."

Source: Winn 1992, 261–63.

writing] a kind of social text on the subject of human decency" (23).

Scott describes the dynamics of this struggle dur-ing the introduction of mechanized rice harvesting in "Sedaka." Traditionally, rice harvesting was manual labor. It regularly allowed poor peasants to earn cash and receive grain from their employers as a tradi-tional form of charitable gift. In the late 1970s, how-ever, the introduction of combine harvesters elimi-nated the rich farmers' need for hired labor, a loss that dealt poor families a severe economic blow. When the rich and poor talked about the harvesters, each side offered a different account of their effect on economic life in the village.

Scott tells us that both sides agreed that using the machines hurt the poor and helped the rich. When each side was asked whether the benefits of the ma-chines outweighed their costs, however, consensus evaporated. The poor offered practical reasons against the use of combine harvesters: They claimed that the heavy machines were inefficient and that their oper-ation destroyed rice paddies. They also offered moral

reasons: They accused the rich of being "stingy," of ignoring the traditional obligation of rich people to help the poor by providing them with work and charity. The rich denied both the practical and the moral objections of the poor. They insisted that using harvesters increased their yield. They accused the poor people of bad faith. They claimed that the poor suffered because they were bad farmers or lazy, and they attributed their own success to hard work and prudent farm management.

Rich rice farmers would never have been able to begin using combine harvesters without the outside assistance of both the national government and the business groups who rented the machines to them at harvest time. Poor peasants were aware of this, yet they directed their critique at the local farmers and not at the government or outside business organiza-tions. After all, the rich farmers "are a part of the com-munity and therefore *ought* not to be indifferent to the consequences of their acts for their neighbors" (Scott 1985, 161). The stinginess of the rich did not just bring economic loss. It also attacked the social identity of

FIGURE 9.8 Until recently, rice harvesting in rural Malaysia was manual labor that regularly allowed poor peasants to earn cash and receive grain from their employers as a traditional form of charitable gift.

the poor, who vigorously resisted being turned into nonpersons. The poor insisted on being accorded the "minimal cultural decencies in this small community" (xviii). The only weapon they controlled in this struggle was their ability, by word and deed, to undercut the prestige and reputation of the rich.

This strategy worked in "Sedaka" because rich local farmers were not ready to abandon the traditional morality that had regulated relations between rich and poor. They had not yet become so Westernized that they no longer cared what other villagers thought of them. A shrewd campaign of character assassination may have caused at least some of the rich to hesitate before ignoring their traditional obligations. The improvement might have been minor in strictly economic terms, but it would have been major in terms of the ability of the poor to defend their claims to citizenship in the local community. In addition, the wider political arena could always change in the future. Scott was convinced that many of the poor peasants he knew might well engage in open, active rebellion if routine repression disappeared.

When disputes are settled in this manner, experience is transformed. As Scott observes, "The key symbols animating class relations in Sedaka—generosity, stinginess, arrogance, humility, help, assistance, wealth and poverty—do not constitute a set of given rules or principles that actors simply follow. They are instead the normative raw material that is created, main-

tained, changed, and above all manipulated by daily human activity" (1985, 309). In a similar way, Rosen refers to such central Moroccan values as intelligence, self-control, and generosity as **essentially negotiable concepts**: "There is an element of uncertainty inherent in these terms, such that their application to any situation by one person can be contested by another" (1984, 43). Bargaining for reality involves just this sort of maneuver: "What is negotiable, then, is less one's view of reality as such than its scope, its impact, and its differential importance" (47). Worldviews articulated in language by different social subgroups aim "not just to convince but to control; better stated, they aim to control by convincing" (Scott 1985, 23).

▼ HISTORY AS A PROTOTYPE OF AND FOR POLITICAL ACTION

When individual actors within a particular cultural and situational context attempt to impose their definition of the situation on those with whom they interact, they draw on elements of a shared tradition of values and beliefs. This shared tradition, however,

essentially negotiable concepts Culturally recognized concepts that evoke a wide range of meanings and whose relevance in any particular context must be negotiated.

does not consist of values and beliefs divorced from experience and history. To some degree, people in all cultures continue to reshape—to bargain over—not merely which part of an agreed-on tradition is relevant in a particular situation but also which version of the tradition ought to be agreed on. The combinations they come up with are sometimes surprising.

Consider the development in the northern Peruvian highlands of rural justice groups, called *rondas campesinas* ("peasants who make the rounds"), beginning in the mid-1970s as discussed by anthropologist Orin Starn (Starn 1992). (See EthnoProfile 9.6: Northern Peru [Rondas Campesinas].) Rondas consist of armed groups of peasants who walk the paths around their hamlets at night, keeping an eye out for animal rustlers (Figure 9.9). The rondas began in one small hamlet in the northern Peruvian department of Cajamarca in 1976. During the 1980s, they spread hundreds of miles within Cajamarca and surrounding departments. At the same time, their functions were radically expanded: they became an alternative justice system with open peasant assemblies to resolve problems ranging from wife-beating to land disputes. By the early 1990s, rondas operated in 3,400 hamlets in the northern Peruvian Andes.

Starn notes that at least five forces spurred campesinos to establish their alternative justice system. First, the theft of animals shot up dramatically with the onset of the Peruvian economic crisis of the mid-1970s. The rise in theft was extremely serious for the poor farmers of the northern Andes, most of whom have small flocks and earn less than $2,000 per year. Second, peasants got no relief from the official justice system. As the economy worsened, many government authorities tried to enlarge their shrinking salaries through bribery, kickbacks, and extortion, and poorer peasants were increasingly unable to pay. Third, the government had only a weak presence in the mountains, providing an opportunity for peasants to develop a new form of community organization. Fourth, country people in northern Peru value toughness and bravery in the face of violence and were able to channel their aggressiveness into the service of order and discipline in the rondas. Fifth, local organizers had outside supporters. In the province where the rondas began, these were activists from the Maoist Red Homeland party. In a neighboring province, peasant catechists trained in liberation theology became early ronda leaders

EthnoProfile 9.6

Northern Peru (Rondas Campesinas)

Region: South America

Nation: Peru

Population: Rondas campesinas now operate in more than 3,400 hamlets across Peru's northern Andes

Environment: Mountainous

Livelihood: Peasant villagers

Political organization: Originally, community-run vigilante patrols that developed by the mid-1980s into an alternative justice system, filling the vacuum created by an ineffectual central government

For more information: Starn, Orin. 1992. I dreamed of foxes and hawks: Reflections on peasant protest, new social movements, and the *rondas campesinas* of northern Peru. In *The making of social movements in Latin America: Identity, strategy, and democracy*, edited by Arturo Escobar and Sonia Alvarez, 89–111. Boulder, CO: Westview.

and were defended by priests and nuns as well as the local bishop.

During the 1980s, rondas were transformed from vigilante groups to dispute-resolution groups. Compared to the expensive, time-consuming, humiliating, and ineffective official justice system, the ronda was inexpensive, efficient, effective, and local. By the late 1980s, rustling was virtually eliminated and rondas in some communities were adjudicating over 100 cases a month. The rondas also involve the elaboration of political identity and culture. Songs and poems celebrate the rondas, and festivals commemorate their anniversaries.

To create the rondas, peasants drew on national and local cultural patterns. Peasants had served on patrols to stop thieves on haciendas before the haciendas were broken up in the late 1960s. Men in the hamlets who had served in the Peruvian military incorporated military strategies and forms into the rondas. The peasants also employed local patterns, keeping the ronda patrols under the collective authority of

FIGURE 9.9 *Rondas campesninas* have become an alternative justice system in highland Peru. Here a group of ronderos pose with a stolen donkey recovered from rustlers in 1986.

the community. Likewise, when the rondas took on adjudication roles, they adopted some forms from the state bureaucracy, using a table like a judge's bench, rubber stamps, a recording secretary with notarized minutes, and so on. But the openness of the ronda system is very different from the state bureaucracy, for the final decision rests on the ronda president's evaluation of the response of the people attending. Assemblies of the ronda are often held outside, where the event occurred, such as a farmyard. All attending have detailed knowledge of some kind that may be brought into play, and everyone jumps in to attempt to settle the dispute.

But the rondas, for all their effective innovation, are sometimes still enmeshed in old practices. First, they are connected with political parties in Peru, and squabbles involving the parties have weakened the ronda movement. Second, although they have challenged the government's monopoly on the administration of justice, they are not working for the overthrow of the state; rather, they see themselves as the genuine upholders of the law and the Peruvian constitution. Third, although constant rotation in many communities discourages permanent leaders, in some rondas the leaders stay on for many years, hoard power, and begin to show favoritism. Fourth, the rondas perpetuate the problems of patriarchy. Many peasant women march in ronda protests, and in some rondas the women oversee the patrol scheduling.

The rondas have given women a place to censure wife-beating, and a number of offenders have received a stern warning or whipping. Nevertheless, only men patrol; female participation in assemblies is limited and mostly passive; and women are never ronda officers. Finally, there is the problem of violence. The ronderos have learned some of the techniques of the Peruvian police, including whipping with barbed wire or hanging accused rustlers by their arms. But it is important to note that the rondas began as a means of creating peace and order in a violent environment. As rustling has been brought under control, cases of harsh physical treatment have diminished. The leaders of rondas have worked within their communities to prevent the use of excessive force. Starn concludes that, on the whole, the rondas have given Peruvian peasants the vision of an alternative modernity and have renewed among them a powerful sense of independent identity.

▼ NEGOTIATING THE MEANING OF HISTORY

The meanings of the central symbols of any cultural tradition are essentially negotiable. That is, each symbol evokes a wide range of meanings among those who accept it. But what that symbol means in any particular situation, as well as the appropriateness of applying that symbol to the situation, is never obvious. Such matters are cultural dilemmas that people struggle creatively to resolve. In the Moroccan example, nobody denied that daughters should allow their fathers to arrange their marriages. The issue was whether this particular daughter, in refusing to marry a particular man, was rejecting the general principle. From her and her mother's perspective she was not; they would accept an arranged marriage if it did not mean taking her far from her family. The family friend, however, insisted on interpreting her behavior as a challenge to her father's authority.

In the Peruvian example, a central question was, Who are the genuine upholders of the law and the Peruvian constitution? The ronderos and the national government gave different answers. Such powerful national symbols as the law and the constitution carry heavy historical freight. The political use to which such symbols are put can be far from negligible. Leftist political parties and Catholic clergy supported the interpretation of the peasants, backing the ronda movement. The rapid spread of the ronda movement suggests that the rondero's account was also strongly persuasive to peasants in many areas of northern highland Peru under the conditions of the late 1970s and 1980s.

The power to invest experience with one's own meanings is a very real power. And yet many anthropologists are divided about the effectiveness of resistance as a solution to the problems of those at the very bottom of society. While there is much ethno-graphic evidence documenting the ability of some individuals and groups to assert themselves and their view of the world in the face of tremendous oppression, there is also much evidence that other individuals and groups have been destroyed by such oppression. Political anthropologist John Gledhill observes that it would be "dangerous to be overoptimistic. 'Counter-hegemonic' movements exist, but much of the world's population is not participating in them" (1994, 198). He is particularly skeptical about the power of everyday forms of peasant resistance: The ability of such practices to undermine the local elite, he warns, may "merely provide the scenario for the replacement of one elite by another, more effective, dominant group" (92).

On the other hand, as Ted Fischer and Peter Benson observe, in the twenty-first century, in places like Guatemala, the way forward is not wholly predictable, and the efforts of Mayan farmers to seek "something better" for themselves and their children by producing broccoli for consumers in the United States should not be despised. Fischer and Benson also suggest what the political anthropology of the twenty-first century may look like. "Our *compromiso* (commitment) as participants as well as observers compels us to pore over the corpus delicti of political violence and the detritus of broken promises, recording what we see and hear so that the horrors will not be forgotten, so that past mistakes can be corrected, and so that reconciliation, if not justice, can be achieved" (2006, 112).

CHAPTER SUMMARY

1. The ability to act implies power. The study of social power in human society is the domain of political anthropology. In most societies at most times, power can never be reduced to physical force, although this is the Western prototype of power. Power in society operates according to principles that are cultural creations. As such, those principles are basically arbitrary, are affected by history, and may differ from one society to another.

2. Western thinkers traditionally assumed that without a state, social life would be chaotic, if not impossible. They believed that people were free agents who would not cooperate unless forced to do so. Anthropologists have demonstrated that power is exercised both by coercive and by persuasive means. People may submit to institutionalized power because they fear punishment, but they may also submit because they believe it is the right thing to do.

3. Anthropologists interested in how power is exercised in states have been influenced in recent

years by the works of Antonio Gramsci and Michel Foucault. Gramsci argued that coercion alone is rarely sufficient for social control. Gramsci distinguished coercive domination from hegemony. Successful hegemonic practice deflects challenges to the coercive power of the ruling group, but hegemony is always the outcome of struggle, and success is never guaranteed. Foucault's concept of governmentality addresses practices developed in Western nation-states in the nineteenth century that aimed to create and sustain peaceful and prosperous social life by exercising power over persons who could be counted, whose physical attributes could be measured statistically, and whose sexual and reproductive behaviors could be shaped by the exercise of state power.

4. Anthropological research in societies without states has shown how social obligations can restrict individuals from pursuing their own self-interest to the detriment of the group. In those societies, power is usually seen to be an independent entity to which one may gain access by supplication, not coercion. Likewise, individuals cannot be coerced but must be persuaded to cooperate. They are not free agents, but they are empowered to resist conforming to another's wishes.

5. All human beings possess the power to invest the world with meaning. Many anthropologists would feel that a discussion of social power is incomplete if it does not also pay attention to the ways individuals make sense of and use the constraints and opportunities for action open to them, however limited they may be. Rulers always face the risk that those they dominate may create new persuasive accounts of their experience of being dominated, organize themselves to defend and disseminate their account, acquire a following, and unseat their rulers.

6. When people bargain for reality, they draw on elements of a shared culture and shared history in order to persuade others of the validity of their position. But they often must bargain over not merely which part of an agreed-on tradition is relevant but also which version of the tradition ought to be agreed on. Much political debate concerns which lessons from the past are relevant to the present. When disputes are settled in this manner, experience is transformed.

KEY TERMS

power
political anthropology
free agency
ideology
domination
hegemony
governmentality
resistance
consensus
persuasion
anomie
alienation
essentially negotiable concepts

SUGGESTED READINGS

Alverson, Hoyt. 1978. *Mind in the heart of darkness*. New Haven: Yale University Press. *Difficult in places, but important and gripping: A classic study of how Tswana miners in apartheid South Africa maintained a sense of who they were under the most hellish circumstances.*

Arens, W., and Ivan Karp, eds. 1989. *Creativity of power: Cosmology and action in African societies*. Washington, DC: Smithsonian Institution Press. *Contains 13 essays exploring the relationship among power, action, and human agency in African social systems and cosmologies.*

Keesing, Roger. 1983. *'Elota's story*. New York: Holt, Rinehart and Winston. *The autobiography of a Kwaio Big Man, with interpretative material by Keesing. First-rate, very readable, and involving. We come to know 'Elota by the end of the book.*

Lewellen, Ted. 1993. *Political anthropology*. 2d ed. Westport, CT: Bergin and Garvey. *A basic text in political anthropology, covering leading theories, scholars, and problems in the field.*

Vincent, Joan, ed. 2002. *The anthropology of politics: A reader in ethnography, theory, and critique*. Malden, MA: Blackwell Publishers. *A bit challenging for beginning students, but an excellent collection of key texts in political anthropology, ranging from the eighteenth-century Enlightenment to twenty-first century critique.*

Chapter 10

Making a Living

People in all societies need to secure the basic material necessities of life, and different societies have developed a variety of ways of doing so. This chapter introduces some of the diversity in human economic practices and also discusses the different ways that anthropologists have tried to explain this economic diversity.

The morning in 1963 after ethnographer Richard Lee arrived in the Dobe Ju/'hoansi area in the central Kalahari Desert of southern Africa, his neighbors, including a man named N!eishi, asked him to give them a ride in his Land Rover to get some food (see EthnoProfile 11.1: Ju/'hoansi). They said there was little left in their area—mostly bitter roots and berries. They wanted to collect mongongo nuts—a staple of their diet and a great favorite—in a nearby grove (Figure 10.1). Lee agreed to take them. "The travel was anything but high-speed, and our destination was anything but near. We ground along for hours in four-wheel drive at a walking pace where no truck had ever been before, swerving to avoid antbear holes and circumventing fallen trees" (1992b, 39).

By the time they stopped, Lee figured they were about 10 miles north of Dobe. Lee was amazed by how fast the Ju/'hoansi, both men and women, were able to gather the nuts. After two hours, they left the grove. He later weighed the food collected in that short time: The women had gathered loads weighing 30 to 50 pounds each; the men, 15 to 25 pounds each. Lee continued:

> That worked out to about 23,000 calories for food for each woman collector, and 12,000 for each man. Each woman had gathered enough to feed a person for ten days and each man enough for five days. Not at all a bad haul for two hours' work!
>
> My first full day of fieldwork had already taught me to question one popular view of hunter-gatherer subsistence: that life among these people was precarious, a constant struggle for existence. My later studies were to show that the Ju/'hoansi in fact enjoyed a rather good diet and that they didn't have to work very hard to get it. As we will see, even without the aid of an anthropologist's truck the Ju/'hoansi had to work only 20 hours a week in subsistence. But what about the fact that N!eishi had come to me that morning saying that they were hungry and that there was no food nearby? Strictly speaking, N!eishi spoke the truth. October is one of the harder months of the year, at the end of the dry season, and the more desirable foods had been eaten out close to Dobe. What N!eishi did not say was that a little farther away food *was* available, and, if not plentiful, there was enough

to see them through until the rains came. When N!eishi came to me with his proposition, he was making an intelligent use of his resources, social and otherwise. Why hike in the hot sun for a small meal, when the bearded White man might take you in his truck for ten large ones? (1992b, 40–41)

It is a stereotype of Western culture that human beings who forage for a living lead lives that, in Thomas Hobbes's famous phrase, are nasty, brutish, and short. Only recently have anthropologists lived closely enough with foraging peoples to discover the inaccuracy of the Hobbesian position. Lee's Ju/'hoansi informants were well nourished, with balanced diets. What is more, they were choosy about what they ate, unwilling to settle for food they disliked when Lee was there to take them to food they preferred. Such behavior is entirely familiar to us and far from brutish. Much has changed in the Dobe area since the 1960s, and the Ju/'hoansi no longer forage as they once did. Until recently, however, the cultural knowledge of the Ju/'hoansi enabled them to live rather well by means of culture in what some see as a marginal environment.

▼ WHAT ARE THE CONNECTIONS BETWEEN CULTURE AND LIVELIHOOD?

Although our physical survival depends on our making adequate use of the material resources around us, the resources themselves do not determine how they must be used. Rather, our cultures suggest a range of options for making a living, as well as furnishing the tools to pursue those options. Anthropologist Richard Wilk has defined **economic anthropology** as "the part of the discipline that debates issues of *human nature* that relate directly to the decisions of daily life and making a living" (1996, xv).

Self-Interest, Institutions, and Morals

Wilk and Cliggett argue that it is possible to identify three theoretical camps in economic anthropology, each of which depends on a different set of assumptions about human nature, and that the "real heat and argument in economic anthropology comes from underlying disagreement over these starting assumptions" (2007, 40).

---

economic anthropology "The part of the discipline [of anthropology] that debates issues of human nature that relate directly to the decisions of daily life and making a living" (Wilk 1996, xv).

FIGURE 10.1 Anthropologist Richard Lee and Ju'/hoansi informants gathering mongongo nuts.

The first model Wilk and Cliggett identify is the *self-interested model*: This model of human nature originated during the Enlightenment and is based on the assumption that individuals are first and foremost interested in their own well-being, that selfishness is natural. Economists since Adam Smith have argued that people's resources (for example, money) are not and never will be great enough for them to obtain all the goods they want. This view of economy also assumes that economic analysis should focus on *individuals* who must maximize their *utility* (or satisfaction) under conditions of scarcity. An economizing individual sets priorities and allocates resources rationally according to those priorities. Economic anthropologists who accept the self-interest model of human behavior should therefore investigate the different priorities set by different societies and study how these priorities affect the maximizing decisions of individuals.

Other economic anthropologists, however, are committed to the *social model* of human nature. This means that they pay attention to "the way people

form groups and exercise power" (2007, 42). This view of human nature assumes that people ordinarily identify with the groups to which they belong and, in many cases, cannot even conceive of having a self with interests that diverge from the interests of the group. This view of human nature suggests that economics ought to focus on **institutions**—stable and enduring cultural practices that organize social life—not on individuals. From an institutional point of view, a society's economy consists of the culturally specific processes its members use to provide themselves with material resources. Therefore, economic processes cannot be considered apart from the cultural institutions in which they are embedded (Halperin 1994).

Wilk and Cliggett's third model of human nature is the *moral model*. Economic anthropologists

institutions Stable and enduring cultural practices that organize social life.

committed to a moral model of human nature assume that people's motivations "are shaped by culturally specific belief systems and values . . . guided by a culturally patterned view of the universe and the human place within it" (2007, 43). People are socialized and enculturated into these values and practices over a lifetime, such that they will experience distress and conflict if tempted to make decisions—including economic decisions—that are contrary to their internalized morality. From the point of view of the moral model, "modern society is one that has lost the morality and ethics that guided behavior in traditional cultures, replacing them with amoral selfishness" (2007, 44). Wilk and Cliggett are unwilling to take any one model as a fact and are more interested in paying close ethnographic attention to the particularities of real human beings in real sociocultural settings. "The problem is explaining why people are guided sometimes by one set of motivations and at other times by others. . . . By suspending our preconceptions about human nature, we can give more direct attention to this fundamental question, which forms the basis of each culture's practical ethics and its distinction between moral and immoral" (2007, 46).

▼ SUBSISTENCE STRATEGIES

Human beings invent ways of using their relationships with one another and with the physical environment to make a living. *Subsistence* is the term often

---

subsistence strategies The patterns of production, distribution, and consumption that members of a society employ to ensure the satisfaction of the basic material survival needs of humans.

food collectors Those who gather, fish, or hunt for food.

food producers Those who depend on domesticated plants or animals for food.

extensive agriculture A form of cultivation based on the technique of clearing uncultivated land, burning the brush, and planting the crops in the ash-enriched soil, which requires moving farm plots every few years as the soil becomes exhausted.

intensive agriculture A form of cultivation that employs plows, draft animals, irrigation, fertilizer, and such to bring much land under cultivation at one time, to use it year after year, and to produce significant crop surpluses.

mechanized industrial agriculture Large-scale farming and animal husbandry that is highly dependent on industrial methods of technology and production.

---

used to refer to the satisfaction of the most basic material survival needs: food, clothing, and shelter. The different ways that people in different societies go about meeting these needs are called **subsistence strategies**.

Anthropologists have devised a typology of subsistence strategies that has gained wide acceptance (Figure 10.2). The basic division is between **food collectors** (those who gather, fish, or hunt) and **food producers** (those who depend on domesticated plants or animals or both). The strategies followed by food collectors depend on the richness of the environments in which they live. Small-scale food collectors, like the Ju/'hoansi through the 1960s, live in environments less well-endowed with resources and are likely to change residence often in search of them. By contrast, complex food collectors live in environments richly endowed with dependable food sources and may even, like the indigenous peoples of the northwest coast of North America, build settlements with permanent architecture. Archaeological evidence shows, moreover, that some of the first food producers in the world continued food collection for many generations, raising a few crops on the side and occasionally abandoning food production to return to full-time foraging.

Food producers may farm exclusively or herd exclusively or do a little of both. Among those who farm, there are again distinctions. Some farmers depend primarily on human muscle power plus a few simple tools such as digging sticks or hoes or machetes. They clear plots of uncultivated land, burn the brush, and plant their crops in the ash-enriched soil that remains. Because this technique exhausts the soil after two or three seasons, the plot must then lie fallow for several years as a new plot is cleared and the process repeated. This form of cultivation is called **extensive agriculture**, emphasizing the extensive use of land as farm plots are moved every few years. Other farmers use plows, draft animals, irrigation, fertilizer, and the like. Their method of farming—known as **intensive agriculture**—brings much more land under cultivation at any one time and produces significant crop surpluses. Finally, **mechanized industrial agriculture** is found in societies in which farming or animal husbandry has become organized along industrial lines. Agribusiness "factories in the field" or animal feedlots transform food production

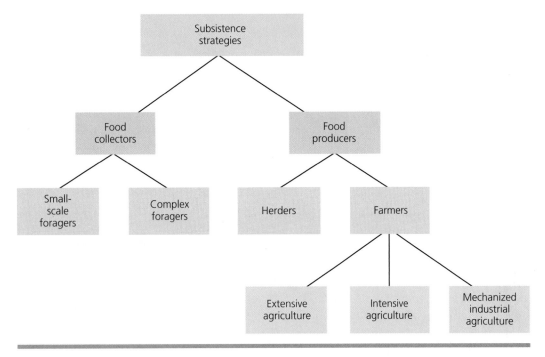

FIGURE 10.2 Subsistence strategies.

into a large-scale, technology-dependent industry of its own.

▼ WHAT ARE PRODUCTION, DISTRIBUTION, AND CONSUMPTION?

Anthropologists generally agree that economic activity is usefully subdivided into three distinct phases: production, distribution, and consumption. **Production** involves transforming nature's raw materials into products useful to human beings. **Distribution** involves getting those products to people. **Consumption** involves using up the products—for example, by eating food or wearing clothing.

When analyzing economic activity in a particular society, however, anthropologists differ in the importance they attach to each phase. For example, the distributive process known as *exchange* is central to the functioning of capitalist free enterprise. Some anthropologists have assumed that exchange is equally central to the functioning of all economies and have tried to explain the economic life of non-Western so-

cieties in terms of exchange. Anthropologists of a Marxian bent, however, have argued that exchange cannot be understood properly without first studying the nature of *production*. They point out that production shapes the context in which exchange can occur, determining which parties have how much of what kind of goods to exchange. Other anthropologists have suggested that neither production nor exchange patterns make any sense without first specifying the *consumption* priorities of the people who are producing and exchanging. Consumption priorities, they argue, are of course designed to satisfy material needs. But the recognition of needs and appropriate ways to satisfy them is shaped by arbitrary cultural patterns. Finally, still others argue that patterns of production, exchange, and consumption are all seriously affected by the kind of *storage* in use in a particular society (Figure 10.3).

production The transformation of nature's raw materials into a form suitable for human use.

distribution The allocation of goods and services.

consumption The using up of material goods necessary for human survival.

FIGURE 10.3 A seventeenth-century drawing of storage warehouses built at the height of the Inka Empire (below). At right, the plan of Huánuco Pampa shows the location of these storage warehouses. Some anthropologists argue that food storage practices buffer a population from ecological fluctuations, making possible considerable cultural manipulation of the economic relations of consumption.

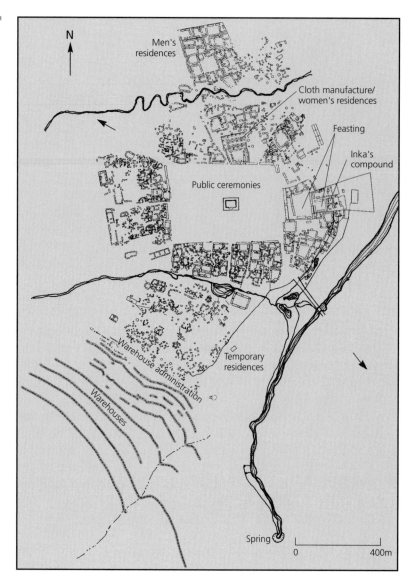

▼ HOW ARE GOODS DISTRIBUTED AND EXCHANGED?

Neoclassical Economics and Capitalism

The discipline of economics was born in the early years of the rise of capitalist industry in western Europe. At that time, such thinkers as Adam Smith and

his disciples struggled to devise theories to explain the profound changes in economic and social life that European society had recently begun to experience. Their work has become the foundation for neoclassical economic theory in the Western world. **Neoclassical economic theory** is a formal attempt to explain the workings of capitalism.

Capitalism differed in many ways from the feudal economic system that had preceded it, but perhaps the most striking difference was how it handled distribution. Feudal economic relations allotted goods and services to different social groups and individuals

---

neoclassical economic theory A formal attempt to explain the workings of capitalist enterprise, with particular attention to distribution.

on the basis of a person's position in society, or *status*. Because lords had high status and many obligations, they had a right to more goods and services. Peasants, with low status and few rights, were allowed far less. This distribution of goods was time-honored and not open to modification. The customs derived from capitalist economic relations, by contrast, were considered "free" precisely because they swept away all such traditional restrictions. As we saw in our discussion of "Sedaka" Village, Malaysia, capitalism also swept away traditional protections (see EthnoProfile 9.5: "Sedaka" Village). In any case, distribution under capitalism was negotiated between buyers and sellers in the market.

In Adam Smith's ideal market, everyone has something to sell (if only his or her willingness to work), and everyone is also a potential buyer of the goods brought to the market by others. Individual buyers and sellers meet in the market to buy from and sell to each other—to engage in economic exchange. Ideally, because there are many buyers, many sellers, and no traditional restrictions governing who should get how much of what, prices can fluctuate depending on levels of supply and demand. Distribution is carried out in line with the preferences of individuals. High demand by individuals for certain items raises the price for those items, as many buyers bargain to obtain few goods. This high demand, in turn, entices more people to produce those goods to take advantage of their higher prices. As competition between suppliers increases, however, prices go down, as each supplier attempts to obtain a greater share of the market. Ideally, prices stabilize as suppliers begin offering desired goods at a cost sufficiently high to allow a profit but sufficiently low for buyers to afford.

Capitalist market exchange of goods for other goods, for labor, or (increasingly) for cash was an important development in Western economic history. It is not surprising, therefore, that Western economic theory was preoccupied with explaining how the capitalist market worked. Markets clearly had a new, decisive importance in capitalist society, which they had not possessed in feudal times. Western neoclassical economics is based on the assumption that market forces are the central forces determining levels of both production and consumption in society.

Modes of Exchange

Some anthropologists have argued, however, that to take self-interested, materialistic decision making in the capitalist market as the prototype of human rationality is both reductionistic and ethnocentric. They pointed out that the capitalist market is a relatively recent cultural invention in human history. Neoclassical economic theory is an equally recent invention, designed to make sense of the capitalist market and its effects, and capitalist market exchange is but one mode of exchange. Western capitalist societies distribute material goods in a manner that is consistent with their basic values, institutions, and assumptions about the human condition. So, too, non-Western,

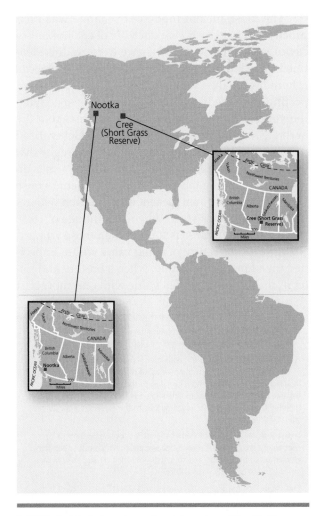

FIGURE 10.4 Locations of societies whose EthnoProfiles appear in chapter 10.

noncapitalist societies have devised alternative modes of exchange that distribute material goods in ways that are in accord with their basic values, institutions, and assumptions about the human condition.

In the early twentieth century, for example, French anthropologist Marcel Mauss (2000 [1950]) had contrasted noncapitalist *gift* exchanges (which are deeply embedded in social relations, and always requiring a return gift) with impersonal *commodity* exchanges typical of the capitalist market (in which nothing links exchange partners but cash). Similarly, Marshall Sahlins (1972) drew on the work of economic historian Karl Polanyi to propose that three **modes of exchange** could be identified historically and cross-culturally: reciprocity, redistribution, and market exchange.

The most ancient mode of exchange was **reciprocity**. Reciprocity is characteristic of egalitarian societies, such as the Ju/'hoansi once were. Sahlins identified three kinds of reciprocity. *Generalized reciprocity* is found when those who exchange do so without expecting an immediate return and without specifying the value of the return. Everyone assumes that the exchanges will eventually balance out. Generalized reciprocity usually characterizes the exchanges that occur between parents and their children. Parents do not keep a running tab on what it costs them to raise their children and then present their children with repayment schedules when they reach the age of 18.

Balanced reciprocity is found when those who exchange expect a return of equal value within a specified time limit (for example, when a brother and sister exchange gifts of equal value with one another at

Christmastime). Lee notes that the Ju/'hoansi distinguish between barter, which requires an immediate return of an equivalent, and *hxaro*, which is a kind of generalized reciprocity that encourages social obligations to be extended into the future (1992b, 103).

Finally, *negative reciprocity* is an exchange of goods and services in which at least one party attempts to get something for nothing without suffering any penalties. These attempts can range from haggling over prices to outright seizure.

Redistribution, the second mode of exchange, requires some form of centralized social organization. Those who occupy the central position receive economic contributions from all members of the group. It is then their responsibility to redistribute the goods they receive in a way that provides for every member of the group. The Internal Revenue Service is probably the institution of redistribution that Americans know best. A classic anthropological example involves the *potlatch* of the indigenous Americans of the northwest coast of North America (Figure 10.5). In the highly stratified fishing and gathering society of the Nootka, for example, nobles sought to outdo one another in generosity by giving away vast quantities of objects during the potlatch ceremony (see Ethno-Profile 10.1: Nootka). The noble giving the potlatch accumulated goods produced in one village and redistributed them to other nobles attending the ceremony. When the guests returned to their own villages, they, in turn, redistributed the goods among their followers.

Market exchange, invented in capitalist society, is the most recent mode of exchange, according to Polanyi (Figure 10.6). Capitalism involves an exchange of goods (*trade*) calculated in terms of a multipurpose medium of exchange and standard of value (*money*) and carried on by means of a "supply-demand-price mechanism" (the *market*). Polanyi was well aware that trade, money, and market institutions had developed independently of one another historically. He also knew that they could be found in societies outside the West. The uniqueness of capitalism was how all three institutions were linked to one another in the societies of early modern Europe.

According to Polanyi, different modes of exchange often coexist within a single society, although only one functions as the society's mode of economic integration. The United States, for example, is integrated by

modes of exchange Patterns according to which distribution takes place: reciprocity, redistribution, and market exchange.

reciprocity The exchange of goods and services of equal value. Anthropologists distinguish three forms of reciprocity: generalized, in which neither the time nor the value of the return are specified; balanced, in which a return of equal value is expected within a specified time limit; and negative, in which parties to the exchange hope to get something for nothing.

redistribution A mode of exchange that requires some form of centralized social organization to receive economic contributions from all members of the group and to redistribute them in such a way that every group member is provided for.

market exchange The exchange of goods (trade) calculated in terms of a multipurpose medium of exchange and standard of value (money) and carried on by means of a supply-demand-price mechanism (the market).

FIGURE 10.5 A classic anthropological case study of redistribution involves the *potlatch* of the Indian people of the northwest coast of North America. Although the potlatch was outlawed in 1904, it continued to be practiced. In 2004, Tlingit clan members, wearing Chilkat and Raven's Tail robes and clan hats, gathered in Sitka, Alaska, for the 100th Anniversary Commemoration of "The Last Potlatch."

the market mode of exchange, yet redistribution and reciprocity can still be found. Within the family, parents who obtain income from the market redistribute that income, or goods obtained with that income, to their children. Generalized reciprocity also characterizes much exchange within the family: As noted earlier, parents provide their children with food and clothing without expecting any immediate return.

Some economic anthropologists, however, argued that exchange could not properly be understood without a prior knowledge of production. Like earlier critics of neoclassical economics, such as Karl Marx, they insisted that people who meet to exchange have different kinds and amounts of resources to use in bargaining with one another. Those differences in resources, Marx argued, are not shaped by the market but rooted in the productive process itself.

▼ DOES PRODUCTION DRIVE ECONOMIC ACTIVITIES?

Some economic anthropologists see production as the driving force behind economic activity. Production creates supplies of goods to which demand must accommodate, and it determines levels of consumption as well. Anthropologists who stress the centrality of production borrow their perspective on economic activity, as well as many key concepts, from the works of Karl Marx. They argue that this perspective is far more insightful than the one taken by neoclassical theorists of market exchange.

Labor

Labor is perhaps the most central Marxian concept these anthropologists have adopted. **Labor** is the activity linking human social groups to the material world around them; human labor is therefore always social labor. Human beings must actively struggle together to transform natural substances into forms they can use. This is clearest in the case of food production but includes the production of clothing and

---

EthnoProfile 10.1

Nootka

Region: North America

Nation: Canada (Vancouver Island)

Population: 6,000 (1970s)

Environment: Rainy, relatively warm coastal strip

Livelihood: Fishing, hunting, gathering

Political organization: Traditionally, ranked individuals, chiefs; today, part of a modern nation-state

For more information: Rosman, Abraham, and Paula G. Rubel. 1971. *Feasting with mine enemy: Rank and exchange among northwest coast societies*. New York: Columbia University Press.

---

labor The activity linking human social groups to the material world around them; from the point of view of Karl Marx, labor is therefore always social labor.

FIGURE 10.6 Shirts for sale at the market in Guider, Cameroon. Markets can be found in many societies, but capitalism links markets to trade and money in a unique way.

shelter and tools. Marx emphasized the importance of human physical labor in the material world, but he also recognized the importance of mental or cognitive labor. Human intelligence allows us to reflect on and organize productive activities. Mentally and physically, human social groups struggle together to ensure their material survival. In so struggling, they reproduce patterns of social organization, production, and thought.

Modes of Production

Marx attempted to classify the ways different human groups carry out production. Each way is called a **mode of production**. Anthropologist Eric Wolf defined a mode of production as "a specific, historically occurring set of social relations through which labor is deployed to wrest energy from nature by means of tools, skills, organization, and knowledge" (1982, 75).

> **mode of production** A specific, historically occurring set of social relations through which labor is deployed to wrest energy from nature by means of tools, skills, organization, and knowledge.
>
> **means of production** The tools, skills, organization, and knowledge used to extract energy from nature.
>
> **relations of production** The social relations linking the people who use a given means of production within a particular mode of production.

Tools, skills, organization, and knowledge constitute what Marx called the **means of production**. The social relations linking human beings who use a given means of production within a particular mode of production are called the **relations of production**. That is, different productive tasks (clearing the bush, planting, harvesting, and so on) are assigned to different social groups, all of which must work together for production to be successful.

The concept of mode of production is holistic, highlighting recurring patterns of human activity in which certain forms of social organization, production practices, and cultural knowledge codetermine one another. Wolf notes that Marx speaks of at least eight different modes of production in his own writings, although he focused mainly on the capitalist mode. Wolf finds the concept of mode of production useful. But like most anthropologists inspired by Marx's work, he does not feel bound to accept Marx's conclusions as a matter of course (Figure 10.7). He suggests that three modes of production have been particularly important in human history: (1) a *kin-ordered mode*, in which social labor is deployed on the basis of kinship relations (for example, husbands/fathers clear the fields, the whole family plants, mothers/wives weed, children keep animals out of the field); (2) a *tributary mode*, "in which the primary

IN THEIR OWN WORDS

"So Much Work, So Much Tragedy . . . and for What?"

Angelita P. C. (the author's surnames were initialed to preserve her anonymity) describes traditional labor for farmers' wives in Costa Rica during the 1930s. Her account was included in a volume of peasant autobiographies published in Costa Rica in 1979.

The life of farmers' wives was more difficult than the life of day laborers' wives; what I mean is that we work more. The wife of the day laborer, she gets clean beans with no rubbish, shelled corn, pounded rice, maybe she would have to roast the coffee and grind it. On the other hand, we farm wives had to take the corn out of the husk, shuck it; and if it was rice, generally we'd have to get it out of the sack and spread it out in the sun for someone to pound it in the mortar. Although we had the advantage that we never lacked the staples: tortillas, rice, beans, and sugar-water. When you had to make tortillas, and that was every day, there were mountains of tortillas, because the people who worked in the fields had to eat a lot to regain their strength with all the effort they put out. And the tortilla is the healthiest food that was eaten—still is eaten—in the countryside. Another thing we had to do often was when you'd get the corn together to sell it, you always had to take it off the cob and dry it in the sun: the men spread it

out on a tarp, maybe two or three sackfuls, and they would go and bring the corn, still in the husks, up from the corn-field or the shack where it was kept. Well, we women had to guard it from the chickens or the pigs that were always in the house, but the rush we had when it started to rain and the men hadn't gotten back! We had to fill the sacks with corn and then a little later haul it in pots to finish filling them; that's if the rain gave us time. If not, all of us women in the house would have to pick up the tarps—sometimes the neighbor-women would get involved in all the bustle—to carry the corn inside. We looked like ants carrying a big worm! The thing was to keep the corn from getting wet.

It didn't matter if you threw out your spine, or if your uterus dropped, or you started hemorrhaging, or aborted, but since none of that happened immediately, it was the last thing we thought of. So much work, so much tragedy and that was so common that it seemed like just a natural thing, and for what? To sell corn at about 20 colones or at most at 24 colones per fanega [about 3 bushels] of 24 baskets! What thankless times for farm people!

Source: Autobiografías campesinas. 1979, 36 (translation from the original Spanish by Robert H. Lavenda).

producer, whether cultivator or herdsman, is allowed access to the means of production while tribute is exacted from him by political or military means" (1982, 79); and (3) the *capitalist mode*. The capitalist mode has three main features: The means of production are property owned by the capitalists; workers are denied access to such ownership and must sell their labor to the capitalists in order to survive; and this labor for capitalists produces surpluses of wealth that capitalists may retain or plow back into production to increase output and generate further surpluses.

An overlap exists between this classification of modes of production and the traditional anthropological classification of subsistence strategies. The

kin-ordered mode of production is found among foragers and those farmers and herders whose political organization does not involve domination by one group. The tributary mode is found among farmers or herders living in a social system that is divided into classes of rulers and subjects. Subjects produce both for themselves and for their rulers, who take a certain proportion of their subjects' product as tribute. The capitalist mode, the most recent to develop, can be found in the industrial societies of North America and Western Europe beginning in the seventeenth and eighteenth centuries.

Thus, in some ways the mode-of-production concept simply recognizes the same variation in the arts

FIGURE 10.7 This drawing from 1562 shows Indian men breaking the soil and Indian women planting, a gender-based division of labor.

of subsistence that Lewis Henry Morgan recognized in the nineteenth century. Yet the concept of mode of production also highlights certain attributes of subsistence strategies that the Morgan approach tended to downplay. For example, modes of production have as much to do with forms of social and political organization as with material productive activities. That is, the kin-ordered mode of production is distinctive as much for its use of the kinship system to allocate labor to production as for the kind of production undertaken, such as farming. In a kin-ordered mode of production, the *relations of kinship* serve as the *relations of production* that enable a particular *mode of production* to be carried out. Compare the differences in the way farm labor is organized in the kin-ordered mode, described here, to the way it is organized in the capitalist mode, where labor is often performed by nonrelatives who are paid a wage.

The Role of Conflict in Material Life

Anthropologists traditionally have emphasized the important links between a society's social organization (kinship groups, chiefdom, state) and the way that society meets its subsistence needs, either to demonstrate the stages of cultural evolution or to display the functional interrelationships between parts of a particular society. In both cases, however, the em-

phasis of the analysis was on the harmonious fashion in which societies either changed or stayed the same. This implied that social stability should not be tampered with. Social change was possible, but it would take place in an equally orderly fashion, in the fullness of time, according to laws of development beyond the control of individual members of society.

Many anthropologists have not been persuaded that social change is orderly or social organization by nature harmonious. They find the Marxian approach useful precisely because it treats conflict as a natural part of the human condition. The concept of mode of production makes a major contribution to economic anthropology precisely because of the very different interpretation it gives to conflict, imbalance, and disharmony in social life.

Marx pointed out, for example, that the capitalist mode of production incorporates the workers and the owners in different and contradictory ways. These groups, which he called *classes*, have different interests, and what is good for one class may not be good for all classes. The workers' desires (for higher wages with which to purchase more goods) are inevitably opposed to the owners' desires (for lower wages to increase the profits they can keep for themselves or reinvest in tools and raw materials).

This does not mean that the different classes engaged in production are always at war; however, it does mean that the potential for conflict is built into the mode of production itself. The more complex and unequal the involvement of different classes in a mode of production, the more intense the struggle between them is likely to be. Such struggle may not always lead to outright rebellion for sound political reasons, as was the case in "Sedaka" Village, Malaysia (see EthnoProfile 9.5: "Sedaka" Village). But we should not be surprised to find the "everyday forms of peasant resistance" that Scott discusses in his analysis of life in "Sedaka." When viewed from a Marxian perspective, such struggles are clearly not just "healthy competition." Marx was one of the first social analysts, and certainly one of the most eloquent, to document the high level of human suffering generated by certain modes of production, particularly the capitalist mode.

Wolf's three modes of production (kin-ordered, tributary, and capitalist) describe not only a society's subsistence strategy but also that society's social organization. As a result, they accent the lines of cleavage along which tension and conflict may develop—or may have developed historically—between different segments of the society: between, say, parents and children or husbands and wives in the kin-ordered mode; between lords and peasants in the tributary mode; and between capitalists and workers in the capitalist mode.

Applying Production Theory to Social and Cultural Life

Economic anthropologists who focus on production as the prime causal force in material life tend to apply the metaphor of production to other areas of social life as well. They see production as involving far more than short-term satisfaction of material survival needs. If a given *mode* of production is to persist over time, the *means* and *relations* of production must also be made to persist.

For example, farmers produce grain and leave behind harvested fields. They exchange some grain with cattle herders for milk and meat, and they permit the herders' cattle to graze in the harvested fields in exchange for manure they need to fertilize their fields. Consequently, farmers and herders alike end up with a mix of foodstuffs to sustain human life (that is, to reproduce the producers). In addition, each group has what it needs in the coming season to re-

new its means of production. Both groups will want to ensure that similar exchanges are carried out by their children; that is, they must find a way to ensure that the next generation will consist of farmers and cattle herders producing the same goods and willing to exchange them. Therefore, not only the means of production itself must be perpetuated but the relations of production as well. The result, then, is the reproduction of society from generation to generation.

People also produce and reproduce *interpretations* of the productive process and their roles in that process. As we have seen in earlier chapters, Marx used the term **ideology** to refer to the cultural products of conscious reflection, such as morality, religion, and metaphysics, that are used to explain and justify the social arrangements under which people live. For Marx, ideology was not independent of the productive process itself, and was intended to explain and justify the relations of production to those who engage in them. He wrote, "Men, developing their material production and their material intercourse, alter, along with this their real existence, their thinking and the products of their thinking. Life is not determined by consciousness, but consciousness by life" (Marx [1932] 1973, 164). Today, even anthropologists sympathetic to Marxian analysis would be unwilling to endorse such a strongly reductionist position. Nevertheless, they have been interested in investigating the kinds of ideas, beliefs, and values that are produced and reproduced in societies with different modes of production. As we saw in "Sedaka," the class in power usually holds to an ideology that justifies its domination. Those who are dominated may assent publicly to the ideology of the rulers, but this does not mean that they accept without question the ruling ideology. In private, as Scott demonstrated, they were likely to be highly critical and to offer alternative interpretations.

The production metaphor has yielded some important insights into social and cultural life. First, it highlights processes and relationships that the exchange metaphor tends to downplay or ignore. For example, exchange theorists are less likely to care why the different parties to an exchange have different

ideology Those products of consciousness—such as morality, religion, and metaphysics—that purport to explain to people who they are and to justify to them the kinds of lives they lead.

Solidarity Forever

Anthropologist Dorinne Kondo, who worked alongside Japanese women in a Tokyo sweets factory, describes how factory managers, almost despite their best efforts, managed to engender strong bonds among women workers.

Our shared exploitation sometimes provided the basis for commonality and sympathy. The paltry pay was often a subject of discussion. . . . My co-workers and I were especially aware, however, of the toll our jobs took on our bodies. We constantly complained of our sore feet, especially sore heels from standing on the concrete floors. And a company-sponsored trip to the seashore revealed even more occupational hazards. At one point, as we all sat down with our rice balls and our box lunches, the part-timers pulled up the legs of their trousers to compare their varicose veins. In our informal contest, Hamada-san and Iida-san tied for first prize. The demanding pace and the lack of assured work breaks formed another subject of discussion. At most of the factories in the neighborhood where I conducted extensive interviews, work stopped at ten in the morning and at three in the afternoon, so workers could have a cup of tea and perhaps some crackers. Nothing of the sort occurred at the Satō factory, although the artisans were, if the pace of work slackened, able to escape the workroom, sit on their haunches, and have a smoke, or grab a snack if they were out doing deliveries or running up and down the stairs to the other divisions. Informal restrictions on the part-timers' movement and time

seemed much greater. Rarely, if ever, was there an appropriate slack period where all of us could take a break. Yet our energy, predictably, slumped in the afternoon. After my first few months in wagashi, Hamada-san began to bring in small containers of fruit juice, so we could take turns having a five-minute break to drink the juice and eat some seconds from the factory. Informal, mutual support enabled us to keep up our energies, as we each began to bring in juice or snacks for our tea breaks.

The company itself did nothing formally in this regard, but informal gestures of thoughtfulness and friendliness among co-workers surely redounded to the company's benefit, for they fostered our sense of intimacy and obligation to our fellow workers. The tea breaks are one example, but so are the many times we part-timers would stop off at Iris, our favorite coffee house, to sip banana juice or melon juice and trade gossip. We talked about other people in the company, about family, about things to do in the neighborhood. On one memorable occasion, I was sitting with the Western division part-timers in a booth near the window. A car honked as it went by, and Sakada-san grimaced and shouted loudly, "Shitsurei yarō—rude bastard!" The offender turned out to be her husband. In subsequent weeks, Sakada-san would delight in recounting this tale again and again, pronouncing shitsurei yarō with ever greater relish, and somehow, we never failed to dissolve in helpless laughter.

Source: Kondo 1990, 291–92.

quantities of resources with which to bargain. Production theorists, by contrast, are interested precisely in this issue. They aim to show that access to resources is determined *before* exchange by the relations of production, which decide who is entitled to how much of what.

In particular, they reject as naive the assumption that access to valued resources is open to anyone with gumption and the spirit of enterprise. Different

modes of production stack the deck in favor of some classes of people and against other classes. This is most clear in the capitalist mode, where owners have disproportionate access to wealth, power, and prestige and where the access of workers to these goods is sharply restricted. Thus, the classes who fare poorly do so not because of any inherent inferiority, laziness, or improvidence. They fail to get ahead because the rules of the game (that is, of the mode of production) were set up in a way that keeps them from winning (Figure 10.8).

Second, a production metaphor provides an especially dynamic perspective on cultural persistence and cultural change. Production theory relates peoples' preferences for different goods to the interests and opportunities of the different classes to which they belong. People buy and sell as they do, not out of idiosyncratic whimsy but because the choices open to them are shaped by the relations of production. From this perspective, poor people do not purchase cheap goods because they have poor taste and cannot recognize quality when they see it; rather, their deprived position within the mode of production provides them with very limited income, and they must make do with the only goods they can afford, however shoddy.

Finally, production theory focuses on people as much as or more than it focuses on the goods they produce. It views human beings as social agents involved in the construction and reconstruction of human society on all levels in every generation. Traditions persist, but only because people labor to reproduce them from one day to the next. To speak of the production (and reproduction) of goods, social relations, and ideologies highlights the contingent nature of social life, even as it suggests how traditions are carried on.

▼ WHY DO PEOPLE CONSUME WHAT THEY DO?

Consumption is usually understood to refer to the using up of material goods necessary for human survival. These goods include—at a minimum—food, drink, clothing, and shelter; they can and often do include much more. Until quite recently, economists and others have neglected the study of consumption, especially when compared to distribution or production. Many observers assumed that there were no interesting questions to ask about consumption. It seemed clear that people either consume goods for obvious reasons (e.g., because they need to eat and drink to survive) or they consume goods as a result of idiosyncratic personal preferences. (I like the flavor of licorice and so I eat a lot of it, but my neighbor hates the flavor and would never put it into his mouth.) In either case, studying consumption seemed unlikely to reveal any interesting patterns.

Anthropologists who make cross-cultural comparisons, however, have always noticed striking differences in consumption patterns in different societies that seemed hard to reconcile with accepted economic explanations. Historically, they have taken three basic approaches to account for these patterns:

FIGURE 10.8 Factory production has displaced traditional household-based production of thread, not just among the Baule of Ivory Coast, but throughout Africa. This man works in a thread factory in Ivory Coast.

the internal explanation, the external explanation, and the cultural explanation.

The Internal Explanation: Malinowski and Basic Human Needs

The internal explanation for human consumption patterns comes from the work of Bronislaw Malinowski. Malinowski's version of functionalist anthropology explains social practices by relating them to the basic human needs that each practice supposedly functions to fulfill. Basic human needs can be biological or psychological. Whatever their origin, if they go unmet, the society might not survive. Malinowski proposed a list of basic human needs, which includes nourishment, reproduction, bodily comforts, safety, movement, growth, and health. Every culture responds in its own way to these needs with some form of the corresponding institutions: food-getting techniques, kinship, shelter, protection, activities, training, and hygiene (Malinowski 1944, 91).

Malinowski's approach had the virtue of emphasizing the dependency of human beings on the physical world in order to survive. In addition, Malinowski was able to show that many customs that appear bizarre to uninitiated Western observers are in fact "rational" because they help people satisfy their basic human needs. However, Malinowski's approach fell short of explaining why all societies do not share the same consumption patterns. After all, some people eat wild fruit and nuts and wear clothing made of animal skins, others eat bread made from domesticated wheat and wear garments woven from the hair of domesticated sheep, and still others eat millet paste and meat from domesticated cattle and go naked. Why should these differences exist?

The External Explanation: Cultural Ecology

A later generation of anthropologists were influenced by evolutionary and ecological studies. They tried to answer this question with an external explanation for the diversity of human consumption patterns.

Ecology has to do with how living species relate to one another and the physical environment. That environment is divided into different **ecozones** formed of the mix of plant and animal species living there. A species adapts to an ecozone by constructing an *econiche*—plants and animals on which it can depend for survival. *Socioecologists* investigate the features of ecozones to explain why a particular animal population—a troop of baboons, for example—organizes itself the way it does in a particular environment.

Cultural ecology is an anthropological attempt to apply socioecology to human beings and their societies. For cultural ecologists, patterns of human consumption (as well as production and distribution) derive from features of the ecozones in which groups live. Every human group must learn to make use of the resources available in its ecozone if it is to survive. Hence, the particular consumption patterns found in a particular society do not depend just on the obvious, internal hunger drive, which is the same for all people everywhere; rather, they depend on the particular external resources present in the ecozone to which a society must adapt.

Why do people *X* raise peanuts and sorghum? The internal, Malinowskian explanation would be to meet their basic human need for food. The external, socioecological explanation would be because peanuts and sorghum are the only food crops available in their ecozone that, when cultivated, will meet their subsistence needs. Both these answers are suggestive, but they are also incomplete. To be sure, people must consume something to survive, and they will usually meet this need by exploiting plant and animal species locally available. However, we might ask whether the local food sources that people *X* choose to exploit are the *only* food sources locally available to them. Ethnographic data show that no society exploits every locally available food source to meet its consumption needs. Quite the contrary, consumption "needs" are selective; in other words, they are culturally shaped.

Economic anthropologist Rhoda Halperin (1994) has recently examined the relationship between ecological anthropology and economic anthropology. Borrowing concepts from Karl Polanyi, she argues that every economic system can be analyzed in terms of two kinds of movements: *locational movements*, or

---

ecology The study of the ways in which living species relate to one another and to their natural environment.

ecozone The particular mix of plant and animal species occupying any particular region of the earth.

"changes of place," and *appropriational movements*, or "changes of hands." In her view, ecological relationships that affect the economy are properly understood as changes of place, as when people must move into the grasslands, gather mongongo nuts, and transport them back to camp. Economic relationships, by contrast, are more properly understood as changes of hands, as when mongongo nuts are distributed to all members of the camp, whether or not they helped to gather them. Thus, ecological (locational) movements involve transfers of energy; economic (appropriational) movements, by contrast, involve transfers of rights (1994, 59). Analyzed in this way, people's rights to consume mongongo nuts cannot be derived from the labor they expended to gather them.

Food Storage and Sharing

Another way of seeing the difference between ecological and economic arrangements is to pay attention to the connection between food storage and food sharing. A socioecologist might argue that those who gather mongongo nuts are obliged to share them out and consume them immediately because they have no way to store this food if it is not eaten. Ecological anthropologist Tim Ingold (1983) agrees that the obligation to share makes storage unnecessary, but he also points out that sharing with others today ordinarily obligates them to share with you tomorrow. Put another way, sharing food can be seen not only as a way of avoiding spoilage but also as a way of storing up IOUs for the future!

Once societies develop ways to preserve and store food and other material goods, however, new possibilities open up. Archaeological evidence indicates that the more food there is to store, the more people invest in storage facilities (such as pits or pottery vessels), and the more quickly they become sedentary. Large-scale food storage techniques involve a series of "changes of place" that buffer a population from ecological fluctuations for long periods of time. But techniques of food storage alone predict nothing about the "changes of hands" that food will undergo once it has been stored. Food storage techniques have been associated with all subsistence strategies, including that of complex food collectors. This suggests that economic relations of consumption, involving the transfer of

rights in stored food, have long been open to considerable cultural elaboration and manipulation (Halperin 1994, 178).

While both ecological and economic transfers are important in any economy, they should not be confused with one another. Indeed, anthropologists have become increasingly aware that economic transfers of rights to material resources cannot be separated from wider political forces that impinge on those rights. According to anthropologist Elliot Fratkin, this awareness has led to "a shift in theoretical understanding from *cultural* ecology to *political* ecology" (1997, 236; italics in original). For example, the current adaptations of eastern African pastoralists and their herds to the semiarid environment is strongly affected by political pressures coming from the nation-states of eastern Africa in which they live. As a result, Fratkin says, contemporary anthropological studies of pastoralists explain human-livestock interactions "less in terms of 'carrying capacity' or 'desertification' and more in terms of loss of common property rights, increased economic differentiation and social stratification, and incorporation and domination of tribal pastoral groups by larger state systems" (236).

▼ HOW DOES CULTURE CONSTRUCT HUMAN NEEDS?

A major shortcoming of both internal and external explanations for human consumption patterns is that they ignore or deny the possibility of agency. Malinowski and many cultural ecologists seem to assume that patterns of consumption are dictated by an iron environmental necessity that does not allow alternatives. From such a perspective, choice of diet is a luxury that non-Western, "primitive" societies cannot afford. Yet to rob non-Western peoples of choice is to dehumanize them.

Marshall Sahlins urged anthropologists to pay close attention to consumption because consumption choices reveal what it means to be a human being. Human beings are *human*, he tells us, "precisely when they experience the world as a concept (symbolically). It is not essentially a question of priority but of the unique quality of human experience as meaningful experience. Nor is it an issue of the reality of the world; it concerns *which worldly dimension becomes pertinent*, and in what way, to a given human group" (1976, 142; emphasis added).

The Original Affluent Society

Many Westerners long believed that foraging peoples led the most miserable of existences, spending all their waking hours in a food quest that yielded barely enough to keep them alive. To test this assumption in the field, Richard Lee went to live among the Dobe Ju/'hoansi, a foraging people of southern Africa (see EthnoProfile 11.1: Ju/'hoansi). Living in the central Kalahari Desert of southern Africa in the early 1960s, the Ju/'hoansi of Dobe were among the few remaining groups of San still able to return to full-time foraging when economic ties to neighboring Tswana or Herero herders became too onerous. Some students of southern African history have argued that contemporary foragers are all dispossessed herders who were forced into this "despised and despicable" way of life as a result of European colonial oppression (for example, Wilmsen 1989, 1991). While dispossession and exploitation have clearly been the lot of most of the original foraging and hunting peoples of southern Africa (see, for example, Gordon 1992), Lee and other ethnographers have been able to show that the Ju/'hoansi were able until very recently to find refuge beyond the reach of these forces (Lee 1992a, 1992b; Solway and Lee 1990). They have also argued powerfully that, for people like the Ju/'hoansi of Dobe, full-time foraging was anything but a "despised and despicable" way of life. Although full-time foraging has been impossible in the Dobe area since the 1980s, and the Dobe Ju/'hoansi have had to make some difficult adjustments, Lee documented a way of life that contrasts vividly with their current settled existence.

As we saw at the beginning of this chapter, Lee accompanied his informants as they gathered and hunted in 1963, and he recorded the amounts and kinds of food they consumed. The results of his research were surprising. It turned out that the Ju/'hoansi provided themselves with a varied and well-balanced diet based on a *selection* from among

affluence The condition of having more than enough of whatever is required to satisfy consumption needs.

the food sources available in their environment. At the time of Lee's fieldwork the Ju/'hoansi classified more than 100 species of plants as edible, but only 14 are primary or major (1992b, 45ff.). Some 70 percent of this diet consisted of vegetable foods; 30 percent was meat. Mongongo nuts, a protein-rich food widely available throughout the Kalahari, alone made up more than one-quarter of the diet. Women provided about 55 percent of the diet, and men provided 45 percent, including the meat. The Ju/'hoansi spent an average of 2.4 working days—or about 20 hours—per person per week in food-collecting activities. Ju/'hoansi bands periodically suffered from shortages of their preferred foods and were forced to resort to less desired items. Most of the time, however, their diet was balanced and adequate and consisted of foods of preference (1992b, 56ff; Figure 10.9).

Marshall Sahlins coined the expression "the original affluent society" to refer to the Ju/'hoansi and other foragers like them. In an article published in 1972, Sahlins challenged the traditional Western assumption that the life of foragers is characterized by scarcity and near-starvation. **Affluence**, he argued, is having more than enough of whatever is required to satisfy consumption needs. There are two ways to create affluence. One, to *produce much*, is the path taken by Western capitalist society. The second is to *desire little*, the option, Sahlins argues, that foragers have taken. Their wants are few, but they are abundantly supplied by nature. Moreover, foragers do not suppress their natural greed; rather, their society simply does not institutionalize greed or reward the greedy. As a result, foragers cannot be considered poor, even though their material standard of living is low by Western standards. Poverty is not an absolute condition, nor is it a relationship between means and ends; it is a relationship between people.

The original affluent society of the Ju/'hoansi reinforces the observation that "needs" is a vague concept. Hunger can be satisfied by beans and rice or steak and lobster. Thirst can be quenched by water or beer or soda pop. In effect, culture defines needs and provides for their satisfaction according to its own logic. And cultural logic is reducible neither to biology nor psychology nor ecological pressure.

By adopting this cultural approach to consumption, the distinctions between needs and wants or necessities and luxuries disappear. Mary Douglas

FIGURE 10.9 Ju/'hoansi women returning from foraging with large quanitites of mongongo nuts.

and Baron Isherwood deplore "the widespread and misleading distinction between goods that sustain life and health and others that service the mind and heart—spiritual goods. . . . The counterargument proposed here is that all goods carry meaning, but none by itself. . . . The meaning is in the relations between all the goods, just as music is in the relations marked out by the sounds and not in any one note" (1979, 72–73). For instance, a good's meaning may have to do with its edibility, but edibility is always culturally determined. Furthermore, the meaning of any individual item of food cannot be explained in isolation. That meaning only becomes clear when the item is compared with other consumption items that are also marked by the culture as edible or inedible.

The Abominations of Leviticus

Consider the prohibition against eating pork. For Jews and Muslims, pork is inedible, culturally speaking. According to Mary Douglas (1966), this has nothing to do with ecological problems associated with pig raising in southwestern Asia nor with defects in the digestive systems of Jews or Muslims. Douglas analyzed the Jewish dietary prohibitions detailed in the biblical Book of Leviticus. She argues that certain animals were prohibited as food because something about them violated the prototypes for edibility recognized in ancient Hebrew culture (Table 10.1).

Prototypically "clean" land animals were supposed to have four legs and cloven hooves and to chew the cud; pigs were an "abomination" because they were four-legged, cloven-hoofed beasts that did not chew the cud. "Clean" beasts of the air were supposed to have feathers and to fly with wings; therefore, hopping insects were "unclean" because they had six legs, neither walked nor flew, and lacked feathers. "Clean" water animals were supposed to have fins and scales; shrimp were forbidden because, although they lived in the sea, they lacked fins and scales.

By itself, Douglas argues, a prohibition against eating pork is meaningless and appears irrational. However, when the prohibition against pork is taken together with other dietary prohibitions in Leviticus, and when these are compared with the foods that were permitted, a pattern emerges. Douglas and Isherwood write, "Goods assembled together in ownership make physical, visible statements about the hierarchy of values to which their chooser subscribes" (1979, 5). Thus, Jews who consume only "clean" foods that meet the ritual requirements laid down by

	CLASS PROTOTYPE	CLEAN EXAMPLES	UNCLEAN EXAMPLES	REASON PROHIBITED
Earth	Four-legged animals that hop, jump, or walk (that is, cloven-hoofed, cud-chewing ungulates)	Cattle, camels, sheep, goats	Hare, hyrax	Cud-chewing but not cloven-hoofed
			Pig	Cloven-hoofed but not cud-chewing
			Weasel, mouse, crocodile, shrew, chameleon, mole	Two legs, two hands, but go about on all fours
Air	Two-legged fowl that fly with wings	Chicken	Grasshoppers	Six legs, cannot walk or fly, and lack feathers
Water	Scaly fish that swim with fins	Carp, whitefish	Shrimp, clams	Possess neither fins nor scales but still live in water

TABLE 10.1   Jewish Dietary Prohibitions

Source: Adapted from Douglas 1966, 41–57.

their tradition are doing more than procuring the means to satisfy their hunger; they are also making a social declaration of solidarity with their religious community, and the care with which they adhere to the dietary laws is a measure of their commitment. Their need for food is being met, but selectively, and the selection they make carries a social message.

Dietary laws deal with food and drink, and so might still be explained in biological or ecological terms. Such explanations are more difficult to construct, however, when we consider the role of banana leaves in the Trobriand Islands.

Banana Leaves in the Trobriand Islands

Anthropologist Annette Weiner traveled to the Trobriand Islands more than half a century after Malinowski carried out his classic research there (see EthnoProfile 3.4: Trobriand Islanders). To her surprise, she discovered a venerable local tradition involving the accumulation and exchange of banana leaves, or women's wealth (Figure 10.10). Malinowski had never described this tradition, even though there is evidence from photographs and writing that it was in force at the time of his fieldwork. There are probably two reasons why Malinowski overlooked these transactions. First, they are carried out by women, and Malinowski did not view women

as important actors in the economy. Second, banana leaves would be an unlikely item of consumption because Malinowski labeled as "economic" only activities that satisfied biological survival needs, and you can't eat banana leaves. However, explaining transactions involving women's wealth turns out to be crucial for understanding Trobriand kinship obligations.

Banana leaves might be said to have a "practical" use in that women make skirts out of them. These skirts are highly valued, but the transactions involving women's wealth more often involve the bundles of leaves themselves. Why bother to exchange great amounts of money or other goods to obtain bundles of banana leaves? This would seem to be a classic example of irrational consumption. And yet, as Weiner demonstrates, banana bundles play exactly the role Douglas and Isherwood have suggested that consumption goods play in society: "As an economic, political, and social force, women's wealth exists as the representation of the most fundamental relationships in the social system" (Weiner 1980, 289).

Trobrianders are matrilineal, and men traditionally prepare yam gardens for their sisters. After the harvest, yams from these gardens are distributed by a woman's brother to her husband. Weiner's research suggests that what Malinowski took to be the *redistribution* of yams, from a wife's kin to her husband, could be better understood as a *reciprocal exchange* of

FIGURE 10.10 In the Trobriand Islands, women's wealth, made from banana leaves, is displayed during a funeral ritual called the *sagali*, which serves to reaffirm the status of the women's kinship group.

yams for women's wealth. The parties central to this exchange are a woman, her brother, and her husband. The woman is the person through whom yams are passed from her own kin to her husband and also the person through whom women's wealth is passed from her husband to her own kin.

Transactions involving women's wealth occur when someone in the woman's kinship group dies. Surviving relatives must "buy back," metaphorically speaking, all the yams or other goods that the deceased person gave to others during his or her lifetime. Each payment marks a social link between the deceased and the recipient, and the size of the payment marks the importance of their relationship. All the payments must be made in women's wealth.

The dead person's status, as well as the status of her or his family, depends on the size and number of the payments made, and the people who must be paid can number into the hundreds. Women make women's wealth themselves and exchange store goods to obtain it from other women, but when someone in their matrilineage dies, they collect it from their husbands. Indeed, a woman's value is measured by the amount of women's wealth her husband provides. Furthermore, "if a man does not work hard enough for his wife in accumulating wealth for her, then her brother will not increase his labor in the yam garden. . . . The production in yams and women's wealth is always being evaluated and calculated in terms of effort and energy expended on both sides of production. The value of a husband is read by a woman's kin as the value of his productive support in securing women's wealth for his wife" (Weiner 1980, 282).

Weiner argues that women's wealth upholds the kinship arrangements of Trobriand society. It balances out exchange relationships between lineages linked by marriage, reinforces the pivotal role of women and matriliny, and publicly proclaims, during every funeral, the social relationships that make up the fabric of Trobriand society. The system has been stable for generations, but Weiner suggests that it could collapse if cash ever became widely substitutable for yams. Under such conditions, men might buy food and other items on the market, they would no longer be dependent on yams from their wives' kin, and they could therefore refuse to supply their wives' kin with women's wealth. This had not yet happened at the time of Weiner's research, but she saw it as a possible future development.

▼ THE CULTURAL CONSTRUCTION OF UTILITY

Just as culture shapes needs, so it also offers standardized ways of satisfying them. No social exchange can occur unless the parties to it are able to

IN THEIR OWN WORDS

Fake Masks and Faux Modernity

Christopher Steiner addresses the perplexing situation all of us face in the contemporary multicultural world: given mass reproduction of commodities made possible by industrial capitalism, how can anybody distinguish "authentic" material culture from "fake" copies? The encounter he describes took place in Ivory Coast, western Africa.

In the Plateau market place, I once witnessed the following exchange between an African art trader and a young European tourist. The tourist wanted to buy a Dan face mask which he had selected from the trader's wooden trunk in the back of the market place. He had little money, he said, and was trying to barter for the mask by exchanging his Seiko wrist watch. In his dialogue with the trader, he often expressed his concern about whether or not the mask was "real." Several times during the bargaining, for example, the buyer asked the seller, "Is it really old?" and "Has it been worn?" While the tourist questioned the trader about the authenticity of the mask, the trader, in turn, questioned the tourist about the authenticity of his watch. "Is this the real kind of Seiko," he asked, "or is it a copy?" As the tourist examined the mask—turning it over and over

again looking for the worn and weathered effects of time—the trader scrutinized the watch, passing it to other traders to get their opinion on its authenticity.

Although, on one level, the dialogue between tourist and trader may seem a bit absurd, it points to a deeper problem in modern transnational commerce: an anxiety over authenticity and a crisis of misrepresentation. While the shelves in one section of the Plateau market place are lined with replicas of so-called "traditional" artistic forms, the shelves in another part of the market place—just on the other side of the street—are stocked with imperfect imitations of modernity: counterfeit Levi jeans, fake Christian Dior belts, and pirated recordings of Michael Jackson and Madonna. Just as the Western buyer looks to Africa for authentic symbols of a "primitive" lifestyle, the African buyer looks to the West for authentic symbols of a modern lifestyle. In both of their searches for the "genuine" in each other's culture, the African trader and the Western tourist often find only mere approximations of "the real thing"—tropes of authenticity which stand for the riches of an imagined reality.

Source: Steiner 1994, 128–29.

assess the value of the items to be exchanged. Because of the openness of culture and the ambiguity inherent in many social situations, values and exchange rates may well be bargained over. Such exchanges ultimately rest on cultural principles for assessing value and fairness.

Once consumption is defined as the use of goods and services to communicate cultural values, a new understanding of wealth and poverty is possible. We have noted Sahlins's comment that foragers with simple needs and ample means of satisfying those needs are affluent—rich, not poor. Douglas and Isherwood also refuse to use the sheer amount of material possessions as a universal measure of wealth or poverty. They write: "Many of the countries that an-

thropologists study are poor on such material criteria—no wall-to-wall carpets, no air conditioning—but they do not regard themselves as poor. The Nuer of the Sudan in the 1930s would not trade with the Arabs because the only things they had to sell were their herds of cattle, and the only things they could possibly want from trade were more cattle" (1979, 17–18; see EthnoProfile 11.3: Nuer). Cattle mattered to the Nuer as much for their use as markers of social relations as for their use as food. To have few or no cattle constituted poverty for the Nuer—though as much for the lack of social relationships it indicated as for the lack of food. "To be rich means to be well integrated in a rich community. . . . To be poor is to be isolated" (160).

Institutionalized Sharing

Capitalist societies have passed laws and created social institutions that reward individuals for accumulating wealth. The economic practices of some noncapitalist societies, by contrast, prevent individual accumulation; the goal is to spread any wealth that exists throughout the community. This pattern is called institutionalized sharing.

People accustomed to capitalist practices are often either incredulous or cynical when it is suggested that institutionalized sharing can be the backbone of economic life. They assume that such widespread "generosity" can only be expected of saintly altruists, not of ordinary human beings. Nevertheless, people in societies with institutionalized sharing are not saints who never experience greed any more than people in capitalist societies are devils who never experience compassion. Both societies, however, make it difficult to get away publicly with practices that undercut established social arrangements.

Institutionalized sharing can be found among the Plains Cree of North America, studied by Niels Braroe (1975, 143ff.) (see EthnoProfile 10.2: Cree [Short Grass Reserve]). In the past, the Cree were bison hunters living in bands. Each band had a leader who provided his followers with the materials necessary for hunting. This leader was the focus of a redistributive mode of exchange, and generosity in redistribution qualified him to be the band leader. At the time of Braroe's fieldwork, the Cree no longer hunted bison, but they still practiced the institutionalized sharing of consumption items such as food, clothing, beer, or cigarettes. For example, Braroe tells us that "it is not considered improper, as it is among Whites, to ask for someone's last cigarette; to refuse a request, however, is frowned upon" (145). Generosity is further reinforced in ceremonies known as "giveaway dances." The central event in those ceremonies is dancing around the room and giving away such material goods as clothing to other guests. Dancers aim to give away more than they receive. It is an insult to shower someone with gifts in the course of such an event.

The Cree ideal is that generosity should be spontaneous and contempt for material goods genuine. Nevertheless, Braroe's informants sometimes

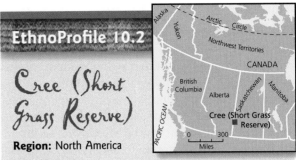

EthnoProfile 10.2

Cree (Short Grass Reserve)

Region: North America

Nation: Canada

Population: About 100

Environment: 3,040 acres of rocky soil and dense aspen brush

Livelihood: Monthly inadequate relief payments; manufacture and sale of fenceposts; casual ranch work

Political organization: Traditionally, consensus of adult males announced by chief; today, part of a modern nation-state

For more information: Braroe, Niels. 1975. *Indian and white*. Stanford: Stanford University Press.

possessed consumption goods or money that they clearly wanted to keep for themselves. Individuals could enjoy such goods in private, but only if their existence were kept a secret. Men sometimes hid beer to avoid having to share it with others. A woman informant once asked Braroe's wife to keep a sizable amount of cash for her so others would not know she had it and demand some. The rule seemed to be that "any visible resource may legitimately be requested by another" (1975, 146), and Braroe reported that direct refusals of such requests were rare.

For the Cree, institutionalized sharing is supposed to ensure that consumption goods are not hoarded but spread out and enjoyed by all in the band. This consumption pattern clashes with that of the capitalist, who views accumulation and consumption by individuals in a positive light. Some individual Cree earned money off the reserve and tried to save it in order to get ahead—by capitalist standards. Those people were considered stingy by other Cree and were resented; they could not hope to gain a position of leadership in the band.

Consumption Studies Today

The foregoing examples focus attention on distinctive consumption practices in different societies, and remind us forcefully not to take the Western market as the measure of all things. These studies also encourage respect for alternative consumption practices that, in different times and places, have worked as well or better than capitalist markets to define needs and provide goods to satisfy those needs. They have also often drawn attention to the way in which the arrival of capitalism, usually in the context of colonialism, has regularly undermined such alternatives, attempting to replace them with new needs and goods defined by the market. This helps explain why, as Daniel Miller summarizes, "much of the early literature on consumption is replete with moral purpose," emphasizing the ways in which vulnerable groups have resisted commodities or have developed ritual means of "taming" them, based on an awareness at some level of their capacity to destroy (1995, 144–45).

In an era of globalization, however, the consumption of market commodities now occurs everywhere in the world. Moreover, the evidence is mounting that not only are Western commodities sometimes embraced by those whom we might have expected to reject them (e.g., video technology by indigenous peoples of the Amazon), but this embrace frequently involves making use of these commodities for local purposes, to defend or to enrich local culture, rather than to replace it (e.g., the increasing popularity of sushi in the United States).

Daniel Miller, a pioneer in this kind of consumption study, has therefore urged anthropologists to recognize that these new circumstances require that they move beyond a narrow focus on the destructive potential of mass-produced commodities to broader recognition of the role commodities play in a globalizing world. "Desire for goods is not assumed to be natural, nor goods per se as either positive or negative. Poverty is regarded as a relative lack of resources rather than the preservation of authenticity" (1995, 143). But this shift does not mean that concern about the negative consequences of capitalist practices disappears. In a global world in which everyone everywhere increasingly relies on commodities provided by a capitalist market, he believes that critical attention needs to be refocused on "inequalities of access and the deleterious impact of contemporary economic institutions on much of the world's population" (143).

Coca-Cola in Trinidad

The change of focus promoted in Miller's writing about anthropological studies of consumption is nowhere better in evidence than in his own research on the consumption of Coca-Cola in Trinidad (1998). He points out that for many observers of global consumption, Coca-Cola occupies the status of a *metasymbol:* "a symbol that stands for the debate about the materiality of culture" (169). That is, Coca-Cola is often portrayed as a Western/American commodity that represents the ultimately destructive global potential of all forms of capitalist consumption, produced by powerful controllers of capitalist market forces who extract profits from dominated peoples by brainwashing them into thinking that drinking Coke will improve their lives, thereby replacing cheaper, culturally appropriate, locally produced, and probably more nutritious beverages with empty calories. Based on his own fieldwork, however, Miller is able to show that this scenario grossly misrepresents the economic and cultural role which Coca-Cola plays in Trinidad, where it has been present since the 1930s.

First, Coca-Cola is not a typical example of global commodification, because it has always spread as a franchise, allowing for flexible arrangements with local bottling plants. Second, the bottling plant that originally produced Coca-Cola in Trinidad was locally owned (as is the conglomerate that eventually bought it). Third, apart from the imported concentrate, the local bottler was able to obtain all the other key supplies needed to produce the drink (e.g., sugar, carbonation, bottles) from local, Trinidadian sources. Fourth, this bottling company exports soft drinks to other islands throughout the Caribbean, making it an important local economic force that accounts for a considerable proportion of Trinidad's foreign exchange earnings. Fifth, the bottler of Coca-Cola also bottled other drinks, and has long competed with several other, local bottling companies. Decisions made by these companies, rather than by Coca-Cola's home office, have driven local production decisions about such matters as the introduction of new flavor lines.

Sixth, and perhaps most importantly, Coca-Cola has long been incorporated into a set of local, Trinidadian understandings about beverages that divides them into two basic categories: "red, sweet drinks" and "black, sweet drinks;" in this framework, Coke is simply an up-market black, sweet drink, and it has traditionally been consumed, like other black sweet drinks, as a mixer with rum, the locally produced alcoholic beverage. Finally, the Trinidadian categories of "sweet drinks" do not correspond to the Coca-Cola company's idea of "soft drinks," a distinction which has baffled company executives. For example, executives were taken by surprise when Trinidadians objected to attempts to reduce the sweetness of Coca-Cola and other beverages, since this did not correspond to the trend they were familiar with from the United States, where taste has shifted away from heavily sugared soft drinks in recent years.

Beverage consumption in Trinidad is connected with ideas of cultural identity, but not in the way that is often presumed (Figure 10.11). "Red, sweet drinks" have been associated with the Trinidadian descendants of indentured laborers originally from the Indian subcontinent, and "black, sweet drinks" with Trinidadian descendants of enslaved Africans. But this does not mean that the drinks are consumed exclusively by those communities. On the contrary, both kinds of sweet drink make sense as elements in a more complex image of what it means to be Trinidadian: "a higher proportion of Indians drink Colas, while Kola champagne as a red drink is more commonly drunk by Africans. Many Indians explicitly identify with Coke and its modern image" while "In many respects the 'Indian' connoted by the red drink today is in some ways the Africans' more nostalgic image of how Indians either used to be or perhaps still should be" (180). There is no simple connection between the political parties which different segments of the Trinidadian population support and the owners of different local bottling companies producing red or black sweet drinks.

Finally, the Trinidadians Miller knew emphatically did *not* associate drinking Coke with trying to imitate

FIGURE 10.11 The soft-drink market in Trinidad is both complex and idiosyncratic, reflecting Trinidadian understandings of beverage categories.

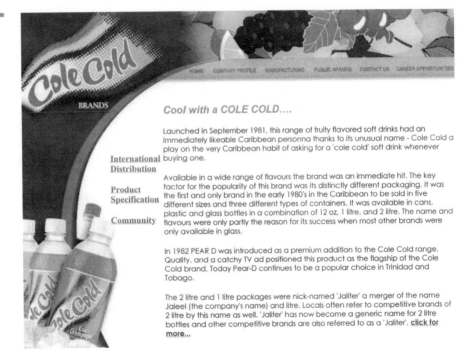

HOME   COMPANY PROFILE   MANUFACTURING   PUBLIC AFFAIRS   CONTACT US   CAREER OPPORTUNITIES

BRANDS

International Distribution

Product Specification

Community

Cool with a COLE COLD....

Launched in September 1981, this range of fruity flavored soft drinks had an immediately likeable Caribbean personna thanks to its unusual name - Cole Cold a play on the very Caribbean habit of asking for a 'cole cold' soft drink whenever buying one.

Available in a wide range of flavours the brand was an immediate hit. The key factor for the popularity of this brand was its distinctly different packaging. It was the first and only brand in the early 1980's in the Caribbean to be sold in five different sizes and three different types of containers. It was available in cans, plastic and glass bottles in a combination of 12 oz, 1 litre, and 2 litre. The name and flavours were only partly the reason for its success when most other brands were only available in glass.

In 1982 PEAR D was introduced as a premium addition to the Cole Cold range. Quality, and a catchy TV ad positioned this product as the flagship of the Cole Cold brand. Today Pear-D continues to be a popular choice in Trinidad and Tobago.

The 2 litre and 1 litre packages were nick-named 'Jaliter' a merger of the name Jaleel (the company's name) and litre. Locals often refer to competitive brands of 2 litre by this name as well. 'Jaliter' has now become a generic name for 2 litre bottles and other competitive brands are also referred to as a 'Jaliter'. **click for more...**

Americans. "Trinidadians do not and will not choose between being American and being Trinidadian. Most reject parochial nationalism or neo-Africanized roots that threaten to diminish their sense of rights of access to global goods, such as computers or blue jeans. But they will fiercely retain those localisms they wish to retain, not because they are hypocritical but because inconsistency is an appropriate response to contradiction" (185). Miller concludes, therefore, that it is a serious mistake to use Coca-Cola as a meta-symbol of the evils of commodity consumption. As we will see in our discussion of globalization in chapter 15, Miller's conclusion is reinforced by studies of consumption that focus on the ways in which global

commodities are incorporated into locally defined cultural practices.

▼ A DIALECTIC BETWEEN THE MEANINGFUL AND THE MATERIAL

Material goods carry culturally defined meanings, and what is viewed as meaningful (as stipulated by culture) can have material consequences. It is out of this dialectic between the meaningful and the material that the modes of livelihood followed by human beings everywhere emerge.

CHAPTER SUMMARY

1. Although our physical survival depends on our making adequate use of the material resources around us, the resources themselves do not determine how they must be used. Rather, our cultures suggest a range of options for making a living, as well as furnishing the tools to pursue those options. Human beings have devised a variety of subsistence strategies to satisfy their material survival needs.

2. Human economic activity is usefully divided into three phases: production, distribution, and consumption. Some anthropologists argue that storage practices affect production, distribution, and consumption. In capitalist societies, market exchange is the dominant mode of distribution, yet many non-Western societies have traditionally carried out distribution without money or markets.

3. Formal neoclassical economic theory developed in an attempt to explain how capitalism works. Building on the emphasis which this theory gives to market exchange, economic anthropologists showed that noncapitalist societies regularly relied on nonmarket modes of exchange, such as reciprocity and redistribution, which still play restricted roles in societies dominated by the capitalist market.

4. Marxian economic anthropologists view production as more important than exchange in determining the patterns of economic life in a society. They argue that societies can be classified in terms of their modes of production. Each mode of production contains within it the potential for conflict between classes of people who receive differential benefits and losses from the productive process.

5. The internal explanation for consumption patterns argues that people produce material goods to satisfy basic human needs. The external explanation argues that consumption patterns depend on the particular external resources available within the ecozone to which a particular society must adapt. Ethnographic evidence demonstrates that both internal and external explanations for consumption patterns are inadequate because they ignore how culture defines our needs and provides for their satisfaction according to its own logic—a logic that is reducible neither to biology nor to psychology nor to ecological pressure.

6. Particular consumption preferences that may seem irrational make sense when considered in the context of other consumption preferences and prohibitions in the same culture. Examples include Jewish dietary prohibitions, the role

of banana leaves in the Trobriand Islands, and institutionalized sharing of consumption goods among the Plains Cree.

7. In an era of globalization, the consumption of Western market commodities is often embraced by those whom we might have expected to reject them. Moreover, this embrace frequently involves making use of market commodities for local purposes, to defend or enrich local culture rather than to replace it. In a global world in which everyone everywhere increasingly relies on commodities provided by a capitalist market, critical attention needs to be focused on inequalities of access and the negative impact of contemporary economic institutions on most of the world's population.

KEY TERMS

economic anthropology
institutions
subsistence strategies
food collectors
food producers
extensive agriculture
intensive agriculture
mechanized industrial agriculture

production
distribution
consumption
neoclassical economic theory
modes of exchange
reciprocity
redistribution
market exchange

labor
mode of production
means of production
relations of production
ideology
ecology
ecozones
affluence

SUGGESTED READINGS

Douglas, Mary, and Baron Isherwood. 1996. *The world of goods: Towards an anthropology of consumption.* Rev. ed. New York: Routledge. *A discussion of consumption, economic theories about consumption, and what anthropologists can contribute to the study of consumption.*

Lee, Richard. 2002. *The Dobe Ju/'hoansi.* 3d ed. Belmont, CA: Wadsworth. *This highly readable ethnography contains important discussions about foraging as a way of making a living.*

Miller, Daniel, ed. 1995. *Acknowledging consumption: A review of new studies.* New York: Routledge. *Groundbreaking essays that reconfigured the study of consumption anthropology.*

Plattner, Stuart, ed. 1989. *Economic anthropology.* Palo Alto, CA: Stanford University Press. *A readable collection of articles by economic anthropologists. Displaying the achievements of formalist-inspired research, it also reconciles with substantivism and recognizes the contribution of Marxian analyses.*

Sahlins, Marshall. 1972. *Stone Age economics.* Chicago: Aldine. *A series of classic essays on economic life, written from a substantivist position. Includes "The original affluent society."*

Wilk, Richard, and Lisa Cligett. 2007. *Economies and cultures.* Boulder, CO: Westview. *A current, accessible "theoretical guidebook" to the conflicting views of human nature that underlie disputes in economic anthropology.*

Chapter 11

Imagined Communities: Kinship and Other Forms of Relatedness

Because human beings need one another to survive and reproduce, they have invented a variety of ways of creating, maintaining, and dissolving social ties with one another. This chapter focuses primarily on a range of forms of face-to-face relatedness that different human groups have imagined and practiced in different times and places.

Martha Macintyre, an Australian anthropologist, did field research on the small island of Tubetube in Papua New Guinea from 1979 to 1983. She writes:

> Like many anthropologists, I was initially taken in as "fictive kin." The explanations given to me for this were several. First, as I was going to stay on the island for a long time, I had to live in an appropriate place. I therefore needed to belong to the totemic "clan" that would enable me to live near to the main hamlet. This was a pragmatic decision. Secondly, as the only person who could translate for me was a young married man, I must become his "elder sister" in order to avoid scandal. Later a *post hoc* explanation emerged which drew on a long tradition of incorporating migrants and exiles into the community. My reddish hair, my habit of running my fingers through my hair when nervous, and the way that I hold my head at a slight angle when I listen to people intently, were indicators of my natural connection to Magisubu, the sea eagle clan. This view gained currency as I was "naturalised," and was proved to everybody's satisfaction when an elderly woman from another island pronounced that the lines on my hand proclaimed me as Magisubu.
>
> An equally pressing reason for incorporating me was the need to minimize the disruption I caused by having no rightful place. People found it difficult to use my first name, as first names are used exclusively by spouses, or in intimate contexts. This left them with the honorific "sinabada," a form of address for senior women that was used in the colonial context for white women. It is now redolent of subservience and I hated being addressed in this way. In making me a part of the Magisubu clan, Tubetube leaders lessened my anomalous status and gave everyone on the island a way of speaking to me. Set in a large lineage with two older sisters, a mother and three powerful men as my mother's brothers, as well as numerous younger siblings, I could be managed, instructed, and guided in ways that did not threaten their dignity or mine. Although I was unaware of it at the time, there was a meeting of people who decided my fate in these terms within days of my arrival.
>
> The adoption by Magisubu people carried with it numerous obligations, most of which were unknown to me until I was instructed as to their nature. In retrospect, they were advantageous to my research in the sense that I was given a role in various events affecting my adoptive family and so learned within a defined context. Usually, before any occasion where I

might be expected to behave in some role appropriate to my (fictive) status, some senior person would explain to me what I should do. So, for example, I was told that I must on no account step over people's belongings nor stand so that I looked down on the head of a senior man or woman, nor sit close to any affines [in-laws]. . . . On neighbouring islands I was treated as an honoured guest, unless I was accompanied by a group of Magisubu people, in which case the hosts would treat me in accordance with my fictive status within that clan. (1993, 51–52)

▼ HOW DO HUMAN BEINGS ORGANIZE INTERDEPENDENCE?

Human life is group life. How we choose to organize ourselves is open to creative variation, as we have seen. But each of us is born into a society that was already established when we arrived. Its political, economic, and cultural practices make some social connections more likely than others. Just knowing the kind of social groups a child is born into tells us much about that child's probable path in life. Such human experiences as sexuality, conception, birth, and nurturance are selectively interpreted and shaped into shared cultural practices that anthropologists call **relatedness**. As we will see in this chapter, relatedness takes many forms—friendship, marriage, parenthood, shared links to a common ancestor, workplace associations, and so on. Furthermore, these intimate everyday relationships are always embedded in and shaped by broader structures of power, wealth, and meaning.

For more than a century, anthropologists have paid particular attention to that form of relatedness believed to be based on shared substance and its transmission (Holy 1996, 171). The shared substance may be a bodily substance, such as blood, semen, genes, or mother's milk. It may be a spiritual substance, such as the soul, spirit, nurturance, or love. Sometimes, more than one substance is thought to be shared. Western anthropologists noted that, like themselves, people in many societies believed that those who share a substance were related to each other in systematic ways and that, like the Western societies to which the anthropologists belonged, members of these societies had developed sets of labels for different kinds of relatives, such as *mother* and *cousin*. They also found that people in many parts of the world linked the

---

relatedness The socially recognized ties that connect people in a variety of different ways.

sharing of substance to conception, the act of sexual intercourse between parents. This collection of similarities was enough to convince early anthropologists that all people base their kinship systems on the biology of reproduction. It was but a short step to conclude that Western beliefs about who counts as relatives are universally valid.

For many decades, kinship studies were based on the assumption that all societies recognize the same basic biological relationships between mothers and fathers, children and parents, and sisters and brothers. But growing ethnographic evidence indicates that quite often people's understanding of their relations to other people is strikingly at odds with these genealogical connections. In other cases, the genealogical connections turn out to form but a small subset of the ways in which people create enduring relationships with one another.

Is there some social glue that ensures social cooperation? In 1968, anthropologist David Schneider argued that North Americans' ideas of kinship generated the feeling of "enduring diffuse solidarity" among all those who understood themselves to be related by ties of blood and sex. In many cases, however, human beings seek to establish (or find themselves belonging to) collectivities organized on regional, national, or global scales. As a result, they come to experience varying degrees of relatedness and solidarity with large numbers of individuals whom they will never meet face to face. As we will see in this chapter, human beings are perfectly capable of establishing and honoring ties of enduring diffuse solidarity that have nothing to do with blood or sex. Sociologist Zygmunt Bauman has argued, in fact, that "all supra-individual groupings are first and foremost processes of collectivization of friends and enemies. . . . More exactly, individuals sharing a common group or category of enemies treat each other as friends" (1989, 152). Although a common enemy surely has the effect of drawing people together, it is rarely sufficient by itself to produce solidarity that endures.

People in all societies have developed patterned social relationships that aim to bind them together for the long term, and some of these reach beyond, and even cut across, ties forged in terms of everyday relatedness. Consider, for example, the way members of Catholic monastic orders, who may neither marry nor bear children, nevertheless refer to one another

as *brother*, *sister*, *father*, and *mother*. They also take as the prototype for these interpersonal relationships the formal role obligations of family members. But religious orders in many cases are large, international institutions fitting into the overall global hierarchy of the Catholic Church. Again, the kinds of connections established among members of such institutions reach far beyond the contexts of everyday, face-to-face relatedness.

As we already noted, anthropologists were the first social scientists to recognize that people in different societies classified their relatives into categories that did not correspond to those accepted in European societies. Coming to understand the complexities of different kinds of formal kin relations helped undermine the ethnocentric assumption that European ways of categorizing relatives were a transparent reflection of natural biological ties. Indeed, beginning anthropology students from many backgrounds regularly assume that the way they grew up classifying their kin reflects the universal truth about human relatedness. For this reason, we devote part of this chapter to introducing some findings from kinship studies in anthropology. Learning to distinguish between cross cousins and parallel cousins, or considering some of the consequences that follow from tracing descent through women rather than men remain useful exercises that help overcome ethnocentric tendencies.

At the same time, it is important to realize that the different classes of relatives identified in a formal kinship system may or may not be considered important in a particular society. Moreover, even when such kin categories remain important, ties of relatedness to people who are not formally kin may be as important as—or more important than—ties to formal kin. Formal kin ties are supplemented by or replaced by other forms of relatedness in many societies, and these forms of relatedness take a variety of forms and operate at different scales. This chapter pays particular attention to local, face-to-face forms of relatedness, including friendship, kinship, and institutions that anthropologists call *sodalities*.

To recognize the varied forms that institutions of human relatedness can take is to acknowledge fundamental openness in the organization of human interdependence. This openness makes possible the elaboration and extension of ties of relatedness to supra-local levels. Structures of relatedness

FIGURE 11.1 Locations of societies whose EthnoProfiles appear in chapter 11.

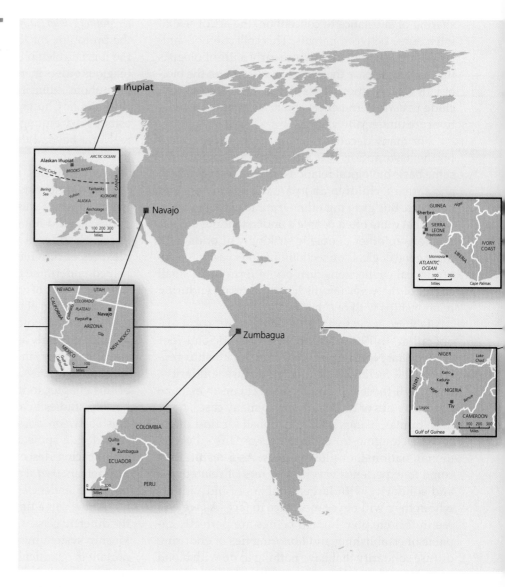

with increasingly vast scope tend to emerge when changed historical circumstances draw people's attention to shared aspects of their lives that more intimate forms of relatedness ignore or cannot handle. New shared experiences offer raw material for the invention of new forms of common identity. Recognition of this process led political scientist Benedict Anderson to invent the term **imagined**

imagined communities Term borrowed from political scientist Benedict Anderson to refer to groups whose members' knowledge of one another does not come from regular face-to-face interactions but is based on shared experiences with national institutions, such as schools and government bureaucracies.

communities to refer to "all communities larger than primordial villages of face-to-face contact (and perhaps even these)" (1983, 6). Anderson originally applied the concept of "imagined communities" to modern nation-states, but anthropologists were quick to note the range of communities included in his definition and have used the concept successfully to study different forms of human relatedness. The concept of imagined communities is important because it emphasizes that the ties that bind people into *all* supra-individual communities are *contingent*: They have not existed since the beginning of time and they may disappear in the future. Put another way, imagined communities are social, cultural, and

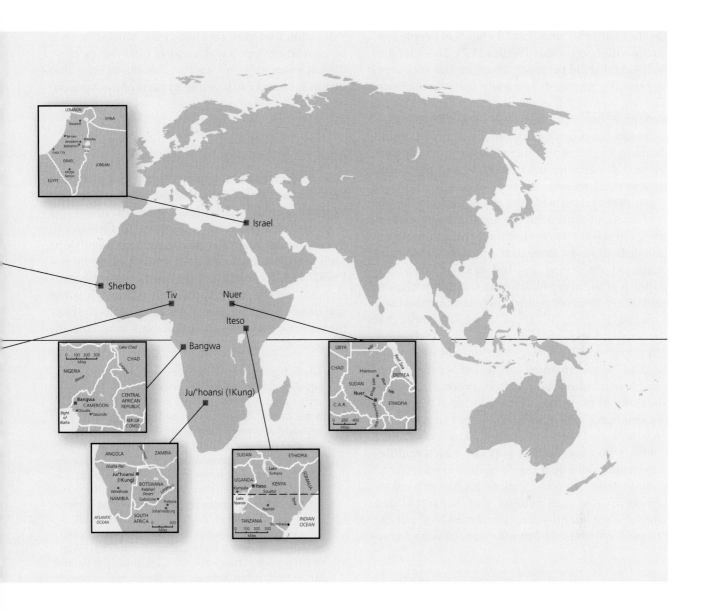

historical constructions. They are the joint outcome of shared habitual practices and of symbolic images of common identity promulgated by group members with an interest in making a particular imagined identity endure.

▼ FRIENDSHIP

Anthropologist Robert Brain cites a dictionary definition of *friend* as "one joined to another in intimacy and mutual benevolence independent of sexual or family love" (1976, 15). He quickly points out that the Western belief that friendship and kinship are separate phenomena often breaks down in practice. Today, for example, some husbands and wives in Western societies consider each other "best friends." Similarly, we may become friends with some of our relatives while treating others the same way we treat nonrelatives. Presumably, we can be friends with people over and above any kinship ties we might have with them. Sandra Bell and Simon Coleman suggest that typical "markers" for **friendship**

friendship The relatively "unofficial" bonds that people construct with one another that tend to be personal, affective, and often a matter of choice.

are the relatively "unofficial" bonds that people construct with one another (Figure 11.2). These tend to be bonds that are personal, affective, and, to a varying extent from society to society, a matter of choice. The line between friendship and kinship is often a very fuzzy one, since there may be an affective quality to kinship relations (we can like our cousins and do the same things with them that we would do with friends), since sometimes friends are seen after a long time as being related, and since some societies have networks of relatedness that can be activated or not for reasons of sentiment, not just for pragmatic reasons. Friendship has been difficult for some anthropologists to study, since in the past they have concentrated on trying to find regular long-term patterns of social organization in societies with noncentralized forms of political organization (Bell and Coleman 1999, 4). Bell and Coleman also note that the importance of friendship seems to be increasing: "In many shifting social contexts, ties of kinship tend to be transformed and often weakened by complex and often contradictory processes of globalization. At the same time new forms of friendship are emerging" (5). This is illustrated in a striking way in Rio de Janeiro by Claudia Barcellos Rezende (1999), who observed the ways in which middle-class women and their maids could come to refer to each other as "friends." Within this hierarchical relationship, the distinctions that separated the women were not questioned in themselves, but the "friendship" consisted of affection, care, and consideration that both sets of women valued in their work relationship. It was a way of establishing trust: "What friendship invokes . . . is the affinity that brings these people together as parts of the same social world" (93).

Bangwa Friendship

How do societies bring strangers together in mutual benevolence? Brain notes that people in many non-Western societies are far less haphazard about this than are Westerners. The Bangwa of Cameroon, among whom Brain did fieldwork, seal friendships with a ritual similar to that of marriage (see Ethno-Profile 11.1: Bangwa). But the obligations of friendship are not the same as the obligations of kinship that derive from marriage. Friendship limits the risks that follow from close relationships with consanguineal kin.

> The Bangwa spoke of ideal friendship as one of equality and complete reciprocity, backed by moral, rather than supernatural and legal, sanctions. He is my friend "because he is beautiful," "because he is good." Although there is in fact a good deal of ceremonial courtesy and gift exchange, it is seen as a relationship of disinterested affection. Youths who are friends spend long hours in each other's company, holding hands when they walk together in the market. As they grow older, friendships become increasingly valued—elders have little else to do but sit around with their friends, chatting about local politics, disputes over land boundaries, trouble with an obstreperous young wife. . . . Friendship is valued far above kinship; between kin there are niggling debts and witchcraft fears. Friendship lasts till death; kinship is brittle and involves inequalities of age and wealth and status. Friendship alone can cancel these out. A chief born on the same day as a slave automatically becomes his "best friend" and is bound to treat him in a friendly manner, at least in some contexts. The son who succeeds to a chief's position depends on the friends he made as a child—not his kin—in the crooked corridors of palace politics (Brain 1976, 35).

Brain recognizes that certain relationships among formal kin may be viewed as prototypes of friendship in some societies. Even for the Bangwa, twins are ideal best friends, and other groups, such as the Kuma of New Guinea, see brothers-in-law as best

FIGURE 11.2 These two young men in Cameroon were the best of friends.

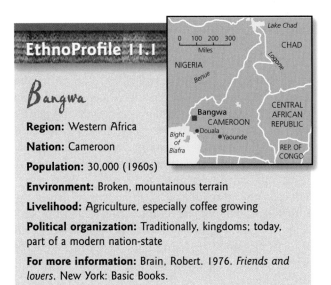

EthnoProfile 11.1

Bangwa

Region: Western Africa

Nation: Cameroon

Population: 30,000 (1960s)

Environment: Broken, mountainous terrain

Livelihood: Agriculture, especially coffee growing

Political organization: Traditionally, kingdoms; today, part of a modern nation-state

For more information: Brain, Robert. 1976. *Friends and lovers*. New York: Basic Books.

friends. But friendship can also be seen as a nonkin link that can correct the defects and limitations of formal kinship.

American College Student Friendship and Friendliness

Between 1977 and 1987, anthropologist Michael Moffatt studied student culture at Rutgers University in New Jersey, where he teaches. Friendship was a central cultural feature for the American college students he knew in the 1980s. Friends were the only freely chosen companions of equal status in their lives; all other social connections—family, religion, work, race, ethnicity—were imposed on the self from the outside. Friends were those with whom you shared "who you really were," your authentic self. But proof of friendship was invisible, which was troubling to the students: "You and I are true friends if and only if both of us consider the other to be a true friend 'in our hearts,' and I am never entirely certain about what you really feel in your heart" (1989, 43). As a result, students spent hours thinking about and discussing the authenticity of their own friendships and those of other people they knew well. Not everyone, of course, could be a friend, but Moffatt found that the students he knew believed that normal Americans should be ready under certain circumstances to extend "real" friendship to any other

person. To be otherwise is to be "snobbish," or to "think you are better than other people."

This attitude reflects what Moffatt sees as a central value of American daily life: friendliness. To act "friendly" is

> to give regular abbreviated performances of the standard behaviors of real friendship—to look pleased and happy when you meet someone, to put on the all-American friendly smile, to acknowledge the person you are meeting by name (preferably by the first name, shortened version), to make casual body contact, to greet the person with one of the two or three conventional queries about the state of their "whole self" ("How are you?" "How's it goin'?" "What's new?") (1989, 43–44).

Moffatt observed that students were friendly to anyone they had met more than once or twice. This was even more strongly required among students who knew one another personally. "To violate 'friendly' in an apparently deliberate way was to arouse some of the strongest sentiments of distrust and dislike in Rutgers student culture" (1989, 43–44).

▼ KINSHIP

Our case studies of friendship in two different societies contrasted the relationships people may develop with friends with other relationships based on kin ties. In this part of the chapter, we want to explore more fully how traditional anthropological studies of kinship contribute to our understanding of the organization of human relatedness. People struggle to find ways to preserve certain ties of relatedness over time, reinforcing them with public affirmations and gift exchanges that aim to provide scaffolding for enduring forms of social solidarity that strengthen the agency that group members can exercise jointly in their encounters with other groups. At the same time, as we saw earlier, such publicly acknowledged forms of relatedness can be experienced as a burden from which individuals try to escape, either by formal affirmation of alternative kinds of relatedness (as in Bangwa institutionalized friendship) or by informal affirmations of relatedness whose value comes precisely from the fact that these ties are freely chosen and unencumbered by formally imposed obligations.

Anthropologists who study formal systems of **kinship** pay primary attention to those publicly recognized sets of social relations that are prototypically derived from the universal human experiences of mating, birth, and nurturance. Anthropologists call relationships based on mating **marriage** (discussed in chapter 12) and those based on birth **descent**. Although nurturance is ordinarily seen to be closely connected with mating and birth, it need not be, and all societies have ways of acknowledging a relationship based on nurturance alone. In the United States, we call this relationship **adoption**.

Although marriage is based on mating, descent on birth, and adoption on nurturance, marriage is not the same thing as mating, descent is not the same thing as birth, and adoption is not the same thing as nurturance. The human experiences of mating, birth, and nurturance are ambiguous. The fascinating thing about systems of relatedness is that different societies choose to highlight some features of those experiences while downplaying or even ignoring others. Europeans and North Americans know that in their societies mating is not the same as marriage, although a valid marriage encourages mating between the married partners. Similarly, all births do not constitute valid links of descent: Children whose parents have not been married according to accepted legal or religious specifications do not fit the cultural logic of descent, and many societies offer no positions that they can properly fill. Finally, not all acts of nurturance are recognized as adoption: Consider, for example, foster parents in the United States, whose custody of foster children is officially temporary. Put another way, through kinship, a culture emphasizes certain aspects of human experience, constructs its own theory of human nature, and specifies "the processes by which an individual comes into being and develops into a complete (i.e., mature) social person" (Kelly 1993, 521).

Marriage, descent, and adoption are thus selective. One society may emphasize women as the bearers of children and base its kinship system on this fact, paying little formal attention to the male's role in conception. Another society may trace connections through men, emphasizing the paternal role in conception and reducing the maternal role. A third society may encourage its members to adopt not only children but also adult siblings, blurring the link between biological reproduction and family creation. Even though they contradict one another, all three understandings can be justified with reference to the panhuman experiences of mating, birth, and nurturance.

Consider the North American kinship term *aunt*. This term seems to refer to a woman who occupies a unique biological position. In fact, an aunt may be related to a person in one of four different ways: as father's sister, mother's sister, father's brother's wife, or mother's brother's wife. From the perspective of North American kinship, all those women have something in common, and they are all placed into a single kinship category. Prototypically, a person's aunts are women one generation older than he or she is and are sisters or sisters-in-law of a person's parents. However, North Americans may also refer to their mother's best friend as *aunt*. By doing so, they recognize the strengths of this system of classification. By way of contrast, in Chile, *tía*, the Spanish term that translates as "aunt," is regularly used by children to refer to female friends of their parents. Indeed, people well into their early adulthood continue to use the term to refer to women who are taking on the role of "mother," but with whom they are not as intimate as they would be with their own mothers. U.S. university students living with Chilean families frequently use the term "*tía*" to address the woman who, in English, would be called their "host mother."

Thus, kinship is an idiom. It is a selective interpretation of the common human experiences of mating, birth, and nurturance. The result is a set of coherent principles that allow people to assign one another group membership. These principles normally cover several significant issues: how to carry out the reproduction of legitimate group members (marriage or adoption); where group members should

---

kinship Social relationships that are prototypically derived from the universal human experiences of mating, birth, and nurturance.

marriage An institution that prototypically involves a man and a woman, transforms the status of the participants, carries implications about sexual access, gives offspring a position in the society, and establishes connections between the kin of the husband and the kin of the wife.

descent The principle based on culturally recognized parent-child connections that define the social categories to which people belong.

adoption Kinship relationships based on nurturance, often in the absence of other connections based on mating or birth.

live after marriage (residence rules); how to establish links between generations (descent); and how to pass on positions in society (succession) or material goods (inheritance). Taken together, kinship principles define social groups, locate people within those groups, and position the people and groups in relation to one another both in space and over time.

Sex, Gender, and Kinship

Kinship is based on but is not reducible to biology. It is a cultural interpretation of the culturally recognized "facts" of human reproduction. One of the most basic of these "facts," recognized in some form in all societies, is that two different kinds of human beings must cooperate sexually to produce offspring (although what they believe to be the contribution of each party to the outcome varies from society to society). Anthropologists use the term **sex** to refer to the observable physical characteristics that distinguish the two kinds of human beings, females and males, needed for reproduction. People everywhere pay attention to *morphological sex* (the appearance of external genitalia and observable secondary sex characteristics such as enlarged breasts in females). Scientists further distinguish females from males on the basis of *gonadal sex* (the presence of ovaries in females, testes in males) and *chromosomal sex* (two X chromosomes in females, one X chromosome and one Y chromosome in males).

At the same time, cross-cultural research repeatedly demonstrates that physical sex differences do not allow us to predict the roles that females or males will play in any particular society. Consequently, anthropologists distinguish sex from **gender**—the cultural construction of beliefs and behaviors considered appropriate for each sex. As Barbara Miller puts it, "In some societies, people with XX chromosomes do the cooking, in others it is the XY people who cook, in others both XX and XY people cook. The same goes for sewing, transplanting rice seedlings, worshipping deities, and speaking in public. Even the exclusion of women from hunting and warfare has been reduced by recent studies from the level of a universal to a generality. While it is generally true that men hunt and women do not, and that men fight in wars and women do not, important counter cases exist" (1993, 5; Figure 11.3).

In fact, the outward physical features used to distinguish females from males may not be obvious either. Sometimes genetic or hormonal factors produce ambiguous external genitalia, a phenomenon called *hermaphroditism*. Steroid 5-alpha reductase deficiency, for example, is a rare hormonal defect that causes males who are otherwise biologically normal to be born with ambiguous genitals, leading some to be categorized as male and others as female. At puberty, however, increased testosterone levels cause these individuals to experience changes typical of males: a deepening voice, muscle development, growth of the penis, and descent of the testicles. Gilbert Herdt (1994) investigated cases of individuals with steroid 5-alpha reductase deficiency in the Dominican Republic and in New Guinea. In both places, the sexually anomalous individuals had been assigned to a locally recognized third sex, called *guevedoche* ("testicles at twelve") in the Dominican Republic and *kwolu-aatmwol* ("changing into a male thing") among the Sambia of New Guinea.

How Many Sexes Are There?

In other cases, however, anthropologists have documented the existence of *supernumerary* (that is, more than the standard two) sexes in cultures where the presence of ambiguous genitalia at birth seem to play no obvious role. In the Byzantine civilization of late antiquity, phenotypic differences were deliberately created in the case of eunuchs, whose testicles were removed or destroyed, often before puberty (Ringrose 1994). In the case of the hijras of Gujarat, India, adult males deliberately cut off both penis and testicles in order to dedicate themselves to the Mother Goddess Bahuchara Mata (Nanda 1994). In both these cases, third gender roles distinct from traditional feminine and masculine gender roles are believed appropriate for third-sexed individuals.

Elsewhere, supernumerary gender roles developed that apparently had nothing to do with morphological sex anomalies. Perhaps the most famous

---

sex Observable physical characteristics that distinguish two kinds of humans, females and males, needed for biological reproduction.

gender The cultural construction of beliefs and behaviors considered appropriate for each sex.

FIGURE 11.3 Cross-cultural research repeatedly demonstrates that physical indicators of sex difference do not allow us to predict the roles that females or males will play in any particular society. In Otavalo, Ecuador, men were traditionally weavers (*a*), while traditional Navajo weavers were women (*b*).

case is that of the so-called *berdache*. Will Roscoe points out that "the key features of male and female berdache roles were, in order of importance, *productive specialization* (crafts and domestic work for male berdaches and warfare, hunting, and leadership roles in the case of female berdaches), *supernatural sanction* (in the form of an authorization and/or bestowal of powers from extrasocietal sources) and *gender variation* (in relation to normative cultural expectations for male and female genders)," commonly but not always marked by cross-dressing (1994, 332). Some berdaches may have engaged in sexual practices that Westerners consider homosexual or bisexual. Berdaches were accepted and respected members of their communities, and their economic and religious pursuits seem to have been culturally more significant than their sexual practices.

The term *berdache* apparently meant "male prostitute" to the early French explorers in the Americas who first used it. For this reason, many gay and lesbian anthropologists refuse to use the term, as do those members of contemporary indigenous societies who want to reclaim this alternative gender role for themselves. No single term, however, has yet reached universal acceptance, although members of Native American societies have begun to use the term *Two Spirits* rather than *gay* or *lesbian*. Perhaps no single term is adequate; after all, male berdaches have been described in almost 150 indigenous North American societies and female berdaches in perhaps half that number.

For many people, the "natural" existence of only two sexes, each with its own gender role, seems too obvious to question. Nevertheless, Thomas Laqueur (1990) has shown that the "two-sex model," which most contemporary Westerners accept as transparently obvious, only took root after the Renaissance. Prior to that, the bodies of all human beings were evaluated in terms of a "one-sex model" based on the Platonic notion that there was one ideal human form, which all actual human beings embodied to greater or lesser degrees. Moreover, as Roscoe points out, "the presence of multiple genders does not require belief in the existence of three or more physical sexes but, minimally, a view of physical differences as unfixed, or insufficient on their own to establish gender, or simply less important than individual and social factors" (1994, 342). These observations sustain the key assertion of Sylvia Yanagisako and Jane Collier: "there are no 'facts,' biological or material, that have social consequences and cultural meanings in and of themselves" (1987, 39).

Herdt's survey of ethnographic literature leads him to conclude that it is difficult for societies to maintain supernumerary sexes or genders. Still, anthropologists can argue convincingly that societies have such statuses when a culture defines for each "a symbolic niche and a social pathway of development into later adult life distinctly different from the cultural life plan set out by a model based on male/female duality" (1994, 68).

Interestingly, supernumerary sexes and genders can coexist alongside strongly marked male-female duality, as among the Sambia, perhaps serving to temper the absolutism of that duality. That male-female duality should be an issue for the Sambia reminds us that no human society is unconcerned about biological and social reproduction. However, kinship institutions, which build on gender duality, do more than provide for reproduction. Kinship not only classifies people, but it also establishes and enforces the conventions by which different classes of people interact with one another. In this way, societies are able to maintain social order without central government.

Understanding Different Kinship Systems

Kinship practices, rather than written statutes, clarify for people what rights and obligations they owe one another. But the first Westerners who encountered different kinship practices found some of them highly unusual. Western explorers discovered, for example, that some non-Western people distinguished among their relatives only on the basis of *age* and *sex*. To refer to people one generation older than the speaker required only two terms: one applying to men and one applying to women. The man who was married to their mother, or whom they believed to be their biological father, although known to them and personally important to them, was socially no more or less significant than that man's brothers or their mother's brothers. The explorers mistakenly concluded that these people were unable to tell the difference between their fathers and their uncles because they used the same kin term for both. They assumed that terms like *father* and *uncle* were universally recognized kinship categories. However, the

people whom the explorers met were no more deluded than English speakers are when they assert that their father's sister and mother's brother's wife are equally their *aunts*.

The categories of feeling these people associated with different kin were as real as, but different from, the emotions Westerners associate with kin. "Just as the word *father* in English means a great deal more than lineal male ancestor of the first ascending generation, *aita* in Basque has many local connotations not reducible to *father*, as we understand the term" (Greenwood and Stini 1977, 333). Because the world of kin is a world of expectations and obligations, it is fundamentally a moral world charged with feeling. In some societies, a man's principal authority figure is his mother's brother, and his father is a figure of affection and unwavering support. A phrase like "God the Father" would not mean the same thing in those societies as it does in a society in which the father has life-and-death control over his children and a mother's brothers are without significant authority.

▼ WHAT IS THE ROLE OF DESCENT IN KINSHIP?

A central aspect of kinship is descent—the cultural principle that defines social categories through culturally recognized parent-child connections. Descent groups are defined by ancestry and so exist in time. Descent involves transmission and incorporation: the transmission of membership through parent-child links and the incorporation of these people into groups. In some societies, descent group membership controls how people mobilize for social action.

Two major strategies are employed in establishing patterns of descent. In the first strategy, the descent group is formed by people who believe they are related to each other by connections made through their mothers and fathers *equally*. That is, they believe themselves to be just as related to their father's side of the family as to their mother's. Anthropologists call this **bilateral descent** (or *cognatic descent*). Two

---

bilateral descent The principle that a descent group is formed by people who believe they are related to each other by connections made through their mothers and fathers equally (sometimes called cognatic descent).

kinds of bilateral kinship groups have been identified by anthropologists. One is made up of people who claim to be related to one another through ties either from the mother's or father's side to a common ancestor. This *bilateral descent group* is rare. The other kind, called a *bilateral kindred*, is much more common and consists of the relatives of one person or group of siblings.

The second major strategy, **unilineal descent**, is based on the assumption that the most significant kin relationships must be traced through *either* the mother *or* the father. Such descent groups are the most common kind of descent group in the world today, based on a count of the number of societies that continue to employ them. Unilineal descent groups that are made up of links traced through a father are called *patrilineal;* those traced through a mother are called *matrilineal.*

Bilateral Kindreds

The **bilateral kindred** is the kinship group that most Europeans and North Americans know. This group forms around a particular individual and includes all the people linked to that individual through kin of both sexes—people conventionally called *relatives* in English (Figure 11.4). These people form a group only because of their connection to the central person or persons, known in the terminology of kinship as *Ego.* In North American society, bilateral kindreds assemble when Ego is baptized, confirmed, bar or bat mitzvahed, graduated from college, married, or buried. Each person within Ego's bilateral kindred has his or her own separate kindred. For example, Ego's father's sister's daughter has a kindred that includes people related to her through her father and his siblings—people to whom Ego is not related. This is simultaneously the major strength and major weakness of bilateral kindreds. That is, they have overlapping memberships and they do not endure beyond the lifetime of an individual Ego. But they are widely extended and can form broad networks of people who are somehow related to one another.

A classic bilateral kindred is found among the Ju/'hoansi (!Kung) of the Kalahari Desert in southern Africa (see EthnoProfile 11.2: Ju/'hoansi [!Kung]). Anthropologist Richard Lee points out that for the Ju/'hoansi, every individual in the society can be linked to every other individual by a kinship term, either through males or through females. As a result, a person can expect to find a relative everywhere there are Ju/'hoansi. When they were full-time foragers, the Ju/'hoansi lived in groups that were relatively small (10 to 30 people) but made up of a constantly changing set of individuals. "In essence, a Ju/'hoan camp consists of relatives, friends, and in-laws who have found that they can live and work well together. Under this flexible principle, brothers may be united or divided; fathers and sons may live together or apart. Further, during his or her lifetime a Ju/'hoan may live at many waterholes with many different groups" (1992b, 62). A wide range of kinspeople makes this flexibility possible. When someone wanted to move, he or she had kin at many different waterholes and could choose to activate any of several appropriate kin ties.

For the Ju/'hoansi, the bilateral kindred provides social flexibility. However, flexible group boundaries become problematic in at least four kinds of social circumstances: (1) where clear-cut membership in a particular social group must be determined, (2) where social action requires the formation of groups that are larger than individual families, (3) where conflicting claims to land and labor must be resolved, and (4) where people are concerned to perpetuate a particular social order over time. In societies that face these dilemmas, unilineal descent groups are usually formed.

Unilineal Descent Groups

Unilineal descent groups are found all over the world. They are all based on the principle that certain kinds of parent-child relationships are more important than others. Membership in a *unilineal descent group* is based on the membership of the appropriate parent in the group. In patrilineal systems, an individual belongs to a group formed through male sex links,

---

unilineal descent The principle that a descent group is formed by people who believe they are related to each other by links made through a father or mother only.

bilateral kindred A kinship group that consists of the relatives of one person or group of siblings.

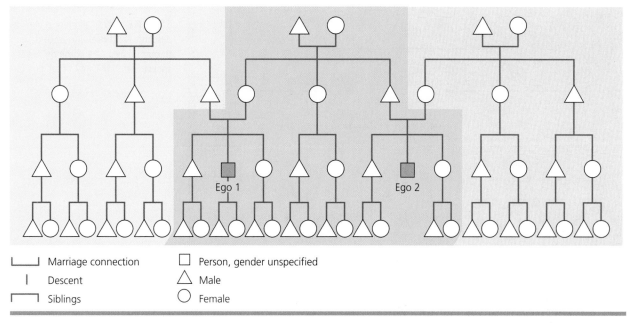

⊐ Marriage connection	□ Person, gender unspecified
∣ Descent	△ Male
⊓ Siblings	○ Female

FIGURE 11.4 A bilateral kindred includes all recognized relatives on Ego's father's and mother's sides. The dark area in the center indicates where the kindreds of Ego 1 and Ego 2 overlap.

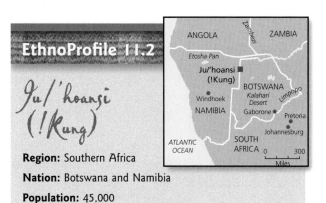

EthnoProfile 11.2

Ju/'hoansi (!Kung)

Region: Southern Africa

Nation: Botswana and Namibia

Population: 45,000

Environment: Desert

Livelihood: Hunting and gathering

Political organization: Traditionally, egalitarian bands; today, part of modern nation-states

For more information: Lee, Richard B. 2002. *The Dobe Ju/'hoansi.* 3d ed. Belmont, CA: Wadsworth.

the lineage of his or her father. In matrilineal systems, an individual belongs to a group formed by links through women, the lineage of his or her mother. *Patrilineal* and *matrilineal* do not mean that only men belong to one and women to the other; rather, the terms refer to the principle by which membership is conferred. In a patrilineal society, women and men belong to a **patrilineage** formed by father-child links (Figure 11.5); similarly, in a matrilineal society, men and women belong to a **matrilineage** formed by mother-child connections (Figure 11.6). In other words, membership in the group is, on the face of it, unambiguous. An individual belongs to only one lineage. This is in contrast to a bilateral kindred, in which an individual belongs to overlapping groups. Nevertheless, as Martine Segalen observes, a pattern of unilineal descent itself is "no more than a kind of external framework," which can support a wide range of cultural variations (1986, 51–52).

patrilineage A social group formed by people connected by father-child links.

matrilineage A social group formed by people connected by mother-child links.

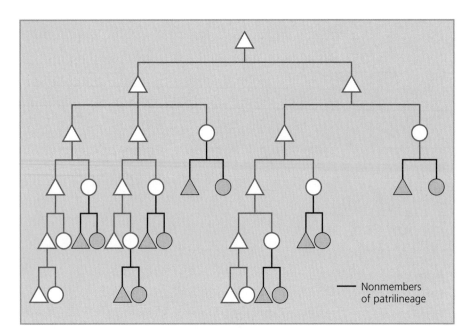

FIGURE 11.5 Patrilineal descent: All those who trace descent through males to a common male ancestor are indicated in white.

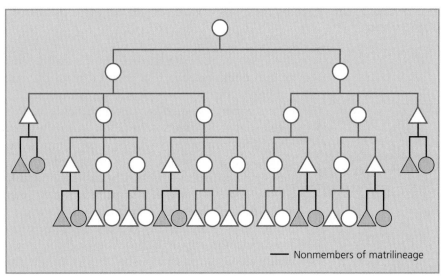

FIGURE 11.6 Matrilineal descent: All those who trace descent through females to a common female ancestor are indicated in white.

▼ WHAT ROLE DO LINEAGES PLAY IN DESCENT?

The -*lineal* in patrilineal and matrilineal refers to the nature of the social group formed. These **lineages** are composed of people who believe they can specify the parent-child links that unite them. Although the ab-

stract kinship diagrams that anthropologists draw include just a few people, lineages in the world vary in size, ranging from 20 or 30 members to several hundred. Before 1949, some Chinese lineages were composed of more than 1,000 members.

Lineage Membership

The most important feature of lineages is that they are *corporate* in organization—that is, a lineage has a single legal personality. As the Ashanti put it, a lineage is

---

lineages The consanguineal members of descent groups who believe they can trace their descent from known ancestors.

"one person" (Fortes 1953). To outsiders, all members of a lineage are equal *in law* to all others. For example, in the case of a blood feud, the death of any opposing lineage member avenges the death of the person who started the feud. Lineages are also corporate in that they control property, especially land, as a unit. Such groups are found in societies where rights to use land are crucial and must be monitored over time.

Lineages are also the main political associations in the societies that have them. Individuals have no political or legal status in such societies except through lineage membership. They have relatives outside the lineage, but their own political and legal status comes through the lineage.

Because membership in a lineage comes through a direct line from father or mother to child, lineages can endure over time and in a sense have an independent existence. As long as people can remember from whom they are descended, lineages can endure. Most lineages have a time depth of about five generations: grandparents, parents, Ego, children, and grandchildren. When members of a group believe that they can no longer accurately specify the genealogical links that connect them but believe that they are "in some way" connected, we find what anthropologists call *clans*.

A **clan** is usually made up of lineages that the society's members believe to be related to each other through links that go back into mythic times. Sometimes the common ancestor of each clan is said to be an animal that lived at the beginning of time. The important point is that lineage members can specify all the generational links back to their common ancestor, whereas clan members ordinarily cannot. The clan is thus larger than any lineage and also more diffuse in both membership and the hold it has over individuals.

The Logic of Lineage Relationships

Lineages endure over time in societies in which no other form of organization lasts. Hence, they provide for the "perpetual exercise of defined rights, duties, office and social tasks vested in the lineage" (Fortes

1953, 165). In other words, in the societies where they are found, the system of lineages becomes the foundation of social life.

While lineages might look solid and unchanging, they are often more flexible than they appear. The memories people have of their ancestry are often transmitted in the form of myth or legend. Rather than accurate historical records, they are better understood in Malinowskian terms as mythical charters, justifications from the invisible world for the visible arrangements of the society (see the discussion of myth in chapter 7).

In showing how this relationship works, Fortes (1953, 165) quotes anthropologists Paul and Laura Bohannan, whose research was among the Tiv of Nigeria (see EthnoProfile 11.3: Tiv). The Bohannans observed that Tiv who had not previously viewed one another as kin sometimes renegotiated their lineage relationships, announcing publicly that they shared some of the same ancestors. Such changes were plausible to the Tiv because they assumed that traditional lineage relationships determined current social arrangements. If current social arrangements and tradition conflicted, therefore, the Tiv concluded that errors had crept into the tradition. Such renegotiation enabled the Tiv to keep their lineage relationships in line with changing legal and political relationships.

Patrilineages

By far the most common form of lineage organization is the patrilineage, which consists of all the people (male and female) who believe themselves related to each other because they are related to a common male ancestor by links through men. The prototypical kernel of a patrilineage is the father-son pair. Women members of patrilineages normally leave the lineages when they marry, but they do not relinquish their interest in their own lineages. In a number of societies, they play an active role in the affairs of their own patrilineages for many years.

An assumption of hierarchy exists in patrilineal societies: Men believe they are superior to women, and many women seem to agree. However, there is a puzzle at the heart of these societies. Women with little power, who are strangers to the lineage, nevertheless marry its members and produce the children who perpetuate the lineage. Ironically, the future of

clan A descent group formed by members who believe they have a common (sometimes mythical) ancestor, even if they cannot specify the genealogical links.

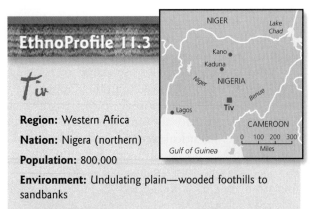

EthnoProfile 11.3

Tiv

Region: Western Africa

Nation: Nigera (northern)

Population: 800,000

Environment: Undulating plain—wooded foothills to sandbanks

Livelihood: Farming

Political organization: Traditionally egalitarian; today, part of a modern nation-state

For more information: Bohannon, Laura, and Paul Bohannon. 1969. *The Tiv of central Nigeria.* 2d ed. London, International African Institute.

EthnoProfile 11.4

Nuer

Region: Eastern Africa

Nation: Ethiopia and Sudan

Population: 300,000

Environment: Open grassland

Livelihood: Cattle herding and farming

Political organization: Traditionally, egalitarian tribes, no political offices; today, part of modern nation-states

For more information: Evans-Pritchard, E. E. 1940. *The Nuer.* Oxford: Oxford University Press; and Hutchinson, Sharon. 1996. *Nuer dilemmas.* Berkeley: University of California Press.

the patrilineage depends on people who do not belong to it! A second irony is that women must leave their own lineages to reproduce the next generation of somebody else's lineage. Women in patrilineal societies are often torn between conflicting interests and loyalties (see Karp 1986). Should they support their own children or their fathers and brothers?

A classic patrilineal system was found among the Nuer of the Sudan and Ethiopia (see EthnoProfile 11.4: Nuer). At the time of his fieldwork in the 1930s, English anthropologist E. E. Evans-Pritchard noted that the Nuer were divided into at least 20 clans. Evans-Pritchard defined *clan* as the largest group of people who (1) trace their descent patrilineally from a common ancestor, (2) cannot marry each other, and (3) consider sexual relations within the group to be incestuous. The clan is divided, or segmented, into lineages that are themselves linked to each other by presumed ties of patrilineal descent. The most basic stage of lineage segmentation is the *minimal lineage*, which has a time depth of three to five generations.

Evans-Pritchard observed that the Nuer kinship system worked in the following way: Members of lin-

eages A and B might consider themselves related because they believed that the founder of lineage A had been the older brother of the founder of lineage B. These two *minimal lineages*, as Evans-Pritchard called them, together formed a *minor lineage*—all those descended from a common father, believed to be the father of the two founders of A and B. Minor lineages connect to other minor lineages by yet another presumed common ancestor, forming *major lineages*. These major lineages are also believed to share a common ancestor and thus form a *maximal lineage*. The members of two maximal lineages believe their founders had been the sons of the clan ancestor; thus, all members of the clan are believed to be patrilineally related.

According to Evans-Pritchard, disputes among the Nuer emerged along the lines created by lineages. Suppose a quarrel erupted between two men whose minimal lineages were in different minor lineages. Each would be joined by men who belonged to his minor lineage, even if they were not in his minimal lineage. The dispute would be resolved when the quarreling minor lineages recognized that they were all part of the same major lineage. Similarly, the minor lineages to one major lineage would ally if a dispute with an opposed major lineage broke out. This process of groups coming together and opposing one another, called **segmentary opposition**, is expressed in kinship terms but represents a very common social process.

---

segmentary opposition A mode of hierarchical social organization in which groups beyond the most basic emerge only in opposition to other groups on the same hierarchical level.

Evans-Pritchard noted that lineages were important to the Nuer for political purposes. Members of the same lineage in the same village were conscious of being in a social group with common ancestors and symbols, corporate rights in territory, and common interests in cattle. When a son in the lineage married, these people helped provide the **bridewealth** cattle. If the son were killed, they—indeed, all members of his patrilineage, regardless of where they lived—would avenge him and would hold the funeral ceremony for him. Nevertheless, relationships among the members of a patrilineage were not necessarily harmonious: "A Nuer is bound to his paternal kin from whom he derives aid, security, and status, but in return for these benefits he has many obligations and commitments. Their often indefinite character may be both evidence of, and a reason for, their force, but it also gives ample scope for disagreement. Duties and rights easily conflict. Moreover, the privileges of [patrilineal] kinship cannot be divorced from authority, discipline, and a strong sense of moral obligation, all of which are irksome to Nuer. They do not deny them, but they kick against them when their personal interests run counter to them" (1951, 162).

Although the Nuer were patrilineal, they recognized as kin people who were not members of their lineage. In the Nuer language, the word *mar* referred to "kin": all the people to whom a person could trace a relationship of any kind, including people on the mother's side as well as those on the father's side. In fact, at such important ceremonial occasions as a bridewealth distribution after a woman in the lineage had been married, special attention was paid to kin on the mother's side. Certain important relatives, such as the mother's brother and the mother's sister, were given cattle. A man's mother's brother was his great supporter when he was in trouble. The mother's brother was kind to him as a boy and even provided a second home after he reached manhood. If he liked his sister's son, a mother's brother would even be willing to help pay the bridewealth so that he could marry. "Nuer say of the maternal uncle that he is both father and mother, but most frequently that 'he is your mother'" (Evans-Pritchard 1951, 162).*

*Readers interested in what has happened to Nuer kinship and relatedness as a consequence of the seemingly unending civil war in the Sudan should look at Hutchinson 1996 or 2002.

Matrilineages

In matrilineages, descent is traced through women rather than through men. Recall that in a patrilineage a woman's children are not in her lineage. In a matrilineage, a man's children are not in his. However, certain features of matrilineages make them more than just mirror images of patrilineages.

First, the prototypical kernel of a matrilineage is the sister-brother pair; a matrilineage may be thought of as a group of brothers and sisters connected through links made by women. Brothers marry out and often live with the family of their wives, but they maintain an active interest in the affairs of their lineage. Second, the most important man in a boy's life is not his father (who is not in his lineage) but his mother's brother, from whom he will receive his lineage inheritance. Third, the amount of power women exercise in matrilineages is still being hotly debated in anthropology. A matrilineage is not the same thing as a *matriarchy* (a society in which women rule); brothers often retain what appears to be a controlling interest in the lineage. Some anthropologists claim that the male members of a matrilineage are supposed to run the lineage even though there is more autonomy for women in matrilineal societies than in patrilineal ones—that the day-to-day exercise of power tends to be carried out by the brothers or sometimes the husbands. A number of studies, however, have questioned the validity of these generalizations. Trying to say something about matrilineal societies in general is difficult. The ethnographic evidence suggests that matrilineages must be examined on a case-by-case basis.

The Navajo are a matrilineal people (see Ethno-Profile 11.5: Navajo). Traditionally, the basic unit of Navajo social organization is the subsistence residential unit composed of a head mother, her husband, and some of their children with their spouses and children (Witherspoon 1975, 82; Figure 11.7). The leader of the unit is normally a man, usually the husband of the head mother. He directs livestock and agricultural operations and is the one who deals with the outside world: "He speaks for the unit at

bridewealth The transfer of certain symbolically important goods from the family of the groom to the family of the bride on the occasion of their marriage. It represents compensation to the wife's lineage for the loss of her labor and childbearing capacities.

FIGURE 11.7 The head mother of a Navajo subsistence residence unit is identified with the land, the herd, and the agricultural fields.

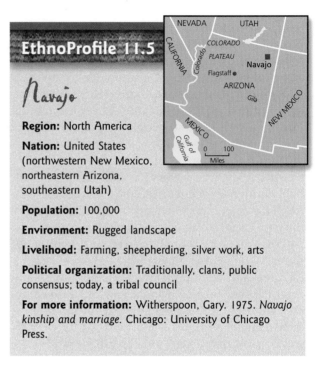

EthnoProfile 11.5

Navajo

Region: North America

Nation: United States (northwestern New Mexico, northeastern Arizona, southeastern Utah)

Population: 100,000

Environment: Rugged landscape

Livelihood: Farming, sheepherding, silver work, arts

Political organization: Traditionally, clans, public consensus; today, a tribal council

For more information: Witherspoon, Gary. 1975. *Navajo kinship and marriage.* Chicago: University of Chicago Press.

community meetings, negotiates with the traders and car salesmen, arranges marriages and ceremonies, talks to visiting strangers, and so on." (Contemporary Navajo women may not be involved in livestock and agricultural operations at all, finding professional and salaried careers outside the residential unit.) He seems to be in charge. But it is the head mother around whom the unit is organized:

> [The head mother] is identified with the land, the herd, and the agricultural fields. All residence rights can be traced back to her, and her opinions and wishes are always given the greatest consideration and usually prevail. In a sense, however, she delegates much of her role and prestige to the leader of the unit. If we think of the unit as a corporation, and the leader as its president, the head mother will be the chairman of the board. She usually has more sheep than the leader does. Because the power and importance of the head mother offer a deceptive appearance to the observer, many students of the Navajo have failed to see the importance of her role. But if one has lived a long time in one of these units, one soon becomes aware of who ultimately has the cards and directs the game. When there is a divorce between the leader and the head, it is always the leader who leaves and the head mother who returns, even if the land originally belonged to the mother of the leader. (Witherspoon, 1975, 82–83)

Overall, evidence from matrilineal societies reveals some domains of experience in which men and women are equal, some in which men are in control, and some in which women are in control. Observers and participants may disagree about which of these domains of experience is more or less central to Navajo life.

In discussing patrilineages, we referred to a patrilineal puzzle. Matrilineal societies also have a paradox, sometimes called the *matrilineal puzzle*—the contradiction between the rule of residence and the rule of inheritance. The contradiction is especially clear in societies that are strongly matrilineal and encourage residence with the wife's matrilineage. Among the Bemba of Zambia, for example, a man is a stranger in his wife's house, where he goes when he marries. A man may feel great affection for his father, but he will not be his father's heir. He will inherit from his mother's brother, who lives elsewhere. And although a father may wish to have his son inherit from him, he must give to his sister's son (Richards 1954).

The classic case of the matrilineal puzzle comes from the Trobriand Islands, and Malinowski interpreted it in the way just described (see EthnoProfile 3.4: Trobriand Islanders). But research on the Trobriand Islanders by anthropologist Annette Weiner calls Malinowski's interpretation into question. Weiner argues that to understand matrilineal kinship in the Trobriand Islanders, one must begin by seeing the sister-brother pair as an integral unit:

> [The sister-brother pair] makes complementary contributions both to a woman's brother's children and

to a woman's own children. . . . In the former instance, a man and his sister (father and father's sister to a child) contribute their own [lineage] resources to the man's children, thus building up these children with resources that they may use, but may not subsequently pass on to their own children. . . . In the latter case, a woman and her brother (mother and mother's brother) contribute to the regeneration of [the matrilineage]—the woman through the process of conception and the man through the control and transmission of [matrilineage] property such as land and palm trees." (1980, 286–87)

The result is that both a man and his sister "give" to the man's children, and his children return things to them later in life.

▼ WHAT ARE KINSHIP TERMINOLOGIES?

People everywhere use special terms to refer to people they recognize as related to them. Despite the variety of kinship systems in the world, anthropologists have identified six major patterns of kinship terminology based on how people categorize their cousins. The six patterns reflect common solutions to structural problems faced by societies organized in terms of kinship. They provide clues concerning how the vast and undifferentiated world of potential kin may be divided up. Kinship terminologies suggest both the external boundaries and internal divisions of the kinship groups, and they outline the structure of rights and obligations assigned to different members of the society.

Criteria for Distinguishing Kin

Anthropologists have identified several criteria that people use to indicate how people are related to one another. From the most common to the least common, these criteria include the following:

- *Generation*. Kin terms distinguish relatives according to the generation to which the relatives belong. In English, the term *cousin* conventionally refers to someone of the same generation as Ego.
- *Gender*. The gender of an individual is used to differentiate kin. In Spanish, *primo* refers to a male cousin and *prima* to a female cousin. In English, cousins are not distinguished on the basis of gender, but *uncle* and *aunt* are distinguished on the basis of both generation and gender.

- *Affinity*. A distinction is made on the basis of connection through marriage, or **affinity**. This criterion is used in Spanish when *suegra* (Ego's spouse's mother) is distinguished from *madre* (Ego's mother). In matrilineal societies, Ego's mother's sister and father's sister are distinguished from one another on the basis of affinity. The mother's sister is a direct, lineal relative; the father's sister is an affine; and they are called by different terms.
- *Collaterality*. A distinction is made between kin who are believed to be in a direct line and those who are "off to one side," linked to Ego through a lineal relative. In English, the distinction of **collaterality** is exemplified by the distinction between mother and aunt or father and uncle.
- *Bifurcation*. The distinction of **bifurcation** is employed when kinship terms referring to the mother's side of the family differ from those referring to the father's side.
- *Relative age*. Relatives of the same category may be distinguished on the basis of whether they are older or younger than Ego. Among the Ju/'hoansi, for example, speakers must separate "older brother" (*!ko*) from "younger brother" (*tsin*).
- *Gender of linking relative*. This criterion is related to collaterality. It distinguishes *cross relatives* (usually cousins) from *parallel relatives* (also usually cousins). Parallel relatives are linked through two brothers or two sisters. **Parallel cousins**, for example, are Ego's father's brother's children or mother's sister's children. Cross relatives are linked through a brother-sister pair. Thus, **cross cousins** are Ego's mother's brother's children or father's sister's children. The gender of either Ego or the cousins does not matter; rather the important factor is the gender of the linking relative (Figure 11.8).

---

affinity Connection through marriage.

collaterality A criterion employed in the analysis of kinship terminologies in which a distinction is made between kin who are believed to be in a direct line and those who are "off to one side," linked to the speaker by a lineal relative.

bifurcation A criterion employed in the analysis of kinship terminologies in which kinship terms referring to the mother's side of the family are distinguished from those referring to the father's side.

parallel cousins The children of a person's parents' same-gender siblings (a father's brother's children or a mother's sister's children).

cross cousins The children of a person's parents' opposite-gender siblings (a father's sister's children or a mother's brother's children).

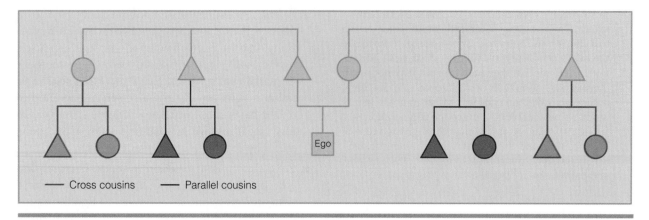

FIGURE 11.8 Cross cousins and parallel cousins: Ego's cross cousins are the children of Ego's father's sister and mother's brother. Ego's parallel cousins are the children of Ego's father's brother and mother's sister.

By the early 1950s, kinship specialists in anthropology had identified six major patterns of kinship terminology, based on how cousins were classified. In recent years, however, anthropologists have become quite skeptical of the value of these idealized models, in large measure because they are highly formalized and do not capture the full range of people's actual practices. Perhaps the main value to come from formal kinship studies is the fact that they took seriously the ways other people classified their relatives and were able to show the logic that informed such classifications. On the model of language, the set of kinship terms can be derived from a small number of principles that direct our attention to the important categories in a society.

▼ KINSHIP AND ALLIANCE THROUGH MARRIAGE

Any society divided into subgroups must devise a way to manage intergroup relations, and its members usually want to make sure that those relations are carried on from one generation to the next. Societies based on kinship attempt to resolve these difficulties by connecting kinship with marriage. By promoting or *prescribing* certain kinds of marriage, such societies both ensure the reproduction of their own memberships and establish long-term alliances with other groups.

Anthropologists find two major types of prescriptive marriage patterns in unilineal societies. One is a man's marriage with the father's sister's daughter. The more common is a man's marriage with the mother's brother's daughter.

In patrilineal societies, a "father's sister's daughter marriage" sets up a pattern of what is called *direct exchange marriage*. In this pattern, a line that has received a wife from another line in one generation gives a wife back in the next generation. That is, if line A receives a wife for one of its members from line B in generation I, line A will provide a wife for a member of line B in generation II. But in generation I, the men of line B cannot marry women from line A. They must find wives from somewhere else, say line C. This pattern reverses itself in the next generation, when the obligation has been fulfilled and the original balance restored. This is called a *father's sister's daughter marriage system* because, from a man's point of view, that woman is the prototypical spouse. However, any woman of the appropriate line is an eligible marriage partner for him. Before the marriage occurs, the men and women of the groom's line negotiate with those of the bride's line to determine the appropriate match.

A *mother's brother's daughter marriage system* sets up a pattern of asymmetrical exchange marriage. Unlike direct exchange systems, this marriage pattern does not balance out after two generations. Instead, one line always gets wives from the same line and gives wives to a different line. Put another way, women always marry into the line their father's sisters married into, and men always find wives in the line their mothers came from. This pattern provides a permanent alliance among the lines involved. The prototypical wife for a man is his mother's brother's daughter. If a man in a matrilineal society actually does marry his mother's brother's daughter, he inherits both what his mother's brother would give him and what his wife's father would give her husband.

Here, then, is the final piece in the lineage puzzle. People recognize certain classes of kin as potential marriage partners, and their kinship terminologies reflect this fact. Hence, if Ego's mother's brother doesn't have a daughter, all is not lost. Ego may not be looking for a literal mother's brother's daughter. Women whom anthropologists refer to as "mother's brother's daughters" are any women of Ego's generation who are members of his mother's patrilineage.

▼ ADOPTION

Kinship systems may appear to be fairly rigid sets of rules that use the accident of birth to thrust people into social positions laden with rights and obligations they cannot escape. Social positions that people are assigned at birth are sometimes called **ascribed statuses**, and positions within a kinship system have long been viewed as the prototypical ascribed statuses in any society. Ascribed statuses are often contrasted with **achieved statuses**, those social positions that people may attain later in life, often as the result of their own (or other people's) effort, such as becoming a spouse or college graduate. All societies have ways of incorporating outsiders into their kinship groups, however, which they achieve by converting supposedly ascribed kinship statuses into achieved ones, thus undermining the distinction between them. We will use the term *adoption* to refer to these practices, which allow people to transform relationships based on nurturance into relations of kinship.

Adoption in Highland Ecuador

Mary Weismantel is an anthropologist who carried out fieldwork among indigenous farmers living outside the community of Zumbagua, in highland Ecuador (1995; see EthnoProfile 11.6: Zumbagua). The farmers' households were based on lifelong heterosexual relationships, but she discovered that Zumbaguans

EthnoProfile 11.6

Zumbagua

Region: South America

Nation: Ecuador

Population: 20,000 (parish)

Environment: Andean mountain valley

Livelihood: Farming

Political organization: Peasant village and parish in modern nation-state

For more information: Weismantel, Mary. 2001. *Food, gender, and poverty in the Ecuadorian Andes.* Prospect Heights, IL: Waveland Press.

recognized kin ties that were very different from those found in European American cultures. Most striking was her discovery that every adult seemed to have several kinds of parents and several kinds of children.

In some societies, like that of ancient Rome, people distinguish between Ego's biological father (or *genitor*) and social father (or *pater*); they may also distinguish between Ego's biological mother (or *genetrix*) and social mother (or *mater*). Social parents are those who nurture a child, and they are often the child's biological parents as well. Zumbaguans use the Quichua term *tayta* for both genitor and pater and *mama* for both genetrix and mater. In their society, however, genitor, pater, genetrix, and mater are often entirely different people.

Weismantel learned that this use of kin terms was related to local forms of adoption, most of which occur within the family. In 1991, for example, a young girl named Nancy moved into the household of her father Alfonso's prosperous, unmarried older sister, Heloisa, whom Nancy called *tía* ("aunt"). By 1993, however, Nancy was calling Heloisa *mama*. Everyone

ascribed statuses Social positions people are assigned at birth.

achieved statuses Social positions people may attain later in life, often as the result of their own (or other people's) effort.

concerned viewed this transition positively, a way of strengthening family solidarity in a difficult economic situation, and no one seemed worried about whether Heloisa was Nancy's "natural" mother or not.

People also often adopted children who were not kin. In both cases, however, the bond of adoption was created through nurturing, symbolized by the provision of food. Heloisa became Nancy's adoptive *mama* because she took care of her, fed her. Men in Zumbagua can also become the adoptive *tayta* of children by feeding them in front of witnesses who verbally proclaim what a "good father" the man is. However, the adoptive relationship does not gain recognition unless the adoptive parent continues feeding the child regularly for a long time. Weismantel discovered that the Zumbaguan family consists of those who eat together. The kinship bond results, they believe, because people who regularly eat the same food together eventually come to share "the same flesh," no matter who gave birth to them. Weismantel points out that feeding children is every bit as biological as giving birth to them: It is simply a different aspect of biology.

Indeed, in Zumbagua, a woman's biological tie to her offspring is given no greater weight than a man's biological tie to his. Many Zumbaguans are closer to their adopted family than they are to their biological parents. If genitor and genetrix are young and poor, moreover, they run a very real risk that they will lose their children to adoption by older, wealthier individuals. In other words, enduring kin ties in Zumbagua are achieved, not merely ascribed, statuses.

▼ HOW FLEXIBLE CAN RELATEDNESS BE?

Negotiation of Kin Ties among the Ju/'hoansi

Michael Peletz observes that many contemporary kinship studies in anthropology "tend to devote considerable analytic attention to themes of contradiction, paradox and ambivalence" (1995, 343). This is true both of Weismantel's study in Zumbagua and Richard Lee's analysis of kinship among the Ju/'hoansi. Lee learned that for the Ju/'hoansi "the principles of kinship constitute, not an invariant code of laws written in stone, but instead a whole series of codes, consis-

tent enough to provide structure but open enough to be flexible." He adds: "I found the best way to look at [Ju/'hoansi] kinship is as a game, full of ambiguity and nuance" (1992b, 62).

The Ju/'hoansi have what seems to be a straightforward bilateral kindred with alternating generations. Outside the nuclear core of the system, the same terms are used by Ego for kin of his or her generation, his or her grandparents' generation, and his or her grandchildren's generation. Likewise, the same terms are used for Ego's parents' generation and children's generation. These terms have behavioral correlates, which Lee calls "joking" and "avoidance." Anyone in Ego's own generation (except opposite-gender siblings) and in the grandparents' generation or the grandchildren's generation is joking kin. Anyone in Ego's parents' generation or children's generation is avoidance kin, as are Ego's same-gender siblings. Relatives in a joking relationship can be relaxed and affectionate and can speak using familiar forms. In an avoidance relationship, however, respect and reserve are required, and formal language must be used. Many of these relationships may be warm and friendly if the proper respect is shown in public: However, people in an avoidance relationship may not marry one another.

The "game," as Lee puts it, in the Ju/'hoansi system begins when a child is named. The Ju/'hoansi have very few names: 36 for men and 32 for women. Every child must be named for someone: A first-born son should get his father's father's name and a first-born daughter her father's mother's name. Second-born children are supposed to be named after the mother's father and mother. Later children are named after the father's brothers and sisters and the mother's brothers and sisters. It is no wonder that the Ju/'hoansi invent a host of nicknames to distinguish among people who have the same name. Ju/'hoansi naming practices impinge upon the kinship system because all people with the same name will claim to be related. A man older than you with your name is called *!kun!a* ("old name") which is the same term used for *grandfather*. A man younger than you with your name is called *!kuna* ("young name"), the same term used for *grandson*. It does not matter how people are "really" related to others with the same name or even if they are related at all according to formal kinship terminology; the name relationship takes precedence.

But the complications do not end here. By metaphorical extension, anyone with your father's name you call *father*, anyone with your wife's name you call *wife*, and so on. Worse, "a woman may not marry a man with her father's or brother's name, and a man may not marry a woman with his mother's or sister's name" (Lee 1992b, 74). Sometimes a man can marry a woman but because his name is the same as her father's she can't marry him! Further, you may not marry anyone with the name of one of your avoidance kin. As a result, parents who do not want their children to marry can almost always find a kinship-related reason to block the marriage. Once again, it does not matter what the exact genealogical relationships are.

The name relationship ties Ju/'hoansi society closer together by making close relatives out of distant ones. At the same time, it makes nonsense of the formal kinship system. How is this dilemma resolved? The Ju/'hoansi have a third component to their kinship system, the principle of *wi*, which operates as follows: relative age is one of the few ways the Ju/'hoansi have of marking distinctions. Thus, in any relationship that can be described by more than one kin relationship, the older party chooses the kin term to be used. For example, a man may get married only to discover that his wife's aunt's husband has the same name he has. What will he and his wife's aunt call each other? According to the principle of *wi*, the aunt decides because she is older. If she calls him *nephew* (rather than *husband*), he knows to call her *aunt*.

The principle of *wi* means that a person's involvement with the kinship system is continually changing over the course of his or her lifetime. For the first half of people's lives, they must accept the kin terms their elders choose, whether they understand why or not. After midlife, however, they begin to impose *wi* on their juniors. For the Ju/'hoansi, kinship connections are open to manipulation and negotiation rather than being rigidly imposed from the outside.

Iñupiaq Relatedness

An example of a society in which relatedness is defined far more broadly than biological kinship is the Iñupiat (EthnoProfile 11.7: Iñupiat; Figure 11.9). The Iñupiat are one of the Inuit peoples of the circumpolar region of North America. Those who live on the

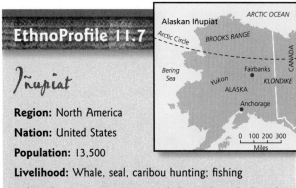

EthnoProfile 11.7

Iñupiat

Region: North America

Nation: United States

Population: 13,500

Livelihood: Whale, seal, caribou hunting; fishing

Political organization: Home rule borough, with elected Iñupiat-controlled Assembly

For more information: Bodenhorn, Barbara. 2000. "He used to be my relative": Exploring the bases of relatedness among Iñupiat of northern Alaska. In *Cultures of Relatedness: New approaches to the study of kinship*, ed. Janet Carsten, 128–48. Cambridge: Cambridge University Press.

North Slope of Northern Alaska are whalers. Barbara Bodenhorn (2000) writes that while there seems to be no term among the Iñupiat that can be translated into English as "family," the term *ilya* was consistently used for the English term "relative." Literally translated, it means "addition," and this is its significance in Iñupiaq relatedness. Iñupiat have a variety of ways of making "additions." One way to be *ilya* is through biology, but there are many other ways. Relatives are very important to the Iñupiat, and they have strong obligations to each other. But not even the bond between biological parent and child provides a fixed basis for a claim to the obligations of relatedness.

Bodenhorn observes that the Iñupiat value individual autonomy very highly and protect it carefully. For example, the organization of hunting is gendered: There are things that men do and things that women do. But once those tasks are fulfilled, men and women are equally free to develop expertise in the other's activities—there are women who are skilled hunters and men who cook and sew well. When the results of the hunt are shared, men and women receive shares equal to the work they have done, not according to gender or age. Iñupiat also extend autonomy to children, whom they believe decide for themselves when they are going to be born, and may even decide which sex they are going to be before they are born.

FIGURE 11.9 Iñupiat whalers prepare to set out to hunt whales. Members of the crew may be related in a variety of different ways.

The Iñupiat calculate kin relations bilaterally, but very flexibly: "anyone considered a relative to anyone you consider a relative may be your relative. And if a clear line is impossible to establish, *kinguvaaqatigiich* (through the generations somehow) will do" (135). Some anthropologists suggest that it is useful to distinguish two domains of kinship terminology among Inuit peoples, one based on how people become the relative, and the other the moral commitments being such a relative entails. Bodenhorn notes that the category of "younger brother" (*nukaaluk*) is one with a number of obligations and commitments. There are three ways to become a younger brother: men can be siblings through having been born of the same woman, through adoption, or through having parents who once had a sexual relationship that they acknowledged publicly. They do not have to be the offspring of such a relationship; in fact, all offspring

of two people who had such a relationship can consider themselves siblings, regardless of who the other partner may have been.

It should be clear that the universe of possible relatives for the Iñupiat is vast! As a result it is useful to distinguish between relatedness that cannot be denied without incurring social disapproval and relatedness by choice. In the former category are parents, grandparents, and siblings; in the latter, everyone else. These are people Bodenhorn describes as "kin who are kin because they—and you—act like kin" (136). She remarks that "it was not uncommon to hear the comment 'he used to be my cousin.'"

Naming is another way in which relatedness is formed among the Iñupiat, and makes an interesting contrast with the Ju/'hoansi case. The Iñupiat believe that names play an important role in transforming babies into real people. This is because names contain personal essence which attaches to the human being who is given the name. The name connects the previous bearer of the name to the baby and shapes the character and person of that baby. Apparently, almost anyone can give a baby a name. They may be relatives, but they do not have to be. It is never just the parents who give names, and in fact, they may have no input at all into the baby's names. Sometimes the names are the names of deceased relatives, but they do not have to be. The person who gives the name sees something in the baby that indicates a specific connection with someone else who is deceased. This can be a facial expression, an apparent familiarity with a place, or seeming to recognize a particular person the first time the baby sees him or her. None of this is based on gender. People can and do inherit names—and the personal essence that goes along with them—from both men and women.

Names also establish how the person with the name will relate to the relatives of the person who gave the name. "Thus a young girl may be addressed as '*aapa*,' grandfather, by those who are grandchildren of the original name provider" (138). All of the personal essences of the names a child is given (and there may be several) are what create any specific person. This means that a person's identity alters depending on the group of people with whom he or she is interacting—to one group she is "grandfather," to another she may be "sister," and to yet a third she may be "cousin." Names, then, have nothing to do with who the person's parents are, or the descent group to which he or she belongs, or his or her gender. They create and extend "additions" from the past into the future.

Finally, adoption, which is very common in the polar region, highlights how the practice of parenting overrides "begetting and bearing." Bodenhorn estimates that most adults have themselves been adopted or have lived in a household in which children have been adopted. People who adopt usually know each other, but do not have to be close kin. The most common reason that people gave Bodenhorn for adopting was that they "wanted to"; or that they had too many boys and wanted a girl (or vice versa); that "all my other brothers and sisters have adopted"; "we kind of exchanged"; or "we had too many kids."

Often adoption occurred because the child wanted to be adopted. In many cases, the shift was to everyone's satisfaction, but even when it was not, the question of where the child should end up was never based on the argument that it naturally belonged with its biological parents. After adoption, the degree to which a relationship is maintained between the birth parents and the child is up to the child, and ranges from no contact to regular shared activities. The point here is that recognition of the biological relationship becomes a matter of choice—there is no social stigma involved if a child ignores its biological parents, but people do disapprove if the child does not act like a son or daughter to its adoptive parents, who are real.

In fact, the tasks of a family are spread out broadly and none of those tasks is seen as naturally the domain of the birth parents. After all, who the child is socially comes from its names; the grandparents often provide the moral upbringing; aunts and uncles are the disciplinarians; everyone who is related nurtures. So what do parents do? Bodenhorn quotes Raymond Neakok, one of her older informants: "My people believed at the time when they were growing up, that parents had only one thing to do with the children—just love . . . their whole heart. They brought me up that way. Though it has changed, it hasn't changed much—the only thing they could give me was love" (141).

From the Iñupiaq perspective, then, the people who do the parenting are the parents—biology does not create parents, but action does. Thus, many kinds of people may play the role of parents. People do not deny biological kinship, but their primary relationships are with the people who brought them up. There seems to be little that is permanent about Iñupiaq relatedness, for people move in and out of relatedness with others. From another perspective, however, it is the possibility of reactivating "additions" at any time that endures. But to reactivate "additions," people have to act, and act intentionally. This is kinship based on agency: "What is real is acted on and mutually recognized" (143). Keeping such ties active is not easy. Because relatedness is not permanent, the maintenance of connections requires constant reciprocal activity: "shared tools, food, labor, political alliance, ceremonial participation, and simply company. . . . It is *this* labor—the work of being related—rather than the labor of giving birth, of the 'fact' of shared substance that marks out the kinship sphere from the potentially infinite universe of relatives who may or may not belong" (143).

European American Kinship and New Reproductive Technologies

Western medicine has developed new reproductive technologies, such as *in vitro* fertilization, sperm banks, and surrogate motherhood, that are creating challenges not only for law and morality, but also for Western concepts of kinship (Figure 11.10). Marilyn Strathern (1992) observes that in the European American world, kinship is understood as the social construction of natural facts, a logic that both combines and separates the social and natural worlds. That is, European Americans recognize kin related by blood and kin related by marriage, but they also believe that the process—procreation—that brings kin into existence is part of nature. "The rooting of social relations in natural facts traditionally served to impart a certain quality to one significant dimension of kin relations. For all that one exercised choice, it was also the

case that these relations were at base non-negotiable" (Strathern 1992, 28). Ties of kinship are supposed to stand for what is unalterable in a person's social world in contrast to what is open to change. Yet the new reproductive technologies make clear that nothing is unalterable: even the world of natural facts is subject to social intervention.

As Janet Dolgin (1995) reports, contemporary ambiguities surrounding kinship in the United States have put pressure on the courts to decide what constitutes biological parenthood and how it is related to legal parenthood. She examined two sets of recent cases, the first involving the paternal rights of unwed putative fathers and the second focusing on the rights of parties involved in surrogate motherhood agreements. In two cases involving putative unwed fathers, courts reasoned that biological maternity automatically made a woman a social mother but biological paternity did not automatically make a man a social father. Because the men in these two cases had failed to participate in rearing their children, their paternity rights were not recognized. In

FIGURE 11.10 In vitro fertilization (IVF), one of the new reproductive technologies, is already having an effect on what it means to be a "natural" parent. Over 1,000 IVF babies gathered in 2003 to celebrate the twenty-fifth anniversary of the birth of the first IVT baby, Louise Brown (center front).

another case, the biological father had lived with his child and her mother for extended periods during the child's early years and had actively participated in her upbringing. However, the child's mother had been married to another man during this period, and the law proclaimed her legal husband to be the child's father. Although the genitor had established a supportive relationship with his daughter, the court labeled him "the adulterous natural father," arguing, in effect, that a genitor can never be a pater unless he is involved in an ongoing relationship with the child's mother, something that was clearly impossible because she was already married to someone else.

The surrogacy cases demonstrate directly the complications that can result from new reproductive technologies. The "Baby M" situation was a traditional surrogacy arrangement in which the surrogate, Mary Beth Whitehead, was impregnated with the sperm of the husband in the couple who intended to become the legal parents of the child she bore. Whitehead was supposed to terminate all parental rights when the child was born, but she refused to do so. The court faced a dilemma. Existing law backed Whitehead's maternal rights, but the court was also concerned that the surrogacy agreement looked too much like babyselling or womb-rental. The court's opinion focused on Whitehead's attempt to break the surrogacy contract to justify terminating her legal rights, although she was awarded visitation rights.

More complicated than traditional surrogacy, *gestational surrogacy* deconstructs the role of genetrix into two roles that can be performed by two different women. In a key case, the Calverts, a childless married couple, provided egg and sperm that were used in the laboratory to create an embryo, which was then implanted in Anna Johnson's uterus. But when Johnson gave birth to the baby, she refused to give it up. As Dolgin points out, this case "provided a context in which to measure the generality of the assumption that the gestational role both produces and constitutes maternity" (1995, 58). As we have seen, several other court cases emphasized the role of gestation in forming an indissoluble bond between mother and child. In this case, however, the court referred to Anna Johnson "as a 'gestational carrier,' a 'genetic hereditary stranger' to the child, who acted like a 'foster parent'" (1995, 59). The court declared the Calverts and the child a family unit on genetic grounds and ruled that the Calverts were the baby's "natural" and legal parents.

Dolgin notes that in all of these cases, the courts awarded legal custody to those parties whose living arrangements most closely approximated the traditional middle-class, North American two-parent family. "Biological facts were called into judicial play only . . . when they justified the preservation of traditional families" (1995, 63). Biological facts that might have undermined such families were systematically overlooked. Perhaps the clear-cut biological basis of North American kinship is not so clear-cut after all.

Compadrazgo in Latin America

An important set of kinship practices in Roman Catholic Latin America is **compadrazgo**, or ritual coparenthood. The baptism of a child requires the presence of a godmother and a godfather as sponsors. By participating in this ritual, the sponsors become the ritual coparents of the child. In Latin America, godparents are expected to take an active interest in their godchildren and to help them wherever possible. However, the more important relationship is between the godparents and the parents. They become *compadres* ("coparents"), and they are expected to behave toward each other in new ways.

Sometimes the godparents are already kin; in recent years, for example, Nicaraguans have been choosing relatives living in the United States as compadres (Lancaster 1992, 66). A couple often chooses godparents whose social standing is higher than their own: the owners of the land they farm, for example, or of the factory where they work. Participating together in the baptism changes these unequal strangers into ritual kin whose relationship, although still unequal, is now personalized, friendlier, more open. The parents will support the godparents when that support is needed (politically, for example), and the godparents will do favors for the parents. They even call each other *compadre* rather than, say, "Señor López" and "José."

compadrazgo Ritual coparenthood in Latin America and Spain, established through the Roman Catholic practice of having godparents for children.

Catherine Allen notes that the bonds of *compadrazgo*, in combination with marriage alliances and kinship, "form constellations of mutual obligation and dependence that shift with time as new compadrazgo relationships are formed, young relatives come of age, and old bonds fall into disuse through death or quarreling. Like kin ties, bonds of compadrazgo can become as much a burden as an asset, and like kin ties they can be ignored or honored in the breach" (1988, 90).

▼ HOW CAN PRACTICES OF RELATEDNESS PRODUCE UNEXPECTED OUTCOMES?

Kinship systems are not straitjackets; as we have seen, they offer a flexible series of opportunities for people to choose how to deal with others. They also provide multiple social vectors along which relations of alliance, association, mutual support, opposition, and hatred may develop—all of which are thrown into high relief under changing social and political contexts.

Conflicting Obligations among the Iteso

In his work on the Iteso of Kenya, Ivan Karp discusses the options for action that a kinship system can provide (principally Karp 1978) (see EthnoProfile 11.8: Iteso). Karp notes that among the Iteso, affinal and **consanguineal** kin have very different and even contradictory rights and obligations to one another. Two people who share links both through marriage and patrilineal descent must choose which tie to emphasize; it is often the affinal tie rather than the consanguineal tie. However, they may be ambivalent about the choice. Close members of a patrilineage often quarrel and may be ritually dangerous to one another, but they will—indeed, must—help one another in ritual and conflict situations. By contrast, affinal relatives are amiable and helpful but cannot be counted on in times of crisis.

Karp recounts a story that serves as an example. An Iteso man who was widowed and had remarried moved away from his lineage and was living with his

---

consanguineal Kinship connections based on descent.

EthnoProfile 11.8

Iteso

Region: Eastern Africa

Nations: Kenya and Uganda

Population: 150,000 in Kenya; 600,000 in Uganda (1970s)

Environment: High-rainfall savanna and hills

Livelihood: Agriculture, both subsistence and cash

Political organization: Traditionally, chiefs, subchiefs, headmen; today, part of modern nation-states

For more information: Karp, Ivan. 1978. *Fields of change among the Iteso of Kenya*. London: Routledge and Kegan Paul.

maternal kin. His daughters by his first marriage were living with their mother's brother. One daughter was bitten by a snake and died. Karp was asked to help bring the body back to her father's house for burial. The father went to all his neighbors—his maternal kin—for help in burying her, but none would help. Only at the last moment did some members of his patrilineage arrive to help with the burial. This story illustrates the drawbacks associated with living apart from one's close lineage mates. The father had left himself open to a lack of support in a crisis by cutting himself off from his lineage and choosing to live with his maternal kin. Moreover, the Iteso kinship system provides no rule for resolving conflicting loyalties to maternal and paternal kin. Indeed, the system almost ensures the creation of overlapping loyalties that are difficult to resolve.

Assisted Reproduction in Israel

Similar unanticipated trajectories that derive from our systems of relatedness are being opened by recent biotechnological advances, such as assisted reproduction; these practices are already transforming and complicating traditional understandings of human connectedness in any society that adopts them. For example, studying assisted reproduction in Israel (see EthnoProfile 11.9: Israel) led Susan Martha Kahn to ask whether Jewish ideas about kinship are or are not usefully understood as "Euro-American," especially since Jews have lived for millennia within the boundaries of many different societies outside Europe and America. Within Israel itself, Euro-American ideas about kinship coexist with other ideas from elsewhere that developed among different Jewish populations long before the state of Israel was founded; moreover, "multiple and often contradictory popular opinions about these matters have always simultaneously co-existed, competed, and conflicted with each other" (Kahn 2000, 161–2). This means that it is important not to equate Jewish ideas about kinship in Israel with "Euro-American kinship thinking" and to recognize that "Jewish" and "Euro-American" conceptual frameworks for imagining kinship make "differing assumptions about genetic relatedness and its role in establishing kinship" (2000, 162–3).

As a result, assisted reproduction has played a very different role in Israel than it has played in the United States. First, Israelis in general are pronatalist: They believe they have a duty to produce children, for a variety of historical and political reasons (2000, 3). Second, through its national health insurance programs, the Israeli state supports both families and unmarried mothers, and this support includes heavily subsidized access to reproductive technologies for all women, married or not. As one Israeli woman told Kahn, "It is considered much worse to be a childless woman than to be an unmarried mother" (2000, 16). Third, Kahn found that most Jews of all backgrounds endorse the idea that Jewishness is passed on to children matrilineally—that is, from one's mother, not from one's father. As a result, "genetic relatedness is a considerably more plastic category in rabbinic thinking about kinship; it can be conceptually erased, made invisible, or otherwise reconfigured" (2000, 165).

One consequence of this is that religious authorities agree that "the specific identity and origin of sperm is conceptualized as irrelevant to Jewish reproduction" (2000, 166). On the one hand, this means that infertile couples are encouraged (and subsidized by the state) to use assisted reproduction. On the other hand, assisted reproduction "has revealed curious and provocative loopholes within the rabbinic imagination of relatedness" that "implicitly allow for and legitimate Jewish children conceived by unmar-

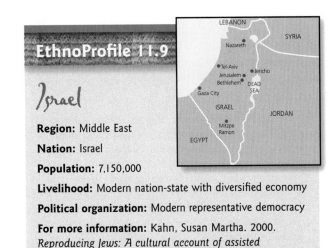

EthnoProfile 11.9

Israel

Region: Middle East

Nation: Israel

Population: 7,150,000

Livelihood: Modern nation-state with diversified economy

Political organization: Modern representative democracy

For more information: Kahn, Susan Martha. 2000. *Reproducing Jews: A cultural account of assisted conception in Israel.* Durham, NC: Duke University Press.

ried Jewish women as well as by infertile Jewish couples who conceive children with reproductive genetic material donated by anonymous non-Jews" (2000, 170).

Organ Transplantation and the Creation of New Relatives

Equally curious and provocative are the new kinds of kin ties that have emerged in the United States, following the increasingly widespread use of biomedical and surgical techniques that allow bodily organs to be salvaged from brain-dead individuals and transplanted into the bodies of others. Lesley Sharp reports that professionals who manage the many steps involved in organ transplantation have, until very recently, attempted to keep the families of organ donors from finding out the identities of organ recipients. The rather paternalistic justification given was that keeping people ignorant would be good for their psychic health. But Sharp reports that donor kin and organ recipients have found ways to find each other and meet face-to-face, and her research contradicted the fears of the professionals: Out of 30 recorded cases of such meetings, only one failed (2006, 191).

An important outcome of the bringing together of donor kin and organ recipients has been the development of kinship relationships linking donor kin to those who received organs from their relatives. Affected individuals struggle with the question of what Sharp calls "donor ownership": "What rights do surviving kin have to trace the whereabouts of the remains of the lost loved one? Can one, for instance, assert claims of access—or postmortem visiting rights?" (2006, 190). Sharp's research showed her that

> donor kin and recipients alike share the understanding that transplanted organs, as donor fragments, carry with them some essence of their former selves, and this persists in the bodies of recipients. The donor then becomes a transmigrated soul of sorts, one that generates compelling dilemmas for involved parties. . . . At risk here is the further shattering of each person's world; yet, as successful encounters reveal, potentially each party is partially healed in the process. (2006, 190)

One example Sharp offers involves Sally and Larry. Both had been involved in activities promoting organ donation and had known each other for several years, before they learned that Sally's son had provided the heart now beating inside Larry's body. When Sharp interviewed them, Sally was in her mid-fifties and a widow; Larry was a dozen years older and married. Right after his transplant surgery, and against the advice of his doctors, Larry had begun trying to find the family of the teenager who had provided his heart, and his wife, "Bulldog," helped him find Sally. Larry and Sally exchanged letters and met

three years later. As they got to know one another, Larry, Sally, and Sally's daughter began to use kin terms to refer to one another.

> For example, Larry addresses Sally's daughter as "Sis," and she calls him "Bro." After Larry's own birth mother died, he then began to address Sally as "Mom," and she now calls him "Son." As Sally explained, Larry now sends her a Mother's Day card. These terms have facilitated the establishment of an elaborate joking relationship. . . . They are mildly troubled by the adulterous overtones of their relationship, one laced, too, I would assert, with the incestuous, given that Larry now harbors part of Charlie inside his body. (188)

Sharp found that, of all kinship statuses, the role of the donor mother was particularly important among those whom she interviewed (Figure 11.11). In this case, emphasizing Sally's role as donor mother helped Sally and Larry deal with the "adulterous" or "incestuous" overtones in their relationship. "In assuming the role of donor mother to Larry, she eliminates the discomfort that arises when one considers their proximity in age. In essence, the mother–son bond trumps age" (2006, 190). Interestingly, traditionally North American understandings about "blood" relations extend to Larry but not to his wife: " Today, Sally, Larry, and Bulldog are dear to one another," but

FIGURE 11.11 The families of organ donors and the recipients of those organs have begun to meet face-to-face in the United States. A heart recipient (center, facing camera) embraces the mother of the young man whose heart he received; his wife (right) and the young man's sister (left) look on.

"there is no special term of address reserved for Bull-dog. . . . Structurally, she is simply 'Larry's wife,' whereas Larry, in embodying Charlie's heart, is now embraced as blood kin" (2006, 190).

▼ KINSHIP AS SOCIAL IDIOM

Kinship may seem awesomely complete and utterly basic to the life of some societies, but, as the preceding discussion makes clear, formalized kinship systems vary in importance between societies and even between subgroups within the same society. As we have seen, more than one system of relatedness may be found in most societies, and these systems can overlap with, contradict, or completely ignore connections based on formal kinship. Some kinds of imagined communities, however, may use kin ties as resources out of which to construct new forms of relatedness at a broader social scale. For example, many societies of foragers, farmers, and herders have developed forms of imagined community that anthropologist Elman Service called *pantribal sodalities* (1962, 113).

Furthermore, formal kinship is only one way of thinking about how people relate themselves to one another. As the case studies of adoption, assisted reproduction, and organ transplantation illustrate, the everyday lived experiences of people can provide them with unanticipated opportunity to create new cultures of relatedness that are meaningful, that enable them to get on with life, that follow their own (sometimes surprising) internal logic, and that frequently allow individuals to evade the attempts of others who would impose systems of organization, control, or analysis on them.

▼ SODALITIES

Sodalities are "special-purpose groupings" that may be organized on the basis of age, sex, economic role, or personal interest. "[Sodalities] serve very different functions—among them police, military, medical, initiation, religious [Figure 11.12], and recreation. Some sodalities conduct their business in secret, others in public. Membership may be assigned at birth, or it may be obtained via inheritance, purchase, attain-

ment, performance, or contract. Men's sodalities are more numerous and highly organized than women's and, generally, are also more secretive and exclusive in their activities" (Hunter and Whitten 1976, 362). Examples of sodalities include military societies of indigenous people of the Great Plains, such as the Cheyenne, and the age set systems found among a number of neighboring peoples in eastern Africa. One distinctive form of sodality—the secret societies—is found in western Africa.

Secret Societies in Western Africa   Several neighboring peoples in western Africa use **secret societies** as a way of drawing members of different kinship groups into crosscutting associations. The most famous secret societies are the Poro and Sande, which are found among the Mende, Sherbro, Kpelle, and other neighboring peoples of Sierra Leone, Ivory Coast, Liberia, and Guinea.

Membership and Initiation   Poro is a secret society for men; Sande is a secret society for women. Poro is responsible for initiating young men into social manhood; Sande is responsible for initiating young women into social womanhood. These sodalities are secret in the sense that members of each have certain knowledge that can be revealed only to initiated members. Both sodalities are hierarchically organized. The higher a person's status within the sodality, the greater the secret knowledge revealed.

Poro and Sande are responsible for supervising and regulating the sexual, social, and political conduct of all members of the wider society. To carry out this responsibility, high-status sodality members impersonate important supernatural figures by donning masks and performing in public. One secret kept from the uninitiated is that these masked figures are not the spirits themselves.

Membership is automatic on initiation, and all men and women are ordinarily initiated. "Until he has been initiated in the society, no Mende man is

sodality A special-purpose grouping that may be organized on the basis of age, sex, economic role, or personal interest.

secret society A form of social organization that initiates young men or women into social adulthood. The "secrecy" concerns certain knowledge that is known only to initiated members of the secret society.

FIGURE 11.12 Members of the Oruro, Bolivia, devil sodality dance.

considered mature enough to have sexual intercourse or to marry" (Little 1967, 245; see EthnoProfile 12.5: Mende). Each community has its own local Poro and Sande congregations, and a person initiated into one community is eligible to participate in the congregations of other communities. Initiates must pay a fee for initiation; if they wish to receive advanced training and progress to higher levels within the sodality, they must pay additional fees. In any community where Poro and Sande are strong, authority in society is divided between a sodality of mature women and one of mature men. Together, they work to keep society on the correct path. Indeed, the relationship between men and women in societies with Poro and Sande tends to be highly egalitarian.

Anthropologist Beryl Bellman (1984) was initiated into a Poro chapter among the Kpelle of Liberia (see EthnoProfile 6.2: Kpelle). He describes initiation as a ritual process that takes place about every 16–18 years, about once a generation (Figure 11.13). One of the Poro's forest spirits, or "devils," metaphorically captures and eats the novices—only for them later to be metaphorically reborn from the womb of the devil's "wife." Marks incised on the necks, chests, and backs of initiates represent the "devil's teeth marks." After this scarification, initiates spend a year

living apart from women in a special village constructed for them in the forest. During this period, they carry out various activities under the strict supervision of senior Poro members. Female Sande initiates undergo a similar experience during their year of initiation, which normally takes place several years after the Poro initiation has been completed.

Use of the Kinship Idiom   In Kpelle society, the relationship between a mother's brother (*ngala*) and a sister's son (*maling*) describes the formal relationship between kin. There is also a metaphoric aspect to this connection that is used to describe relationships between patrilineages, sections of a town, and towns themselves. "Besides the serious or formal rights and obligations between *ngala* and *maling*, other aspects of the relationship are expressed as joking behavior between kinsmen. . . . The *ngala–maling* relationship is also the basis of labor recruitment, financial assistance, and a general support network" (Bellman 1984, 22–23). This kinship idiom is used within the Poro society to describe the relationships between certain members. For example, two important Poro officials involved in initiation are the *Zo* and the *kwelebah*. The Zo directs the ritual, and the kwelebah announces both the ritual death and the ritual rebirth

FIGURE 11.13 Young men returning from their initiation into the Poro secret society in March 2007.

of the initiates to the community at large. The Zo is said to be the ngala of the kwelebah, and the kwelebah is said to be the maling of the Zo.

The Thoma Secret Society: A Microcosm Anthropologist Carol MacCormack (1980) studied secret societies among the Sherbro (see EthnoProfile 11.10: Sherbro). In addition to Poro and Sande congregations, the Sherbro have a third secret society called *Thoma*, which initiates both men and women. Members of one society cannot be initiated into the others, and families with several children usually try to initiate at least one child into each.

MacCormack writes: "With Poro and Sande, the contrastive gender categories are split apart and the uniqueness of each gender is emphasized, but always with the final view that the complementarity of the two constitute human society, the full cultural unity. Thoma is a microcosm of the whole. Its local congregations or chapters are headed by a man and a woman, co-equal leaders who are 'husband and wife' in a ritual context but are not married in mundane life" (1980, 97). The Sherbro are concerned with the reproduction of their society. *Reproduction* here means not just production of children but also continuation of the division of labor between men and women. The Sherbro say that the ritual function of the Thoma

sodality is to "wash the bush"—that is, "to cleanse the land and the village from evil and restore its fertility and well-being" (98).

The purpose of Thoma initiation is to transform uninitiated, protosocial beings into initiated, fully

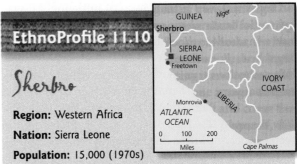

EthnoProfile 11.10

Sherbro

Region: Western Africa

Nation: Sierra Leone

Population: 15,000 (1970s)

Environment: Rainy, swampy coastal area with sandy soil

Livelihood: Shallow-water fishing and hoe cultivation of rice

Political organization: Chiefdoms that are part of a modern nation-state

For more information: MacCormack, Carol. 1980. Protosocial to adult: A Sherbro transformation. In *Nature, culture, and gender*, ed. Carol MacCormack and Marilyn Strathern, 95–118. Cambridge: Cambridge University Press.

social adult human beings. The Thoma society has four masks representing two pairs of spirits: an animal pair and a humanoid pair. The masks, which are considered very powerful, appear when initiates are nearing the end of their ritual seclusion in the forest. They "symbolize that 'wild,' unsocialized children are being transformed into cultured adults, but will retain the fertile vigour of the animal world" (MacCormack 1980, 100). The humanoid masks represent male and female ancestral spirits who appear when the initiates are about to be reborn into their new, adult status. "Human beings must abide by ancestral rules of conduct if they are to be healthy and fertile. Indeed, they wish to be as healthy and strong as forest animals which give birth in litters. Only by becoming fully 'cultural,' vowing to live by ancestral laws, may they hope to avoid illness and barrenness" (116).

The Meaning of Secrecy in a Secret Society   Bellman was interested in the secrecy that surrounded membership in Poro and other, similar sodalities. He argued that Poro (and Sande) initiation rituals are primarily concerned with teaching initiates how to keep a secret. Discretion—knowing when, how, and even whether to speak about various topics—is a prized virtue among the Kpelle and is required of all mature members of their society. So learning how to "practice secrecy" is a central lesson of initiation. "It was always crucial for members to be certain whether they have the right to talk as well as the right to know. The two are not necessarily related. Nonmembers very often know some of the secrets of membership; yet they must maintain a description of the event comparable to that of nonmembers" (1984, 51).

Based on this interpretation of "secrecy" in the secret society he knew, Bellman analyzed what the secret societies meant to outsiders. What do the uninitiated actually believe about these societies? In the case of the Poro, the women speak of devils killing and eating novices as though they believe this to be literally true. Bellman and his informants believe that the women know perfectly well what is "really" happen-

ing when Poro novices are taken away into the forest. But women are not allowed to talk about what they know except in the language of ritual metaphor. In the context of the initiation ritual, participation of the "audience" of women and other noninitiates is as important as the participation of the Poro elders and the initiates themselves. In playing their appropriate ritual role, women show respect for traditional understandings concerning which members of society have the right to speak about which topics, in which manner, and under which circumstances. "The enactment of Poro rituals serves to establish the ways in which that concealed information is communicated. . . . It offers methods for mentioning the unmentionable" (1984, 141).

▼ THE DIMENSIONS OF GROUP LIFE

The discussion of relatedness in this chapter as well as of the kinds of imagined communities that different forms of relatedness can produce provides a context within which to approach a form of imagined community that often depends on and sustains other kinds of social groupings: families. Imagined communities that anthropologists and others identify as families regularly depend for their social legitimacy on a particular form of relatedness that anthropologists and others call *marriage*. Anthropological approaches to issues of marriage and family are the focus of chapter 12.

But anthropological studies of imagined communities do not end there. The forms of imagined community we have described in this chapter all developed in societies whose component groups were roughly equal to one another in terms of wealth, power, and prestige—**egalitarian societies**. Many anthropologists would argue that a broad threshold is crossed once social organization becomes hierarchical and social inequality becomes permanent. Social organization based on class or caste marks a change not just in degree of complexity but also in kind of complexity, with important consequences for the kinds of community relationships that can be forged. For example, we have seen that in egalitarian societies like those of the Mende and the Sherbro, gender relations

---

egalitarian society A society in which no great differences in wealth, power, or prestige divide members from one another.

were not characterized by vast differences in wealth, power, or prestige, but this situation often changes in the face of hierarchy and other forms of social inequality. At the same time, complex forms of social organization do not develop in a vacuum. Many of the social organizational complexities of the contemporary world, including hierarchies based on race, ethnicity, and nationality, took shape during the 500 years of European imperial expansion. Moreover, at the beginning of the twenty-first century, the group life of all societies—what goes on locally in face-to-face communities—is everywhere affected by forces that originate elsewhere in the world. These themes are the focus of chapter 14.

CHAPTER SUMMARY

1. Human life is group life; we depend on one another to survive. All societies invent forms of relatedness to organize this interdependence. People in all societies recognize that they are connected to certain other people in a variety of ways and that they are not connected to some people at all. Anthropologists have traditionally paid closest attention to those formal systems of relatedness called kinship systems. But anthropologists also draw attention to other forms of relatedness, like friendship, that may provide ways of counterbalancing relations with kin. It is important to remember that all forms of relatedness are always embedded in and shaped by politics, economics, and worldviews.

2. To recognize the varied forms that institutions of human relatedness can take is to acknowledge fundamental openness in the organization of human interdependence. New shared experiences offer raw material for the invention of new forms of common identity. Anthropologists now argue that all communities—even face-to-face communities—larger than a single individual are contingent, "imagined" communities. That is, all human communities are social, cultural, and historical constructions. They are the joint outcome of shared habitual practices and of symbolic images of common identity promulgated by group members with an interest in making a particular imagined identity endure.

3. Friendships are relatively "unofficial" bonds of relatedness that are personal, affective, and, to a varying extent from society to society, a matter of choice. Nevertheless, in some societies, friendships may be so important that they are formalized like marriages. Depending on the society, friendships may be developed to strengthen kin ties or to subvert kin ties, because friendship is understood as the precise opposite of formal kin ties. This illustrates the ways in which people everywhere struggle to find ways to preserve certain ties of relatedness without being dominated by them.

4. The system of social relations that is based on prototypical procreative relationships is called kinship. Kinship principles are based on but not reducible to the universal human experiences of mating, birth, and nurturance. Kinship systems help societies maintain social order without central government. Although female–male duality is basic to kinship, many socities have developed supernumerary sexes or genders.

5. Patterns of descent in kinship systems are selective. Matrilineal societies emphasize that women bear children and trace descent through women. Patrilineal societies emphasize that men impregnate women and trace descent through men. Adoption pays attention to relationships based on nurturance, whether or not they are also based on mating and birth.

6. Descent links members of different generations with one another. Bilateral descent results in the formation of groups called *kindreds* that include all relatives from both parents' families. Unilineal descent results in the formation of groups called *lineages* that trace

descent through either the mother or the father. Unlike kindreds, lineages are corporate groups. Lineages control important property, such as land, that collectively belongs to their members. The language of lineage is the idiom of political discussion, and lineage relationships are of political significance.

7. Kinship terminologies pay attention to certain attributes of people that are then used to define different classes of kin. The attributes most often recognized include from most to least common, generation, gender, affinity, collaterality, bifurcation, relative age, and the gender of the linking relative.

8. Anthropologists recognize six basic terminological systems according to their patterns of classifying cousins. In recent years, however, anthropologists have become quite skeptical of the value of these idealized models, because they are highly formalized and do not capture the full range of people's actual practices.

9. By prescribing certain kinds of marriage, lineages establish long-term alliances with one another. Two major types of prescriptive marriage patterns in unilineal societies are a father's sister's daughter marriage system (which sets up a pattern of direct exchange marriage) and a mother's brother's daughter marriage system (which sets up a pattern of asymmetrical exchange marriage).

10. Achieved kinship statuses can be converted into ascribed ones by means of adoption. In Zumbagua, Ecuador, most adults have several kinds of parents and several kinds of children, some adopted and some not. Zumbaguan adoptions are based on nurturance—in this case, the feeding by the adoptive parent of the adopted child.

11. From the complexities of Ju/'hoansi kinship negotiations to the unique features of *compadrazgo* in Latin America to the dilemmas created by new reproductive technologies and organ transplantation, anthropologists have shown clearly that kinship is a form of relatedness, a cultural construction that cannot be reduced to biology.

12. Many egalitarian societies have developed sodalities that build on formal kinship institutions to create imagined communities of wider scope. Members of sodalities, such as western African secret societies, ordinarily take on responsibility for various public functions of a governmental or ritual nature. Membership in such sodalities is often a mark of adulthood and may be connected with initiation rituals.

KEY TERMS

relatedness	unilineal descent	bifurcation
imagined communities	bilateral kindred	parallel cousins
friendship	patrilineage	cross cousins
kinship	matrilineage	ascribed statuses
marriage	lineages	achieved statuses
descent	clan	*compadrazgo*
adoption	segmentary opposition	consanguineal
sex	bridewealth	sodalities
gender	affinity	secret societies
bilateral descent	collaterality	egalitarian societies

SUGGESTED READINGS

Anderson, Benedict. 2006. *Imagined communities: Reflections on the origin and spread of nationalism*, Rev. ed. London: Verso. *Although Anderson's goal is to address the origin of nationalism, his insistence that all human communities—even those based on kinship—are imagined communities marks an important breakthrough for the study of human social forms. It can be read with profit not only in connection with this chapter, but also with the next.*

Bell, Sandra, and Simon Coleman, eds. 1999. *The anthropology of friendship*. Oxford: Berg. *A recent collection of articles on friendship, with contributions on Europe, Asia, Africa, and South America.*

Collier, Jane, and Sylvia Yanagisako, eds. 1987. *Gender and kinship: Essays toward a unified analysis*. Stanford: Stanford University Press. *An important collection of work on the connections between gender and kinship.*

Ginsburg, Faye D. 1998. *Contested lives: The abortion debate in an American community*. Updated ed. Berkeley: University of California Press. *A study of gender and procreation in the context of the abortion debate in Fargo, North Dakota, in the 1980s.*

Ginsburg, Faye D., and Rayna Rapp, eds. 1995. *Conceiving the new world order: The global politics of reproduction*. Berkeley: University of California Press. *An important collection of articles by anthropologists who address the ways human reproduction is structured across social and cultural boundaries.*

Kahn, Susan Martha. 2000. *Reproducing Jews: A cultural account of assisted conception in Israel*. Durham, NC: Duke University Press. *An exceptionally interesting ethnographic study of the effects of new reproductive technologies on kinship in Israel.*

Sharp, Lesley. 2006. *Strange harvest: Organ transplants, denatured bodies, and the transformed self*. Berkeley: University of California Press. *In addition to her discussion of posttransplant forms of kinship, Sharp addresses a range of related issues raised by organ transplantation, all of which—as her subtitle indicates—call into question traditional Western notions of natural bodies and autonomous selves.*

Smith, Mary F. [1954] 1981. *Baba of Karo*. Reprint. New Haven, CT: Yale University Press. *A remarkable document: The autobiography of a Hausa woman born in 1877 in what is today northern Nigeria. A master storyteller, Baba provides much information about Hausa patterns of friendship, clientage, adoption, kinship, and marriage.*

Stone, Linda. 2005. *Kinship and gender*, 3d ed. Boulder, CO: Westview. *A recent discussion of human reproduction and the social and cultural implications of male and female reproductive roles.*

Stone, Linda, ed. 2001. *New directions in anthropological kinship*. Lanham, MD: Rowman & Littlefield. *An excellent collection of recent articles on kinship.*

Chapter 12

Marriage and Family

All societies try to find ways not only to organize daily life and social relations among individuals, but also to locate individual groups in space and to sustain and perpetuate those relations over time. The cultural practices discussed in this chapter illustrate both commonalities and variation in the way these goals are achieved in different human groups.

The distinguished Indian novelist R. K. Narayan (1906–2001) writes in his autobiography about falling in love and getting married.

In July 1933, I had gone to Coimbatore, escorting my elder sister, and then stayed on in her house. There was no reason why I should ever hurry away from one place to another. I was a free-lance writer and I could work wherever I might be at a particular time. One day, I saw a girl drawing water from the street-tap and immediately fell in love with her. Of course, I could not talk to her. I learned later that she had not even noticed me passing and repassing in front of her while she waited to fill the brass vessels. I craved to get a clear, fixed, mental impression of her features, but I was handicapped by the time factor, as she would be available for staring at only until her vessels filled, when she would carry them off, and not come out again until the next water-filling time. I could not really stand and stare; whatever impression I had of her would be through a side-glance while passing the tap. I suffered from a continually melting vision. The only thing I was certain of was that I loved her, and I suffered the agonies of restraint imposed by the social conditions in which I lived. The tall headmaster, her father, was a friend of the family and often dropped in for a chat with the elders at home while on his way to the school, which was at a corner of our street. The headmaster, head-master's daughter, and the school were all within geographical reach and hailing distance, but the re-straint imposed by the social code created barriers. I attempted to overcome them by befriending the headmaster. He was a booklover and interested in lit-erary matters, and we found many common subjects for talk. We got into the habit of meeting at his school after the school-hours and discussing the world, seated comfortably on a cool granite *pyol* in front of a little shrine of Ganesha in the school compound. One memorable evening, when the stars had come out, I interrupted some talk we were having on political matters to make a bold, blunt announcement of my affection for his daughter. He was taken aback, but did not show it. In answer to my proposal, he just turned to the god in the shrine and shut his eyes in prayer. No one in our social condition could dare to proceed in the manner I had done. There were for-malities to be observed, and any talk for a marriage proposal could proceed only between the elders of the families. What I had done was unheard of. But the headmaster was sporting enough not to shut me up immediately. Our families were known to each other, and the class, community, and caste require-ments were all right. He just said, "if God wills it,"

and left it at that. He also said, "Marriages are made in Heaven, and who are we to say Yes or No?" After this he explained the difficulties. His wife and wom-enfolk at home were to be consulted, and my parents had to approve, and so on and so forth, and then the matching of the horoscopes—this last became a great hurdle at the end. . . .

What really mattered was not my economic out-look, but my stars. My father-in-law, himself an adept at the study of horoscopes, had consultations with one or two other experts and came to the con-clusion that my horoscope and the girl's were incom-patible. My horoscope had the Seventh House occu-pied by Mars, the Seventh House being the one that indicated . . . nothing but disaster unless the part-ner's horoscope also contained the same flaw, a case in which two wrongs make one right. . . .

In spite of all these fluctuations and hurdles, my marriage came off in a few months, celebrated with all the pomp, show, festivity, exchange of gifts, and the overcrowding, that my parents desired and expected.

Soon after my marriage, my father became bed-ridden with a paralytic stroke, and most of my mother's time was spent at his side upstairs. The new entrant into the family, my wife Rajam, was her deputy downstairs, managing my three younger brothers, who were still at school, a cook in the kitchen, a general servant, and a gigantic black-and-white Great Dane ac-quired by my elder brother, who was a dog-lover. She kept an eye on the stores, replenishing the food-stuffs and guarding them from being squandered or stolen by the cook. Rajam was less than twenty, but managed the housekeeping expertly and earned my mother's praise. She got on excellently with my brothers. This was one advantage of a joint family system—one had plenty of company at home. (1974, 106–10)

Narayan had fallen in love, gotten married, and set up housekeeping with his wife. These are familiar phases in the relationship of a man and a woman, yet the details of his description may seem extraordinary to many North Americans. Narayan's essay illustrates how the patterns of courtship, marriage, and house-keeping in India engage people in the wider patterns of Indian life. They channel emotion and economic ac-tivity. They also link previously unrelated people while binding individuals firmly to groups. One in-dividual, Narayan, fell in love with and married an-other, Rajam. But they could never have become a married couple without knowing how to maneuver within the cultural patterns that shaped their society. Neither could they have gotten married without the active intervention of the wider social groups to which they belonged—specifically, their families.

Getting married involves more than just living together or having sexual relations, and nowhere in the world is marriage synonymous with *mating*. In most societies, marriage also requires involvement and support from the wider social groups to which the spouses belong—first and foremost from their families. *Marriage* and *family* are two terms anthropologists use to describe how different societies understand and organize mating and its consequences.

▼ HOW DO ANTHROPOLOGISTS DEFINE MARRIAGE?

A prototypical **marriage** (1) transforms the status of the participants; (2) stipulates the degree of sexual access the married partners are expected to have to each other, ranging from exclusive to preferential; (3) perpetuates social patterns through the production or adoption of offspring; (4) creates relationships between the kin of the partners; and (5) is symbolically marked in some way, from an elaborate wedding to simply the appearance of a husband and wife seated one morning outside her hut.

Ordinarily, a prototypical marriage involves a man and a woman. But what are we to make of the following cases? Each offers an alternative way of understanding the combination of features that define appropriate unions in a particular society.

Woman Marriage and Ghost Marriage among the Nuer

Among the Nuer, as E. E. Evans-Pritchard observed during his fieldwork in the 1930s, a woman could marry another woman and become the "father" of the children the wife bore (see EthnoProfile 11.3: Nuer). This practice, which also appears in some other parts of Africa, involves a distinction between *pater* and *genitor* (see chapter 11). The female husband (the pater) had to have some cattle of her own to use for bridewealth payments to the wife's lineage. Once the bridewealth had been paid, the marriage was established. The female husband then got a male kinsman, friend, or neighbor (the genitor) to impregnate the wife and to help with certain tasks around the homestead that the Nuer believed could be done only by men.

Generally, Evans-Pritchard (1951) noted, a female husband was unable to have children herself, "and for this reason counts in some respects as a man." Indeed, she played the social role of a man. She could marry several wives if she was wealthy. She could demand damage payment if those wives engaged in sexual activity without her consent. She was the pater of her wives' children. On the marriage of her daughters, she received the portion of the bridewealth that traditionally went to the father, and her brothers and sisters received the portions appropriate to the father's side. Her children were named after her, as though she were a man, and they addressed her as *Father*. She administered her compound and her herds as a male head of household would, and she was treated by her wives and children with the same deference shown a male husband and father.

More common in Nuer social life was what Evans-Pritchard called the *ghost marriage*. The Nuer believed that a man who died without male heirs left an unhappy and angry spirit who might trouble his living kin. The spirit was angry because a basic obligation of Nuer kinship was for a man to be remembered through and by his sons: His name had to be continued in his lineage. To appease the angry spirit, a kinsman of the dead man—a brother or a brother's son—would often marry a woman "to his name." Bridewealth cattle were paid in the name of the dead man to the patrilineage of a woman. She was then married to the ghost but lived with one of his surviving kinsmen. In the marriage ceremonies and afterwards, this kinsman acted as though he were the true husband. The children of the union were referred to as though they were the kinsman's—but officially they were not. That is, the ghost husband was their pater, and his kinsman their genitor.

As the children got older, the name of their ghost father became increasingly important to them. The ghost father's name, not his stand-in's name, would be remembered in the history of the lineage. The social union between the ghost and the woman took precedence over the sexual union between the ghost's surrogate and the woman.

marriage An institution that prototypically transforms the status of a man and a woman, carries implications about permitted sexual access, gives the offspring a position in society, and establishes connections between the kin of the husband and the kin of the wife.

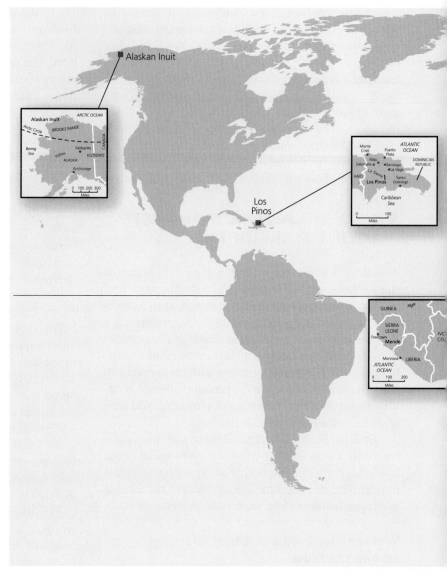

FIGURE 12.1 Location of societies whose EthnoProfiles appear in chapter 12.

Ghost marriage serves to perpetuate social patterns. Although it was common for a man to marry a wife "to his kinsman's name" before he himself married, it became difficult, if not impossible, for him to marry later in his own right. His relatives would tell him he was "already married" and that he should allow his younger brothers to use cattle from the family herd so they could marry. Even if he eventually accumulated enough cattle to afford to marry, he would feel that those cattle should provide the bridewealth for the sons he had raised for his dead kinsman. When he died, he died childless because the children he had raised were legally the children of the ghost. He was then an angry spirit, and someone else (in fact, one of the sons he had raised for the ghost) had to marry a wife to *his* name. Thus the pattern continued, as, indeed, it does into the present day.

▼ MARRIAGE AS A SOCIAL PROCESS

Like all formal definitions, our definition of marriage is somewhat rigid, especially if we think of marriage as a ritual action that accomplishes everything at a single point in time. However, if we think of marriage as a

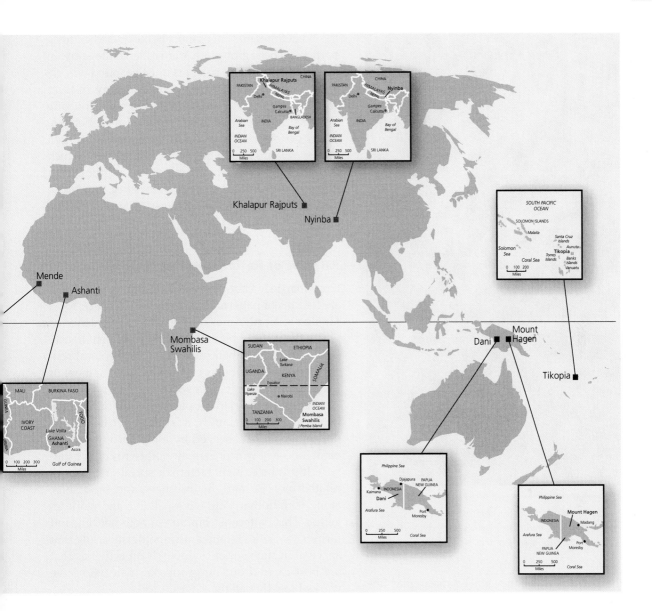

social process that unfolds over time, we find that our definition allows us to account for a wider range of marriage practices (Figure 12.2). For example, a marriage ritual may join spouses together, but their production of offspring who mature into recognized members of a particular social group takes time and cannot be assured in advance. Traditionally in some societies, a couple were not considered fully married until they had a child. Similarly, marriage set up new relations between the kin of both spouses, called **affinal** relationships (based on *affinity*—that is, created through marriage). As we saw in chapter 11, these contrast with descent-based **consanguineal** relationships (from the

Latin words for "same blood"). But a married couple's relationships with their affinal kin again develop over time, and whether they get along well and cooperate or become hostile to one another cannot be predicted or controlled when a marriage is first contracted. How successfully the married couple, their children, and their other relatives are able to manage the many challenges that emerge over time (economic transactions such as bridewealth payments, births, deaths, divorces)

affinal Kinship connections through marriage, or affinity.
consanguineal Kinship connections based on descent.

FIGURE 12.2 Marriage is a social process that creates social ties and involves more than just the people getting married. This is an elaborate marriage in Rajasthan, India.

affects the extent to which they will be able to play important roles in the wider society to which they belong. The lives of all are transformed, though not all at the same time or with the same outcome—shaping the future of the community as a whole.

endogamy Marriage within a defined social group.

exogamy Marriage outside a defined social group.

neolocal A postmarital residence pattern in which a married couple sets up an independent household at a place of their own choosing.

patrilocal A postmarital residence pattern in which a married couple lives with (or near) the husband's father.

matrilocal A postmarital residence pattern in which a married couple lives with (or near) the wife's mother.

avunculocal A postmarital residence pattern in which a married couple lives with (or near) the husband's mother's brother (from avuncular, "of uncles").

Sometimes marriages must be contracted within a particular social group, a pattern called **endogamy**. In other cases, marriage partners must be found outside a particular group, a pattern called **exogamy**. In Nuer society, for example, a person had to marry outside his or her lineage. Even in North American society, we prefer people to marry within the bounds of certain groups. We are told to marry "our own kind," which usually means our own ethnic or racial group, religious group, or social class. In all societies, some close kin are off limits as spouses or as sexual partners. This exogamous pattern is known as the *incest taboo*.

Patterns of Residence after Marriage

Once married, a couple must live somewhere. There are four major patterns of postmarital residence. Most familiar to North Americans is **neolocal** residence, in which the new couple sets up an independent household at a place of their own choosing. Neolocal residence tends to be found in societies that are more or less individualistic in their social organization.

When the married couple lives with (or near) the husband's father's family, it is called **patrilocal** residence, which is observed by more societies in the contemporary world than any other residence pattern. It produces a characteristic social grouping of related men: A man, his brothers, and their sons, along with in-marrying wives, all live and work together. This pattern is common in both herding and farming societies; some anthropologists argue that survival in such societies depends on activities that are best carried out by groups of men who have worked together all their lives.

When the married couple lives with (or near) the family in which the wife was raised, it is called **matrilocal** residence, which is usually found in association with matrilineal kinship systems. Here, the core of the social group consists of a woman, her sisters, and their daughters, together with in-marrying men. This pattern is most common among horticultural groups.

Less common, but also found in matrilineal societies, is the pattern known as **avunculocal** residence. Here, the married couple lives with (or near) the husband's mother's brother. The most significant man in a boy's matrilineage is his mother's brother, from whom he will inherit. Avunculocal residence emphasizes this relationship.

There are other, even less common patterns of residence. In *ambilocal* residence, the couple shifts residence, living first with the family of one spouse and later with the family of the other. At some point, the couple usually has to choose which family they want to affiliate with permanently. *Duolocal* residence is found where lineage membership is so important that husbands and wives continue to live with their own lineages even after they are married. The Ashanti of Ghana observe duolocal residence (see EthnoProfile 12.1: Ashanti). We will see later how this residence pattern affects other aspects of Ashanti social and cultural life.

Single and Plural Spouses

The number of spouses a person may have varies cross-culturally. Anthropologists distinguish forms of marriage in terms of how many spouses a person may have. **Monogamy** is a marriage form in which a person may have only one spouse at a time, whereas **polygamy** is a marriage system that allows a person to have more than one spouse. Within the category of polygamy are two subcategories: **polygyny**, or multiple wives, and **polyandry**, or multiple husbands. Most societies in the world permit polygyny.

Monogamy Monogamy is the only legal spousal pattern of the United States and most industrialized nations. (Indeed, in 1896, a condition of statehood for the territory of Utah was the abolition of polygyny, which had been practiced by Mormon settlers for nearly 50 years.) There are variations in the number of times a monogamous person can be married. Before the twentieth century, people in western European societies generally married only once unless death intervened. Today, some observers suggest that we practice *serial monogamy;* we may be married to several different people but only one at a time.

Polygyny Polygynous societies vary in the number of wives a man may have. Islam permits a man to have as many as four wives but only on the condition that he can support them equally. Some Muslim authorities today argue, however, that equal support must be emotional and affective, not just financial. Convinced that no man can feel the same toward each of his wives, they have concluded that monogamy must be the rule. Other polygynous societies have no

limit on the number of wives a man may marry. Nevertheless, not every man can be polygynous. There is a clear demographic problem: For every man with two wives, there is one man without a wife. Men can wait until they are older to marry and women can marry very young, but this imbalance cannot be completely eliminated. Polygyny is also expensive, for a husband must support all his wives as well as their children (Figure 12.3).

Polyandry Polyandry is the rarest of the three marriage forms. In some polyandrous societies, a woman may marry several brothers. In others, she may marry men who are not related to each other and who all will live together in a single household. Sometimes a woman is allowed to marry several men who are not related, but she will live only with the one she most recently married. Recent studies of polyandry have shed new light on the dynamics of polygyny and monogamy.

EthnoProfile 12.1

Ashanti

Region: Western Africa

Nation: Ghana

Population: 200,000

Environment: Slightly inland, partly mountainous

Livelihood: Farming, fishing, market trading (women)

Political organization: Traditionally, a kingdom; today, part of a modern nation-state

For more information: Fortes, Meyer. 1950. Kinship and marriage among the Ashanti. In *African systems of kinship and marriage*, ed. A. R. Radcliffe-Brown and Daryll Forde. Oxford: Oxford University Press.

monogamy A marriage pattern in which a person may be married to only one spouse at a time.

polygamy A marriage pattern in which a person may be married to more than one spouse at a time.

polygyny A marriage pattern in which a man may be married to more than one wife at a time.

polyandry A marriage pattern in which a woman may be married to more than one husband at a time.

FIGURE 12.3 The wives and children of a polygynous family.

Polyandry, Sexuality, and the Reproductive Capacity of Women

Different marriage patterns reflect significant variation in the social definition of male and female sexuality. Monogamy and polygyny are in some ways similar because both are concerned with controlling women's sexuality while giving men freer rein. Even in monogamous societies, men (but not women) are often expected to have extramarital sexual adventures. Polyandry is worth a closer look; it differs from polygyny or monogamy in instructive ways.

Polyandry is found in three major regions of the world: Tibet and Nepal, southern India and Sri Lanka, and northern Nigeria and northern Cameroon. The forms of polyandry in these areas are different, but all involve women with several husbands.

Fraternal Polyandry The traditional anthropological prototype of polyandry has been found among some groups in Nepal and Tibet, where a group of brothers marry one woman. This is known as *fraternal polyandry*. During one wedding, one brother, usually the oldest, serves as the groom. All brothers (including those yet to be born to the husbands' parents) are married by this wedding, which establishes public recognition of the marriage. The wife and her husbands live together, usually patrilocally. All brothers

have equal sexual access to the wife, and all act as fathers to the children. In some cases—notably among the Nyinba of Nepal (Levine 1980, 1988)—each child is recognized as having one particular genitor, who may be a different brother than the genitor of his or her siblings (see EthnoProfile 12.2: Nyinba). In other cases, all the brothers are considered jointly as the father, without distinguishing the identity of the genitor.

There appears to be little sexual jealousy among the men, and the brothers have a strong sense of solidarity with one another. Levine (1988) emphasizes this point for the Nyinba. If the wife proves sterile, the brothers may marry another woman in hopes that she may be fertile. All brothers also have equal sexual access to the new wife and are treated as fathers by her children. In societies that practice fraternal polyandry, marrying sisters (or *sororal polygyny*) may be preferred or permitted. In this system, a group of brothers could marry a group of sisters.

According to Levine, Nyinba polyandry is reinforced by a variety of cultural beliefs and practices (1988, 158ff.). First, it has a special cultural value. Nyinba myth provides a social charter for the practice because Nyinba legendary ancestors are polyandrous, and they are praised for the harmony of their family life. Second, the solidarity of brothers is a central kinship ideal. Third, the corporate, landholding

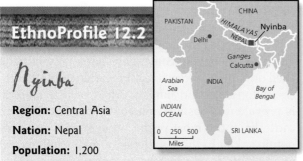

EthnoProfile 12.2

Nyinba

Region: Central Asia

Nation: Nepal

Population: 1,200

Environment: Valleys

Livelihood: Agriculture, herding

Political organization: Traditionally, headmen; today, part of a modern nation-state

For more information: Levine, Nancy. 1988. *The dynamics of polyandry: Kinship, domesticity, and population on the Tibetan border.* Chicago: University of Chicago Press.

household, central to Nyinba life, presupposes polyandry. Fourth, the closed corporate structure of Nyinba villages is based on a limited number of households, and polyandry is highly effective in checking the proliferation of households. Finally, a household's political position and economic viability increase when its resources are concentrated.

Associated Polyandry   A second form of polyandry, known as *associated polyandry*, refers to any system in which polyandry is open to men who are not necessarily brothers (Levine and Sangree 1980). There is some evidence that associated polyandry was an acceptable marriage variant in parts of the Pacific and among some indigenous peoples of North and South America. The best-described form of associated polyandry, however, is from Sri Lanka (see EthnoProfile 7.6: Sinhalese). Among the Sinhalese of Sri Lanka, a woman may marry two men, but rarely more than two. Unlike fraternal polyandry, which begins as a joint venture, Sinhalese associated polyandry begins monogamously. The second husband is brought into the union later. Also unlike fraternal polyandry, the first husband is the principal husband in terms of authority. A woman and her husbands live and work together, although economic resources are held independently. Both husbands are considered fathers to any children the wife bears.

This system allows many individual choices. For example, two husbands and their wife may decide to take another woman into the marriage—often the sister of the wife. Thus, their household becomes simultaneously polygynous and polyandrous, a marriage pattern called *polygynandry*. Thus, depending on relative wealth and the availability of economic opportunity, a Sinhalese household may be monogamous, polyandrous, or polygynandrous.

As we mentioned at the beginning of the chapter, one important aspect of marriage is the creation of ties between the bride's and the groom's families. The two forms of polyandry just discussed sharply curtail the potential network of ties created by marriage. This is particularly true where fraternal polyandry occurs with preferred or permitted sororal polygyny. For example, in a Tibetan household of four brothers married to one woman, the entire household is tied affinally only to the family of the wife. If these same brothers take another wife by marrying a sister of their first wife, they would be giving up the possibility of establishing ties with other households in favor of fortifying the relationship already established by the first marriage. Nancy Levine and Walter Sangree call this *alliance intensifying* (1980).

Secondary Marriage   The final form of polyandry, sometimes referred to as *secondary marriage*, is found only in northern Nigeria and northern Cameroon. In secondary marriage, a woman marries one or more secondary husbands while staying married to all her previous husbands (Levine and Sangree 1980, 400). The woman lives with only one husband at a time, but she retains the right to return to a previous husband and to have legitimate children by him at a later date. No divorce is permitted in the societies that practice secondary marriage; marriage is for life.

In this system, men are polygynous and women polyandrous. A man marries a series of women and lives with one or more of them at his homestead. At the same time, the women independently pursue their own marital careers. Secondary marriage is really neither polyandry nor polygyny but rather a combination of the two, resulting from the overlap of men seeking several wives and women seeking several husbands. Secondary marriage is the opposite of Tibetan fraternal polyandry. It is *alliance proliferative*, serving to connect rather than to concentrate groups as people build extensive networks of marriage-based ties throughout a region.

The Distinction Between Sexuality and Reproductive Capacity   Polyandry demonstrates how a woman's sexuality can be distinguished from her reproductive capacity. This distinction is absent in monogamous or purely polygynous systems, in which polyandry is not permitted; such societies resist perceiving women's sexual and reproductive capacities as separable (except, perhaps, in prostitution), yet they usually accept such separation for men without question. "It may well be a fundamental feature of the [world-view] of polyandrous peoples that they recognize such a distinction for *both* men and women" (Levine and Sangree 1980, 388). In the better-known polyandrous groups, a woman's sexuality can be shared among an unlimited number of men, but her childbearing capacities cannot be. Indeed, among the Nyinba (Levine 1980), a woman's childbearing capacities are carefully controlled and limited to one husband at a time. But she is free to engage in sexual activity outside her marriage to the brothers as long as she is not likely to get pregnant.

▼ MARRIAGE AND ECONOMIC EXCHANGE

In many societies, marriage is accompanied by the transfer of certain symbolically important goods. Anthropologists have identified two major categories of marriage payments, usually called *bridewealth* and *dowry*.

Bridewealth is most common in patrilineal societies that combine agriculture, pastoralism, and patrilocal marriage, although it is found in other types of societies as well (Figure 12.4). When it occurs among matrilineal peoples, a postmarital residence rule (avunculocal, for example) usually takes the woman away from her matrilineage.

The goods exchanged have significant symbolic value to the people concerned. They may include shell ornaments, ivory tusks, brass gongs, bird feathers, cotton cloth, and animals. Bridewealth in animals is prevalent in eastern and southern Africa, where cattle have the most profound symbolic and economic value. In these societies, a man's father, and often his entire patrilineage, give a specified number of cattle (often in installments) to the patrilineage of the man's bride. Anthropologists view bridewealth as a way of compensating the bride's relatives for the loss of her labor and childbearing capacities. When the bride leaves her home, she goes to live with her husband and his lineage. She will be working and producing children for his people, not her own.

Bridewealth transactions create affinal relations between the relatives of the wife and those of the husband. The wife's relatives, in turn, use the bridewealth they receive for her to find a bride for her brother in yet another kinship group. In many societies in eastern and southern Africa, a woman gains power and influence over her brother because her marriage brings the cattle that allow him to marry and continue their lineage. This is why Jack Goody describes bridewealth as "a societal fund, a circulating pool of resources, the movement of which corresponds to the movement of rights over spouses, usually women" (Goody and Tambiah 1973, 17). Or, as the Southern Bantu put it, "cattle beget children" (Kuper 1982, 3).

Dowry, by contrast, is typically a transfer of family wealth, usually from parents to their daughter, at the time of her marriage. It is found primarily in the agricultural societies of Europe and Asia but has been brought to some parts of Africa with the arrival of religions like Islam that support the practice. In societies where both women and men are seen as heirs to family wealth, dowry is sometimes regarded as the way women receive their inheritance. Dowries are often considered the wife's contribution to the establishment of a new household, to which the husband may bring other forms of wealth. In stratified societies, the size of a woman's dowry often ensures that when she marries she will continue to enjoy her accustomed style of life, and the dowry can be reclaimed by the woman in the

---

bridewealth The transfer of certain symbolically important goods from the family of the groom to the family of the bride on the occasion of their marriage. It represents compensation to the wife's lineage for the loss of her labor and her childbearing capacities.

dowry The transfer of wealth, usually from parents to their daughter, at the time of her marriage.

IN THEIR OWN WORDS

Outside Work, Women, and Bridewealth

Judith M. Abwunza took life histories from and interviewed many women among the Logoli of western Kenya about their lives, and has allowed many of those women to speak for themselves in her 1997 book, Women's Voices, Women's Power: Dialogues of Resistance from East Africa. *Here, Abwunza introduces us to Alice, a 24-year-old secondary school teacher.*

Alice's father is relatively affluent, as all his children are in school or working, his land is well-kept and fully utilized and the yard has cows, chickens, and goats. Alice's motivation to get a job was that she wanted to assist her family. She said that everyone in the family depends upon her for money, a burden that she finds to be "overwhelming." Alice has been living with her husband, who is also a teacher, since January, 1987. They have seven-month-old twins, a boy and a girl. Uvukwi [bridewealth] discussion has taken place and her in-laws and her relatives have agreed on 23,000 shillings and five cows. A 3,000 shilling "down payment" has been given, and her marriage occurred in January, 1988. Alice discusses her situation in English:

> We live in a house supplied by the school. We have electricity and water and a gas cooker. We have a small house plot in my husband's yard at Bunyore, and six acres in the scheme in Kitale. We hire people to dig there, as we are teaching. So far, we have not sold cash crops. We are only beginning. On the schemes, workers are paid between five and six hundred shillings a month to dig, so it is expensive. There is no need of paying uvukwi. Am I a farm to be bought? It is unfortunate the parents are poor. Parents ought to contribute to the newly married to start them off. But there is nothing we can do; it's a custom. Also uvukwi is not the end of assistance to parents. Some men mistreat after buying, that is paying uvukwi. Some men refuse to help parents any more after uvukwi, think that's enough. On the other hand, if you don't pay uvukwi, the husbands think you are not valued by parents. You are cheap. It's a tug of war.
>
> People who get jobs in Kenya have been to school, these are the elite. They are able to integrate various situations. They are analytical

and choosing courses of action. They have developed decision-making skills; this gives access to wage labour. Most women are not this; many men are not. Things have changed for women, but still it is very difficult; they must work very hard. In the old days, customs did not allow men in the kitchen; now they do. It's absurd to see milk boiling over in the kitchen while I'm taking care of the baby and he is reading. A more even distribution of labour is needed. Women need a word of appreciation for their hard work, in the home and caring for children. Here in Maragoli we cannot develop: the population is too high. The government is suggesting that maternity leave will not be given after the fourth child. This is a good thing but it has not been passed yet. I will not be abused in my marriage. I will leave. My job is difficult. Children are beaten, sent from school for fees, for harambee this, harambee that. Seldom do I have my entire class to teach. Some are always missing. I have had to chase them for fees. This is not my role; my job is to teach them, so they may better their lives. I refuse to beat them. I try not to upset them. I want them to learn. But many do not want to. Girls only want to chase boys, and boys the girls. But a few learn. Teaching is difficult.

[Abwunza concludes:] Alice takes a different position from most Logoli women. She complains of having to follow traditional ways in these difficult economic times, even as she adheres to them. Although many people complained about the "high cost" of uvukwi, on no other occasion did women suggest that parents should assist a newly married couple and not follow the custom of uvukwi. Alice's feeling is not typical of Logoli people. It comes about at least in part because Alice's uvukwi is quite high and both she and her husband will have to contribute to its payment, as she says, "at the expense of our own development." She sees that she is caught in a bind. Not following the traditions will place her in a position of being without a good reputation and thus at risk in the community.

Source: Abwunza 1997, 77–78.

FIGURE 12.4 This photograph illustrates a bridewealth ceremony in southern Africa. Bridewealth is usually understood as a way of compensating the bride's relatives for the loss of her labor and childbearing capacities. Cash may be used for bridewealth, as here among the Lese of the Democratic Republic of Congo.

event of divorce, to avoid destitution. The goods included in dowries vary in different societies and may or may not include land (Goody and Tambiah 1973). There is perhaps a carryover from the European dowry in the Western practice of the bride's family paying for her wedding.

Leigh Minturn (1993), who worked among the Khalapur Rajputs of northern India, studied how dowries fit into their marriage system (see Ethno-Profile 12.3: Khalapur Rajputs). To begin with, all land is held and inherited by men, who live together in a patrilocal *joint family* centering on a group of brothers with their wives and children. Rajput marriages are not only village exogamous but also *hypergamous:* that is, women normally marry into lineages of higher status than the ones into which they were born. This means that women must leave their home villages to live in another village as low-ranking outsiders in the households of their husbands. How well they marry and how well they are treated by their in-laws depend on the size of their dowries. Rajputs told Minturn that "It is best to have two sons and one daughter, because then you will receive two dowries, but give only one" (1993, 130). Poor people whose sons cannot attract women with dowries often engage in a practice called "buying a wife," in which the husband's family gives money

to the bride's family to purchase her dowry goods. Rajput dowries consisted exclusively of transportable items such as money, jewelry, clothing, and household decorations.

In the 1950s, when Minturn first visited Khalapur, new Rajput wives were under the strict control

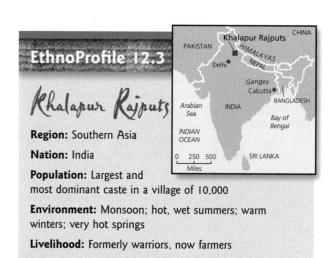

EthnoProfile 12.3

Khalapur Rajputs

Region: Southern Asia

Nation: India

Population: Largest and most dominant caste in a village of 10,000

Environment: Monsoon; hot, wet summers; warm winters; very hot springs

Livelihood: Formerly warriors, now farmers

Political organization: Village in modern nation-state

For more information: Minturn, Leigh. 1993. *Sita's daughters: Coming out of purdah.* Oxford: Oxford University Press.

IN THEIR OWN WORDS

Dowry Too High.
Lose Bride and Go to Jail

In some parts of the world, discussions of bridewealth or dowry seem so divorced from reality as to appear "academic." But elsewhere, these topics remain significant indeed. In May 2003, news media all over the world reported the story of a bride in India who called the police when a battle erupted over demands for additional dowry payments at her wedding. The New York Times *reports.*

Noida, India, May 16—The musicians were playing, the 2,000 guests were dining, the Hindu priest was preparing the ceremony and the bride was dressed in red, her hands and feet festively painted with henna.

The, the bride's family says, the groom's family moved in for the kill. The dowry of two televisions, two home theater sets, two refrigerators, two air-conditioners and one car was too cheap. They wanted $25,000 in rupees, now, under the wedding tent.

As a free-for-all erupted between the two families, the bartered bride put her hennaed foot down. She reached for the royal blue cellphone and dialed 100. By calling the police, Nisha Sharma, a 21-year-old computer student, saw her potential groom land in jail and herself land in the national spotlight as India's new overnight sensation.

"Are they marrying with money, or marrying with me?" Ms. Sharma asked today, her dark eyes glaring under arched eyebrows. In the next room a fresh wave of reporters waited to interview her, sitting next to the unopened boxes of her wedding trousseau.

After fielding a call from a comic-book artist who wanted to bring her act of defiance last Sunday night to a mass market, she said, "I'm feeling proud of myself."

"It Takes Guts to Send Your Groom Packing," a headline in *The Times of India* read.

Rashtriya Sahara, a major Hindi daily, said in a salute, "Bravo: We're Proud of You."

"She is being hailed as a New Age woman and seen as a role model to many," the newspaper *Asian Age* wrote next to a front-page drawing of Ms. Sharma standing in

Nisha Sharma, surrounded by some of the dowry with which her family had intended to endow her.

front of red and green wedding pennants while flashing a V sign to cameras and wearing a sash over her blue sari with the words *Miss Anti-Dowry*.

"This was a brave thing for a girl dressed in all her wedding finery to do," said Vandana Sharma, president of the Women's Protection League, one of many women's rights leaders and politicians to make a pilgrimage this week to this eastern suburb of Delhi. "This girl has taken a very dynamic step." India's new 24-hour news stations have propelled Nisha Sharma to Hindi stardom. One television station set up a service allowing viewers to "send a message to Nisha." In the first two days, 1,500 messages came in.

Illegal for many decades in India, dowries are now often disguised by families as gifts to give the newlyweds a start in life. More than a media creation, Ms. Sharma and her dowry defiance struck a chord in this nation, whose expanding middle class is rebelling against a dowry tradition that is being overfed by a new commercialism.

(continued on next page)

Dowry Too High. Lose Bride and Go to Jail
(continued)

"Advertisements now show parents giving things to make their daughters happy in life," Brinda Karat, general secretary of the All India Democratic Women's Association, a private group, said, referring to television commercials for products commonly given in dowries.

"It is the most modern aspects of information technology married to the most backward concepts of subordination of women," Ms. Karat continued in a telephone interview. Last year, she said, her group surveyed 10,000 people in 18 of India's 26 states. "We found an across-the-board increase in dowry demand," she said.

Much of the dowry greed is new, Ms. Karat added. In a survey 40 years ago, she noted, almost two-thirds of Indian communities reported that the local custom was for the groom to pay the bride's family, the reverse of the present dominant custom. According to government statistics, husbands and in-laws angry over small dowry payments killed nearly 7,000 women in 2001.

When Ms. Sharma's parents were married in 1970, "my father-in-law did not demand anything," her mother, Hem Lata Sharma, said while serving hot milk tea and cookies to guests.

For the Sharma family, the demands went far beyond giving the young couple a helping hand.

Dev Dutt Sharma, Nisha's father, said his potential in-laws were so demanding that they had stipulated brands. "She specified a Sony home theater, not a Philips," Mr. Sharma, an owner of car battery factories, said of Vidya Dalal, the mother of the groom, Munish Dalal, 25.

Sharma Jaikumar, a telecommunications engineer and friend of the Sharma family, said as the press mob ebbed and flowed through the house: "My daughter was married recently and there was no dowry. But anyone can turn greedy. What can be more easy money than a dowry? All you have to do is ask."

Source: Brooke 2003.

---

of their mothers-in-law, who assigned them tasks, limited their contact with their husbands, and controlled their dowries. Every time a wife visited her parents, moreover, she was expected to return with more gifts for her husband's family. In 1961, the government of India passed a law prohibiting dowries, but it has proven impossible to enforce. Nevertheless, by 1975, attitudes and practices regarding dowries had changed, especially among educated Rajputs. Many believed that dowries were a woman's rightful inheritance from her parents, and educated brides refused to relinquish control of theirs to their mothers-in-law. Indeed, following the passage of a law in 1956 that permitted daughters, widows, and mothers to inherit land, the size of dowries in Khalapur increased in order to discourage daughters from claiming family land. Much was at stake, and Minturn knew of wives who had been killed to keep them from withdrawing their husband's portion of the land from traditional joint holdings. The practice of dowry continues to be controversial in India.

▼ BROTHERS AND SISTERS IN CROSS-CULTURAL PERSPECTIVE

The brother–sister relationship and its link to marriage deserves special attention. In North American society, we tend to interpret all relationships between men and women in terms of the prototypical relationship between husbands and wives. Such an interpretation is unnecessarily limiting and overlooks significant variations in how people view relationships (see Sacks 1979). In some cultures, the most important relationships a man and a woman have are those with their opposite-sex siblings. This is perhaps clearest in matrilineal societies, where, for example, a man's closest ties to the next generation are with his sister's children.

Brothers and Sisters in a Matrilineal Society

A classic illustration comes from the Ashanti of Ghana, as described by Meyer Fortes in the late 1940s. The central legal relationship in Ashanti society is the tie between brother and sister. A brother has power over his sister's children because he is their closest male relative and because Ashanti legal power is vested in males (Fortes 1950). A sister has claims on her brother because she is his closest female relative and represents the only source of the continuity of his lineage. In patrilineal societies like that of the Nuer, a man is centrally concerned with his own ability to produce children. Among the Ashanti, a man is centrally concerned with his *sister's* ability to produce children (Figure 12.5). "Men find it difficult to decide which is more important to them, to have children or for their sisters to have children. But after discussion most men conclude that sad as it may be to die childless, a good citizen's first anxiety is for his lineage to survive" (274–75).

More than this, the Ashanti brother and sister are supposed to be close confidants:

> Quoting their own experiences, men say that it is to his sister that a man entrusts weighty matters, never to his wife. He will discuss confidential matters, such as those that concern property, money, public office, legal suits, and even the future of his children or his matrimonial difficulties with his sister, secure in the knowledge that she will tell nobody else. He will give his valuables into her care, not his wife's. He will use her as go-between with a secret lover, know-

ing that she will never betray him to his wife. His sister is the appropriate person to fetch a man's bride home to him, and so a sister is the best watch-dog of a wife's fidelity. Women, again, agree that in a crisis they will side with their brothers against their husbands. There is often jealousy between a man's sister and his wife because each is thinking of what he can be made to do for her children. That is why they cannot easily live in the same house. Divorce after many years of marriage is common, and is said to be due very often to the conflict between loyalties towards spouse and towards sibling. (Fortes 1950, 275)

Because Ashanti women may be sisters and wives simultaneously, they often experience conflict between these two roles. In the United States, the relationship of husband and wife ordinarily takes precedence over the brother-sister relationship, which is attenuated at marriage. But for the Ashanti, the lineage comes first. In part, the closeness of brothers and sisters is reinforced by the Ashanti residence pattern: people live in their matrilineages' neighborhoods, and often husbands and wives do not live together.

Since the late 1940s, the status of women within Ashanti matrilineages has eroded, according to Gracia Clark, who did fieldwork in Kumasi, Ghana, in the 1980s (Clark 1994). The market women she knew could still turn to their matrilineages for support

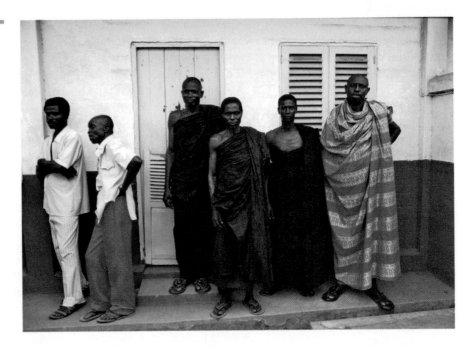

FIGURE 12.5 Ashanti men, living in a matrilineal society, were more likely to trust their sisters with important information than their wives.

against the risks of divorce, illness, or bankruptcy. At the same time, support beyond subsistence level is not automatic and must be negotiated between a woman and her kin. Clark concludes that Ashanti girls and women "unfortunately seem to be increasingly marginalized within their lineages, in leadership, residence, and inheritance" (1994, 335).

Brothers and Sisters in a Patrilineal Society

The relationship of brother and sister is important in patrilineal societies, too, and even in some contemporary urban nation-states. Thomas Belmonte notes that in the slums of Naples, Italy, a brother still maintains a moral control over his sister that her husband does not have (1978, 193). In patrilineal societies, the strength of the relationship depends on how the kinship group is organized. Where sisters do not move too far from home upon marriage and where they are not incorporated into their husbands' lineages, a group of brothers and sisters may control the lineage and its economic, political, social, and religious aspects. The senior members of the lineage—males and females alike—exercise control over the junior members. Although the brothers generally have more control than the sisters (in part because they are the ones who stay in place while the sisters move when they marry), sisters still have influence.

In the Mount Hagen area of the New Guinea highlands, for example, women marry into many different subtribes, usually within a two-hour walk from home (see EthnoProfile 12.4: Mount Hagen). However, they retain rights to the wealth of their own lineages and to its disposal. A clan sister married outside the clan is believed to remain under the control of her clan ghosts. At her death, in association with them, she is able to influence the affairs of her own lineage. Nevertheless, over the course of time, a woman becomes more interested and involved in the affairs of her husband's clan. As this happens, it is believed that she comes increasingly under the control of her husband's clan ghosts. After her death, in addition to her influence on her own clan as a ghostly sister, she is believed to have influence on her husband's clan as a ghostly mother (Strathern 1972, 124).

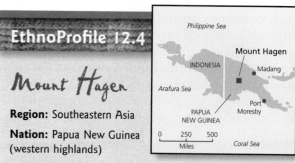

EthnoProfile 12.4

Mount Hagen

Region: Southeastern Asia

Nation: Papua New Guinea (western highlands)

Population: 75,000 (1960s)

Environment: Forested mountain slopes, grassy plains

Livelihood: Farming, pig raising

Political organization: Traditionally, some men of influence but no coercive power; today, part of a modern nation-state

For more information: Strathern, Marilyn. 1972. *Women in between*. London: Academic Press.

▼ HOW DO ANTHROPOLOGISTS THINK ABOUT FAMILY STRUCTURE?

The process by which a woman becomes gradually involved in her husband's clan or lineage was recorded by Evans-Pritchard during his fieldwork among the Nuer (see EthnoProfile 11.4: Nuer). Affinal ties gradually become kinship ties: *Ruagh* (in-law relationship) became *mar* (kinship; Evans-Pritchard 1951, 96). The birth of a child gave the wife kinship with her husband's relatives, and it gave the husband kinship with the wife's relatives. In many patrilineal societies, a woman begins to identify with and become more interested in the affairs of her husband's lineage, partly because she has been living there for many years and comes to be more intimate with the details of her husband's lineage. More significantly, however, what had been her *husband's* lineage becomes her *children's* lineage. The children create a link to the lineage that is independent of her husband. This is one example of how family relationships inevitably transform over time. The transformations people experience vary from one society to the next according to how families are defined and organized.

The Family Defined

What is a family? A minimal definition of a **family** would be that it consists of a woman and her dependent children. While some anthropological definitions require the presence of an adult male, related either by marriage or descent (husband or brother, for example), recent feminist and primatological scholarship has called this requirement into question. As a result, some anthropologists prefer to distinguish the **conjugal family**, which is a family based on marriage—at its minimum, a husband and wife (a spousal pair) and their children—from the **nonconjugal family**, which consists of a woman and her children. In a nonconjugal family, the husband/father may be occasionally present or completely absent.

Nonconjugal families are never the only form of family organization in a society and, in fact, cross-culturally are usually rather infrequent. In some large-scale industrial societies including the United States, however, nonconjugal families have become increasingly common. In most societies, the conjugal family is coresident—that is, spouses live in the same dwelling, along with their children—but there are some matrilineal societies in which the husband lives with his matrilineage, the wife and children live with theirs, and the husband visits his wife and children.

The Nuclear Family

The structure and dynamics of neolocal monogamous families are familiar to North Americans. They are called *nuclear families*, and it is often assumed that most North Americans live in them (although in 2000, only about one-quarter of North Americans did). For anthropologists, a **nuclear family** is made up of two generations: the parents and their unmarried children. Each member of a nuclear family has a series of evolving relationships with every other member: husband and wife, parents and children, and children with each other. These are the lines along which jealousy, competition, controversy, and affection develop in neolocal monogamous families; sibling rivalry, for example, is a form of competition characteristic of nuclear families that is shaped by the relationships between siblings and between siblings and their parents.

The Polygynous Family

Polygynous families are significantly different in their dynamics. Each wife has a relationship with her cowives as individuals and as a group (Figure 12.6). Cowives, in turn, individually and collectively, interact with the husband. These relationships change over time, as the authors (EAS and RHL) were once informed during our fieldwork in Guider, northern Cameroon (see EthnoProfile 8.1: Guider). The nine-year-old daughter of our landlord announced one day that she was going to become Lavenda's second wife. "Madame [Schultz]," she said, "will be angry at first, because that's how first wives are when their husbands take a second wife. But after a while, she will stop being angry and will get to know me and we will become friends. That's what always happens."

The differences in internal dynamics in polygynous families are not confined to the relationships of husband and wives. An important distinction is made between children with the same mother and children with a different mother. In Guider, people ordinarily refer to all their siblings (half and full) as brothers or sisters. When they want to emphasize the close connection with a particular brother or sister, however, they say that he or she is "same father, same mother." This terminology conveys a relationship of special intimacy and significance. Children, logically, also have different kinds of relationships with their own mothers and their fathers' other wives—and with their fathers as well.

Where there is a significant inheritance, these relationships serve as the channels for jealousy and conflict. The children of the same mother, and especially the children of different mothers, compete with one another for their father's favor. Each mother tries to protect the interests of her own children, sometimes at the expense of her cowives' children.

family Minimally, a woman and her dependent children.

conjugal family A family based on marriage; at a minimum, a husband and wife (a spousal pair) and their children.

nonconjugal family A woman and her children; the husband/father may be occasionally present or completely absent.

nuclear family A family made up of two generations: the parents and their unmarried children.

FIGURE 12.6 Cowives in polygynous households frequently cooperate in daily tasks, such as food preparation.

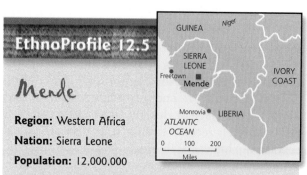

Competition in the Polygynous Family   Although the relationships among wives in a polygynous society may be very close, among the Mende of Sierra Leone, cowives eventually compete with each other (see EthnoProfile 12.5: Mende). Caroline Bledsoe (1993) explains that this competition is often focused on children: how many each wife has and how likely it is that each child will obtain things of value, especially education. Husbands in polygynous Mende households should avoid overt signs of favoritism, but wives differ from one another in status. First, wives are ranked by order of marriage. The senior wife is the first wife in the household, and she has authority over junior wives. Marriage-order ranking structures the household but also lays the groundwork for rivalries. Sec-

ond, wives are also ranked in terms of the status of the families from which they came. Serious problems arise if the husband shows favoritism toward a wife from a high-status family by educating her children ahead of older children of other wives or children of wives higher in the marriage-order ranking.

The level of her children's education matters intensely to a Mende woman because her principal claim to her husband's land or cash, and her expectations of future support after he dies, comes through her children. She depends not only on the income that a child may earn to support her but also on the rights her children have to inherit property and positions of leadership. Nevertheless, education requires a significant cash outlay in school fees, uniforms, books, and so on. A man may be able to send only one child to school, or he may be able to send one child to a prestigious private school only if he sends another to a trade apprenticeship. These economic realities make sense to husbands but can lead to bitter feuds—and even divorce—among cowives who blame the husband for disparities in the accomplishments of their children. In extreme cases, cowives are said to use witchcraft to make their rivals' children fail their exams. To avoid these problems, children are frequently sent to live with relatives who will send them to school. Such competition is missing in monogamous households unless they include adopted children or spouses who already have children from a previous marriage.

FIGURE 12.7 In a joint family in Rajasthan, six daughters of four mothers pose for a portrait.

Extended and Joint Families

Within any society, certain patterns of family organization are considered proper. In American nuclear families, two generations live together. In some societies, three generations—parents, married children, and grandchildren—are expected to live together in a vertical **extended family**. In still other societies, the extension is horizontal: Brothers and their wives (or sisters and their husbands) live together in a **joint family**, as we saw among the Khalapur Rajputs. These are ideal patterns, which all families may not be able or willing to emulate (Figure 12.7).

Individual families also change in their basic structures over time. In a polygynous society with extended families, consider a recently married husband and wife who set up housekeeping by themselves. They are monogamous. After a while, a child is born, and they become a monogamous nuclear family. Some time later, elderly parents come to live with them, and they become an extended family. Later the husband takes another wife, and the family becomes polygynous. Then the elderly parents die, and the family is no longer extended. After a time, the husband's younger brother and his wife and children move in, creating a joint household. One wife leaves, and the husband is monogamous again. His brother and his wife and children leave, the husband takes another wife, and the family is polygynous again. The eldest son marries and brings his wife to live in the household, and the household is once again an extended family. One wife dies, and the children all move away, and there is now a monogamous couple living in the household. Finally, with the death of the husband, there is a solitary widow who is supported by her eldest son but lives alone.

In this example, each household structure is different in its dynamics. These are not several nuclear families that overlap. Extended and joint families are fundamentally different from an extended family with regard to the relationships they engender.

▼ HOW DO FAMILIES CHANGE OVER TIME?

As we just saw, families change over time. They have a life cycle and a life span. The same family takes on different forms and provides different opportunities

---

extended family A family pattern made up of three generations living together: parents, married children, and grandchildren.

joint family A family pattern made up of brothers and their wives or sisters and their husbands (along with their children) living together.

Law, Custom, and Crimes Against Women

John van Willigen and V. C. Channa describe the social and cultural practices surrounding dowry payments that appear to be responsible for violence against women in some parts of India.

> A 25-year-old woman was allegedly burnt to death by her husband and mother-in-law at their East Delhi home yesterday. The housewife, Mrs. Sunita, stated before her death at the Jaya Prakash Narayana Hospital that members of her husband's family had been harassing her for bringing inadequate dowry.
>
> The woman told the Shahdara subdivisional magistrate that during a quarrel over dowry at their Pratap Park house yesterday, her husband gripped her from behind while the mother-in-law poured kerosene over her clothes.
>
> Her clothes were then set ablaze. The police have registered a case against the victim's husband, Suraj Prakash, and his mother.
>
> —*Times of India*, February 19, 1988

This routinely reported news story describes what in India is termed a "bride-burning" or "dowry death." Such incidents are frequently reported in the newspapers of Delhi and other Indian cities. In addition, there are cases in which the evidence may be ambiguous, so that deaths of women by fire may be recorded as kitchen accidents, suicides, or murders. Dowry violence takes a characteristic form. Following marriage and the requisite giving of dowry, the family of the groom makes additional demands for the payment of more cash or the provision of more goods. These demands are expressed in unremitting harassment of the bride, who is living in the household of her husband's parents, culminating in the murder of the woman by members of her husband's family or by her suicide. The woman is typically burned to death with kerosene, a fuel used in pressurized cook stoves, hence the use of the term "bride-burning" in public discourse.

Dowry death statistics appear frequently in the press and parliamentary debates. Parliamentary sources report the following figures for married women 16 to 30 years of age in Delhi: 452 deaths by burning for 1985; 478 for 1986 and 300 for the first six months of 1987. There were 1,319 cases reported nationally in 1986 (*Times of India*, January 10, 1988). Police records do not match hospital records for third degree burn cases among younger married women; far more violence occurs than the crime reports indicate.

There is other violence against women related both directly and indirectly to the institution of dowry. For example, there are unmarried women who commit suicide so as to relieve their families of the burden of providing a dowry. A recent case that received national attention in the Indian press involved the triple suicide of three sisters in the industrial city of Kanpur. A photograph was widely published showing the three young women hanging from ceiling fans by their scarves. Their father, who earned about 4000 Rs. [rupees] per month, was not able to negotiate marriage for his oldest daughter. The grooms were requesting approximately 100,000 Rs. Also linked to the dowry problem is selective female abortion made possible by amniocentesis. This issue was brought to national attention with a startling statistic reported out of a seminar held in Delhi in 1985. Of 3000 abortions carried out after sex determination through amniocentesis, only one involved a male fetus. As a result of these developments, the government of the state of Maharashtra banned sex determination tests except those carried out in government hospitals.

Source: van Willigen and Channa 1991, 369–70.

for the interaction of family members at different points in its development. New households are formed and old households change through divorce, remarriage, the departure of children, and the breakup of extended families.

Divorce and Remarriage

Most human societies make it possible for married couples to separate. In some societies, the process is long, drawn out, and difficult, especially when bridewealth must be returned; a man who divorces a wife in such societies, or whose wife leaves him, expects some of the bridewealth back. But for the wife's family to give the bridewealth back, a whole chain of marriages may have to be broken up. Brothers of the divorced wife may have to divorce to get back enough bridewealth from their in-laws. Sometimes a new husband will repay the bridewealth to the former husband's line, thus letting the bride's relatives off the hook.

Divorce in Guider   In other societies, divorce is easier. Marriages in Guider, for example, are easily broken up (see EthnoProfile 8.1: Guider). The Fulbe of Guider prefer that a man marry his father's brother's daughter. In many cases, such marriages are contracted simply to oblige the families involved; after a few months, the couple splits up. In other cases, a young girl (12 or 13 years old) is married to a man considerably her senior, despite any interest she may have had in men closer to her own age. Here too the marriage may not last long. In general, there is enough dissatisfaction with marriage in Guider to make household transformation through divorce quite common.

Among Muslims in Guider, divorce is controlled by men; women are not allowed legally to initiate divorces. A man wanting a divorce need only follow the simple procedure laid down in the Qur'an and sanctioned by long practice in Guider: He appears before two witnesses and pronounces the formula "I divorce you" three times. He is then divorced, and his wife must leave his household. She may take an infant with her, but any children at the toddler stage or older stay with the father. If she takes an infant, she must return the child to the father's household by the time the child is six to eight years old. In case she was pregnant at the time of the divorce, a woman must wait three months after she is divorced before she can remarry. After this time, the vast majority of women remarry.

Do women in Guider, then, have no power to escape from marriages that are unsatisfactory? Legally, perhaps not. But several conventionally recognized practices allow a woman to communicate her desire for a divorce. She can ask her husband for a divorce, and in some cases he will comply. If he does not or if she is unwilling to confront him directly, she can neglect household duties—burn his food or stop cooking for him entirely or refuse to sleep with him. She

can also leave, going to live in the compound of her father or brother.

Grounds for Divorce   Depending on the society, nagging, quarreling, cruelty, stinginess, or adultery may be cited as causes for divorce. In almost all societies, childlessness is grounds for divorce as well. For the Ju/'hoansi, most divorces are initiated by women, mainly because they do not like their husbands or do not want to be married (Lee 1992b; Shostak 1981; see EthnoProfile 11.1: Ju/'hoansi). After what is often considerable debate, a couple that decides to break up merely separates. There is no bridewealth to return, no legal contract to be renegotiated. Mutual consent is all that is necessary. The children go with the mother. Ju/'hoansi divorces are cordial, Richard Lee (1992b) tells us, at least compared with the Western norm. Ex-spouses may continue to joke with each other and even live next to each other with their new spouses.

There are very few societies in which divorce is not recognized. In ancient Rome, for example, divorce was impossible. This followed from legal consequences of the marriage ritual. When she married, a woman was cut off from the patrilineage into which she was born and incorporated into her husband's patrilineage. Were she to leave her husband, she would have no place to go and no lineage to protect her.

Separation among Inuit   Among the northwestern Inuit, the traditional view is that all kin relationships, including marital ones, are permanent (Burch 1970) (see EthnoProfile 12.6: Alaskan Inuit). Thus, although it is possible to deactivate a marriage by separating, a marriage can never be permanently dissolved. (Conversely, reestablishing the residence tie is all that's needed to reactivate the relationship.) A husband and wife who stop living together and having sexual relations with each other are considered to be separated and ready for another marriage. If each member of a separated couple remarried, the two husbands of the wife would become cohusbands; the two wives of the husband, cowives; and the children of the first and second marriages, cosiblings. In effect, a "divorce" among the Inuit results in more, not fewer, connections. Not all contemporary Inuit, especially those who are Christians, continue to follow this practice. (The consequences of this approach, as well as some additional details, are found in chapter 11,

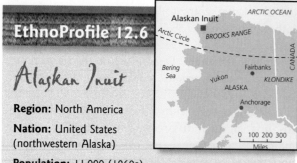

EthnoProfile 12.6

Alaskan Inuit

Region: North America

Nation: United States (northwestern Alaska)

Population: 11,000 (1960s)

Environment: Arctic: mountains, foothills, coastal plain

Livelihood: Hunting, wage labor, welfare

Political organization: Traditionally, families; today, part of a modern nation-state

For more information: Burch, Ernest S., Jr. 1975. *Eskimo kinsmen: Changing family relationships in northwest Alaska.* American Ethnological Society Monograph, no. 59. St. Paul: West.

in the discussion of relatedness among the Iñupiat, also in northwestern Alaska.)

Blended Families   In recent years in the United States, anthropologists have observed the emergence of a new family type: the **blended family**. A blended family is created when previously divorced or widowed people marry, bringing with them children from their previous marriages. The internal dynamics of the new family—which can come to include his children, her children, and their children—may resemble the dynamics of polygynous families, as the relations among the children and their relations to each parent may be complex and negotiated over time.

Breaking Up Complex Households

The formation of new households following the breakup of extended families is best illustrated in joint families. In a joint family, the pressures that build up among coresident brothers or sisters often increase dramatically on the death of the father. In theory, the eldest son inherits the position of head of

the household from his father, but his younger brothers may not accept his authority as readily as they did their father's. Some younger brothers may decide to establish their own households, and gradually the joint family splits. Each brother whose household splits off from the joint stem usually hopes to start his own joint family; eventually, his sons will bring their wives into the household, and a new joint family emerges out of the ashes of an old one.

Something similar happens among the Nyinba, the polyandrous people of Nepal discussed earlier (see EthnoProfile 12.2: Nyinba). In a family with many brothers widely separated in age, the corporation of brothers may take a second wife. At first, all brothers have equal sexual access to her, but in time the brothers will tend to form groups around each wife, with some preferring the first and others preferring the second. At this point, the time is ripe for splitting the household in two. The Nyinba recognize that bringing a second fertile wife into the house sets in motion the transformation of the family into two polyandrous households and the division of land ownership. Hence, family systems contain within them the seeds of their own transformation.

International Migration and the Family

Migration to find work in another country has become increasingly common worldwide and has important effects on families. Anthropologist Eugenia Georges (1990) examined its effects on people who migrated to the United States from Los Pinos, a small town in the Dominican Republic (see EthnoProfile 12.7: Los Pinos). Migration divided these families, with some members moving to New York and some remaining in Los Pinos. Some parents stayed in the Dominican Republic while their children went to the United States. A more common pattern was for spouses to separate, with the husband migrating and the wife staying home. Consequently, many households in Los Pinos were headed by women. In most cases, however, the spouse in the United States worked to bring the spouse and children in Los Pinos there.

This sometimes took several years because it involved completing paperwork for the visa and saving money beyond the amount regularly sent to Los Pinos. Children of the couple who were close to working age also came to the United States, frequently

blended family A family created when previously divorced or widowed people marry, bringing with them children from their previous families.

EthnoProfile 12.7

Los Pinos

Region: Caribbean

Nation: Dominican Republic

Population: 1,000

Environment: Rugged mountain region

Livelihood: Peasant agriculture (tobacco, coffee, cacao) and labor migration

Political organization: Part of a modern nation-state

For more information: Georges, Eugenia. 1990. *The making of a transnational community: Migration, development, and cultural change in the Dominican Republic.* New York: Columbia University Press.

FIGURE 12.8 As migration from the Dominican Republic to the United States has increased, more Dominicans are staying and bringing their families or creating families in the United States. Such celebrations of ethnic pride as Dominican Day in New York have increased in recent years.

with their mother, and younger children were sent for as they approached working age. Finally, after several years in the United States, the couple who started the migration cycle would often take their savings and return home to the Dominican Republic. Their children stayed in the United States and continued to send money home. Return migrants tended not to give up their residence visas, and therefore had to return to the United States annually. Often they stayed for a month or more to work. This also provided them with the opportunity to buy clothing and household goods at a more reasonable cost, as well as other items—clothing, cosmetics, and the like—to sell to neighbors, friends, and kin in the Dominican Republic (Figure 12.8).

Georges observes that the absent family member maintained an active role in family life despite the heavy psychological burden of separation. Although he might be working in a hotel in New York, for example, the husband was still the breadwinner and the main decision maker in the household. He communicated by visits, letters, and occasional telephone calls. Despite the strains of migration, moreover, the divorce rate was actually slightly lower in migrant families. In part, this was because the exchange of information between Los Pinos and New York was both dense and frequent, but also because strong ties

of affection connected many couples. Finally, "the goal of the overwhelming majority of the migrants [from Los Pinos] I spoke with was permanent return to the Dominican Republic. Achievement of this goal was hastened by sponsoring the migration of dependents, both wives and children, so that they could work and save as part of the reconstituted household in the United States" (Georges 1990, 201). This pressure also helped keep families together.

In recent years, the Internet has come to play an increasingly important role in the lives of families that are separated by migration, education, work, and so on. Daniel Miller and Don Slater (2000) studied Internet use in Trinidad, finding that e-mail and instant messaging have considerably strengthened both the nuclear and extended families, allowing closer relations between distant parents and children, among siblings, and among other relatives as well. They remark on the experiences of a widow they knew who, depressed after her husband's death, was convinced by relatives to learn to use e-mail to contact a beloved grandchild who had gone abroad. This experience was so valuable to her that she began to contact other relatives abroad and in Trinidad, that younger members of her family "swear it has given 'new lease of life'" (Miller and Slater 2000, 61). Overall, the use of the Internet offers anthropologists the opportunity to observe how family separation can be moderated, and offers people around the world opportunities for relaxed, expansive, and everyday forms of communication that seem to have important effects on family life.

Not all migrants to the United States share the same financial constraints or family pressures. A contrasting case comes from Japanese corporate wives in the United States. Anthropologist Sawa Kurotani, born and raised in Japan and trained and now working in the United States, discusses the situation of middle-class Japanese women who accompany their husbands when the husband's corporate employer sends him to work in the United States for up to five years. Kurotani (2005) observes that, traditionally, domestic management was the job of the wife. In Japan there is a sharp division of labor and of interest: Husbands and wives know little about the other's world and do not engage in many activities together. But when removed from the social context of work, family, and neighbors that surrounds them in Japan and placed in the position of expatriates living in the United States—a position that some of the women liken to a "long vacation"—a space is opened for changes in family dynamics.

Kurotani studied corporate wives in three places in the United States where there were substantial but different communities of expatriate Japanese: a place in the Midwest she calls "Centerville," New York City, and the Research Triangle in North Carolina. The three cases were different in important ways, in terms of the availability of Japanese products, Japanese schools and restaurants, and in terms of the degree to which the major Japanese corporations provided for the families of their Japanese employees on assignment in the United States. But there were some experiences in common. As Kurotani remarks, "During their long vacation, Japanese corporate wives also experience several profound changes in their lives that, in some cases, permanently change their relation to their domesticity, their family and to Japan. Although the vacation will come to an end sooner or later, its transformative potential goes far beyond wishful thinking in some critical instances" (2005, 182). Not only are husbands and wives thrown together in ways that are unfamiliar to them, they are also forced to deal with life in the United States and with neighbors, friends, coworkers, teachers, or

other parents who defamiliarize the things about everyday life that the Japanese wives had always previously taken for granted.

Many women find that their relationships with their children change as a result of residence in the United States: Mothers feel that they have an improved understanding of their children because the isolation and difficulty they faced together have made them more like partners. But a much larger change can occur in the conjugal relationship, beginning in ways that seem trivial—a husband begins to take out the trash and bring the trash bin back from the end of the driveway; a husband begins to cook on the barbecue grill in warm weather. But Kurotani observes that "it was often through everyday practices in and around their home that they begin to renegotiate their domestic relationships" (189).

One of the consequences of this renegotiation was that male Japanese workers spent more time at home with the family, took on additional responsibilities at home, and often found themselves enjoying both as well as coming to depend on their wife's support. The wives appreciated a greater sense of closeness and egalitarian partnership with their husbands. "Expatriate Japanese husbands and wives in the United States not only depend on each other to share the responsibility of work, but also seek personal support and camaraderie in each other—in many cases, for the first time in their marriage. Once established, this sense of partnership seems to last. To many of my informants, this is 'the best thing' that happened to them during [their stay abroad]" (191). Although the return to Japan was difficult and many of the changes the women underwent in the United States had to be put on hold, the changes in the conjugal relationships have called into question the "naturalness" of the division between men's and women's work.

Families by Choice

In spite of the range of variation in family forms that we have surveyed, some readers may still be convinced that family ties depend on blood and that blood is thicker than water. It is therefore instructive to consider the results of research carried out by Kath Weston (1991) on family forms among gays and lesbians in the San Francisco Bay Area during the 1980s.

Why Migrant Women Feed Their Husbands Tamales

Brett Williams suggests that the reasons Mexican migrant women feed their husbands tamales may not be the stereotypical reasons that outside observers often assume.

Because migrant women are so involved in family life and so seemingly submissive to their husbands, they have been described often as martyred purveyors of rural Mexican and Christian custom, tyrannized by excessively masculine, crudely domineering, rude and petty bullies in marriage, and blind to any world outside the family because they are suffocated by the concerns of kin. Most disconcerting to outside observers is that migrant women seem to embrace such stereotypes: they argue that they should monopolize their foodways and that they should not question the authority of their husbands. If men want tamales, men should have them. But easy stereotypes can mislead; in exploring the lives of the poor, researchers must revise their own notions of family life, and this paper argues that foodways can provide crucial clues about how to do so.

The paradox is this: among migrant workers both women and men are equally productive wage earners, and husbands readily acknowledge that without their wives' work their families cannot earn enough to survive. For migrants the division of labor between earning a living outside the home and managing household affairs is unknown; and the dilemma facing middle-class wives who may wish to work to supplement the family's income simply does not exist. Anthropologists exploring women's status cross-culturally argue that women are most influential when they share in the production of food and have some control over its distribution. If such perspectives bear at all on migrant women, one might be led to question their seemingly unfathomable obsequiousness in marriage.

Anthropologists further argue that women's influence is even greater when they are not isolated from their kinswomen, when women can cooperate in production and join, for example, agricultural work with domestic duties and childcare. Most migrant women spend their lives within large, closely knit circles of kin and their work days with their kinswomen. Marriage does not uproot or isolate a woman from her family, but rather doubles the relatives each partner can depend on and widens in turn the networks of everyone involved. The lasting power of marriage is reflected in statistics which show a divorce rate of 1 percent for migrant farmworkers from Texas, demonstrating the strength of a union bolstered by large numbers of relatives concerned that it go well. Crucial to this concern is that neither partner is an economic drain on the family, and the Tejano pattern of early and lifelong marriages establishes some limit on the whimsy with which men can abuse and misuse their wives.

While anthropology traditionally rests on an appreciation of other cultures in their own contexts and on their own terms, it is very difficult to avoid class bias in viewing the lives of those who share partly in one's own culture, especially when the issue is something so close to home as food and who cooks it. Part of the problem may lie in appreciating what families are and what they do. For the poor, public and private domains are blurred in confusing ways, family affairs may be closely tied to economics, and women's work at gathering and obligating or binding relatives is neither trivial nor merely a matter of sentiment. Another problem may lie in focusing on the marital relationship as indicative of a woman's authority in the family. We too often forget that women are sisters, grandmothers, and aunts to men as well as wives. Foodways can help us rethink both of these problematic areas and understand how women elaborate domestic roles to knit families together, to obligate both male and female kin, and to nurture and bind their husbands as well.

Source: Williams 1984.

A lesbian herself, Weston knew that a turning point in the lives of most gays and lesbians was the decision to announce their sexual orientation to their parents and siblings. If blood truly were thicker than water, this announcement should not destroy family bonds, and many parents have indeed been supportive of their children after the announcement. Often enough, however, shocked parents have turned away, declaring that this person is no longer their son or daughter. Living through—or even contemplating—such an experience has been enough to force gays and lesbians to think seriously about the sources of family ties.

By the 1980s, some North American gays and lesbians had reached two conclusions: (1) that blood ties *cannot* guarantee the "enduring diffuse solidarity" supposedly at the core of North American kinship (Schneider 1968); and (2) that new kin ties *can* be created over time as friends and lovers demonstrate their genuine commitment to one another by creating families of choice. "Like their heterosexual counterparts, most gay men and lesbians insisted that family members are people who are 'there for you,' people you can count on emotionally and materially" (Weston 1991, 113). Some gay kinship ideologies now argue that "whatever endures is real" as a way of claiming legitimacy for chosen families that were not the product of heterosexual marriages. Such a definition of family is compatible with understandings of kinship based on nurturance described in chapter 11. Gay and lesbian activists have used this similarity as a resource in their struggles to obtain for long-standing families by choice some of the same legal rights enjoyed by traditional heterosexual families, such as hospital visiting privileges, joint adoption, and property rights (Weston 1995, 99).

▼ THE FLEXIBILITY OF MARRIAGE

It is easy to get the impression that marriage rules compel people to do things they really do not want to do. Younger people, for example, seem forced by elders to marry complete strangers of a certain kin category belonging to particular social groups; or women appear to be pawns in men's games of prestige and power. Marriage rules, however, are always subject to some negotiation, as illustrated by the marriage practices of the Ju/'hoansi of the Kalahari Desert (see

EthnoProfile 11.1: Ju/'hoansi [!Kung]). Richard Lee (1992b) notes that all first marriages are set up by means of a long-term exchange of gifts between the parents of a bride and groom.

As we saw in chapter 11, the Ju/'hoansi kinship system is as simple or as complex as people want to make it, and the game of kinship is extended to marriage. A girl may not marry a father, brother, son, uncle, or nephew, or a first or second cousin. A girl may also not marry a boy with her father's or brother's name, and a boy may not marry a girl with his mother's or sister's name. In addition, neither a boy nor girl should marry someone who stands in an avoidance relationship.

Consequently, for the Ju/'hoansi, about three-quarters of a person's potential spouses are off limits. In practice, parents of girls tend to be quite choosy about whom their daughter marries. If they are opposed to a particular suitor, they will come up with a kin or name prohibition to block the match. Because the parents arrange the first marriage, it appears that the girl has very little to say about it. If she has an objection and protests long and hard, however, her parents may well call it off. This clear and insistent assertion of displeasure is not uncommon in the world. Even when a young woman follows the wishes of her parents for her first marriage, that first marriage may not be her last if dissatisfaction persists. Despite the parents' quest to find ideal spouses for their children, close to half of all first marriages among the Ju/'hoansi fail. However, as in many societies, only about 10 percent of marriages that last five years or longer end in divorce (Lee 1992b, 83).

Sometimes the contrast between the formal rules of marriage and the actual performance of marriage rituals can be revealing. Ivan Karp (1978) asks why Iteso women laugh at marriage ceremonies (see EthnoProfile 11.4: Iteso). During his fieldwork, Karp was struck by a paradox. The marriage ritual is taken very seriously by the patrilineal Iteso; it is the moment of creation for a new household, and it paves the way for the physical and social reproduction of Iteso patrilineages. But the ritual is carried out entirely by women who are not consanguineal members of the patrilineage! Despite the seriousness of the occasion and although they are carrying out the ritual for the benefit of a lineage to which they do not belong, Iteso women seem to find the ceremony enormously funny.

To explain this apparently anomalous behavior, Karp suggests that the meaning of the marriage ritual needs to be analyzed from two different perspectives: that of the men and that of the women. The men's perspective constitutes the official (or hegemonic) ideology of Iteso marriage. It emphasizes how marriage brings the bride's sexuality under the control of her husband's lineage. It distinguishes between women of the mother-in-law's generation and women of the wife's own generation. It stresses the woman's role as an agent of reproduction who is equivalent, in a reproductive sense, to the bridewealth cattle.

The women's perspective constitutes an unofficial (or counterhegemonic) ideology. For the men and women of a given lineage to succeed in perpetuating that lineage, they must control women's bodies. But the bodies they must control belong to female outsiders who marry lineage men. These same female outsiders direct the two ritual events crucial to lineage reproduction: marriage and birth. And men of the lineage are not allowed to attend either of these rituals. In sum, female outsiders control the continued existence of a patrilineage whose male members are supposed to control them!

Iteso women, Karp says, can see the irony in this: They are at once controlled and controlling. In the marriage ritual itself, they comment on this paradox through their laughter. In so doing, they reveal two things. First, they show that they know the men are dependent on them. Second, even as the men assert their control over women's bodies, the women's ritual actions escape the men's control. The official ideology of male control is subverted, at least momentarily, by the women's laughter. Even as they ensure that lineages will continue, they are able to comment on the paradoxical relation of women to men. It should be remembered, however, that all the women could do was comment on those relations; they did not have the power to change them.

▼ HOW DO SEXUAL PRACTICES DIFFER?

Some anthropologists seem to regard marriage as an abstract formal system, having little if anything to do with human sexuality. As a result, their discussions tend to ignore its carnal aspects. But sexual intercourse is part of almost all marriages. And because in many societies marriage is the formal prerequisite for becoming sexually active (at least for females), a desire for sex is a strong motivation for getting married (Spiro 1977, 212).

Heterosexual Practices

The range of sexual practice in the world is vast. In many Oceanian societies—Tikopia, for example—the young are expected to have a great deal of sexual experience before marriage (see EthnoProfile 12.8: Tikopia). Young men and young women begin having sexual relations at an early age, and having several lovers is considered normal for the young. Getting married, as in many societies, is considered the final step (or the beginning of the final step) in becoming an adult. The distinguished British anthropologist Sir Raymond Firth notes that for the Tikopia, marriage represents a great change for both partners in this regard. The woman must abandon sexual freedom, but she replaces it with what Firth calls "a safe and legalized sexual cohabitation" ([1936] 1984, 434). The man is theoretically free to continue to have affairs, but in practice he will "settle down." This pattern is quite common cross-culturally.

The Ju/'hoansi also begin sexual activity at an early age (see EthnoProfile 11.1: Ju/'hoansi [!Kung]). As a result, the social and sexual constraints of marriage represent quite a shock at first, especially for young women. Some Ju/'hoansi are strictly faithful to one another, but a significant minority take lovers. The Ju/'hoansi have no double standard. Both men and women are free to take lovers, and women are sometimes eloquent about the time they spend with lovers. However, discretion is necessary when taking a lover because both husbands and wives can become very jealous and start fights. Sexual satisfaction is important to the Ju/'hoansi: Female orgasm is known, and women expect both husbands and lovers to satisfy them sexually.

Not all societies have the same attitude. Robert Murphy and Yolanda Murphy (1974) note that for the Mundurucu, a group of about 1,250 gardening and hunting people in the Brazilian Amazon, female orgasm is more accidental than expected. Many societies require a woman's virginity at marriage; in some Arab societies, for example, bloodstained sheets must be

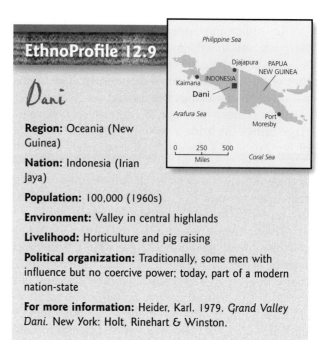

EthnoProfile 12.8

Tikopia

Region: Oceania (Polynesia)

Nation: Solomon Islands

Population: 1,200 (1928)

Environment: Tropical island

Livelihood: Horticulture and pig raising

Political organization: Traditionally, chiefs; today, part of a modern nation-state

For more information: Firth, Raymond. [1936] 1984. *We, the Tikopia.* Reprint. Stanford, CA: Stanford University Press.

EthnoProfile 12.9

Dani

Region: Oceania (New Guinea)

Nation: Indonesia (Irian Jaya)

Population: 100,000 (1960s)

Environment: Valley in central highlands

Livelihood: Horticulture and pig raising

Political organization: Traditionally, some men with influence but no coercive power; today, part of a modern nation-state

For more information: Heider, Karl. 1979. *Grand Valley Dani.* New York: Holt, Rinehart & Winston.

produced the morning after the consummation of a marriage to demonstrate that the bride was a virgin.

Karl Heider (1979) studied the Dani, a people of highland New Guinea (see EthnoProfile 12.9: Dani). Heider discovered that the Dani have extraordinarily little interest in sex. For five years after the birth of a child, the parents do not have sexual intercourse with each other. This practice, called a *postpartum sex taboo*, is found in all cultures, but in most societies it lasts for a few weeks or months. (In North America, we say that the mother needs time to heal; other societies have other justifications.) In a few cases, the postpartum sex taboo is two years long, which is considered a very long time.

Five years is hard to believe. What could explain why the Dani had such a low level of sexuality? Heider himself cannot, but his work illustrates the extraordinary range of human sexual behavior.

Heider points out that Westerners assume that the sex drive is perhaps the most powerful biological drive of all, and that if this drive is not satisfied directly in sexual activity, then some other outlet will be found. In fact, some suggest that the Dani's high levels of outgroup aggression may be connected with their low level of sexual intercourse. The Dani are not celibate, and they certainly have sexual intercourse often enough to reproduce biologically, yet they do not seem very interested in sex (1979, 78–81). The Dani, who are not abnormal physically or mentally, represent an extreme in the cultural construction of sexuality.

Other Sexual Practices

The traditional anthropological focus on what European Americans call heterosexual relationships is understandable. People in every society are concerned about perpetuating themselves, and most have developed complex ideological and ritual structures to ensure that this occurs. The fact that such elaborate cultural constructions seem necessary to encourage heterosexual practices, however, suggests that human sexual expression would resist such confinement if it were not under strict control. As we saw in the previous chapter, anthropological information about supernumerary sexes and genders undermines the "two-sex model" that is hegemonic in European American cultures.

Anthropologists Evelyn Blackwood and Saskia Wieringa have studied cultural shaping of female desires. They examined how female bodies are assigned cultural meanings in different historical and ethnographic settings—and how those meanings affect the way females relate to other females. They found a wide range of "varied and rich cultural identities and same-sex practices between those with female bodies" (Blackwood and Wieringa 1999, ix). This research does not assume that having a male body or a female body necessarily determines any individual's traits, feelings, or experiences (Blackwood and Wieringa 1999, x). As a result, it provides a vital comparative context which can illuminate our understanding of sexual practices that European Americans call *homosexuality* and *bisexuality*.

Female Sexual Practices in Mombasa

Anthropologist Gill Shepherd shows that traditional patterns of male-female interaction among Swahili Muslims in Mombasa, Kenya, make male and female homosexual relationships perfectly intelligible (1987) (see EthnoProfile 12.10: Mombasa Swahilis; Figure 12.9). For one thing, men and women in Muslim Mombasa live in very different subcultures. For women, the most enduring relationship is between mothers and daughters, mirrored in the relationship between an older married sister and a younger unmarried sister. By contrast, relationships between mothers and sons and between brothers and sisters are more distant. Except in the case of young, modern, educated couples, the relationship between husband and wife is often emotionally distant as well. Because the worlds of men and women overlap so little, therefore, relationships between the sexes tend to be one-dimensional. Men and women join a variety of sex-segregated groups for leisure-time activities such as dancing or religious study. Within these same-sex groups, individuals compete for social rank.

EthnoProfile 12.10

Mombasa Swahilis

Region: Eastern Africa

Nation: Kenya

Population: 50,000 Swahili among 350,000 total population of city (1970s)

Environment: Island and mainland port city

Livelihood: Various urban occupations

Political organization: Part of a modern nation-state

For more information: Shepherd, Gil. 1987. Rank, gender and homosexuality: Mombasa as a key to understanding sexual options. In *The cultural construction of sexuality,* ed. Pat Caplan, 240–70. London: Tavistock.

Of the some 50,000 Swahili in Mombasa, about 5,000 could be called homosexual. The number is misleading, however, because men and women shift between what European Americans call *homosexuality* and *heterosexuality* throughout their lives. Women are allowed to choose other women as sexual partners only after they have been married. Therefore, all such women in Mombasa are married, widowed, or divorced. Both men and women are open about their same-sex relationships, and "nobody would dream of suggesting that their sexual choices had any effect on their work capabilities, reliability, or religious piety" (Shepherd 1987, 241).

Because women in many all-female households do not have sexual relationships with one another, Shepherd uses the term *lesbian* to imply an overt sexual relationship between two women. Lesbian couples in Mombasa are far more likely to live together than are male homosexual couples. In addition to having private, sexual relationships with other women, they also form clublike groups that meet regularly in one another's houses. Each group is composed of an inner circle of relatively wealthy older women who are friends. The rule is that younger, lower-status women visit older, higher-status women. Wealthy lesbian women hold court in the afternoons, when Swahili women have the chance to go visiting. Women in the inner circle compete for status by, for example, trying to outdo one another by dressing their lovers as opulently as possible.

Many women were quite clear about the practical reasons that had led them into sexual relationships with other women. Women with little money are unlikely to marry men who can offer them jewelry, shoes, new dresses, status, or financial security, but a wealthy lesbian lover can offer them all these things. Also, a poor young woman in an unhappy marriage may have no way to support herself if she leaves her husband unless she has a lesbian lover. Very occasionally a wealthy lesbian woman will help a girl who has remained single after all her peers have married. Adult status and freedoms come only with marriage, but a woman who is well-educated or from a high-status family may still be unmarried in her late twenties or early thirties due to her parents' intimidation of potential suitors. A wealthy lesbian who wants to help such a woman finds a man willing to make a marriage of convenience and finances his marriage to the woman. The couple are divorced

FIGURE 12.9 View of Mombasa, Kenya.

shortly thereafter, and the girl goes to live with her lesbian benefactress.

According to Islamic law, a wealthy, high-ranking Muslim woman can only marry a man who is her equal or superior. A marriage of this kind brings a great deal of seclusion, and her wealth is administered by her husband. The wealthy partner in a lesbian relationship, however, is freed from these constraints. "Thus if she wishes to use her wealth as she likes and has a taste for power, entry into a lesbian relationship, or living alone as a divorced or widowed woman, are virtually her only options" (Shepherd 1987, 257). Financial independence for a woman offers the chance to convert wealth to power. If she pays for the marriages of other people or provides financial support in exchange for loyalty, a woman can create a circle of dependents. Shepherd points out that a few women, some lesbians, have achieved real political power in Mombasa in this way (1987, 257).

Still, it is not necessary to be a lesbian to build a circle of dependents. Why do some women follow this route? The answer, Shepherd tells us, is complicated. It is not entirely respectable for a woman under 45 or 50 to be unmarried. Some women can maintain autonomy by making a marriage of convenience to a man who already lives with a wife and then living apart from him. Many women, however, find this arrangement both lonely and sexually unsatisfying. Living as a lesbian is less respectable than being a second, nonresident wife, but it is more respectable than not being married at all. The lesbian sexual relationship does not reduce the autonomy of the wealthy partner "and indeed takes place in the highly positive context of the fond and supportive relationships women establish among themselves anyway" (1987, 258).

Shepherd suggests that the reason sexual relationships between men or between women are generally not heavily stigmatized in Mombasa is because social rank takes precedence over all other measures of status. Rank is a combination of wealth, the ability to claim Arab ancestry, and the degree of Muslim learning and piety. Rank determines marriage partners, as well as relations of loyalty and subservience, and both men and women expect to rise in rank over a lifetime. Although lesbian couples may violate the prototype for sexual relations, they do not violate relations of rank. Shepherd suggests that a marriage between a poor husband and a rich wife might be more shocking than a lesbian relationship between a dominant rich woman and a dependent poor one. It is less important that a woman's lover be a male than it is for her to be a good Arab, a good Muslim, and a person of wealth and influence.

Anthropologists working in Africa have described a range of relations between females, such as woman marriage, that have been likened to European or American models of lesbian relationships, but disputes have arisen about whether such relationships included an erotic involvement between the female partners. In a survey of this evidence, Blackwood and Wieringa note that woman marriage can take many forms, some of which are more likely than others to have included sexuality between the female partners. Among those where such sexual relations appear more likely are cases like that described by Shepherd, "in which a woman of some means, either married (to a man) or unmarried, pays bride-price for a wife and establishes her own compound" (Blackwood and Wieringa 1999, 5). Such evidence is not merely of academic interest. In the contemporary world of intensified global communication and exchange, Western and non-Western same-sex practices are becoming increasingly entangled with one another, leading to the emergence of local movements for "lesbian" and "gay" rights in Africa and elsewhere. In this context, the presidents of Zimbabwe, Kenya, and Namibia recently declared that homosexuality is "un-African." Based on the ethnographic evidence, however, Blackwood and Wieringa side with those arguing that, on the contrary, it is homophobia that is "un-African:" "President Mandela from South Africa is a striking exception to the homophobia of his colleagues. The South African constitution specifically condemns discrimination on the basis of sexual orientation" (1999, 27).

Male Sexual Practices in Nicaragua

Anthropologist Roger Lancaster spent many months during the 1980s studying the effects of the Sandinista Revolution on the lives of working people in Man-agua, Nicaragua. While he was there, he learned about *cochones*. *Cochón* could be translated into English as *homosexual*, but this would be highly misleading. As Lancaster discovered, working-class Nicaraguans interpret sexual relations between men differently than North Americans do, and their interpretation is central to the traditional Nicaraguan ideas about masculinity that have been called *machismo*.

To begin with, a "real man" (or *macho*) is widely admired as someone who is active, violent, and dominant. In sexual terms, this means that the penis is seen as a weapon used violently to dominate one's sexual partner, who is thereby rendered passive, abused, and subordinate. North Americans typically think of machismo as involving the domination of women by men, but as Lancaster shows, the system is equally defined by the domination of men over other men. Indeed, a "manly man" in working-class Nicaragua is defined as one who is the active, dominant, penetrating sexual partner in encounters with women *and* men. A "passive" male who allows a "manly man" to have sexual intercourse with him in this way is called a cochón.

A North American gay man himself, Lancaster found that Nicaraguan views of male-male sexual encounters differ considerably from contemporary North American ideas about male homosexuality. In Nicaragua, for example, the people Lancaster knew assumed that men "would naturally be aroused by the idea of anally penetrating another male" (1992, 241). Only the "passive" cochón is stigmatized, whereas males who always take the "active" role in sexual intercourse with other males and with females are seen as "normal." Nicaraguans, moreover, find hate crimes such as gay-bashing inconceivable: Cochones may be made fun of, but they are also much admired performers during Carnival. In the United States, by contrast, the active-passive distinction does not exist, and anal intercourse is not the only form that male homosexual expression may take. Both partners in same-sex encounters are considered homosexual and equally stigmatized, and gay-bashing is a sometimes deadly reality, probably because it is *not* assumed that "normal" males will naturally be aroused by the idea of sex with another man.

In Nicaragua, public challenges for dominance are a constant of male-male interaction even when sexual intercourse is not involved. The term *cochón* may be used as an epithet not only for a man who yields publicly to another man, but also for cats that don't catch mice, or indeed anything that somehow fails to perform its proper function. In Lancaster's view, cochones are made, not born: "Those who consistently lose out in the competition for male status . . . discover pleasure in the passive sexual role or its social status: these men are made into cochones. And those who master the rules of conventional masculinity . . . are made into machistas" (1992, 249).

These ideas about gender and sexuality created an unanticipated roadblock for Sandinistas who wanted to improve the lives of Nicaraguan women and children. The Sandinista government passed a series of New Family Laws, which were designed to encourage men to support their families economically and to discourage irresponsible sex, irresponsible parenting, and familial dislocation. When Lancaster interviewed Nicaraguan men to see what they thought of these laws, however, he repeatedly got the following response: "First the interrogative: 'What do the Sandinistas want from us? That we should all become cochones?' And then the tautological: 'A man has to be a man.' That is, a man is defined by what he is not—a cochón" (1992, 274).

▼ SEXUALITY AND POWER

The physical activity that we call sexual intercourse is not just doing what comes naturally. Like so much else in human life, sex does not speak for itself, nor does it have only one meaning. Sexual practices can be used to give concrete form to more abstract notions we have about the place of men and women in the world. They may serve as a metaphor for expressing differential power within a society. This is particularly clear in the sexual practices that embody Nicaraguan machismo or North American date rape and family violence. That is, sexual practices can be used to enact, in unmistakable physical terms, the reality of differential power. This is equally clear in the arguments over "gay marriage" in the United States, since marriage in a nation-state has legal consequences and protections, as well as embodying the legitimacy of the couple's commitment to each other. This reminds us that marriages, families, and sexual practices never occur in a vacuum but are embedded in other social practices such as food production, political organization, and kinship.

CHAPTER SUMMARY

1. Marriage is a social process that transforms the status of a man and woman, stipulates the degree of sexual access the married partners may have to each other, establishes the legitimacy of children born to the wife, and creates relationships between the kin of the wife and the kin of the husband.
2. Woman marriage and ghost marriage highlight several defining features of marriage and also demonstrate that the roles of husband and father may not be dependent on the gender of the person who fills it.
3. There are four major patterns of postmarital residence: neolocal, patrilocal, matrilocal, and avunculocal.
4. A person may be married to only one person at a time (monogamy) or to several (polygamy). Polygamy can be further subdivided into

polygyny, in which a man is married to two or more wives, and polyandry, in which a woman is married to two or more husbands.
5. The study of polyandry reveals the separation of a woman's sexuality and her reproductive capacity, something not found in monogamous or polygynous societies. There are three main forms of polyandry: fraternal polyandry, associated polyandry, and secondary marriage.
6. Bridewealth is a payment of symbolically important goods by the husband's lineage to the wife's lineage. Anthropologists see this as compensation to the wife's family for the loss of her productive and reproductive capacities. A woman's bridewealth payment may enable her brother to pay bridewealth to get a wife.
7. Dowry is typically a transfer of family wealth from parents to their daughter at the time of her marriage. Dowries are often considered the

wife's contribution to the establishment of a new household.

8. In some cultures, the most important relationships a man and a woman have are with their opposite-sex siblings. Adult brothers and sisters may see one another often and jointly control lineage affairs.

9. Different family structures produce different internal patterns and tensions. There are three basic family types: nuclear, extended, and joint. Families may change from one type to another over time and with the birth, growth, and marriage of children.

10. Most human societies permit marriages to end by divorce, although it is not always easy. In most societies, childlessness is grounds for divorce. Sometimes nagging, quarreling, adultery, cruelty, and stinginess are causes. In some societies, only men may initiate a divorce. In very few societies is divorce impossible.

11. Families have developed ingenious ways of keeping together even when some members live abroad for extended periods. Gays and lesbians in North America have created families by choice, based on nurturance, which they believe are as enduring as families based on marriage and birth.

12. Marriage rules are subject to negotiation, even when they appear rigid. This is illustrated by Iteso marriage. The Iteso depend upon women from the outside to perpetuate their patrilineages, and the women express their ironic awareness of this fact through ritualized laughter at marriage.

13. Sexual practices vary greatly worldwide, from the puritanical and fearful to the casual and pleasurable. In some societies, young men and women begin having free sexual relations from an early age until they are married. Sexual practices that North Americans call *homosexuality* or *bisexuality* may be understood very differently in different societies. In the contemporary globalizing world, Western and non-Western same-sex practices are becoming increasingly entangled with one another, leading to the emergence of local movements for "lesbian" and "gay" rights on many continents.

KEY TERMS

marriage	patrilocal	polyandry	nuclear family
affinal	matrilocal	bridewealth	extended family
consanguineal	avunculocal	dowry	joint family
endogamy	monogamy	family	blended family
exogamy	polygamy	conjugal family	
neolocal	polygyny	nonconjugal family	

SUGGESTED READINGS

Bohannan, Paul, and John Middleton. 1968. *Marriage, family, and residence.* New York: Natural History Press. *A classic collection, with important and readable articles.*

Lancaster, Roger. 1992. *Life is hard.* Berkeley: University of California Press. *A stunning analysis of machismo in Nicaragua, in which sexual practices North Americans consider homosexual are interpreted very differently.*

Sacks, Karen. 1979. *Sisters and wives.* Urbana: University of Illinois Press. *A Marxian analysis of the notion of sexual equality. This book includes very important data and analysis on sister-brother relations.*

Shostak, Marjorie. 1981. *Nisa: The life and words of a !Kung woman.* New York: Vintage. *A wonderful book. The story of a Ju/'hoansi (!Kung) woman's life in her own words. Shostak provides background for each chapter. There is much here on marriage and everyday life.*

Suggs, David, and Andrew Miracle, eds. 1993. *Culture and human sexuality.* Pacific Grove, CA: Brooks/Cole. *A collection of important articles from a variety of theoretical perspectives on the nature and culture of human sexuality.*

Chapter 13

Dimensions of Inequality in the Contemporary World

The ethnographic and historical records show that societies in which people enjoy relatively equal relations with one another have flourished in different times and places. But cultural constructions of human differences and the use of such cultural constructions to build societies based on unequal social relations also have a long history. This chapter discusses some key forms of social and cultural inequality in the contemporary world to which anthropologists have devoted attention.

In the previous chapter, we described some of the distinctive forms of face-to-face social organization invented by societies that, at one time, were relatively egalitarian in political organization. But anthropologists have also long been interested in documenting the various forms of social stratification that human beings have invented. **Stratified societies**, you will recall, are societies made up of permanently ranked subgroups, in which the higher-ranking groups have disproportionately greater access to wealth, power, and prestige than do lower-ranking groups. As we saw in an earlier chapter, in those societies that anthropologists call *chiefdoms*, stratification is minimal. Perhaps only the office of chief is a permanently superior status (with the chief's relatives sharing it), and social and economic relations among nonchief members of society may remain relatively egalitarian. More elaborate social stratification is found in societies classified as *states*, which are not only much larger than chiefdoms but also employ a variety of mechanisms to bind together different subgroups into a hierarchy that regulates each group's access to wealth, power, and prestige.

All people in the world today, even refugees, must deal with the authority of one or another nation-state, and all nation-states are socially stratified. But inequality within nation-states may be constructed out of multiple categories arranged in different, and sometimes contradictory, hierarchies of stratification. In this chapter we discuss six such categories: gender, class, caste, race, ethnicity, and nationality. It is important to emphasize from the outset that *every one of these categories is a cultural invention* designed to create boundaries around one or another imagined community. *None* of these categories maps onto unambiguous biological subdivisions within the human species, although members of societies that employ these categories often will invoke "nature" to shore up their legitimacy.

Some of these patterns (i.e., gender, class, caste) reach back thousands of years into human history. Others (i.e., race, ethnicity, and nationality) are far more recent in origin and are closely associated with

changes that began in Europe some 500 years ago. The spread of capitalism and colonialism introduced new forms of stratification into formerly autonomous, egalitarian societies, and these also reshaped forms of stratification that predated their arrival. Anthropologists and other social scientists have argued with one another about how these categories should be defined and whether or not they can be usefully applied cross-culturally, and we will look at some of their arguments.

▼ GENDER

Anthropological research on issues involving sex and gender increased enormously in the last third of the twentieth century, especially in the work of feminist anthropologists. Research focused not only on reproductive roles and sexuality, but also on the question of gender inequality. Beginning in the 1970s, feminist anthropologists dissatisfied with gender inequality in their own societies closely examined the ethnographic record to determine whether male dominance is a feature of all human societies.

Early work seemed to suggest that male dominance is in fact universal. For example, Sherry Ortner suggested that male dominance was rooted in a form of binary cultural thinking that opposed male to female. Males were then ranked higher than females because females were universally seen as "closer to nature," by virtue of the fact that they gave birth and nursed their young (Ortner 1974). Yet Jane Collier, Michelle Rosaldo, and Sylvia Yanagisako (1997) were able to show that the roles of men and women within families—even the very idea of what constituted a "family"—varied enormously, cross-culturally and historically. They concluded that the "nuclear family" of father, mother, and children was far from universal and was in fact best understood as a relatively recent historical consequence of the rise of industrial capitalism in western European societies. Attention to history also led Marxist-feminist anthropologists like Eleanor Leacock to argue that women's subordination to men was not inevitable but could be connected explicitly to the rise of private property and the emergence of the state. She used ethnographic and historical evidence from North and South America, Melanesia, and Africa to show how

---

stratified societies Societies in which there is a permanent hierarchy that accords some members privileged access to wealth, power, and prestige.

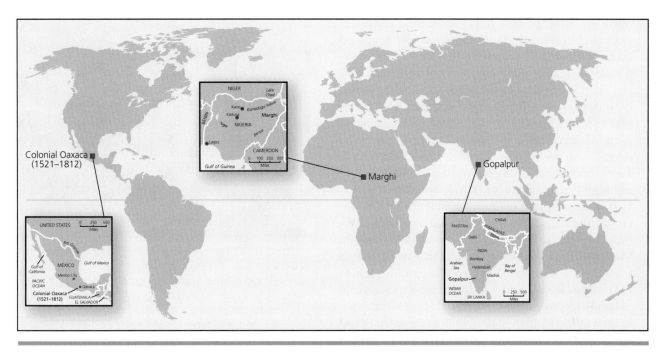

FIGURE 13.1 Location of societies whose EthnoProfiles appear in chapter 13.

Western capitalist colonization had transformed egalitarian precolonial indigenous gender relations into unequal, male-dominated gender relations (Leacock 1983).

More recently, anthropologists like Marilyn Strathern (1988) have argued that the particular relations between males and females in society need to be recognized as just one example of gender *symbolism*. Strathern defines **gender** as "those categorizations of persons, artifacts, events sequences, and so on which draw upon sexual imagery—upon the ways in which the distinctiveness of male and female characteristics make concrete people's ideas about the nature of social relations" (1988, ix). Thinking of gender in this way helps explain why people in some societies not only apply gendered forms of inequality to phenotypic males and females but may also use gender categories to structure relations between hierarchically ranked categories of men, as in the Nicaraguan contrast between "manly men" and *cochones* described in chapter 12. Similarly, Roy Richard Grinker found that male village-dwelling Lese householders of the Democratic Republic of Congo distinguished themselves from their forest-dwelling Efe pygmy trading partners using the same unequal gender categories that they used to distinguish themselves from their wives. From the point of view of Lese men, both Efe partners and Lese wives were subordinate to them because both had been incorporated within the households of Lese men (Grinker 1994).

Anthropologist Ann Stoler has compared Dutch colonialism in Indonesia with colonialism elsewhere. She found that white European colonizers conceived of their relationship to indigenous males in terms of both "racial" and gender inequality. The colonizers constructed a "racial" divide between colonizer and colonized, ranking "white" colonial males above the "nonwhite" indigenous males whom they had conquered. At the same time, they violently punished any hint of sexual involvement between indigenous males and "white" women while allowing themselves unrestricted sexual access to indigenous women. In this way, white male colonizers "feminized" indigenous males, constructing them as less than fully male because they had been unable to defend their land or "their women" against more powerful white

gender The cultural construction of beliefs and behaviors considered appropriate for each sex.

outsiders. Stoler points out that white male colonizers struggled to shore up these racialized and gendered colonial hierarchies whenever indigenous males organized politically and threatened colonial rule.

Haiti began as a colony of France and achieved its independence following a successful revolt of black slaves against their white colonial masters. As Nina Glick Schiller and Georges Fouron argue, however, "Haiti has its own particular and mixed messages about gender that give to women and men both rights and responsibilities to family and nation" (2002, 133). Women appear in official stories about the Haitian revolution, some even portrayed as heroines. Yet most are portrayed as silent wives and mothers. Moreover, the founders of the Haitian state borrowed from their former French masters "a patriarchal idea of family as well as a civil code that gave men control of family life, wealth, and property" (134). Women belonged to the Haitian nation, but "state officials and the literate elite envisioned women as able to reproduce the nation only in conjunction with a Haitian man" (134). Until recently, Haitian women who married foreigners lost their Haitian citizenship. High-status Haitian women are those who are supported economically by their Haitian husbands and who stay home with their children. Schiller and Fouron argue that many Haitians "still believe that to live by these values is to uphold not only family but also national honor" (135) (Figure 13.2).

By contrast, Haitian women who cannot live by these values are accorded low status. On the one hand, this means that they are not confined to the domestic sphere. On the other hand, for this very reason they are assumed to be always sexually available. "Men in Haiti see women alone or in the workplace as willing and able to trade their sexuality for other things they need. Men may ask rather than take, but often they are making an offer that women cannot afford to refuse" (139–40). This well describes the structural constraints with which Acéphie Joseph had to contend; options open to women of higher social class position were not available to her. To understand why, however, we need to look

FIGURE 13.2 The founders of the Haitian state borrowed from their former French masters an idea of gender that gave men control of family life. Women belonged to the Haitian nation, but until recently Haitian women who married foreigners lost their Haitian citizenship and their children would not be Haitians.

more closely at what anthropologists have to say about the connections between social class and social inequality.

▼ CLASS

In general, **classes** are hierarchically arranged social groups defined on economic grounds. That is, higher-ranked social classes have disproportionate access to sources of wealth in the society, whereas the members of low-ranked classes have much more limited access to wealth (Figure 13.3).

The concept of class has a double heritage in modern anthropology, one stemming from Europe, the other from the United States. European social scientists lived in states with a long history of social class divisions reaching back into the Middle Ages and, in some cases, even into Roman times. In their experience, social classes are well entrenched and relatively closed groups. The Industrial Revolution and the French Revolution promised to end the oppressive privileges of the ruling class and to equalize everyone's access to wealth. However, class divisions did not wither away in Europe during the nineteenth century; they just changed their contours. Followers of Marx judged that, at best, an old ruling class had

class A ranked group within a hierarchically stratified society whose membership is defined primarily in terms of wealth, occupation, or other economic criteria.

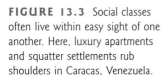

FIGURE 13.3 Social classes often live within easy sight of one another. Here, luxury apartments and squatter settlements rub shoulders in Caracas, Venezuela.

been displaced by a new one: feudal aristocrats by bourgeois capitalists. The lowest level in European societies—rural peasants—were partially displaced as well, with the appearance of the urban working class. But the barriers separating those at the top of the class hierarchy from those on the bottom seemed just as rigid as ever.

As we saw in an earlier chapter, Marx defines classes in terms of their members' different relations to the means of production. This means that as long as a particular set of unequal productive relations flourishes in a society, the classes defined by these unequal roles in the division of labor will also persist. The French Revolution had triggered the displacement of aristocrats and peasants who had played the key roles in European feudalism. They were replaced by new key classes—industrial entrepreneurs and the industrial working class—who were linked together within the capitalist mode of production. In time, Marx predicted, these industrial workers would become the new "leading class," rising up to oust capitalists when the socialist revolution came.

As Marx was well aware, all those who are linked to the means of production in the same way (e.g., as workers) often do not recognize what they have in common and may therefore fail to develop the kind of solidarity among themselves—the "class consciousness"—that could, in Marx's view, lead to

revolution. Indeed, the possibility of peasant- or working-class solidarity in many of the stratified societies studied by anthropologists is actively undercut by institutions of **clientage**. According to anthropologist M. G. Smith, clientage "designates a variety of relationships, which all have inequality of status of the associated persons as a common characteristic" ([1954] 1981, 31). Clientage is a relationship between individuals rather than groups. The party of superior status is the patron, and the party of inferior status is the client. Stratified societies united by links of clientage can be very stable. Low-status clients believe their security depends on finding a high-status individual who can protect them. For example, clientage is characteristic of *compadrazgo* relationships, especially when the ritual parents are of higher social status than the biological parents. In fact, the Latin American societies in which compadrazgo flourishes are class societies, and parents who are peasants or workers often seek landowners or factory owners as *compadres*.

Marx's view of class is clearly different from the view of class hegemonic in the United States. For generations the "American dream" has been that in

clientage The institution linking individuals from upper and lower levels in a stratified society.

the United States individuals may pursue wealth, power, and prestige unhampered by the unyielding class barriers characteristic of "Old World" societies. As a result, many social scientists trained in the United States (including cultural anthropologists) have tended to define social classes primarily in terms of income level and to argue that such social classes are open, porous, and permeable, rather than rigid and exclusionary. Upward class mobility is supposed to be, in principle, attainable by all people, regardless of how low their social origins are. Even poor boys like Abraham Lincoln, born in a log cabin on the frontier, can grow up to be president.

But the promise of the American Dream of equal opportunity for upward class mobility has not been realized by all those living in the United States. In the early twentieth century, both black and white social scientists concluded that an unyielding "color bar" prevented upward class mobility for U.S. citizens with African ancestry. One participant in these studies, an anthropologist named W. Lloyd Warner, argued in 1936 that the color bar looked more like the rigid barrier reported to exist between castes in India than the supposedly permeable boundary separating American social classes. That is to say, membership in a **caste** is ascribed at birth and each ranked caste is closed, such that individuals are not allowed to move from one caste into another. Membership in social classes is also ascribed at birth, according to Warner, but unlike castes, classes are not closed and individual social mobility from one class into another is possible (Harrison 1995, 1998; Sharma 1999, 15; Warner 1936). Warner's distinction between caste and class became standard for decades in American cultural anthropology.

Is this a plausible contrast? The aspect of caste that impressed Warner was the reported rigidity of the barrier between castes, which seemed much like the barrier separating blacks and whites in the United States. But in 1948, an African American sociologist named Oliver Cromwell Cox rejected an equation between caste and race. Cox pointed out that many authorities on caste in India claimed that Hindu castes were harmoniously integrated within a *caste system*

> **caste** A ranked group within a hierarchically stratified society that is closed, prohibiting individuals to move from one caste to another.

shaped by Hindu religious beliefs about purity and pollution. Most importantly, it appeared that members of low-ranked "impure" castes did not challenge the caste system even though it oppressed them. If this were true, Cox concluded, caste relations were *unlike* race relations in the United States, because whites had imposed the color bar by force and only by force had they been able to repress black resistance to the injustice of the system. Ursula Sharma (1999) points out, however, that both Warner and Cox were relying on an understanding of Hindu castes that today is considered highly misleading.

▼ CASTE

The world *caste* comes from the Portuguese word *casta*, meaning "chaste." Portuguese explorers applied it to the stratification systems they encountered in South Asia in the fifteenth century. They understood that these societies were divided into a hierarchy of ranked subgroups, each of which was "chaste" in the sense that sexual and marital links across group boundaries were forbidden. That is, in anthropological terms, castes were *endogamous*, and many anthropologists agree that caste is fundamentally a form of kinship (Guneratne 2002).

Most Western scholars have taken the stratification system of India as the prototype of caste stratification, and some insist that caste cannot properly be said to exist outside India. Others, however, do find value in applying the term to forms of social stratification developed elsewhere that bear a family resemblance to the South Asian pattern. One important example, which we examine later in this chapter, comes from Nigeria.

Caste in India

The term *caste*, as most Western observers use it, collapses two different South Asian concepts. The first term, *varna*, refers to the widespread notion that Indian society is ideally divided into priests, warriors, farmers, and merchants—four functional subdivisions analogous to the estates of medieval and early modern Europe (Guneratne 2002; Sharma 1999). The second term, *jati*, refers to localized, named, endogamous groups. Although jati names are frequently the names of occupations (e.g., farmer, saltmaker), there is no agreed upon way to group the many local jatis within one or the other of the four varnas, which is why jati members can disagree with others about where their own jati ought to belong. In any case, varna divisions are more theoretical in nature, whereas jati is the more significant term in most of the local village settings where anthropologists have traditionally conducted fieldwork.

Villagers in the southern Indian town of Gopalpur defined a jati for anthropologist Alan Beals (see EthnoProfile 13.1: Gopalpur). They said it was "a category of men thought to be related, to occupy a particular position within a hierarchy of jatis, to marry among themselves, and to follow particular practices and occupations" (Beals 1962, 25). Beals's informants compared the relationship between jatis of different rank to the relationship between brothers. Ideally, they said, members of low-ranking jatis respect and obey members of high-ranking jatis, just as younger brothers respect and obey older brothers.

Villagers in Gopalpur were aware of at least 50 different jatis, although not all were represented in the village. Because jatis have different occupational specialties that they alone can perform, villagers were sometimes dependent on the services of outsiders. For example, there was no member of the Washerman jati in Gopalpur. As a result, a member of that jati from another village had to be employed when people in Gopalpur wanted their clothes cleaned ritually or required clean cloth for ceremonies.

Jatis are distinguished in terms of the foods they eat as well as their traditional occupations. These features have a ritual significance that affects interactions between members of different jatis. In Hindu belief, certain foods and occupations are classed as pure and others as polluting. In theory, all jatis are ranked on a scale from purest to most polluted (Figure 13.4). Ranked highest of all are the vegetarian Brahmins, who are pure enough to approach the gods. Carpenters and Blacksmiths, who also eat a vegetarian diet, are also assigned a high rank. Below the vegetarians are those who eat "clean," or "pure," meat. In Gopalpur, this group of jatis included Saltmakers, Farmers, and Shepherds, who eat sheep, goats, chicken, and fish but not pork or beef. The lowest-ranking jatis are "unclean" meat eaters, who include Stoneworkers and Basketweavers (who eat pork) and Leatherworkers (who

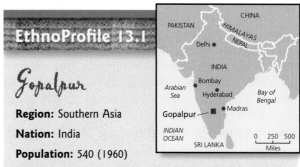

EthnoProfile 13.1

Gopalpur

Region: Southern Asia

Nation: India

Population: 540 (1960)

Environment: Center of a plain, some fertile farmland and pasture

Livelihood: Intensive millet farming, some cattle and sheep herding

Political organization: Caste system in a modern nation-state

For more information: Beals, Alan. 1962. *Gopalpur, a south Indian village.* New York: Holt, Rinehart, & Winston.

eat pork and beef). Occupations that involve slaughtering animals or touching polluted things are themselves polluting. Jatis that traditionally carry out such activities as butchering and washing dirty clothing are ranked below jatis whose traditional work does not involve polluting activities.

FIGURE 13.4 Gautam Ganu Jadhao, a city worker, removes a cart full of sewage waste from a Bombay neighborhood in July 2005. People like him, whose occupations are characterized as polluting, are ranked at the bottom of Hindu caste society.

Hindu dietary rules deal not only with the kinds of food that may be eaten by different jatis but also with the circumstances in which members of one jati may accept food prepared by members of another. Members of a lower-ranking jati may accept any food prepared by members of a higher-ranking jati. Members of a higher-ranking jati may accept only certain foods prepared by a lower-ranking jati. In addition, members of different jatis should not eat together.

In practice, these rules are not as confining as they appear. In Gopalpur, "'food' referred to particular kinds of food, principally rice. 'Eating together' means eating from the same dish or sitting on the same line. . . . Members of quite different jatis may eat together if they eat out of separate bowls and if they are facing each other or turned slightly away from each other" (Beals 1962, 41). Members of jatis that are close in rank and neither at the top nor at the bottom of the scale often share food and eat together on a daily basis. Strict observance of the rules is saved for ceremonial occasions.

The way in which non-Hindus were incorporated into the jati system in Gopalpur illuminates the logic of the system. For example, Muslims have long ruled the region surrounding Gopalpur; thus, political power has been a salient attribute of Muslim identity. In addition, Muslims do not eat pork or the meat of animals that have not been ritually slaughtered. These attributes, taken together, led the villagers in Gopalpur to rank Muslims above the Stoneworkers and Basketweavers, who eat pork. All three groups were considered to be eaters of unclean meat because Muslims do eat beef.

There is no direct correlation between the status of a jati on the scale of purity and pollution and the class status of members of that jati. Beals noted, for example, that the high status of Brahmins meant that "there are a relatively large number of ways in which a poor Brahmin may become wealthy" (1962, 37). Similarly, members of low-status jatis may find their attempts to amass wealth curtailed by the opposition of their status superiors. In Gopalpur, a group of Farmers and Shepherds attacked a group of Stoneworkers who had purchased good rice land in the village. Those Stoneworkers were eventually forced to buy inferior land elsewhere in the village. In general, however, regardless of jati, a person who wishes to advance economically "must be prepared

to defend his gains against jealous neighbors. Anyone who buys land is limiting his neighbor's opportunities to buy land. Most people safeguard themselves by tying themselves through indebtedness to a powerful landlord who will give them support when difficulties are encountered" (Beals 1962, 39).

Although the interdependence of jatis is explained in theory by their occupational specialties, the social reality is a bit different. For example, Saltmakers in Gopalpur are farmers and actually produce little salt, which can be bought in shops by those who need it. It is primarily in the context of ritual that jati interdependence is given full play. Recall that Gopalpur villagers required the services of a Washerman when they needed *ritually* clean garments or cloth; otherwise, most villagers washed their own clothing. "To arrange a marriage, to set up the doorway of a new house, to stage a drama, or to hold an entertainment, the householder must call on a wide range of jatis. The entertainment of even a modest number of guests requires the presence of the Singer. The Potter must provide new pots in which to cook the food; the Boin from the Farmer jati must carry the pot; the Shepherd must sacrifice the goat; the Crier, a Saltmaker, must invite the guests. To survive, one requires the cooperation of only a few jatis; to enjoy life and do things in the proper manner requires the cooperation of many" (Beals 1962, 41).

Caste Struggle in Contemporary India

Beals's study of Gopalpur documented three dimensions of caste relations in India that have become increasingly significant over time. First, Beals describes a rural village in which jati membership mattered most on ritual occasions. In the last 30 years, cultural practices associated with caste in village India have become even more attenuated or have disappeared as increasingly large numbers of Indians have moved to large cities where they are surrounded by strangers whose caste membership they do not know (Sharma 1999, 37). They still use the idiom of purity and pollution to debate the status of particular castes, but otherwise their understanding of caste usually has nothing to do with ritual status.

Second, Beals describes members of middle-ranking jatis in Gopalpur who treated one another as equals outside of ritual contexts. Subrata Mitra points out that "By the 1960s, electoral mobilization had led to a new phenomenon called horizontal mobilization whereby people situated at comparable levels within the local caste hierarchy came together in caste associations," many of which formed new political parties to support their own interests (1994, 61). Moreover, increased involvement of Indians in capitalist market practices has led to "a proliferation of modern associations that use traditional ties of *jati* and *varna* to promote collective economic well-being" (65). For example, a housing trust set up for Brahmins in the Indian state of Karnataka recruits Brahmins from throughout the Karnataka region, in an effort to overcome "*jati*-based division into quarrelling sects of Brahmins" (66). The interests that draw jatis into coalitions of this kind "often turn out to be class interests. . . . This does not mean that caste and class are the same, since commentators note caste as blurring class divisions as often as they express them. Rather it tells us that class and caste are not 'inimical' or antithetical" (Sharma 1999, 68).

Third, Beals showed that middle-ranking jatis in Gopalpur in the 1960s were willing to use violence to block the upward economic mobility of members of a low-ranking jati. Similar behavior was reported in the work of other anthropologists like Gerald Berreman, who did fieldwork in the late 1950s in the peasant village of Sirkanda in the lower Himalayas of North India. Berreman observed that low-caste people in Sirkanda "do not share, or are not heavily committed to, the 'common official values' which high-caste people affect before outsiders. . . . Low-caste people resent their inferior position and the disadvantages which inhere in it" while "high castes rely heavily on threats of economic and physical sanctions to keep their subordinates in line," such that when low-caste people do publicly endorse "common official values," they do so only out of fear of these sanctions (1962, 15–16).

In recent years, a number of low-caste groups in urban India have undertaken collective efforts to lift themselves off the bottom of society, either by imitating the ritual practices of higher castes (a process called "Sanskritization") or by converting to a non-Hindu religion (such as Buddhism or Christianity) in which caste plays no role. According to Dipankar Gupta, this should not surprise us. His research has shown that "castes are, first and foremost, discrete

entities with deep pockets of ideological heritage" and that "the element of caste competition is, therefore, a characteristic of the caste order and not a later addition. . . . This implies that the caste system, as a system, worked primarily because it was enforced by power and not by ideological acquiescence" (2005, 412–13).

These challenges have had little effect in changing the negative stereotypes of so-called untouchables held by the so-called clean castes. However, the constitution of India prohibits the practice of untouchability, and the national government has acted to improve the lot of the low castes by regularly passing legislation designed to improve their economic and educational opportunities. In some cases, these measures seem to have succeeded, but violent reprisals have been common. In rural areas many disputes continue to be over land, as in Gopalpur. However, even worse violence has been seen in urban India, as in 1990, when unrest was triggered by publication of a report recommending increases in the numbers of government jobs and reserved college places set aside for members of low castes. At the end of the twentieth century, relations between low-caste and high-caste Hindus were described as "conflictual rather than competitive in some localities" with "caste violence . . . recognized as a serious problem in contemporary India" (Sharma 1999, 67).

Caste in Western Africa

Anthropologists often use the term *caste* to describe societies outside India when they encounter one of two features: (1) endogamous occupational groupings, whose members are looked down on by other groups in the society or (2) an endogamous ruling elite who set themselves above those over whom they rule. Anthropologist James Vaughan (1970; see also Tamari 1991) reviewed the data on western African caste systems. The presence of endogamous, stigmatized occupational groupings was common in all societies of the Sahara and in the western Sudan (the band of territory between Senegal and Lake Chad that lies south of the Sahara and north of the coastal rain forest). Vaughan also found castes in a second culture area located in the mountain ranges that lie along the modern border between Nigeria and Cameroon. In this region, many societies had endogamous groups of "blacksmiths" whose status was distinct from that of other members of society. These "blacksmiths" were not despised, however; if anything, they were feared or regarded with awe.

Vaughan studied such a caste of blacksmiths in a kingdom of the Marghi, whose traditional territory was in the mountains and nearby plains south of Lake Chad in present-day Nigeria (see EthnoProfile 13.2: Marghi; see also http://www.indiana.edu/margi). Members of the caste, who were called *ingkyagu*, were traditional craft specialists whose major occupation was the smithing of iron. They made a variety of iron tools for ordinary Marghi, the most important of which were the hoes used for farming. They also made weapons and iron ornaments of various kinds. They worked leather, fashioning traditional items of apparel, leather-covered charms, and slings in which infants were carried. They worked wood, making beds and carving stools. They were barbers, incising traditional tribal markings on Marghi women, and were responsible in some Marghi kingdoms for shaving the head of a newly installed king. They were morticians, responsible for assisting in the preparation of a body for burial, digging the grave, and carrying the corpse from the household to the grave. They were musicians, playing a distinctive drum played by no one else. Some were diviners and "doctors." And female caste members were the potters of Marghi society.

Vaughan stresses that although regular Marghi and ingkyagu both recognized that ingkyagu were different, in most ways the ingkyagu did not stand out from other Marghi. All the same, Marghi and ingkyagu did not intermarry and would not share the same food. In an interesting parallel to the Indian case described earlier, ingkyagu could drink beer brewed by Marghi women as long as they provided their own drinking vessel. Marghi, however, would not drink beer brewed by female ingkyagu.

When Marghi described the differences between themselves and ingkyagu to Vaughan, they said that caste members were "different" and "strange." In Vaughan's opinion, this has to do in large part with the fact that ingkyagu do not farm: "To be a Marghi means to be a farmer. . . . A person who does not farm cannot in the Marghi idiom be considered an altogether normal person" (1970, 71). By contrast, ingkyagu attribute the difference between themselves

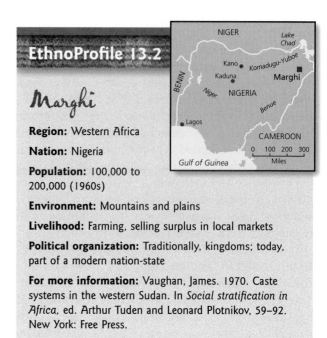

EthnoProfile 13.2

Marghi

Region: Western Africa

Nation: Nigeria

Population: 100,000 to 200,000 (1960s)

Environment: Mountains and plains

Livelihood: Farming, selling surplus in local markets

Political organization: Traditionally, kingdoms; today, part of a modern nation-state

For more information: Vaughan, James. 1970. Caste systems in the western Sudan. In *Social stratification in Africa*, ed. Arthur Tuden and Leonard Plotnikov, 59–92. New York: Free Press.

and other Marghi to the division of labor and point out that both groups depend on one another. Marghi do their own smelting, but they require ingkyagu to use their skills as smiths to turn the smelted ore into implements. Thus, Marghi rely on members of the caste for their farming tools, but ingkyagu rely on Marghi for food.

Vaughan suggested that this division of labor and interdependence is not only practical but also part of the Marghi worldview, revealed in the domains of politics and ritual. For example, a curious relationship linked ingkyagu to Marghi kings. The most remarkable feature of this relationship was that Marghi kings traditionally took a female member of the caste as a bride, thereby violating the rule of endogamy. Recall the role a member of the caste plays during the investiture of a new king; it was even more common for ingkyagu to bury deceased Marghi kings seated on an iron stool, surrounded by charcoal, which is the way ingkyagu themselves were buried. In addition, of all Marghi clans, only the ngkyagu clans were exempt from participating in the choice of a new Marghi king. Indeed, traditionally they had their own "king," the *ptil ingkyagu*, who decided disputes among ingkyagu without recourse to the legal advisers of the Marghi king.

All this suggests that the two categories Marghi and ingkyagu formed the foundation of Marghi

IN THEIR OWN WORDS

Europe's Walls for Gypsies

The New York Times *published the following editorial on October 24, 1999, drawing attention to the tragic fate of Gypsies who have been caught in the war between Serbs and ethnic Albanians in Kosovo, a province in the former Yugoslavia. On October 28, 1999, a letter to the editor from Michael Ratner, vice president of the Center for Constitutional Rights in New York City, argued that ethnic Albanians had been responsible for most of the violence against Gypsies in Kosovo. He agreed, however, with the main point of the editorial, writing: "It is curious that the countries that engaged in a war over 'ethnic cleansing' by Serbs have remained almost silent about the expulsion of the Gypsies."*

Ten days ago, the Czech town of Usti nad Labem managed to symbolize both of Europe's 20th-century pathologies—Communism and Nazism—when it erected a six-foot high concrete wall to separate a Gypsy neighborhood from one of ethnic Czechs. The wall, called a "law and order" measure by the town's mayor, has been condemned by the Czech Republic's government and Parliament, and by President Vaclav Havel. But it still stands, and is very popular in Usti nad Labem.

The wall is a sign of both the increasing problems faced by Gypsies, or Roma, as they call themselves, and the half-hearted efforts of the former Communist countries to solve them. The most recent tragedy took place in Kosovo, where Gypsies lost a war they did not even fight. Virtually all the region's 100,000 Gypsies have been driven out of their homes and hundreds have been killed—by Serbs during the war and by ethnic Albanians afterward.

The fall of Communism has not been kind to the east bloc's five million Gypsies. As the work force has lost its guaranteed employment, Gypsies have been among the first fired. Newly permitted nationalism has brought to the surface widespread prejudice against Gypsies and given rise to dozens of racial killings and attacks, which are often treated lightly by police.

Czech workers under police protection building a wall to separate a Gypsy neighborhood from an ethnic Czech neighborhood in Usti nad Labem, October 1999.

One of the least visible but most basic problems for Gypsies in the Czech Republic, Slovakia and Hungary is that they are disproportionately shunted into special schools for the mentally retarded. According to the Czech government, half of Gypsy children go to these schools, and Czech Gypsy leaders say the figure is 70 percent.

Children in these schools are even more walled off than the Gypsies of Usti nad Labem. They cannot acquire a high school education or the skills for good jobs. The

(continued on next page)

Europe's Walls for Gypsies
(continued)

label of "retarded" discourages employers from hiring Gypsies even for unskilled work. Their status as unemployable outsiders contributes to the Gypsies' high rates of crime. The special schools, in use for decades, have also insured that new generations are raised in families with little education.

Last June, 12 Gypsy families in the Czech city of Ostrava sued the Ostrava school board and the country's constitutional court to try to stop the practice. They were aided by the European Roma Rights Center in Budapest, which is financed in part by George Soros.

Children are supposed to be put in special schools only after extensive tests and with parental consent. But a study by the Roma Rights Center found that some are transferred from regular schools because teachers consider them disruptive, and others are considered retarded due to linguistic

problems. Many Gypsy children do not speak Czech at home, or use a dialect of Czech.

Gypsy parents are often intimidated and not informed that such transfers are nearly always permanent, the Roma Rights Center argues. Some readily agree to send their children to the heavily Gypsy special schools because the children are targets of bullying in regular schools.

When Social Democrats took over the Czech government last year, they acknowledged the problem of special schools. They have begun some programs to give Gypsy children extra attention in regular schools. But more energy is needed to solve a hidden problem that dooms Gypsy children to a lifetime of disadvantage and discrimination.

Source: New York Times, October 24, 1999, A14.

society. They were mutually interdependent. The ritual prohibitions that divided them, however, suggest that this interdependence carried symbolic overtones. According to Vaughan, the caste distinction allows the Marghi to resolve a paradox. They are a society of farmers who need to support full-time toolmaking nonfarmers in order to farm. Marghi disliked being dependent on others, yet their way of life required them to depend on ingkyagu. The ritual prohibitions that separated ingkyagu from other Marghi also seemed designed to ensure that there would always be some caste specialists around to provide Marghi with the goods they could not make themselves.

The Value of Caste as an Analytic Category

Vaughan's study is but one example of how a generalized concept of caste can illuminate anthropological understanding of social systems with no historical connections to India. The concept of caste has been applied by anthropologist Jacques Maquet (1970) to describe the closed, endogamous ranked strata Tutsi, Hutu, and Twa in the central African kingdom of Rwanda prior to 1959. Pierre van den Berghe (1970)

documents the history of caste-like relationships dating from the beginnings of white settlement in southern Africa that culminated in the twentieth-century "color caste" system distinguishing Whites, Asians, Coloreds, and Bantu that was enforced in apartheid South Africa. De Vos and Wagatsuma (1966) used the term *caste* to describe the *burakamin* of Japan, low-ranking endogamous groups traditionally associated with polluting occupations, who have been subject to dehumanizing stereotypes and residential segregation from other Japanese (Figure 13.5). Ursula Sharma suggests that the concept of caste might be fruitfully used to characterize the relations between the Rom (or Gypsies) of Europe and their non-Rom neighbors, who for centuries have subjected the Rom to stigmatization, social segregation, and economic exclusion (1999, 85–86).

A key element recognized by all anthropologists who use the concept of caste is the endogamy that is enforced, at least in theory, on the members of each ranked group. As van den Berghe put it, membership in such groups is "determined by birth and for life" (1970, 351). Sharma notes the significance of this link between descent and caste, observing that "in societies

FIGURE 13.5 A burakumin man in Japan. De Vos and Wagatsuma argue that the term *caste* is an accurate term to apply to the burakumin.

where descent is regarded as a crucial and persistent principle (however reckoned, and whatever ideological value it is given) almost any social cleavage can become stabilized in a caste-like form" (1999, 85). She suggests the term *castification* to describe a political process by which ethnic or other groups become part of a rank order of some kind, probably orchestrated from the top, but which need not result in the construction of a caste system (92–93).

But the principle of descent has also played a central role in the identification and persistence of race, ethnicity, and nation. As noted above, these three categories are all closely bound up with historical developments over the past 500 years that built the modern world. Indeed, these categories are particularly significant in nation-states, and many contemporary nation-states are of very recent, post-colonial origin. Clearly, to make sense of contemporary postcolonial forms of social stratification, we will also need some understanding of the categories of race, ethnicity, and nation.

▼ RACE

As we saw in chapter 4, the concept of **race** developed in the context of European exploration and conquest, beginning in the fifteenth century. Europeans conquered indigenous peoples in the Americas and

established colonial political economies that soon depended on the labor of Africans imported as slaves. By the end of the nineteenth century, light-skinned Europeans had established colonial rule over large territories inhabited by darker-skinned peoples, marking the beginnings of a global racial order (see Harrison 1995; Köhler 1978; Smedley 1995, 1998; Sanjek 1994; Trouillot 1994). European intellectuals wished both to explain the existence of the human diversity they had encountered and to justify the domination of indigenous peoples and the enslavement of Africans. They argued that the human species was subdivided into "natural kinds" of human beings called "races" that could be sharply distinguished from one another on the basis of physical (or *phenotypic*) appearance. Biological anthropologists contrast an organism's genetic inheritance, or *genotype*, with its observable external appearance, or *phenotype*, which is shaped by environmental as well as genetic influences. All individuals assigned to the same race were assumed to share many common features, of which phenotype was only the outward index.

Race as a Social Category

Belief in the existence of biologically distinct races (sometimes called **racialism**) was then joined to an ancient Western notion called the Great Chain of Being, which proposed that all "natural kinds" could be ranked in a hierarchy, from lowest to highest. In the latter half of the nineteenth century, European thinkers, including many early anthropologists, devised schemes for ranking the "races of Mankind" from lowest to highest. Not surprisingly, the "white" Northern Europeans at the apex of imperial power were placed at the top of this global hierarchy. Darker-skinned peoples like the indigenous inhabitants of the Americas or of Asia, were ranked somewhere in the middle. But Africans, whom Europeans had bought and sold as slaves and whose homelands in Africa were later conquered and incorporated into European empires, ranked lowest of all.

race A human population category whose boundaries allegedly correspond to distinct sets of biological attributes.

racialism Belief in the existence of biologically distinct races.

On the Butt Size of Barbie and Shani
Dolls and Race in the United States

Anthropologist Elizabeth Chin writes about race and Barbie dolls, based on some hands-on research.

The Shani line of dolls introduced by Mattel in 1991 reduces race to a simulacrum consisting of phenotypical features: skin color, hair, and butt. Ann DuCille . . . has discussed much of their complex and contradictory nature, highlighting two central issues: derriere and hair. According to DuCille's interviews with Shani designers, the dolls have been remanufactured to give the illusion of a higher, rounder butt than other Barbies. This has been accomplished, they told her, by pitching Shani's back at a different angle and changing some of the proportions of her hips. I had heard these and other rumors from students at the college where I teach: "Shani's butt is bigger than the other Barbies' butts," "Shani dolls have bigger breasts than Barbie," "Shani dolls have bigger thighs than Barbie." DuCille rightly wonders why a bigger butt is necessarily an attribute of blackness, tying this obsession to turn-of-the-century strains of scientific racism.

Deciding I had to see for myself, I pulled my Shani doll off my office bookshelf, stripped her naked, and placed her on my desk next to a naked Barbie doll that had been cruelly mutilated by a colleague's dog (her arms were chewed off and her head had puncture wounds, but the rest was unharmed). Try as I might, manipulating the dolls in ways both painful and obscene, I could find no difference between them, even after prying their legs off and smashing their bodies apart. As far as I have been able to determine, Shani's bigger butt is an illusion (see photo). The faces of Shani and Barbie dolls are more visibly different than their behinds, yet still, why these differences could be considered natural indicators of race is perplexing. As a friend of mine remarked acidly, "They still look like they've had plastic surgery." The most telling difference between Shani and Barbie is at the base of the cranium, where Shani bears a raised mark similar to a branding iron scar: © 1990 MATTEL INC. Barbie's head reads simply © MATTEL INC. Despite claims of redesign, both Barbie and Shani's torsos

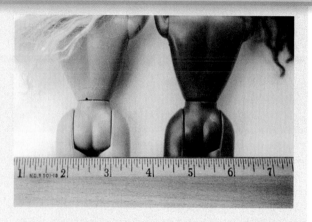

Barbie and Shani from behind.

bear a 1966 copyright, and although DuCille asserts that Shani's legs are shaped differently than Barbie's, their legs are imprinted with the same part numbers. This all strongly suggests that despite claims and rumors to the contrary, Shani and Barbie are the same from the neck down.

These ethnically correct dolls demonstrate one of the abiding aspects of racism: that a stolid belief in racial difference can shape people's perceptions so profoundly that they will find difference and make something of it, no matter how imperceptible or irrelevant its physical manifestation might be. If I had to smash two dolls to bits in order to see if their butts were different sizes, the differences must be small indeed: holding them next to each other revealed no difference whatsoever—except color—regardless of the positioning (crack to crack or cheek to cheek). With the butt index so excruciatingly small, its meaning as a racial signifier becomes frighteningly problematic. Like the notion of race itself, Shani's derriere has a social meaning that is out of all proportion to its scientific measurement.

Source: Chin 1999, 311–13.

In this way, the identification of races was transformed into **racism**: the systematic oppression of one or more socially defined "races" by another socially defined "race" that is justified in terms of the supposedly inherent biological superiority of the rulers and the supposed inherent biological inferiority of those they rule.

It is important to emphasize once again that all the so-called races of human beings are *imagined communities*. The racial boundaries that nineteenth-century European observers thought they had discovered do *not* correspond to major biological discontinuities within the human species. Although our species as a whole does exhibit variation in phenotypic attributes such as skin color, hair texture, or stature, these variations do *not* naturally clump into separate populations with stable boundaries that can be sharply distinguished from one another. Put another way, *the traditional concept of race in Western society is biologically and genetically meaningless.*

But even though the concept of race is biologically meaningless, racial thinking persists at the beginning of the twenty-first century. This can only mean that *racial categories have their origins not in biology but in society.* And in fact, anthropologists have long argued that race is a culturally constructed social category whose members are identified on the basis of certain selected phenotypic features (such as skin color) that all of them are said to share. The end result is a highly distorted but more or less coherent set of criteria that members of a society can use to assign people they see to one or another culturally defined racial category. Once this happens, members of society can treat racial categories *as if* they reflect biological reality, using them to build institutions that include or exclude particular culturally defined races. In this way, race can become "real" in its consequences, even if it has no reality in biology.

The social category of race is a relatively recent invention. Audrey Smedley reminds us that in the worlds of European classical antiquity and through the Middle Ages, "no structuring of equality . . . was associated with people *because of their skin color*" (1998, 693; emphasis in original), and Faye Harrison points out that "phenotype prejudice was not institutionalized before the sixteenth century" (1995, 51). By the nineteenth century, European thinkers (some early anthropologists among them) were attempting to classify all humans in the world into a few, mutually exclusive racial categories. Significantly, from that time until this, as Harrison emphasizes, "blackness has come to symbolize the social bottom" (1998, 612; see also Smedley 1998, 694–95).

White domination of European American racial hierarchies has been a constant, but some anthropologists who study the cultural construction of whiteness point out that even in the United States "whiteness" is not monolithic and that the cultural attributes supposedly shared by "white people" have varied in different times and places. Some members of white ruling groups in the southern United States, for example, have traditionally distanced themselves from lower-class whites, whom they call "white trash"; and the meaning of whiteness in South Africa has been complicated by differences of class and culture separating British South Africans from Afrikaners (Hartigan 1997). Moreover, the sharp "caste-like" racial divide between blacks and whites in the United States is currently being complicated by new immigrants identified with so-called brown/Hispanic and yellow/Asian racial categories. Harrison and others recognize that racial categorization and repression take different forms in different places. As we shall see, anthropologists working in Latin America and the Caribbean have described racial practices that do not match those characteristic of the United States.

Race in Colonial Oaxaca

Anthropologist John Chance studied the development of ideas about race and class in the city of Oaxaca, Mexico (see EthnoProfile 13.3: Colonial Oaxaca [1521–1812]). Oaxaca (known as *Antequera* during the period of Spanish colonial domination) is a highland city founded in an area that was densely populated prior to the Spanish conquest by indigenous people who participated in Mexican high civilization. Chance (1978) examined how social stratification changed from the period of Spanish conquest, in 1521, to the early years of the Mexican war of independence, in 1812. He used an anthropological

---

racism The systematic oppression of one or more socially defined "races" by another socially defined "race" that is justified in terms of the supposedly inherent biological superiority of the rulers and the supposed inherent biological inferiority of those they rule.

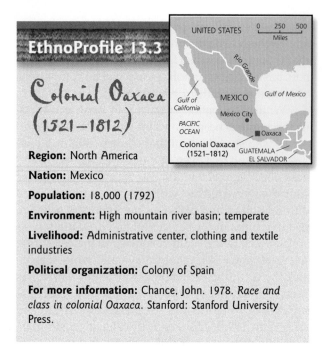

EthnoProfile 13.3

Colonial Oaxaca (1521–1812)

Region: North America

Nation: Mexico

Population: 18,000 (1792)

Environment: High mountain river basin; temperate

Livelihood: Administrative center, clothing and textile industries

Political organization: Colony of Spain

For more information: Chance, John. 1978. *Race and class in colonial Oaxaca.* Stanford: Stanford University Press.

perspective to interpret census records, wills, and other archival materials preserved in Mexico and Spain. As a result, he was able to show that changes occurred both in the categories used to describe social groups and in the meanings attached to those categories, with associated changes in the dynamics of social stratification itself.

When the Spanish arrived in Mexico in 1521, they found a number of indigenous societies organized into states. The Aztecs, for example, were divided into an upper ruling stratum of nobles and a lower, commoner stratum. The Spanish conquerors also came from a society stratified into a system of *estates*, which were legally recognized social categories entitled to a voice in government. European estates prototypically included the nobility, the clergy, and the common people. By 1529, African slaves had been brought to New Spain. The colonizers in colonial Oaxaca reworked the European notion of estates to accommodate these new cleavages by assigning people membership into one or another estate on the basis of their outward phenotypes, the key criterion that is used to define *race*.

In theory, the clergy and nobility were reserved for the "white" Spanish; all "nonwhite" indigenous groups were merged together to form the common people, and "black" African slaves formed a final

layer at the bottom of the colonial hierarchy. There were exceptions to this system, however. Indigenous nobles were given special status in postconquest society and were used by the colonial administration to control their own people.

Moreover, the conquistadors, who brought no Spanish women with them, soon established sexual relationships with local indigenous women. In the early years, if these unions involved marriage, the offspring were usually considered Spanish. If they were casual or clandestine, however, the offspring were more likely to be considered indigenous. Europeans, indigenous peoples, and Africans interbred, and a population of mixed descent was created.

According to the system of estates, people of mixed ancestry were not supposed to exist. By the mid–sixteenth century, however, their numbers and their economic importance made them impossible to ignore. As a result, the rulers of New Spain developed the *sistema de castas* to classify all people of mixed racial heritage (Figure 13.6). The first castas recognized were *mestizos* (people of mixed Spanish and indigenous descent) and *mulatos* (people who showed evidence of African ancestry).

As soon as there were enough mestizos and mulatos to attract attention, the colonial government tried to limit their social mobility by legal means. Yet their status was ambiguous. Mestizos were ranked above mulatos because they had no African ancestry but were ranked below the Spanish because of their "illegitimacy." In cases where indigenous and Spanish people were legally married, their children were called *españoles* (creoles). They were distinguished from *españoles europeos* (Spaniards born in Spain). In later years, the term *creole* (*criollo*) was also used to refer to people of presumably "pure" European ancestry who were born in America. Some mestizos managed to obtain elite privileges, such as the right to carry arms. Most mulatos were classed with Africans and could be enslaved. Yet free mulatos could also apply for the right to carry arms, which shows that even their status was ambiguous.

During the seventeenth century, the castas were acknowledged as legitimate strata in the system of colonial stratification. A number of new castas were recognized: *castizo* (a person of mixed Spanish and mestizo descent), *mulato libre* ("free mulatto"), *mulato esclavo* ("mulatto slave"), *negro libre* ("free black"),

FIGURE 13.6 By the late eighteenth century, the number of castas recognized in Mexico had proliferated. This contemporary painting displays 16 different outcomes of various cross-casta matings. Note that a castizo (with three español [Spanish] grandparents) and an española (with four Spanish grandparents) produce offspring considered español (seven out of eight great-grandparents are españoles). The painting attempts to represent not only the phenotypes of different castas but also the relative social statuses their members might occupy, as suggested by the clothing they wear (note especially the presence or absence of shoes).

and *negro esclavo* ("black slave"). Perhaps most striking is the castizo category. This seems to have been designed by the colonial elite to stem the tide of ever "whiter" mestizos who might be mistaken for genuine Spaniards. Chance points out that racial mixing was primarily an urban phenomenon and that the castas perceived themselves, and were perceived by the elite, as belonging to Hispanic rather than indigenous society (1978, 126). It is perhaps not surprising that lighter-skinned castas became increas-

ingly indistinguishable from middle-class and lower-class creoles. In fact, census records in Oaxaca list creoles as the largest segment of the city's population throughout the entire colonial period.

Other Stratification Systems As if the sistema de castas were not enough, colonial society recognized three additional systems of classification that cut across the castas. One distinguished groups required to pay tribute to the Spanish crown (indigenous groups, Africans, and mulattos) from everyone else. The second distinguished *gente de razon* ("rational people," who practiced the Hispanic culture of the city) from *indios* (the rural, culturally distinct indigenous population). And a third distinguished *gente decente* ("respectable people") from *la plebe* (the "common people"). Chance suggests that the last distinction, which made most sense in the urban setting, represented an embryonic division into socio-economic classes (1978, 127).

Mobility in the Casta System Throughout the colonial period, the boundaries of the stratification system in Oaxaca were most rigid for those of "unmixed" indigenous, African, and European descent. Paradoxically, those of mixed background had the most ambiguous status—and the greatest opportunity to improve it. For example, when a couple married, the priest decided the casta membership of the bride and groom. The strategy for upward mobility called for choosing a marriage partner who was light-skinned enough for the priest to decide that both spouses belonged in a high-ranking casta. Over time, such maneuvering swelled the ranks of the creoles.

The growth of the casta population coincided with the transformation of the colonial economy from one based on tribute and mining to one based on commercial capitalism. The prosperity this transformation brought to Oaxaca was greatest in the eighteenth century, when the city became the center of an important textile and dye-manufacturing industry. Many castas were able to accumulate wealth, which together with a light skin and adoption of the urban culture made it possible for them to achieve the status of creole.

Chance argues that during the late colonial period racial status had become an achieved, rather than an ascribed, status. By that time, the increasing rate of legitimacy in all castas meant that descent lost its importance as a criterion of group membership. Creole status could be claimed by anyone who was able to show that his or her ancestors had not paid tribute. At the same time, in a dialectical fashion, people's image of what high-status people looked like had changed. As people with indigenous and African ancestry moved up the social scale, their phenotypes widened the range of phenotypes considered prototypical for creoles.

Chance concludes that the sistema de castas is best understood as "a cognitive and legal system of ranked socioracial statuses" (1978, viii). Anthropologists have used the term **social race** to describe the system of ranking to which it eventually gave birth. The stratification system in Oaxaca was a hybrid, beginning with closed, caste-like racial categories whose "purity" could not be maintained, and ending up with open, classlike categories with racial labels.

Colorism in Nicaragua

Some observers might expect that once race becomes an achieved status racism has disappeared. But the situation is not so simple. Let us compare the case of Oaxaca, Mexico, with that of Managua, Nicaragua. Roger Lancaster argues that in Nicaragua racism exists but that it is "not as absolute and encompassing a racism as that which one encounters in the United States" even though it remains, in his opinion, "a significant social problem" (1992, 215). One dimension of Nicaraguan racism contrasts the Spanish-speaking mestizo majority of the highlands with the indigenous Miskitos and African Caribbeans along the Atlantic coast. Highland mestizos whom Lancaster knew tended to regard these coastal groups as backward, inferior, and dangerous—notions overlain with political suspicions deriving from the fact that some Miskito factions had fought with the contras against the Sandinistas.

But Lancaster came to see racism toward the coastal peoples as simply an extension of the pattern of race relations internal to highland mestizo culture that he calls **colorism**: a system of color identities negotiated situationally along a continuum between white and black (Figure 13.7). In colorism, no fixed race boundaries exist. Instead, individuals negotiate their color identity anew in every social situation they enter, with the result that the color they might claim or be accorded changes from situation to situation.

Lancaster's informants used three different systems of color classification. The first, or "phenotypic" system, has three categories—*blanco* (white), *moreno* (brown), and *negro* (black)—that people use to describe the various skin tones that can be seen among Nicaraguan mestizos: "Nicaraguan national culture is mestizo; people's physical characteristics are primarily indigenous; and in the terms of this phenotypic system, most people are moreno. In this system, *negro* can denote either persons of African ancestry or sometimes persons of purely indigenous appearance, whether they are culturally classified as Indio or mestizo" (1992, 217).

Lancaster calls the second system Nicaraguans use the "polite" system, in which all the colors in the phenotypic system are "inflated." That is, Europeans are called *chele* (a Mayan word meaning "blue," referring to the stereotypically blue eyes of people of European ancestry), morenos are called blanco, and negros are called moreno. Polite terms are used in the presence of the person about whom one is speaking, and Lancaster was told that it was "a grave and violent offence to refer to a black-skinned person as *negro*" (1992, 217). In rural areas, for similar reasons, Indians are called *mestizos* rather than *Indios*.

Lancaster calls the third system of color terms the "pejorative and/or affectionate" system. This system has only two terms, *chele* (fairer skin and lighter hair) and *negro* (darker skin, darker hair). When the less powerful person in an interaction feels he is being imposed upon by the more powerful person, the former might express his displeasure by addressing the latter as *chele* or *negro*, both of which would be heard as insulting. Paradoxically, members of families call one another *negro* or *negrito mio* as affectionate and intimate terms of address, perhaps precisely because these terms are "informal" and violate the rules of polite discourse (1992, 218).

Lancaster discovered that "Whiteness is a desired quality, and polite discourse inflates its descriptions of

---

social race An achieved status with a racial label in a system of stratification that is composed of open, classlike categories to which racial labels are assigned.

colorism A system of social identities negotiated situationally along a continuum of skin colors between white and black.

FIGURE 13.7 This photograph of Brazilian children shows a range of skin tones. In some parts of Latin America, such as Nicaragua and Brazil, such variation is used to create a system of classification based on lightness or darkness of skin tone that assigns people with relatively lighter skin to higher status, a phenomenon that anthropologist Roger Lancaster calls *colorism*.

people" (1992, 219). People compete in different settings to claim whiteness. In some settings, individuals may be addressed as *blanco* if everyone else has darker skin; but in other settings, they may have to yield the claim of whiteness to someone else with lighter skin than theirs and accept classification as *moreno*.

Because it allows people some freedom of maneuver in claiming higher-status color for themselves, Nicaraguan colorism may seem less repressive than the rigid black-white racial dichotomy traditional in the United States. Lancaster points out, however, that all three systems of colorist usage presuppose white superiority and black inferiority. "Africanos, Indios, and lower-class mestizos have been lumped together under a single term—*negro*—that signifies defeat" (1992, 223). Of course, the achieved social races of Oaxaca also oscillated along a continuum with whites on top and blacks on the bottom. Lancaster is not optimistic about the possibilities of successfully overturning this system any time soon in Nicaragua. Similarly, Harrison argues that racial solidarity and rebellion are hard to achieve or sustain in societies where social race is present, and she is not optimistic that adoption of a similar system in the United States would improve race relations. On the contrary, she fears that a "more multi-shaded discourse" would be more likely to con-

tribute to "an enduring stigmatization of blackness" than to "democratization and the dismantling of race" (1998, 618–19).

▼ ETHNICITY

For anthropologists, **ethnic groups** are social groups whose members distinguish themselves (and/or are distinguished by others) in terms of **ethnicity**. That is, in terms of distinctive cultural features, such as language, religion, or dress. Ethnicity, like race, is a culturally constructed concept. Many anthropologists today would agree with John and Jean Comaroff that ethnicity is created by historical processes that incorporate distinct social groups into a single political structure under conditions of inequality (1991, 55–57; see also Williams 1989 and Alonso 1994). The Comaroffs point out that ethnic consciousness existed in precolonial and precapitalist societies; however, they

ethnic groups Social groups that are distinguished from one another on the basis of ethnicity.

ethnicity A principle of social classification used to create groups based on selected cultural features such as language, religion, or dress. Ethnicity emerges from historical processes that incorporate distinct social groups into a single political structure under conditions of inequality.

and most contemporary anthropologists have been more interested in forms of ethnic consciousness that were generated under capitalist colonial domination.

Ethnicity develops as members of different groups try to make sense of the material constraints they experience within the single political structure that confines them. This is sometimes described as a struggle between *self-ascription* (that is, *insiders'* efforts to define their own identity) and *other-ascription* (that is, *outsiders'* efforts to define the identities of other groups). In the Comaroffs' view, furthermore, the ruling group turns both itself and the subordinated groups into *classes* because all subordinated social groupings lose independent control "over the means of production and/or reproduction" (1991, 56).

One outcome of this struggle is the appearance of new ethnic groups and identities that are not continuous with any single earlier cultural group (Comaroff and Comaroff 1991, 56). In northern Cameroon, for example, successive German, French, and British colonial officials relied on local Muslim chiefs to identify significant local social divisions for them. They adopted the Muslim practice of lumping together all the myriad non-Muslim peoples of the hills and plains and calling them *Haabe* or *Kirdi*—that is, "Pagans." To the extent, therefore, that Guidar, Daba, Fali, Ndjegn, or Guiziga were treated the same by colonial authorities and came to share a common situation and set of interests, they developed a new, more inclusive level of ethnic identity, like the young man we met in Guider who introduced himself to us as "just a Kirdi boy." This new, postcolonial "Kirdi" identity, like many others, cannot be linked to any single precolonial cultural reality but has been constructed out of cultural materials borrowed from a variety of non-Muslim indigenous groups who were incorporated as "Pagans" within the colonial political order.

The Comaroffs argue that a particular structure of nesting, opposed identities was quite common throughout European colonies in Africa. The least inclusive consisted of local groups called "tribes," who struggled to dominate one another within separate colonial states. The middle levels consisted of a variety of entities that crossed local boundaries, sometimes called *supertribes*, or *nations*. For example, the British administered the settler colony of Southern Rhodesia (later to become Zimbabwe) according to the policy of "indirect rule," which used indigenous "tribal" authorities to maintain order on the local

level. The effect of indirect rule was thus both to reinforce "tribal" identities where they existed and to create them where they had been absent in precolonial times. Two such tribal identities, those of the Shona and Ndebele, became preeminent, and each gave rise to its own "(supratribal) nationalist movement."

Both movements joined together in a "patriotic front" to win a war of independence fought against white settlers. This confrontation took place at the highest level of the ethnic hierarchy, which the Comaroffs call *race*. At this level, "Europeans" and "Africans" opposed one another, and each group developed its own encompassing ethnic identity. For example, Africans dealing regularly with Europeans began to conceive of such a thing as "African culture" (as opposed to European culture) and "pan-African solidarity" (to counter the hegemony of the European colonizers). Conversely, in the British settler colonies of southern and eastern Africa, European immigrants defined themselves in opposition to Africans by developing their own "settler-colonial order" based on a caricature of aristocratic Victorian English society (1991, 58).

Ethnicity in Urban Africa

Because ethnic groups are incorporated into the colony on unequal terms (and, if we follow the Comaroffs, in different class positions), it is not surprising to discover that many individuals in colonies attempted to achieve upward mobility by manipulating ethnicity. Anthropological studies of such attempts at ethnic mobility constitute, as the Comaroffs put it, "the very stuff of the ethnography of urban Africa" (1991, 63), and one of us (EAS) investigated ethnic mobility in the northern Cameroonian town of Guider (Figure 13.8).

Guider began as a small settlement of non-Muslim Guidar. In 1830 it was brought into the Muslim Fulbe empire of Yola and remained a Fulbe stronghold under subsequent colonial rule. The Fulbe remained numerically dominant in town until after World War II; by 1958, individuals from over a dozen non-Fulbe groups had migrated to town, primarily from the neighboring countryside. By 1976, 83 percent of household heads in town were recent migrants, and 74 percent did not claim Fulbe origins.

In the Comaroffs' terms, all these groups, including the Fulbe, had lost political and economic

The Politics of Ethnicity

Stanley Tambiah reflects on the late-twentieth-century upsurge in ethnic conflict that few people predicted because many assumed that ethnic particularisms would disappear within modern nation-states.

The late-twentieth-century reality is evidenced by the fact that ethnic groups, rather than being mostly minority or marginal subgroups at the edges of society, expected in due course to assimilate or weaken, have figured as major "political" elements and major political collective actors in several societies. Moreover, if in the past we typically viewed an ethnic group as a subgroup of a larger society, today we are also faced with instances of majority ethnic groups within a polity or nation exercising preferential or "affirmative" policies on the basis of that majority status.

The first consideration that confirms ethnic conflict as a major reality of our time is not simply its ubiquity alone, but also its cumulative increase in frequency and intensity of occurrence. Consider these conflicts, by no means an exhaustive listing, that have occurred since the sixties (some of them have a longer history, of course): conflicts between anglophone and francophone in Canada; Catholic and Protestant in Northern Ireland; Walloon and Fleming in Belgium; Chinese and Malay in Malaysia; Greek and Turk in Cyprus; Jews and other minorities on the one hand and Great Russians on the other in the Soviet Union; and Ibo and Hausa and Yoruba in Nigeria; the East Indians and Creoles in Guyana. Add, to these instances, upheavals that became climactic in recent years: the Sinhala–Tamil war in Sri Lanka, the Sikh–Hindu, and Muslim–Hindu, confrontations in India, the Chackma–Muslim turmoil in Bangladesh, the actions of the Fijians against Indians in Fiji, the Pathan–Bihari clashes in Pakistan, and last, but not least, the inferno in Lebanon, and the serious erosion of human rights currently manifest in Israeli actions in Gaza and the West Bank. That there is possibly no end to these eruptions, and that they are worldwide has been forcibly brought to our attention by a century-old difference that exploded in March 1988 between Christian Armenians and Muslim Azerbaijanis in the former U.S.S.R.

Most of these conflicts have involved force and violence, homicide, arson, and destruction of property. Civil-

ian riots have evoked action by security forces: sometimes as counteraction to quell them, sometimes in collusion with the civilian aggressors, sometimes both kinds of action in sequence. Events of this nature have happened in Sri Lanka, Malaysia, India, Zaire, Guyana, and Nigeria. Mass killings of civilians by armed forces have occurred in Uganda and in Guatemala, and large losses of civilian lives have been recorded in Indonesia, Pakistan, India, and Sri Lanka.

The escalation of ethnic conflicts has been considerably aided by the amoral business of gunrunning and free trade in the technology of violence, which enable not only dissident groups to successfully resist the armed forces of the state, but also civilians to battle with each other with lethal weapons. The classical definition of the state as the authority invested with the monopoly of force has become a sick joke. After so many successful liberations and resistance movements in many parts of the globe, the techniques of guerrilla resistance now constitute a systematized and exportable knowledge. Furthermore, the easy access to the technology of warfare by groups in countries that are otherwise deemed low in literacy and in economic development—we have seen what Afghan resistance can do with American guns—is paralleled by another kind of international fraternization among resistance groups who have little in common save their resistance to the status quo in their own countries, and who exchange knowledge of guerrilla tactics and the art of resistance. Militant groups in Japan, Germany, Lebanon, Libya, Sri Lanka, and India have international networks of collaboration, not unlike—perhaps more solidary than—the diplomatic channels that exist between mutually wary sovereign countries and the great powers. The end result is that the professionalized killing is no longer the monopoly of state armies and police forces. The internationalization of the technology of destruction, evidenced in the form of terrorism and counterterrorism, has shown a face of free-market capitalism in action unsuspected by Adam Smith and by Immanuel Wallerstein.

Source: Tambiah 1989, 431–32.

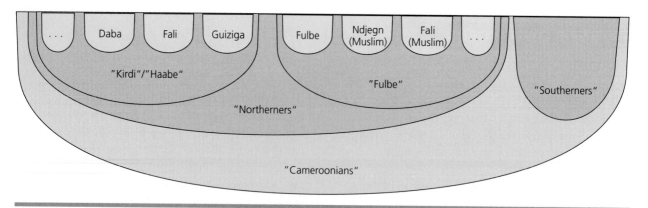

FIGURE 13.8 Nesting identities in northern Cameroon (1976).

independence with the coming of colonial rule and, under conditions of inequality, were incorporated as ethnic groups into first the German and later the French colony of Cameroon. The colonizers uniformly admired the political, cultural, and religious accomplishments of the Muslim Fulbe. In their own version of indirect rule, they allowed Fulbe chiefs to administer territories they had controlled prior to colonization and, in some cases, handed over to them additional territories whose residents had successfully resisted Fulbe domination in precolonial times.

In 1976, the local ethnic hierarchy in Guider placed Fulbe at the top and recent non-Muslim, non-Fulfulde-speaking migrants from rural areas at the bottom. But in the middle were numerous individuals and families of Fulfulde-speaking Muslims who could claim, and in some cases be accorded, recognition as Fulbe by others in the town. For example, two young men whom I hired as field assistants first described themselves to me as "100 percent Fulbe." As I got to know them better, however, I learned that the family of one was Ndjegn, and the family of the other was Fali. Neither young man saw anything contradictory about being both Fulbe and Ndjegn, or Fulbe and Fali. And in fact, each ethnic identity was emphasized in different situations. Ndjegn and Fali ethnicity mattered to them in the domain of family and kinship; these ethnic identities nested within the broader Fulbe ethnicity that mattered in urban public settings, especially high-status ones associated with education and cash salaries.

Indeed, by 1976, Fulbe identity had become an achieved status; it was the ethnicity claimed by the upwardly mobile in Guider. People born outside the dominant Fulbe ethnic group could achieve Fulbe status in their lifetimes (Schultz 1984). To do this, they had to be successful in three tasks: they had to adopt the Fulbe language (Fulfulde), the Fulbe religion (Islam), and the Fulbe "way of life," which was identified with urban customs and the traditional high culture of the western Sudan. Many Fulbe claimed that descent from one or another Fulbe lineage was needed in order to claim Fulbe identity. Nevertheless, they seemed willing to accept "Fulbeized Pagans" as Fulbe (for example, by giving their daughters to them as brides) because those people were committed defenders of the urban Fulbe way of life. Those who were "Fulbeizing," however, came from societies in which descent had never been an important criterion of group membership. For those people, ethnic identity depended on territorial affiliation of the group to which they were currently committed. In becoming Fulbe, they had simply chosen to commit themselves to Fulfulde, Islam, and life in "Fulbe territory," the town.

This example illustrates some of the key attributes often associated with ethnicity: it is *fluid* and *malleable*, something that can be *voluntarily* embraced or successfully ignored in different situations. Ambitious individuals and groups in an ethnically stratified society can manipulate ethnicity as a resource in order to pursue their interests. When nesting identities are present, people may regularly alternate between different identities in different contexts. Ethnic Fulbeization in northern Cameroon might be described as the formation of a "supertribe." Like the

The Emergence of a New Political Paradigm

John Matthiasson first went to Baffin Island, in the Canadian Arctic, to do fieldwork among the Inuit in 1963. He returned a decade later to carry out additional fieldwork and has kept up with events in the Canadian Arctic since then. Here he writes about a people's name.

The names by which we refer to ourselves or others can also be used to manipulate our identity and to align with or isolate ourselves from others, as well as to rationalize our treatment of others. When I lived with the Aullativikmiut in the 1960s they referred to themselves as Eskimos, as did all of the Tununermiut. By the 1970s many of them had ceased to use the term, which was now considered pejorative. (Its etymological origins have always been murky, although many sources claim that it means "eaters of raw meat.") It was, of course, replaced in both singular and plural by Inuk and Inuit, for "a person," and "the people." The change in terminology of self-reference had, I am convinced, enormous political significance.

Not everyone accepted the change readily, and in some instances it was never adopted. One elderly man who had lived virtually all of his life in the camps told me in 1973, "I was born an Eskimo and I will die an Eskimo." However, his was to become a minority position. Others—even of his generation—soon saw the political significance of rejecting the term, and certainly that man's children and grandchildren did. This change, which was so important in the construction of new individual and group identities, was the work of The Inuit Tapirisat of Canada (ITC), or Inuit Brotherhood, a new organization that sought to create a pan-Inuit consciousness. The ITC was external to the Tununermiut, but when it offered them a new political agenda they responded, and in the process took further steps towards a renewed sense of self-determination.

Source: Matthiasson 1992, 161–62.

---

formation of caste alliances in India, it involves the expansion of group boundaries, allowing for the creation of stronger solidarity linkages among more people of different backgrounds. When such expanded alliances actually achieve increased success in political, economic, and social struggles, they may affect the very structures that gave rise to them (as the Shona-Ndebele alliance did in Zimbabwe) (Comaroff and Comaroff 1991, 61).

Ethnicity and Race

For dominant groups, however, defense of ethnic identity can be a way of defending privilege. They may be threatened rather than flattered by subordinate groups who master elite cultural practices. Members of the dominant ethnic group may stress their cultural superiority and question the eligibility (and even the humanity) of subordinate groups who challenge them.

At this point, anthropologists like Faye Harrison would argue that ethnicity becomes *racialized*. In her view, race differs from ethnicity precisely because it is used to "mark and stigmatize certain peoples as essentially and irreconcilably different, while treating the privileges of others as normative. This quality of difference, whether constructed through a biodeterminist or culturalist idiom, is what constitutes the social category and material phenomenon of 'race'" (Harrison 1998, 613). Racialization in Western societies would thus bear a family resemblance to castification in South Asian societies.

Harrison argues that by the middle of the nineteenth century white Northern Europeans, connecting their growing colonial power with their whiteness, began to racialize ethnic, religious, or class stereotypes associated with other Europeans (e.g., Irish, Jews, Italians, Poles, Slavs), viewing them as less human or, at any rate, differently human from themselves and attributing this difference to biologically inherited factors (1995, 52). Conversely, some racialized ethnic groups, such as the Irish, were able to reverse this process once they moved to the United States, shedding their stigma and *ethnicizing* into just another American ethnic group.

Some social scientists might argue, or at any rate hope, that all racialized groups should be able to ethnicize sooner or later. But such a perspective risks ignoring the plight of racialized groups whose status never seems to change. Historians argue, for example, that the Irish were able to ethnicize precisely because they accepted the racialization of black Americans (Allen 1994–97). Indeed, operating under material conditions that presuppose white privilege, nonwhite races in the United States "historically have defined layers of the social bottom vis-à-vis several successive waves of immigrants" (Harrison 1995, 49; see also Smedley, 1998, 690).

For these reasons, Harrison argues that attempts to interpret race relations in the United States as ethnic relations "euphemized if not denied race" by failing to address the social, political, and economic factors responsible for keeping groups like African Americans excluded and stigmatized at the bottom of society (1995, 48). Harrison agrees that African Americans do engage in "ethnicizing practices emphasizing cultural heritage," but in her view such practices have never been able to overcome the "caste-like assumptions of the most systematically oppressive racial orders" like that of the United States (1998, 613; 1995, 54; see also Sharma 1999, 91).

As we have seen, anthropologists have argued about which technical terms ought to be used to describe which forms of identity under which circumstances. We would agree with Ursula Sharma that social scientists should use a particular term only if it highlights a dimension of social relationships that would otherwise go unnoticed (1999, 93). Thus, ethnicity probably needs to be supplemented by the notion of race in order to distinguish the dehumanizing confinement of certain social groups to the bottom layers of society. Similarly, caste's emphasis on endogamy and hierarchical ranking highlights features of social organization that elude the usual scope of race, class, or ethnicity.

Anthropologist Pnina Werbner (1997) argues that in order to make progress in analyzing ethnic vio-

lence as a social force, practices of "everyday" ethnic identification need to be distinguished from racism. Based on her research on multicultural social relations in Britain, Werbner distinguishes two different social processes, objectification and reification. *Objectification* simply refers to the intentional construction of a collective public identity; it is the process that produces "everyday" or "normal" ethnicity. Ethnic identities are distinguished by the fact that they are "evoked situationally . . . highlighted pragmatically, and objectified relationally and contingently." Further, they develop around two key issues: "a demand for ethnic rights, including religious rights, and a demand for protection against racism" (1997, 241). Social relations between objectified ethnic groups are based on a "rightful performance" of multiple, shifting, highly valued forms of collective identification, based on religion, dress, food, language, and politics. Interaction between groups that differentiate themselves along such lines ordinarily does not lead to violent confrontations (1997, 229).

Reification, by contrast, is a form of negative racial or ethnic absolutism that encourages the violent elimination of targeted groups, and is central to the practice of racism. Reification "distorts and silences"; it is "essentialist in the pernicious sense" (1997, 229). It is violence that differentiates racism from everyday ethnicity, and if ethnic confrontation becomes violent, then it turns into a form of racism (1997, 234–35). For Werbner, making this distinction is crucial in multiethnic situations. When people fail to distinguish nonviolent forms of everyday ethnicity from racism, they are, in effect, criminalizing valid ethnic sentiments and letting racists off the hook (1997, 233).

▼ NATION AND NATION-STATE

As we saw earlier, state societies are not new social forms. Nation-states, however, are a far more recent invention. Prior to the French Revolution, European states were ruled by kings and emperors whose access to the throne was officially believed to have been ordained by God. After the French Revolution in 1789, which thoroughly discredited the divine right of kings, rulers needed to find a new basis on which to found legitimate state authority.

The solution that was eventually adopted rooted political authority in **nations**: groups of people believed to share the same history, culture, language, and even the same physical substance. Nations were associated with territories, as were states, and a **nation-state** came to be viewed as an ideal political unit in which national identity and political territory coincided.

Nationalities and Nationalism

The building of the first nation-states is closely associated with the rise and spread of capitalism and its related cultural institutions during the nineteenth century. Following the demise of European colonial empires and the end of the Cold War, the final decades of the twentieth century witnessed a scramble in which former colonies or newly independent states struggled to turn themselves into nation-states capable of competing successfully in what anthropologist Liisa Malkki has called a "transnational culture of nationalism" (Malkki 1995).

On the one hand, the ideology of the nation-state implies that every nation is entitled to its own state. On the other hand, it also suggests that a state containing heterogeneous populations *might be made into a nation* if all peoples within its borders could somehow be made to adopt a common **nationality**: a sense of identification with and loyalty to the nation-state. The attempt made by government officials and state institutions to instill into the citizens of a state this sense of nationality has been called **nation-building**, or **nationalism**.

As we learned in our discussion of ethnicity, states are the very political structures that generate ethnic identities among the various cultural groupings unequally incorporated within them. Thus, anthropologists studying state formation often find themselves studying ethnicity as well as nationalism (Alonso 1994). However, groups with different forms of identity that continue to persist within the boundaries of the nation-state often are viewed as obstacles to nationalism. If such groups successfully resist assimilation into the nationality that the state is supposed to represent, their very existence calls into question the legitimacy of the state. Indeed, if their numbers are sufficient, they might well claim that they are a separate nation, entitled to a state of their own!

To head off this possibility, nationalist ideologies typically include some cultural features of subordinate cultural groups. Thus, although nationalist traditions are invented, they are not created out of thin air. The prototype of national identity is usually based on attributes of the dominant group, into which are integrated specially chosen elements of the cultural practices of other, subordinated groups. That is, those who control the nation-state will try to define nationality in ways that "identify and ensure loyalty among citizens . . . the goal is to create criteria of inclusion and exclusion to control and delimit the group" (Williams 1989, 407). The hope seems to be that if at least some aspects of their ways of life are acknowledged as essential to national identity subordinated groups will identify with and be loyal to the nation. Following Gramsci, Brackette Williams calls this process a **transformist hegemony** in which nationalist ideologues are attempting to "create purity out of impurity" (Williams 1989, 429, 435).

National leaders will measure the trustworthiness and loyalty of citizens by how closely they copy (or refuse to copy) the cultural practices that define national identity (Williams 1989, 407). Unfortunately, the practices of subordinated groups that do not get incorporated into nationalist ideology are regularly marginalized and devalued, and continued adherence to such practices may be viewed as subversive. Some groups, moreover, may be totally ignored. Alonso points out, for example, that Mexican nationalism is "mestizo nationalism" rooted in the official doctrine that the Mexican people are a hybrid of European whites and the indigenous people they conquered. As we saw in colonial Oaxaca, African slaves were also a part of early colonial Mexican society. Nationalist ideology, however, erases their presence entirely (1994, 396).

---

nation A group of people believed to share the same history, culture, language, and even the same physical substance.

nation-state An ideal political unit in which national identity and political territory coincide.

nationality A sense of identification with and loyalty to a nation-state.

nation-building, or nationalism The attempt made by government officials to instill into the citizens of a state a sense of nationality.

transformist hegemony A nationalist program to define nationality in a way that preserves the cultural domination of the ruling group while including enough cultural features from subordinated groups to ensure their loyalty.

Australian Nationalism

Australia began its existence as a settler colony of Great Britain. Over the past 200 years, the prototype of Australian national identity was based on the racial and cultural features of the settler population. The phenotypically distinct indigenous people, called *Aborigines* by the settlers, were completely excluded from citizenship. Settlers' claims to land and other resources rested on the doctrine of *terra nullius*: the idea that, before their arrival, the land had been owned by nobody.

In European capitalist terms, "ownership" meant permanent settlement and "improvement" of the land by clearing it and planting crops or grazing animals. Since the Aboriginal peoples living on the continent of Australia were foraging peoples who did not depend on domesticated plants or animals, European settlers felt justified in displacing them and "improving" the land as they saw fit. Aborigines were viewed as a "dying race," and white settler domination was taken as a foregone conclusion.

But times change, and currently Australians are seriously rethinking the nature of Australian national identity. Indeed, according to Robert Tonkinson (1998), two kinds of nation-building are going on at the same time. First, an intense national debate has developed in recent years that would favor creating a new Australian Republic whose constitution would affirm the existence and rights of the country's indigenous peoples. For that to happen, however, "the nation as a whole must reimagine itself via a myth-making process, in which the search for distinctively Australian national symbols may well include elements drawn from indigenous cultures" (Tonkinson 1998, 287–88).

And this will not be easy, because such a myth-making process (or transformist hegemony) immediately runs up against a second, alternative myth-making process generated by Australia's indigenous minorities, who have for decades struggled to construct for themselves a sense of "pan-Aboriginal" identity. Since the 1970s, a central theme in this struggle has been the demand for land rights, which was given an enormous boost by the decision handed down by the High Court of Australia in 1992 in the case of *Eddie Mabo and others* v. *the State of Queensland*. The so-called *Mabo* decision rejected the doctrine of *terra nullius*, proclaiming that the native title of Aus-

tralia's indigenous people was part of Australian common law.

The symbolic significance of the *Mabo* decision has been enormous. For those Australians who want to remake Australian nationalism, *Mabo* clears ground for constructing a multicultural national identity. The Australian federal government has therefore made reconciliation with indigenous minorities a major policy goal, well aware that "unless Australia achieves a formal and lasting reconciliation with its indigenous people, its self-image as a fair and just land will continue to be mocked by the history of its oppression of them" (Tonkinson 1998, 291). Many white Australians and the national government are seeking ways of incorporating Aboriginality into Australian national identity. A measure of success is indicated by increasing interest on the national level in the artistic, literary, and athletic accomplishments of Aboriginal people. As a popular reconciliation slogan puts it, "White Australia has a Black History" (Figure 13.9).

While all this might augur favorably for a reconstructed Australian national identity that includes Aboriginal people, many problems remain. Some come from white Australians who reject a multicultural national identity or who see their economic interests threatened by the *Mabo* decision. But even Aboriginal people may criticize the *Mabo* decision because of its limitations and unresolved complexities.

FIGURE 13.9 Australian Aboriginal people marching in protest over the Australian Bicentennial celebrations, which, they argued, did not pay appropriate attention to them.

For example, the only lands eligible for indigenous claims turn out to be those that have demonstrable historical connection to contemporary Aboriginal groups who continue to practice "traditional" Aboriginal customs. This not only exempts most of Australia from indigenous land claims, but it also means that most of Australia's quarter of a million Aboriginal people will be barred from making land claims because they live in Australia's large towns and cities and have been separated from the lands of their ancestors for generations.

Since the *Mabo* decision, however, expressions of Aboriginality seem to be moving toward "a more culture-centered—and to non-Aboriginal Australians more easily accommodated—emphasis on Aboriginal commonalities, continuity and survival" (Tonkinson 1998, 289). The *Mabo* decision has ratified the legitimacy and revival not only of Aboriginal land rights but also of Aboriginal customs. This has stimulated the explosion of Aboriginal cultural expression that white Australians have come to appreciate, as well as numerous programs that have brought urban Aboriginals into remote areas to work, to learn about rural Aboriginal traditions, and to contribute to the growth of biculturalism among rural Aboriginal people. Even in a multicultural Australia, however, many Aboriginal people would insist that they must not be lumped together with other "ethnic minorities," given their special status as descendants of the original inhabitants and victims of centuries of exploitation. Tonkinson concludes that, at the end of the twentieth century, "despite the limitations of Mabo . . . its symbolic force is such that it may provide the basis for reconciliation between indigenous and other Australians" (300).

Naturalizing Discourses

We have emphasized more than once in this chapter that all the social categories under discussion—class, caste, race, ethnicity, and nation—are culturally created and cannot be justified with reference to biology or nature. At the same time, many members of the societies anthropologists study argue just the opposite, employing what some anthropologists call **naturalizing discourses**. That is, they regularly represent particular identities as if they were rooted in biology or nature, rather than in history and culture, thereby making them appear eternal and unchanging.

Naturalizing discourses rely on the imaginary reduction, or *conflation*, of identities to achieve persuasive power (Williams 1989). For example, every one of the forms of identity we have discussed in this chapter has been described or justified by someone at some time in terms of *shared bodily substance*. Thus, living within the same borders is conflated with having the same ancestors and inheriting the same culture, which is conflated with sharing the same blood or the same genes. Culture is reduced to blood, and "the magic of forgetfulness and selectivity, both deliberate and inadvertent, allows the once recognizably arbitrary classifications of one generation to become the given inherent properties of reality several generations later" (Williams 1989, 431).

Nation-states frequently use trees as national symbols, rooting the nation in the soil of its territory (Figure 13.10). Sometimes they use kinship imagery, referring to the nation-state as a "motherland" or "fatherland"; sometimes the territory of a nation-state itself can be a unifying image, especially when portrayed on a map (Alonso 1994). The case of Australia shows, however, that doctrines like *terra nullius* enable newcomers to deny the "natural" links to the land of indigenous inhabitants while specifying how newcomers may proceed to establish their own "natural" links to the land through "improvement."

The Paradox of Essentialized Identities

The struggle of Aboriginal people to defend themselves and claim their rights after centuries of exploitation and neglect has been extraordinarily important in making the *Mabo* decision possible. In response to dominant groups that attempted to conflate their humanity with a narrow, unflattering stereotype, they chose to accept the racial designation, but to view it as a positive *essence*, an "inner something or distinctive 'spirituality' possessed by

naturalizing discourses The deliberate representation of particular identities (caste, class, race, ethnicity, and nation, for example) as if they were a result of biology or nature, rather than history or culture, making them appear eternal and unchanging.

FIGURE 13.10 Nation-states frequently use trees as national symbols, rooting the nation in the soil of its territory. The treelike symbol at the center of the Mexican national seal (the cactus on which an eagle perches holding a snake in its beak) is a preconquest Aztec symbol. Other versions of the image are encircled by the Spanish words *Estados Unidos Mexicanos* (United Mexican States). These combined elements stand for the officially mixed—*mestizo*—Mexican people the state is supposed to represent, the offspring of Spanish conquerors and the indigenous people they conquered.

everyone who is Aboriginal" (Tonkinson 1998, 294–95). Similar kinds of essentialist rhetoric have helped many stigmatized groups build a positive self-image and unite politically.

Many anthropologists and other observers would argue that the essentialist rhetoric of Aboriginal activists does not, in fact, reflect their beliefs about Aboriginality at all. They would describe what the activists are promoting as *strategic essentialism:* that is, essentialist rhetoric is being used as a conscious political strategy. Most activists are perfectly aware that essentialized racial or ethnic identities are simplistic and of dubious validity. Nevertheless, they press their claims, hoping that by stressing their difference they may be able to extract concessions that the national government cannot refuse without violating its own laws and sense of justice. The concessions may be substantial, as in the case of the *Mabo* decision. At the same time, strategic essentialism is troubling to many observers and participants in these struggles, for those who promote it as a political strategy risk "reproducing the same logic that once oppressed them" (Hale 1997, 547) and, rather than bringing about a more just society, may simply "serve to per-

petuate an ethnically ordered world" (Comaroff and Comaroff 1991, 62).

Nation-Building in a Postcolonial World: Fiji

While the citizens of nation-states need to construct a shared public identity, they also need to establish concrete legal mechanisms for taking group action to influence the state. That is, as John Kelly and Martha Kaplan (2001) argue, nation-states are more than imagined communities; they are also *represented* communities. For this reason, nation-building involves more than constructing an image of national unity; it also requires institutions of political representation that channel the efforts of citizens into effective state support.

But what happens when citizens of a nation-state do not agree about exactly what nation they are building, or what kinds of legal and political structures are necessary to bring it about? One answer to these questions can be seen in the South Pacific island nation of Fiji, which became independent from Britain in 1970, and has experienced two political coups since 1987.

At independence, the image of the Fijian nation was that of a "three-legged stool"; each "leg" was a separate category of voters: "general electors" (a minority of the population including Europeans), "Fijians" (ethnic Fijians, descended from the original inhabitants of the island), and "Indians" (or Indo-Fijians, descendents of indentured laborers brought to Fiji by the British from Bombay and Calcutta in the nineteenth century). Kelly and Kaplan show that these three categories have deep roots in the colonial period, where they were said to correspond to separate "races." In the British Empire, race was an accepted way to categorize subordinated peoples, even though in many cases—as in the case of the Indo-Fijians—the people so labeled had shared no common identity prior to their arrival in Fiji.

These racial distinctions were concretized in colonial law, and the legal status of the ethnic Fijians was different from the legal status of Indo-Fijians. The status of ethnic Fijians was determined by the Deed of Cession, a document signed by some Fijian chiefs with the British in 1874, which linked ethnic

Fijians to the colonial government through their hierarchy of chiefs. The status of Indo-Fijians, by contrast, was determined by the contracts of indenture (*girmit*) which each individual laborer had signed in order to come to Fiji. Thus, ethnic Fijians were accorded a hierarchical, collective legal identity, whereas the Indo-Fijians had the status of legal individuals, with no legally recognized ties to any collectivity.

Inspired by the Freedom Movement in India in the early twentieth century, Indo-Fijians began to resist racial oppression and struggle for equal rights in Fiji, but their efforts were repeatedly quashed by the British. When it became possible for them to vote after 1929, for example, Indo-Fijians lobbied for equal citizenship and the abolition of separate racial voting rolls, and they lost: The voting rolls were divided by race in order to limit representation for Indo-Fijians in government. At the time of World War II, Indo-Fijians agreed to serve in the armed forces, but only if they were treated as equals with white soldiers, and their efforts were resisted: They spent the war serving in a labor battalion for very low wages, while ethnic Fijians joined a Fijian Defense Force. It was primarily Indo-Fijians who pushed for independence in the late 1960s, and once again they engaged in difficult negotiations for equal citizenship and a common voting roll, but finally consented to separate race-based voting rolls in 1969, in order to obtain independence.

> Thus, when Fiji's independence became real in 1970, the constitution insisted that races still existed in Fiji and had to vote separately. Since then parties have generally and increasingly followed racial lines, and the army has remained an enclave of indigenous Fijians. When political parties backed mostly by Indo-Fijian voters won Fiji's 1987 election, this army took over the country after only a month. The constitution that was then installed in 1990 returned to even more naked discrimination against IndoFijians in regard to voting rights. (Kelly and Kaplan 2001, 77)

The constitution was revised yet again, in a manner that favored ethnic Fijian chiefly interests and seemed guaranteed to prevent parties backed by Indo-Fijian voters from winning control of the government in the 1999 election. To everyone's surprise, parties backing ethnic Fijians lost again. On May 19, 2000, came a second coup. Finally, after new elections

in 2001, ethnic Fijians won control of the government (Figure 13.11).

What lessons does this history suggest about nation-building in postcolonial states? The issues are many and complex. But Kelly and Kaplan emphasize that the image of a united Fijian nation projected at independence was severely undermined by legal mechanisms of political representation carried over from the colonial period, particularly the race-based voting rolls. What became apparent in the years after independence was the fact that Indo-Fijians and ethnic Fijians had imagined very different national communities. Indo-Fijians had supported the image of a Fijian nation in which all citizens, Indo-Fijian or ethnic Fijian or "general elector," would have equal status, voting on a single roll, working together to build

FIGURE 13.11 A Fijian citizen reads a newspaper on the day of the military coup in May 2000.

a constitutional democracy. However, "few among the ethnic Fijians have yet come to see themselves as partners with immigrants" (2001, 41). Ever since independence, and particularly after each coup, ethnic Fijians worked to construct an image of the Fijian nation based solely on chiefly traditions in which Indo-Fijians had no meaningful place. Thus, Kelly and Kaplan conclude, in Fiji (and in many other parts of the world) "'the nation' is a contested idea, not an experienced reality" (2001, 142).

Nationalism and Its Dangers

The most horrifying consequence of nation-building movements in the twentieth century has been the discovery of just how far the ruling groups of some nation-states are willing to go in order to enforce their version of national identity.

After World War II, the world was shocked to learn about Nazi programs to "liquidate" Jews, Gypsies, and other groups that failed to conform to Nazi ideals of Aryan purity (Linke 1997). Many people hoped that the Nazi Holocaust was exceptional, but subsequent developments suggest that it may have been only the most dramatic example of an exterminationist temptation that accompanies all drives to

nationalism. Sociologist Zygmunt Bauman argued in his book *Modernity and the Holocaust* (1989) that modern nation-states with rationalized bureaucracies and industrial technology were the first societies in history to make efficient mass extermination of deviants technically possible. In a transnational culture of nationalism, not to belong to a nation-state made up of loyal, ambitious, like-minded citizens is a severe, possibly fatal handicap. Using violence against all citizens who undermine claims of national homogeneity and common purpose may thus be a peculiarly modern way for insecure rulers of embattled nation-states to try to bring about solidarity and stability.

In the late twentieth century, warring nationalities in the former Yugoslavia deployed selective assassinations and forced migration to rid their fledgling nation-states of unwanted others, a policy known as *ethnic cleansing* (Figure 13.12). Thus, rather than relics of a barbarian past, ethnic cleansing, *ethnocide* (the destruction of a culture), and *genocide* (the extermination of an entire people) may constitute a series of related practices that are all signs of things to come. All are measures of the high stakes for which rulers of these nation-states see themselves competing.

FIGURE 13.12 Relatives of 8,000 Muslim men and boys slaughtered in the 1995 Srebrenica massacre walk between rows of coffins next to freshly dug graves, looking for those belonging to their relatives, in a field in the town March 31, 2003.

Inevitably, such policies create populations of immigrants and refugees whose social status is anomalous and ambiguous in a world of nation-states and whose presence as new pockets of heterogeneity in a different nation-state sets the stage for new rounds of social struggle that may lead to violence. As we will see in the next chapter, the economic, political, and cultural processes that made this possible have undergone important shifts in the last few years.

CHAPTER SUMMARY

1. All people in the world today, even refugees, must deal with the authority of one or another nation-state, each of which contains multiple and sometimes contradictory hierarchies of stratification. Every one of these hierarchies is a cultural invention designed to create boundaries around different kinds of imagined communities. Some patterns of stratification may reach back thousands of years, but others are closely associated with the rise of European capitalism and colonialism.

2. Gender stratification draws on sexual imagery to create and rank categories of people. Stratification by gender regularly subordinates phenotypic females to phenotypic males, but it is often applied more widely to other categories of people, artifacts, or events: to structure relations between different categories of men, for example, or between ethnic groups of "races."

3. The concept of class in anthropology has a double heritage: Europeans tended to view class boundaries as closed and rigid, whereas North Americans tended to view them as open and permeable. Class solidarity may be undercut by clientage relations that bind individuals to one another across class boundaries.

4. The stratification system of India has been taken as the prototype of caste stratification, although anthropologists also have applied the concept to social hierarchies encountered elsewhere in the world. Local caste divisions in village India adhere to rules of purity and pollution defined in terms of the occupations their members perform and the foods they eat, and which govern whom they may marry. Members of jatis of similar rank do not observe such distinctions with one another, especially in urban settings. Caste associations in large cities of India use jati ties to promote their members' economic well-being. The use of violence by higher-ranking jatis to block the advance of lower-ranking jatis has also increased in recent years. Contemporary anthropologists reject views of caste in India that portray it as internally harmonious and uncontested by those at the bottom of the caste hierarchy, pointing to the rise in caste violence in recent years.

5. The contemporary concept of race developed in the context of European exploration and conquest beginning in the fifteenth century, as light-skinned Europeans came to rule over darker-skinned peoples in different parts of the world. The so-called races whose boundaries were forged during the nineteenth century are imagined communities; human biological variation does not naturally clump into separate populations with stable boundaries. Despite variations in opinions and practices regarding race over the centuries, a global hierarchy persists in which whiteness symbolizes high status and blackness symbolizes the social bottom.

6. Although ethnic consciousness existed in precolonial and precapitalist societies, contemporary anthropologists have been most interested in forms of ethnicity that were generated under capitalist colonial domination, when different groups were subordinated within a single political structure under conditions of inequality. This process can produce ethnic groups not continuous with any single earlier group and is

often characterized by nesting, opposed identities that individuals often manipulate in order to achieve upward mobility. When dominant ethnic groups feel threatened, they may attempt to stigmatize subordinate groups by "racializing" them.

7. Nation-states were invented in nineteenth-century Europe, but they have spread throughout the world along with capitalism, colonialism, and eventual political decolonization. Nationalist thinking aims to create a political unit in which national identity and political territory coincide, and this has led to various practices designed to force subordinate social groups to adopt a national identity defined primarily in terms of the culture of the dominant group. When subordinate groups resist, they may become the victims of genocide or ethnic cleansing. Alternatively, the dominant group may try to recast its understanding of national identity in a way that acknowledges and incorporates

cultural elements belonging to subordinate groups. If the creation of such an imagined hybrid identity is not accompanied by legal and political changes that support it, however, the end result may be political turmoil, as shown in the recent history of Fiji.

8. Because membership in social categories such as class, caste, race, ethnicity, and nation can determine enormous differences in peoples' life chances, much is at stake in defending these categories, and all may be described as if they were rooted in biology or nature, rather than culture and history. Conceptualizing these forms of identity as essences can be a way of stereotyping and excluding, but it has also been used by many stigmatized groups to build a positive self-image and as a strategic concept in struggles with dominant groups. Although strategic essentialism may be successful in such struggles, it also risks repeating the same logic that justifies oppression.

KEY TERMS

stratified societies	racialism	nation
gender	racism	nation-state
class	social race	nationality
clientage	colorism	nation-building, or nationalism
caste	ethnic groups	transformist hegemony
race	ethnicity	naturalizing discourses

SUGGESTED READINGS

Anderson, Benedict. 2006. *Imagined communities*, Rev. ed. London: Verso. *Based on the recognition that all community ties between people are culturally constructed, Anderson identifies the cultural processes that make it possible for citizens of a nation-state who have never seen one another to develop the personal and cultural feeling of belonging to a nation.*

Hinton, Alexander Laban. 2002. *Annihilating difference: The anthropology of genocide*. Berkeley: University of California Press. *A recent collection of articles probing the ways in which anthropology can help explain and perhaps contribute to the prevention of genocide. Case studies include Nazi Germany,*

Cambodia under the Khmer Rouge, Rwanda, Guatemala, and the former Yugoslavia.

Malkki, Liisa. 1995. *Purity and exile: Memory and national cosmology among Hutu refugees in Tanzania*. Chicago: University of Chicago Press. *This ethnography chronicles a recent example in Africa of the bloody consequences of nationalist politics and explores the connections between the conditions of refugee resettlement and the development of refugee identities.*

Nash, Manning. 1989. *The cauldron of ethnicity in the modern world*. Chicago: University of Chicago Press. *Nash looks at ethnicity in the postcolonial world and sees more of a seething cauldron than* a melting pot. He examines the relations between Ladinos and Maya in Guatemala, Chinese and Malays in Malaysia, and Jews and non-Jews in the United States.

Sharma, Ursula. 1999. *Caste*. Philadelphia: Open University Press. *A brief, up-to-date survey of recent anthropological scholarship dealing with caste in South Asia.*

Smedley, Audrey. 1998. *Race in North America: Origin and evolution of a worldview.* 2d ed. Boulder, CO: Westview Press. *This book offers a comprehensive historical overview of the development of the concept of race in North America, beginning in the* late eighteenth century. *The second edition includes additional coverage of developments in the nineteenth and twentieth centuries. Smedley shows how the concept of race is a cultural construct that over time has been used in different ways, for different purposes.*

Strathern, Marilyn. 1988. *The gender of the gift.* Berkeley: University of California Press. *This is a challenging volume but a classic. Strathern expands the notion of "gender" beyond the traditional bounds of feminist anthropology in order to make sense of the complexities of Melanesian cultural practices.*

Chapter 14

A Global World

Human groups have never lived in total isolation from one another, but by the end of the twentieth century their interconnections had become more intense and more complex than ever before in human history. This chapter examines the processes that have led to intensified forms of global interconnection, explores the cultural consequences of such interconnection, and presents some of the ways these intensified cultural processes have drawn anthropologists into new understandings of culture, citizenship, and human rights.

Orlando, Claudio, and Leonardo Villas Bôas were middle-class Brazilians who took part in an expedition that explored central Brazil in the early 1940s. Their experiences led the three brothers to dedicate their lives to protecting Brazil's indigenous peoples from the ravages of contact with Western society. They were instrumental in persuading the government to create in 1952 the Xingu National Park, a large area in the state of Mato Grosso where indigenous groups could live undisturbed by outsiders. Since that time, they have worked to contact threatened indigenous groups and to persuade them to move to Xingu.

One such group was the Kréen-Akaróre, now known as the Panará, whose existence was menaced by a highway being built through their traditional territory. In February 1973, after years of avoiding outsiders, the Panará finally made contact with Claudio Villas Bôas, who had been following them in hopes of finding them before the highway builders did. Shortly after this, Orlando Villas Bôas gave a press conference in which he forcefully urged that a reserve be created for the Panará by the Brazilian government. The reserve was not located in traditional Panará territory, however, and it was bounded by the Santarém-Cuiabá Highway. Within months, the 300 remaining Panará settled there had abandoned their gardens; sick and in despair, they were begging for food from truck drivers. Finally, in October 1974, the Villas Bôas brothers were able to fly the 135 surviving Panará to the Xingu National Park (Davis 1977, 69–73). Within a year, there were only 79 left.

Disease, devastation, and misery have been all too common for indigenous peoples who have encountered Western expansion. Many observers, including anthropologists, have long feared that indigenous Amazonian peoples were destined for extinction. After all, of a population of 5 million in 1500, only 280,000 remain today, and some groups have already died out (Gomes 1996).

Recent history, however, suggests a reversal of fortune. During the last 30 to 40 years, the surviving 220 indigenous groups have seen their populations grow. Although some still strive to keep free of outside entanglements, others have been educated and live in cities; one has even been elected to the Brazilian National Congress (Gomes 1996). Even the Panará population has rebounded to over 160 people,

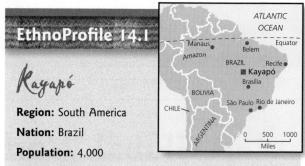

EthnoProfile 14.1

Kayapó

Region: South America

Nation: Brazil

Population: 4,000

Environment: Rain forest and savanna; wet and dry seasons

Livelihood: Extensive agriculture and hunting and gathering

Political organization: Headmen with no formal power; age grades

For more information: Rabben, Linda. 1999. *Unnatural Selection: The Yanomami, the Kayapó and the onslaught of civilisation.* London: Pluto Press.

and they recently received title to a 1.2 million acre tract of the land they had originally inhabited, as well as a legal settlement for damages resulting from unsupervised contact with outside society. This was the first time that the Brazilian state has had to pay an indigenous people for pain and suffering (S. Schwartzman, 1998; Rainforest Foundation 2003; see EthnoProfile 14.1: Kayapó).

This remarkable and heartening turn of events is illustrated by more recent events involving the Kayapó. In March 1989, the *Anthropology Newsletter* published a report from anthropologist Terence Turner describing how indigenous Amazonians had organized themselves to resist outside encroachment on their traditional lands. They were the people most directly affected by continued destruction of the Amazonian rain forest, but no one could have imagined that they might be leaders in defense of the environment, working successfully with national and international allies. Yet they brought some 28 indigenous nations together in a huge intertribal village built in the path of a proposed hydroelectric dam complex at Altamira, on the Xingu River.

The Kayapó leader Payakan combined traditional indigenous political skills with a knowledge of Portuguese and a keen understanding of the international media. He and other Kayapó chiefs, such as

Amazon Indians Honor an Intrepid Spirit

New York Times writer Larry Rohter reports on ceremonies held in Yawalapiti, Brazil, in July 2003 to honor the memory of Orlando Villas Bôas.

Yawalapiti, Brazil, July 20—Traveling for hours by boat and on foot, the chiefs, shamans and warriors arrived from all over the southeastern Amazon. For two days they danced, sang, chanted and reminisced around a painted tree trunk, decorated with a feathered headdress, that represented the soul of a recently departed friend.

The trunk was placed in the large open space that is the focus of community life here and implanted almost directly above the burial site of a former tribal leader, so he could help guide the spirit to the "village in the stars."

After daubing their bodies and hair with designs in black and red dye, scores of nearly naked men and boys paraded past the totem, whooping and stamping their feet in unison as they moved back and forth.

This elaborate quarup, or traditional Indian ceremony of lamentation for those of noble lineage, has been performed in the splendid isolation of the jungle for time uncounted. The farewell ceremony is normally an insular event performed before members of the community in honor of one of their own.

But the departed friend this time was Orlando Villas Bôas, who died eight months ago at the age of 88 and was buried in São Paulo.

. . . "This is the biggest quarup we have ever had, and maybe our last one ever for a white man," said Aritana, 54, the village chief. "It is hard to imagine that any other white man in the future could be a friend of ours as wise and courageous and dedicated as Orlando was."

. . . "This park [The Xingu Indigenous Park] is Orlando's legacy to us, and this quarup is our way of paying him back for the gift he made," said Itiamã, a tribal shaman who believes his age to be 56. "I loved Orlando. After my father died he became like a father to me and always used to tell me that he wanted us to have our own land and to be able to eat what we wanted."

Some anthropologists have criticized the brothers' approach as paternalistic, and the brothers themselves often had mixed feelings about their work. "Each time we contact a tribe we contribute to the destruction of what is most pure in it," Orlando Villas Bôas often said.

Western encroachments are indeed visible here. A painting of Spiderman adorns the entrance to one large thatched-roof lodge where a gas stove is also in use, a photograph of the Eiffel Tower hangs in another and some Indians now travel from village to village on bicycles, and even motorcycles.

But the Indians themselves argue that their situation today would have been much worse had the Villas Bôas brothers not intervened on their behalf. They have been able to retain their original language and religion, and smoked fish and manioc continue to dominate their diet.

"Orlando used to warn us about his concerns for the future, and everything he predicted has come to pass," said Paié, a member of the Kayabi tribe who is the director of the park and came nearly 800 miles from Brasilia to attend the ceremony. "Fortunately he trained us and prepared us to deal with the white man and his world."

. . . "We owe not just the preservation of our language and our culture to Orlando, but also our very existence today as a people," Aritana, the village chief, said. "He arranged the marriage of my father and my mother, and he saw me born, so he was always a part of the life of the Yawalapiti and my life."

Source: Rohter 2003.

Raoni, toured Europe and appeared publicly with well-known celebrities such as the rock musician Sting, who supported their cause (Figure 14.1). The Brazilian government, moreover, has still not built its dam. As anthropologist Terence Turner observes, "The boldness and global vision of this project are breathtaking; nothing like such a concerted action by even a few, let alone 28 unrelated Indian societies has ever taken place in the Amazon. The Indians are trying to tell us something important; we should listen" (T. Turner 1989, 21–22).

By 1992, the Kayapó had established legal and physical control of 28.4 million acres of their traditional land. However, some Kayapó had been illegally selling very valuable mahogany trees, in part to buy boats and radios to protect their borders. In that year, one Kayapó village began working with Conservation International to create a sustainable and income-generating research station to replace cutting trees. By 2002, all fifteen Kayapó villages had signed agreements with Conservation International for conservation-based development projects, and Conservation International was also helping to develop a system for effective border surveillance (Conservation International 2003).

Peoples like the Panará and the Kayapó have struggled with the effects of European contact for over 500 years, but rather than disappear forever,

they have now moved out of the forest and into the thick of Brazilian national life. Indeed, they and other indigenous people elsewhere in the world have been able to create global alliances by making use of contemporary Internet technology (e.g., Niezen 2003, 10). Anthropological research on Amazonian peoples has also changed. Today, Mercio Gomes observes, "one's living objects of research are easy to find, not more than a few hours away by plane, at the most a few days away by boat. They are on the outskirts of cities, in hospitals and medical centers, and even in the corridors of the National Congress. . . . They will also be available in the future" (1996, 19).

In this chapter, we take up again the story of how the Western world and the societies where anthropologists work are interrelated, how those interrelationships have changed over the last fifty years, and with what consequences. We will be looking at ourselves as much as we look at the traditional subjects of anthropological research.

In this chapter we take up again the story of changes in the world that have affected not only peoples like the Kayapó and the Panará, but also the anthropologists who work among them. Since the end of the Cold War in 1989, the entire globe has been—and continues to be—reshaped by powerful social, cultural, and political processes on an ever-intensifying scale. The term *globalization* has been used by many observers to describe these processes, which have left nobody and no territory untouched. The outcomes of these processes are often portrayed as unambiguously positive. As we will see, however, anthropologists who study globalization have shown that its outcomes are not positive for everyone. Finding ways to cope with these processes is an ongoing challenge for anthropologists and the people with whom they work.

▼ WHAT HAPPENED TO THE GLOBAL ECONOMY AFTER THE COLD WAR?

In 1989, the Cold War came to an end. The Soviet Union and its satellite states collapsed, and China began to encourage some capitalist economic practices. These radical changes in the global political economy left no part of the world unaffected. For some, this period of uncertainty offered a chance to challenge

FIGURE 14.1 To publicize their opposition to a proposed hydroelectric dam complex that threatened to flood their traditional territories, indigenous Amazonian peoples, under the leadership of the Kayapó, engaged in a variety of activities. Here, Kayapó chief Payakan (left) and British rock star Sting hold a press conference.

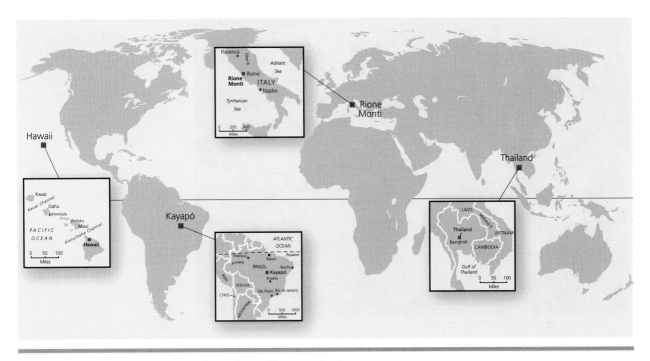

FIGURE 14.2 Location of societies whose EthnoProfiles appear in chapter 14.

long-unquestioned truths about development and underdevelopment that had guided government policies throughout the Cold War. New social movements questioned both the importance of market capitalism and the need for socialist revolution. From vigilante movements such as the *rondas campesinas* of Peru to squatter movements in cities, to movements defending the rights of women and homosexuals and movements to preserve rain forests, people attempted to construct entirely new social institutions that often bypassed national governments or development agencies (see Figure 14.3; EthnoProfile 9.6: Northern Peru [Rondas Campesinas]). Anthropologist Arturo Escobar (1992) argued that the new social movements in Latin America were struggles over meanings as well as over material conditions.

At the same time Escobar and others, such as James Ferguson, attacked previous notions of development. They argued that Western governments and international aid agencies created an "antipolitics machine": It persuades citizens in "underdeveloped" countries that the source of their problems is to be found in their technological backwardness rather than in the exploitative nature of their political systems. When this persuasion succeeds, the governments and agencies supplying development aid are transformed into "a machine for reinforcing and expanding the exercise of bureaucratic state power, which incidentally takes 'poverty' as its point of entry" (Ferguson 2001 [1990], 407).

This work continued the critique of Western Cold War efforts at modernization through development. It offered the hope that new social movements might promote less exploitative forms of society in generations to come. But such a world was already disappearing. The breakdown of communism led to a crisis of confidence among many who had been inspired by key tenets of Marxian thought. At the same time, the apparent triumph of capitalism reanimated the traditional Cold War supporters of modernization theory. Under the new conditions of an emerging global capitalism, they now began to offer a new view of the future, called *neoliberalism*. Modernization theory had urged nation-states to seek self-sufficient prosperity while avoiding communist revolution. Neoliberalism, by contrast, relied on international institutions like the World Bank and the International Monetary Fund to encourage nation-states to achieve prosperity by finding a niche in

FIGURE 14.3 Following the Cold War, a number of "new social movements" developed around the world, including Wangari Maathai's Green Belt Movement, a tree-planting project in Kenya, run mostly by women.

the growing global capitalist market. Market discipline would force state bureaucrats to support economic enterprises that would bring them income. However, it would also eliminate state institutions and subsidies that had provided a safety net for the poor. Western leaders embraced with enthusiasm the beckoning opportunity to bring the entire world within the compass of the capitalist economy. Less enthusiastic observers began to suspect that forces unleashed at the end of the Cold War were remaking the global political economy in unprecedented new ways, with outcomes that no one could predict or control.

▼ CULTURAL PROCESSES IN A GLOBAL WORLD

Modernization theory and other Cold War–era theories presupposed a world with relatively clear-cut geographic and cultural boundaries. Only then does it make sense to distinguish developed from underdeveloped nations, cores from peripheries, or local cultures from global social processes. The worldwide political, economic, and technological changes

globalization Reshaping of local conditions by powerful global forces on an ever-intensifying scale.

of recent decades, however, have caused many social scientists to question these distinctions. The cybernetics revolution has led to advances in manufacturing, transportation, and communications technology. It has also removed the seemingly insuperable barriers to communication and contact, a phenomenon called "space-time compression" (Harvey 1990). These changes made it easier, cheaper, and faster to move people and things around the world than ever before; they also made it possible to stretch social relationships of all kinds over huge distances that previously would have been unbridgeable (Giddens 1990). With the end of the Cold War, all parts of the world were drawn into these processes of **globalization**. Globalization suggests a world full of movement and mixture, contacts and linkages, and persistent cultural interaction and exchange" (Inda and Rosaldo 2002, 2).

Globalization is understood and evaluated differently by different observers. Anthropologists ordinarily approach globalization from the perspective of those among whom they do their research. From this point of view, it has been apparent for some time that the effects of globalization are *uneven:* "There are large expanses of the planet only tangentially tied to the webs of interconnection that encompass the globe" (Inda and Rosaldo 2002, 4). As a result, global processes are interpreted and experienced in contradictory ways by different groups and actors.

IN THEIR OWN WORDS

The Ethnographer's Responsibility

French ethnographers Jacques Meunier and A. M. Savarin reflect on the role they can play in Europe to affect the policies of Latin American governments toward the indigenous peoples living within their borders.

At the most fundamental level, the history of thought about primitive people—are they human, overgrown children, or replicas of early stages of Western civilization?—provides a summary of the changes that have taken place in our own culture: the West knows that it can no longer hold exclusive power, but it still considers itself the dominant power. Western ignorance follows from this error. Our taste for exoticism and our morality stem from it, as does the deadly intolerance that seems lodged in our hearts. Centuries of culture and well-intentioned unreasonableness, centuries of humanism have led to the most heinous of all crimes: genocide.

Entire communities forced to abandon their lands, children kidnapped, people treated barbarously, degraded mentally and physically, punitive expeditions launched against them. . . . With genocide, with racism, we confront horror itself. We have spoken of the fragility of traditional societies, of the blind intolerance of our civilization toward the Indians, of the lack of understanding that has led the Amazonians—white, creole, and mestizo—to the organized extermination of the Indians. But there is one question that haunts us, that emerges through the pages of this case like the recurring notes of a flute, forcing us to

weigh an unpleasant possibility: aren't we just as guilty of exploiting the Indians, aren't we indulging in a lot of useless discussion? But when we use the word genocide, we have no intention of turning ourselves into defenders of a lost cause; we do not see our roles as charity and moralism. We are not writing off the Indians; we do not believe that genocide should be considered an inevitable calamity.

Ethnographers must organize; they must enact plans to safeguard the threatened minorities—this is important. But if they do not capture public opinion, their projects will not produce results. More than anything, ethnographers need to launch an information campaign, a sound and systematic campaign. The general public has the right to know. The right and the duty. To accept this atrocity, to allow these terrible crimes to be committed, is to become an accomplice in them.

Do not misjudge us: our indignation is not mere posturing. We are convinced that it is possible to affect the policy of Latin American governments. Especially since these countries, while dependent on the United States economically, still turn toward Europe culturally. We can say to them without paternalism: the sense Latin Americans have of their countries still comes from Europe. Why shouldn't they learn a respect for their indigenous populations from Europe, just as they have acquired a taste for pre-Columbian antiquities and folklore? In our view, the salvation of the Indian must begin here and now.

Source: Meunier and Savarin 1994, 128–29.

Faye Ginsburg and Rayna Rapp, for example, describe the global process of *stratified reproduction*, in which some categories of people are empowered to nurture and reproduce, while others are not: "Low-income African American mothers, for example, often are stereotyped as undisciplined 'breeders' who sap the resources of the state through incessant demands on welfare. But historically and in the present, they were 'good enough' nurturers to work as child-

care providers for other, more privileged class and ethnic groups" (1995, 3). Globalization has created new opportunities for some groups, like the Kayapó and other indigenous peoples, to build worldwide organizations to defend their interests (Niezen 2003; Kearney 1995). At the same time, global forces can also reinforce old constraints. Evaluating the record of new social movements in Latin America, for example, John Gledhill writes that "to date the challenge

Protest Disrupts Tour de France

Globalization, however defined, is controversial. In France, José Bové has become famous for leading protests against trade liberalization, the introduction of genetically modified seeds, and mass-produced fast food. In July 2003, he led a protest at one of Europe's premier sporting events.

A protest by supporters of jailed French anti-globalisation activist Jose Bove has disrupted the world's premier cycling race.

Demonstrators sat down in the middle of the road during the 10th stage of the Tour de France, about 70km (43 miles) away from the city of Marseille.

The *peloton*, or main pack of riders, was forced to halt for two minutes before police dragged the protesters away.

Mr. Bové, a prominent critic of trade liberalisation and mass-produced food, is currently serving two separate prison terms for destroying genetically modified crops of maize and rice in the late 1990s.

He also leads a militant group of farmers called the Confederation Paysanne, which champions smaller producers, and is considered by many in France to be a hero for his stand against big business.

Tour officials ruled that the protest was "a normal race incident," meaning that riders would have to suffer the penalties of being caught in the protest.

But the protest did not have any affect on the result of the Tuesday's stage.

Although the group affected included four-time winner and current race leader, Lance Armstrong, all his closest rivals were held up in the group with him so his lead did not suffer.

Bové is nicknamed Asterix by the French, both for his moustachioed resemblance to the cartoon character and his determination to repel what he sees as foreign invaders—whether they be a McDonald's restaurant or GM crops.

Protesters had hoped that Bové would be granted clemency during the country's Bastille Day celebrations.

However French President Jacques Chirac said that activists did not have the right to break the law, although he did shorten Bove's sentence.

On Monday protesters held several demonstrations in Paris on behalf of Bové, which included draping banners across the Louvre and a protest picnic in the shadow of the Eiffel Tower.

Source: BBC News 2003.

---

that popular forces have been able to mount to the remorseless progress of the neoliberal, neomodernization agenda, has remained limited" (1994, 198).

It would be difficult to find any research project by contemporary cultural anthropologists that does not in some way acknowledge the ways in which global forces affect the local societies in which they work. In this respect, globalization studies emphasize the ways in which *the global articulates with the local:* anthropological studies of globalization aim to show "how globalizing processes exist in the context of, and must come to terms with, the realities of particular societies" (Inda and Rosaldo 2002, 4). The consequences are that "while everyone might continue to live local lives, their phenomenal worlds have to some extent become global" (Inda and Rosaldo 2002, 9).

Globalization is seen in the growth of transnational corporations that relocate their manufacturing operations from core to periphery or that appropriate local cultural forms and turn them into images and commodities to be marketed throughout the world (Figure 14.4). It is seen in tourism, which has grown into the world's largest industry, and in migration from periphery to the core on such a massive scale that observers now speak of the "deterritorialization" of peoples and cultures that, in the past, were presumed to be firmly attached to specific geographical locations.

FIGURE 14.4 One dimension of globalization involves the appropriation of local cultural forms and their use on a variety of widely sold commodities. For example, the image of "Kokopelli," taken from ancient rock art of the southwestern United States, has been reproduced on many items with no connection to its region or culture of origin, including this mailbox flag from Albuquerque, New Mexico. Such items are readily available on the Internet.

Not only that: Deterritorialized people always "reterritorialize" in a new location. Such reterritorialization regularly sparks social conflicts and generates new forms of cultural identity, as nation-states try to retain control over citizens living beyond their borders and as relocated populations struggle both for recognition in their new homes and for influence in their places of origin. Globalization has drawn the attention of many anthropologists to regions such as the borderland between northern Mexico and the southwestern United States, where struggles with contradictory social practices and ambiguous identities have long been the rule, rather than the exception. Such contexts exhibit a "diffusion of culture traits gone wild, far beyond that imagined by the Boasians" (Kearney 1995, 557). Since borderland conditions are now becoming worldwide, they undermine views of culture that depend upon settled peoples with distinct cultural attributes.

Such heterogeneous and unstable cultural spaces also call into question views like that of sociologist Immanuel Wallerstein, which portrays global processes as part of a world *system*. Anthropologist Arjun Appadurai claims, to the contrary, that ever-intensifying global flows of people, technology, wealth, images, and ideologies are highly contradictory, generating global processes that are fundamentally disorganized and unpredictable (1990).

Jonathan Friedman, by contrast, argues that the disorder may be real but is also a predictable consequence of the breakdown of Western global hegemony. As European colonial empires dissolved, capitalist economic accumulation has decentralized, from Europe and North America to parts of the world such as the Pacific Rim (1994). In his view, these developments exemplify a pattern of commercial expansion and contraction that began at least 5,000 years ago with the rise of the first commercial civilizations—world systems in Wallerstein's sense—each of which was characterized by its own form of "modernity." Recognition of this pattern makes Friedman even more pessimistic than Wallerstein about possibilities for the future. He sees current changes in the capitalist world system as simply the latest example of "a more cyclically sinister history of civilizational systems" that have risen and fallen repeatedly throughout history (1994, 99; cf. Janet Abu-Lughod 1991). He does not claim that "there are not local structures, no autonomous cultural schemes" (1994, 190). But he remains unmoved by those who would suggest that anything new or hopeful might emerge from the current state of the world: "The capacity to even conceive of consciously changing the world for the better lies, perhaps, in changing the system as a whole, a system whose more general properties have eluded the storms of innumerable revolutions and cataclysm" (1994, 41).

Not all anthropologists accept Friedman's conclusions. But even if Friedman's overall schema of civilizational cycles seems plausible, it cannot by itself account for the "local structures" and "autonomous cultural schemes" that appear at any point in the cycle. It is this historically specific local detail—what Inda and Rosaldo (2002, 27) call "the conjunctural and situated character of globalization"—that anthropologists aim to document and analyze. In the rest of the chapter, we examine three important areas of study in the anthropology of globalization: the effect of global forces on nation-states, human rights as the emerging discourse of globalization, and debates about cultural hybridization, cosmopolitanism, and the emergence of new global assemblages.

▼ GLOBALIZATION AND THE NATION-STATE

Are Global Flows Undermining Nation-States?

In the second half of the twentieth century, one of the fundamental suppositions about global social organization was that it consisted of an international order of independent nation-states. This assumption has roots that can be traced back to nineteenth-century nationalist struggles in Europe, but it seems to have come fully into its own after World War II, with the final dissolution of European empires, as former colonies achieved independence. The United Nations (UN), created in 1945, presupposed a world of nation-states. Social theorists and activists alike assumed that the world was a mosaic of nations that, one way or another, were entitled to self-determination and a state of their own (Figure 14.5).

The flows of wealth, images, people, things, and ideologies unleashed by globalization have undermined the ability of nation-states to police their boundaries effectively, and have seemed to suggest that the conventional ideas about nation-states require revision. Many observers have suggested that globalization inevitably undermines the power and sovereignty of nation-states. National governments are virtually powerless to control what their citizens read or watch in the media: Satellite services and telecommunications and the Internet elude state-ordered censorship. Nation-states allow migrants or students or tourists to cross their borders because they need their labor or tuition or vacation expenditures, but in so doing states must contend with the political values or religious commitments or families that these outsiders bring with them. Some people have argued that to weaken boundaries between states is a good thing, since border restrictions and censorship need to be overcome. Since 1989, however, as we witness the ways that forces of globalization have made weakened states vulnerable to chaos and violence, the ability of the nation-state to protect its citizens from such destruction has led some to ask whether stronger nation-states might not have at least some points in their favor.

Massive global displacements of people have characterized Western modernity, starting with the slave trade and the movement of indentured labor to the colonies. In the nineteenth century, developing capitalist markets pushed and pulled waves of European and Asian emigrants out of their homelands and installed them in different parts of the globe. At the same time, colonial authorities revived the institution of indentured labor to rearrange population within their dominions. A hundred years earlier, when volumes of immigration were lower and moved at a slower pace and jobs were plentiful, the possibility of assimilation into the society of reterritorialization was often possible. Today, however, desperate economic and political situations in migrants' home territories plus ease of transportation have increased the volume and speed of migration. Meanwhile, market crises in the countries where migrants have settled have sharply reduced the economic opportunities available once they arrive.

Migrants often find themselves caught. On the one hand, they now form a sizeable and highly visible minority in the countries of settlement, often in the poorer areas of cities. There they find opportunities for economic survival and political security, encouraging them to stay. On the other hand, hostility and sometimes violence is directed against them whenever there is a local economic downturn. Many migrants conclude that the possibility of permanent assimilation is unrealistic, which encourages them to maintain ties to the homeland or to migrant communities elsewhere.

FIGURE 14.5 Queen Elizabeth II at Nigerian Independence ceremonies, January 1956.

Cofan

Story of the Forest People and the Outsiders

Randy Borman is president of the Centro Cofan Zabalo. He was born to missionary parents and grew up in Cofan culture in the Ecuadorian Amazon. Borman briefly attended school in North America and then returned to Ecuador to become a leader in the Cofan fight for economic and cultural survival. He has written in Cultural Survival Quarterly *about the development of ecotourism in the Cofan area of Ecuador. The results of tourism elsewhere in the world are not always as positive as they have been for the Cofan people, in part because tourism is often imposed from the outside.*

I had the fortune to grow up as a forest person, enjoying the clean rivers and unlimited forests, learning the arts and skills of living comfortably in a wonderland of the marvelous, beautiful, and deadly. I experienced first hand both the good and the bad of a world, which will never again be possible, at least in the foreseeable future. And I also experienced the crushing physical, psychological, and spiritual impact of the invasion of the outside that erased our world.

In 1955, the Cofan people were the sole inhabitants of more than 1,000,000 hectares of pristine forest in northeastern Ecuador. By 1965, oil exploration and exploitation had begun. And by 1975, the forest was fast disappearing before a massive mestizo colonization, which was brought in by roads created to access vast quantities of oil. The rivers were fouled with chemicals and raw crude; the animals disappeared; boom towns sprung up all over; and the Cofan struggled to survive on less than 15,000 hectares of badly degraded forest. The old life was gone forever, and my companions and I faced the numbing prospect of discarding our culture and way of life, and becoming peasant farmers like so many others, trying to eke out a living from crops and animals which were never meant to grow in this environment. We had been powerless to maintain our forests in the face of outsider pressures to make every given piece of land profitable. If we were to save any-

thing from the wreckage we needed alternatives, and quickly. . . .

[As the only member of his community with an outsider education, Borman worked with the community in trying to develop strategies for community survival, including those associated with marketing forest products. These strategies did not work.]

As we were wrestling with these possible alternatives, we were also acting as boatmen for the slowly increasing economy on the river. Several of us had managed to buy outboard motors with carefully saved returns from corn fields, animal skins, and short stints as trail makers with the oil companies. We had a long tradition of carving dug-outs, and soon our canoes were traveling up and down the rivers with loads of lumber, corn, and coffee; occasional trips carrying cattle provided excitement and variety. This was not an alternative for the entire community, and it was only viable until roads were built, but it worked as a stop-gap measure for some of us. And unexpectedly, it led us directly into the alternative, which we have adopted as our own in the years since.

Travelers were coming to our region. The roads made it easier than at any previous time, and people from First World countries—the USA, Canada, England, Germany, Israel, Italy—began to come, searching for the vanishing rain forest. Most of them were primarily interested in seeing wildlife. This fit with our view of the situation precisely. We had our motorboats. There was still a lot of good forest out there, but it was hard to access with regular paddling and poling expeditions. So when these travelers arrived and wanted to go to "wild jungle," we were delighted to take them. They paid the transportation cost, and we took our shotguns and spears along to go hunting. Our attitude was that if the traveler wanted to go along with us, and didn't mind that we were hunting, why, we were happy to have them along to help carry the game home! From such a pragmatic beginning, we slowly developed our concept of tourism.

(continued on next page)

Cofan
Story of the Forest People and the Outsiders
(continued)

There were changes. We soon learned that the traveler had a lot more fun if we modified our normal hunting pattern a bit, and we even got paid extra for it. We found out that the average tourist didn't mind if we shot birds that looked like chickens, even if they were rare. But if we shot a toucan they were outraged, despite the fact that toucans are very common. Tourists preferred a board to a stick as a seat in the canoe, and a pad made them even happier. Tourists' food needed to be somewhat recognizable, such as rice, rather than the lumpy, thick manioc beer we normally eat and drink. But the community as a whole decided early that our role would be that of guides and service providers for tourists interested in the forest. We would not dress up and do dances, or stage fake festivals, or in any way try to sell our traditions and dress. We would not accept becoming the objects of tourism—rather, we would provide the skills and knowledge for the tourist to understand our environment. We would sell our education, at a price that was in line with the importance to the outsiders who wanted to buy it, such as lawyers, biologists, doctors, teachers, and other professionals the world over do.

Being guides for the tourism experience, not the objects of it, has provided both a very real economic alternative and a very solid incentive for the younger generation to learn the vast body of traditional knowledge, which lies at the heart of our culture. A deep conservation ethic—the roots of which lie at the hearts of most cultures who maintain a viable relation with their environments—has helped the Cofan community to create a number of projects which combine outsider science with our traditional knowledge. Interestingly enough, this has also turned out to be an economic success, as many of our projects began to receive funding in recognition of their innovation and replicability in other communities throughout Amazonia.

At present, the Cofan community most involved in both tourism and conservation is my community, Zabalo. Located in what is now part of the Cuyabeno Wildlife Reserve near the northern border of Ecuador with Peru, this community owns and manages over 100,000 hectares of forest in coordination with the Ecuadorean national parks system. With four community-operated cabins, an interpretation center, and a series of trails and camps both in deep forest and on the black water streams of the area, Zabalo plays host in varying scale to over 3000 visitors annually. Most of these visitors come via an Ecuadorean tourism agency, Metropolitan Touring, which operates a floating hotel in the region (appropriately the Flotel), and spend only a few hours at the interpretation center and market. However, perhaps 200 visitors per year spend up to 10 days enjoying the village's programs—trekking, canoeing, birding, wildlife watching; learning to know the forest intimately in the company of Cofan guides, cooks, and administrators. Both the cabins and the interpretation center generate income for the community. Working as crew and as guides for the groups provides individual income. And the sale of crafts both directly to tourists and to retailers elsewhere in the country is a steady and important source of cash for the families of the community. . . .

Tourism is not for everyone. Some of our experiences have been negative. One of our biggest and most constant headaches is effective commercialization. To operate a community-based tourism business while maintaining our cultural heritage is not possible using the outsider formula of a tour operator. The implied hierarchy of manager, finance department, buyers, transport specialists, etc., all working eight hours a day, five days a week, with an office and a fax machine is clearly not applicable. Instead, we rely on teams, which rotate in their work, leaving time for farms, family duties, crafts, fishing, hunting and the garden. But the lack of a full-time office makes it difficult to commercialize effectively, and we walk the precarious line between too much tourism (no time left over to live a normal life, and possible loss of our cultural way of life) and too little (not enough jobs, not enough income, lack of attraction for a forest-based life and education for our young people). If we commercialize effectively, we run the risk of the operation snowballing, with more and more tourists arriving, and eventually, we are all wealthy in outsider goods and income but without our culture's wealth of time and

Cofan
Story of the Forest People and the Outsiders
(continued)

interpersonal relationships that we all value so much now. If we don't commercialize effectively, we will wake up tomorrow back at the beginning, with the need to destroy our forest for short-term survival.

But in the overall scheme of things, our experiment with tourism has been overwhelmingly positive. Contact with people who wish to know what we can teach, who

value our forests and are willing to pay to help us maintain them has been very important. Our increased awareness of the conservation imperatives facing us has led to many changes in our way of life, all aimed at preserving core values for future generations.

Source: Borman 1999, 48–50.

Migration, Transborder Identities, and Long-Distance Nationalism

The term *diaspora* is commonly used to refer to migrant populations with a shared identity who live in a variety of different locales around the world, but Nina Glick Schiller and Georges Fouron point out that not all such populations see themselves in the same way. Schiller and Fouron describe different types of "transborder identities" that characterize different groups of migrants. They prefer to use the term **diaspora** to identify a form of trans-border identity that does not focus on nation-building. Should members of a diaspora begin to organize in support of nationalist struggles in their homeland, or to agitate for a state of their own, they become **long-distance nationalists** (Schiller and Fouron 2002, 360–61). Long-distance nationalism is a term coined by political scientist Benedict Anderson to describe the efforts of émigrés to offer moral, economic, and political support to the nationalist struggles of their countries of origin. In his original discussion, Anderson emphasized the dangerous irresponsibility of the "citizenshipless participation" of the long-distance nationalists: "while technically a citizen of the state in which he comfortably lives, but to which he may feel little attachment, he finds it tempting to play identity politics by participating (via propaganda, money, weapons, any way but voting) in the conflicts of his imagined *Heimat* [homeland]" (2002, 269–70).

Schiller and Fouron argue, however, that the conditions of globalization have led to new forms of long-distance nationalism that do not correspond to Anderson's original description. They point to the

emergence of the **trans-border state**: a form of state "claiming that its emigrants and their descendants remain an integral and intimate part of their ancestral homeland, even if they are legal citizens of another state" (Schiller and Fouron 2002, 357).

Trans-border states did not characterize periods of mass emigration in the nineteenth and twentieth centuries. At that time, nations sending emigrants abroad regarded permanent settlement elsewhere as national betrayal. They encouraged emigrants to think of migration as temporary, expecting them eventually to return home with new wealth and skills to build the nation. But in today's global world, political leaders of many states sending emigrants accept the likelihood that those emigrants will settle permanently elsewhere. They may even insist that émigrés retain full membership in the nation-state from which they came. This form of long-distance nationalism creates what Schiller and Fouron call a **trans-border citizenry**: "Citizens residing within the

---

diaspora Migrant populations with a shared identity who live in a variety of different locales around the world; a form of trans-border identity that does not focus on nation building.

long-distance nationalism Members of a diaspora begin to organize in support of nationalist struggles in their homeland, or to agitate for a state of their own.

trans-border state A form of state in which it is claimed that those people who left the country and their descendents remain part of their ancestral state, even if they are citizens of another state.

trans-border citizenry A group made up of citizens of a country who continue to live in the homeland plus the people who have emigrated from the country and their descendants, regardless of their current citizenship.

territorial homeland and new emigrants and their descendants are part of the nation, whatever legal citizenship the émigrés may have" (Schiller and Fouron 2002, 358).

Trans-border states and trans-border citizenries are more than symbolic identities: They have become concretized in law. For example, several Latin American countries, including Mexico, Colombia, the Dominican Republic, Ecuador, and Brazil, permit emigrants who have become naturalized citizens in countries such as the United States to retain dual nationality and even voting rights in their country of origin (Figure 14.6). Special government ministries are set up to address the needs of citizens living abroad. This is very different from Anderson's notion of "citizenshipless participation." Schiller and Fouron stress that trans-border states and citizenries "cannot be seen as top-down fostering of elite beliefs" but that they spring instead "from the life experiences of migrants of different classes" and are "rooted in the day to day efforts of people in the homeland to live lives of dignity and self-respect that compel them to include those who have migrated" (Schiller and Fouron 2002, 359).

But some trans-border citizenries face difficulties. First, their efforts at nation-building are sometimes blocked by political forces in the homeland who do not welcome their contributions. This has been the case for Haitians living abroad while Haiti was ruled by the Duvalier dictatorship and for Cubans living abroad whose efforts are blocked by Fidel Castro's revolutionary government. Second, the states in which immigrants have settled may not welcome the continued involvement of trans-border citizens in the affairs of another state. Such involvement has often been seen as even more threatening since terrorists destroyed the World Trade Center and attacked the Pentagon on September 11, 2001. Yet in an era of globalization, attempts to control migration threaten to block the flows of people that keep the global economy going. Moreover, the vulnerability of trans-border citizens in these circumstances often increases the appeal of long-distance nationalism (Schiller and Fouron 2002, 359–60).

FIGURE 14.6 The Dominican Republic permits emigrants who have become naturalized citizens of the United States to vote in Dominican elections. Here, a Dominican woman in New York campaigns in 2004 for a second term for President Hipólito Mejía.

The globalizing forces that produce long-distance nationalism and trans-border states and citizens have undermined previous understandings of what a world made up of nation-states should look like. In addition, unacknowledged contradictions and weaknesses of actual nation-states are revealed. For example, the existence and strength of trans-border states and citizenries show that some nation-states—especially those sending migrants—are actually what Schiller and Fouron call *apparent states*: They have all the outward attributes of nation-states (government bureaucracies, armies, a seat in the United Nations), but in fact they are unable to meet the needs of their people (Schiller and Fouron 2002, 363). The strength of long-distance nationalism and trans-border citizenries also exposes inconsistencies and paradoxes in the meaning of citizenship in the nation-states where migrants settle.

Schiller and Fouron contrast legal citizenship with what they call substantive citizenship, and point out that, for trans-border citizens, the two often do not coincide. As we saw, **legal citizenship** is accorded by state laws and can be difficult for migrants to obtain. But even those trans-border citizens who obtain legal citizenship often experience a gap between what the legal citizenship promises and the way they are treated by the state. For example, people of color and women who are United States citizens are not treated

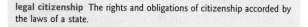

legal citizenship The rights and obligations of citizenship accorded by the laws of a state.

by the state the same way white male citizens are treated. By contrast, **substantive citizenship** is defined by the actions people take, regardless of their legal citizenship status, to assert their membership in a state and to bring about political changes that will improve their lives. Some trans-border citizenries call for the establishment of fully fledged **transnational nation-states**. That is, "they challenge the notion that relationships between citizens and their state are confined within that territory" and work for the recognition of a new political form that contradicts the understandings of political theory, but which reflects the realities of their experiences of national identity (Schiller and Fouron 2002, 359).

Anthropology and Multicultural Politics in the New Europe

One of the more interesting things about the early twenty-first century is that Europe, the continent that gave birth to the Enlightenment and colonial empires and to anthropology itself (along with North American contributions) has now itself become a key setting for the anthropological study of social and cultural changes. During the last half of the twentieth century, the countries of Europe, including Italy, were the target of large waves of migration from all over the world.

Visitors to Rome regularly make stops at the ancient ruins in the center of the city. One venerable working-class Roman neighborhood, only a short walk from the Coliseum, is Rione Monti, which has a fascinating history of its own (EthnoProfile 14.2). In 1999 anthropologist Michael Herzfeld moved into Rione Monti to do fieldwork exploring social change in the uses of the past (2003). Longtime residents of Monti share a common local culture, which includes use of the *romanesco* dialect rather than standard Italian, and a strong sense of local identity that distinguishes them from "foreigners," including diplomats and non-Roman Italians Their identity survived Mussolini's demolition of part of the neighborhood in the early twentieth century. They successfully dealt with a local criminal underworld by mastering a refined urbane code of politeness. The underworld had faded away by the 1970s, but beginning in the 1980s, residents began to face two new challenges to their community. First, historic Roman neighborhoods be-

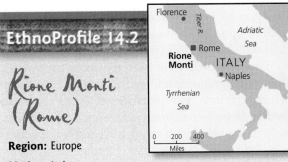

EthnoProfile 14.2

Rione Monti (Rome)

Region: Europe

Nation: Italy

Population: 15,300

Environment: Central neighborhood in Rome

Livelihood: Urban occupations, ranging from tourism and factory work to restaurants, small businesses, bureaucratic, executive

Political organization: Neighborhood in a modern nation-state

For more information: http://www.rionemonti.net/

came fashionable, and well-to-do Italians began to move into Rione Monti, pushing many workers into cheaper housing elsewhere. And then, in the 1990s, another group of newcomers arrived: immigrants from Eastern Europe.

Italy is one of the more recent destinations of immigration into Europe, reversing the country's historical experience as a source, rather than a target, of immigration. However, after Germany, France, and Britain passed laws curtailing immigration in the 1970s, Italy became an increasingly popular destination for immigrants from Africa, Asia, and Latin America; after the end of the Cold War came immigrants from outside the European Union, including Eastern Europe. Until recently, laws regulating immigration were few, and the country appeared welcoming. But this is changing. "Italy has not historically been a racist country, but intolerant attitudes towards immigrants have increased. To a large extent, this seems to be the result of a long-standing underestimation of the magnitude of the changes and

substantive citizenship The actions people take, regardless of their legal citizenship status, to assert their membership in a state and to bring about political changes that will improve their lives.

transnational nation-state A nation-state in which the relationships between citizens and their states extend to wherever citizens reside.

thus poor policy implementation for a lengthy period, in spite of the best intentions officially proclaimed" (Melotti 1997, 91).

Umberto Melotti contrasts the distinctive ways in which immigration is understood by the governments of France, Britain, and Germany. According to Melotti, the French project is *ethnocentric assimilationism:* Since early in the nineteenth century, when French society experienced a falling birthrate, immigration was encouraged and immigrants were promised all the rights and privileges of native-born citizens as long as they adopted French culture completely, dropping other ethnic or cultural attachments and assimilated the French language, culture, and character (1997, 75). The British project, by contrast, is *uneven pluralism:* that is, the pragmatic British expect immigrants to be loyal and law-abiding citizens, but they do not expect immigrants to "become British" and they tolerate private cultivation of cultural differences as long as these do not threaten the British way of life (1997, 79–80). Finally, Melotti describes the German project as *the institutionalization of precariousness,* by which he means that despite the fact that Germany has within its borders more immigrants than any other European country, and began receiving immigrants at the end of the nineteenth century, its government continues to insist that Germany is not a country of immigrants. Immigrants were always considered "guest workers," children born to guest workers are considered citizens of the country from which the worker came, and it still remains very difficult for guest workers or their children born in Germany to obtain German citizenship. (This contrasts with France, for example, where children of immigrants born on French soil automatically become French citizens.) A very different pattern can be found in Belgium, where the Dutch-speaking Flemings in the north and the French-speaking Walloons in the south enjoy considerable autonomy and the state's role is to protect the rights of each community in the public sphere. This system, known as *pillorization,* bears some similarity to the way separate religious communities were organized under the Ottoman Empire (Modood 1997, 22–23).

Coming to terms with increasing numbers of Muslims living in countries where Christianity has historically been dominant is a central theme in multicultural debates within Europe, as we saw in chapters 8 and 15. Although all European states consider themselves secular in orientation, the relation between religion and state is far from uniform. France is unusual because of its strict legal separation between religion and state. In Britain, the combination of a secular outlook with state funding of the established Anglican Church has allowed citizens to support forms of religious inclusion that first involved state funding of Catholic schools for Irish immigrants and now involve state funding of Muslim schools for Muslim immigrants (Lewis 1997; Modood 1997). In Germany, where a secular outlook also combines with state-subsidized religious institutions, the state has devised curricula for elementary schools designed to teach all students about different religious traditions, including Islam, in ways that emphasize the possibility of harmonizing one's religious faith with one's obligations as a citizen. Although this approach may be seen as presumptuous or paternalistic, its supporters counter that its advantages outweigh its costs. Perhaps as a result of their own history, many contemporary Germans have less faith than the British that a civic culture of religious tolerance will automatically lead to harmony without state intervention, and less faith than the French in the existence of a separate secular sphere of society from which religion can be safely excluded (Schiffauer 1997).

These are, of course, thumbnail sketches of more complex attitudes and practices. But they illustrate the fact that there is no single "European" approach to the challenges posed by immigration. In a way, each European state, with its own history and own institutions, is experimenting with different ways of coping with the challenges of multiculturalism, and their failures and successes will influence the kinds of multicultural relations and institutions that develop in the twenty-first century. This is particularly significant in light of the fact that European nation-states have joined together in the European Union, a continent-wide super-state with 25 members. Reconciling the diverse interests and needs of member states poses enormous challenges for EU members, and multicultural issues are among them.

Many scholars and activists hope that solutions can be found that will involve extensions of social justice throughout the EU (e.g., Ben-Tovim 1997; Brewin 1997). But there is still a lot of work to be done, and no guarantees about the outcome. Tariq Modood points out, for example, that European multiculturalism requires supporting conceptions of citizenship that allow the "right to assimilate" as well as conceptions of citizenship that allow "right to have one's 'difference' . . . recognized and supported in the public and the private spheres"; multiculturalism must recognize that "participation in the public or national culture is necessary for the effective exercise of citizenship" while at the same time defending the "right to widen and adapt the national culture" (1997, 20). The potential and actual contradictions among some of these goals are apparent, but insofar as they are seen as necessary, the challenge becomes one of finding ways to move forward. And here, with no blueprint to follow, all parties find themselves involved in creating new cultural practices. Based on her experience in France, Dembour is convinced that "we need to accept the discomfort of moving in-between, as a pendulum" (Dembour 2001, 71–72). Modood agrees: "There is indeed a tension here, and perhaps it can only be resolved in practice through finding and cultivating points of common ground between dominant and subordinate cultures, as well as new syntheses and hybridities. The important thing is that the burdens of change . . . are not all dependent on one party to this encounter" (1997, 20).

Anthropologists inevitably are drawn into these discussions, not only because they carry out research in the communities struggling for resolution, but also because many of them are citizens of the societies whose future depends on the solutions that are implemented. As a result, theoretical debates in the field are intertwined with political debates in society, and scholars can disagree with one another just as political activists do. For example, Norwegian anthropologist Thomas Eriksen reports on the outcome of a formal debate organized by the Department of Anthropology at the University of Oslo in 1997, in which the thesis to be contested was the assertion that cultural freedom protects not only a group but also the rights of every individual within a group (Eriksen 2001, 144). "Speaking from very different ethnographic horizons, the antagonists not only reached opposite conclusions but also failed to engage in a proper dialogue: they tended to depict each other . . . as

hopeless Romantics and cynical modernists, respectively" (2001, 144). In the end, Eriksen observes, the debate raised the same kinds of issues, and provoked the same kinds of responses, and standoffs, that can be found in the wider society. After the debate, the audience was invited to vote for the side they thought had made the best case. The results were 78 in favor of the motion, 75 against. This almost perfect standoff is, Eriksen points out, very different from what the outcome would likely have been ten or fifteen years earlier, when there would, he says, have been "almost certainly a massive 'yes' vote . . . perhaps the tide will turn again" (145).

Thus, the struggles and dilemmas facing residents of Rione Monti are widespread across the new Europe. But the specifics of their situation, and the cultural resources at their disposal, have their own particularity. Thus, the traditionally left-wing Monti residents have resisted attempts by neofascist politicians to get them to turn against immigrant families in the neighborhood. Still, they are unhappy with the location of the Ukranian church in a building that overlooks the neighborhood's central square, because church-goers gather there twice a week, invading "their" space (Herzfeld 2003, 4) (Figure 14.7). Herzfeld reports that the residents of Monti, like other Romans claim not to be racist (which accords with Melotti's views of Italians in general), and that they seem less hostile to immigrants of color than to Ukranians. But Ukranians are more numerous in Monti, and more threatening, because they look like local people but in fact are competing with local people for work and space in the neighborhood (5). At the same time, the Monti code of politeness "underlies the facility with which democratically inclined residents today construct a popular street democracy, a system of neighbourhood associations" (2). Currently, immigrants are not able to deploy this code, a fact that signals their outsider status and can lead to misunderstandings and bad feelings. If they could learn to use the code, however, fresh opportunities for political cooperation might be forged. This could be decisive, for the code of politeness is the foundation of local democratic processes and "may also eventually be the only generally available means of denying access to manipulative party politics and land speculation alike" (6).

FIGURE 14.7 Rione Monti is a neighborhood in central Rome where longtime residents and new immigrants are negotiating new forms of relationship.

Flexible Citizenship and the Postnational Ethos

Schiller and Fouron's observations about the way globalization has undermined the stability of conventional nation-states exposes contradictory and ambiguous practices associated with such basic concepts as "national identity" and "citizenship." Their contrast between formal and substantive citizenship suggests that conventional notions of citizenship that previously seemed straightforward begin to break down in the context of globalization. Another way of addressing these contradictions and ambiguities is suggested by anthropologist Aihwa Ong, who speaks of **flexible citizenship**: "the strategies and effects of mobile managers, technocrats, and professionals seeking both to circumvent *and* benefit from different nation-state regimes by selecting different sites for investment, work, and family relocation" (2002, 174). Ong's research concerns diaspora communities of elite Chinese families who have played key roles in the economic successes of the Pacific Rim in recent

flexible citizenship The strategies and effects employed by managers, technocrats, and professionals who move regularly across state boundaries who seek both to circumvent and benefit from different nation-state regimes.

years. Although their success is often attributed by outsiders to "Chinese culture," Ong's research calls this simplistic explanation into question. Ong documents the ways in which Chinese families have responded creatively to opportunities and challenges they have encountered since the end of the nineteenth century, as they found ways to evade or exploit the governmentality of three different kinds of institutions: Chinese kinship and family, the nation-state, and the marketplace.

The break from mainland Chinese ideas of kinship and Confucian filial piety came when Chinese first moved into the capitalist commercial circuits of European empires. Money could be made in these settings, but success required Chinese merchant families to cut themselves off from ties to mainland China and to reinforce bonds among family members and business partners in terms of *guanxi* ("relationships of social connections built primarily upon shared identities such as native place, kinship or attending the same school" [Smart 1999, 120]).

The family discipline of overseas Chinese enabled them to become wealthy, and provided the resources to subvert the governmentality of the nation-state. The orientation of these wealthy families toward national identity and citizenship, Ong explains, is "market-driven." In Hong Kong, for example, in the years leading up to its return to mainland China in 1997, many wealthy Chinese thought of citizenship "not as the right to demand full democratic representation, but as the right to promote familial interests apart from the well-being of society" (Ong 2002, 178). None of the overseas Chinese she knew expressed any commitment to nationalism, either local or long-distance. This understanding of citizenship could not be more different from the committed trans-border citizenship of long-distance nationalists described by Schiller and Fouron.

Quite the contrary. Relying on family discipline and loyalty, and buttressed by considerable wealth and strong interpersonal ties, they actively worked to evade the governmentality of nation-states. For example, Chinese from Hong Kong who wanted to migrate to Britain in the 1960s were able to evade racial barriers that blocked other "colored" immigrants because of their experience with capitalism and their reputation for peaceful acquiescence to British rule. When the British decided to award citizenship to some Hong Kong residents in the 1990s, they used a point system that favored applicants with education, fluency in English, and training in professions of value to the economy, such as accountancy and law. These attributes fitted well the criteria for citizenship valued under the government of Margaret Thatcher, while other applicants for citizenship who lacked such attributes were excluded. Citizenship, or at least a passport, could be purchased by those who had the money: "well-off families accumulated passports not only from Canada, Australia, Singapore and the United States but also from revenue poor Fiji, the Philippines, Panama and Tonga (which required in return for a passport a down payment of U.S. $200,000 and an equal amount in installments" (2002, 183) (Figure 14.8).

Although wealthy overseas Chinese families had thus managed to evade or subvert both the governmentality of Chinese kinship and family and the governmentality of nation-states, they remained vulnerable to the discipline of the capitalist market. To be sure, market discipline under globalization was very different from the market discipline typical in the 1950s and 1960s. Making money in the context of globalization required the flexibility to take advantage of economic opportunities wherever and whenever they appeared. Ong describes one family in which the eldest son remained in Hong Kong to run part of the family hotel chain located in the Pacific region while his brother lived in San Francisco and managed the hotels located in North America and Europe. Children can be separated from their parents when they are, for example, installed in one country to be educated while their parents manage businesses in other countries on different continents.

FIGURE 14.8 Overseas Chinese are to be found in many parts of the world, as here in Tahiti. They are not always millionaire businesspeople but are shopkeepers and small businesspeople as well.

The Postnational Ethos

These flexible business arrangements are not without costs. "Familial regimes of dispersal and localization . . . discipline family members to make do with very little emotional support; disrupted parental responsibility, strained marital relations, and abandoned children are such common circumstances that they have special terms." At the same time, individual family members truly do seem to live comfortably as citizens of the world. A Chinese banker in San Francisco told Ong that he could live in Asia, Canada, or Europe: "I can live anywhere in the world, but it must be near an airport" (2002, 190).

The values and practices to which overseas Chinese adhere, and which seem responsible for their tremendous achievements in a globalized capitalist economy, suggest to Ong that, for these elite Chinese, the concept of nationalism has lost its meaning. Instead, she says, they seem to subscribe to a **postnational ethos** in which they submit to the governmentality of the capitalist market while trying to evade the governmentality of nation-states, ultimately because their only true loyalty is to the family business (2002, 190). Ong notes, however, that flexible citizenship informed by a postnational ethos is not an option for nonelite migrants: "whereas for bankers, boundaries are always flexible, for migrant workers, boat people, persecuted intellectuals and artists, and other kinds of less well-heeled refugees, this . . . is a harder act to follow" (2002, 190).

She also points out that, on the way to their success, contemporary Chinese merchants "have also revived premodern forms of child, gender, and class oppression, as well as strengthened authoritarianist regimes in Asia" (2002, 190). Yet neither the positives nor the negatives should, she insists, be attributed to any "Chinese" essence; instead, she thinks these strategies are better understood as "the expressions of a habitus that is finely tuned to the turbulence of late capitalism" (2002, 191).

---

postnational ethos An attitude toward the world in which people submit to the governmentality of the capitalist market while trying to evade the governmentality of nation-states.

human rights A set of rights that should be accorded to all human beings everywhere in the world.

▼ ARE HUMAN RIGHTS UNIVERSAL?

Globalization has stimulated discussions about **human rights**: powers, privileges, or material resources to which people everywhere are justly entitled by virtue of being human. Rapidly circulating capital, images, people, things, and ideologies juxtapose, and thereby at least implicitly challenge, different understandings about what it means to be human, or what kinds of rights people are entitled to under radically changed conditions of everyday life. It is in multicultural settings—found everywhere in today's globalized world—that questions of rights become salient, and different cultural understandings of what it means to be human and what rights humans are entitled to become the focus of contention.

Human Rights Discourse as the Global Language of Social Justice

Discourses about human rights have proliferated in recent decades, stimulated by the original United Nations Declaration on Human Rights in 1948, and followed by numerous subsequent declarations. For example, in 1992, the Committee for the Elimination of Discrimination against Women (CEDAW) declared that violence against women was a form of gender discrimination that violated the human rights of women. This declaration was adopted by the UN General Assembly in 1993 and became part of the rights platform at the Fourth World Conference on Women in Beijing, China, in 1995 (Figure 14.9). Anthropologist Sally Merry observes that this declaration "dramatically demonstrates the creation of new rights—rights which depend on the state's failure to protect women rather than its active violation of rights. . . . The emergence of violence against women as a distinct human rights violation depends on redefining the family so that it is no longer shielded from legal scrutiny" (Merry 2001, 36–37).

Although CEDAW has proved particularly contentious, other human rights documents have been signed without controversy by many national governments. Signing on to a human rights declaration ostensibly binds governments to take official action to implement changes in local practices that might be

FIGURE 14.9 Women marching against violence at the Fourth World Conference on Women in Beijing, 1995.

seen to violate the rights asserted in the declarations. Human rights discourses are common currency in all societies, at all levels. As Jane Cowan, Marie-Bénédicte Dembour, and Richard Wilson write, it is "no use imagining a 'primitive' tribe which has not yet heard of human rights. . . . What it means to be 'indigenous' is itself transformed through interaction with human rights discourses and institutions" (2001, 5).

Because of the wide adoption of human rights discourses throughout the world, some people have come to speak of an emerging "culture of human rights" which has now become "the preeminent global language of social justice" (Merry 2001, 38). These developments mean that anthropologists need to take note of the important influence this discourse is having in the various settings where they do their research.

What counts as "human rights" has changed over time, and not only because of international bodies like the United Nations. An increasing number of nongovernmental organizations (NGOs) have become involved in various countries of the world, many of them deeply committed to projects designed to improve people's lives and protect their rights (Figure 14.10). As Sally Merry says, these developments "have created a new legal order," which has given birth to new possibilities throughout the world

for the elaboration and discussion of what human rights are all about (Merry 2001, 35).

In addition, because the "culture of human rights" is increasingly regarded, in one way or another, as the "culture of globalization," the topic seems well-suited to anthropological analysis in itself. This is because, as we shall see, human rights

FIGURE 14.10 Mejgon Amoni (left), 16, and skills trainer Shakoofah Rahmi, wait for another resident after participating in literacy classes provided by the shelter run by Women Activities and Social Services in Afghanistan (WASSA), an NGO run by Afghan women in Herat.

discourse is not as straightforward as it seems. On the face of things, defending human rights for all people would seem unproblematic. Few people who are aware of the devastation wrought by colonial exploitation, for example, would want to suggest that the victims of that exploitation did not have rights that needed to be protected at all costs. And yet, when we look closely at particular disputes about human rights, the concept no longer seems so simple.

Cowan and her colleagues have noted that there are two major arguments that have developed for talking about the way human rights and culture are related. The first involves arguments that *human rights are opposed to culture*, and that the two cannot be reconciled. The second involves arguments that a key universal human right is precisely one's *right to culture*. We will consider each in turn.

Rights versus Culture

Arguments that pit human rights against culture depend on two assumptions. First, that "cultures" are homogeneous, bounded, and unchanging sets of ideas and practices. Second, each society has only one culture, which its members are obligated to follow. As we saw in chapter 2, this view of culture has been severely criticized by cultural anthropologists. But such a view of culture is very much alive in many human rights disputes. If people have no choice but to follow the rules of the culture into which they were born, international interference with customs said to violate human rights would seem itself to constitute a human rights violation: disrupting a supposedly harmonious way of life and preventing those who are committed to such a way of life from observing their own culturally specific understandings about rights. Thus, cultures should be allowed to enjoy absolute, inviolable protection from interference by outsiders.

This has been the position adopted, for example, by some national governments that have refused to sign the CEDAW declaration that violence against women violates women's human rights. "Many states have opposed this conception of human rights on cultural or religious grounds, and have refused to ratify treaties. . . . By 1997, 160 countries had ratified CEDAW but it has more substantive reservations against it than any other international treaty" (Merry 2001, 37).

Sometimes the reasons for defending culture against rights discourses is explicitly linked to the nineteenth-century struggle between defenders and opponents of the European Enlightenment. Thus, representatives of non-Western nation-states may feel free to dismiss rights talk as an unwelcome colonial imposition of ideas that, far from being universal, reflect ethnocentric European preoccupations. But such dismissal of human rights discourse needs to be closely examined.

In the case of the right of women to protection from violence, for example, Merry points out that although some forms of violence against women may be culturally sanctioned in some societies, violence against women can take many forms even in those societies, and not all of these are accorded the same amount of cultural support. As we saw in chapter 2, female genital cutting could be justified in the past in some circumstances as an appropriate cultural action, but it is now being questioned and even outlawed in the societies where it was traditional. This suggests "culture values" cannot be held responsible for everything that people do in any society, and that members of the same society can disagree about these matters, and sometimes change their minds.

As talk about human rights has become incorporated into local cultural discussions in recent decades, anthropologists are not surprised to discover that the notion undergoes transformation as people try to make sense of what it means in their own local contexts (Cowan et al. 2001, 8). Being forced to choose between rights *or* culture, however, seems increasingly unviable in a globalizing, multicultural world. In their own anthropological work on these matters, Cowan and her colleagues are convinced that the rights-versus-culture debate exaggerates cultural differences. Like many cultural anthropologists today, they find that "it is more illuminating to think of culture as a field of creative interchange and contestation" (2001, 4). Such a view of culture makes the possibility of finding points of connection between the defense of certain human rights and the defense of particular cultural values.

Finally, it is worth asking if "culture" is sometimes used as a scapegoat to mask the unwillingness of a government to extend certain rights to its citizens for reasons that have nothing to do with culture. Cowan, Dembour, and Wilson observe that states like

Indonesia and Singapore, which position themselves as stout defenders of "Asian values," have welcomed Western industrial capitalism. To reject human rights discourse because it contradicts "Asian values" would, at the very least, suggest "an inconsistent attitude toward westernization." This, in turn, feeds suspicions that the defense of "Asian values" may be a political tactic designed "to bolster state sovereignty and resist international denunciations of internal repression and political dissent" (Cowan et al. 2001, 6–7).

Rights to Culture

A second popular argument about the relationship between rights and culture begins from very different premises. This argument does not view universal "human rights" as alien and opposed to "cultures." Instead, it says that all peoples have a universal human right to maintain their own distinct cultures. The *right to culture* has already been explicit in a number of international rights documents.

This argument is interesting because it seems to concede that such things as universal human rights do exist after all. The list of universal rights is simply amended to include the right to one's culture. It draws strength from the idea that cultural diversity is intrinsically valuable, and people should be able to observe their own cultural practices free from outside interference. However, it calls into question the common understanding that people frequently have to be *freed* from the constraints of local cultures in order to enjoy their full human rights. A right to culture therefore shows how the very idea of rights and culture is transformed and contested by globalization.

One key issue in the struggle to protect the right to culture is shared by *any* claim to human rights. It concerns the kinds of legal mechanisms needed to ensure protection. The great promise of international documents like the UN Declaration on Human Rights seems to be that people are now free to bring allegations of human rights abuses to an international forum to seek redress. But in fact this is not the case. First, as human rights activists have discovered, human rights are legally interpreted as *individual* rights, not group rights. Second, people must then demand that the *governments of the nation-states in which they are citizens* recognize and enforce the individual rights defended in international documents. International institutions like the United Nations have been unwilling to challenge the sovereignty of individual nation-states.

The defense of all human rights, including a right to culture, thus depends on the policies of national governments. Some activists see this reliance as a serious contradiction in human rights discourse that undermines its effectiveness. Talal Asad recounts, for example, how Malcolm X argued in the 1960s that African Americans who wanted redress for abuses of their human rights should go directly to the United Nations and press their case *against* the government of the United States: "When you expand the civil-rights struggle to the level of human rights, you can then take the case of the black man in this country before the nations in the UN" (quoted in Asad 2003, 141).

In fact, however, this is not the way the system was intended to work. Asad reminds us that "*The Universal Declaration of Human Rights* begins by asserting 'the inherent dignity' and the 'equal and inalienable rights of all members of *the human family*,' and then turns immediately to the state. In doing so, it implicitly accepts the fact that the universal character of the rights-bearing person is made the responsibility of sovereign states" (Asad 2003, 137). In this legal universe, African Americans (and similarly situated groups in other nation-states) occupied an anomalous position: "they were neither the bearers of national rights nor of human rights" (Asad 2003, 144). The recognition of the human rights of African Americans thus depended on persuading the *United States government* to recognize those rights; the United Nations might use its persuasive power to urge such changes, but it had no coercive power to force the United States—or any other national government—to come into compliance.

Martin Luther King's strategy, Asad points out, took a very different tack, drawing on prophetic religious discourse and the discourse of American liberalism (Figure 14.11). His movement aimed at "mobilizing American public opinion for change," and it was effective in pressing for social change compatible with the division of labor set forth by the UN Declaration (2003, 146). In a globalizing world, however, this division of human rights labor—international bodies propose, but nation-states implement—is being challenged. For example, trans-border citizenries

FIGURE 14.11 Martin Luther King and Malcolm X, shown here in a photograph from 1964, had different strategies for involving the United Nations Universal Declaration of Human Rights in the civil rights struggle in the United States.

lack any forum in which their status and their demands are clearly accorded legitimacy. The right-to-culture movement has succeeded in recent years in highlighting such anomalies, and eroding the traditionally recognized right of nation-states to determine the kinds of rights their citizens will be accorded (Cowan et al. 2001, 8–9). As in the case of the rights-versus-culture argument, however, the right-to-culture argument can be "called upon to legitimate reactionary projects as easily as progressive ones . . . the uses to which culture can be put in relation to rights are evidently multiple" (Cowan et al. 2001, 10).

Anthropological disciplinary commitments have allowed anthropologists to approach debates about rights and culture in ways that contribute something new to the discussion. These anthropological contributions can be seen in two ways. First, anthropologists have addressed the ways in which human rights discourse can itself be seen as culture. Second, their own struggles with the concept of culture allow them to mount a critique of some of the ways

that this concept has been mobilized in the discussion of human rights.

Rights as Culture

The tools that anthropologists have developed to study cultural patterns are well suited to investigate the extent to which a "culture of human rights" has now emerged. Like other cultures, the culture of human rights is based on ideas about human beings, their needs, and their ability to exercise agency as well as the kinds of social connections between human beings that are considered legitimate and illegitimate. The entire question of "legitimacy" in human rights discourse points to the central role played by *law*, both as a way of articulating specific human rights, and as a tool for defending those rights. Cowan, Dembour, and Wilson have drawn on earlier anthropological work in which systems of law were analyzed as cultural systems.

One important source has been the *law and culture* framework developed by anthropologists Clifford Geertz, Laura Nader, and Lawrence Rosen and nonanthropologists like Boaventura de Sousa Santos. In this framework, "law is conceived as a worldview or structuring discourse . . . 'facts' . . . are socially constructed through rules of evidence, legal conventions, and the rhetoric of legal actors" (Cowan et al. 2001, 11). Analysts who talk about a "culture of human rights" as the new culture of a globalizing world point out that human rights have their clear origins in Western secular discourse: It focuses on the rights of individuals; it proposes to relieve human suffering through technical rather than ethical solutions, and it emphasizes rights over duties or needs (Cowan et al. 2001, 11).

To the extent that this is the case, human rights culture is well designed to function as James Ferguson's "anti-politics machine" (2002, 407). As we noted, Ferguson saw this as a bad thing in the context of 1970s programs sponsored by the United States Agency for International Development. In the early twentieth-first century, however, we live in a globalizing world where state structures are under stress and the dynamics of transnational and multicultural living sometimes provoke violent and bloody political confrontations. In such a world, a human-rights discourse—or discourses—capable of "depoliticizing" such confrontations might have an important role.

In the meantime, most anthropologists would probably agree that anthropology can clarify the idea of a "culture of human rights" (Cowan et al. 2001, 13). An understanding of culture as open, heterogeneous, and supple can become an effective analytic tool to help us understand how human rights processes work.

▼ HOW CAN CULTURE HELP IN THINKING ABOUT RIGHTS?

To use the culture concept as a tool for analyzing human rights means looking for "patterns and relationships of meaning and practice between different domains of social life" that are characteristic of the culture of human rights (Cowan et al. 2001, 13). Since human rights are articulated in legal documents and litigated in courts, one of the most important patterns that become visible in the culture of human rights is the way in which rights accommodate the law. Groups and individuals who assert that their human rights have been violated regularly take their cases to courts of law. But in order to get the courts to take them seriously, they need to understand how the law operates. They must be aware of the kinds of claims that the law pays attention to and the kinds of claims that will be dismissed.

Looking at human rights law as culture reveals that only certain kinds of claims are admissible. As we saw, the culture of human rights is currently best suited to redress the grievances of individuals, not groups. It also provides technical, not ethical, remedies, and it emphasizes rights over duties or needs. Plaintiffs are therefore likely to have a difficult time if they want to claim that their group rights have been violated, that they want the violator exposed and punished, or that the state itself has failed to fulfill its responsibilities. A claim to human rights therefore involves learning how to craft cases that will fit the laws. This can be tricky if the categories and identities recognized in human rights law do not correspond to categories and identities that are meaningful to the plaintiffs.

Anthropologists have worked with many social groups struggling with national governments to practice their culture freely. These political struggles regularly include claims about distinct and unchanging values and practices. As we saw in a previous

chapter, arguments for a right to culture are often cases of "strategic essentialism." That is, the unity and unchanging homogeneity of a particular "culture" is deliberately constructed in order to build group solidarity and to engage the state in a focused and disciplined way. But the "essentialism" that often comes to dominate discussions of group rights is not due entirely to the strategies of activists. Once they choose to make their case in a court of law, they become subject to the "essentializing proclivities of the law" (Cowan et al. 2001, 11).

Because human rights law recognizes only certain kinds of violations, groups with grievances must tailor those grievances to fit. According to Merry, for example, groups like the Hawaiian Sovereignty Movement have successfully achieved some of their political goals by making claims based on the requirements of their "traditional culture." But they live in a society that is "willing to recognize claims on the basis of cultural authenticity and tradition but not reparations based on acts of conquest and violation" (Merry 2001, 42–43).

Outside the courtroom, many members of indigenous groups think of their culture in the same way as contemporary anthropologists: There are some common patterns, but culture is basically unbounded, heterogeneous, and open to change. But human rights law ordinarily recognizes cultural rights only if the culture in question is bounded, homogenous, and unchanging. As a result, indigenous peoples are often forced to portray themselves and their cultures in ways that are very different from their own everyday understandings of who they are. While doing so may enable them to win legal judgments in their favor, it also can reshape their ideas about what their culture is. Groups that enter into the human rights process thus are entering into ethically ambiguous territory that is "both enabling and constraining" (Cowan et al. 2001, 11).

Violence against Women in Hawaii

Merry has studied how changing legal regimes in Hawaii over nearly two centuries have reshaped local understandings of Hawaiian culture (see Ethno-Profile 14.3: Hawaii). Part of her work has addressed the ways "local human rights activists are struggling to create a new space which incorporates

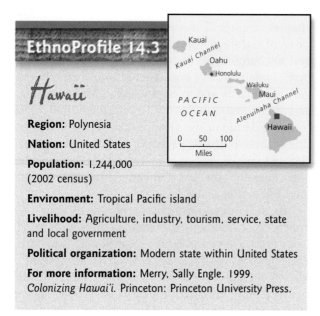

EthnoProfile 14.3

Hawaii

Region: Polynesia

Nation: United States

Population: 1,244,000 (2002 census)

Environment: Tropical Pacific island

Livelihood: Agriculture, industry, tourism, service, state and local government

Political organization: Modern state within United States

For more information: Merry, Sally Engle. 1999. *Colonizing Hawai'i*. Princeton: Princeton University Press.

both cultural differences and transnational conceptions of human rights" (2001, 32). Hawaii is a particularly interesting setting for such a study, since for much of the nineteenth century it was located "at the crossroads of a dizzying array of peoples and at the center of a set of competing cultural logics" (2001, 44). Its setting is thus very much like the globalized, multicultural settings increasingly common today.

Over the course of the century, Hawaiian law went through two important periods of "legal transplantation." The first, between 1820 and 1844, involved the adoption of a Christianized Hawaiian law. The second, between 1845 and 1852, involved the adoption of a secularized Western law. Although these legal transformations involved colonial imposition, they also depended upon active collaboration by Hawaiian elites (2001, 43–44). Indeed, Merry says that these legal changes are best understood as a process of *transculturation* in which subjugated Hawaiians received and adopted forms of self-understanding imposed by the Christian West, even as the Christian West was modified in response to this reception and adoption.

Because the Hawaiians were not passive in this process, and tried to make use of Christianity and Western ideas for purposes of their own, the process, Merry argues, was fraught with frustration and failure. Missionaries and rulers who wanted to turn Hawaii into a "civilized" place were forced to try to impose their will in stages, rather than all at once, and the end result still bore many Hawaiian traces

that, to their dismay, seemed to evade the civilizing process (Figure 14.12).

In this uncertain process of cultural appropriation, change comes in fits and starts, and it requires constant adjustment as circumstances change. It is very similar, Merry argues, to how contemporary Hawaiians are claiming human rights (2001, 46–47). For the past decade she has studied a feminist program in Hilo, Hawaii, that "endeavors to support women victims of violence and retrain male batterers" (48). This program is based on one originally created in Duluth, Minnesota, and it works closely with the courts. In 1985, the courts adopted the language of rights in dealing with violence against women. This means that the law supports the notion of gender equality, and when husbands are found guilty of battering their wives, calls for separation of the couple. By contrast, Hawaiian couples who participate in the program are often conservative Christians who do not believe in divorce.

It might seem that this is a classic example of the conflict between "rights" and "culture," but in fact "local adaptations of the rights model do take place" (2001, 47). This was done by tailoring the program's curriculum to local circumstances by using Hawaiian images and examples. Particularly interesting was the way the part of the program designed to teach anger management to batterers was made locally relevant by combining Christian ideas with ideas from Hawaiian activists that connected male anger to the losses they have suffered as a consequence of conquest. Merry visited a similar kind of program in New Zealand, based on the same Minnesota model, that had been locally modified for Maori men in a way that linked their anger to Maori experiences of racism and loss. "Although all of these programmes share a similar commitment to a rights-based approach that works in conjunction with the criminal justice system, each has developed a local accommodation of the curriculum, a reframing which takes into account local problems and cultural practices" (2001, 49).

Child Prostitution in Thailand

Reaching successful accommodations between human rights discourse and local cultural practices is not always easy. A particularly difficult set of issues must be confronted when attempting to enforce the

FIGURE 14.12 The Hawaiian Sovereignty Movement has emphasized Hawaii's traditional culture and has taken action more broadly. Here members lead a march protesting the Asian Development Bank.

rights of children. Anthropologist Heather Montgomery did field research in a slum settlement in Thailand that was located near a prosperous seaside resort catering to foreign tourists (2001; see Ethno-Profile 14.4: Thailand). Those who lived in this settlement had broken all ties to other kin and other places from which they had migrated, which meant, Montgomery tells us, that the bonds linking parents and children in the settlement had become especially strong. Of overriding importance among these families was the duty of children to work to help support their families. Children did their best to fulfill this duty as soon as they were able, trying many different jobs, including begging. But none of these options earned very much. And so, sooner or later, children began working as prostitutes for wealthy foreign tourists who visited the resort. At the time of her research, 65 children in the community were working as prostitutes.

Children could earn as much as five times the money working as prostitutes as they could get from begging, plus they were able to visit fancy hotels and were well fed. Many of the clients, moreover, developed long-term relationships with the families of the child prostitutes, often lending them large sums of money—in one case, enough to rebuild the family home of one girl. It was friends and neighbors of the children, not their mothers, who recruited children into prostitution. When faced with the reality of the nature of their children's employment, mothers were able to claim that they had not found out until it was too late, and they interpreted the children's acts as evidence of their strong sense of filial duty in fulfilling obligations to help support the family.

"Both adult and child were aware of the child's duties, but there was a degree of unease about how far a child had to go to fulfill them" (Montgomery

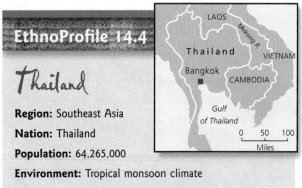

EthnoProfile 14.4

Thailand

Region: Southeast Asia

Nation: Thailand

Population: 64,265,000

Environment: Tropical monsoon climate

Livelihood: Agriculture, industry, tourism, service

Political organization: Constitutional monarchy; modern state

For more information: van Esterik, Penny. 2000. *Materializing Thailand*. Oxford: Berg.

2001, 90). The children claimed not to hate the men whom they worked for, especially those who kept in touch even when not in Thailand and who continued to send money to the children. Because of the financial generosity and long-term involvement of these men with their children, mothers said they felt the men were trustworthy. The actual sexual acts for which the children are paid take place outside the settlement and are never publicly discussed, and the bleeding and tearing the children experience is ignored.

Commercial sex and even child prostitution are not new in Thailand, but in recent years many Thais working in the media and for NGOs have denounced child sex tourism and have tried to force the national government to put a stop to it. Human rights discourse—particularly discourse about the rights of the child—have played a prominent role in this campaign (Figure 14.13). Montgomery points out that, since 1924, international bodies have issued nine separate documents dealing with human rights and the rights of the child.

Children's rights, like human rights in general, are based on Western middle-class ideas about what constitutes an acceptable human childhood, and on Western ideas of when childhood begins and ends. For example, the 1989 Convention on the Rights of the Child defines a child as anyone under 18 years of age, and AntiSlavery International has claimed that child-marriage is a form of slavery and therefore violates human rights. But as Montgomery observes, "it does not take an anthropologist to recognize that a child marrying at 15 in full accordance with traditional norms and local custom in India is very different from a child marrying at 15 in the UK" (2001, 82). In common with other forms of human rights discourse, declarations on the rights of the child normally emphasize the importance of rights over duties, although this is not universal. But this is the issue that needs to be emphasized, Montgomery argues, in order to talk

FIGURE 14.13 Doctors Without Borders runs a rehabilitation center for child prostitutes in Thailand.

meaningfully about the rights of the children working as prostitutes in the Baan Nua slum.

The model of ideal Western childhood contained in the UN Convention on the Rights of the Child includes the idea that, as Montgomery puts it, "every child has a right to a childhood that is free from the responsibilities of work, money and sex" (2001, 83). The problem with this standard is that it fits so poorly with understandings of childhood in which, for example, children are expected (or needed) to work for money to support the family, and it seems unable to imagine situations in which the entire support of a family depends on a child's earnings from prostitution. Yet that is an accurate description for many families and children in Baan Nua.

Local Thai activists have been particularly interested in enforcing Article 34 of the Convention which aims to protect children "from all forms of sexual exploitation and sexual abuse" (2001, 86). But the Convention also recognizes many other children's rights, including the notion that the child's best interests must always be kept uppermost and that they have a right to live with their families. The problem is that "how these rights are prioritized is not culturally neutral. . . . Too often . . . Article 34 is quoted in isolation, decontextualizing sexual abuse and presenting it as the paramount difficulty that poor children face, without linking it to global issues of poverty, cultural background, and discrimination" (2001, 85–87). The child's best interests are certainly compromised through prostitution, but they are also compromised when children are removed from their families and communities, or when they have nothing to eat.

This is particularly poignant in the case of the children of Baan Nua, many of whom claimed that they were not exploited, and all of whom were strongly motivated to engage in prostitution based on the cultural belief that children are obliged to support their parents. Montgomery concludes:

> By ensuring that their families could stay together and have a sustainable income, it would be possible to eradicate child prostitution without enforcing punitive measures against their parents. . . . Thailand's positions in globalized political and economic relations are as important as cultural specificities in perpetuating that sexual exploitation. . . . Article 34 would be redundant if the other rights enshrined in the convention . . . could be reliably enforced." (2001, 97–98)

These and other examples suggest two important conclusions. First, it is possible to find ways of accommodating the universal discourse of human rights to the particularities of local conditions. Second, no single model of the relationship between rights and culture will fit all cases. Moreover, as the culture of human rights becomes better established, it increasingly becomes enmeshed in political and legal institutions that go beyond the local level. As activists become more experienced operating in globalized circumstances, they are likely to become more sophisticated about making use of these different settings as they plan their human rights strategies (Cowan et al. 2001, 21). Struggles over human rights are hardly likely to go away; indeed, along with struggles over global citizenship, they can be seen as the prime struggles of our time (Mignolo 2002). Anthropologists are well positioned to help make sense of these complex developments as they unfold.

▼ CULTURAL IMPERIALISM OR CULTURAL HYBRIDIZATION?

The *impact* of the global spread of images, ideas, people, things, and ideologies in local social settings has clearly been profound, as illustrated by the preceding examples. But how should anthropologists characterize the processes by which these changes have come about?

Cultural Imperialism

One explanation, formulated during the Cold War, was **cultural imperialism**. Cultural imperialism is based on two notions. First, it says some cultures dominate other cultures. In recent history, the culture(s) of Europe or the United States or "the West" have come to dominate all other cultures of the world, owing to the spread of colonialism and capitalism. Second, cultural domination by one culture leads inevitably to the destruction of subordinated cultures and their replacement by the culture of those

cultural imperialism The idea that some cultures dominate other cultures, and that cultural domination by one culture leads inevitably to the destruction of subordinated cultures and their replacement by the culture of those in power.

in power. Thus, Western cultural imperialism is seen as responsible for destroying, for example, local music, technology, dress, and food traditions and replacing them with rock and roll, radios, flashlights, cell phones, T-shirts, blue jeans, McDonalds hamburgers, and Coca-Cola (Figure 14.14). The inevitable outcome of Western cultural imperialism is seen as "the cultural homogenization of the world," with the unwelcome consequence of "dooming the world to uniformity" (Inda and Rosaldo 2002, 13, 14).

The idea of cultural imperialism developed primarily outside anthropology, but anthropologists could not ignore it, because it purported to describe what was happening to the people they studied. Anthropologists, too, were aware that Western music, fashion, food, and technology had spread among those they worked with. But cultural imperialism did not seem to explain this spread, for at least three rea-sons (Inda and Rosaldo 2002, 22–24). First, cultural imperialism denies *agency* to non-Western peoples who make use of Western cultural forms. It assumes that they are passive and without the resources to resist anything of Western origin that is marketed to them. Second, cultural imperialism assumes that non-Western cultural forms never move "from the rest to the West." But this is clearly false. Non-Western music and food and material culture have large and eager followings in Western Europe and the United States. Third, cultural imperialism ignores that cultural forms and practices sometimes move from one part of the non-Western world to other parts of the non-Western world, bypassing the West entirely. Movies made in India have been popular for decades in northern Nigeria (Larkin 2002), Mexican soap operas have large followings in the Philippines, and karaoke is popular all over the world.

Cultural Hybridity

Dissatisfied with the discourse of cultural imperialism, anthropologists began to search for alternative ways of understanding global cultural flows. From the days of Boas and his students, anthropologists had not only recognized the significance of cultural borrowing. They had also emphasized that borrowing cultural forms or practices from elsewhere always involves *borrowing-with-modification*. That is, people never adopt blindly, but always adapt what they borrow for local purposes. Put another way, people rarely accepted ideas or practices or objects from elsewhere without *domesticating* or *indigenizing* them—finding a way of reconciling them with local practices in order to serve local purposes.

In the 1980s, for example, weavers in Otavalo, Ecuador, were making a lot of money selling textiles to tourists. They could then organize small production firms and purchase television sets to entertain their employees while they worked at their looms. In addition, some men had so much business that they encouraged their wives to take up weaving, even though women were not traditionally weavers. In order to spend more time weaving, women started to use indoor cookstoves, which relieved them from the time-consuming labor of traditional meal preparation over an open fire (Colloredo-Mansfeld 1999). From the perspective of anthropologist Rudi Colloredo-

FIGURE 14.14 People line up outside a McDonald's in Cairo.

How Sushi Went Global

Talk of "global flows" can seem abstract and divorced from everyday life, but one of the strengths of anthropology is its ability to capture the articulation of the local with the global. As sushi swept the United States, anthropologist Theodore Bestor looked at the trade in tuna.

A 40-minute drive from Bath, Maine, down a winding two-lane highway, the last mile on a dirt road, a ramshackle wooden fish pier stands beside an empty parking lot. At 6:00 P.M. nothing much is happening. Three bluefin tuna sit in a huge tub of ice on the loading dock.

Between 6:45 and 7:00, the parking lot fills up with cars and trucks with license plates from New Jersey, New York, Massachusetts, New Hampshire, and Maine. Twenty tuna buyers clamber out, half of them Japanese. The three bluefin, ranging from 270 to 610 pounds, are winched out of the tub, and buyers crowd around them, extracting tiny core samples to examine their color, fingering the flesh to assess the fat content, sizing up the curve of the body.

After about 20 minutes of eyeing the goods, many of the buyers return to their trucks to call Japan by cellphone and get the morning prices from Tokyo's Tsukiji market—the fishing industry's answer to Wall Street where the daily tuna auctions have just concluded. The buyers look over the tuna one last time and give written bids to the dock manager, who passes the top bid for each fish to the crew that landed it.

The auction bids are secret. Each bid is examined anxiously by a cluster of young men, some with a father or uncle looking on to give advice, others with a young woman and a couple of toddlers trying to see Daddy's fish. Fragments of concerned conversation float above the parking lot: "That's all?" "Couldn't we do better if we shipped it ourselves?" "Yeah, but my pickup needs a new transmission now!" After a few minutes, deals are closed and the fish are quickly loaded onto the backs of trucks in crates of crushed ice, known in the trade as "tuna coffins." As rapidly as they arrived, the flotilla of buyers sails out of the parking lot—three bound for New York's John F. Kennedy Airport, where their tuna will be airfreighted to Tokyo for sale the day after next.

Bluefin tuna may seem at first an unlikely case study in globalization. But as the world rearranges itself—around silicon chips, Starbucks coffee, or sashimi-grade tuna—new channels for global flows of capital and commodities link far-flung individuals and communities in unexpected new relationships. The tuna trade is a prime example of the globalization of a regional industry, with intense international competition and thorny environmental regulations; centuries-old practices combined with high technology; realignments of labor and capital in response to international regulation; shifting markets; and the diffusion of culinary culture as tastes for sushi, and bluefin tuna, spread worldwide. . . .

Culture Splash

Just because sushi is available, in some form or another, in exclusive Fifth Avenue restaurants, in baseball stadiums in Los Angeles, at airport snack carts in Amsterdam, at an apartment in Madrid (delivered by motorcycle), or in Buenos Aires, Tel Aviv, or Moscow, doesn't mean that sushi has lost its status as Japanese cultural property. Globalization doesn't necessarily homogenize cultural differences nor erase the salience of cultural labels. Quite the contrary, it grows the franchise. In the global economy of consumption, the brand equity of sushi as Japanese cultural property adds to the cachet of both the country and the cuisine. A Texan Chinese-American restauranteur told me, for example, that he had converted his chain of restaurants from Chinese to Japanese cuisine because the prestige factor of the latter meant he could charge a premium; his clients couldn't distinguish between Chinese and Japanese employees (and often failed to notice that some of the chefs behind his sushi bars were Latinos).

(continued on next page)

How Sushi Went Global
(continued)

The brand equity is sustained by complicated flows of labor and ethnic biases. Outside of Japan, having Japanese hands (or a reasonable facsimile) is sufficient warrant for sushi competence. Guidebooks for the current generation of Japanese global *wandervogel* sometimes advise young Japanese looking for a job in a distant city to work as a sushi chef; U.S. consular offices in Japan grant more than 1,000 visas a year to sushi chefs, tuna buyers, and other workers in the global sushi business. A trade school in Tokyo, operating under the name Sushi Daigaku (Sushi University), offers short courses in sushi preparation so "students" can impress prospective employers with an imposing certificate. Even without papers, however, sushi remains firmly linked in the minds of Japanese and foreigners alike with Japanese cultural identity. Throughout the world, sushi restaurants operated by Koreans, Chinese, or Vietnamese maintain Japanese identities. In sushi bars from Boston to Valencia, a customer's simple greeting in Japanese can throw chefs into a panic (or drive them to the far end of the counter).

On the docks, too, Japanese cultural control of sushi remains unquestioned. Japanese buyers and "tuna techs" sent from Tsukiji to work seasonally on the docks of New England laboriously instruct foreign fishers on the proper techniques for catching, handling, and packing tuna for export. A bluefin tuna must approximate the appropriate *kata*, or "ideal form," of color, texture, fat content, body shape, and so forth, all prescribed by Japanese specifications. Processing requires proper attention as well. Special paper is sent from Japan for wrapping the fish before burying them in crushed ice. Despite high shipping costs and the fact that 50 percent of the gross weight of a tuna is unusable, tuna is sent to Japan whole, not sliced into salable portions. Spoilage is one reason for this, but form is another. Everyone in the trade agrees that Japanese workers are much more skilled in cutting and trimming tuna than Americans, and no one would want to risk sending botched cuts to Japan.

Not to impugn the quality of the fish sold in the United States, but on the New England docks, the first determination of tuna buyers is whether they are looking at a "domestic" fish or an "export" fish. On that judgment hangs several dollars a pound for the fisher, and the supply of sashimi-grade tuna for fishmongers, sushi bars, and seafood restaurants up and down the Eastern seaboard. Some of the best tuna from New England may make it to New York or Los Angeles, but by way of Tokyo—validated as top quality (and top price) by the decision to ship it to Japan by air for sale at Tsukiji, where it may be purchased by one of the handful of Tsukiji sushi exporters who supply premier expatriate sushi chefs in the world's leading cities.

Source: Bestor 2000.

Mansfeld, these uses of Western technology could not be understood as the consequences of Western cultural imperialism, because they clearly had nothing to do with trying to imitate a Western lifestyle. It made more sense to interpret these changes as Otavalan *domestication* or *indigenization* of televisions and cookstoves, since these items from elsewhere were adopted precisely in order to promote indigenous Otavalan weaving. Put yet another way, borrowing-with-modification always involves *customizing* that which is borrowed to meet the purposes of the borrowers, which may be quite remote from the purposes of those among whom the form or practice originated (Inda and Rosaldo 2002, 16). This form of cultural change is very different from having something from elsewhere forced upon you, against your will (Figure 14.15).

At the same time, the consequences of borrowing-with-modification can never be fully controlled. Thus, Otavalan weavers may start watching television because local reruns of old American television series relieve the tedium of weaving. However, once television watching becomes a habitual practice, it also exposes them to advertising and news broadcasts, which

FIGURE 14.15 Musical performance has become an important part of the Otavalo Indian economy, as musicians from Otavalo travel throughout the world performing and selling woven goods. They have domesticated CD production as well and have been quite successful in selling CDs of their music to tourists in Otavalo and to listeners abroad.

in relationships with donors even as they are made to serve new goals by recipients (Thomas 1991). People in multicultural settings must deal on a daily basis with tempting cultural alternatives emanating from more powerful groups. It is therefore not surprising that they regularly struggle to control processes of cultural borrowing and to contain domesticated cultural practices within certain contexts, or in the hands of certain people only.

Many social scientists have borrowed a metaphor from biology to describe this complex process of globalized cultural exchange and speak of *cultural hybridization* or *hybridity*. Anthropologist Ulf Hannerz, by contrast, objects to the "biologistic" overtones of hybridity metaphors and prefers to borrow the concept of *creolization* from linguistics (see chapter 5). "Creolist concepts suggest that cultural mixture is not necessarily deviant, second-rate, unworthy of attention, matter out of place. . . . What is at the core of the concept of creole culture, I think, is a combination of diversity, interconnectedness, and innovation, in the context of global center-periphery relations" (1996, 66–67). Both cultural hybridization and creolization were meant to highlight forms of cultural borrowing that produced something new that could not be collapsed or subsumed, either within the culture of the donor or within the culture of the recipient. In addition, both terms stressed the positive side of cultural mixing: Rather than indicating a regrettable loss of original purity, hybridity and creolization draw attention to positive processes of cultural creativity.

The move from talk of dependency and cultural imperialism to talk about globalization and cultural hybridization is widely seen as a move from *modernist* discourse to *postmodernist* discourse. Modernist discourse embodies Enlightenment assumptions about rationality, science, progress, capitalism, and democracy. Postmodernist discourse calls all these Enlightenment assumptions into question. The "writing against culture" movement in anthropology discussed in chapter 2 was a postmodernist critique of modernist social science assumptions that portrayed "authentic" non-Western societies and cultures as bounded, orderly, and unchanging. Postmodernists argued, on the contrary, that all social and cultural borders were porous, and thus open to people, ideas, and practices from elsewhere.

may stimulate other local changes that nobody can predict. The domestication or indigenization of cultural forms from elsewhere *both* makes it possible to do old things in new ways *and* leaves open the possibility of doing new things as well. Put another way, cultural borrowing is double-edged; borrowed cultural practices are both amenable to domestication and yet able to escape it. No wonder that cultural borrowing is often viewed with ambivalence.

The challenges are particularly acute in globalizing conditions, colonial or postcolonial, where borrowed ideas, objects, or practices remain entangled

This postmodern position is not confined to academic contexts, but has had important implications regarding everyday cultural choices. For example, if hybridity is a normal part of all human social experience, then the idea that "authentic" traditions never change can legitimately be challenged. For members of a social group who wish to revise or discard cultural practices that they find outmoded or oppressive, hybridity talk is liberating. Choosing to revise or discard, borrow or invent *on terms of one's own choosing* also means that one possesses agency, the capacity to exercise at least some control over one's life. And exercising agency calls into question charges that one is succumbing to cultural imperialism or losing one's cultural "authenticity."

The Limits of Cultural Hybridity

However, as anthropologist Nicholas Thomas puts it, "hybridity is almost a good idea, but not quite" (1996, 9). Close examination of talk about cultural hybridization or creolization reveals at least three problems. First, it is not clear that either concept actually frees anthropologists from the modernist commitment to the existence of bounded, homogeneous, unchanging "cultures." That is, the idea of **cultural hybridity** is based on the notion of cultural mixing. But what is it that is mixed? Two or more non-hybridized, original, "pure" cultures! But such "pure" homogeneous, bounded, unchanging cultures are not supposed to exist.

Thus we are caught in a paradox. For this reason Jonathan Friedman, among others, is highly critical of discussions of cultural hybridity; in his view, cultures have *always* been hybrid and it is the existence of *boundaries*, not cultural borrowing, that anthropologists need to explain. Besides, hybrid cultural mixtures often get transformed into new, unitary cultural identities. This process can be seen, he argues, in the way in which the "mixed race" category in the United States has been transformed into a "new, unitary group of mixtures for those who feel 'disenfranchised' by the current single-race categories" (1997, 83). Friedman also points out that hybrid identities are not liberating when they are thrust upon people rather than

---

being adopted freely. He draws attention to cases in Latin America where the "mestizo" identity has been used "as a middle-/upper-class tool" against indigenous groups by "'creolizing' them from above": that is, criticizing their claims to a common Indian identity in order to undermine their sense of solidarity as members of a single group. "We are all part-Indian, say members of the elite who have much to lose in the face of minority claims" (1997, 81–82).

These examples highlight a second difficulty with hybridity talk: Those who celebrate cultural hybridization often ignore the fact that its effects are experienced differently by those with power and those without power. As Friedman says, "the question of class becomes crucial" (1997, 81). The complexity of this issue is seen in many popular discussions of "multiculturalism" that celebrate cultural hybridization and that, in the context of globalizing capitalism, turn hybridity into a marketable commodity. The commodification of hybridity is problematic because it smooths over differences in the experience of cultural hybridization, offering multiculturalism as an array of tempting consumables for outsiders. "Multiculturalism is aimed at nourishing and perpetuating the kind of differences which do not [threaten]," writes Nira Yuval-Davis (1997, 197). International Folk Festivals, Festivals of Nations, and the like—events that emphasize costume, cuisine, music, and dance—spring to mind. But the troubling fact is that cultural hybridity is experienced as both nonthreatening and very threatening, depending on the terms on which it is available.

Because of power differences among groups challenged by cultural hybridization, any globalized "multicultural" setting reveals active processes of cultural hybridization *together with* the defense of discrete cultural identities that seem to *resist* hybridization (Werbner 1997, 3). Cultural hybridization is unobjectionable when actors perceive it to be under their own control, but cultural hybridization is resisted when it is "perceived by actors themselves to be potentially threatening to their sense of moral integrity" (Werbner 1997, 12). The threat is greatest for those with the least power who feel unable to control forms of cultural hybridization that threaten to undermine the fragile survival structures on which they depend in an unwelcoming multicultural setting.

---

cultural hybridity Cultural mixing.

And this leads to a third problem with the concept of cultural hybridization. Fashionable hybridity talk hides the differences between elite and nonelite experiences of multiculturalism. Anthropologist John Hutnyk, for example, deplores the way "world music" is marketed to middle-class consumers, because such sales strategies divert attention "from the urgency of anti-racist politics" (1997, 122). When cultural hybridization becomes fashionable, it easily turns the experiences of hybridized elites into a hegemonic standard suggesting that class exploitation and racial oppression are easily overcome or no longer exist. But to dismiss or ignore continuing nonelite struggles with cultural hybridization can spark dangerous confrontations that can quickly spiral out of control.

Anthropologist Peter van der Veer argues that such a dynamic ignited the furor in Britain that followed the publication of Salman Rushdie's novel *The Satanic Verses*. Rushdie is an elite, highly educated South Asian migrant to Britain who experienced cultural hybridity as a form of emancipation from oppressive religious and cultural restrictions. His novel contained passages describing Islam and the Prophet Muhammad that, from this elite point of view, embodied "transgression" that was liberating. But migrants from South Asia in Britain are not all members of the elite. Most South Asian Muslim immigrants in Britain are workers, and they saw *The Satanic Verses* not as a work of artistic liberation but as a deliberate attempt to mock their beliefs and practices. "These immigrants, who are already socially and culturally marginalized, are thus doubly marginalized in the name of an attack on 'purity' and Islamic 'fundamentalism'" (1997, 101–2).

Even more important, however, may be the way popular interpretations of their objections in the press and among Western intellectuals ignored these immigrants' own, very different but very real, *nonelite* experiences of cultural hybridization. Van der Veer stresses that British Muslims who objected to the novel were

> not necessarily fundamentalists at all; their religious ideas are just as hybrid and syncretic as those of the author. They, too, are migrants, but the sources of their identity are authenticated not by profane literary texts but by what are to them sacred religious traditions. It is ironic, therefore, to find that migrants

who are at the vanguard of political resistance to the assimilationist tendencies of the nation-state, who have their own cultural project for living hybrid cultural lives in a non-Islamic nation expressed, for example, in demand for state-funded Muslim schools or the extension of the blasphemy laws—are condemned, while the postmodernist hybrid novelist is celebrated by liberals and the state, extolled for his struggle against that very oppositional resistance, against the supposed "backwardness" of the "fundamentalist" British Muslim community. (1997, 102)

Put simply, elites experience cultural hybridization in ways that are often very different from the way nonelites experience cultural hybridization. We all ignore this fact at our peril.

▼ CAN WE BE AT HOME IN A GLOBAL WORLD?

The current globalization is an era of uncertainty and insecurity. Possibilities for emancipatory new ways of living are undercut by sharpening economic and political differences and the looming threat of violence. Is it possible, in the midst of all this confusion and conflict, to devise ways of coping with our circumstances that would provide guidance in the confusion, moderation to the conflict? No one expects such efforts to be easy. But anthropologists and other concerned scholars are currently struggling to come up with concepts and practices that might be helpful.

Cosmopolitanism

Our era is not the first to have faced such challenges. Walter Mignolo argues that multiculturalism was born in the sixteenth century when Iberian conquest in the New World first raised troubling issues among Western thinkers about the kinds of relationships that were possible and desirable between the conquerors and the indigenous peoples whom they had conquered. During the ensuing centuries, the challenges posed by a multicultural world did not disappear. In the context of eighteenth-century Enlightenment promises of human emancipation based on *The Rights of Man and the Citizen*, philosopher Immanuel Kant concluded that the achievements of the Enlightenment offered individuals new opportunities for developing ways of being at home in the world wherever they were.

To identify this orientation, he revived a concept that was first coined by the Stoic philosophers of ancient Rome: **cosmopolitanism** (Mignolo 2002). Kant's cosmopolitanism was firmly embedded within the values and practices of Enlightenment civilization, which meant, in the terms of our preceding discussion, that it was embedded in Western elite forms of cultural hybridization. That is, Kantian cosmopolitanism "by and large meant being versed in Western ways and the vision of 'one world' culture was only a sometimes unconscious, sometimes unconscionable, euphemism for 'First World' culture" (Abbas 2002, 210). To the extent that discussions of cosmopolitanism continue to focus on Western elites only, they would seem to offer little to anthropologists and others who are interested in finding a place for nonelite and non-Western experiences of cultural hybridization. Perhaps it is for this reason that Jonathan Friedman has written that those who celebrate their own cultural hybridity are simply "all those who can afford a cosmopolitan identity" (1997, 81).

But is it possible to rework our understandings of cultural hybridity to stretch the notion of cosmopolitanism beyond its traditional association with privileged Western elites? Many anthropologists have become comfortable talking about "alternative" or "minority modernities" that depart from the Western European norm. In a similar fashion, any new anthropological understanding of cosmopolitanism would have to be plural, not singular, and it would have to include nonelite experiences of cultural hybridization—"minoritarian" or "discrepant" cosmopolitanisms—that reflect the experiences of those who have been the victims of modernity (Abu-Lughod 1997, 134; Pollock et al. 2002, 6,8). The goal would be to develop new concepts and new skills enabling one to handle difficult cultural situations with grace "by juggling with multiple perspectives" (Abbas 1999, 223); new ways of thinking "beyond the local" or "ways of living at home abroad or abroad at home—ways of inhabiting multiple places at once, of being different beings simultaneously, of seeing the larger picture stereoscopically with the smaller" (Pollock et al. 2002, 1, 10–11) (Figure 14.16).

---

cosmopolitanism Being at ease in more than one cultural setting.

Does anthropological talk about a world of "cosmopolitanisms" offer any advantage over earlier anthropological talk about a world of "cultures?" It might, if anthropologists can find a way to think about cultural hybridization (and resistance to hybridization) that moves beyond the current stalemate. Pnina Werbner suggests that this might be possible if we can think about cultural hybridization as a *process*, rather than as a series of momentary, shocking "transgressive" challenges that periodically disrupt the ongoing tense standoff among defenders of different cultural positions. Rather than assuming that all hybridity (or all resistance to hybridity) is the same—either all "good" or all "bad"—Werbner's approach would make it possible to distinguish *different processes* of cultural hybridization and cultural resistance.

To illustrate, Werbner insists on distinguishing between cultural processes that lead to ethnicity and cultural processes that lead to racism (see chapter 13). A processual theory of cultural hybridization "must differentiate . . . between a politics that proceeds from the legitimacy of difference [ethnicity] and a politics that rests on coercive unity [racism]" and it "must explain how and why cultural hybrids are still able to disturb and 'shock' . . . in a postmodern world that celebrates difference" (Werbner 1997, 21). Previous anthropological work can suggest how such a processual analysis might proceed. For example, Victor Turner's analysis of rites of passage (see chapter 7) demonstrated that "liminality is itself structured processually . . . categories are exaggerated and caricatured *in order to be worked upon and reconfigured*. . . . By analogy we need to think . . . of the way discourses interact to create bridges or precipitate polarizing processes" (Werbner 1997, 21; emphasis added).

Friction

Pnina Werbner emphasized that open-ended negotiation across cultural and political divides could lead to cosmopolitan cultural practices but also to polarization. As Marie-Bénédicte Dembour observes, we should not be surprised when negotiations over volatile issues like female genital cutting in France turn out to be full of conflict and contradiction. Dembour concludes that "we need to accept the discomfort of

IN THEIR OWN WORDS

Destructive Logging and Deforestation in Indonesia

WALHI, Wahana Lingkungan Hidup Indonesia, *Friends of the Earth Indonesia, is an Indonesian umbrella organization for nongovernment and community-based organizations. It is represented in 25 provinces and has over 438 member organizations (as of June 2004). According to their website (http://www.eng.walhi.or.id/) it "stands for social transformation, people's sovereignty, and sustainability of life and livelihoods. WALHI works to defend Indonesia's natural world and local communities from injustice carried out in the name of economic development." In late March 2007, they issued the following release.*

The deforestation problem in Indonesia is spreading. Illegal and destructive logging is a major cause. In addition, conversion of forest areas for the development of oil palm and the pulp and paper industry has been substantial. Since the beginning of this decade, as much as 2.8 million ha of Indonesia's forests have been lost each year to illegal and destructive logging. This has led to US $4 billion or 40 trillion rupiah in losses to the State per year.

If we put two and two together, forest conversion and the pulp and paper industry are also causal factors in the rising rate of deforestation. We know that some 15.9 million ha of natural tropical forest has been cleared for forest conversion. The conversion of forests for oil palm development is a contributing factor to the increase in deforestation in Indonesia. From being prime land, 15.9 million ha of natural tropical forests have been cleared. On the contrary, there has been no meaningful increase in planted land area. Plantation area has only increased to 5.5 million ha in 2004, from 3.17 million ha in 2000. More than 10 million ha of forest have been abandoned after the harvest of the wood crop growing there.

Similarly, the pulp and paper industry have also brought problems. This industry needs at least 27 million cubic meters of timber each year (Department of Forestry, 2006). Since plantation forests can only supply 30 percent of the total demand for pulp, this industry continues logging activities in natural forests, harvesting some 21.8 million cubic meters in order to fulfill its annual requirement. The timber obtained from natural forests is owned by company affiliates or taken from the concessions of its partners. This is not mentioning plywood or other trades, for which only 25% of timber requirements are supplied by plantation forests.

The negative impacts of forestry crime in Indonesia are described above. Economic losses from forestry crimes such as illegal logging, conversion of natural forests, and so on are calculated to reach 200 trillion rupiah. This loss does not include ecological disasters caused by illegal logging activities, such as floods and landslides, which now occur frequently in all corners of the Archipelago.

WALHI deduces that the ecological degradation caused by forestry crimes is caused, at least, by two major factors: (1) differences in the outlooks and value systems upheld by the community, the forestry department, and the government (both local and central); and (2) erosion of the judicial process due to corruption, collusion and nepotism. At this point, enforcement of the law is inconsistent.

Inconsistency in the judicial process is caused by the viruses of corruption, collusion and nepotism, which intricately bind the immediate interests of law enforcers (and even bureaucratic officers) throughout the judicial process, starting with the police, attorneys and the judiciary. The result is that anti-illegal logging operations in Papua Province (March 2005) failed to catch top-rung criminals or their protectors in the police force and military. From this operation, 186 suspects were arrested. But, until January 2007, only 13 suspects had been successfully prosecuted and not one syndicate leader has been caught. From the 18 major cases that have reached court, all accused have been released.

Furthermore, differences in the outlooks and value systems upheld by the community, the forestry department

(*continued on next page*)

Destructive Logging and Deforestation in Indonesia *(continued)*

and the government (both local and central) have been a major factor in the increasing rate of forestry crime. From the community's perspective, forests function to protect people from high winds, drought and erosion. The forestry department also recognises the ecological functions of the forests; however, illegal clearing and logging are allowed to continue in accordance with the economic calculations maintained by the forestry department. Similarly, the government's stance also draws from economic aspects of forests rather than its ecological functions. For them, the forests are a resource with abundant natural resource wealth that must be extracted for the national income. Unfortunately, the development policies that are implemented do not favour forest sustainability.

As we track the rate of forestry crime (illegal logging, conversion of forests without replanting, the unlimited thirst of the pulp and paper industry for wood), it is clear that the government needs to halt several forms of forestry crime that have the potential to trigger a series of ecological disasters, such as floods, landslides, and drought. In addition, community involvement (especially the traditional community) in securing forest conservation is highly necessary. Moreover, the seriousness of all law enforcers (starting with the police force, attorneys, and judges) is crucial to stopping deforestation associated with forestry crimes. Without the serious involvement of all parties in carrying out surveillance, it is quite possible that Indonesia's forests will be completely cleared in the not-too-distant future.

Finally, deforestation as a consequence of illegal logging is caused, at least, by three major factors, that is, the lack of acknowledgement by the government of people's rights to manage their forest resources, widespread corruption in various sectors of forest resource management, and the large gap between supply and demand. If these three factors are not immediately overcome—make no mistake—Indonesia's forests will be rapidly cleared within a short timeframe.

Source: WALHI, 2007

FIGURE 14.16
Cosmopolitanism is no longer only for Western elites. Otavalo Indian tourist José María Cotachaci, visiting the San Francisco Bay Area, November 2000. Otavalos have created their own form of modernity.

moving in between, as a pendulum." She is insisting that these difficulties are to be expected—a phenomenon that anthropologist Anna Lowenhaupt Tsing has called *friction*. Tsing defines **friction** as "the awkward, unequal, unstable aspects of interconnection across difference" (2005, 4).

Tsing has worked in Indonesia for many years, investigating exactly the kinds of intereactive processes that concern Werbner and Dembour. She seeks to understand how capitalist interests brought about the destruction of the Indonesian rain forests in the 1980s and 1990s as well as how environmental movements emerged to defend the forests and the people who live in them. Discussions of cultural imperialism assume that processes of global change will be smooth and unstoppable, that "globalization can be predicted in advance" (2005, 3). After the Cold War, for example, a number of politicians and social theorists predicted "an inevitable, peaceful transition" to global integration of the capitalist market (2005, 11). On the contrary, her research showed that the encounters between Japanese lumber traders and Indonesia government officials that turned Indonesia into the world's largest tropical lumber producer by 1973 were "messy and surprising" (2005, 3). She points out that "Indonesian tropical rain forests were not harvested as industrial timber until the 1970s" because "large-scale loggers prefer forests in which one valuable species predominates; tropical rain forests are just too biologically diverse" (2005, 14). However, in the 1970s the Japanese trading companies that began negotiations with the Indonesian New Order regime of President Suharto did not want access to valuable hardwoods; instead, they wanted "large quantities of cheaply produced logs," which they intended to turn into plywood.

The Japanese traders did not get what they wanted right away, however. Rather, as Tsing points out, this could not happen until three specific transformations had occurred. First, the forest had to be "simplified." Japanese lumber traders and Indonesian officials ignored species diversity, recognizing as valuable only those species that could be turned into plywood and regarding everything else—"the rest of the trees, fungi, and fauna . . . the fruit orchards, rattans, and other human-tended plants of forest dwellers"—as waste (2005, 16). Second, to make such forest simplification politically palatable, forests were reconfigured as a

"sustainable resource" that could be replaced later by industrial tree plantations. However, once the Japanese traders were successful, Indonesian businessmen built their own plywood industry, based on the Japanese model. This led to the development of links between destruction of the forest and nation-building, as the state came to depend on income from selling forest concessions to favored political cronies. Once this alliance was forged, legal and illegal forms of forest exploitation could no longer be distinguished from one another, and it became impossible for forest dwellers to defend their own, preexisting property rights. "Either official or unofficial alone could be challenged, but together they overwhelmed local residents. . . . Together they transform the countryside into a free-for-all frontier" (2005, 17). But the production of such a frontier was not inevitable. It was the outcome of contingent encounters that people reworked in order to produce desired outcomes, along with additional, unintended consequences.

In response to rain forest destruction, a strong Indonesian environmental movement came into existence (Figure 14.17). Once again, however, this cannot be understood as a simple, predictable extension of Western environmentalist practices into Indonesia. On the contrary, "the movement was an amalgam of odd parts: engineers, nature lovers, reformers, technocrats" (2005, 17). In fact, activists who were dissatisfied with other features of President Suharto's New Order regime decided to focus on environmental issues, because these seemed to be issues less likely to trigger government censorship and repression. In any case, as Tsing says, "the movement was organized around difference" (2005, 17). It was not centralized, but "imagined itself as coordinating already existing but scattered and disorganized rural complaints. Activists' jobs, as they imagined it, involved translating subaltern demands into the languages of the powerful" and "translating back to let people know their rights" (2005, 18). It was messy, but this did not deter activists. "Within the links of awkwardly transcended difference, the environmental movement has tried to offer an alternative to forest destruction and the erosion of indigenous rights."

---

friction The awkward, unequal, unstable aspects of interconnection across difference.

FIGURE 14.17 Heavy logging activity has led to destruction of the rain forest in Kalimantan and to the emergence of a strong Indonesian environmental movement.

Like the alliance between businessmen and New Order government officials, the environmental movement emerged out of relationships forged by unlikely parties who struggled to find ways of working together to achieve overlapping but nonidentical goals. Thus, friction in the struggle to bridge differences makes new things possible: "Rubbing two sticks together produces heat and light; one stick alone is just a stick. As a metaphorical image, friction reminds us that heterogeneous and unequal encounters can lead to new arrangements of culture and power" (2005, 3–5). And these arrangements, while potentially dangerous, may also be seen as a source of hope: "Just as the encounter of Japanese trading companies and Indonesian politicians produced simplified dipterocarp forests, these activist-inspired encounters may yet produce different kinds of forests" (2005, 18).

Border Thinking

Tsing's understanding of "friction" as an unavoidable and productive feature of the process of cultural hybridization has much in common with what Walter Mignolo calls *border thinking*. For Mignolo, in a globalized world, concepts like "democracy" and "justice" can no longer be defined within a single Western logic—or, for that matter, from the perspective of the

political left or the political right. Border thinking involves detaching these concepts from their hegemonic "Western" meanings and practices. It means using them as "connectors," tools for imagining and negotiating new, cosmopolitan forms of democracy or justice informed by the ethical and political judgments of nonelites (Mignolo 2002, 179, 181).

Finally, in reimagining what cosmopolitanism might mean, it is important not only to go beyond Kantian limitations, but also to go beyond standard anthropological orientations to other ways of life. An understanding of cosmopolitanism that is limited to being open to other cultures or to being inclusive—the traditional orientation of cultural relativism—is insufficient to cope with the challenges presented by a globalizing world. For one thing, "Otherness has lost its innocence as a result of the colonial experience" (Abbas 2002, 226). For another, "silenced and marginalized voices are bringing themselves into the conversation of cosmopolitan projects, rather than waiting to be included" (Mignolo 2002, 174).

The hope is that border thinking can produce a *critical cosmopolitanism* capable of negotiating new understandings of human rights and global citizenship in ways that can dismantle barriers of gender and race that are the historical legacies of colonialism (Mignolo 2002, 161, 180). In many cases this may require seriously revising Western modernist ideas and practices, if that is the only honorable way of overcoming power differentials and threats to moral integrity experienced by nonelites. But because cosmopolitanism involves border thinking, ideals and practices with Enlightenment credentials may also turn out to be valuable counterweights to extremism and violence.

This is apparent in the stance taken by those citizens of Bombay (Mumbai), India, who resist attempts by radical Hindus to banish Muslims from the city and to turn India into a Hindu state. Relationships between Hindus and Muslims in India took a severe turn for the worse after Hindu vandals destroyed a mosque in the city of Ayodhya in 1992. Arjun Appadurai, who has followed these developments closely, notes that the brutal Hindutva movement pushing to turn India into a Hindu state "violates the ideals of secularism and interreligious harmony enshrined in the constitution" (Appadurai 2002, 73–74). Appadurai writes of Indians from many walks of life, rich and poor, Muslim and Hindu, who have shown "extraordinary displays of courage and critical imagination in Mumbai," who have "held up powerful images of a cosmopolitan, secular, multicultural Bombay." Their "radical moderation" in resisting violent religious polarization is, he argues, neither naïve nor nostalgic: "These utopian visions and critical practices are resolutely modernist in their visions of equity, justice, and cultural cosmopolitanism" (Appadurai 2002, 79). Secularism, as we saw in chapter 7, is a notion with impeccable Enlightenment credentials that arrived in India with British colonialism. And yet it is this "situated secularism"—indigenized, customized, domesticated, *Indian* secularism, opposed to *Indian* interreligious violence—that Appadurai and many other Indian citizens see as a key element of a form of local Indian cosmopolitanism that have been effective in preventing religious strife in the past and may be able to do so again.

Many of the cases in this chapter demonstrate the human ability to cope creatively with changed life circumstances. They remind us that human beings are not passive in the face of the new, that they actively and resiliently respond to life's challenges. Nevertheless, the example of the Panará reminds us that successful outcomes are never ensured. Modes of livelihood that may benefit some human groups can overwhelm and destroy others. Western capitalism and modern technology have exploded into a vortex of global forces that resist control. A critical cosmopolitanism involving concerted practical action to lessen violence and exploitation may be all that can prevent these forces from destroying us all.

CHAPTER SUMMARY

1. Anthropologists have made use of a variety of theoretical perspectives to explain the relationship between the West and the rest of the world. During the Cold War, anthropologists debated the relative merits of modernization theory and dependency theory. Later, they were influenced by world system theory, which divided the territories controlled by capitalism into core, periphery and semiperiphery, and argued that the relationships between these regions had been established during the years when capitalism first was introduced outside Europe.

2. The end of the Cold War and the fall of communism led to a crisis in Marxian thought, and many of the tenets of modernization theory were revived in neoliberal economic theory, which promised to bring prosperity to any nation-state to find its niche in the globalizing capitalist market.

3. Globalization is understood and evaluated differently by different observers, but most anthropologists agree that the effects of globalization are uneven. In a globalizing world, wealth, images, people, things, and ideologies are deterritorialized. Some groups in some parts of the world benefit from global flows, contacts, and exchanges, whereas others are bypassed entirely.

4. Anthropologists and others disagree about whether these global processes are or are not systemic, or whether they are only the latest in a series of expansions and contractions that can be traced back to the rise of the first commercial

civilizations several thousand years ago. But none of these overall schemas can by itself account for the historically specific local details of the effects of global forces in local settings, which is what most anthropologists aim to document and analyze.

5. The flows unleashed by globalization have undermined the ability of nation-states to police their boundaries effectively, suggesting that conventional ideas about nation-states require revision. Contemporary migrants across national borders have developed a variety of trans-border identities. Some become involved in long-distance nationalism that leads to the emergence of trans-border states claiming emigrants as trans-border citizens of their ancestral homelands even if they are legal citizens of another state. Some trans-border citizenries call for the establishment of fully fledged transnational nation-states.

6. The contrasts between formal and substantive citizenship suggest that conventional notions of citizenship are breaking down in the context of globalization. Diaspora communities of elite Chinese families have developed a strategy of flexible citizenship that allows them both to circumvent and benefit from different nation-state regimes by investing, working, and settling their families in different sites. For these elite Chinese, the concept of nationalism has lost its meaning, and they seem to subscribe instead to a postnational ethos in which their only true loyalty is to the family business.

7. Discussions of human rights have intensified as global flows juxtapose and at least implicitly challenge different understandings of what it means to be human, or what kinds of rights people may be entitled to under radically changed conditions of everyday life. But different participants in this discourse have different ideas about the relationship that human rights and culture have with one another. As talk about human rights becomes incorporated into local cultural discussions, the notion is transformed to make sense in local contexts. Sometimes, "culture" may be used as a scapegoat for a government unwilling to extend certain rights to its citizens.

8. Some arguments about human rights include the right to one's culture. One of the key issues involved concerns the kinds of legal mechanisms needed to ensure such protection. But most international human rights documents only protect individual human rights, not group rights. And even those who seek to protect their individual rights are supposed to appeal to the governments of their own nation-states to enforce rights defended in international documents. Many activists and others view this factor as a serious contradiction in human rights discourse that undermines its effectiveness.

9. Some anthropologists argue that a "culture of human rights" has emerged in recent years that is based on certain ideas about human beings, their needs, and their abilities that originated in the West. Some consider this culture of human rights to be the culture of a globalizing world that emphasizes individual rights over duties or needs, and that proposes only technical rather than ethical solutions to human suffering. Anthropologists disagree about the value of such a culture of human rights in contemporary circumstances.

10. Groups and individuals who assert that their human rights have been violated regularly take their cases to courts of law. But because human rights law only recognizes certain kinds of rights violations, groups with grievances must tailor those grievances to fit the violations that human rights law recognizes. Groups that enter into the human rights process are entering into ethically ambiguous territory that is both enabling and constraining.

11. Debates about women's rights in Hawaii and children's rights in Thailand show both that it is possible to accommodate the universal discourse of human rights to local conditions and that no single model of the relationship between rights and culture will fit all cases. Struggles over human rights, along with struggles over global citizenship, can be seen as the prime struggles of our time.

12. The discourse of cultural imperialism, which developed primarily outside anthropology, tried to explain the spread of Western cultural forms outside the West. But anthropologists

reject cultural imperialism as an explanation because it denies agency to non-Western peoples, because it assumes that cultural forms never move "from the rest to the West," and because it ignores flows of cultural forms that bypass the West entirely.

13. Anthropologists have developed alternatives to the discourse of cultural imperialism. They speak about borrowing-with-modification, domestication, indigenization, or customization of practices or objects imported from elsewhere. Many anthropologists describe these processes as examples of cultural hybridization or hybridity.

14. Talk of cultural hybridization has been criticized because the very attempt to talk about cultural mixtures assumes that "pure" cultures existed prior to mixing. Others object to discussions of cultural hybridization that fail to recognize that its effects are experienced differently by those with power and those without power. Cultural hybridization is unobjectionable when actors perceive it to be under their own control, but is resisted when they see it threatening their moral integrity.

15. Some anthropologists are working to devise ways of coping with the uncertainties and insecurities of globalization. Some would like to revive the notion of cosmopolitanism originally associated with Western elite forms of cultural hybridization and rework it in order to be able to speak about alternative or discrepant cosmopolitanisms that reflect the experiences of those who have been the victims of modernity. The ideal end result would be a critical cosmopolitanism capable of negotiating new understandings of human rights and global citizenship in ways that can dismantle barriers of gender and race that are the historical legacies of colonialism.

KEY TERMS

globalization	legal citizenship	human rights
diaspora	substantive citizenship	cultural imperialism
long-distance nationalism	transnational nation-states	cultural hybridity
trans-border state	flexible citizenship	cosmopolitanism
trans-border citizenry	postnational ethos	friction

SUGGESTED READINGS

Hobart, Mark, ed. 1993. *An anthropological critique of development*. London: Routledge. *Anthropologists from Britain, Holland, and Germany challenge the notion that Western approaches to development have been successful. They use ethnographic case studies to demonstrate how Western experts who disregard indigenous knowledge contribute to the growth of ignorance.*

Inda, Jonathan Xavier and Renato Rosaldo, eds. 2002. *The anthropology of globalization: A reader*. Malden, MA: Blackwell. *A recent, comprehensive collection of articles by anthropologists who* address the process of globalization from varied points of view and different ethnographic situations.

Wallerstein, Immanuel. 1974. *The modern world-system*. New York: Academic Press. *A difficult but tremendously influential work that started the world-system approach to understanding and explaining patterns of social change in recent world history.*

Wolf, Eric. 1999. *Peasant wars of the twentieth century*. Reprint. Norman: University of Oklahoma Press. Originally published in 1969. *An important, readable study of the commonalities of the twentieth century's major wars of revolution.*

Chapter 15

Anthropology in Everyday Life

More than ever, anthropologists are applying their understandings of human nature, human culture, and the human past in settings outside the university. This chapter introduces some of the unique contributions anthropologists can make as they use their analytical and practical skills to tackle real-world problems in a variety of different contexts.

▼ ANTHROPOLOGY BEYOND THE UNIVERSITY

Do anthropologists do anything other than teach at universities? The answer is yes. Anthropology is attractive to many students in the form of college coursework, and they know that many anthropologists spend their careers as fieldworkers and university professors. But many of the ethnographic examples we have offered in the course of this book were produced by anthropologists who have taken their ethnographer's skills into a variety of different settings outside the university.

Today, anthropologists are working in everything from law, health, and medicine to marketing and advertising, agriculture, environmental impact, migration and resettlement, education, and aging. A particularly important field for archaeologists in the private sector is cultural resource management (CRM), which is mandated by federal law in the United States.

A number of anthropologists are actively involved in *international development*, sometimes working with the U.S. Agency for International Development (AID), the principal instrument of U.S. foreign development assistance. Their work includes projects dealing with such issues as appropriate technology, fuelwood shortages, agricultural credit, new-lands development, feasibility studies for dams and other projects, bilingual education, livestock improvement and range management, and the like (for more examples, see Partridge 1984; van Willigen 1991).

Other anthropologists are in *medical anthropology*, an important and growing field. Some are involved in gerontology, designing programs for the elderly and doing research on aging in different cultures. Others work in public or community health, medical education, nursing, or hospital planning. Another important area of work is in medical care delivery to distinct cultural groups. This is related to applied anthropological work in international health, which includes demographics, epidemiology, planning and development of health programs, family planning, environmental health, and the like. Many applied anthropologists are also working on AIDS-related projects. A few anthropologists are psychotherapists, employing the insights of anthropologist Gregory Bateson and others on family systems and family therapy. Others are cross-cultural social workers.

Some anthropologists have gone into *public policy and planning* as interpreters, mediators, civil servants, or urban planners. Others have begun to work with indigenous people's organizations or with human rights organizations such as Survival International and Cultural Survival, itself founded by anthropologists

FIGURE 15.1 The business world has discovered that the skills of anthropologists can be very valuable. Anthropologists Alexandra Mack, left, and Jill Lawrence, right, are workplace anthropologists at Pitney Bowes Inc. Lawrence and Mack observe company customers to help improve product design.

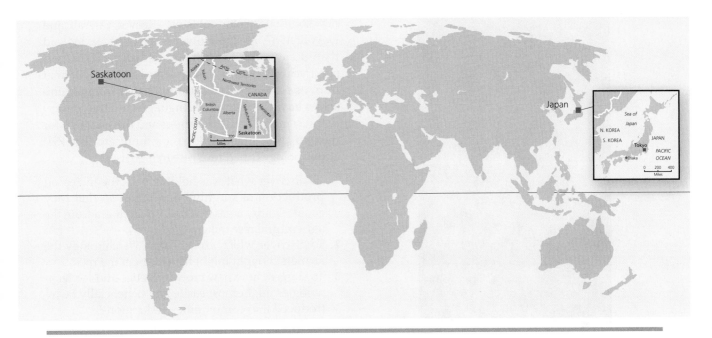

FIGURE 15.2 Locations of societies whose EthnoProfiles appear in chapter 15.

David Maybury-Lewis and Pia Maybury-Lewis. Recently the business world has discovered how valuable the observational and analytic skills of anthropologists can be in marketing, market research, executive training for international assignments, and management (Figure 15.1).

As we noted in chapter 1, at least half of all new anthropology Ph.D.s in the twenty-first century will be making careers in fields such as these. Although what they do is still called "applied anthropology" in some settings, anthropologists who pursue such careers have increasingly called what they do "the anthropology of practice." We shall examine several cases of the anthropology of practice, highlighting not only the way the anthropological perspective and ethnographic skills transfer into such fields as development work, business, and human rights advocacy.

Sorghum and Millet in Honduras and the Sudan

Applied anthropologists carry out much work in international development, often in agricultural programs. The U.S. Agency for International Development (AID) is the principal instrument of U.S. foreign development assistance. One new direction taken by AID in the mid-1970s was to create multidisciplinary research programs to improve food crops in developing countries. An early research program dealt with sorghum and millet, important grains in some of the poorest countries in the world (Figure 15.3). This was the International Sorghum/Millet Research Project (INTSORMIL). Selected American universities investigated one of six areas: plant breeding, agronomy, plant pathology, plant physiology, food chemistry, and socioeconomic studies.

Anthropologists from the University of Kentucky, selected for the socioeconomic study, used ethnographic field research techniques to gain first-hand knowledge of the socioeconomic constraints on the production, distribution, and consumption of sorghum and millet among limited-resource agricultural producers in the western Sudan and in Honduras. They intended to make their findings available to INTSORMIL as well as to scientists and government officials in the host countries. They believed sharing such knowledge could lead to more effective research and development. This task also required ethnographic research and anthropological skill.

The principal investigators from the University of Kentucky were Edward Reeves, Billie DeWalt,

FIGURE 15.3 INTSORMIL has been involved in the improvement of the cultivation of sorghum and millet. This is sorghum.

and Katherine DeWalt. They took a holistic and comparative approach, called *Farming Systems Research* (FSR). This approach attempts to determine the techniques used by farmers with limited resources to cope with the social, economic, and ecological conditions under which they live. FSR is holistic because it examines how the different crops and livestock are integrated and managed as a system. It also relates farm productivity to household consumption and off-farm sources of family income (Reeves, DeWalt, and DeWalt 1987, 74). This is very different from the traditional methods of agricultural research, which grow and test one crop at a time in an experiment station. The scientists at INTSORMIL are generally acknowledged among the best sorghum and millet researchers in the world, but their expertise comes from traditional agricultural research methods. They have spent little time working on the problems of limited-resource farmers in Third World countries.

The anthropologists saw their job as facilitating "a constant dialog between the farmer, who can tell what works best given the circumstances, and agricultural scientists, who produce potentially useful

new solutions to old problems" (Reeves, DeWalt, and DeWalt 1987, 74–75). However, this was easier said than done in the sorghum/millet project. The perspectives of farmers and scientists were very different from one another. The anthropologists found themselves having to learn the languages and the conceptual systems of both the farmers and the scientists for the two groups to be able to communicate. The FSR anthropologists had four research goals:

1. To discover what was holding back the increased production of sorghum and millet so that they could identify areas that needed attention from the agricultural researchers
2. To discover which aspects of new technology the farmers thought might benefit them the most
3. To suggest how new crop "varieties and/or technologies might most easily and beneficially be introduced into communities and regions"
4. "To suggest the long-term implications that changing production, distribution, and consumption patterns might have on these communities" (1987, 74)

The anthropologists began research in June 1981 in western Sudan and in southern Honduras. They were in the field for 14 months of participant-observation and in-depth interviewing, as well as survey interviewing of limited-resource farmers, merchants, and middlemen. They discovered that the most significant constraints the farmers faced were uncertain rainfall, low soil fertility, and inadequate labor and financial resources (Reeves, DeWalt, and DeWalt 1987, 80). Equally important were the social and cultural systems within which the farmers were embedded. Farmers based their farming decisions on their understanding of who they were and what farming meant in their own cultures.

As a result of the FSR group's research, it became increasingly clear that "real progress in addressing the needs of small farmers in the Third World called for promising innovations to be tested at village sites and on farmers' fields under conditions that closely approximated those which the farmers experience" (Reeves, DeWalt, and DeWalt 1987, 77). Convincing the scientists and bureaucrats of this required the anthropologists to become advocates for the limited-resource farmers. Bill DeWalt and Edward Reeves ended up negotiating INTSORMIL's contracts with the Honduran and Sudanese governments and succeeded

What Can You Learn from an Anthropology Major?

The Career Development Center at SUNY Plattsburgh developed a document that highlights what students typically learn from a major in anthropology.

1. Social agility	In an unfamiliar social or career-related setting, you learn to quickly size up the rules of the game. You can become accepted more quickly than you could without this anthropological skill.
2. Observation	You must often learn about a culture from within it, so you learn how to interview and observe as a participant.
3. Analysis and planning	You learn how to find patterns in the behavior of a cultural group. This awareness of patterns allows you to generalize about the group's behavior and predict what they might do in a given situation.
4. Social sensitivity	Although other people's ways of doing things may be different from your own, you learn the importance of events and conditions that have contributed to this difference. You also recognize that other cultures view your ways as strange. You learn the value of behaving toward others with appropriate preparation, care, and understanding.
5. Accuracy in interpreting behavior	You become familiar with the range of behavior in different cultures. You learn how to look at cultural causes of behavior before assigning causes yourself.
6. Ability to appropriately challenge conclusions	You learn that analyses of human behavior are open to challenge. You learn how to use new knowledge to test past conclusions.
7. Insightful interpretation of information	You learn how to use data collected by others, reorganizing or interpreting the data to reach original conclusions.
8. Simplification of information	Because anthropology is conducted among publics as well as about them, you learn how to simplify technical information for communication to nontechnical people.
9. Contextualization	Although attention to details is a trait of anthropology, you learn that any given detail might not be as important as its context and can even be misleading when the context is ignored.
10. Problem solving	Because you often function within a cultural group or act on culturally sensitive issues, you learn to approach problems with care. Before acting, you identify the problem, set your goals, decide on the actions you will take, and calculate possible effects on other people.

(continued on next page)

IN THEIR OWN WORDS

What Can You Learn from an Anthropology Major? (continued)

| 11. Persuasive writing | Anthropologists strive to represent the behavior of one group to another group and continually need to engage in interpretation. You learn the value of bringing someone else to share—or at least understand—your view through written argument. |
| 12. Assumption of a social perspective | You learn how to perceive the acts of individuals and local groups as both shaping and being shaped by larger sociocultural systems. The perception enables you to "act locally and think globally." |

Source: Omohundro 2000.

in representing the farmers. They had to learn enough about the bureaucracies and the agricultural scientists so they could put the farmers' interests in terms the others could understand.

As a result of the applied anthropologists' work, INTSORMIL scientists learned to understand how small farmers in two countries made agricultural decisions. They also learned that not all limited-resource farmers are alike. The poorest third of the Sudanese farmers, for example, have to decide during the cropping season whether to weed their own gardens or someone else's for a wage. If they choose the former, they realize a long-term gain but they and their families go hungry. The latter choice enables them to buy food in the short run but lowers their own harvests later. The decisions farmers make, and the needs they have, are context-sensitive.

Together with INTSORMIL, the Honduran and Sudanese governments have increased funding for projects aimed at limited-resource farmers. Staff have been assigned to work with INTSORMIL, new programs have begun, and the research results of the anthropologists are guiding the breeding of sorghum.

Reeves, DeWalt, and DeWalt warn that it is too early to demonstrate gains in sorghum or millet production and use in either country. "Nevertheless, INTSORMIL scientists are clearly coming to accept the farming systems research goals and the value of anthropological fieldwork. The FSR Group has argued that on-site research is both desirable and nec-

essary for the problems of farmers to be correctly identified and that eventually on-farm testing of new plant varieties and technologies will be essential to ensure that farmers are going to accept them" (1987, 79).

The INTSORMIL staff was so impressed by the anthropologists' work that it has begun funding long-term research directed at relieving the constraints that limited-resource farmers face. Rather than trying to develop and then introduce hybrids, INTSORMIL research is now aimed at modifying existing varieties of sorghum. The goal is better-yielding local varieties that can be grown together with other crops.

In summary, Reeves, DeWalt, and DeWalt point out that without the anthropological research, fewer development funds would have been allocated to research in Sudan and Honduras. More important, the nature of the development aid would have been different.

Lead Poisoning among Mexican American Children

In the summer of 1981, a Mexican American child was treated for lead poisoning in a Los Angeles emergency room. When the child's stomach was pumped, a bright orange powder was found. It was lead tetroxide, more than 90 percent elemental lead. Lead in that form is not usually found in lead poisoning cases in the United States. When questioned by health professionals, the mother revealed that her child had been given a folk remedy in powdered form—*azarcón*. Azarcón was used to treat an illness called *empacho*, part of the Mexican American set of culturally recognized diseases. Empacho is believed to be a combination of indigestion and constipation.

This case prompted a public health alert that was sent out nationally to clinics and physicians. The alert turned up another case of lead poisoning from azarcón in Greeley, Colorado. A nurse had read about the Los Angeles case and asked if the mother was treating the child for empacho. She was. Additional questioning in Los Angeles and Greeley turned up what appeared to be widespread knowledge of azarcón in both Mexican American communities. The U.S. Public Health Service decided that an anthropological study of azarcón would be useful.

The Public Health Service in Dallas called Dr. Robert Trotter, who had done research on Mexican American folk medicine. Trotter had never heard of azarcón, and could not find it in south Texas. But a short time later, he received information from the Los Angeles County Health Department, which had discovered that azarcón was not the only name for the preparation. When he asked for *greta*, he was sold a heavy yellow powder that turned out to be lead oxide with an elemental lead content of approximately 90 percent. The shop owners said it was used to treat empacho. Here was confirmation that two related lead-based remedies were being used to treat empacho. Trotter discovered that a wholesale distributor in Texas was selling greta to over 120 herb shops.

Trotter was asked to work in a health education project designed to reduce the use of these lead-based remedies. Because of the complex nature of the problem, he had six different clients with somewhat different needs and responsibilities. The first client was the Public Health Service office in Dallas, which sponsored the first study he did.

The second client was the task force that had been formed to create and implement a health education project in Colorado and California. Task force members wanted to reduce the use of azarcón—but they did not want to attack or denigrate the folk medical system that promoted its use. They knew that attacking folk beliefs would produce strong resistance to the entire health campaign and make people ignore the message, no matter how important it was. The task force hoped Trotter's ethnographic data could help design a health awareness campaign that would encourage a switch to nonpoisonous remedies.

The goal of the task force became product substitution—to convince people to switch from greta or azarcón to another, harmless remedy for empacho that was already part of the folk medical system. This strategy was based on an old advertising technique: It is easier to get people to switch from one product to another when both products perform the same function; it is difficult or impossible to get people to stop using a product they think they need, regardless of its known danger, unless an acceptable alternative is provided.

The Food and Drug Administration (FDA), Trotter's third client, decided it needed basic ethnographic information on the use of greta. The staff wanted to know who used it, what it was used for, how it was used, and where it could be purchased. The FDA had never considered that lead oxide could be a food additive or a drug, and it needed verifiable data that the compound was being used in this way. As a result of Trotter's research, the FDA concluded that greta was a food additive. It issued a Class I recall to ban the sale of greta as a remedy.

Client number four was the Texas regional office of the Department of Health and Human Services. It needed assistance in creating and carrying out a survey along the United States–Mexico border to discover what people knew about greta and azarcón and how many people used them. Trotter's survey indicated that as many as 10 percent of the Mexican American households along the border had at one time used greta or azarcón. The survey also turned up several other potentially toxic compounds that were in use.

Trotter's fifth client was the Hidalgo County Health Care Corporation, a local migrant clinic. It needed a survey that would compare the level of greta and azarcón usage in the local population in general with the level of usage among the people who came to the clinic. Trotter found that the two groups did not differ significantly in their knowledge about and use of the two preparations; however, the clinic population was more likely to treat folk illnesses with folk medicines than was the population at large.

The sixth client was the Migrant Health Service. It needed to know whether it was necessary to design a nationwide lead project. Based on the research that Trotter and others did, it became clear that such a major project was not necessary; rather, health projects were targeted and health professionals notified in the areas of high greta and azarcón use only.

Because Trotter had several clients, his work led to a variety of outcomes. The health education project resulted in considerable media exposure on the dangers of greta and azarcón. Public service announcements were broadcast on Spanish-language radio stations, special television programs aired in Los Angeles County, and information packets were sent to migrant clinics. Trotter commissioned Mexican American students at the Pan American University to design a culturally appropriate poster warning of the dangers of greta and azarcón. The poster, using the culturally powerful symbol of *La Muerte* (a skeleton) to warn of the dangers, has been placed in over 5,000 clinics and other public access sites (Trotter 1987, 152).

The various health education measures may be judged successful by the fact that, two years after the project began, both greta and azarcón were hard to find in the United States. In addition, the various surveys Trotter carried out led to better screening procedures for lead poisoning. Information on traditional medications is now routinely gathered when lead poisoning is suspected, and several other potentially toxic compounds have been discovered. Health professionals were able to learn about the current use of traditional medications in their areas and about the specific health education needs of their clients.

"Perhaps the most important overall result of the project was an increased awareness of the utility of anthropology in solving culturally related health care problems in at least one segment of the medical care delivery system. . . . Our discovery of the use of greta and azarcón and the subsequent discoveries that similar remedies are causing lead poisoning in Hmong, Saudi Arabian, and Chinese communities have finally demonstrated a clear link between anthropological research and the dominant biophysical side of modern medicine. Anthropological knowledge, research methods, and theoretical orientations are finally being used to solve epidemiological problems overlooked by the established disciplines" (Trotter 1987, 154).

Trotter brought to the project the skills of the anthropologist; his principal focus was on culture. He took a holistic, comparative approach, and he was willing to innovate, to look for explanations in areas that investigators from other disciplines had not thought to look. This is typical for medical anthropologists, who struggle with the friction generated when biomedical approaches encounter cultural practices that begin with different assumptions about the way the world works.

Caring for Infibulated Women Giving Birth in Norway

Female genital cutting has generated enormous publicity—and enormous conflict. As we observed in chapters 2 and 14, coping with this practice across difference is complex. People in Western societies often have very little grasp of how the operation fits into the cultural practices of those who perform it. Even women from societies with the tradition find themselves on opposing sides: Some seek asylum to avoid it, while others are prosecuted because they seek to have it performed on their daughters. Many governments have declared it a human rights violation.

Norway has struggled with these issues ever since 1991, when it became the home of a large number of refugees from civil war in Somalia (Figure 15.4). Norwegian health care is free, and Norway has one of the lowest infant mortality rates in the world. Nevertheless, despite the efforts of dedicated health care workers to be culturally sensitive, outcomes for Somali women are not always optimal. Medical anthropologist R. Elise B. Johansen tried to find out why (Johansen 2006, 516).

In contemporary Norway, Johansen reports, giving birth is considered a positive, "natural" process that women are expected to be able to handle with minimal medical intervention. As a result, "midwives are preferred to obstetricians, medication and incisions are avoided whenever possible, partners are allowed to be present in the delivery room to support the birthing mother, newborns are immediately placed on the mother's belly, and mothers are encouraged to breast feed immediately" (2006, 521). At the same time, Norwegian health workers believe that giving birth "naturally" is hard for Norwegian women, because their "natural female essence" is "buried under layers of modernity" (521). Norwegian women nevertheless support "natural" birth practices out of concern for the health of the child, and they expect to

FIGURE 15.4 These Somali women are returned refugees. Political turmoil in their country has led many Somalis to flee to other countries, including Norway.

manage the pain of unmedicated labor assisted by nothing more than their own physical stamina. Midwives also usually leave women alone until the explusion phase of labor begins, a practice connected to their idea of what constitutes a "natural" delivery: "Women are expected to take charge of their own deliveries. Health workers explained restricted interference as a gesture of respect for women's strength and ability to deliver by themselves," an attitude that is possibly also reinforced by the Norwegian values of independence and privacy (538).

What happens when midwives with these expectations encounter Somali women about to give birth? The high value they place on "natural" birthing has led some to regard African immigrant women as "more natural than most Norwegians" and "in closer contact with their female essence" (2006, 521). As a result, health care workers sometimes assume that African women are "naturally" equipped with the skills they need to deliver and care for their babies. "What could then be more natural than African women giving birth?" (522). Only "modern" Norwegian women require such things as medication or child care instruction.

At the same time, Somali women present a paradox: They are African, but they have been infibulated, and infibulation is thought by most health workers to be "the ultimate expression of female oppression and male dominance" (522). As a result, "infibulated women in the delivery ward present a confusing mixture because 'the natural wild' has culturally constructed genitals." Johansen saw this paradox as "central to understanding the challenges facing health workers in looking after infibultated women during delivery" (522).

Midwives thought of infibulation as a social stigma: It marked infibulated women "as incomplete, disfigured, and oppressed." It marked them as " 'victims of culture' rather than as self-assertive individuals,"—despite the fact that actual Somali women were often "both strong-willed and demanding" (523). At the same time, many health care workers refused to talk about infibulation with Somali women. The workers assumed that "Somali women are ashamed of their infibulation and share the health workers' negative understanding of the practice." Yet, again, those who *did* ask Somali women about infibulation found them open and eager to discuss the matter (523). Johansen concludes that health care workers are at once troubled by infibulation and concerned that this discomfort not interfere with their "professionalism." Their solution is simply *not to speak about infibulation*, a decision that "seems to increase discomfort in both health workers and birthing women. It also reduces the parties' chances of exchanging vital information" (523).

Although the midwives Johansen interviewed knew about infibulation, they had not been formally trained to provide care for infibulated women giving birth, because guidelines were not yet available. This lack of training, coupled with the midwives' unwillingness to talk with Somali women about infibulation, had two unfortunate, interconnected effects. First, it made many Somali women unsure about whether they would be properly cared for during their deliveries, adding to their own anxieties about childbirth. Second, it allowed health care workers to draw their own silent, *mistaken* conclusions about the "cultural meaning" of infibulation for Somali women. Midwives assumed without asking, for example, that Somali women would not want to be defibulated—that is, to have the infibulation scar cut to widen the vaginal opening. They further assumed without asking that Somali women would also oppose the use of *episiotomies*—cuts used to widen the vaginal passage for the child during delivery. Such cuts, which are sewn up afterwards, are a standard practice in Western obstetrics.

Paradoxically, health care workers understood that defibulation would make delivery easier and safer but were generally unwilling to perform defibulations during delivery. In fact, when Somali women *asked* to be defibulated, many midwives ignored their request, interpreting it as a by-product of "Westernization" and not an expression of "authentic" Somali practice. Yet, Johansen observed, "there is no evidence that reinfibulation has ever been a customary practice among the Somali" (528).

Since many health care workers assumed that Somali values dictated that Somali women remain infibulated through life, they were concerned that defibulation would violate those values. Why had one midwife chosen to perform three episiotomies to avoid defibulating one Somali woman, even though episiotomies involve cutting through muscular and blood-filled tissue? Had the midwife asked the woman if she preferred defibulation? The surprised midwife replied, "No! Of course she wants to remain the way she is " (526). Because the midwife assumed that Somali women want to remain infibulated and

because the midwife wanted to respect this wish, to ask this Somali woman if she wanted defibulation made no sense to the midwife.

Sometimes, however, Somali women were defibulated while giving birth, and this presented the midwives with a different dilemma: Should they reinfibulate the women after their babies were delivered? As we saw earlier, midwives believed that cutting open the infibulation scar would be beneficial for the woman giving birth, and yet respecting Somali women required them to preserve the infibulation scar. Furthermore, after 1995, reinfibulation became illegal in Norway. The midwives who defibulated a woman during delivery would break the law if they closed the defibulation incision afterwards. Struggling with such conflicting directives, some midwives decided "to avoid defibulation altogether to avoid the dilemma of whether to restitch or not. In a few cases, health workers actually performed reinfibulations, either because of ignorance of the law or because they saw reinfibulation as a medical necessity, or as an act of respect for what they perceived to be the best way to secure women's cultural and bodily integrity" (527).

Had the midwives actually spoken with Somali women, Johansen reports, much discomfort and misunderstanding could have been avoided on both sides. Midwives would have learned that almost all Somali women *wanted* to be defibulated and *did not want* to be reinfibulated—and that nearly two-thirds of their husbands did not want their wives to be reinfibulated either (527). Midwives would also have learned that Somali infibulation practices were different from infibulation practices elsewhere in Africa. As we saw from Boddy's ethnography in chapter 2, lifelong infibulation is a traditional practice in Sudan. Johansen discovered that "infibulation as practiced in Sudan has been taken to represent infibulation in general, so that the practice of reinfibulation in Sudan is taken as evidence that reinfibulation must also be common in all other societies practicing infibulation. However, as we have seen, this is not always the case" (529).

Johansen's research shows how even attempts to be culturally sensitive can generate a wall of misconceptions. These can circumvent actual conversation with those individuals whose culture is the focus of attention. There is no question that the midwives were trying to do right by the women they attended.

Ironically, however, from a Norwegian perspective, to respect the dignity and autonomy of Somali women meant that one left Somali women alone and *did not ask them questions*. In situations like this, medical anthropologists can play an important role as cultural brokers who see situations from a fresh perspective, ease the friction, and help to build a bridge across difference.

Doing Business in Japan

Anthropologist Richard Reeves-Ellington (1993) designed and implemented a cross-cultural training program for a North American company doing business in Japan (see EthnoProfile 15.1: Japan). He found that many of the traditional methods of anthropology—cultural understanding, ethnographic data, and participant-observation—helped managers conduct business in Japan. Reeves-Ellington began the training program by having employees first gather general cultural information artifacts ("How are things classified or what are the artifacts of an agreed classification system?"), social knowledge ("What are proper principles for behavior? What are the values that drive the categories and artifacts?"), and cultural logic. Social knowledge or values are based on an underlying, taken-for-granted cultural logic. Coming to understand Japanese cultural logic is of great importance to foreigners wishing to live and work in Japan.

The managers at the company decided to learn how to carry out introductions, meetings, leave-taking, dinner, and drinking in Japan (Figure 15.5). Each practice was analyzed according to the framework of artifacts, social knowledge, and cultural logic and was taught by a combination of methods that included the general observations that the managers collected while visiting Japanese museums, theaters, shrines, baseball games, and business meetings. The managers analyzed these observations and discussed stories that show how badly things can go when cultural knowledge is not sufficient. For example, one thing Reeves-Ellington's students needed to learn about introductions involved the presentation of the business card (*meishi*). The proper presentation and use of the meishi is the central element in the practice of making introductions at business meetings. Reeves-Ellington explained that, to a Japanese businessperson, the meishi is an extension of the self. Damage to the card is damage to the individual. Therefore, mistreatment of a meishi will ruin a relationship. Reeves-Ellington notes that his colleagues did not fully appreciate the consequences of these beliefs until he told them a story:

> A major U.S. company was having problems with one of its distributors, and the parties seemed unable to resolve their differences. The president of the U.S. company decided to visit Japan, meet with his counterpart in the wholesaler organization, and attempt to resolve their differences. The two had not met previously and, upon meeting, each followed proper *meishi* ritual. The American, however, did not put the Japanese counterpart's *meishi* on the table; instead he held on to it. As the conversation became heated, the American rolled up the *meishi* in his hand. Horror was recorded on the face of the Japanese businessman. The American then tore the *meishi* into bits. This was more than the Japanese could stand; he excused himself from the meeting. Shortly afterward the two companies stopped doing business with each other. (209)

Table 15.1 shows the information regarding introductions and the use of the meishi that Reeves-Ellington's students derived from their work based on their analytic framework of artifacts, social knowledge, and cultural logic.

On three critical measures—effective working relationships with Japanese executives, shortened project times, and improved financial returns—the anthropologically based training program that Reeves-Ellington

EthnoProfile 15.1

Japan

Region: Northeastern Asia

Nation: Japan

Population: 118,000,000

Environment: Temperate climate

Livelihood: Full range of occupations to be found in a core industrial nation-state

Political organization: Highly urbanized nation-state

For more information: Kondo, Dorinne, 1990. *Crafting selves*. Chicago: University of Chicago Press.

FIGURE 15.5 Japanese and North American businesspeople negotiating pickup. Japanese and U.S. business people negotiate better when they understand something of each other's culture.

designed was a success. Both employees and their Japanese counterparts felt more comfortable in working with each other. Prior to the program, joint projects required an average of fifteen months to complete; projects run by executives applying the methodologies of the program cut completion time to an average of eight months. Financial returns based on contracts negotiated by personnel who had not participated in the program averaged gross income of 6 percent of sales whereas those negotiated by personnel applying the anthropological techniques averaged gross income equal to 18 percent of sales.

Urban Social Planning and Restructuring in Canada

Alexander Ervin is an anthropologist in Saskatoon, Saskatchewan, in Canada, who has had considerable experience in collaborative, community-based research in social service and health agencies (see

Table 15.1 **Introductions at Business Meetings**		
ARTIFACTS	**SOCIAL KNOWLEDGE**	**CULTURAL LOGIC**
Technology ■ Business cards ■ Meishi Visual behavior ■ Presentation of meishi by presenting card, facing recipient. ■ Senior people present meishi first. ■ Guest presents first, giving name, company affiliation, and bowing. ■ Host presents meishi in same sequence. ■ Upon sitting at conference table, all meishi are placed in front of recipient to assure name use.	■ Once given, a card is kept—not discarded. ■ Meishi are not exchanged a second time unless there is a position change. ■ Before the next meeting between parties, the meishi are reviewed for familiarization with the people attending the meeting. ■ The meishi provides status for the owner.	Human relations ■ Meishi provide understanding of appropriate relations between parties. ■ Meishi take uncertainty out of relationships. Environment ■ Meishi help establish insider/outsider environment. ■ Meishi help establish possible obligations to environment. Human activity ■ Meishi help to establish human activities.

Source: Reeves-Ellington 1993.

EthnoProfile 15.2

Saskatoon

Region: North America

Nation: Canada

Population: 186,000

Environment: Northern plains

Livelihood: Industrial, commercial, agricultural, educational center

Political organization: City in contemporary nation-state

For more information: http://duke.usask.ca/~lowey/saskatoon/about_saskatoon/index.html

EthnoProfile 15.2: Saskatoon). In his view, anthropologists seem to be particularly well-suited for this kind of applied work, since they "have been trained conceptually and methodologically to seek linkages among behaviors, institutions, and values, and to attempt to construct integrated overviews of whatever is the phenomenon under investigation" (1996, 324). As government policymakers move to cut costs by downsizing, few policy disciplines are able to provide information about how the different social service providers and their services fit together, nor are they able to listen effectively to grassroots perceptions of issues, needs, and solutions. Anthropologists, however, are trained to do precisely these things.

To illustrate, Ervin discusses his work with the Saskatoon Social Planning Council. The council was established in 1992 with a push from activists from the approximately 200 human service delivery organizations in Saskatoon. In Canada, social planning councils focus attention on local social issues. They are involved with an extremely wide range of policies and issues and carry out policy research, including needs assessment, program evaluations, and problem-focused investigations. Ervin's main task has been to design a plan for an annual investigation of a specific policy domain or issue to be carried out by the council. The goal of the research would be to provide the data that the human service organizations could use to solve effectively some of the problems the research identified.

The pilot investigation has been a multidimensional study of the well-being of children in the city in relation to poverty, hunger, recreation, education, family, native and immigrant issues, substance abuse, and general health concerns. Several organizations collaborated in the project, including the regional health board, the Catholic and public school boards, and the social services district office. A working group of representatives of each organization has been formed to analyze the data, much of which was collected by three anthropology students at the University of Saskatchewan. When the report of the research has been written, the council will call together those organizations and people that are involved with children's issues in Saskatoon to consider the results and discuss possible solutions.

Ervin believes that anthropologists can make important contributions in urban policy contexts, especially in needs assessment, "the process of identifying and seeking solutions to problems of particular populations, irrespective of whether programs have already been designed to address them" (330). Anthropologists seem particularly well placed for these projects, given their commitment to participatory research and holism. Indeed, from his point of view, the major need in the kinds of urban policy research that he has been engaged in is for flexible generalists—anthropologists who can move from one policy domain to another and construct integrated overviews of the phenomenon under investigation.

▼ HOW CAN ANTHROPOLOGY INFLUENCE POLICY?

Anthropology's role in policymaking has waxed and waned. During World War II, anthropologists worked in government. By the 1970s, however, during the Vietnam War, many were unwilling to support policies that not only contradicted their own personal convictions, but also might require them to abandon their professional judgments. Anthropologists are necessarily aware of the costs of policies that disregard cultural practices. They have been critical of technical experts who make decisions without consulting the people whose lives will be affected. Anthropologists realize that no change benefits everyone equally: Some gain as others lose. Even if they help plan a program, its implementation may depend on factors over which they have no control—cash flow problems to the AID office, fear over a legislator's response, political issues, elections, budget reductions, lack of interest, and so on.

As we saw in chapter 4, however, there is a trend among anthropologists to engage in policy work as partners with other groups. Their support and expertise can enable the people most affected by government policies to become effective advocates for their own causes. Even beyond ethnography, an anthropologist may act as advocate, observer, and witness in the cause of democracy and human rights, as we see next.

Anthropology and Democracy

The end of the Cold War marked a turning point in world politics. Capitalism spread to all parts of the globe, and many observers assumed that other Western institutions were bound to follow. The fall of dictatorial political regimes in a number of Latin American and central European countries, for example, was viewed as an opportunity to introduce Western political practices, including political parties and formal elections. Many members of the Western political and economic elite eagerly proclaimed the arrival of democracy as soon as the first elections were held and have often been very suspicious of political movements—such as some of the new social movements we described in the previous chapter—that challenge formal electoral institutions in the name of democracy.

But anthropologists and other social scientists working in these same countries are often able to present a different perspective on the "transition" to democracy. Fieldwork brings them into close regular contact with citizens who have their own ideas about what kinds of social institutions do or do not operate in a democratic fashion. Taking these observations seriously has drawn anthropologists into a growing debate about what democracy has been and can be. In particular, their work has helped to show that formal Western electoral politics may produce less democratic outcomes than other, traditional institutions.

For example, anthropologist Serge Tcherkézoff (1998) followed policy debates about the shape democracy ought to take in the independent nation of Samoa

(see EthnoProfile 5.2: Samoa). Traditionally, Samoa had been a land of villages, each of which was governed by a council of *matai*, or "sacred chiefs." This system survived Christian missionaries, German colonization, and the effects of 42 years as a protectorate of New Zealand. A referendum sponsored by the United Nations in 1962 led to independence, and the people of what was called Western Samoa until 1997 voted to set up a parliamentary system of national government (Figure 15.6). However, their constitution specified that only matai could vote and run for office. In 1990, the law was changed to allow all citizens to vote, but matai were still the only ones allowed to run for office.

Does this hybrid of Western parliamentary system and the Samoan *faamatai*, or "chief-system," represent an undemocratic attempt by chiefly "aristocrats" to maintain power within formally democratic political institutions? In Tcherkézoff's opinion, the question is deeply misleading because it rests on a fundamental misunderstanding of how the Samoan chief-system functions. He points out that if outsiders insist on thinking of matai as aristocrats, then there are no families in Samoa who are not aristocratic. This is because each matai or chief is actually the head of an extended family. Each extended family is held together by kinship connections, joint ownership of land, and joint participation in rituals directed to their founding ancestor.

Matai, in fact, means "the one who bears the family name," and members of each extended family choose the person who will be ritually invested with this title. It is the job of each matai to serve his family and his matai name by leading worship directed to the ancestor and engaging in other activities designed to elevate the reputation of his extended family. If a matai fails to live up to these expectations, his extended family can strip him of his title and give it to someone else. Every family has a matai, which is why Tcherkézoff says that there are no families that are not chiefly families; and matais serve at the will of the kin who choose them, which is why, he tells us, that "when Samoans heard about 'democracy,' they said that they 'already have it'" (1998, 423).

So why are Samoans arguing about the connection between the matai system and democracy? As Tcherkézoff explains, this debate involves a variety of different ideas about what democracy means and

FIGURE 15.6 The parliament building in Samoa. Samoans today are taking part in a debate that involves a variety of ideas about what democracy means and what kinds of institutional arrangements are most likely to ensure it.

which kinds of institutional arrangements are most likely to ensure it. Those who want universal suffrage favor a view of democracy in which the emphasis is on individual freedom: Anyone can run for office, and anyone can vote. They point out, for example, that traditionally nobody becomes a matai until he has served his family for many years and his predecessor has died, which limits the field of possible parliamentary candidates to one (relatively) old man per extended family. How can it be democratic to restrict the opportunities of younger people to run for office? These sorts of arguments fit well with traditional Western arguments that speak of democracy in connection with individual freedom from arbitrary restrictions.

But those Samoans who want the matai system to continue stress that it is more democratic than universal suffrage. It creates representatives who can never forget that they are responsible to those who elected them—the other members of their extended family. In thinking about democracy in this way, these Samoans are refusing to reduce democratic citizenship to the right to vote. Rather, they take the

view that democracy involves not just being treated as an equal by others. It also obligates those who make political decisions for others to remain accountable and accessible to those whom they represent (O'Donnell and Schmitter 1986; Rubin 1997). Thus, the matai system ensures that every extended family will be represented in some form in the electoral process, and any matais elected to parliament will not be able to ignore the wishes of those who put them in office.

Politics in Samoa also has a regional dimension. Tcherkézoff points out that Samoa primarily has been a nation of villages but that the capital city has been growing in size in recent years. Many of those who live in the growing urban area depend more on wage labor and less on agriculture and fishing, the activities central to village life where matais traditionally exercised their authority. Thus, those who want to preserve the matai system also defend it as a way of maintaining equality between those who live in the city and those who still live in rural areas. They fear that if parliamentary elections were to operate in terms of universal suffrage, Samoa would be fractured into two societies: an urban sector with a Western political system and no way to hold their parliamentary representatives accountable and a rural sector in which matais still exist but have become powerless guardians of local folklore. Should this happen, "then some Samoans say that 'democracy' will not be achieved and will even go backwards" (1998, 427).

As Tcherkézoff makes clear, the policy debate about democracy in Samoa is complex and subtle: Samoans have a sophisticated understanding of the advantages and drawbacks of different democratic political forms, some of which are indigenous to Samoa and some of which came there from elsewhere. "The problem is that Samoa has the chance to build its future on ideas and experiences that come both from the faamatai tradition and from the Western tradition of democracy and to maybe create a new synthesis where the advent of democracy will not just be the replacement of hierarchy (in the faamatai) by inequality (in the Western-style politics). There lies the real question of the future of the country" (1998, 430).

Anthropology and Human Rights

Anthropologists have been involved in expanding the understanding of human rights and are increasingly participating in organizations for the defense of human rights. In particular, they have contributed to the recognition by human rights legal advocates that the collective rights of groups (such as indigenous peoples) deserve as much attention as the rights of individuals. Ellen Messer observes that anthropologists have examined, and continue to examine, the "contexts of human rights abuses, to understand how the political economic conditions that create cultural customs such as infanticide, underfeeding of women and children, and other abuses of women might be improved and make the customs of less evident utility. They also continue to work with interpreters of local traditions, so that through persuasion and contextualization, and by drawing on the authority of multiple traditions, people might be empowered to improve human rights in their own lives" (1993, 24). For example, anthropologist Carolyn Nordstrom (1993) has written about the efforts of the Ministry of Education in Mozambique and the Mozambican Woman's Organization to assist children and women traumatized, raped, displaced, and impoverished by 16 years of war. She discusses how indigenous healers have come to develop specialties in war trauma, "to take the violence out of people," and are being brought into the national health care system. One of the foremost anthropologically oriented organizations involved with human rights is Cultural Survival, founded in 1972 by anthropologists Pia Maybury-Lewis and David Maybury-Lewis (Figure 15.7) and dedicated to helping indigenous people and ethnic minorities deal as equals in their encounters with industrial society, and this includes struggles for indigenous rights (E. Lutz 2006).

Settings where indigenous rights are debated and policies are formulated have become sites for ethnographic research, much of it multisited. For example, anthropologist Ronald Niezen began his career in the time-honored fashion of carrying out single-sited research on Islamic reform in Mali. Later he undertook community-based research with the eastern James Bay Crees in northern Québec, Canada. Nevertheless, he writes, "the James Bay Crees also introduced me to international politics." In 1994, he traveled as an observer delegate with the Grand Council of the Crees to a meeting of the Working Group on Indigenous Populations at the United Nations in Geneva, Switzerland. People on the reservation were also learning via the Internet about the struggles of other indigenous communities for rights and were starting to "see themselves as leading a cause for justice directly analogous to (and without distinguishing among) a variety of liberation movements, including the American civil rights movement and resistance to South African apartheid" (2003, xiii). As his involvement with the James Bay Crees increased, Niezen found that the Crees valued his ability to provide a link between their own aboriginal government and the government of Canada. He was called on to perform many roles in addition to that of participant-observer: During the first two years he found himself acting "as an observer, witness, advocate, author—roles that were pretty much informally developed as needs became felt" (xiv). As he moved back and forth from reservation to government meetings, he came to realize that a global movement of indigenous peoples had come into existence and was getting noticed at places like the United Nations. His earlier research in Mali also became relevant in a new way when, during one of his trips to Geneva, he encountered delegates from West Africa who were coming to identify themselves as indigenous peoples and who were

FIGURE 15.7 Anthropologists have become increasingly involved in the defense of human rights. David Maybury-Lewis (pictured here with Xavante informants in Brazil) and Pia Maybury-Lewis founded Cultural Survival, an organization dedicated to helping indigenous peoples and ethnic minorities deal as equals in their encounters with industrial society.

working "to develop human rights standards appropriate to their concerns" (xiv).

Indigeneity is supposed to refer to a primordial identity that preceded the establishment of colonial states. Yet the very possibility that groups from West Africa, Latin America, and North America might come together as indigenous peoples "is predicated upon global sameness of experience, and is expressed through the mechanisms of law and bureaucracy" (2003, 2–3). "Indigenous peoples" is not just a badge of identity, but also a legal term that has been included in international conventions issued by the International Labor Organzation. "Today, the term is both a fragile legal concept and the indefinite unachievable sum of the historical and personal experiences of those gathered in a room who share, at the very least, the notion that they have all been oppressed in similar ways for similar motives by similar state and corporate elites" (4).

According to Niezen, it is important to distinguish what he calls *ethnonationalism*, from *indigenism*. Ethnonationalism, he believes, describes a movement of people who "have defined their collective identities with clear cultural and linguistic contours and who express their goals of autonomy from the state with the greatest conviction and zeal, sometimes with hatreds spilling over into violence." For example, in Canada the advocates of sovereignty for Quebec have pushed for an independent French-speaking nation-state (8). Indigenism, by contrast, "is not a particu-

larized identity but a global one, . . . grounded in international networks" (9). What connects specific groups to this identity, whether they live in dictatorships or democratic states, "is a sense of illegitimate, meaningless, and dishonorable suffering" (13). Their tactics and strategies do not conform to the "everyday forms of resistance" described by James Scott among peasants in Sedaka, who were not formally organized with explicit policy goals. Nor do they correspond to groups like the Zapatistas in Chiapas, Mexico, who have taken up arms to resist the central government (Figure 15.8).

Unlike ethnonationalists, indigenous rights activists do not seek to form breakaway states of their own. Their approach is entirely different: "Indigenous representatives are taking their complaints to international forums, striving to be involved at the highest level possible in international politics" (16). Indigenous delegates lobby for their rights by using "the international bodies of states to overcome the domestic abuse of states themselves," a strategy that, in Niezen's opinion, "shows some indigenous leaders to be, despite their limited power and resources, some of the most effective political strategists on the contemporary national and international scenes" (2003, 16). Their goal is to get nation-states to live up to their responsibilities and promises to indigenous people, which are often explicitly stated in treaties. Thus, they seek affirmation of their rights to land and

FIGURE 15.8 Sidney Hill, Tadodaho Chief of the Haudenosaunee, speaking at the United Nations Permanent Forum on Indigenous Issues

compensation for past losses and suffering; they seek cultural self-determination and political sovereignty. The goal of indigenous liberation thus involves the recognition of *collective rights*. These go beyond the individual rights traditionally recognized in such documents as the UN Declaration of Human Rights, discussed in chapter 14.

While Niezen urges us to acknowledge the daring and effectiveness of the indigenous movement, he also warns against romanticizing it: "Significant obstacles remain to be overcome before a new order of relations between indigenous peoples and the state can be said to have truly arrived" (2003, 23). For example, the United Nations has been less responsive than many indigenous delegates might have hoped, because some of its member states continue to equate the movement for indigenous sovereignty with ethnonationalism. Hence the UN Permanent Forum on Indigenous Issues is not called the UN Permanent Forum on Indigenous *Peoples* (160–164).

Some liberal human rights theorists are also concerned that the recognition of collective rights would serve as a green light to despotic governments, who could use the rights of distinct cultures as an excuse for repression. Niezen concluded that

> if indigenous claims to self-determination are to avoid playing into the hands of despotic governments, they must have individual rights built into

them. . . . Human rights do not offer protection of cultural practices that themselves violate individual rights. The concept of 'indigenous peoples,' developed principally within Western traditions of scholarship and legal reform . . . has transcended its symbolic use by acquiring legal authority. . . . It has been taken control of by its living subjects—reverse-engineered, rearticulated, and put to use as a tool of liberation. (219–221)

▼ AWARENESS AND UNCERTAINTY

Why study anthropology? The second part of our answer is personal.

Studying cultural anthropology brings students into contact with different ways of life. It makes them aware of just how arbitrary their own understanding of the world is as they learn how other people have developed satisfying but different ways of living. In addition, if they are from Western countries that were responsible for colonialism and its consequences, it makes them painfully aware of just how much their own tradition has to answer for in the modern world.

Knowing and experiencing cultural variety gives rise, perhaps inevitably, to doubt. We come to doubt the ultimate validity of the central truths of our own cultural tradition, which have been ratified

United Nations Declaration on the Rights of Indigenous Peoples

In September 2007, after much debate and negotiation, the United Nations General Assembly adopted a document on the rights of indigenous peoples. The Declaration is lengthy, consisting of a Preamble and 46 articles. Here is the Preamble section and the first three articles of the Declaration. The full Declaration can be found at the United Nations web site: http://daccessdds.un.org/doc/UNDOC/LTD/N07/498/30/PDF/N0749830.pdf?OpenElement.

Affirming that indigenous peoples are equal to all other peoples, while recognizing the right of all peoples to be different, to consider themselves different, and to be respected as such,

Affirming also that all peoples contribute to the diversity and richness of civilizations and cultures, which constitute the common heritage of humankind,

Affirming further that all doctrines, policies, and practices based on or advocating superiority of peoples or individuals on the basis of national origin, racial, religious, ethnic, or cultural differences are racist, scientifically false, legally invalid, morally condemnable, and socially unjust,

Reaffirming also that indigenous peoples, in the exercise of their rights, should be free from discrimination of any kind,

Concerned that indigenous peoples have suffered from historic injustices as a result of, inter alia, their colonization and dispossession of their lands, territories, and resources, thus preventing them from exercising, in particular, their right to development in accordance with their own needs and interests,

Recognizing the urgent need to respect and promote the inherent rights of indigenous peoples which derive from their political, economic, and social structures and from their cultures, spiritual traditions, histories, and philosophies, especially their rights to their lands, territories, and resources,

Further recognizing the urgent need to respect and promote the rights of indigenous peoples affirmed in treaties, agreements, and other constructive arrangements with States,

Welcoming the fact that indigenous peoples are organizing themselves for political, economic, social, and cultural enhancement and in order to bring an end to all forms of discrimination and oppression wherever they occur,

Convinced that control by indigenous peoples over developments affecting them and their lands, territories, and resources will enable them to maintain and strengthen their institutions, cultures, and traditions, and to promote their development in accordance with their aspirations and needs,

Recognizing also that respect for indigenous knowledge, cultures, and traditional practices contributes to sustainable and equitable development and proper management of the environment,

Emphasizing the contribution of the demilitarization of the lands and territories of indigenous peoples to peace, economic and social progress and development, understanding, and friendly relations among nations and peoples of the world,

Recognizing in particular the right of indigenous families and communities to retain shared responsibility for the upbringing, training, education, and well-being of their children, consistent with the rights of the child,

Recognizing also that indigenous peoples have the right freely to determine their relationships with States in a spirit of coexistence, mutual benefit, and full respect,

Considering that the rights affirmed in treaties, agreements, and constructive arrangements between States and indigenous peoples are, in some situations, matters of international concern, interest, responsibility, and character,

Also considering that treaties, agreements, and other constructive arrangements, and the relationship they represent, are the basis for a strengthened partnership between indigenous peoples and States,

Acknowledging that the Charter of the United Nations, the International Covenant on Economic, Social,

(continued on next page)

IN THEIR OWN WORDS

United Nations Declaration on the Rights of Indigenous Peoples
(continued)

and Cultural Rights and the International Covenant on Civil and Political Rights affirm the fundamental importance of the right of self-determination of all peoples, by virtue of which they freely determine their political status and freely pursue their economic, social, and cultural development,

Bearing in mind that nothing in this Declaration may be used to deny any peoples their right of self-determination, exercised in conformity with international law,

Convinced that the recognition of the rights of indigenous peoples in this Declaration will enhance harmonious and cooperative relations between the State and indigenous peoples, based on principles of justice, democracy, respect for human rights, nondiscrimination, and good faith,

Encouraging States to comply with and effectively implement all their obligations as they apply to indigenous peoples under international instruments, in particular those related to human rights, in consultation and cooperation with the peoples concerned,

Emphasizing that the United Nations has an important and continuing role to play in promoting and protecting the rights of indigenous peoples,

Believing that this Declaration is a further important step forward for the recognition, promotion, and protection of the rights and freedoms of indigenous peoples and in the development of relevant activities of the United Nations system in this field,

Recognizing and reaffirming that indigenous individuals are entitled without discrimination to all human rights recognized in international law, and that indigenous peoples possess collective rights which are indispensable for their existence, well-being, and integral development as peoples,

Solemnly proclaims the following United Nations Declaration on the Rights of Indigenous Peoples as a standard of achievement to be pursued in a spirit of partnership and mutual respect,

Article 1

Indigenous peoples have the right to the full enjoyment, as a collective or as individuals, of all human rights and fundamental freedoms as recognized in the Charter of the United Nations, the Universal Declaration of Human Rights, and international human rights law.

Article 2

Indigenous peoples and individuals are free and equal to all other peoples and individuals and have the right to be free from any kind of discrimination, in the exercise of their rights, in particular that based on their indigenous origin or identity.

Article 3

Indigenous peoples have the right of self-determination. By virtue of that right they freely determine their political status and freely pursue their economic, social, and cultural development.

and sanctified by the generations who preceded us. We doubt because a familiarity with alternative ways of living makes the ultimate meaning of any action, of any object, a highly ambiguous matter. Ambiguity is part and parcel of the human condition. Human beings have coped with ambiguity from time immemorial by means of culture, which places objects and actions in contexts and thereby makes their meanings plain. This doubt can lead to anxiety, but it can also be liberating.

▼ FREEDOM AND CONSTRAINT

Why study anthropology? The third part of our response is, for want of a better word, humanistic.

All human beings, ourselves included, live in culturally shaped worlds, enmeshed in webs of interpretation and meaning that we have spun. It has been the particular task of anthropology and its practitioners to go out into the world to bear witness to and record

Into the Warp and Woof of Multicultural Worlds

Changes in the contemporary world are producing what anthropologist George Marcus calls "transcultural 'traditional' peoples," whose members live in many different places and whose sense of cultural identity involves a mix of many cultural elements.

The power of global cultural homogenization in the late twentieth century challenges the conventions and rationales by which anthropology has so far produced its knowledge of other cultures. The reorganization of the world economy through technological advances in communication, production processes, and marketing has thoroughly deterritorialized culture. For example, the Tongan islanders of Polynesia that I studied in the early 1970s now constitute a diaspora of communities in locales around the Pacific rim. As many, if not more, Tongans now live permanently in Australia, New Zealand, and the United States as in the islands themselves. One might fairly ponder where both the cultural and geographical center of the Tongan people resides. Their identity is produced in many locales and through the mix of many cultural elements. And their conditions are similar to those of numerous other peoples that anthropologists have traditionally studied. It is no longer just the most powerful, large-scale, and most modern societies, such as the United States and Japan, that exist in international, transcultural science.

Among such transcultural "traditional" peoples, levels of cultural self-consciousness and alternatives increase. The authenticity of performances, rituals, or apparently deep seated norms like those of kinship cannot be merely assumed, either by locals or by visitors such as anthropologists. To some extent, media documentaries have absorbed anthropology's function of presenting vividly the lifeways of other cultures to Euro-American publics that themselves can no longer be considered as homogeneous or mainstream. And, finally, the subjects of anthropological study independently and articulately translate their own perspectives with sensitivity to the effects of different media.

Peoples who in particular have become classic anthropological subjects, such as the Samoans, Trobriand Islanders, Hopi, and Todas of India, know their status well, and have, with some ambivalence, assimilated anthropological knowledge about them as part of their sense of themselves. A recent example was the visit of a Toda woman to Houston. A trained nurse among her people as well as a cultural broker, she was on tour in the United States, giving talks about the Todas, of the sort that anthropologists might have given in past decades. By chance, she was visiting the home of a colleague just as a British documentary about the Todas appeared on the television—a documentary in which the visitor was featured prominently as the filmmaker's prime source of information. The visitor's comments as she watched the program along with my colleague did not much concern the details of Toda culture, but rather dealt with the ironies of the multiple representations of her people—by herself, by anthropologists, and by the British Broadcasting Corporation.

The lesson of this story is compelling. The penetrations of a world economy, communications, and the effects of multiple, fragmented identities on cultural authenticity, once thought restricted to advanced modernity, have increased markedly among most local and regional cultures worldwide. They have thus engendered an ethnography in reverse among many peoples who not only can assimilate the professional idioms of anthropology but can relativize them among other alternatives and ways of knowledge. This does not mean that the traditional task of anthropology to represent distinctive and systematic cultural forms of life has been fundamentally subverted by its own subjects. Rather, anthropology's traditional task is now much more complicated, requiring new sensibilities in undertaking fieldwork and different strategies for writing about it.

Source: Marcus 1990, 254–55.

the vast creative diversity in world-making that has been the history of our species. In our lifetimes, we will witness the end of many of those ways of life—and if we are not careful, of all ways of life. This loss is tragic, for as these worlds disappear, so too does something special about humanity: variety, creativity, and awareness of alternatives.

Our survival as a species and our viability as individuals depend on the possibility of choice, of perceiving and being able to act on alternatives in the various situations we encounter during our lives. If, as a colleague has suggested, human life is a minefield, then the more paths we can see and imagine through that minefield, the more likely we are to make it through—or at least to have an interesting time trying. As alternatives are destroyed, wantonly smashed, or thoughtlessly crushed, *our* own human possibilities are reduced. A small group of men and women have for the last century labored in corners of the world, both remote and nearby, to write the record of human accomplishment and bring it back and teach it to others.

Surely our greatest human accomplishment is the creation of the sometimes austerely beautiful worlds in which we all live. Anthropologists have rarely given in to the romantic notion that these other worlds are all good, all life-enhancing, all fine or beautiful. They are not. Ambiguity and ambivalence are, as we have seen, hallmarks of the human experience. There are no guarantees that human cultures will be compassionate rather than cruel or that people will agree they are one or the other. There are not even any guarantees that our species will survive. But all anthropologists have believed that these are *human* worlds that have given those who have lived in them the ability to make sense out of their experiences and to derive meaning for their lives, that we are a species at once bound by our culture and free to change it.

This is a perilous and fearsome freedom, a difficult freedom to grasp and to wield. Nevertheless, the freedom is there, and in this dialectic of freedom and constraint lies our future. It is up to us to create it.

Bibliography

Abbas, Akhbar. 2002. Cosmopolitan description: Shanghai and Hong Kong. In *Cosmopolitanism*, ed. Carol Breckenridge, Sheldon Pollock, Homi Bhaba, and Dipeesh Chakrabarty, 209–28. Durham, NC: Duke University Press.

Abu-Lughod, Janet. 1989. *Before European hegemony: The world system A.D. 1250–1350*. New York: Oxford University Press.

Abu-Lughod, Lila. 1991. Writing against culture. In *Recapturing anthropology*, ed. Richard Fox, 137–62. Santa Fe, NM: SAR Press.

Abu-Lughod, Lila. 1995. The objects of soap opera: Egyptian television and the cultural politics of modernity. In *Worlds apart: Modernity through the prism of the local*, ed. Daniel Miller, 190–210. London: Routledge.

Abusharaf, Rogaia Mustafa. 2000. Female circumcision goes beyond feminism. *Anthropology News* 41(March): 17–18.

Abwunza, Judith M. 1997. *Women's voices, women's power: Dialogues of resistance from East Africa*. Peterborough, ON: Broadview Press.

Adams, Richard Newbold. 1979. *Energy and structure: A theory of social power*. Austin: University of Texas Press.

Agar, Michael. 1996. *The professional stranger*, 2d ed. San Diego: Academic Press.

Alland, Alexander. 1977. *The artistic animal*. New York: Doubleday Anchor.

Allen, Catherine J. 1988. *The hold life has: Coca and cultural identity in an Andean community*. Washington, DC: Smithsonian Institution Press.

Allen, Theodore. 1994–1997. *The invention of the white race*, 2 vols. London: Verso.

Alonso, Ana María. 1994. The politics of space, time, and substance: State formation, nationalism, and ethnicity. *Annual Review of Anthropology* 23: 379–405.

Alverson, Hoyt. 1977. Peace Corps volunteers in rural Botswana. *Human Organization* 36(3): 274–81.

Alverson, Hoyt. 1978. *Mind in the heart of darkness*. New Haven, CT: Yale University Press.

Alverson, Hoyt. 1990. Guest editorial. In *Cultural anthropology: A perspective on the human condition*, Emily Schultz and Robert Lavenda. St. Paul, MN: West.

Anderson, Benedict. 1983. *Imagined communities*. London: Verso.

Anderson, Richard L. 1990. *Calliope's sisters: A comparative study of philosophies of art*. Englewood Cliffs, NJ: Prentice Hall.

Apfel, Roberta, and Bennett Simon. 2000. Mitigating discontents with children in war: An ongoing psychological inquiry. In *Cultures under siege: Collective violence and trauma*, ed. Antonius C. G. M. Robben and Marcelo M. Suárez-Orozco, 271–84. Cambridge: Cambridge University Press.

Appadurai, Arjun. 1990. Disjuncture and difference in the global cultural economy. In *Global culture*, ed. Mike Featherstone, 295–310. London: Sage.

Appadurai, Arjun. 2002. Grassroots globalization and the research imagination. In *The anthropology of politics*, ed. Joan Vincent, 271–84. Malden, MA: Blackwell.

Asad Talal. 1973. *Anthropology and the colonial encounter*. New York: Humanities Press.

Asad, Talal. 2002. From the history of colonial anthropology to the anthropology of Western hegemony. In *The anthropology of politics*, ed. Joan Vincent, 133–42. Malden, MA: Blackwell.

Asad, Talal. 2003. *Formations of the secular: Christianity, Islam, modernity*. Stanford, CA: Stanford University Press.

Aufderheide, Patricia. 1993. Beyond television. *Public Culture* 5: 579–92.

Autobiografías Campesinas. 1979. Heredia, Costa Rica: Editorial de la Universidad Nacional.

Baer, Hans, Merrill Singer, and Ida Susser. 2003. *Medical anthropology and the world system*, 2d ed. Westport, CT: Praeger.

Bakhtin, M. M. 1981. *The dialogic imagination: Four essays*. Ed. Michael Holquist. Trans. Michael Holquist and Caryl Emerson. Austin: University of Texas Press.

Barad, Karen. 1999. Agential realism: Feminist interventions in understanding scientific practices. In *The science studies reader*, ed. Mario Biagioli, 1–11. New York: Routledge.

Basham, Richard. 1978. *Urban anthropology*. Palo Alto, CA: Mayfield.

Bateson, Gregory. 1972. A Theory of Play and Fantasy. In *Steps to an ecology of mind*, ed. Gregory Bateson. 1955, 177–93. New York: Ballantine Books.

Bauman, Zygmunt. 1989. *Modernity and the Holocaust*. Ithaca, NY: Cornell University Press.

BBC News. 2003. Protest disrupts Tour de France. July 15. http://news.bbc.co.uk/1/hi/world/europe/3068985.stm. Accessed 15 July 2003.

Beals, Alan. 1962. *Gopalpur, a south Indian village*. New York: Holt, Rinehart & Winston.

Beidelman, Thomas. 1982. *Colonial evangelism*. Bloomington: Indiana University Press.

Bell, Sandra, and Simon Coleman. 1999. The anthropology of friendship: Enduring themes and future possibilities. In *The anthropology of friendship*, ed. Sandra Bell and Simon Coleman, 1–19. Oxford: Berg.

Bellman, Beryl. 1984. *The language of secrecy*. New Brunswick, NJ: Rutgers University Press.

Belmonte, Thomas. 1978. *The broken fountain*. New York: Columbia University Press.

Ben-Tovim, Gideon. 1997. Why "positive action" is "politically correct." In *The politics of multiculturalism in the new Europe: Racism, identity, and community*, ed. Tariq Modood and Pnina Werbner, 209–22. London: Zed Books.

Bernard, H. Russell. 2006. *Research methods in anthropology*. 4th ed. Thousand Oaks, CA: Sage.

Berreman, Gerald. 1962. *Behind many masks: Ethnography and impression management in a Himalayan village*. Lexington, KY: Society for Applied Anthropology.

Bestor, Theodore. 2000. How sushi went global. *Foreign Policy* (November–December): 54–63.

Bickerton, Derek. 1981. *Roots of language*. Ann Arbor, MI: Karoma.

Bigenho, Michelle. 2002. *Sounding indigenous: Authenticity in Bolivian music performance*. New York: Palgrave Macmillan.

Blackwood, Evelyn, and Saskia E. Wieringa. 1999. Preface. In *Female desires: Same-sex relations and transgender practices across cultures*, ed. Evelyn Blackwood and Saskia E. Wieringa, ix–xiii. New York: Columbia University Press.

Blanchard, Kendall, and Alyce Cheska. 1985. *The anthropology of sport*. South Hadley, MA: Bergin & Garvey.

Bledsoe, Caroline. 1993. The politics of polygyny in Mende education and child fosterage transactions. In *Sex and gender hierarchies*, ed. Barbara Diane Miller, 170–92. Cambridge: Cambridge University Press.

Boaz, Noel T., and Linda Wolfe, eds. 1995. *Biological anthropology: The state of the science*. Bend, OR: International Institute for Human Evolutionary Research.

Bock, Philip. 1994. *Rethinking psychological anthropology: Continuity and change in the study of human action*. 2d ed. Prospect Heights, IL: Waveland.

Boddy, Janice. 1997. Womb as oasis: The symbolic context of pharaonic circumcision in rural northern Sudan. In *The Gender/Sexuality Reader*, edited by Roger Lancaster and Micaela De Leonardo, 309–24. New York: Routledge.

Bodenhorn, Barbara. 2000. "He used to be my relative": Exploring the bases of relatedness among Iñupiat of northern Alaska. In *Cultures of relatedness: New approaches to the study of kinship*, ed. Janet Carsten, 128–48. Cambridge: Cambridge University Press.

Boesch-Ackermann, H., and C. Boesch. 1994. Hominization in the rainforest: The chimpanzee's piece of the puzzle. *Evolutionary Anthropology* 3(1): 9–16.

Bohannan, Paul, and Fred Plog, eds. 1967. *Beyond the frontier*. Garden City, NY: Natural History Press.

Borman, Randy. 1999. Cofan: Story of the forest people and the outsiders. *Cultural Survival Quarterly* 23(2): 48–50.

Bourgois, Philippe. 1995. *In search of respect: Selling crack in El Barrio*. New York: Cambridge University Press.

Bowen, John, ed. 1998. *Religion in culture and society*. Needham Heights, MA: Allyn & Bacon.

Bowen, John. 2002. *Religions in practice: An approach to the anthropology of religion*. 2d ed. Needham Heights, MA: Allyn & Bacon.

Bowie, Fiona. 2006. *The anthropology of religion: An introduction*. 2d ed. Malden, MA: Blackwell.

Bradburd, Daniel. 1998. *Being there: The necessity of fieldwork*. Washington, DC: Smithsonian Institution Press.

Brain, Robert. 1976. *Friends and lovers*. New York: Basic Books.

Braroe, Neils. 1975. *Indian and white*. Stanford, CA: Stanford University Press.

Brenneis, Donald, and Ronald Macaulay, eds. 1996. *The matrix of language: Contemporary linguistic anthropology*. Boulder, CO: Westview Press.

Brewin, Christopher. 1997. Society as a kind of community: Communitarian voting with equal rights for individuals in the European Union. In *The politics of multiculturalism in the new Europe: Racism, identity, and community*, ed. Tariq Modood and Pnina Werbner, 223–39. London: Zed Books.

Briggs, Jean. 1980. Kapluna daughter: Adopted by the Eskimo. In *Conformity and conflict*. 7th ed., ed. by James Spradley and David McCurdy, 44–62. Boston: Little, Brown.

Bromberger, Christian. 1995. *Le match de football: Etnologie d'une passion partisane à Marseille, Naples et Turin*. Paris: Éditions de la Maison des sciences de l'homme.

Brooke, James. 2003. Dowry too high: Lose bride and go to jail. *New York Times*, May 17.

Broom, Leonard, Bernard J. Siegel, Evon Z. Vogt, and James B. Watson. 1954. Acculturation: An exploratory formula. *American Anthropologist* 56: 973–1000.

Brown, Michael F. 1997. *The channeling zone: American spirituality in an anxious age*. Cambridge, MA: Harvard University Press.

Burch, Ernest. 1970. Marriage and divorce among the North Alaska Eskimos. In *Divorce and after*, ed. Paul Bohannan, 152–81. Garden City, NY: Doubleday.

Caplan, Pat. 2003. Introduction: Anthropology and ethics. In *The ethics of anthropology: Debates and dilemmas*, ed. Pat Caplan, 1–33. London: Routledge.

Carter, Thomas. 2001. Baseball arguments: *Aficionismo* and masculinity at the core of *Cubanidad*. *International Journal of the History of Sport* 18(3): 117–38.

Chance, John. 1978. *Race and class in colonial Oaxaca*. Stanford, CA: Stanford University Press.

Chin, Elizabeth. 1999. Ethnically correct dolls: Toying with the race industry. *American Anthropologist* 101(2): 305–21.

Chomsky, Noam. 1957. *Syntactic structures*. Cambridge, MA: MIT Press.

Chomsky, Noam. 1965. *Aspects of the theory of syntax*. Cambridge, MA: MIT Press.

Clark, Gracia. 1994. *Onions are my husband*. Chicago: University of Chicago Press.

Clastres, Pierre. 1977. *Society against the state*. Trans. Robert Hurley. New York: Urizen Books.

Cole, Michael. 1994. *Cultural psychology: A once and future discipline*. Cambridge, MA: Harvard University Press.

Cole, Michael, and Sylvia Scribner. 1974. *Culture and thought: A psychological introduction*. New York: Wiley.

Collier, Jane, Michelle Z. Rosaldo, and Sylvia Yanagisako. 1997. Is there a family?: New anthropological views. In *The gender/sexuality reader*, ed. Roger Lancaster and Michaela Di Leonardo, 71–81. New York: Routledge.

Collier, Jane, and Sylvia Junko Yanigasako, eds. 1987. *Gender and kinship*. Stanford, CA: Stanford University Press.

Colloredo-Mansfeld, Rudi. 1999. *The native leisure class: Consumption and cultural creativity in the Andes*. Chicago: University of Chicago Press.

Colson, Elizabeth. 1977. Power at large: Meditation on "The symposium on power." In *The anthropology of power: Ethnographic studies from Asia, Oceania, and the New World*, ed. Raymond Fogelson and Richard N. Adams, 375–86. New York: Academic Press.

Comaroff, John, and Jean Comaroff. 1991. *Of revelation and revolution*. Chicago: University of Chicago Press.

Condry, Ian. 2001. Japanese hip-hop and the globalization of popular culture. In *Urban life: Readings in the anthropology of the city*, ed. George Gmelch and Walter Zenner, 357–87. Prospect Heights, IL: Waveland Press.

Conservation International. 2003. Kayapó indigenous territories: Preserving ancestral lands. *Conservation International Online*. Http://www.conservation.org/xp/frontlines/2003/fall/features/parkprofiles/parkprofile5.xml. Accessed 13 September 2003.

Cowan, Jane. 1990. *Dance and the body politic in northern Greece*. Princeton, NJ: Princeton University Press.

Cowan, Jane, Marie-Bénédicte Dembour, and Richard A. Wilson. 2001. Introduction. In *Culture and rights: Anthropological perspectives*, ed. Jane Cowan, Marie-Bénédicte Dembour, and Richard A. Wilson, 1–26. Cambridge: Cambridge University Press.

Cox, Oliver Cromwell. 1948. *Caste, class, and race: A study in social dynamics*. Garden City, NY: Doubleday.

Crehan, Kate. 2002. *Gramsci and cultural anthropology*. Berkeley: University of California Press.

Crick, Malcolm. 1976. *Explorations in language and meaning: Towards a semantic anthropology*. New York: Wiley.

Crystal, David. 1987. *The Cambridge encyclopedia of language*. Cambridge: Cambridge University Press.

Csikszentmihalyi, Mihalyi. 1981. Some paradoxes in the definition of play. In *Play as context*, ed. Alyce Cheska, 14–25. West Point, NY: Leisure Press.

Daly, Mary. 1978. *Gyn/Ecology: The Metaethics of Radical Feminism*. Boston: Beacon Press.

da Matta, Robert. 1994. Some biased remarks on interpretism. In *Assessing cultural anthropology*, ed. Robert Borofsky, 119–32. New York: McGraw-Hill.

D'Andrade, Roy G. 1992. Cognitive anthropology. In *New directions in psychological anthropology*, ed. Theodore Schwartz, Geoffrey M. White, and Catherine A. Lutz, 47–58. Cambridge: Cambridge University Press.

Daniel, E. Valentine. 1997. Suffering nation and alienation. In *Social suffering*, ed. Arthur Kleinman, Veena Das, and Margaret Lock, 309–58. Berkeley: University of California Press.

Das, Veena, and Arthur Kleinman. 2000. Introduction. In *Violence and subjectivity*, ed. Veena Das, Arthur Kleinman, Mamphela Ramphele, and Pamela Reynolds, 1–18. Berkeley: University of California Press.

Davis, Shelton. 1977. *Victims of the miracle*. Cambridge: Cambridge University Press.

Deacon, Terrence. 1997. *The symbolic species: The coevolution of language and the brain.* New York: W. W. Norton.

Deacon, Terrence. 2003. The hierarchic logic of emergence: Untangling the interdependence of evolution and self-organization. In *Evolution and learning: The Baldwin effect reconsidered*, ed. Bruce H. Weber and David J. Depew, 273–308. Cambridge, MA: MIT Press.

Dembour, Marie-Bénédicte. 2001. Following the movement of a pendulum between universalism and relativism. In *Culture and rights: Anthropological perspectives*, ed. Jane Cowan, Marie-Bénédicte Dembour, and Richard A. Wilson, 26–79. Cambridge: Cambridge University Press.

De Vos, George, and Hiroshi Wagatsuma. 1966. *Japan's invisible race.* Berkeley: University of California Press.

DeWalt, Kathleen, and Billie DeWalt. 2002. *Participant observation.* Walnut Creek, CA: AltaMira Press.

Dolgin, Janet. 1995. Family law and the facts of family. In *Naturalizing power*, ed. Sylvia Yanagisako and Carol Delaney, 47–67. New York: Routledge.

Douglas, Mary. 1966. *Purity and danger.* London: Routledge and Kegan Paul.

Douglas, Mary. 1970. Introduction. In *Witchcraft confessions and accusations*, ed. Mary Douglas, vi–xxxviii. London: Tavistock.

Douglas, Mary, and Baron Isherwood. 1979. *The world of goods: Towards an anthropology of consumption.* New York: W. W. Norton.

Drewal, Margaret Thompson. 1992. *Yoruba ritual: Performers, play, agency.* Bloomington: Indiana University Press.

Duranti, Alessandro. 1994. *From grammar to politics.* Berkeley: University of California Press.

Durham, William H. 1991. *Coevolution: Genes, culture, and human diversity.* Stanford, CA: Stanford University Press.

Elliot, Alison. 1981. *Child language.* Cambridge: Cambridge University Press.

Ericksen, Thomas Hylland. 2001. Between universalism and relativism: A critique of the UNESCO concept of culture. In *Culture and rights: Anthropological perspectives*, ed. Jane Cowan, Marie-Bénédicte Dembour, and Richard A. Wilson, 127–48. Cambridge: Cambridge University Press.

Errington, Shelly. 1998. *The death of authentic primitive art and other tales of progress.* Berkeley: University of California Press.

Ervin, Alexander M. 1996. Collaborative and participatory research in urban social planning and restructuring: Anthropological experiences from a medium-sized Canadian city. *Human Organization* 55(3): 324–33.

Escobar, Arturo. 1992. Culture, economics, and politics in Latin American social movements theory and research. In *The making of social movements in Latin America*, ed. Arturo Escobar and Sonia Alvarez, 62–85. Boulder, CO: Westview Press.

Evans, N. 2001. The last speaker is dead—Long live the last speaker! In *Linguistic fieldwork*, ed. P. Newman and M. Ratliff, 250–81. Cambridge: Cambridge University Press.

Evans-Pritchard, E. E. [1937] 1976. *Witchcraft, oracles, and magic among the Azande.* Abridged ed. Prepared Eva Gillies. Oxford: Oxford University Press.

Evans-Pritchard, E. E. 1951. *Kinship and marriage among the Nuer.* Oxford: Oxford University Press.

Evans-Pritchard, E. E. 1963. *Social anthropology and other essays.* New York: Free Press.

Fagen, Robert. 1981. *Animal play behavior.* New York: Oxford University Press.

Fagen, Robert. 1992. Play, fun, and the communication of well-being. *Play & Culture* 5(1): 40–58.

Farmer, Paul. 2002. On suffering and structural violence: A view from below. In *The anthropology of politics*, ed. Joan Vincent, 424–37. Malden, MA: Blackwell.

Ferenczi, Thomas. 1996. L'école doit accepter d'assumer une éducation civique et morale. *Le Monde*, 15 October.

Ferguson, James. 2002. The anti-politics machine. In *The anthropology of politics*, ed. Joan Vincent, 399–408. Malden, MA: Blackwell.

Fernandez, James. 1977. The performance of ritual metaphors. In *The social use of metaphor*, ed. J. D. Sapir and J. C. Crocker. Philadelphia: University of Pennsylvania Press.

Fernandez, James. 1980. Edification by puzzlement. In *Explorations in African systems of thought*, ed. Ivan Karp and Charles Bird, 44–69. Bloomington: Indiana University Press.

Fernandez, James. 1982. *Bwiti: An ethnography of the religious imagination.* Princeton, NJ: Princeton University Press.

Fernandez, James W. 1990. "Guest Editorial." In *Cultural anthropology: A perspective on the human condition*, Emily Schultz and Robert Lavenda. St Paul, MN: West.

Field, Les. 2004. Beyond "applied" anthropology. In *A companion to the anthropology of American Indians*, ed. Thomas Biolsi, 472–89. Malden, MA: Blackwell.

Firth, Raymond. [1936] 1984. *We, the Tikopia.* Reprint. Stanford, CA: Stanford University Press.

Fischer, Edward F., and Peter Benson. 2006. *Broccoli and desire: Global connections and postwar struggles in Mayan Guatemala*. Stanford, CA: Stanford University Press.

Foley, Douglas. 1989. *Learning capitalist culture: Deep in the heart of Tejas*. Philadelphia: University of Pennsylvania Press.

Forge, Anthony. 1967. The Abelam artist. In *Social organization: Essays presented to Raymond Firth*, ed. Maurice Freedman, 65–84. London: Cass.

Fortes, Meyer. 1950. Kinship and marriage among the Ashanti. In *African systems of kinship and marriage*, ed. A. R. Radcliffe-Brown and Daryll Forde. Oxford: Oxford University Press.

Fortes, Meyer. 1953. The structure of unilineal descent groups. *American Anthropologist* 55: 25–39.

Foucault, Michel. [1980] 1991. Governmentality. In *The Foucault effect: Studies in governmentality*, ed. Graham Burchell, Colin Gordon, and Peter Miller, 87–104. Chicago: University of Chicago Press.

Franklin, Sarah. 1995. "Science as culture, cultures of science." *Annual Review of Anthropology* 24: 163-84.

Fratkin, Elliot. 1997. Pastoralism: Governance and development issues. *Annual Review of Anthropology* 26: 235–61.

Friedman, Jonathan. 1994. *Cultural identity and global process*. London: Sage.

Friedman, Jonathan. 1997. Global crises, the struggle for cultural identity and intellectual porkbarrelling: Cosmopolitans versus locals, ethnics and nationals in an era of dehegemonisation. In *Debating cultural hybridity: Multicultural identities and the politics of anti-racism*, ed. Pnina Werbner and Tariq Modood, 70–89. London: Zed Books.

Gampel, Yoland. 2000. Reflections of the prevalence of the uncanny in social violence. In *Cultures under siege: Collective violence and trauma*, ed. Antonius C. Robben and Marcelo M. Suárez-Orozco, 48–69. Cambridge: Cambridge University Press.

Geertz, Clifford. 1960. *The religion of Java*. New York: Free Press.

Geertz, Clifford. 1973. *The interpretation of cultures*. New York: Basic Books.

Geertz, Hildred, and Clifford Geertz. 1975. *Kinship in Bali*. Chicago: University of Chicago Press.

Georges, Eugenia. 1990. *The making of a transnational community: Migration, development, and cultural change in the Dominican Republic*. New York: Columbia University Press.

Giddens, Anthony. 1979. *Central problems in social theory*. Berkeley: University of California Press.

Giddens, Anthony. 1990. *The consequences of modernity*. Stanford, CA: Stanford University Press.

Gilligan, Carol. 1982. *In a different voice*. Cambridge, MA: Harvard University Press.

Gillman, Neil. 1992. *Sacred fragments: Recovering theology for the modern Jew*. New York: Jewish Publication Society.

Gilsenan, Michael. 1982. *Recognizing Islam: Religion and society in the modern Arab world*. New York: Pantheon.

Ginsburg, Faye, and Rayna Rapp. 1995. *Conceiving the new world order: The global politics of reproduction*. Berkeley: University of California Press.

Gledhill, John. 1994. *Power and its disguises*. London: Pluto Press.

Gomes, Mercio. 1996. *Indians and Brazil: Holocaust and survival of a native population.* Unpublished translation of *Os indios e o Brasil*, 2d ed. Petropolis, Brazil: Editora Vozes.

Goody, Jack, and Stanley Tambiah. 1973. *Bridewealth and dowry*. Cambridge: Cambridge University Press.

Gordon, Colin. 1991. Governmental Rationality: An introduction. In *The Foucault effect: Studies in governmentality*, ed. Graham Burchell, Colin Gordon, and Peter Miller, 1–52. Chicago: University of Chicago Press.

Gordon, Robert. 1992. *The bushman myth: The making of a namibian underclass*. Boulder, CO: Westview Press.

Gottlieb, Alma. 1988. American premenstrual syndrome: A mute voice. *Anthropology Today* 4(6).

Gottlieb, Alma. 1989. Witches, kings, and the sacrifice of identity *or* The power of paradox and the paradox of power among the Beng of Ivory Coast. In *Creativity of power: Cosmology and action in African societies*, ed. W. Arens and Ivan Karp, 245–72. Washington, DC: Smithsonian Institution Press.

Gould, Stephen J. 1996. *Full circle*. New York: Harmony Books.

Gramsci, Antonio. 1971. *Selections from the Prison Notebooks*. Translated by Q. Hoare and G. N. Smith. New York: International.

Greenwood, David, and William Stini. 1977. *Nature, culture, and human history*. New York: Harper & Row.

Gregory, Joseph, compiler. 1999. World briefing. *New York Times*, 22 October.

Gregory, Richard. 1981. *Mind in science: A history of explanations in psychology and physics*. Cambridge: Cambridge University Press.

Grinker, Roy Richard. 1994. *Houses in the rainforest: Ethnicity and inequality among farmers and foragers in central Africa*. Berkeley: University of California Press.

Gudeman, Stephen. 1990. Guest editorial. In *Cultural anthropology: A perspective on the human condition*, 2d ed., by Emily A. Schultz and Robert H. Lavenda, 458–59. St. Paul, MN: West.

Guneratne, Arjun. 2002. Caste and state. In *South Asian folklore: An encyclopedia*, ed. Peter Claus and Margaret Mills. New York: Garland.

Gupta, Akhil, and James Ferguson. 1997. Discipline and practice: "The field" as site, method, and location in anthropology. In *Anthropological locations: Boundaries and grounds of a field science*, ed. Akhil Gupta and James Ferguson, 1–46. Berkeley: University of California Press.

Gupta, Dipankar. 2005. Caste and politics: Identity over system. *Annual Review of Anthropology* 34: 409–27.

Gutierrez Muñíz, José, Josefina López Hurtado, and Guillermo Arias Beatón. n.d. *Un estudio del niño cubano*. Havana: Empresa Impresoras Gráficas MINED.

Hacking, Ian. 1991. How should we do the history of statistics? In *The Foucault effect: Studies in governmentality*, ed. Graham Burchell, Colin Gordon, and Peter Miller, 181–96. Chicago: University of Chicago Press.

Hale, Charles. 1997. Cultural politics of identity in Latin America. *Annual Review of Anthropology* 26: 567–90.

Halperin, Rhoda H. 1994. *Cultural economies: Past and present*. Austin: University of Texas Press.

Handelman, Don. 1977. Play and ritual: Complementary frames of meta-communication. In *It's a funny thing, humour*, ed. A. J. Chapman and H. C. Foot, 185–92. London: Pergamon.

Hanks, William. 1996. *Language and communicative practices*. Boulder, CO: Westview Press.

Hann, Christopher. 2002. "All kulturvölker now? Social anthropological reflections on the German-American tradition." In *Anthropology beyond culture*, ed. Richard Fox and Barbara J. King, 259–76. Oxford: Berg.

Hannerz, Ulf. 1996. *Transnational connections: Culture, people, places*. London: Routledge.

Haraway, Donna. 1989. *Primate Visions*. New York: Routledge.

Haraway, Donna. 1991. *Simians, cyborgs and women: The reinvention of nature*. New York: Routledge.

Harding, Sandra. 1991. *Whose science? Whose knowledge?: Thinking from women's lives*. Ithaca, NY: Cornell University Press.

Harrison, Faye. 1995. The persistent power of "race" in the cultural and political economy of racism. *Annual Review of Anthropology* 24: 47–74.

Harrison, Faye. 1998. Introduction: Expanding the discourse on "Race." *American Anthropologist* 100(3): 609–31.

Hartigan, John, Jr. 1997. Establishing the fact of whiteness. *American Anthropologist* 99(3): 495–504.

Harvey, David. 1990. *The condition of postmodernity*. Malden, MA: Blackwell.

Heider, Karl. 1979. *Grand Valley Dani*. New York: Holt, Rinehart & Winston.

Herdt, Gilbert, ed. 1994. *Third sex, third gender: Beyond sexual dimorphism in culture and history*. New York: Zone Books.

Herrnstein, Richard, and Charles Murray. 1994. *The bell curve*. New York: Free Press.

Herskovits, Melville. 1973. *Cultural relativism*. New York: Vintage Books.

Herzfeld, Michael. 1987. *Anthropology through the looking glass*. Cambridge: Cambridge University Press.

Herzfeld, Michael. 2001. *Anthropology: Theoretical practice in culture and society*. Malden, MA: Blackwell.

Herzfeld, Michael. 2003. Competing diversities: Ethnography in the heart of Rome. *Plurimundi* 3(5): 147–54.

Hess, David J. 1997. *Science studies: An advanced introduction*. New York: New York University Press.

Hill, Jane, and Judith Irvine, eds. 1992. *Responsibility and Evidence in Oral Discourse*. Cambridge: Cambridge University Press.

Hockett, Charles. 1966. The problems of universals in language. In *Universals of language*, ed. J. H. Greenberg, 1–29. Cambridge, MA: MIT Press.

Holm, John. 1988. *Pidgins and Creoles*. Vol. 1 of *Theory and structure*. Cambridge: Cambridge University Press.

Holy, Ladislav. 1996. *Anthropological perspectives on kinship*. London: Pluto Press.

Horton, Robin. 1982. Tradition and modernity revisited. In *Rationality and relativism*, ed. M. Hollis and Steven Lukes, 201–60. Cambridge, MA: MIT Press.

Hudson, R. A. 1980. *Sociolinguistics*. Cambridge: Cambridge University Press.

Hultkrantz, Åke. 1992. *Shamanic healing and ritual drama: Health and medicine in Native North American religious traditions*. New York: Crossroads.

Hunter, David, and Phillip Whitten. 1976. *Encyclopedia of anthropology*. New York: Harper & Row.

Hutchinson, Sharon. 1996. *Nuer dilemmas*. Berkeley: University of California Press.

Hutchinson, Sharon. 2002. Nuer ethnicity militarized. In *The anthropology of politics*, ed. Joan Vincent, 39–52. Malden, MA: Blackwell.

Hutnyk, John. 1997. Adorno at Womad: South Asian crossovers and the limits of hybridity talk. In *Debating cultural hybridity: Multicultural identities and the politics of anti-racism*, ed. Pnina Werbner and Tariq Modood, 106–36. London: Zed Books.

Hymes, Dell. 1972. On communicative competence. In *Sociolinguistics: Selected readings*, ed. J. B. Pride and J. Holmes, 269–93. Baltimore: Penguin.

Inda, Jonathan Xavier, and Renato Rosaldo. 2002. Introduction: A world in motion. In *The anthropology of globalization*, ed. Jonathan Xavier Inda and Renato Rosaldo, 1–34. Malden, MA: Blackwell.

Ingold, Tim. 1983. The significance of storage in hunting societies. *Man* 18: 553–71.

Ingold, Tim. 1994. General introduction. In *Companion encyclopedia of anthropology*, ed. Tim Ingold, xiii–xxii. London: Routledge.

Ingold, Tim. 2000. *The perception of the environment: Essays in livelihood, dwelling and skill*. London: Routledge.

Johansen, R. Elise B. 2006. Care for infibulated women giving birth in Norway: An anthropological analysis of health workers' management of a medically and culturally unfamiliar issue. *Medical Anthropology Quarterly* 20(4): 516–44.

Jones, J. S. 1986. The origin of *Homo sapiens*: The genetic evidence. In *Modern trends in primate and human evolution*, ed. B. Wood, L. Martin, and P. Andrews, 317–30. Cambridge: Cambridge University Press.

Jourdan, Christine. 1991. Pidgins and Creoles: The blurring of categories. *Annual Review of Anthropology* 20: 187–209.

Kahn, Susan Martha. 2000. *Reproducing Jews: A cultural account of assisted conception in Israel*. Durham, NC: Duke University Press.

Kapferer, Bruce. 1983. *A celebration of demons*. Bloomington: Indiana University Press.

Karp, Ivan. 1978. *Fields of change among the Iteso of Kenya*. London: Routledge and Kegan Paul.

Karp, Ivan. 1986. Laughter at marriage: Subversion in performance. In *Transformations of African marriage*, ed. David Parkin and David Nyamwaya. Manchester: Manchester University for the International African Institute.

Karp, Ivan. 1990. Guest editorial. *In Cultural anthropology: A perspective on the human condition*, 2d ed., by Emily A. Schultz and Robert H. Lavenda, 74–75. St. Paul, MN: West.

Karp, Ivan, and Martha B. Kendall. 1982. Reflexivity in Field Work. In *Explanation in social science*, ed. P. Secord. Los Angeles: Sage.

Kearney, Michael. 1995. The local and the global: The anthropology of globalization and transnationalism. *Annual Review of Anthropology* 24: 547–65.

Keesing, Roger. 1982. *Kwaio religion: The living and the dead in a Solomon Island society*. New York: Columbia University Press.

Keesing, Roger. 1983. *'Elota's story*. New York: Holt, Rinehart & Winston.

Keesing, Roger. 1992. *Custom and confrontation: The Kwaio struggle for cultural autonomy*. Chicago: University of Chicago Press.

Keller, Evelyn Fox. 1997. Secrets of God, nature, and life. In *The gender/sexuality reader*, ed. Roger Lancaster and Micaela di Leonardo, 209–18. New York: Routledge.

Kelly, John D., and Martha Kaplan. 2001. *Represented communities: Fiji and world decolonization*. Chicago: University of Chicago Press.

Kelly, Raymond. 1993. *Constructing inequality: The fabrication of a hierarchy of virtue among the Etoro*. Ann Arbor: University of Michigan Press.

Khazanov, Anatoly. 1993. State and violence in the ex-Soviet Union. Paper presented at 92d annual meeting of the American Anthropological Association. Chicago, IL.

Knorr Cetina, Karin. 2000. *Epistemic cultures*. Cambridge, MA: Harvard University Press.

Kondo, Dorinne K. 1990. *Crafting selves: Power, gender, and discourses of identity in a Japanese workplace*. Chicago: University of Chicago Press.

Köhler, G. 1978. *Global apartheid*. New York: Institute for World Order.

Kuhn, Thomas. 1970. *The structure of scientific revolutions*. Chicago: University of Chicago Press.

Kuhn, Thomas. 1979. Metaphor in science. In *Metaphor and thought*, ed. Andrew Ortony, 409–19. Cambridge: Cambridge University Press.

Kuipers, Joel. 1986. Talking about troubles: Gender differences in Weyéwa speech use. *American Ethnologist* 13(3): 448–62.

Kumar, Nita. 1992. *Friends, brothers, and informants: Field-work memories of Banaras*. Berkeley: University of California Press.

Kuper, Adam. 1982. *Wives for cattle: Bridewealth and marriage in southern Africa*. London: Routledge and Kegan Paul.

Kuper, Adam. 1999. *Culture: The anthropologist's account*. Cambridge, MA: Harvard University Press.

Kurotani, Sawa. 2005. *Home away from home: Japanese corporate wives in the United States*. Durham, NC: Duke University Press.

Labov, William. 1972. *Language in the inner city: Studies in the black English vernacular*. Philadelphia: University of Pennsylvania Press.

Lakoff, George, and Mark Johnson. 1980. *Metaphors we live by*. Berkeley: University of California Press.

Lancaster, Roger. 1992. *Life is hard: Machismo, danger, and the intimacy of power in Nicaragua*. Berkeley: University of California Press.

Langer, Lawrence L. 1997. The alarmed vision: Social suffering and Holocaust atrocity. In *Social suffering*, ed. Arthur Kleinman, Veena Das, and Margaret Lock, 47–65. Berkeley: University of California Press.

Laqueur, Thomas. 1990. *Making sex*. Cambridge, MA: Harvard University Press.

Larkin, Brian. 2002. Indian films and Nigerian lovers: Media and the creation of parallel modernities. In *The anthropology of globalization*, ed. Jonathan Xavier Inda and Renato Rosaldo, 350–78. Malden, MA: Blackwell.

Lassiter, Luke Eric. 2001. From "Reading over the shoulders of natives" to "Reading alongside natives," literally: Toward a collaborative and reciprocal ethnography. *Journal of Anthropological Research* 57: 137–49.

Lassiter, Luke Eric, Clyde Ellis, and Ralph Kotay. 2002. *The Jesus road: Kiowas, Christianity, and Indian hymns*. Lincoln: University of Nebraska Press.

Lassiter, Luke Eric. 2004. Music. In *A companion to the anthropology of American Indians*, ed. Thomas Biolsi, 196–211. Malden, MA: Blackwell.

Lave, Jean. 1988. *Cognition in practice*. Cambridge: Cambridge University Press.

Leach, J. W., and G. Kildea, directors. 1974. *Trobriand cricket: An ingenious response to colonialism*. Berkeley: University of California Extension Media Center.

Leacock, Eleanor. 1983. Interpreting the origins of gender inequality: Conceptual and historical problems. *Dialectical Anthropology* 7(4): 263–84.

Lederman, Rena. 2005. Unchosen grounds: Cultivating cross-subfield accents for a public voice. In *Unwrapping the sacred bundle*, ed. Daniel Segal and Sylvia Yanagisako, 49–77. Durham, NC: Duke University Press.

Lee, Richard B. 1992. Art, science, or politics? The crisis in hunter-gatherer studies. *American Anthropologist* 94: 31–54.

Lee, Richard B. 2002. *The Dobe Ju/'hoansi*, 3d ed. Belmont, CA: Wadsworth.

Lever, Janet. 1983. *Soccer madness*. Chicago: University of Chicago Press.

Levine, Nancy. 1980. Nyinba polyandry and the allocation of paternity. *Journal of Comparative Family Studies* 11(3): 283–88.

Levine, Nancy. 1988. *The dynamics of polyandry: Kinship, domesticity, and population on the Tibetan border*. Chicago: University of Chicago Press.

Levine, Nancy, and Walter Sangree. 1980. Women with many husbands. *Journal of Comparative Family Studies* 11(3): 385–410.

Lévi-Strauss, Claude. [1962] 1967. *Structural anthropology*. Trans. Claire Jacobson and Brooke Grundfest Schoepf. New York: Doubleday Anchor.

Lewellen, Ted C. 1993. *Political anthropology*, 2d ed. South Hadley, MA: Bergin and Garvey.

Lewis, Philip. 1997. Arenas of ethnic negotiations: Cooperation and conflict in Bradford. In *The politics of multiculturalism in the new Europe: Racism, identity, and community*, ed. Tariq Modood and Pnina Werbner, 126–46. London: Zed Books.

Lewontin, Richard, Steven Rose, and Leon J. Kamin. 1984. *Not in our genes*. New York: Pantheon.

Lienhardt, Godfrey. 1961. *Divinity and experience*. Oxford: Oxford University Press.

Linke, Uli. 1997. Gendered difference, violent imagination: Blood, race, nation. *American Anthropologist* 99(3): 559–73.

Little, Kenneth. 1967. *The Mende of Sierra Leone*. London: Routledge and Kegan Paul.

Livingstone, F. B. 1964. On the nonexistence of human races. In *The Concept of Race*, ed. M. F. Ashley-Montagu, 46–60. New York: Collier.

Lutz, Catherine A. 1988. *Unnatural emotions: Everyday sentiments on a Micronesian atoll and their challenge to Western theory*. Chicago: University of Chicago Press.

Lutz, Ellen. 2006. Fighting for the right rights. *Cultural Survival Quarterly* 30(4): 3–4.

MacCormack, Carol P. 1980. Proto-social to adult: A Sherbro transformation. In *Nature, culture, and gender*, ed. Carol P. MacCormack and Marilyn Strathern, 95–118. Cambridge: Cambridge University Press.

Macintyre, Martha. 1993. Fictive kinship or mistaken identity? Fieldwork on Tubetube Island, Paupua New Guinea. In *Gendered field: Women, men and ethnography*, ed. Diane Bell, Pat Caplan, and Wazir Jahan Karim, 44–62. London: Routledge.

Malinowski, Bronislaw. [1926] 1948. *Magic, science, and religion, and other essays*. New York: Doubleday Anchor.

Malinowski, Bronislaw. 1944. *A scientific theory of culture and other essays*. Oxford: Oxford University Press.

Malkki, Liisa H. 1995. Refugees and exile: From "refugee status" to the national order of things. *Annual Review of Anthropology* 24: 495–523.

Mandler, George. 1975. *Mind and emotion*. New York: Wiley.

Maquet, Jacques. 1970. Rwanda castes. In *Social stratification in Africa*, ed. Arthur Tuden and Leonard Plotnikov. New York: Free Press.

Marcus, George. 1990. Guest editorial. In *Cultural anthropology: A perspective on the human condition*. 2d ed., by Emily A. Schultz and Robert H. Lavenda, 254–55. St. Paul, MN: West.

Marcus, George. 1995. Ethnography in/of the world system: The emergence of multi-sited ethnography. *Annual Review of Anthropology* 24: 95–117.

Marks, Jonathan. 1995. *Human biodiversity*. New York: Aldine.

Martin, Emily. 1995. *Flexible bodies: Tracking immunity in American culture from the days of polio to the age of AIDS*. Boston: Beacon Press.

Martin, Laura. 1986. Eskimo words for snow: A case study in the genesis and decay of an anthropological example. *American Anthropologist* 88(2): 418–19.

Marx, Karl. [1932] 1973. *The German ideology*. In *Karl Marx: Selected writings*. Selections reprinted. Ed. David McLellan. Oxford: Oxford University Press.

Marx, Karl. 1963. *The 18th brumaire of Louis Bonaparte*. New York: International.

Matthiasson, John S. 1992. *Living on the land: Change among the Inuit of Baffin Island*. Peterborough, ON: Broadview Press.

Mauss, Marcel. [1950] 2000. *The gift: The form and reason for exchange in archaic societies*. New York: W. W. Norton.

Mayr, Ernst. 1982. *The growth of biological thought*. Cambridge, MA: Harvard University Press.

McKinnon, Susan, and Sydele Silverman, eds. 2005. *Complexities: Beyond nature and nurture*. Chicago: University of Chicago Press.

Mead, George Herbert. 1934. *Mind, self, and society*. Chicago: University of Chicago Press.

Meisch, Lynn. 2002. *Andean entrepreneurs: Otavalo merchants and musicians in the global arena*. Austin: University of Texas Press.

Melotti, Umberto. 1997. International migration in Europe: Social projects and political cultures. In *The politics of multiculturalism in the new Europe: Racism, identity, and community*, ed. Tariq Modood and Pnina Werbner, 73–92. London: Zed Books.

Merry, Sally Engle. 2001. Changing rights, changing culture. In *Culture and rights: Anthropological perspectives*, ed. Jane Cowan, Marie-Bénédicte Dembour, and Richard A. Wilson, 31–55. Cambridge: Cambridge University Press.

Merry, Sally Engle. 2003. Human-rights law and the demonization of culture. *Anthropology News* 44(2).

Messer, Ellen. 1993. Anthropology and human rights. *Annual Review of Anthropology* 22: 221–49.

Meunier, Jacques, and A. M. Savarin. 1994. *The Amazon chronicles*, trans. Carol Christensen. San Francisco: Mercury House.

Miers, Suzanne, and Igor Kopytoff. 1977. Ethnography. In *Slavery in Africa*, ed. Igov Kopytoff and Suzanne Miers. Madison: University of Wisconsin Press.

Mignolo, Walter D. 2002. The many faces of cosmo-polis: Border thinking and critical cosmopolitanism. In *Cosmopolitanism*, ed. Carol Breckenridge, Sheldon Pollock, Homi Bhaba, and Dipeesh Chakrabarty, 157–87. Durham, NC: Duke University Press.

Miller, Barbara Diane. 1993. The anthropology of sex and gender hierarchies. In *Sex and gender hierarchies*, ed. Barbara Diane Miller, 3–31. Cambridge: Cambridge University Press.

Miller, Daniel. 1995. Consumption and commodities. *Annual Review of Anthropology* 24 : 141–61.

Miller, Daniel. 1998. Coca-Cola: A black sweet drink from Trinidad. In *Material cultures: Why some things matter*, ed. Daniel Miller, 169–88. Chicago: University of Chicago Press.

Miller, Daniel, and Don Slater. 2000. *The Internet: An ethnographic approach*. Oxford: Berg.

Minturn, Leigh. 1993. *Sita's daughters: Coming out of Purdah*. Oxford: Oxford University Press.

Miracle, Andrew. 1991. Aymara joking behavior. *Play & Culture* 4(2): 144–52.

Mitchell-Kernan, Claudia. 1972. On the status of black English for native speakers: An assessment of attitudes and values. In *Functions of language in the classroom*, ed. C. Cazden, V. John, and D. Hymes, 195–210. New York: Teachers College Press.

Mitra, Subrata. 1994. Caste, democracy and the politics of community formation in India. In *Contextualizing caste: Post-Dumontian approaches*, ed. Mary Searle-Chatterjee and Ursula Sharma, 49–71. Oxford: Blackwell/The Sociological Review.

Modood, Tariq. 1997. Introduction: The politics of multiculturalism in the new Europe." In *The politics of multiculturalism in the new Europe: Racism, identity, and community*, ed. Tariq Modood and Pnina Werbner, 1–25. London: Zed Books.

Moffatt, Michael. 1989. *Coming of age in New Jersey: College and American culture*. New Brusnswick, NJ: Rutgers University Press.

Moll, Luis, ed. 1990. *Vygotsky and education*. Cambridge: Cambridge University Press.

Molnar, Stephen. 2001. *Human variation*. New York: Prentice-Hall.

Montgomery, Heather. 2001. Imposing rights? A case study of child prostitution in Thailand. In *Culture and rights: Anthropological perspectives*, ed. Jane Cowan, Marie-Bénédicte Dembour, and Richard A. Wilson, 80–101. Cambridge: Cambridge University Press.

Moore, Sally Falk. 2005. Comparisons: Possible and impossible. *Annual Review of Anthropology* 34: 1–11.

Morgan, Marcyliena. 1995. Theories and politics in African American English. *Annual Review of Anthropology* 23: 325–45.

Morgan, Marcyliena. 1997. Commentary on Ebonics. *Anthropology Newsletter* 38(3): 8.

Morgan, Marcyliena. 2002. *Language, discourse, and power in African American culture*. Cambridge: Cambridge University Press.

Murphy, Robert, and Yolanda Murphy. 1974. *Women of the forest*. New York: Columbia University Press.

Myerhoff, Barbara. 1974. *Peyote hunt: The sacred journey of the Huichol Indians*. Ithaca, NY: Cornell University Press.

Nanda, Serena. 1994. An alternative sex and gender role. In *Third sex, third gender*, Gilbert Herdt, 373–417. New York: Zone Books.

Narayan, R. K. 1974. *My days*. New York: Viking.

Nash, June. 1979. *We eat the mines, and the mines eat us*. New York: Columbia University Press.

Niezen, Ronald. 2003. *The origins of indigenism: Human rights and the politics of identity*. Berkeley: University of California Press.

Nordstrom, Carolyn. 1993. Treating the wounds of war. *Cultural Survival Quarterly* 17(2) (summer): 28–30.

Odling-Smee, F. J. 1994. Niche construction, evolution and culture. In *Companion encyclopedia of anthropology: Humanity, culture, and social life*, ed. Tim Ingold, London: Routledge.

O'Donnell, Guillermo, and Philippe Schmitter. 1986. *Tentative conclusions about uncertain democracies*. Baltimore: Johns Hopkins University Press.

Omohundro, John. 2000. *Careers in anthropology*. New York: McGraw-Hill.

Ong, Aihwa. 2002. The Pacific shuttle: Family, citizenship, and capital circuits. In *The anthropology of globalization*, ed. Jonathan Xavier Inda and Renato Rosaldo, 172–97. Malden, MA: Blackwell.

Ortner, Sherry. 1973. On key symbols. *American Anthropologist* 75(5): 1338–46.

Ortner, Sherry. 1974. Is female to male as nature is to culture? In *Woman, culture, and society*, ed. Michelle Zimbalist Rosaldo and Louise Lamphere. Stanford, CA: Stanford University Press.

Ortony, Andrew. 1979. Metaphor: A multidimensional problem. In *Metaphor and thought*, ed. Andrew Ortony, 1–18. Cambridge: Cambridge University Press.

Oyama, Susan. 1985. *The ontogeny of information*. Cambridge: Cambridge University Press.

Parkin, David. 1984. Mind, body, and emotion among the Giriama. Paper presented at *Humanity as creator* lecture series, St. Cloud State University.

Parkin, David. 1990. Guest editorial. In *Cultural anthropology: A persepctive on the human condition*, 2d ed., by Emily A. Schultz and Robert H. Lavenda, 90–91. St. Paul, MN: West.

Partridge, William L., ed. 1984. *Training manual in development anthropology*. Special Publication of the American Anthropological Association and the Society for Applied Anthropology, Number 17. Washington, DC: American Anthropological Association.

Peletz, Michael. 1995. Kinship studies in late twentieth-century anthropology. *Annual Review of Anthropology* 24: 343–72.

Pfaff, Gunter, cinematographer, and Ronald A. Simons, psychiatric consultant. 1973. *Floating on the air, followed by the wind*. A film distributed by Indiana University Instructional Support Services. East Lansing, MI: Michigan State University.

Pickering, Andrew. 1995. *The mangle of practice: Time, agency and science*. Chicago: University of Chicago Press.

Pinker, Steven. 1999. *How the mind works*. New York: W. W. Norton & Company.

Poewe, Karla. 1989. On the metonymic structure of religious experiences: The example of charismatic Christianity. *Cultural Dynamics* 2(4): 361–80.

Pollock, Sheldon, Homi Bhaba, Carol Breckenridge, and Dipeesh Chakrabarty. 2002. Cosmopolitanisms. In *Cosmopolitanism*, ed. Carol Breckenridge, Sheldon Pollock, Homi Bhaba, and Dipeesh Chakrabarty, 1–14. Durham, NC: Duke University Press.

Potts, Rick. 1996. *Humanity's descent*. New York: William Morrow.

Rabinow, Paul. 1977. *Reflections on fieldwork in Morocco*. Berkeley, CA: University of California Press.

Rabinow, Paul. 1993. Reflections on fieldwork in Alameda. In *Perilous states: Conversations on culture, politics, and nation*, 259–372. Chicago: University of Chicago Press.

Rabinow, Paul. 1996. *Making PCR*. Chicago: University of Chicago Press.

Rainforest Foundation US. 2003. The Panará. *Rainforest Foundation US Online*. http://www.rainforestfoundation.org/1panara.html. Accessed 13 September 2003.

Redfield, Robert, Ralph Linton, and Melville Herskovits. 1936. Memorandum for the study of acculturation. *American Anthropologist* 38: 149–52.

Redford, Kent H. 1993. The ecologically noble savage. In *Talking about people*, ed. William Haviland and Robert Gordon, 11–13. Mountain View, CA: Mayfield.

Reeves, Edward, Billie DeWalt, and Kathleen DeWalt. 1987. The International Sorghum/Millet Research Project. In *Anthropological praxis*, ed. Robert Wolfe and Shirley Fiske, 72–83. Boulder, CO: Westview Press.

Reeves-Ellington, Richard H. 1993. Using cultural skills for cooperative advantage in Japan. *Human Organization* 52(2): 203–16.

Rezende, Claudia Barcellos. 1999. Building affinity through friendship. In *The anthropology of friendship*, ed. Sandra Bell and Simon Coleman, 79–97. Oxford: Berg.

Richards, Audrey. 1954. *Chisungu*. London: Methuen.

Richerson, Peter J., and Robert Boyd. 2006. *Not by genes alone*. Chicago: University of Chicago Press.

Ringrose, Katheryn. 1994. Living in the shadows: Eunuchs and gender in Byzantium. In *Third sex, third gender*, ed. Gilbert Herdt, 85–109. New York: Zone Books.

Rodriguez, Clara. 1994. Challenging racial hegemony: Puerto Ricans in the United States. In *Race*, ed. Stephen Gregory and Roger Sanjek, 131–45. New Brunswick, NJ: Rutgers University Press.

Rohter, Larry. 2003. Amazon Indians honor an intrepid spirit. *New York Times*, July 26.

Ronan, Colin A., and Joseph Needham. 1978. *The shorter science and civilisation in China*. Cambridge: Cambridge University Press.

Roscoe, Will. 1994. How to become a Berdache: Toward a unified analysis of gender diversity. In *Third sex, third gender*, ed. Gilbert Herdt, 329–72. New York: Zone Books.

Rosen, Lawrence. 1984. *Bargaining for reality: The construction of social relations in a Muslim community*. Chicago: University of Chicago Press.

Rubin, Jeffrey W. 1997. *Decentering the regime: Ethnicity, radicalism, and democracy in Juchitán, Mexico*. Durham, NC: Duke University Press.

Sacks, Karen. 1979. *Sisters and wives*. Westport, CT: Greenwood Press.

Sahlins, Marshall. 1972. *Stone Age economics*. Chicago: Aldine.

Sahlins, Marshall. 1976. *Culture and practical reason*. Chicago: University of Chicago Press.

Sanjek, Roger. 1994. The enduring inequalities of race." In *Race*, ed. Stephen Gregory and Roger Sanjek, 1–17. New Brunswick, NJ: Rutgers University Press.

Sapir, Edward. [1933] 1966. *Culture, language, and personality*, ed. David Mandelbaum. Berkeley: University of California Press.

Scheper-Hughes, Nancy. 1994. Embodied knowledge: Thinking with the body in critical medical anthropology. In *Assessing cultural anthropology*, ed. Robert Borofsky, 229–42. New York: McGraw-Hill.

Schiffauer, Werner. 1997. Islam as a civil religion: Political culture and the organisation of diversity in Germany. In *The politics of multiculturalism in the new Europe: Racism, identity, and community*, ed. Tariq Modood and Pnina Werbner, 147–66. London: Zed Books.

Schiller, Nina Glick, and Georges Fouron. 2002. Long-distance nationalism defined. In *The anthropology of politics*, ed. Joan Vincent, 356–65. Malden, MA: Blackwell.

Schneider, David. 1968. *American kinship*. Englewood Cliffs, NJ: Prentice-Hall.

Schultz, Emily. 1984. From Pagan to Pullo: Ethnic identity change in northern cameroon. *Africa* 54(1): 46–64.

Schultz, Emily. 1990. *Dialogue at the margins: Whorf, Bakhtin, and linguistic relativity*. Madison: University of Wisconsin Press.

Schwartzman, Helen. 1978. *Transformations: The anthropology of children's play*. New York: Plenum Press.

Schwartzman, Steven. 1998. Success story in Brazil: The return of the Panará. *The Aisling Magazine*. http://www.aislingmagazine.com/Anu/articles/TAM23/Success.html. Accessed 13 September 2003.

Scott, James. 1985. *Weapons of the weak*. New Haven, CT: Yale University Press.

Scott, James C. 1990. *Domination and the arts of resistance*. New Haven, CT: Yale University Press.

Segal, Daniel, and Sylvia Yanagisako, eds. 2005. *Unwrapping the sacred bundle: Reflections on the disciplining of anthropology*. Durham, NC: Duke University Press.

Segalen, Martine. 1986. *Historical anthropology of the family*. Cambridge: Cambridge University Press.

Service, Elman. 1962. *Primitive social organization*. New York: Random House.

Sharma, Ursula. 1999. *Caste*. Buckingham, UK: Open University Press.

Sharp, Lesley. 2006. *Strange harvest: Organ transplants, denatured bodies, and the transformed self*. Berkeley: University of California Press.

Sheehan, Elizabeth A. 1997. "Victorian clitoridectomy: Isaac Baker Brown and his harmless operative procedure. In *The gender/sexuality reader*, ed. Roger Lancaster and Micaela De Leonardo, 324–34. New York: Routledge.

Shepherd, Gil. 1987. Rank, gender, and homosexuality: Mombasa as a key to understanding sexual options. In *The cultural construction of sexuality*, ed. Pat Caplan, 240–70. London: Tavistock.

Shostak, Marjorie. 1981. *Nisa: The life and words of a !Kung woman*. New York: Vintage.

Silverstein, Michael. 1976. Shifters, linguistic categories, and cultural description. In *Meaning in anthropology*, ed. Keith Basso and Henry Selby, 11–55. Albuquerque: University of New Mexico Press.

Silverstein, Michael. 1985. The functional stratification of language and ontogenesis. In *Culture, communication, and cognition: Vygotskian perspectives*, ed. James Wertsch, 205–35. Cambridge: Cambridge University Press.

Singer, Merrill. 1998. The development of critical medical anthropology: Implications for biological anthropology. In *Building a new biocultural synthesis*, ed. Alan H. Goodman and Thomas L. Leatherman, 93–123. Ann Arbor: University of Michigan Press.

Singer, Natasha. 2007. Is looking your age now taboo? *New York Times*, 1 March, E1, E3.

Smart, Alan. 1999. Expressions of interest: Friendship and *guanzi* in Chinese societies. In *The anthropology of friendship*, ed. Sandra Bell and Simon Coleman, 119–36. Oxford: Berg.

Smedley, Audrey. 1995. *Race in North America: Origin and evolution of a worldview*. Boulder, CO: Westview Press.

Smedley, Audrey. 1998. "Race" and the construction of human identity. *American Anthropologist* 100(3): 690–702.

Smith, Andrea. 1994. For all those who were Indian in a former life. *Cultural Survival Quarterly* (Winter): 71.

Smith, Alex Duval. 2004. France divided as headscarf ban is set to become law. *The Observer*, 1 February. http://observer.guardian.co.uk/international/story/0,6903,1136434,00.html. Accessed 6 March 2004.

Smith, Gavin A., and R. Brokke Thomas. 1998. What could be: Biocultural anthropology for the next generation. In *Building a new biocultural synthesis*, ed. Alan H. Goodman and Thomas L. Leatherman, 451–73. Ann Arbor: University of Michigan Press.

Smith, M. G. [1954] 1981. Introduction. In *Baba of Karo*, by Mary Smith. New Haven, CT: Yale University Press.

Smith, Wilfred Cantwell. 1982. *Towards a world theology*. Philadelphia: Westminster Press.

Solway, Jacqueline, and Richard Lee. 1990. Foragers, genuine or spurious: Situating the Kalahari San in history. *Current Anthropology* 31: 109–46.

Sonntag, Selma K. 2002. *The local politics of global English*. Lanham, MD: Lexington Books.

Spencer, Jonathan. 2000. On not becoming a "Terrorist": Problems of memory, agency, and community in the Sri Lankan conflict. In *Violence and subjectivity*, ed. Veena Das, Arthur Kleinman, Mamphela Ramphele, and Pamela Reynolds, 120–40. Berkeley: University of California Press.

Spiro, Melford. 1977. *Kinship and marriage in Burma: A cultural and psychodynamic account*. Berkeley: University of California Press.

Starn, Orin. 1992. "I dreamed of foxes and hawks": Reflections on peasant protest, new social movements, and the *Rondas Campesinas* of northern Peru. In *The making of social movements in Latin America: Identity, strategy, and democracy*, ed. Arturo Escobar and Sonia E. Alvarez, 89–111. Series in Political Economy and Economic Development in Latin America. Boulder, CO: Westview Press.

Stearman, Allyn. 1989. *The Yuqui*. New York: Holt, Rinehart and Winston.

Steiner, Christopher. 1994. *African art in transit*. Cambridge: Cambridge University Press.

Stewart, Charles, and Rosalind Shaw. 1994. *Syncretism/antisyncretism*. London: Routledge.

Stocks, Anthony. 2005. Too much for too few: Problems of indigenous land rights in America. *Annual Review of Anthropology* 34: 85–104.

Strathern, Marilyn. 1988. *The gender of the gift*. Berkeley: University of California Press.

Strathern, Marilyn. 1992. *Reproducing the future: Anthropology, kinship, and the new reproductive technologies*. New York: Routledge.

Suárez-Orozco, Marcelo M., and Antonius C. G. M. Robben. 2000. Interdisciplinary perspectives on violence and trauma. In *Cultures under siege: Collective violence and trauma*, ed. by Antonius C. G. M. Robben and Suárez-Orozco, 1–41. Cambridge: Cambridge University Press.

Sutton-Smith, Brian. 1992. Notes towards a critique of twentieth-century psychological play theory. In *Homo ludens: Der spielende Mensch*, Vol. 2, ed. Günther G. Bauer, 95–108. Munich-Salzburg: Muskiverlag Emil Katzbichler.

Tamari, Tal. 1991. The development of caste systems in west Africa. *Journal of African History* 32: 221–50.

Tannen, Deborah. 1990. *You just don't understand: Women and men in conversation*. New York: Ballantine Books.

Taylor, Julie. 1987. Tango. *Cultural Anthropology* 2(4): 481–93.

Tcherkézoff, Serge. 1998. Is aristocracy good for democracy? A contemporary debate in western Samoa. In *Pacific answers to western hegemony: Cultural practices of identity construction*, ed. Jürg Wassmann, 417–34. Oxford: Berg.

Thomas, Nicholas. 1991. *Entangled objects*. Cambridge, MA: Harvard University Press.

Thomas, Nicholas. 1996. Cold fusion. *American Anthropologist* 98: 9–25.

Tonkinson, Robert. 1998. National identity: Australia after Mabo. In *Pacific answers to western hegemony: Cultural practices of identity construction*, ed. Jürg Wassmann, 287–310. Oxford: Berg.

Trotter, Robert. 1987. A case of lead poisoning from folk remedies in Mexican American communities. In *Anthropological praxis*, ed. Robert Wolfe and Shirley Fiske, 146–59. Boulder, CO: Westview Press.

Trouillot, Michel-Rolph. 1991. Anthropology and the savage slot: The poetics and politics of otherness. In *Recapturing anthropology*, ed. Richard Fox, 17–44. Santa Fe, NM: SAR Press.

Trouillot, Michel-Rolph. 1994. Culture, color and politics in Haiti. In *Race*, ed. Stephen Gregory and Roger Sanjek, 146–74. New Brunswick, NJ: Rutgers University Press.

Trouillot, Michel-Rolph. 2002. Adieu, culture: A new duty arises. In *Anthropology beyond culture*, ed. Richard Fox and Barbara J. King, 37. Oxford: Berg.

Tsing, Anna Lowenhaupt. 2005. *Friction: An ethnography of global connection*. Princeton, NJ: Princeton University Press.

Turnbull, Colin. 1961. *The forest people*. New York: Simon & Schuster.

Turner, Terence. 1989. Amazonian Indians fight to save their forest. *Anthropology Newsletter* 30(3): 21–22.

Turner, Victor. 1969. *The ritual process*. Chicago: Aldine.

Tylor, E. B. [1871] 1958. *Primitive culture*. New York: Harper & Row.

Valentine, Bettylou. 1978. *Hustling and other hard work*. New York: The Free Press.

Valentine, Charles. 1978. Introduction. In *Hustling and other hard work*, by Bettylou Valentine, 1–10. New York: Free Press.

van den Berghe, Pierre. 1970. Race, class, and ethnicity in South Africa. In *Social stratification in Africa*, ed. Arthur Tuden and Leonard Plotnikov, 345–71. New York: Free Press.

van der Veer, Peter. 1997. The enigma of arrival: Hybridity and authenticity in the global space. In *Debating cultural hybridity: Multicultural identities and the politics of anti-racism*, ed. Pnina Werbner and Tariq Modood, 90–105. London: Zed Books.

Van Gennep, Arnold. 1960. *The rites of passage*. Chicago: University of Chicago Press.

van Willigen, John. 1991. *Anthropology in use: A source book on anthropological practice*. Boulder, CO: Westview Press.

van Willigen, John, and V. C. Channa. 1991. Law, custom, and crimes against women. *Human Organization* 50(4): 369–77.

Vaughan, James. 1970. Caste systems in the western Sudan. In *Social stratification in Africa*, ed. Arthur Tuden and Leonard Plotnikov, 59–92. New York: Free Press.

Vaughan, James. 1973. Engkyagu as artists in Marghi society. In *The traditional artist in African societies*, ed. Warren d'Azevedo, 162–93. Bloomington: Indiana University Press.

Vincent, Joan. 2002. Introduction. In *The anthropology of politics*, ed. Joan Vincent, 1–13. Malden, MA: Blackwell.

Vogel, Susan M. 1997. *Baule: African art/western eyes*. New Haven, CT: Yale University Press.

Voloshinov, V. N. [1926] 1987. Discourse in life and discourse in art. In *Freudianism*, by V. N. Voloshinov, ed. and trans. I. R. Titunik, in collaboration with Neil H. Bruss. 93–116. Bloomington: Indiana University Press.

Vygotsky, Lev. 1978. *Mind in society: The development of higher psychological processes*. Cambridge, MA: Harvard University Press.

Walker, Alice. 1992. *Possessing the secret of joy*. New York: Pocket Books.

Wallace, Anthony F. C. 1966. *Religion: An anthropological view*. New York: Random House.

Wallace, Anthony F. C. 1972. *The death and rebirth of the Seneca*. New York: Vintage.

Wallerstein, Immanuel. 1974. *The modern world system: Capitalist agriculture and the origins of the European world economy in the sixteenth century*. New York: Academic Press.

Wallman, Joel. 1992. *Aping language*. Cambridge: Cambridge University Press.

Walsh, Michael. 2005. Will indigenous languages survive? *Annual Review of Anthropology* 34: 293–315.

Warner, W. Lloyd. 1936. American caste and class. *American Sociological Review* 42(2): 237–57.

Weiner, Annette. 1976. *Women of value, men of renown*. Austin: University of Texas Press.

Weiner, Annette. 1980. Stability in banana leaves: Colonization and women in Kiriwina, Trobriand Islands. In *Women and colonization: Anthropological perspectives*, ed. Mona Etienne and Eleanor Leacock, 270–93. New York: Praeger.

Weiner, Annette. 1988. *The Trobrianders of Papua New Guinea*. New York: Holt, Rinehart & Winston.

Weiner, Annette. 1990. Guest editorial. In *Cultural anthropology: A Perspective on the human condition*, 2d ed., by Emily A. Schultz and Robert H. Lavenda. St. Paul, MN: West.

Weinker, Curtis. 1995. Biological anthropology: The current state of the discipline. In *Biological anthropology: The state of the science*, ed. Noel T. Boaz and Linda Wolfe. Bend, OR: International Institute for Human Evolutionary Research.

Weismantel, Mary. 1995. Making kin: Kinship theory and Zumbagua adoptions. *American Ethnologist* 22(4): 685–709.

Werbner, Pnina. 1997. Aferword: Writing multiculturalism and politics in the new Europe. In *The politics of multiculturalism in the new Europe: Racism, identity, and community*, ed. Tariq Modood and Pnina Werbner, 261–67. London: Zed Books.

Weston, Kath. 1991. *Families we choose: Lesbians, gays, kinship*. New York: Columbia University Press.

Weston, Kath. 1995. Forever is a long time: Romancing the real in gay kinship ideologies. In *Naturalizing power*, ed. Sylvia Yanagisako and Carol Delaney, 87–110. New York: Routledge.

Whiteley, Peter. 2004. Ethnography. In *A companion to the anthropology of American Indians*, ed. Thomas Biolsi, 435–71. Malden, MA: Blackwell.

Whorf, Benjamin Lee. 1956. *Language, thought, and reality*. Ed. John B. Carroll. Cambridge, MA: M.I.T. Press.

Wilk, Richard. 1996. *Economies and cultures: Foundations of economic anthropology*. Boulder, CO: Westview Press.

Wilk, Richard, and Lisa Cliggett. 2007. *Economies and cultures: Foundations of economic anthropology*. Boulder, CO: Westview Press.

Williams, Brackette F. 1989. A class act: Anthropology and the race to nation across ethnic terrain. *Annual Review of Anthropology* 18: 401–44.

Wilmsen, Edwin. 1989. *Land filled with flies: A political economy of the Kalahari*. Chicago: University of Chicago Press.

Wilmsen, Edwin. 1991. Pastoro-foragers to "Bushmen": Transformation in Kalahari relations of property, production and labor. In *Herders, warriors, and traders: Pastoralism in Africa*, ed. John G. Galaty and Pierre Bonte, 248–63. Boulder, CO: Westview Press.

Wilson, R. A., ed. 1997. *Human rights, culture and context*. London: Pluto Press.

Winn, Peter. 1992. *Americas*. New York: Pantheon.

Witherspoon, Gary. 1975. *Navajo kinship and marriage*. Chicago: University of Chicago Press.

Wolcott, Harry F. 1999. *Ethnography: A way of seeing*. Walnut Creek, CA: AltaMira Press.

Wolf, Eric. 1969. *Peasant wars of the twentieth century*. New York: Harper and Row.

Wolf, Eric. 1982. *Europe and the people without history*. Berkeley: University of California Press.

Wolf, Eric. 1994. Facing power: Old insights, new questions. In *Assessing cultural anthropology*, ed. Robert Borofsky, 218–28. New York: McGraw-Hill.

Wolf, Eric. 1999. *Envisioning power: Ideologies of dominance and resistance*. Berkeley: University of California Press.

Wolfe, Linda. 1995. Current research in field primatology. In *Biological anthropology: The state of the science*, ed. Noel T. Boaz and Linda Wolfe, 149–67. Bend, OR: International Institute for Human Evolutionary Research.

Woolard, Kathryn A. 1998. Introduction: Language ideology as a field of inquiry. In *Language ideologies: Practice and theory*, ed. Bambi Schieffelin, Kathryn Woolard, and Paul V. Kroskrity, 3–47. New York: Oxford University Press.

Woost, Michael D. 1993. Nationalizing the local past in Sri Lanka: Histories of nation and development in a Sinhalese village. *American Ethnologist* 20(3): 502–21.

Yanagisako, Sylvia, and Jane Collier. 1987. Towards a unified analysis of gender and kinship. In *Gender and kinship: Essays toward a unified analysis*, ed. Jane Collier and Sylvia Yanagisako, 14–50. Stanford, CA: Stanford University Press.

Yuval-Davis, Nira. 1997. Ethnicity, gender relations, and multiculturalism. In *Debating cultural hybridity: Multicultural identities and the politics of anti-racism*, ed. Pnina Werbner and Tariq Modood. London: Zed Books.

Credits

Boldface page numbers indicate glossary terms.

Fouron, Georges, 362, 405, 406, 410
Fourth World Conference on Women, 412
Framing, **167**
France, 79, 173, 226, 362, 428
    attitude toward immigrants, 408
Franklin, Sarah, 47
Fratkin, Elliot, 275
Free agency, **236**
Free will, 23
Freedom, 458
French (language), 103, 108
French Revolution, 35, 224, 225, 362, 363, 382
Freud, Sigmund, 132, 150
Friction, **431**–32
Friedman, Jonathan, 401, 426, 428
Friendliness, 293
Friends of the Earth Indonesia, 429
Friendship, 288, **291**–92
    American college students, 293
    Bangwa, 292
    kinship and, 291
Fulbe, 345, 378, 380
Fulfulde, 18, 104, 106, 109
Functional cognitive systems, **141**, 151
Functionalism, **206**
    Malinowskian, 274
Fur trade, 80
Furst, Peter, 213

Gabon, 7, 210, 221
Galton, Francis, 6
Gay marriage, arguments over, 356
Gay rights movements, 355
Gays, families by choice, 348, 350
Gbagba dance, 182–84
Geertz, Clifford, 27, 28, 416
Gender, 14, **295**, 360, **361**,
    dance and, 184
    in kinship terminology, 305
Gender of linking relative, 305
Gender relations, 320, 361
Generation, 305
Genes, 4
Genetrix, 307
Genital cutting, 30, 31–34, 414, 428, 444
Genitor, 307, 313, 327
Genocide, 29, 158, 232, 388
Genotype, 371
Georges, Eugenia, 346, 347
Germany, attitude toward immigrants, 408
Gerontology, 438

Ghana, 331, 338, 339
Ghost Dance movement, 220
Gift exchanges, 266
Gilligan, Carol, 154
Gilsenan, Michael, 161
Ginsburg, Faye, 399
Giriama, 148, 149
Giveaway dances, 281
Gledhill, John, 256, 399
Global assemblages, 401
Global citizenship, 421
Global displacements of people, 402
Global flows, 401, 402
Global style, **142**
Globalization, 98, 155, 234, 282, 396, **398**, 399, 400, 401, 402
    culture of, 413
    human rights and, 412–13
Gluckman, Max, 233
Godparents, Latin American, 313
Gomes, Mercio, 396
Goods, meaning of, 277
Gopalpur, India, 365–67
Gordon, Colin, 242
Gottlieb, Alma, 152
Government, 242
Governmentality, **242**, 243, 246, 411, 412
Grammar, **112**, 117
Gramsci, Antonio, 234, 235, 238, 239, 241, 244, 246, 248, 383
Great Chain of Being, 371
Greece, 88, 184
Green Belt Movement, 398
Greenwich Village, 194
Gregory, Richard, 138
Grief, 149
Grinker, Roy Richard, 361
Guatemala, 97, 126, 232, 241–42, 256
Gudeman, Stephen, 70
Guevedoche, 295
Guha, Ranajit, 241
Guider, 2, 67, 170, 200, 209, 220, 223, 341, 378, 380
Guinea, 317
Gujarat, India, 295
Guneratne, Arjun, 96
Gypsies (Roma), 369–70

Habitual knowledge, 117
Habitus, 18, 116, 412
Hacking, Ian, 242
Haiti, 156, 157, 159, 362, 406
Halloween, 169, 194
Halperin, Rhoda, 274

Hannerz, Ulf, 425
Haraway, Donna, 51
Harding, Sandra, 52
Harrison, Faye, 373, 377, 381, 382
Hawaii, 97
    law, 418
    violence against women in, 417–18
Hawaiian Creole, 118, 119
Hawaiian Pidgin English, 118, 119
Hawaiian Sovereignty Movement, 417
Headscarves, France, case of, 226–27
Hegemony, **238**, 239, 241, 242, 244, 248
    global, 401
Heider, Karl, 352
Herdt, Gilbert, 297
Herero, 276
Hermaphroditism, 295
Hermeneutics, 53
Herskovits, Melville, 82
Herzfeld, Michael, 407, 409
Hess, David, 70
Heteroglossia, 117, 119, 122, 123
Heterosexuality, 352, 353
Hidden transcripts, 248
Hijras, 295
Hilmiyya Nights, 186, 187
Hindus, 433
    religious beliefs, 209, 364
Hip-hop, Japan, 181–82
History, human, 23
HIV/AIDS, 8, 64
Hobbes, Thomas, 236, 260
Hockett, Charles, 105, 106, 114, 117
Hofriyat, 31, 33, 34
Holism, **3, 24**, 23
Holland, 79
Holocaust, 388
Homosexuality, 353
Honduras, 439, 440, 442
Hong Kong, 411
Horton, Robin, 206
Household breakup, 346
Huánuco Pampa, 264
Huichol, 209, 212–15, 245
Human nature
    moral model, 262
    self-interested model, 261
    social model, 261
Human rights, 97, 401, **412**, 413, 414, 421, 453
    activists, 417, 418
    advocacy, 439
    against culture, 414, 416
    anthropology and, 452
    child prostitution, 420
    culture as, 416
    culture of, 417